Child welfare and
social policy

To my students at the University of Southern Denmark

"The test of the morality of a society is what it does for its children." (Dietrich Bonhoeffer)

Child welfare and social policy

An essential reader

Edited by Harry Hendrick

First published in Great Britain in March 2005 by

The Policy Press
University of Bristol
Fourth Floor, Beacon House
Queen's Road
Bristol BS8 1QU
UK

Tel +44 (0)117 331 4054
Fax +44 (0)117 331 4093
e-mail tpp-info@bristol.ac.uk
www.policypress.org.uk

British Library Cataloguing in Publication Data
A catalogue record for this book is available from the British Library

Library of Congress Cataloging-in-Publication Data
A catalog record for this book has been requested

ISBN 1 86134 566 6 paperback

A hardback version of this book is also available.

Cover design by Qube Design Associates, Bristol.
Front cover: photograph supplied by www.JohnBirdsall.co.uk and posed by models.
Printed and bound in Great Britain by Hobbs the Printers Ltd, Southampton.

Contents

Sources of extracts

Acknowledgements

It would not have been possible to compile this Reader without the cooperation of the contributors and their publishers, which has been much appreciated. I'm particularly grateful to Vicki Coppock, Barry Goldson, Lucinda Platt, and Paul Daniel and John Ivatts for revising and updating previously published material.

I owe a special thanks to Mike Daly, John Macnicol, Klaus Petersen and John Stewart, each of whom, in his different way, has been encouraging and supportive during the two years in which this volume has been in the making.

In addition, it is a pleasure to say 'thank you' to the following colleagues and friends for references, criticisms and advice: Tom Cockburn, Nick Frost, Barry Goldson, Adrian James, Jane Lewis, Nigel Parton, Alan Prout, Elaine Sharland, Nigel Thomas and Jane Tunstill.

Tom Pettitt never tired of my enquires regarding points of grammar and style and his erudition in these matters has saved me from making numerous blunders. I am in his debt.

As usual, the staff in the inter-library loan section of the University of Southern Denmark library were unfailingly helpful and pleasant as they responded to my hundreds of requests.

With regard to financial assistance, the University History Institute willingly supported me in making several trips to UK libraries. I am also very grateful to the Wellcome Trust for twice awarding me a Wellcome Research Travel Grant.

Few travel awards, however, can cover the full costs of hotels and living expenses in cities such as London and Oxford. The burden was greatly lessened by the regular hospitality of John and Sue Stewart and especially that of Mike Daly who on two fraught occasions gave me the run of his house and his computer.

For a second time, Dawn Rushen has been my editor at The Policy Press. I trust my politically incorrect opinions on feminism and the daycare issue have not caused her too much distress!

Finally, I must mention Elaine Sharland who, besides sending me her unpublished paper on young people and risk, during the course of several email communications, (unknowingly) reminded me why I do this stuff. I hope this volume meets with her broad approval.

List of contributors

Saul Becker is Professor of Social Care and Health at the Institute of Applied Social Studies, University of Birmingham, UK.

Andrew Bibby is a freelance writer and journalist (www.andrewbibby.com).

Terry Carney is Professor of Law and Director of Research at the Faculty of Law, University of Sydney, Australia.

Vicki Coppock is Senior Lecturer in Social Sciences, Edge Hill College of Higher Education, Ormskirk, UK.

Mairian Corker was a freelance researcher, writer and trainer on all issues affecting the lives of deaf and disabled people, until her death in 2004.

Paul Daniel is Senior Lecturer in Social Policy at Roehampton University, London, UK.

John Davis is Lecturer/Coordinator in BA Childhood Studies at the Moray House School of Education, University of Edinburgh, UK.

Barry Goldson is Senior Lecturer in Sociology and Director of Research at the Department of Sociology, Social Policy and Social Work Studies, University of Liverpool, UK.

Harry Hendrick is Associate Professor in the Institute of History, University of Southern Denmark, Odense.

Malcolm Hill, is Director of the Glasgow Centre for the Child and Society, University of Glasgow, UK.

John Ivatts is Visiting Lecturer in Social Policy at Roehampton University, London, UK.

Adrian James is Professor of Social Work in the Department of Sociological Studies, University of Sheffield, UK.

Allison James is Professor of Sociology in the Department of Sociological Studies, University of Sheffield, UK.

Michael King is Professor in the School of Social Sciences and Law, and Co-Director of the Centre for Law, the Child and the Family, Brunel University, UK.

Gerison Lansdown is an international consultant in children's rights.

Penelope Leach is a developmental child psychologist and writer on childcare.

Ruth Lister is Professor of Social Policy in the Department of Social Sciences, Loughborough University, UK.

Virginia Morrow is Lecturer in Childhood Studies at the Institute of Education, University of London, UK.

Peter Moss is Professor of Early Childhood Provision in the Thomas Coram Research Unit, University of London, UK.

Kwame Owusu-Bempah is Reader in Psychology in the School of Social Work, University of Leicester.

Nigel Parton is Professor in Child Care and Director of the Centre for Applied Childhood Studies at the School of Human and Health Sciences, University of Huddersfield, UK.

Pat Petrie is Professor of Education in the Thomas Coram Research Unit, University of London, UK.

Christine Piper is Reader in the School of Social Sciences and Law, and Co-Director of the Centre for Law, the Child and the Family, Brunel University, UK.

Lucinda Platt is Lecturer in the Department of Sociology, University of Essex, UK.

Alan Prout is Professor of Sociology in the Department of Applied Social Science, University of Stirling, UK.

Tess Ridge is Lecturer in the Department of Social and Policy Sciences, University of Bath, UK.

Jeremy Roche is Director of the Health and Social Care Programme and Senior Lecturer in Law in the School of Health and Social Welfare, The Open University, UK.

Tom Shakespeare is Principal Research Associate in the School of Geography, Politics and Sociology, University of Newcastle, UK.

Anne Skevik is Research Fellow at NOVA Norwegian Social Research, Oslo, Norway.

Nigel Thomas is Senior Lecturer in Childhood Studies at the University of Wales, Swansea, UK.

Kay Tisdall is Senior Lecturer in the Social Policy Department, School of Social and Political Studies, University of Edinburgh, UK.

Sally Tomlinson is Professor in the Department of Educational Studies, University of Oxford, UK.

Nick Watson is Director of the Strathclyde Centre for Disability Research, Department of Sociology, Anthropology and Applied Social Science, University of Glasgow, UK.

Introduction

In compiling this Reader, I have four general intentions. First, the multiplicity of themes, debates and agendas surrounding 'child welfare' can make it difficult for 'non-experts' to identify and evaluate policies, practices and principles. With this in mind, many of the chapters have been chosen because they provide a broad framework whereby some of the complexities and ambiguities concerning children's well-being may be observed. For example:

- 'good intentions' and 'social action' (King, Chapter Three);
- rights and welfare (Lansdown, Chapter Six);
- children's participation in the family/state relationship (Thomas, Chapter Nine);
- race, culture and child rearing (Owusu-Bempah, Chapter Ten);
- the different and often contradictory assumptions made about children by the Law (Piper, Chapter Thirteen);
- communitarianism and the control of children (James and James, Chapter Fifteen);
- moral obligations and the daycare of young children (Leach, Chapter Twenty-Four);
- the 'social investment' strategy and childhood as 'the future' (Lister, Chapter Twenty-Five);
- children's agency and the tension between control and self-realisation in late modernity (Prout, Chapter Twenty-Six).

These chapters focus on, and draw attention to, influential and often controversial issues that are fundamental to the analytic study both of children in relation *to* social policy and of the ramifications of social policy *for* children.

The second intention is that as the Reader proceeds, we should be able to recognise many of the commonalities that exist between the different concepts and approaches, and to assess the extent to which they may or may not have been put into practice through particular policies. Among the more pervasive and important themes are children's rights, the significance of governmental/state attitudes, the role of law, the idea of 'justice' in child–adult relations, notions of deviance and marginalisation, and children as investments for the future. The interplay between the governing subject areas, as they are lodged within 'theory and practice', not only illustrates the multidisciplinary nature of social policy, but also reveals the ways in which such thematic contexts impinge on children's interests, often obliquely and usually irreverently.

The third intention is to identify what I call the 'messy interconnectedness' of welfare matters, not at the level of cooperation between different groups of professionals and their agencies, or between different departments of government – currently referred to as 'holistic' or 'joined-up government' (Newman, 2001, pp 104-26), but in the sense that, for example, poverty, disability, delinquency, ill-health and child abuse can only be properly understood, and the problems tackled, if they are seen *organically* rather than as discrete areas confined within their respective boundaries (for current developments in multidisciplinary children's services resulting from the government's Green Paper, *Every child matters*, DfES, 2003, see Williams, 2004). Furthermore, 'interconnectedness' is also used to refer to the symbiotic relations between, on the one hand, the idea of 'child welfare' and social constructions of children/childhood and, on the other, the correlation between a number of different theories and paradigms involving the family, 'social capital', welfare and liberty rights, cultural relativism, 'advanced liberalism' and risk and individualisation.

Fourth, I want to suggest that in order to understand and analyse what is happening *now* in the realm of child welfare, it is often necessary to think 'sideways on', by which I mean we should make greater use of the methodologies and concerns of what is still known as the 'new social studies of childhood' (although it is nearly two decades old), as directly evidenced by Moss and Petrie (Chapter Four) and Prout (Chapter Twenty-Six). Both provide a sociological consideration of children/childhood in late modernity with social policy in mind (for a pioneering attempt to combine the new social studies with policy case studies, see James and James, 2004). This sociologically informed perspective is useful in helping us to clarify our conceptual awareness since too often 'social policy' (as academic study) seems to forget its alleged commitment to a broad contextual analysis and retreats into 'social administration', with its more restricted interest in policy process and delivery.

My hope is that by opening this volume with two historical chapters (Part 1), readers will be made aware of the antecedents of many current debates, particularly:

- the temporal (time) specificity of 'moral' attitudes;
- the anxiety, if not fear, surrounding uncertainties about the *nature* of children and of childhood;
- the ever-present tensions and contradictions involved in the relationship between the family and the state;
- the influence of national economic and political priorities;
- the continual reformulation of children as 'victims' and 'threats'.

The chapters should serve as a reminder that not everything in the approach of the New Labour government to children and social policy is as 'new' or as 'modern' as the style of presentation would have us believe.

In Part 2 the focus is on 'concepts and approaches', and here policy analysts from several different academic disciplines discuss the ways in which children have been perceived and categorised in relation to 'welfare' (see especially Chapters Three to Six, Eight, Nine and Eleven), and critical attention is paid to those contexts in which children are the subjects of professional (legal, medical, social work, and socioeconomic) discourses (Chapters Seven, Nine, Ten; also chapters in Part 3). As a group, these chapters deal with concepts of children *in* welfare, approaches to policy formulation with respect to children, and epistemological considerations of the constitution of child welfare.

The Reader is *not* intended to be merely a guide to present policies and debates; hopefully, it will be helpful in the urgent task of conceptually and practically 'rethinking' the formative processes involved in framing 'children' within 'social policy'. It would be foolish, however, to ignore the politics of the contemporary restructuring of the welfare state that is going on all around us. If we look at the chapters in Part 2 with this in mind, then clearly they are instructive and suggestive in respect of certain tensions that exist between New Labour and a number of policy activists and researchers (Fawcett et al, 2004, p 158). For instance, it would be hard to find more topical subjects than:

- Ridge (Chapter Five) on the significance of recognising children's experiences of poverty;
- Lansdown (Chapter Six) on the importance of 'rights' in the provision of welfare;
- Goldson (Chapter Fourteen) and James and James (Chapter Fifteen) on communitarianism, anti-social behaviour and troubled/troublesome children.

Other chapters (although also concerned with current trends) are more discursive as they invite us to think about either long-term developments and/or profoundly political matters such as:

- the fundamental and continuously perplexing problem of translating 'good intentions' into 'social actions' (King, Chapter Three);
- the sociologically oriented question (with significant political and policy consequences): 'Children – who do we think they are?' (Moss and Petrie, Chapter Four);
- Morrow's critique of 'social capital' in relation to children's well-being (Chapter Eight),
- the complex and historically evolving relationship between children, family and the state (Thomas, Chapter Nine);
- the legitimacy of 'cultural relativism' in evaluating child-rearing styles among minority ethnic groups (Owusu-Bempah, Chapter Ten);
- the search for an appropriate political model to put into practice the moral values necessary to advance children's welfare (Carney, Chapter Eleven).

In many respects, these chapters illustrate the different ways in which child welfare is 'imagined' in competing, but by no means uniform, governmental, professional and academic dialogues.

The focus shifts in Part 3 to those perspectives apparent in either specific policies or policy areas that, by their nature, are of current interest:

- the extent of children's rights in the 1989 Children Act (Roche, Chapter Twelve);
- contemporary penal policy and childhood (Goldson, Chapter Fourteen);
- government attempts to extend control and surveillance of children (James and James, Chapter Fifteen);

- the treatment and identification of 'emotionally disturbed' children (Coppock, Chapter Sixteen);
- children's health (Hill and Tidsall, Chapter Seventeen);
- disability and childhood (Davis et al, Chapter Eighteen);
- children as members of 'the family' rather than as individual figures in the social security system (Skevik, Chapter Nineteen);
- ethnicity and means-tested benefits (Platt, Chapter Twenty);
- the effects of housing policy on children (Daniel and Ivatts, Chapter Twenty-One);
- social policy for young carers (Bibby and Becker, Chapter Twenty-Two);
- education in a post-welfare society (Tomlinson, Chapter Twenty Three);
- ethical issues involved in the daycare of children aged three and under (Leach, Chapter Twenty-Four).

The intention here is to provide concrete examples of how and why children are treated as they are in a number of principal policy areas. And, as the writers are critically disposed, implicit in each chapter are suggestions as to how child welfare *ought* to be conceived and administered. In choosing these examples of specific policy areas, the chapters offer the necessary empirical information which, when combined with the insights derived from Part 2, will provide students with sufficient material for an informed debate around the difficult and controversial topics and themes.

Part 4 raises questions concerning the current status of children's well-being and, more particularly, what it might be in the future. The emphasis is on children in what has recently come to be known as the 'social investment' state, that is, a state which prioritises investment in "*human capital* wherever possible, rather than direct provision of economic maintenance" (Giddens, quoted in Lister, Chapter Twenty-Five; original emphasis). The essence of social investment is that social and economic policies are inextricably linked, and that the former is subservient to the latter. Broadly speaking, the government wishes: to see individuals investing in themselves as lifelong learners in order to maintain relevant employment skills (to be able to adjust to constantly changing employer demands); to facilitate those citizenship skills it deems necessary to create and sustain ordered communities; and to promote 'responsible' (a key word) parenting of the kind that exercises 'discipline' at home and takes an active interest in the children's school work and in their behaviour in public places. In this way, children become an investment in the well-being of the state – their lives seen primarily in terms of futurity.

Lister (Chapter Twenty-Five) marks out the growing significance of 'social investment' as a developing concept. Her account, which should be read in conjunction with the historical chapters in Part 1, where the notion of 'investment' in children was first observed, also points to malleability of the idea, according to government policies. Prout (Chapter Twenty-Six) adopts a more sociological approach to express his concern with children in late modernity, particularly the tension between control and self-realisation. On the one hand, children are increasingly recognised as people in their own right (at least by the majority of social policy professionals); on the other, there is the equally potent tendency by the government to extend control and surveillance over them. Prout considers this tension in relation to the emergence of children as 'human capital' which, as it is moulded, constitutes a means of controlling the future.

So, what then, are the aims and objectives of this collection?

- To offer a coherent and representative selection of writings, that will assist students in their study of social policy (and teachers with preparation of lectures and seminar programmes).
- To stimulate critical thinking about the relationship between children and social policy and vice versa.
- To encourage students to question their assumptions about child welfare.
- To make students aware of the wide range of policies involving children.
- To broaden the student perspective on 'social policy'.
- To encourage students to look for continuities and discontinuities between theory and practice both within and between different policy arenas.

Having worked through the Reader, students (and their teachers) should:

- Be conversant with a number of approaches and concepts used by academics in analysing children in/and social policy.
- Be aware of the ramifications of social policy for children.
- Be able to identify a number of conceptual frameworks through which government and professionals perceive children in social policy.
- Be able to analyse such frameworks in so far as they constitute guides in the formulation of specific areas of policy areas.
- Be able to identify and understand different interpretations of children's 'best interests', and how such meanings are put together, and by whom.
- Be able to make comparisons – both empirical and theoretical – between different approaches to, and outcomes of, social policies involving children.
- Be able to assess the significance of children's voices in relevant policy areas.

Part 1: Child welfare: the historical background

Our ignorance of history causes us to slander our own times.
(Gustave Flaubert)

Can we learn from history? Probably not directly since the post-modern suspicion of anything resembling a 'grand narrative' seems to suggest that we find connecting with the 'the past' a somewhat confusing not to say obfuscatory experience, unless it can be cut and packaged as a televised 'History of Britain', a costume drama or on a visit to a heritage museum. When, however, we historians have our collective back to the ropes and the baying crowd is shouting at us to reveal the utilitarian value of History, we are apt to resort to a certain solemnity (critics would say pomposity) as, in the manner of one of those loveable but slightly irritating and ineffectual characters from a 19th-century novel, we inhale and, metaphorically speaking, rise towards the Heavens and begin to expound: "Well, you see, just as an individual without a memory would be insane, so, too, would be society. History is our collective memory: it helps us to know where we came from and how we came to be here. It offers us the opportunity to contemplate ourselves and, who knows, with 'reflexivity' in mind, perhaps to make improvements here and there. It gives us a point of reference for the future". By now, of course, the crowd has long since dispersed in order to watch the latest episode of a docu-soap.

But *does* History matter? In his famous novel, *The go-between* (1953), L.P. Hartley wrote: "The past is a foreign country. They do things differently there". These two historical chapters suggest that neither statement is necessarily wholly accurate. As Piper (Chapter One) and Hendrick (Chapter Two) show, many of our current interests and difficulties surrounding child welfare would not have been unfamiliar to earlier generations. Both authors provide us with something akin to an episodic diary, whereby not only may we trace journeys begun and abandoned, and travels made with little consequence on arrival, but also rediscover destinations that have changed the meaning and practice of social policy. If properly appreciated, such recollections can help us to understand the present as we bring to it a discriminatory perspective.

Around the end the end of the 18th century, in a kind of combined effort (although with differing emphases), Rousseau, the Romantics and the Evangelicals cast children into the Enlightenment melting pot and, from the standpoints of Nature, 'feeling' as virtue, and a belief in God's hold on redemption, identified childhood as a crucial stage in the evolution of the imaginative process; what in one sense has been termed 'human interiority' (Steedman, 1995; see also Coveney, 1967; Hendrick, in James and Prout, 1990/97; Andrews, 1994; Cunningham, 1995). While it is true that the antecedents of looking to children/childhood as a resource through which the adult life-trajectory might better be understood can be found prior to the 18th century, it is nevertheless around this time that we can date 'a new world for children' (Plumb, 1975; Cunningham, 1995, pp 41-60). During the late 18th-early 19th centuries, a series of 'agendas', moral and otherwise, concerning child labour, the 'Order of Nature' (code for patriarchal and familial relations), and the 'Self' in an industrialising world, began to be composed, often in an acute manner (Coveney, 1967; Cunningham, 1990; Andrews, 1994; Steedman, 1995; Berry, 1999). These agendas grew throughout the 1800s to a point where they became critical to the *apparently* larger questions of social class, gender and nation (Hendrick, in James and Prout, 1990/97; Hendrick, 1994; see also Piper, Chapter One). 'Apparently', because in the agonised debates and social and political upheavals that characterised so many of these years, groups of social reformers – often of a religious persuasion (including some far-sighted and self-interested employers and politicians) – came to think of 'childhood' as socially and politically significant in itself and, therefore, that children were far from being merely of incidental relevance to the social culture that helped to preserve society (New Labour may be the first government to put children at the *centre* of a social investment strategy, but it is by no means the first to use children for its own – and the Nation's ends – see below).

History, as is indicated in the chapters here, points towards the significance of fundamental 'cultural' paradigms such as 'the sanctity of the home', with its authoritarian predisposition, the ambivalence of 'Progress', the importance of soul-saving, and, not least, the Victorian ambiguity about children: were they figures of sensibility, or were they 'little savages' to be rescued and tamed? By the 1880s, following Taine's article 'On the acquisition of language by children' and Darwin's 'A biographical sketch of an infant', the Child Study movement was beginning to promote childhood as a key to unlocking the story of human development (Hendrick, 1990/97; Andrews, 1994; Wooldridge, 1995). We know that as the Victorian state evolved through the processes of industrialisation and urbanisation, so, too, did conceptions of the family and childhood in relation to, and this is the important point, the evolution of what by the closing decades of the century, was being referred to as 'the Nation'. The state of, say, the 1840s was not that of 1900. By the latter date, a partial democracy and imperialism sat, or rather posed, side-by-side, accompanied by all of their social and economic (not to say political) consequences. It was a period of fostering national identities, the outcome of which saw the invention of Englishness (Harris, 1993; Heathorn, 2000).

As these changes in culture and politics proceeded from the 1830s onwards, they were accompanied by an increasingly reflexive response – that is, an awareness of the spectre of uncertainty – on the part of individuals and institutions with regard to matters concerning in particular child labour, juvenile delinquency, compulsory schooling and, lastly, child protection (the 1889 Prevention of Cruelty to Children Act). Etched into this evolving child–adult relationship was the 'child-saving' impulse (in some respects, perhaps the social exclusion debate of its day), which would take children from the streets (and very often from their 'unsuitable' parents) and either institutionalise them or send them off to labour-hungry lands of the Empire (Rose, 1989). What is evident are the different uses – political, social, economic and cultural – to which children/childhood were put, both literally and metaphorically. This was done partly in order to assist in resolving anxieties arising from pressing political tensions associated with the creation of a liberal democracy – one area being 'social welfare', but also in order to understand and resolve a series of disputed relationships, personal, ideological and institutional, between: male and female, social classes, religion and atheism, and (a continuing theme today) the use of the child in the search for personal (adult) authenticity: 'the hero of my own life' (*David Copperfield*) – the first chapter of any autobiography (Hendrick, 1990/97 and 1994; Steedman, 1990/95; Andrews, 1994; Berry, 1999; on the desire to be a parent, a form of emotional 'authenticity', see Archard, 2003, pp 76-86).

Piper (Chapter One), for instance, through her focus on infanticide, the creation of the delinquent child, and the successful anti-cruelty campaigns of the 1880s, contrasts the struggles between reformers and politicians and considers the ways in which certain moral issues became embedded in political (and legal) arenas. During the course of these and other associated struggles, notions of 'innocence' and 'evil' evolved, as did political perceptions not only of what was the proper 'moral' approach to children, but also to their parents – thus shifting the boundaries between children, parents and the state (usually in favour of the latter), although always at pains not to undermine the cultural and political value of the family as a social form. Perhaps most significantly, Patriarchy changed its practice as legislation gradually forced fathers to concede more and more of their power over women and children to the law (Pinchbeck and Hewitt, 1973; Behlmer, 1982; for a clear examination of the current moral and political status of children, see Archard, 2003; see also Thomas, Chapter Nine). The so-called 'natural order', always hand in glove with power and authority, found it had to accommodate itself to new interests, not least those of an imperial Nation under threat from internal dissension and possibly urban degeneration, and economic and political competition from European rivals. Added to which was a certain anxiety about the hitherto endurable nature of Progress. By, say, 1900, Modernism (social and cultural), as "confusing multiplicity" (Jervis, 1998, p 10; also Hutcheon, 1989) and, therefore, the harbinger of self-doubt, was poised to unsettle old indubitabilities.

Hendrick's survey (Chapter Two) begins with a brief account of theoretical approaches to understandings of child welfare (some of which overlap with Piper), paying particular attention to the interplay of welfare activities in relation to children's bodies and minds and to the perception of children as victims and threats, often at one and the same time. The chapter, which then divides the period 1880-1990 into time-specific sections in order to provide a narrative of continuity and change in attitudes and policies, emphasises the importance of political agendas in shaping welfare reform. For example:

- the call for a programme of social amelioration for 'the children of the Nation' at a time of concern about the security of the Empire (1890s-early 1900s);

- the political controversies surrounding child health during the interwar Depression – a period of capitalism versus collectivism;
- the social elevation of the child in 'the family' in the post-war social democratic welfare state;
- the gradual disillusionment with that state as the 1960s ended and 'new' social problems appeared (often articulated in terms of gender, race, disability and sexuality), just as many of the older ones (notably poverty and the consequences of social inequality) were found to be still in existence.

What we see here are a number of recurring concerns/controversies around children, although rarely formulated in quite the same way (in other words, exhibiting features of discontinuity): the changing emphasis between body and mind, the child as human capital, as victim and as threat, as innocent and vulnerable, and as representational figures in the inter-war controversy concerning levels of malnutrition in areas of high unemployment. There is also evidence of further varying levels of discontinuity, as witnessed in the evolving relationship between children, the family and the state through legislation: 1889 Prevention of Cruelty to Children Act, and the Children Acts of 1908, 1948, 1975 and 1989. On the other hand it could be argued that this legislation is an expression of the continual search to resolve what is known as the 'liberal dilemma': "the unresolved problem is how child rearing can be made into a matter of public concern and its qualities monitored without destroying the ideal of the family as a counterweight to state power, a domain of voluntary self regulating actions" (Dingwall et al, 1983, p 214). A clearer example of discontinuity, influenced by medical and political experiences of the two world wars (aggression, totalitarianism, nervous breakdown, social psychiatry, creating a stable democracy), was the emergence and growth of the Child Guidance movement from the late 1920s onwards, with its emphasis on the child as a feeling subject, as much 'mind' as 'body', an individual, sensitive to wishes and anxieties (Thom, 1992; Urwin and Sharland, 1992). This identity was more or less officially recognised in the 1948 Act (Hendrick, 1994, 2003).

The desire to better understand children and childhood was even more apparent by the 1960s, with the beginning of a Children's Rights campaign, in the progressive tendency within primary education, and in a continuing willingness to adopt a liberal 'treatment', rather than punitive, approach to juvenile delinquency (although the party political urge to be seen to be 'tough on crime' was never far beneath the surface). The rediscovery of child physical and sexual abuse in the 1970s and 1980s, which was accompanied by moral panics (Parton, 1985), and the contemporaneous debates surrounding relations between children, state and family (Fox Harding, 1997), helped to destroy the post-war consensus in social politics (Parton, 1991) and culminated in the 1989 Children Act, much proclaimed by its admirers, although it has hardly lived up to all or even many of their expectations (Hendrick, 1993; see also Roche, Chapter Twelve).

Perhaps the fundamental issue governing the post-1960s relationship between children and social policy can be expressed as the 'failure' of the welfare state to produce the harmonious society, free of poverty, vice and conflict – some would say the failure was in fact the result of the *success* of that state in reducing gross poverty, ill health, and economic inequality so that citizens' expectations rose to a level beyond what the political system could or was willing to provide. Whatever the cause, the post-war 'consensus', heralded by a chorus of complaints, eventually collapsed into factions, as it witnessed the erosion of the concept of 'the public' in favour of, as Mrs Thatcher famously expressed it, "individuals and their families". The 'classic' welfare state had sought in its own muddled and somewhat hypocritical manner to defend the weak (including children). From the end of the 1970s no such illusion prevailed; for much of the time the weak were left to their own devices, and so child poverty rates in Britain increased from 10% in 1979 to 35% in 1998/99 – it is important to understand that children become 'poor' by virtue of their *parents'* economic situation, that is, they live in households with incomes less than 50% of the average equivalent income (on 'familialisation' and child poverty, see Skevik, Chapter Nineteen and Platt, Chapter Twenty; see also Daniel and Ivatts, 1998; Bradshaw, 2002).

Both of these historical chapters suggest that 'the past' is neither 'a foreign country', nor do they always 'do things differently there'. Angst is not the privilege of late-modernity! As to the value of history, Gerda Lerner, one of the most inspiring of the American feminist historical school, has written:

> History is not a recipe book; past events are never replicated in the present in quite the same way. Historical events are infinitely variable and their interpretations are a constantly shifting process. There are no certainties to be found in the past.... [However] ... We can learn from history how past generations thought and acted, how they responded to the demands of their time and how they solved their problems. We can learn by analogy, not by example, for our circumstances will always be different than theirs were. The main thing history can teach us is that human actions have consequences and that certain choices, once made, cannot be undone. They foreclose the possibility of making other choices and thus they determine future events. (Lerner, 1997, pp 199-213)

It is this matter of 'human actions' and 'certain choices' – à la *condition humaine* – that occupies (so problematically) the centre-point of social policy in its role as a forum for the working out of 'moral agendas': of what it means to act ethically and, therefore, it might be worth keeping in mind how our forebears tried and very often failed in this endeavour, but not always.

Moral campaigns for children's welfare in the nineteenth century

Christine Piper

As the clouds of pessimism gathered in the late 1980s and 1990s, it was increasingly accepted that there was an historical legacy that needed to be better understood. (Cox, 1996, p 4)[1]

Introduction

The construction of child abuse and, in particular, child sexual abuse, as a major social problem in the last quarter of the 20th century has led to renewed interest in historical material about child abuse and neglect. In particular, it has stimulated a re-examination of what have been referred to as 'moral campaigns' against child cruelty which occurred in the 19th century. The implication of that title is that what was happening to children was morally wrong – an evil to be eradicated. Several generations of school children have therefore learnt about children climbing chimneys, going down mines, working in factories and living on the streets, and of the efforts of people such as Lord Shaftesbury, Mary Carpenter and Dr Barnardo to give them homes and improve their conditions of work, or to remove them from employment or imprisonment. A quotation from a children's book of the 1950s gives the flavour of this approach:

> Many of the changes in our lives have been made not by rulers or statesmen but by reformers – men and women who realised that something was seriously wrong and who strove to set it right....
>
> In the early factories the workers were badly treated. Men, women and even young children were forced to toil for many hours each day in dreadful conditions. Two great reformers led the way to overcoming these evils. Lord Shaftesbury got laws passed limiting the hours and regulating the conditions of work: Robert Owen ran his factory on humane lines, and encouraged cooperative enterprise rather than competition. (*Odhams Encyclopaedia for children*, c 1954, p 204)

Study of those campaigns has, therefore, until relatively recently, been in a liberal historical tradition which, beginning with the historians of the Enlightenment, had focused on cause and consequence[2]. Historians with that approach looked for signs of progress, analysed who was responsible for achieving the reforms and assumed that, as knowledge accumulated within the historical period under review, there would be further progress towards a possible utopia where all evils were overcome. The assimilation of Marxist and sociological approaches to historical research led only to a change of emphasis from individual agents to those economic conditions which facilitated or provoked change and those class- and gender-based interests through which change occurred[3]. Questions of how and why certain actions were labelled evil and why there was a focus on a particular evil at any point in time continued to be begged. The influence on historical research of postmodernism – with its undermining of optimism and the role of 'grand theory' – was therefore immense[4].

In particular, analysis of time- and place-specific discourses which constrain and mould patterns of thought (as exemplified by the work of Foucault)[5] and the work of sociologists of deviance (who focused on responses to 'nonconforming' behaviour as defining that behaviour) have allowed of very different interpretations of the nature of moral campaigns against child cruelty in the 19th century. Research such as that of Becker (1963) and Gusfield (1963)[6] introduced a focus on the processes by which evil and morality themselves were constructed: what is right or wrong at any point in time could no longer be taken for granted. The nature of the analytical exercise then becomes that of constructing contemporary meanings for the terms 'moral crusades' and 'moral entrepreneurs' and defining the nature and influence of the 'moral' element as it relates to the focus for reform. As a result, my aim is not to determine whether humanitarian reformers and religious zeal *or* economic change determined the nature, timing and outcome of the 'crusades' in the relation to the welfare of children. This chapter is a more modest exercise. Its aim is to find out what (and why) particular moral truths were being constructed and drawn upon to influence outcomes in relevant decades.

There is now historical material available to answer this question: the genesis of, and moral frameworks for, both institutionalised philanthropic activity and legislation addressing the welfare of children in the Victorian and Edwardian periods have been analysed from several standpoints. Current interest in the origins of concern about child abuse has generated further documentary research on individuals and societies campaigning against child cruelty at the end of the 19th century. Theoretical interest in forms of social control and regulation has led to analysis (using notions of normalisation and tutelage) of the role of 'lady visitors' and, later, health visitors, school medical inspections and delinquency prevention projects, for example. This particular focus has led to a concentration (for example, in the work of Eekelaar and Dingwall[7]) on the effect of such intervention on the distinction between the public and the private. Writers such as Becker (1963) and Platt (1969) have researched responses to juvenile deviance to analyse class-based moralities and struggles to confirm status. More recently, material from these periods has been plundered, particularly by those writing under the aegis of the Institute of Economic Affairs, to explain the nature of Victorian values and virtues, or the advantages of charitable rather than state organisation of 'welfare' (for example, Himmelfarb, 1995 and Whelan, 1996). In addition, work on concepts of childhood (Stainton Rogers and Stainton Rogers, 1992; Cunningham, 1995; Cox, 1996) and on children's rights (Freeman, 1983; Archard, 1993) offer new perspectives on the wealth of material in standard sociological histories of childhood, notably Pinchbeck and Hewitt (1969, 1973).

What this chapter aims to do is to use the insights provided by these different approaches to analyse in more detail the nature of the moral agendas being pursued, and to identify more clearly different historical perceptions of how children were being 'wronged': what did reformers construct as 'seriously wrong' and who were the 'enemies' of children that the reformers were fighting? This chapter, therefore, seeks to disaggregate the perceived consensual Victorian moral agenda for the improvement of the welfare of children and to show how far and in what ways the 'wrongs' to be put right related to perceived moral needs of the reformers and society as well as identified wrongs done to children.

The visible Victorian child

It would be quite misleading to suggest that the child was ignored and invisible before the 19th century. However, the development of ideas of innocence and malleability in connection with children replacing, at least to an extent, a concept of original sin, together with a much clearer sense of the separation of childhood and adulthood, led to a greater focus on the role of childhood and to the treatment of children[8]. In that sense, as Behlmer points out, "the mid-Victorian generation gave unprecedented attention to children and the problems facing them" (Behlmer, 1982, p 3). The image of the child which resulted was a sentimental image of a child who was frequently portrayed as a vulnerable victim. Behlmer draws attention particularly to the work of Charles Dickens for images of children as "reservoirs of sensitivity" and to the speeches of Lord Shaftesbury for examples of what he refers to as the "politics of pathos" (ibid). The popular pictures of children – even those of children who had not been neglected – are images of children who are especially sensitive and often physically weak. As Hendrick (1994) argues, by the last quarter of the 19th century the focus of philanthropic and state attention was on the body (as opposed to the mind) of the child, but the image of the child which had by then become authoritative was one which evoked the physical fragility of the child – the reverse of the developing image of the 'muscular Christian' adult male.

These weak, sensitive, vulnerable children have no 'voice' of their own, however. Elizabeth Barrett Browning's *The cry of the children* (1843)[9], Andrew Mearn's *The bitter cry of outcast London* (1883) and John Spargo's *The bitter cry of the children* ([1906] 1969)[10] all evoke an image of those who silently 'cry'; who are victims because they have no ability or power to articulate 'aloud' their needs[11]. The powerlessness of the child is what, paradoxically, gives the image such power. As Sadler expressed it, when urging support for the 1832 Ten Hours Bill, "I wish I could bring a group of these little ones to [the] bar [of the House of Commons] – I am sure their silent appearance would plead more forcibly in their behalf than the loudest eloquence"[12].

Childhood had not only become accepted as a separate and different first stage of life but the concern, as Cunningham points out, became one which focused on "children without a childhood"[13]. Before the 1880s the powerful images of the victim/child were those of children who were both most visibly and most publicly being denied a childhood – children who were 'outside' the family because they were working in factories and mines. The existence of large numbers of such children was a relatively new development[14] resulting from industrialisation. Social and economic developments which are both new and visible provoke fear: a notable example occurred in Tudor times. The existence of a new class of wandering landless labourers in the 16th century caused widespread panic reflected in the first two lines of a nursery rhyme – 'Hark, hark, the dogs do bark,/The beggars are coming to town' – and became a major influence on the nature of Poor Law legislation. By the early 19th century, industrialisation was similarly being feared as a force which threatened to destroy rural life and family-, or quasi-family-centred life, which people knew and understood[15]. As 'moral panic' theorists have made clear[16], where such social fear of changing conditions exists there is receptive ground for those who argue for action against a perceived resulting evil. Those campaigning in the early and middle part of the 19th century to better the lives of children therefore tackled what was the most easily seen evil – that produced by the workplace, particularly the new workplaces[17] which put children beyond the reach of protection by their parents. Not only that, the evil was two-headed: the potential or actual harm to children was both physical and moral. The new workplaces were seen as the source of deprivation and depravity.

And so legislation to protect children first dealt with apprentices, servant girls, chimney sweeps and then factory owners[18]. Nor did agitation for, or implementation of, such employment legislation cease when the main focus of concern later became that of cruelty to children in the home. Concern with the protection of children from the cruelties inflicted by capitalism continued throughout the century: in the 20 years after the inaugural meeting of the Liverpool Society for the Prevention of Cruelty to Children, in 1883, were passed the 1887 Coal Mines and Stratified Ironstone Mines Amendment Act, the Factory and Workshop Amending Acts of 1891 and 1901, the 1892 Shop Hours Act, the 1900 Mines (Prohibition of Child Labour Underground) Act and the 1903 Employment (Children) Act.

The same concern was apparent in other jurisdiction facing similar stages of industrialisation. For example, the introduction to *The bitter cry of the children* (Spargo [1906] 1969) pointed out that the aim of the book's author – a Cornishman who had emigrated to the US – was "to make us see that 'this great nation in its commercial madness devours its babes'". This image of 'babes' is invoked throughout his book, although the author is referring to the 1.7 million children and young people under 16 who were gainfully employed according to the 1900 Census in the US, rather than to 'babies' as the late 20th century would use the term. Again the image is of a child so physically weak and dependent that 'babe' is an appropriate image.

This idea of physical dependency, in conjunction with the 'urban disenchantment' which Platt discusses in relation to influences on 19th-century images of North American children (Platt, 1969, pp 36-43), fed also into ideas of the inherent evil of the very streets which children outside the family experience[19].

What emerged was the idea that children should not be publicly visible: that it is wrong to allow a child to act as an adult, either by working in particular places or by being 'independent' on the streets – an idea which is still powerful in relation to campaigns to protect 'street children' in developing countries[20].

That the protection of children from the evils of employment was a priority for reformers, and subsequently for the state, from the end of the 18th century is, therefore, relatively understandable. The more difficult questions are why intervention in the family to protect children occurred as late as it did and why it occurred to protect delinquent children earlier than abused children. Here there is a problem, for my purposes, with some of the literature. The aim, for example, of the analysis by Dingwall et al (1984) of the historical origins of legislation relating to child care and protection is to specify which motives (of campaigners and/or the government) explain satisfactorily the introduction, passage and implementation of legislation. They therefore draw particularly, as does Hendrick (1994), on the apparently dichotomous images of the child as victim or threat, and focus on the importance of the moral socialisation of children in a liberal state.

The fear of inadequate socialisation of children was undoubtedly an impetus for reform throughout the 19th century: the comments of factory and child welfare reformers make that clear.

> The saving of the industrial child reflects a moral concern: the presence of women and children in industry was repeatedly linked to *their* depravity. The picture of vice and indecency in factories and mines was drawn as much to point to the dangers of a demoralised working class ... as to protest on behalf of child victims. (Cannan, 1992, p 53)

The motivations of politicians would of necessity include concern for the future needs of the state: "Children were thought to be unformed enough to be saveable. The represented the future" (Cunningham, 1995, p 135). But as Gordon points out in her study of the Massachusetts' Society for the Prevention of Cruelty to Children,

> The fit between child-saving and other social anxieties was an historical fact, not a causal explanation. Their concern about children was not merely a mask for intervention whose 'real' purposes were other.... However, their own values and anxieties made that cruelty more visible and disturbing than it had once been. (Gordon, 1988, p 30)

This suggests that it may be both unhelpful and impossible to try and disentangle motivations to decide whether the concern was for the unhappy child per se or for the future demoralised citizen. Instead, my focus will be on isolating those particular anxieties that allowed for shifts in the Victorian moral framework held by those classes whose support in the passage and implementation of legislation was crucial. The rest of this chapter will look more closely at the campaigns responding to child criminality (culminating in the 1857 Industrial Schools Act) and to cruelty to infants and children (culminating in the 1872 Infant Life Preservation Act and the 'anti-cruelty' Act of 1889) to see how significant shifts occurred in the 1850s and 1880s. Why did a concern for the effective moral socialisation of children lead to different successful campaigns at different times? Dingwall et al said of the industrial schools movement: "For reasons which are not altogether clear ... there was no major legislation until the middle of the century" (1984, p 215). To shed light on those reasons it is helpful to start with a look at why legislation to protect children from cruelty within their families did not reach the statute book until the end of the 1880s.

The lesser of two evils?

The assumption has been made that parental abuse was at this time simply constructed as excessive discipline[21] and was therefore not considered evil. Recent research would suggest that this is not true: there was acknowledgement that domestic abuse occurred by the mid-19th century and violence in the family was no longer being constructed socially as normal. Pollock's analysis of newspaper accounts of prosecutions of parents for cruelty suggests they were not uncommon in the period 1784 to 1860, and she quotes magisterial comment which explicitly rebuts the idea that "the father had a right to do as he pleased" (Pollock, 1983, pp 62-4[22]). It was therefore something to be denounced and one example of such denunciation was the 1853 Act for Better Prevention of Aggravated Assaults although, as Behlmer points out, it was used more to protect women: research shows little evidence of prosecution of offenders under this Act in regard to assaults on children.

The evil of cruelty to children within the family was apparent before the 1880s. Within the context of moral imperatives for action, therefore, the answer appears simple – interfering with parents' rights was at that time constructed as a greater evil than that of child abuse. What is often quoted in support of this conclusion is the reply of Lord Shaftesbury in 1871 to a letter asking for his support for legislation to protect children from parental cruelty, in which he wrote

> the evils you state are enormous and indisputable, but they are of so private, internal and domestic a character as to be beyond the reach of legislation, and the subject, indeed, would not, I think, be entertained by either House of Parliament[23].

The same attitude is apparent in those philanthropists responding to family poverty. For example, the 1889 Annual Report of the Charity Organisation Society said "everything should be done to help distress in such a way that it does not become a matter rather of public than of private concern" and C.S. Loch, who was appointed honorary secretary of the COS in 1875, wrote, "not to give arms but to keep alive the saving health of the family becomes its problem"[24].

Those who, in support of the moral necessity of family autonomy, suggested the state had never interfered in the family were of course wrong, as Pinchbeck and Hewitt point out when quoting Cooke Taylor's comment of 1874: "That unit, the family, is the unit upon which a constitutional Government has been raised which is the administration and envy of mankind. Hitherto, whatever the laws have touched, they have not invaded this sacred precinct…" (Pinchbeck and Hewitt, 1973, p 359).

The state had intervened to restrict or remove the rights of the parents and guardians of both rich and poor children via the wardship powers of the courts and the duties of the Poor Law Authorities. Restrictions on the parental rights of the economically dependent clearly did not 'count'[25]. Parental cruelty to children was therefore simply not wicked enough to balance out the evils of interference with parental control and, particularly, of interference with the rights of a wage-earning father.

On one level this appears quite incomprehensible to the late 20th-century mind because religion no longer has the authority which it had for the Victorians. The prevalent Victorian Christian religious truth was that the father is the 'natural' head of the family, and that he requires the moral, religious and actual authority of that position to ensure the family is run as a unit which transmits the moral values of society. This divinely ordered system would achieve the welfare of the greatest number of children and families. Without unfettered power and responsibility to organise and discipline for the good of the family, the father could not fulfil that role properly: it was therefore seen as too dangerous to risk intervening in families to investigate abuse of the parental power.

The Victorian moral crusaders were part of a society that took this particular system of morality for granted. When these crusaders spoke of the need to change people's ideas in order to protect the child, they spoke within a system of morality that was taken as unchallengeable. It would therefore be wrong to assume that, until the 1880s, those campaigning to eradicate the evils of child abuse were frustrated by a system of morality to which they did not subscribe[26]. They upheld the need for an autonomous family unit as essential to the moral health of the nation.

That the crusaders so constrained themselves is clear from the following speech in the House of Commons by Lord Ashley[27] (later Lord Shaftesbury) in 1844. He discussed child labour before moving on to the question of female labour, referring to the report of the Medical Officer of Stockport which stated that "it has been the practice in mills, gradually to dispense with the labour of males". He then made the following point which I will extract at some length:

> But listen to another fact and one deserving of serious attention; that the females not only perform the labour but occupy the places of men; they are forming various clubs and associations, and gradually acquiring all those privileges which are held to be the proper portion of the male sex…. Here is a dialogue which occurred in one of these clubs, from an eyewitness: 'A man came into one of these clubrooms, with a child in his arms; "Come lass," said he addressing one of the single women, "come home for I cannot keep this bairn quiet, and the other one I have left

crying at home": "I won't go home, idle devil", she replied, "I have thee to keep and the bairns too, and if I can't get a pint of ale quietly, it is tiresome.... I won't go home yet"'. Whence is it that this singular and unnatural change is taking place? Because that on women are imposed the duty and burden of supporting their husbands and family, a perversion as it were of nature, which has the inevitable effect of introducing into families disorder, insubordination and conflict....

No, Sir, these sources of mischief must be dried up; every public consideration demands such an issue, the health of the females; the care of their families; their conjugal and parental duties; the comfort of their homes; the decency of their lives; the rights of their husbands; the peace of society; and the laws of God[28].

The thoroughly interwoven mix of all the themes deemed necessary to the established social and moral order makes more understandable the fear and trepidation provoked by even the possibility that one of those constituent parts could be undermined and the whole edifice crumble. The issue of infanticide, however, did not provoke such fears.

Infanticide

The visible Victorian child was vulnerable and weak – the more dependent and innocent the more influential the image – but that factor alone cannot explain 'the discovery' of infanticide and the successful passage of the 1872 Infant Life Protection Act with its apparent focus on children when they are most dependent on parents. What the campaigners saw as seriously wrong were the births and deaths of infants which took place in very particular circumstances where regulation posed no serious challenge to the autonomy of the 'normal' family. According to the supporters of the legislation, babies needed protection against the immoral behaviour of those women – often single and unmarried – who left their (illegitimate) babies with 'baby farmers'[29], and also against the commercial nurses themselves. Those who opposed the original Bill that was placed before Parliament did so because it would also have caught in its net nurses in manufacturing districts who took children for the day, in other words, childminders who took in children of parents living in the type of unit defined as 'a family'. This would, as the National Society for Women's Suffrage expressed it, "interfere in a most mischievous and oppressive way with domestic arrangements" (Pinchbeck and Hewitt, 1973, p 617[30]). Therefore, pressure from women to preserve their traditional authority over 'mothering' gained strength from, and further buttressed, notions of family autonomy:

The responsibility for the child in infancy as in later life, lies with [parents], and we emphatically deny that the State has any right to dictate to them the way it shall be fulfilled ... the State should forbear to limit their perfect freedom in this, as in all matters connected with the rearing and maintaining of families. (The Committee for Amending the Law in Points where it is Injurious to Women, quoted in Pinchbeck and Hewitt, 1973, p 618)

As a result, the Bill was limited in its scope to those children under one year old who were 'boarded out' for more than 24 hours[31]. In this campaign the construction of the enemy of children had been successfully confined to those who did not live in normal families. The prevalent morality still did not allow of it being defined as seriously wrong for 'normal' parents to use childminders whose standards of care might be seriously deficient.

Moral abuse: the delinquent child

The focus on the factory child and the minded/fostered baby had generally not required prosecutions against parents. Parents continued to be seen as the protectors, not the enemies, of children. Constructing the child as a victim of a known evil such as parental cruelty was insufficient if intervention threatened the dominant moral system. Something more was required: a threat to the moral system itself – an evil within the system emanating from the family unit that was greater than the threat posed by intervening in that family. This indeed occurred when parents were constructed as 'wicked' *specifically* because they were making their children wicked[32]. In other words, the image of the child was of one who was the victim of the parent, not because of physical and emotional harm done to him, but because of the moral evil inflicted on the child. In this sense constructing the child as evil does, not, of itself, bar that child from victim status, because that evil is not the child's fault: innocence is imputed to him because his depravity is a result of his deprivation of proper paternal moral authority and control, and because that depravity is no longer seen as unchangeable[33]. The harm that the child is being protected from is the possibility that the child will be made permanently evil. As a result it became morally acceptable that the father who is not exerting proper moral control over his children should forfeit his paternal rights to control those children.

This shift in thinking about morality occurred over a number of years: major philanthropic societies with programmes to respond to juvenile criminality (or the risk of it) had been formed in 1788 and 1815 but parliamentary Bills based on their programmes failed in the 1820s (see Dingwall et al, 1984, p 214ff). The social anxiety which acted to quicken the pace of the moral shift was the fact that the 1840s was a period of political instability. As the historian Kitson-Clarke states, "[Industrialization] had brought insecurity to all: by 1840 the bounding prosperity which the new industry had conferred had largely disappeared" (Kitson-Clarke, 1962, p 88). Recovery began in the 1850s but the events of the 1840s – Chartist agitation, revolutions in several European states in 1848, the repeal of the Corn Laws, the Irish famine and subsequent Irish immigration into England – had facilitated the idea that it was morally justifiable to intervene in the family to remove children deemed at risk of (re-)offending, and to send such children to industrial schools for training. Similarly, convicted young offenders were seen to need reformatories – to compensate for the lack of moral training by their parents – rather than penal establishments. The shift was also justified in relation to the moral health of the abuser: "The evil was as much the spiritual harm which befell the abusers as the physical or moral damage sustained by their victims" (Dingwall et al, 1984, p 218).

What this shift led to was a series of Industrial School Acts, 1857-1889[34], to save children from being taught to be immoral in their families or on the streets, and to impose substitute parental discipline. Such schools could be eligible for grants from public funds. Similarly the 1854 Youthful Offenders Act[35] made reformatory schools an alternative to adult prisons and houses of correction for juvenile offenders, and gave the voluntary societies who established and managed reformatories powers of compulsion over such children. This moral shift by the 1850s did not, however, justify the removal of children who had been physically abused by their parents: the fear of causing moral harm to the family by intervention weighed more heavily in the balance than the evil of parental cruelty.

What moral agenda explains the success of the cruelty campaigns in the 1880s?

> There is some dispute about the background to the anti-cruelty movement.... (Dingwall et al, 1984, p 218)

The moral system of the 1850s to 1870s allowed no moral justification for intervention in the family against physical cruelty. When Dingwall et al refer to the 'neglected continuities' between the campaign for factory laws and the campaign against family cruelty (Dingwall et al, 1984, p 218) they give a misleading impression. Certainly there were continuities of personnel in campaigns to prevent animal and child cruelty[36] but attention to these 'slack resources' (of 'spare' campaigners) sheds light only on how, technically, reform could be accomplished, not on how, morally, it became a social and political possibility. Morally, thinking in regard to the balancing of evils could be transformed in two ways: by a reduction in the moral authority of the traditional Victorian family; and by an increase in the 'volume' of evil which child abuse signified. The latter possibility has been refuted in so far as it relies on a false assumption that domestic violence was not seen as 'wrong' until the 1880s. However, the physical condition of children had become more visible (to the state's teachers and inspectors) since the 1870 Education Act, which led to the setting up of 'Board' (that is, state) elementary schools[37]. 'Unsocialised' children were also more visible to other parents: "The rakings of the human cesspool are brought into the school room and mixed up with your children.... Childish innocence is very beautiful; but the bloom is soon destroyed"[38].

As regards the former possibility, Behlmer's thesis is that respect for family integrity and paternal authority was still widespread and strong in the 1880s, and so the reason for the growth in the acceptability of intervention against parental cruelty has to be found elsewhere (Behlmer, 1982, ch 3)[39]. He provides evidence that belief in the 'sanctity of the home' was not weakening, citing literature on moral improvement in the later Victorian period which places the home at the centre of social and religious life. In 1849 John Ruskin had written, "Our God is a household God as well as a heavenly one. He has an altar in every man's dwelling"[40]. In 1883 similar sentiments were still being published:

> Estimate the healing, comforting, purifying, elevating influence which is ever flowing from the fountain, and you will understand the sacred ministry of the home to the higher culture of mankind. It is a mighty restraint of the selfish passions. It is the centrifugal force which continually widens the orbit of life, and bears us into the light of distant suns[41].

Indeed, the furore over the 1906 Education (Provision of Meals) Act, 23 years after the above was written, testifies to the continuing strength of the belief in the moral importance of family autonomy. The Charity Organisation Society, for example, denounced the proposal in its report, 'The better way of assisting school children'[42].

> It is better, in the interests of the community, to allow ... the sins of the parents to be visited on the children, than to impair the principle of the solidarity of the family and run the risk of permanently demoralising large numbers of the population by the offer of free meals to their children[43].

Instead, an understanding of how changes in perceptions of the moral framework became possible in the 1880s must focus on the social anxiety and the national moral crisis. First, from 1875 onwards, as in the decade before the passing of the first Industrial Schools Act, an economic recession led to perceptions of social and political instability. These social anxieties should not be underestimated. Historically, recessions had been accompanied by riots (for example, in the 1810s and 1840s) and the 1880s themselves saw popular disturbances.

This social anxiety was also again linked to specific fears about urbanisation. As Hendrick points out[44], "There was the 'condition of England' question, first raised in the 1830s and 1840s, and rediscovered in the 1880s" (Hendrick, 1994, p 50). The worst excesses of early urbanisation had been ameliorated by legislation about housing, sanitation and public health but the increased geographical segregation of the rich and the poor which had occurred by the 1880s meant that the poorest lived in slums far removed from the dwellings of the rich; the 'distant' urban masses were more frightening than known neighbours. A later development (by the end of the century) feeding into this pre-existent fear was eugenics (see Behlmer, 1982, p 204). The result was that the urban poor perceived as a threat became labelled as 'a race apart', as 'the submerged tenth', and the areas of the United Kingdom in which they lived referred to as 'Darkest England'[45].

Anxiety was also engendered because of a relatively sudden loss of faith in 'progress'. Environmental measures had been passed in the belief that such legislation, given time, would 'solve' the social problems. It appeared that they would not. As a result, "The environmentalism which had such an influence over social reform in mid-century began to give way again to a revived evangelicalism which emphasised depravity rather than deprivation" (Cox, 1996, p 149). There was a sense that change must occur: "We have made for ourselves strange gods, and we live in a state of transition to a yet unknown order", wrote Escott in 1885 in his introduction to *England: Her people, polity and pursuits*[46].

These various social and political anxieties prompted the construction of intervention in the family as a lesser evil than undermining the entire moral framework of society which is what might happen unless selected families were regulated. The moral role of the family – feeding as it did into religion, social order, the health of a democracy and, therefore, the economic and political well-being of the country – became too important to leave to the family. A gradual reconstruction of the particular moral order to which the Victorians had been committed had occurred sufficiently by the end of the 1880s for the 'undisciplined' family (in which child abuse could happen and criminality could be encouraged) to be perceived as one which produced a moral imperative to intervene in that family[47]. Where life in particular families was not in practice sacred and moral, whether its immorality was evidenced by moral or physical abuse of children, it was no longer deemed to carry moral authority:

> The cruelties he warned against were unseen, ... and public feeling resented any invasion of what was considered the sanctity of the home. To change this feeling it was necessary to show how little of the sacredness of family life existed among the more depraved, and the manner in which a man exercised his right to do what he would with his own. (Said of Benjamin Waugh, the congregational minister who became honorary secretary of the London Society for the Prevention of Cruelty to Children in Tuckwell, 1894)[48]

This process of focusing on how moral authority was exercised was one which absorbed, and was accelerated by, a redefining of Christian duty in relation to children. The 1886 NSPCC tract, *The child of the English savage*, added a particular gloss on the innocence of childhood: "of all [God's] creatures [the child] is the most like Himself in its early purity, beauty, brightness and innocence" and so, by harming a child the Christian failed in his religious duty (Behlmer, 1982, p 87).

The general anxiety that moral structures were failing and that drastic action was necessary for the greater good allowed for a rebalancing of evils. The outcome of this rebalancing was never a foregone conclusion: the draft anti-cruelty Bill produced by the London SPCC in 1886 did not receive Home Office sponsorship; the first Bill presented to parliament in August 1888 met extensive opposition and was withdrawn despite the fact that the NSPCC did not support it because it was too weak a measure; the eventually successful Bill was sponsored by Mundella in February 1889 but, when passed, incorporated amendments[49]. Nevertheless, agitation did culminate in the Act for the Prevention of Cruelty to and Better Protection of Children in 1889. The NSPCC, in its report for 1895-96, looking back to the passage of that Act, said that "it was nothing less than a national education which was undertaken ... it was a crusade primarily to the intellect of the nation, preaching the existence and magnitude of the work to be done for needlessly suffering children". When the Act was strengthened in further legislation in 1894, Lord Herschell, speaking in the House of Lords on the Bill, said "there was not a few who at that time entertained some apprehensions with regard to entrusting powers so large – fears were expressed lest it might involve so much interference with parental control as to lead to dangerous results"[50].

Later legislation in relation to child welfare and protection depended for its success on the same moral balancing exercise, although, as mentioned above, the social and political anxiety was heightened by a belief that "The problem of the child is the problem of the race"[51]; that

> Children thus hungered, thus housed, and thus left to grow up as best they can without being fathered or mothered, are not, educate them as you will, exactly the most promising material for the making of the future citizens and rulers of the Empire. (Booth, 1890, pp 65-6)

Lord Rosebery's call for a party of 'National Efficiency' was based on this belief that "in the rookeries and slums which still survive, an imperial race cannot be reared"[52]. This fear increased at the time of the Boer War in England. To quote Spargo:

> In England the high infantile mortality has occasioned much alarm and caused forth much agitation. There is a world of pathos and rebuke in the grim truth that the knowledge that is becoming increasingly difficult to get suitable recruits for the army and navy has stirred the nation in a way that the fate of the children themselves and their inability to become good and useful citizens could not do.... No figures can adequately represent the meaning of this phase of the problem which has been so picturesquely named 'race suicide'. Only by gathering them all into one vast throng would it be possible to conceive vividly the immensity of this annual slaughter of the babies in a Christian land. (Spargo [1906] 1969, pp 9, 10)

The concerns of the Edwardians, therefore, moved on from parental cruelty to issues of child poverty, education, hygiene and diet, but these new moral agendas for the early 20th century cannot be pursued within the confines of this chapter.

Conclusion

Victorians campaigning for the welfare of children were driven by two sets of moral needs: needs stemming from their own personal and political anxieties, and also the perceived needs of selected children. For much of the century their motivation to improve the morality and personal responsibility of the poor and their children was religious. As late as 1890, William Booth, for example, in a chapter entitled 'On the verge of the abyss', asserted, "at the risk of being misunderstood", that "it is primarily and mainly for the sake of saving the soul that I seek the salvation of the body". By the end of the century religious duty was joined by social guilt as a motivation for action. Simey, in her analysis of philanthropy in 19th-century Liverpool, has referred to the period 1875 to 1890 as one of 'Personal Service', when "[t]his sense of guilt was a new element in the relationship between rich and poor" (Simey, 1951)[53].

With these normal imperatives to act the campaigners designated particular harms to children – cruelty by the owners of factories, mines and baby nurseries, by single mothers and by fathers of delinquent children – as wrongs which required state-backed action at least partly because the morals of the children were also at risk. Intervention to prevent and punish physical cruelty required, therefore, a very radical shift in thinking. Parents themselves had to be seen as the enemies of children and the state, and voluntary organisations seen as their saviours. Such a shift in thinking has had far-reaching consequences for 20th-century family policy. Once it had become possible to label particular parents as the source of the harm suffered by their child, then the way was open for other harms to justify not only intervention in the family but also the rescue of children from other sources of harm. Despite the refocusing on parental responsibility in the last quarter of the 20th century, there is no longer social and governmental reticence in blaming parents for harms inflicted on, and by, their children.

Notes

[1] The context for this quotation is an introductory chapter on 'The child in history' and, in particular, a discussion of historical perceptions of children, rather than the experiences of children in different historical periods.

[2] For further discussion, see Tosh (1995, p 114).

[3] So, for example, Carson (1974) analysed the genesis of the 19th-century Factory Acts through a study of the employer interest in productivity and healthier employees. Feminist historians looked at the role of male trade unions in seeking reform of working conditions for women and children, which would, as a side-product, increase the male wage and further improve the terms of employment for men.

[4] For further discussion, see Tosh (1995, pp 178-9).

[5] At its simplest, a discourse is a social process in which, through language (used in its broadest sense to include all semiotic systems) we makes sense of the world around us, but also the process by which the world makes sense to us. (Cox, 1996, p 6, referring to O'Sullivan et al, 1994)

[6] Becker's research looked at responses to marijuana users, dealing specifically with moral crusaders/entrepreneurs in chapter 8; Gusfield researched the Prohibition movement in the USA, discussing 'status politics' in chapter 7, where he focuses on the meaning inherent in political action and discourse.

[7] For example, Eekelaar et al (1982); Dingwall et al (1984, 1995).

[8] The first wave of evangelical reformers – from the end of the 18th century – were, as Hendrick points out, "the foremost in an appreciation of the importance of childhood". In particular, he quotes Hannah More, a founder of the Sunday School movement: "Where are the half-naked, poor, forlorn, wretched, ignorant creatures we used to find lying about on Sunday…?" (Hendrick, 1994, p 8).

[9] Referred to by Behlmer (1982, p 3) and Cunningham (1995, p 143). The latter text excerpts a verse of that poem, the last two lines of which are: "They are weeping in the playtime of the others,/ In the Country of the free".

[10] Originally published in the USA and reprinted in 1969.

[11] This elision of victim and voiceless statuses is not simply a product of Victorian sentimentality: those pressing for 'rights' for victims of crime in the 1980s and 1990s have also constructed the lack of voice as a key element of victim status. See, for example, Sarat (1997).

[12] *Memoirs of the life and writings of Michael Thomas Sadler, MP, FRS, &c,* 337/379 1842, excerpted on page 102 of Ward (1970).

[13] The phrase used by Douglas Jerrold, one of the founders of *Punch,* in 1840 to describe factory children. Quoted by Cunningham (1995, p 144).

[14] This is not an entirely accurate statement in that the 'sending away' of children, of all classes, to work in the households of relatives or strangers was a common occurrence in earlier centuries, notably the 16th and 17th (for example, see Pinchbeck and Hewitt, 1969, pp 25-30 regarding upper-class girls and pp 223-59 regarding the Poor Law apprenticeship system). The novelty is in the extent and nature of this out-of-family working.

[15] In fact, the numbers of people living in the countryside may have increased rather than declined in the early 19th century and the numbers of people living in towns were still lower than those in rural areas by the 1851 Census (Kitson-Clarke, 1961, pp 117-18). The 'fact' underlying the sense of unease was that the numbers in towns had increased comparatively quickly. For example, the population of Manchester and Salford rose from 95,000 in 1801 to 238,000 in 1831 (Pinchbeck and Hewitt, 1973, p 389).

[16] See, for example, Cohen (1972).

[17] It should not be forgotten, however, that there was considerable cruelty to children in the 'old' workplace, that is in agriculture, especially with the development of the gang labour system in the second quarter of the 19th century; see Pinchbeck and Hewitt, 1973, pp 391-5).

[18] See Cunningham (1995, pp 138-45).

[19] Jane Addams, an American philanthropist born in 1859, wrote: "let us know the modern city in its weakness and wickedness, and then seek to rectify and purify it" (quoted in Platt, 1969, p 96).

[20] See the article by Bar-On (1997) analysing research done in Ghana, Namibia and Zambia.

[21] Referred to by Dingwall et al (1984, p 219).

[22] Quoted on p 622 of Pinchbeck and Hewitt (1973).

[23] Both quoted in C.I. Mowat (1961, pp 21 and 71 respectively).

[24] An impression given by Pinchbeck and Hewitt (1969, pp 302-6).

[25] I am grateful to Stephen Cretney for suggesting this perspective CFLQ Seminar, All Souls, Oxford, 1 July 1997.

[26] Pinchbeck and Hewitt do, however, refer to a 'radical group' who campaigned from the 1860s for state action to break the link between the employment of mothers and the early death of their children (1973, pp 358-9).

[27] On 15 March in the debate in committee on the Factories Bill dealing with hours of labour in factories.

[28] Quoted on pp 68-9 of Cairns (1965).

[29] See Behlmer (1982, ch 2) for a very good account of the context of this Act.

[30] Their argument was that, while they approved of licensing, they did not feel it right to compel parents to employ only licensed minders.

[31] This age limit was not raised to five years until 1897 and to seven years until 1908.

[32] When discussing the Maloney Report of 1927 Dingwall et al note the same concern: "The neglect that is being talked about, however, is not a want of physical care but an attention to the control and moral education of children" (1984, p 216).

[33] To quote Cunningham again, "Children were thought to be unformed enough to be saveable" (1995, p 135).

[34] Industrial schools had been set up since the 18th century both under the Poor Law and by charitable bodies, although compulsion to attend could generally be only on the children of families claiming poor relief or on orphans. For a full discussion, see Pinchbeck and Hewitt (1973, pp 530-2).

[35] See Pinchbeck and Hewitt (1973, ch 16) for a full discussion, including details of the 1854 Act as pp 476-7. By 1859 50 reformatory schools had been established.

[36] See Behlmer (1982, p 67ff).

[37] See Hendrick (1994, pp 29-33 and p 50). An example of how the state acquired information about its children can be found in the Final Report of the Royal Commission on the Elementary Education Acts (1988, c 5495) which noted in Part IV under the heading 'Physical Training': "care however must always be taken in applying such training to delicate and underfed children".

[38] W. Booth (1890, ch VIII: 'The children of the lost', pp 63-4).

[39] Although not directly relevant to this analysis, it is worth noting that Behlmer also argues that there was no economic explanation in that children were of diminishing economic importance in that period: in 1851 they constituted 6.9% of the workforce whereas in 1881 only 4.5% (1982, p 46).

[40] J. Ruskin (1849) *The seven lambs of architecture* (1st edn), p 184, quoted in Himmelfarb (1995, p 56).

[41] J.B. Brown (1883) *The home: In its relation to man and society*, p 47, quoted in Behlmer (1982, p 46).

[42] See Mowat (1961, pp 74-5 and pp 154-5).

[43] Quoted by Pinchbeck and Hewitt (1973, p 358).

[44] In the context of arguing for the 'condition of England' as the most influential factor influencing the construction of child abuse as 'a major social disease' in the 1880s.

[45] General William Booth of the Salvation Army produced a book of evidence about the poor entitled *In darkest England and the way out* and referred to the population under scrutiny as 'the submerged tenth'.

[46] An entry in Beatrice Webb's Diary for November 1886 reveals the same questioning of long-held beliefs: "There are times when one loses all faith in laisser-faire and would

suppress the poison at all regards for it eats the life of the nation". Webb was referring to her East End of London research and, in particular, to the 'poison' of 'drink' (quoted in ch 6 of Webb, *My apprenticeship*, 1926).

[47] As Cox notes, "the bourgeoisie as a class was one that always sensed a threat from within, in terms of a failure of its own cultural reproduction, and from without, through the external threat of mass society" (Cox, 1996, p 200).

[48] Gertrude Tuckwell (1894) *The state and its children*, p 127, quoted in Pinchbeck and Hewitt (1973, pp 622-3).

[49] See Behlmer (1982, ch 4) for details. The amendments which were accepted to promote the passage of the Act were that the age limit for jurisdiction under the Act was lowered from 16 to 14 for boys and that less tight restrictions were imposed on street trading by children.

[50] *Hansard*, 1894, xxiv, col 1609, quoted Pinchbeck and Hewitt (1973, p 629).

[51] H.D. Chapin in *The theory and practice of infant feeding*, quoted in Spargo. Spargo enlarges on this statement "the physician traces the weakness and disease of the adults to defective nutrition in early childhood; the penologist traces moral perversion to the same cause; the pedagogue finds the same explanation for his failures" (Spargo, [1906] 1969, pp 2-3).

[52] Taken from a speech by Rosebery in 1901 and quoted in Semmel (1960, p 62).

[53] The resolution produced in November 1883 to announce the intention of setting up a Fabian Society said that its ultimate aim would be "the reconstruction of society in accordance with the highest moral possibilities". Quoted in M. Cole (1961) *The story of Fabian socialism*.

Children and social policies

Harry Hendrick

[...] In pursuit of a broad conceptual framework, it has been tentatively suggested that the history of child welfare might be usefully examined through, on the one hand, two 'dualisms': bodies/minds and victims/threats and, on the other, through the notion of children as investments. Taking its cue from Armstrong's claim that the body came to be the subject of "various techniques of detail which analysed, monitored and fabricated it" and from Bryan Turner's observation that "the body is the location for the exercise of will over desire", the argument is that much of the history of child welfare has been the imposition of adult will upon children's bodies through four primary forms: food and feeding (the School Meals Service); medical inspection and treatment (the School Medical Service, infant welfare clinics and the growth of paediatric medicine); the ordering of the body in movement and control of the tongue in speech (in Poor Law institutions, schools, orphanages, reformatories, child guidance clinics, hospitals, courts); and the punitive use of physical pain in welfare institutions such as schools and residential homes (Hendrick, 1994, pp 1-15).

The role of the body was of special importance during the period 1880 to 1918, partly through the work of the NSPCC, but more significantly as the working-class child came to be 'known' through the observation, inspection and treatment of its body (medically and socially) by infant welfare personnel, and in the classroom after the introduction of compulsory education. For many scholars the child's body is an indispensable component of the Edwardian programme of national public health. And it has continued to be a central feature of numerous identities of childhood since that time – such as those arising from inter-war controversies around 'malnutrition' and the effects of unemployment on health and welfare and from the emergence of paediatrics as a distinct branch of medicine, which accompanied the growing interest in children's diseases as peculiar to them alone rather than as adult diseases in children's bodies. Furthermore, both 'the body' and images associated with it have also featured in debates since the 1960s on child poverty, in the 'rediscovery' of child abuse beginning in the 1970s, and in the current anxiety about the health of poor children (Behlmer, 1992; Armstrong, 1983; Sutherland, 1984; B.Harris, 1995; Hurt, 1985; Bradshaw, 1990; Mayall, 1996).

Besides the emphasis on bodies, children were also being perceived through their minds/emotions. Roy Porter, the medical historian, has observed that the body in relation to mind "differs notably according to century, class, circumstances and culture" (Porter, 1991, p 218). We need to be sensitive to this warning as we trace the progress of the mind/emotion perception from the child study movement of the late 19th century through to the child guidance clinics of the 1930s and beyond, as interests moved along a spectrum of psychosocial and psychoanalytical concerns, none of which were mutually exclusive. Among the interests and concerns were 'feeble-mindedness', causes of juvenile delinquency, developmental psychology, child-rearing advice, 'maladjustment', and post-1945 notions of maternal deprivation and 'bonding' within families. However, it should be stressed that it was not a question of two separate domains – body and mind – but rather that they came to be viewed together in order to constitute the child as a medico- and psychological being who inhabited a special position in the population (Rose, 1985; Urwin and Sharland, 1992; Hendrick, 1994; Wooldridge, 1994).

The second dualism, 'victims and threats', derives from the sociolegal writings, but is also influenced, if somewhat loosely, by sociological debates concerning the definition of social problems, in particular those associated with 'blaming the victim' and 'labelling theory' (Eekelaar et al, 1982; Hulley and Clarke, 1991; Margan and Zedner, 1992). The classic definition of the latter is that "deviance is *not* a quality of the act a person commits but rather a consequence of the application by others of rules and sanctions to an 'offender'". With reference to the history of child welfare, the argument is that children have traditionally been seen as 'threats', either because they were convicted delinquents, or because they were regarded as *potentially* threatening to society, usually as a result of some form of neglect – in effect when they were objectively 'victims'. In practice it was not necessary to have committed a criminal offence, merely the possibility of doing so justified their being identified as a threat. In the words of an inter-war government report: "there is little or no difference in character and needs between the neglected and the delinquent child.... Neglect leads to delinquency and delinquency is often the direct outcome of neglect" (quoted in Eekelaar et al, 1982, p 73). Further legislation and reports confirmed this view. Thus, as Eekelaar et al have argued: "the language of welfare rather than punishment is overtly being used to achieve the same ends as a penal regime: the protection of an existing order by the containment and, at least theoretically, reform of potentially disruptive citizens" (Eekelaar et al, 1982, p 73).

Where children as investments are concerned, few historians would deny that this has been the dominant perspective of them in the policy-making process, usually in relation to programmes of a racial, educational, familial, medical, social and political nature. It is well known that the period 1880-1914 witnessed a surge of interest in health and illness which expressed a political concern for the condition of the nation (Sutherland, 1984). As part of this concern, the rhetoric from the 19th century child-saving movement, with its emphasis on a sentimental depiction of victims, was transformed into a "medico-social discourse of children at risk that expanded the concepts of victimisation, exploitation and abuse" (Rooke, 1995, pp 176-7). As a consequence, children were moved towards the centre of the political agenda so that in 'saving the child', states had other motivations besides the child's welfare: " concern about population levels; worry about the level of 'civilization' of the masses; desire to breed a race capable of competing in the twentieth century". Accordingly, Rose can claim with some certainty that the health, welfare and rearing of children have been linked to the destiny of the nation and the responsibilities of the state (Rose, 1990; Hendrick, 1994).

Much less pronounced in the literature is an awareness of the importance of generation (or *age*) in the history of child welfare. While gender, social class and race are widely regarded as crucial to a proper analysis of social policy, *age* is almost entirely neglected. Frost and Stein are among the few authors who recognise that within the context of 'the family as a power relationship' generation is a 'key dimension' and the child 'can have interests separate from the mother'. Consequently, their explanatory framework is broadly based on the theme of "inequality as manifested in differences in social class, gender, ethnicity, (dis)ability and generation" (Frost and Stein, 1989).

Integral to this analysis is the view that children have become 'objects of welfare interventions', which can be explained by looking "at the state–family relationship and how this has changed over time". One example of this approach, provided by Jacques Donzelot, maintains that the relationship between families and the state has taken a particular gendered form primarily through an alliance between mothers and state agencies in pursuit of child health, education and development (Donzelot, 1980). This means that through what is called the 'welfare apparatus', a 'supervisory' regime, staffed by welfare professionals, is created. Although ostensibly always 'caring', it has a coercive role that derives its authority from the law, and can, in extreme circumstances, impose its will upon both parents and children. Similarly, it has been argued that children are conventionally viewed through the concept of familialisation, meaning "the fusion of childhood into the family institution to such an extent that it becomes an inseparable unit, which obstructs the social visibility of its weaker parts as a separate entity". Furthermore, in terms of welfare policies, the institution of the family is said to be subject to "Covert control by the state". For these commentators, then, welfare cannot be explained simply as "an expression of our collective goodwill" (Frost and Stein, 1989, p 9).

For the final word on overarching approaches, we can turn to the analysis of Lorraine Fox Harding, who has examined historical and contemporary child care law and policy from four different 'value perspectives': *laissez-faire*; state paternalism; defence of the birth family; and children's rights (Fox Harding, 1991/97). The *laissez-faire* perspective is associated with patriarchy and advocates that the state intervene in family relationships only in extreme circumstances. It was common in the 19th century, and has enjoyed some revival in the late 20th century. State paternalism refers to the growth of state intervention from the late 19th century onwards. In this perspective the intervention 'may be authoritarian and biological family bonds undervalued'. The defence of the birth family (and parents' rights) has become popular since the establishment of the welfare state in 1945, as the state has intervened in order to support the birth family which, in practice, has often meant assisting financially disadvantaged families. The children's rights perspective holds that the child should be treated as a subject, as an independent person with rights which 'in the extreme form of this position' are similar to adult rights. On occasions this perspective has been influential, but overall its effect on policy has been marginal....

1880-1918

All scholars agree that this was a critical period for child welfare programmes, and for the emergence of state social policies. How can so much legislative activity be explained? There is no easy answer to this question, and it would be a vulgar methodological procedure to look for a set of straightforward relationships. Instead, the heightened focus on children of all classes, especially those from the working class, has to be seen as part of a much larger interest in science and in social welfare, which was itself a response to that composition of economic, political, racial, imperial and social crises so well known to historians of the period (Freeden, 1978; Soffer, 1978; Harris, 1993).

Recent work identifies a shift, beginning around the 1870s, from a simple concern with child reformation and rescue, usually by placing children in either philanthropic or Poor Law institutional care, to a far more complex notion and practice of welfare. The latter pursued the national interest in the broadest sense and, therefore, looked to children's physical and mental development, to their education, their protection from uncivilised and neglectful behaviour, and to their instruction in matters of hygiene, personal responsibility and 'citizenship'. In line with anxieties about poverty, the effects of slum life, foreign competition and 'national efficiency', these children were given a new social and political identity; they became, the words of a contemporary reformer "Children of the Nation" (Hendrick, 1994, 2003).

Perhaps the first important locus of activity to emanate from the growing awareness of the social and scientific significance of children concerned infant welfare. The initial campaign focused on 'infant protection' from 'baby farmers' (women who took in infants to nurse or rear in exchange for payment). Broadly speaking the reform movement concerned itself with the complex problem of 'infanticide', with community child care networks for working-class mothers, and with informal adoptions (there was no legal adoption until 1926). We may note Jean Heywood's view on the growth of protective legislation for children, in this instance a series of Acts (1872, 1897, 1908) to protect babies, often illegitimate, from being exploited "as a means of private profit", although the root of much of the problem lay in the inadequate financial support given to single mothers (Heywood, 1965). Other scholars link the problem to abortionist midwives and suggest that the practices of wet-nursing and baby farming were closely related to infanticide (Rose, 1986). Ellen Ross, however, who admits that London infants were "being abandoned and killed as a slow but regular rate throughout the later nineteenth century", stresses that murderous baby farmers, each of whom had a dozen or more babies, were a rarity and that the death rate of infants cared for by paid nurses was no higher than that of other groups of bottle-fed babies (Ross, 1993).

Even more worrying for contemporaries was the decline in the birth rate as it fell from 35.5 per 1,000 population in 1871-75 to 29.3 in 1896-1900; the largest fall in Europe (except for France). Imperialists in particular were anxious about the implications of the decline for the defence and administration of the Empire. But it was the rise in the infant mortality rate (IMR) from 146 per 1,000 live births in 1876 to 156 in 1897, alongside a decline in the general mortality rate, that raised the level of concern and anxiety among many political and medical groups (Dwork, 1987). Understanding the problem of infant mortality proved difficult. In general, politicians and medical personnel focused upon two issues: the feeding of infants and the promotion of mothering skills, known as 'mothercraft', which led to the opening of various kinds of infant welfare centres (Lewis, 1980). The major development occurred in 1914 when the Local Government Board offered a grant in aid of local expenditure for maternity and child welfare. This made it possible for local authorities to take over voluntary centres, while the passing of the Maternity and Child Welfare Act in 1918 gave the local authorities powers to provide a range of services. The IMR had been falling since the early 1900s, and it fell sharply during the war (from 152:1,000 in 1900 to 96:1,000 in 1917). Accounting for the decline has proved controversial. The range of factors considered includes environmental and nutritional improvements (such as the rising standard of living, better housing and healthier dried milk powder), the promotion of breast feeding and the development of health visiting. As for the medical contribution to the decline, while some authors see improved medical attention for premature babies as playing a part, more recent research concludes that it was "limited and late" (Lewis, 1980, p 107; Ross, 1993, pp 124-7).

The issue of infant welfare has been of particular interest to feminist historians, who have written about the topic from the mothers' outlook. The emphasis on 'mothercraft' in the official programmes has particularly angered these scholars for two main reasons. First, it reinforced the view that the child was the mother's responsibility rather than a joint parental responsibility, while encouraging the view that the proper role of women was in the home looking after their babies. Second, it implied that mothers were ignorant, careless and often indifferent to the conditions of their infants. According to Jane Lewis, "Attitudes and policies concerning poverty ... ran counter to the demands of women's groups for direct economic assistance", as did their call for policies to deal with "low levels of nutrition [and] the inability of women and children to afford medical treatment". Lewis argues strongly that given the government's promotion of the "ideology of motherhood", neither "changes in medical practice nor in social policy ... can be assumed to have been benevolent" (Lewis, 1980, pp 17, 21). Deborah Dwork, on the other hand, claims that the feminists are too dependent upon the social control thesis. Regarding their analyses, she says, "one begins to doubt the sincerity of official concerns with the problem of infant mortality: everyone appears to have been more concerned with controlling women than saving babies" (Dwork, 1987, p 228).

Although the pivotal role of the mother is acknowledged by certain sociomedical writers, they approach the issue through the Foucauldian notion of 'biopower', which means the power to control life "in order to optimise the capacities of individuals and populations" (Baistow, 1995). This is achieved through submitting the body/ies to scrutiny, surveillance and numeration. These scholars put the emphasis on seeing the infant welfare movement as a clear example of this process in action since infant care is said to be socially constructed as a 'medical problem'

(Wright, 1988), instead of, say, as a problem of poverty. Moreover, as infant mortality was 'invented' – in the sense that infant deaths only appeared in the Census as 'infant mortality rate' in 1877 – it is argued that the appearance of this new statistic signified the emergence of the infant as an object of sociological and medical interest (Armstrong, 1986).

One revealing sidelight on the relationship between children and society, which also pointed to the developing state interest in all areas of child care, focused on the education of the 'handicapped' child. This matter came to public attention partly as a consequence of mass elementary education, and partly in response to the social and political issues arising from the 'condition of England' debate in the 1880s (Pritchard, 1963; Sutherland, 1984; Hurt, 1988). The Report of the Royal Commission on the Blind, the Deaf and the Dumb (1889) concluded that, if left uneducated, handicapped people, including "the educable class of imbeciles", were likely to become a burden to the state by swelling "the great torrent of pauperism". Consequently, in 1893 the Elementary Education (Blind and Deaf Children) Act made it a duty for local education authorities (LEAs) to provide the children with an 'efficient and suitable' education. The situation for the otherwise physically handicapped, however, was much less enviable, with the main effort on their behalf being philanthropic until the 1918 Education Act compelled LEAs to provide for them.

Legislation for the mentally 'defective' child was politically controversial, for in an age of European imperial rivalries mental defectiveness was an important feature of the wide-ranging debates about racial deterioration, physical efficiency and eugenics (the science of proper breeding). The issue was first raised with reference to the condition of school pupils as revealed by compulsory attendance. However, a government committee on 'defective and epileptic' children (1896) had difficulty in defining the terms, and the matter was left largely unresolved. None the less, in 1899 the Elementary Education (Defective and Epileptic Children) Act was passed, although the permissive nature of the Act meant that 10 years later only 133 out of 228 LEAs were providing educational facilities for these pupils. In the eugenicist climate of the early 1900s there was an unsuccessful attempt to exclude 'mentally defective' children from the 1899 Act, since eugenicists saw normal education as pointless, preferring instead to provide vocational education in order to assist them to contribute towards their upkeep. It was 1914 before the 1899 Act was made obligatory on LEAs. While there has been some debate as to the extent to which Social Darwinism and the eugenics movement influenced policy for the mentally handicapped (Rose, 1985; Sutherland, 1984; Hurt, 1988), the important point is that more money was spent on reformatory and industrial schools than on schools for all the handicapped: "The maintenance of law and order had financial priority over compassion for the physically and mentally disadvantaged" (Hurt, 1988, p 152).

By the 1890s the government was turning its attention towards a much more complex issue: cruelty to children. In the closing decades of the century parental authority began to be reduced as it found itself in conflict with the state over such issues as infant life protection, compulsory schooling, and child-rearing practices. Historians see the 1889 Prevention of Cruelty to Children Act as representing a 'progressive' step forward in the humane treatment of children and in their protection by the state. They also agree that the work of the National Society for the Prevention of Cruelty to Children (NSPCC), incorporated in 1884, helped to establish in the public mind that children had 'rights' against their parents. All the same, the degree to which the NSPCC and the legislation was simultaneously concerned with attempting 'to patrol family life', and inculcating 'civilised' values, rather than simply to protect children, should not be underestimated (Behlmer, 1982; Hendrick 1994).

When, in 1881, Lord Shaftesbury, England's premier philanthropist, was first approached by a Liverpool clergyman for his support in promoting legislation to protect children against parental cruelty, he thought the matter "of so private, internal and domestic a character as to be beyond the reach of legislation". But within three years he would help to start a London Society. This change of heart, and the interest of other leading reformers, can be explained with reference to the significance of the 1880s as a decade in which social distress, economic uncertainties, and political developments involving working-class consciousness were causing a shift in opinion among the philanthropic middle and upper classes. Many of them felt that the 'respectable' working class, and those who aspired to that status, were being undermined. It seemed that the ideal of the bourgeois family – self-contained, private, loving, religious, hierarchical and cultured – was at risk, especially from those families of Irish extraction who made up a large proportion of the urban poor. Child cruelty was one of the specific threats, exemplifying as it did irresponsibility, callousness and brutality.

It was through the combined efforts of Thomas Agnew, a Liverpool merchant and banker, and Samuel Smith, the Liberal MP for the city, that the first Society was founded. On returning from a trip to New York in 1882, where he had come into contact with a Society for the Prevention of Cruelty to Children, Agnew approached Smith, who was active in the YMCA and in child emigration schemes, with the idea for such a Society in Liverpool. Soon afterwards Smith attended a meeting of the RSPCA where he converted a proposal for a dog's home into a call for the defence of children, and on 19 April 1883, the Liverpool Society was established. By 1884 the Liverpool example had been followed in Bristol, Birmingham and London.

The credit for the passing of the 1889 Act is given to the London Society with its three-pronged campaign of 'legislative analysis, wrenching propaganda, and organised growth'. Their early experiences convinced members of the societies that child abuse included a range of offences, involving several different causes, few of which were adequately covered by the law. And they knew that a number of obstacles stood in the way of reform. Poor Law guardians were reluctant to punish parents for wilful neglect; women were unable to give evidence against their husbands; the father had an 'absolute right' to custody of his children; schoolteachers feared the abolition of their right to inflict corporal punishment upon pupils; the liquor trade objected to fines on the sale of alcohol to children; the Band of Hope temperance movement feared that clauses to restrict the employment of children would interfere with their use of juveniles in campaigns;

and the Home Office was lukewarm, although it was interested in prosecuting neglectful parents and in curbing child street trading.

Several scholars tend to portray the NSPCC as unproblematically benevolent with references to the "rousing of the public conscience" and to "those whose life-work it was to protect those weaker than themselves" (Allen and Morton, 1961; Heywood, 1965; Pinchbeck and Hewitt, 1983). George Behlmer sees its roots as lying both in the "slow spread of humane sentiment" and the creation of "a new moral vision in which justice for the young took precedence over the claims of parenthood". He also acknowledges that the architects of this vision succeeded "by arguing that the security of the home demanded it. The Englishman's castle was to be breached for the good of the castle, and, ultimately, for the good of the Englishman as well. Thus, child savers laboured also to save parents" (Behlmer, 1982, pp 2-3, 16). Similarly, Harry Ferguson sees the Society and the protective legislation as being part of struggles which not only helped to create modern child protection practice, but also identified how neglectful and cruel parents should be "judged, helped, punished, and treated". As he says, such parents began to feel "the weight of new social practices and powers" which broke with "traditional Victorian strategies of administering welfare, regulating households, and punishing deviations" (Ferguson, 1990, pp 126, 132). It is, then, important to see the prevention of cruelty to children movement (including legal intervention in matters of juvenile sexuality through the raising of the age of consent to 16 [1885] and the punishment of incest [1908]) as part of a larger enterprise identified by Jose Harris, among others, as "a major restructuring of the legal relations between husbands and wives, parents and children, the family and the state" (Harris, 1993, p 75).

The same sort of legal relations were also prominent in the *permissive* Acts allowing LEAs to feed necessitous school children (1906), and to provide for the medical inspection and treatment of all elementary pupils (1907). The first reform was extremely controversial because to many contemporaries it signified the ending of parental responsibility for the basic care of children. But it is not an issue that has aroused much disagreement among scholars, most of whom take the view that despite there having been various philanthropic schemes for feeding hungry children since at least the 1860s, and acknowledging the socialist campaigns for school meals at the end of the century, the single most influential factor leading to legislation was the post-Boer war (1899-1902) 'national efficiency' movement. The 'efficiency group' (politicians, academics, journalists, professionals) were concerned about a wide range of issues relating to Britain's apparent declining status as a great military and economic power. However, central to their activities was the fear of racial deterioration, which gave the whole area of social reform the status of a respectable political question. With specific reference to young people, this transformation was greatly assisted by the Report of the Interdepartmental Committee on Physical Deterioration (1904), with its call for limited schemes of school feeding and school medical attention.

But not everyone is satisfied with this explanation. Roger Cooter refers approvingly to Dwork for locating a sense of unease about racial deterioration back in the mid-19th century (Cooter, 1992). And, given that the child study movement developed out of a growing anxiety, from the 1860s onwards, about the health and efficiency of the population as a whole (Wooldridge, 1994), it is clear that the effects of the Boer War need to be placed in perspective. This is especially so when the importance of the "rediscovery of the condition of England question" in the 1880s is borne in mind, since it led to a number of investigations and soon became central to political debate. The point being made by Cooter is that we need to pay much more attention to political and ideological goals in the history of child health and welfare. We should recognise that social policy initiatives were part of a wider socio-economic and cultural change involving, for example, the ideology of the family, motherhood, an idealised 'childhood', and specific medical, political and economic interests. It was these concerns that legitimised the partial break with the *laissez-faire* approach to child care policy, and which marked children out as "England's most precious resource" (Gilbert, 1966). In this respect, state paternalism and child protection were joined together.

There is a certain amount of debate as to whether or not the establishment of the school medical service aroused much less controversy than did the school meals legislation. The older historical view, associated with Bentley Gilbert, that the service "came peacefully because it came secretly" has been rejected by younger scholars, who see the legislation as being fully discussed and understood by Parliament (Gilbert, 1966, p 117; Hirst, 1989; Harris, 1995, pp 61-4). Likewise, his view that the growth of medical *treatment* was not fully appreciated by Parliament has also been contradicted.

The origins of the service may be found in five areas: foreign examples; sanitation reform and public health concerns; the 'over-pressure controversy of the mid-1880s (the fear that children's health would be damaged by too much schoolwork); administrative and legislative developments in education since the 1890s; and fears of racial deterioration. While all these are relevant, it remains true that as with feeding hungry school children, "the rather casual public interest in the health of schoolchildren suddenly became a widespread fear over the apparent physical deterioration of the British working class. A healthy working-class child was precious in a way he had not been before" (Gilbert, 1966, p 120). The development of inspection schemes was fairly rapid, but medical treatment in school clinics and hospitals had to overcome a considerable amount of institutional and medical hostility before the 1918 Education Act imposed a 'duty' on LEAs to provide for the health and physical condition of all their children.

Another important feature of the changing relationship between the state and the family was developed in the 1908 Children Act. The creation of a separate juvenile justice system (the central feature of the Act), is said to have "reflected a revolutionary change of attitude from the days when the young offender was regarded as a small adult, fully responsible for his crime". The Act "aimed at a more comprehensive and child-oriented legal system and at more generous and liberal provisions for children in all walks of life" (Pinchbeck and Hewitt, 1983, pp 492-4; Hendrick, 2003, pp 82-6). Other scholars, though not denying its 'welfare' aspects, point more emphatically to different motivating sentiments behind the Act, the two most influential being the desire to better regulate families and children and the perception of children as a national asset in which investment was the prudent course (Eekelaar et al, 1982; Rose, 1985). Furthermore, sociolegal writers, who are concerned with the evolution of the 'welfare model' of juvenile justice, point out that as the juvenile court dealt with both the criminal child *and* the needy child and, therefore, fused the notions of depravation and deprivation, so the court itself "became a *locus* for conflict and confusion" (Eekelaar et al, 1982; Harris and Webb, 1987; Frost and Stein, 1989).

1918-1939

The undoubted rise in the standard of living between the wars has led several historians to write in terms of what Charles Webster has criticised as "the 'myth' of the Hungry Thirties" (Webster, 1982, 1985). Part of the difficulty in assessing children's health and welfare during the period is that different historians begin from different assumptions. It is true that all the relevant health statistics show a continuing 'improvement'. The infant mortality rate for England and Wales (IMR: usually seen as a significant indicator of general health) fell from 80:1,000 live births in 1920 to 53:1,000 in 1938. Similarly, among those under 15 years of age, the death rate from scarlet fever, diphtheria, whooping cough and measles also declined dramatically. Equally significant was the increase in the height and weight of children, and the earlier onset of puberty. The reduction in ill-health and mortality was accredited by a contemporary survey to 'improvements in housing, sanitation, hygiene, and medical skill'. A better diet, brought about by rising real wages and cheaper food prices, was another crucial influence (Winter, 1983; Stevenson, 1994). All the same, a number of scholars, in common with government critics during the 1930s, look behind the general statistical picture to cast doubt on both the efficacy and the comprehensive nature of inter-war welfare services (Webster, 1982, 1985; Mitchell, 1985).

Although the decline in the IMR seems to offer incontrovertible proof of an improvement in the standard of health, historians have debated the reliability and meaning of the statistics (Crowther, 1988, pp 67-71). J.M. Winter tends to accept the official view that the economic depression had only a slight effect on the downward trend in infantile mortality. (However, he also points to the possibility of a higher IMR among children of mothers who were born during the worst years of the depression, thereby suggesting that the effects on health may have been delayed.) Webster distrusts the official health figures and argues that the decline in the IMR during the 1930s was much less rapid than in previous decades and from 1940 onwards. Webster also claims that rather than use national statistics, a better guide to the effects of unemployment on infant mortality would be to take the rates for depressed areas. Such regions, he says, show a worsening IMR in the early 1930s (Winter, 1979, 1983, 1986; Webster, 1982, 1985).

One of the most controversial issues at the time concerned malnutrition and involved the extent to which school meals (both free and charged) – including milk – were provided. No one denies that throughout the inter-war period there was a substantial increase in the number of children being fed, however the most rapid growth occurred in the provision of milk and nutritional supplements, such as cod liver oil. Government statistics claimed to show that whereas dietary deficiency had affected between 15% and 20% of school children prior to 1914, by 1925 the figure had fallen to below 5%, and during the period 1925-32 'malnutrition requiring treatment' fell to only 1% of school pupils. Even within official circles these optimistic data were contested and remained so throughout the 1930s (Hurt, 1985; Harris, 1995).

The three main criticisms of official statistics were, first, that different medical officers used different systems of classification; second, there was little connection between the nutritional classification and the identification process of malnourished children; and, third, the standards adopted by medical officers were subject to wide variation. There was also the problem of an incomplete knowledge of nutritional science. The government's response was to mount a huge propaganda campaign to convince the general public that there had been a decline in malnutrition and that there was no real connection between ill-health and unemployment.

In the mid-1980s, the weight of research seemed to tend towards the view that despite the undoubted improvements in conditions for the majority of working-class children, substantial numbers continued to experience severe and increasing deprivation through the effects of long-term unemployment. This view has been qualified to a certain extent by the recent work of Bernard Harris who, using anthropometric data (heights and weights of individuals), has tried to measure child health in relation to unemployment and stature. He concludes that "changes in the average rate of unemployment did have an effect on the average value of children's heights even though the strength of this relationship varied from area to area". This, he says, identifies "the importance of the local context within which unemployment occurred", since those with the highest levels of unemployment were also usually badly provided for in terms of social and health amenities (Harris, 1995, pp 140-2).

With the controversy surrounding child health and welfare in mind, few scholars would disagree with Fox Harding when she declares that during the 1920s and 1930s, children were not a major focus of government policy (Fox Harding, 1997). None the less, government officials *were* enthusiastic about tackling juvenile delinquency. Indeed, it is a striking fact that that major piece of 'welfare' legislation for young people at this time was an Act based on the recommendations of a government committee whose main concern was with juvenile offenders. The 1933 Children and Young Persons Act was a consolidating measure, the main provisions of which included the forging of a closer link between the care of delinquent and neglected children and LEAs; abolishing the distinction between reformatories and industrial schools as both were merged to become 'approved' schools; removing neglected children from the care of the Poor Law; amending the constitution and procedures of the juvenile court system; and broadening the definition of children being in need of care and protection. It has been claimed that the Act was concerned to make the welfare of the child a paramount concern, and that it set "a standard of welfare and rehabilitation for the delinquent and the neglected children and those in need of care which had never previously been approached" (Heywood, 1965, p 130). In similar vein, Victor Bailey, an authority on the Act, rejects the view that the measures within it were "designed as coercive instruments by the governing class" (Bailey, 1987).

A very different view of the Act is proposed by Frost and Stein who see it as essentially "a reactionary measure with no vision of prevention or indeed a return to a 'rehabilitated' family" (Frost and Stein, 1989, p 32). Humphries accepts that the authorities began to see the incarceration of erring children from respectable families as counter-productive, but this did not apply to those from families considered to be morally and physically degenerate (Humphries, 1981). Bailey, on the other hand, emphasises the Act's recognition of the importance of the home environment which, in most cases, could be found in the *natural* home, under the supervision of a probation officer (but he is probably excluding households which were viewed as being in need of rehabilitation). Rose agrees that domestic circumstances were seen as crucial, but says that was because they offered the best prospect for combating juvenile delinquency. Unlike Bailey, he emphasises the disciplinary and control functions of the legislation (Rose, 1985). Sociolegal writers, who focus on the nature of the legislation from the perspective of how it affected children, rather than parents, have argued that while the Act did offer greater care and protection to certain groups, it was at the expense of irredeemably intertwining them with other children who were regarded as "virtually inseparable from delinquent children". Furthermore, it was the threat of delinquency that governed the legislation and which led in this Act, and in others, to the "apparent disappearance of concern for child victims" (Dingwall et al, 1984, p 223).

When it comes to children's psychological well-being, there is little doubt that this was distinctly secondary. All the same, the growing significance of psychosocial treatments, especially child guidance, needs to be considered (Rose, 1985; Thom, 1992; Hendrick, 2003). The movement got properly under way with the formation of the Child Guidance Council in 1927, although a few clinics had opened prior to this time; by the late 1930s progressive LEAs were funding their own clinics. The young clients were usually aged between 8 and 14, and the commonest reason for referral was behaviour likely to bring them into conflict with authority, rather than proper delinquency. Children were rarely referred for emotional disturbances. However, when the children were diagnosed, the position was almost completely reversed. Diagnosis also revealed habit disorders such as speech defects, enuresis (bed wetting), and sleep and eating difficulties. The treatment was said to be of the order of 'common-sense conversation' rather than anything resembling psychoanalysis, which was viewed with some suspicion within the medical fraternity and by the general public.

The clinic was one of the most significant ways in which 'society' (in the form of psychiatrists, social workers, psychologists, educators, magistrates and penal administrators) came to 'know' children and to seek to 'adjust' them to what was regarded as normal behaviour. Here there developed what Rose calls "a second institutional location [the juvenile court being the first] for this new way of thinking about and acting upon the child and the family". The clinic would deal with a variety of disturbed children: "backward children, nervous children, stammerers, liars, truants, the unmanageable, the neglected, and the delinquent.

Within its precincts the troubles of childhood would be diagnosed, norms of adjustment and maladjustment would be produced and refined, and normalization would be undertaken". And as such, it would become "the centre of a web of preventive and therapeutic child welfare embracing the nursery, the home, the school, the playground, and the courts" (Rose, 1985, p 154).

1939-1960s

The evacuation process, the first wave of which began in September 1989, saw 826,959 unaccompanied English and Welsh children, 523,670 mothers with pre-school children, and 7,000 handicapped children sent to reception areas in the South and South West, the East and West Midlands, and North Wales. This mass movement of children gave rise to what Angus Calder has described as the English tendency to confuse matters with morals as children were accused of being infested, incontinent, bad mannered and ungrateful (Calder, 1971). The memories of evacuees who were billeted with families are mixed, and although there is no doubt that many thousands of children suffered in such a way as to condition them adversely for the rest of their lives, many others recall kindness and affection and even love bestowed on them by their hosts (Wicks, 1988; Inglis, 1989).

In terms of health and welfare, evacuation revealed the wider influence of inter-war poverty in a way that the official statistical aggregates could no longer conceal. The Commission of the Churches reported: "The country was undoubtedly electrified to discover the dirt, poverty and ignorance, particularly of home hygiene, that still exists in large towns". The government at first simply reiterated the view that it had propounded throughout the 1930s, namely, that needy children were the responsibility of their parents. But this negative attitude changed under critical pressure and from late 1941 the number of children receiving school dinners increased dramatically. Bob Holman has argued that the evacuation process aroused a new sense of compassion among the middle class, accompanied by a determination to take action to challenge poverty (Holman, 1995, p 142). John Macnicol offers a different emphasis: "Evacuation ... marks the conceptual transition from the 'social problem group' of the inter-war years to the 'problem family' of the 1940s and 1950s ... the latter [was] seen as amenable to character reform through intensive social work intervention" (Macnicol, 1986, p 156).

Whatever the motives behind them, welfare principles certainly came into prominence. In addition to specific influences, such as the development of child guidance services, the general significance of evacuation was threefold. First, it revealed the destitute circumstances of a substantial minority of children, as well as putting into context the extent to which inter-war housing schemes had failed to eradicate the slums with the attendant problem of overcrowding, verminous conditions, and lack of toilet and washing facilities. Second, it showed the variability of local authority provision in infant welfare clinics, nursery schools, health services, and educational opportunities. Third, it stimulated the expansion of statutory provision of a number of health and welfare services (Crosby, 1986; Harris, 1995; Holman, 1995).

Perhaps the single most important consequence of evacuation was the centring of 'the family' in all future policies for children's welfare. Indeed, Heywood is not alone in claiming that after relative neglect during the inter-war years, it was the war itself which "rediscovered for the nation the value of the family", including the social significance of Macnicol's 'problem family' (Heywood, 1965, p 133). In the inter-war period, deprived and delinquent children had often been cared for in institutions, which meant that "the problem child and the problem parent had become separated, instead of connected entities" (Heywood, 1965, p 134). Now the war, in particular the lessons learned from the trauma of evacuees being separated from their families, provided the opportunity for a range of new social policies (Rose, 1985; Holman, 1995).

In March 1945 the government appointed the Curtis Committee to be the first inquiry "directed specifically to the care of children deprived of a normal home life". The Report's findings led to the landmark 1948 Children Act, whose main principles were: the establishment of local authority Children's Departments (under the supervision of the Home Office); a new emphasis on boarding out in preference to residential homes; restoration of children in care to their natural parents; greater emphasis on adoption; and the partial responsibility of the Children's Departments for young offenders. The duty of local authority Children's Departments to restore the child to the natural parents as soon as possible emphasised the importance of family casework in the new service (this was a feature that expanded rapidly over the next 20 years). Ideally, and significantly, every child in care was to be treated as an individual, with access to the same facilities as any other child in the community, thereby removing the last shred of 'less eligibility' which had survived since the Poor Law Amendment Act of 1834. In broad terms, the Act initiated a child care service which tried to help those children "whose homes had failed them; lessen or prevent the trauma of separation ... or grossly inadequate parenting; provide substitute, family-type care whether in institutions or foster homes; forestall emotional stunting in institutions and give the children a better start in life than they would otherwise have had" (Boss, 1971, p vii; Packman, 1981 Heywood, 1985; Hendrick, 1994/2003).

There is no doubt that the Act, although originally envisaged as not much more than "a comparatively minor service for neglected and deprived children", turned out to be a significant piece of child welfare legislation, which has been unjustly neglected in standard histories of the welfare state. If its meaning is to be fully appreciated, it has to be seen in relation to the series of post-war welfare statutes regarded as underpinning the Welfare State: the 1945 Family Allowances Act, the 1946 National Health Service (NHS) Act, the 1946 National Insurance Act, and the 1948 National Assistance Act. With the passing of the NHS Act, the SMS, renamed the school health service, passed on many of its services to the NHS. As a consequence of these Acts, the deprived child and the failing parents were viewed as an interrelated whole, with the objective of the child care service being the restoration of the child to the family.

Unsurprisingly, many commentators view the legislation as benign; it is regarded as part of a more comprehensive breaking down of class barriers and the transformation of political differences from those of ends to those of means. The 1948 Act is said to have strengthened and supported the family as never before albeit that the intention of the legislation of the 1940s was "to impose middle-class values on the working class and thereby reinforce the tendency for class differences of family structure to diminish" (Pinchbeck and Hewitt, 1983, pp 651-3). In Heywood's view the duty of a local authority to provide for the proper development of a child's character and abilities was "perhaps unmatched for its humanity in all our legislation" (Heywood, 1965, pp 158-9). For Fox Harding, the Act "reflected an entirely new ethos ... [it] set new and higher standards of welfare for children in care" (Fox Harding, 1997, pp 136-7).

Other scholars, however, tend to focus on the family within a broader political context. Four main reasons have been suggested to explain why the family was seen as crucial for effective child rearing. First there was growing concern about the reproductive rate of the population, described by a Mass Observation report as "the coming problem for Western Civilisation", which produced a programme of pronatalism. Second, the Act's emphasis on the personal care of children reflected not simply the advice of the Curtis Report, but that of psychologists such as John Bowlby and Anna Freud who were concerned for children's healthy emotional development in post-war democracies. Bowlby's research pointed to the dangers of sudden and chaotic separation of small children from mother figures and, therefore, emphasised emotional attachment, security and continuity. Third, the impact of child guidance contributed towards a view of the family, what Rose calls a "therapeutic agent", as the perfect environment for future democratic citizens. Fourth, the experience of evacuation produced not greater bonding between the classes, but a more detailed understanding of the extent and consequences of physical and mental poverty, and the indentification of 'problem' families (Riley, 1963; Rose, 1985, 1990; Frost and Stein, 1989). Of course, these interpretations do not deny the progressive features of the Act, but they place less emphasis on the humanitarian aspects, preferring instead to pay close attention to the interests and agendas of professional bodies, religious and moral pressure groups, industry and political parties, which are seen to have influenced the legislation and the subsequent development of local authority child care provision.

1960s-1980s

With the establishment of the child care service under the 1948 Act it soon became clear that child welfare could not be confined to those in care since the really difficult area involved *prevention*, that is, working with families in order to keep children from coming into care. Although preventive work was performed during the 1950s, it was not until the 1963 Children and Young Persons Act, that local authorities were given the duty to promote the welfare of children through such an approach. And even then, this was achieved by combining strategies for combating child neglect with those intended to counter juvenile delinquency (Packman, 1981).

The fear of juvenile delinquency had been the main concern of the Ingleby Report (1960), several of whose recommendations appeared in the 1963 Act. The report reflected professional interest in the *treatment* as opposed to the punishment model of juvenile justice as it dealt with deprivation and depravation. Jacques Donzelot has argued that as 'welfare' permeated the judicial process with the social services collaborating with the courts, so the judicial influence was extended into the social life of children and their families (Donzelot, 1979). Nevertheless, the Act confirmed that the focus of the 1948 Children Act, on meeting the needs of children in care, had shifted to providing support for families in order to avert the need for care and to prepare children for 'citizenship'. Thus the way was prepared for 'a family service' in which, under the 1970 Local Authority Social Services Act, Children's Departments were merged into Social Services Departments.

The latter 1969 Children and Young Persons Act, while retaining what Jean Packman calls 'a basic conservatism', drew heavily on the family-oriented approach with its emphasis on the 'treatment' of the delinquent through a "more 'welfare' oriented jurisdiction" (Packman, 1981, pp 154-5). Wherever possible offending children were to be 'treated' in their own home, rather than prosecuted through the juvenile court. The intention was to reduce the number of offenders appearing in court by substituting 'care proceedings' for criminal prosecution – the court was to become a place of last resort. It is noticeable that once again there is a concentration on delinquency at the expense of cruelty and neglect. Indeed, child offenders were to be treated in almost exactly the same manner as those who were neglected in some way or another. In some respects this could be seen as a progressive and humanitarian attempt to understand the causes of delinquency. For John Pitts, however, the issues are those of class politics: "The debate about justice versus welfare" was "ultimately a debate about means rather than ends.... Stripped of their philosophical and theoretical trappings the parliamentary politics of the 1960s concerned productivity and conformity" (Pitts, 1988, p 12).

By the end of the 1960s, a new problem had arrived: child abuse. At that time child physical abuse was regarded as being caused by individual pathology, that is, the character or personality of the abusing parent. It was perceived as essentially a medical problem, with an emphasis on 'disease', 'treatment', 'identification' and 'prevention'. Matters began to change from the late 1970s, when theorists such as Nigel Parton began to open up a new understanding of the problem through a social structural analysis using contemporary conceptual perspectives drawn from the sociology of deviance. Parton, among others, claimed that debates about child abuse, although presented as being about technical and professional matters, were in fact political. Child abuse, he said, involved social inequality and poverty. Thus the medical model, in focusing on individual pathology, ignored the economic and social position of the family. Nor did it consider the wider institutional abuse of children through pollution, poor health services, and bad housing (Parton, 1985).

While Parton, and those who share his views, are explicitly sympathetic to children's separate interests from their parents, Fox Harding shrewdly observes that such defences of what is called the 'birth family' tend to "de-emphasise the extent and seriousness of child abuse as an actual problem….The *actual* abuse of children and its effects are somewhat marginalized" (Fox Harding, 1991, p 124). In a later self-critical essay Parton acknowledged that one of the weaknesses of his earlier work was that it failed "to recognize the child in child abuse" (Parton, 1990). It has also been argued that social structural explanations of child abuse are incomplete because they fail to take account of 'ageism' and the generally low status of children throughout society, not least the widespread physical punishment to which they are habitually subjected. Furthermore, these explanations do not account for the relative absence of child abuse from the headlines between the early 1900s and its re-emergence in the 1960s.

The slowly developing interest in child abuse in the press and among professionals exploded with the report of an inquiry into the death of Maria Colwell – killed by her step-father (the first of 34 into the deaths of children known to Social Services Departments between 1972 and 1987). It is universally held that this report established the issue as a major social problem and led to fundamental changes in policy and practice. The reactions to the case have been described as constituting a 'moral panic' – that is, child abuse was seen as 'a threat to societal values and interests' – which can be explained by contemporary debates about 'permissiveness' and the perceived fear of violence in society. The case was bound up with a multitude of concerns relating to the role of social workers, the nature of the welfare state, and the extent of liberalism and permissiveness throughout the social services in their dealings with the poor and the deviant. In effect, Maria Colwell was taken to be the innocent victim destroyed by alien forces that were threatening 'the British way of life': radical social workers, feminists, Marxists, divorcées, pro-abortionists, homosexuals, and all those in favour of anti-authoritarianism, pop culture, drugs, and sexual and social libertarianism. The panic, then, concerned far more than the risk of injury to children (Parton, 1985).

The Inquiry Report criticised the child care system for its failure to protect Maria Colwell, but it also implicitly criticised the policies, especially the emphasis given by child care workers to maintaining the 'natural' family through their adherence to the principle of the 'blood-tie'. Critics argued that in child care practice the focus on the child, which was prominent in 1948, had been blurred by the increasing attention paid to the maintenance of the 'natural' or 'birth' family. The killing of Maria in her 'natural' family more or less halted this policy. So it was that state paternalism was reintroduced in the later 1970s, with a greater emphasis on substitute care and on protecting children from their families. These sentiments, legislated in the 1975 Children Act, placed much more emphasis on the child's welfare, now to be given 'first consideration'.

The 1980s was a decade during which long-established tensions between child care policy, parental responsibility and rights, and the jurisdiction of the state finally snapped. Fox Harding sees the decade as one "in which both the paternalist and birth parent perspectives were in evidence, while laissez-faire and child liberation had a more minor influence" (Fox Harding, 1991, p 230). With a somewhat different emphasis, Michael Freeman, a prominent family lawyer, sees the period as marked by "a precipitate over-reliance on coercive measures" (Freeman, 1992, p 2). The problem was generally perceived as one of a lack of proper balance between too much and too little intervention by social workers. Increasingly the call was made for a new *partnership* between parents and the state, especially after the Cleveland affair (1987), where a large number of children were compulsorily taken into care on the suspicion that they had been sexually abused by their parents (sexual abuse was *the* child protection issue from about 1984), and the subsequent report of the inquiry, published in 1988. English child care policy during these years has been described as an "uneasy synthesis ... a pragmatic response reflecting a number of different, often conflicting positions ... laissez-faire, paternalism, the support of the family, and children's rights" (Fox Harding, 1991, p 224).

Where the 1989 Children Act is concerned, Fox Harding claims that each of her four value perspectives can be found among its sections. She sees paternalism and defence of the birth family's rights as the most prominent, whereas for Freeman the 'non-interventionist strand in the Act' is seen as dominant. Notwithstanding this dispute, the Act is concerned with 'parental responsibility', 'support for children and families' and 'partnership' (between parents and the state), and it reiterates the Cleveland Inquiry's famous proclamation that "the child is a person and not an object of concern". The most fundamental of the new concepts introduced was the replacement of parental rights and duties by 'parental responsibility'. Besides a new emphasis on the family, the Act also introduced a number of new orders relating to family assistance, education supervision, emergency protection and child assessment. Children 'in need' were legislatively defined for the first time and they were recognised as legitimate participants in proceedings affecting their interests. The main provisions of the Act sought to bring together public and private law involving children in areas covering child care, child protection, wardship and divorce. Old concepts such as custody, care and control and access were abolished, as were 'voluntary care', custodianship or the assumption of parental rights, the 'place of safety' order and criminal care orders. In addition, the use of wardship by local authorities was restricted, while in divorce cases the court's ability to scrutinise arrangements for the care of children was reduced (Dingwall et al, 1983; Fox Harding, 1991; Freeman, 1992).

With respect to the broader area of the socio-economic welfare of children, there is widespread agreement among commentators and children's organisations that from the 1960s onwards a widening gulf has developed between the majority of children whose standard of living has risen and a substantial and growing minority who appear to be living in deepening poverty. Some of the causes of child poverty are the result of long-term economic trends, others relate more immediately to government policies throughout the 1980s. Moreover, "Rising poverty, job insecurity, unequal shares in economic growth and changing family structures are affecting every child and every parent from all sections of society." There has been a sixfold increase in divorce since the 1960s; an increase in the proportion of babies born out of wedlock since 1961 from 6% to 32%; 1 in 5 children live in single-parent families now compared with 1 in 13 in the early

1970s; while the proportion of dependent children living in households with less than half the average net income rose from 1 in 10 to 1 in 3 between 1979 and 1992; and one million children are living in housing unfit for human habitation (Mayall, 1994; Oppenheim and Lister, 1996).

In the field of child health there had been a considerable improvement between 1945 and the mid-1970s; this was reflected in the decline of infant and child mortality, and in the improvement in children's heights and general condition. The main cause was obviously to be found in higher wage rates, full employment, state welfare services, the creation of the NHS and their development of new vaccines. Nonetheless, there were nagging doubts about Britain's falling position in the world infant mortality table, the mental condition of between 5 and 10% of children, dental dilapidation, and domestic and road accidents. The Court Committee (1977), which enquired into child health services, felt that they had not responded sufficiently to the changing nature of health and disease. Moreover, the report expressed a "profound anxiety about the state of child health in this country" (quoted in Allsop, 1984, p 157). Further studies, while agreeing that children were healthier in the 1970s than in the 1940s, pointed to serious social inequalities in all aspects of their fitness and argued that in explaining these a key concept was material deprivation. This was reiterated in the famous Black Report (1980) which, in the light of its depressing findings, argued (vainly) for "the abolition of child poverty [to] be adopted as a national goal for the 1980s". Furthermore, a recent study (1991) has concluded that with reference to chronic illness and disability and handicap, which are regarded as crucial features of child health, "The part played by medicine in the prevention and management of these conditions reveals mixed messages about how we value children". Without for a moment disregarding the tremendous advances made in combating children's illnesses and in preventive medicine throughout the century, the consensus of opinion appears to be that in this field, as in so many other areas of social welfare, "Children have not been a focus of policy" (Kurtz and Tomlinson, 1991, p 216; Mayall, 1994, p 165).

This chapter [slightly edited] was taken from Hendrick, H. (1997) *Children, childhood and English society, 1880-1990*, Cambridge: Cambridge University Press. The right of Harry Hendrick to be identified as author of this chapter has been asserted by him in accordance with the 1988 Copyright, Designs and Patents Act.

Part 2: Identifying and exploring concepts and approaches

Implicit in any theory is a set of underlying assumptions and methods that are rarely questioned.... (Johnson, 1995, p 327)

By 'concepts', I have in mind something theoretical – although in the 'soft' rather than the 'hard' sense: as in "a general notion; an abstract idea" (*Oxford English Dictionary*). 'Approaches' is taken to imply means of access, avenues: mapped out pathways along which academics, professionals, and government, proceed. Concepts and approaches are not entirely distinct from each other – they usually function symbiotically. Furthermore, it is important to see that 'concepts and approaches' is used here in two senses. First the chapters identify and discuss a selection of the different perceptions, understandings, assumptions and theories that have governed the ways in which 'child welfare' (as a social category) and children *in* welfare have been presented in the formulation of policies (and the supporting analyses) and in professional practice. Second, in their critique of existing concepts and approaches, the chapters implicitly (and sometimes explicitly) suggest new paradigms through which contentious theories and customs of child welfare may be better examined and even resolved. In other words, the chapters in this section, and indeed throughout the Reader, are often engaged in an *is/ought* dialogue: they seek to present contemporary practices (and their underlying assumptions and beliefs) in opposition to what they claim *ought* to be.

Michael King (Chapter Three) offers a complex chapter that is informed by the sociological theory of 'self-referential systems', meaning that each system – law, science, politics, economics – "is closed to its external world in the sense that information from that world cannot penetrate the system in a direct manner. Before it can be recognised by the system, it has to be reproduced in the system's own terms. Only then can it enter the system's programme". So, in a postmodern mode, King claims social systems exist and function as "distinct and often conflicting sites of authority", as 'truth' and 'valid knowledge' have become fragmented. This, he says, represents a fundamental change in the nature of society that seriously undermines the widely held view that personal morality may be "galvanised into social action through reforming attitudes and interpersonal behaviour". King raises one of the primary conundrums underlying so much of the debate among advocates of children's rights in relation to children's well-being: why, given that this is a 'golden age' for children's rights, do children still suffer exploitation, cruelty and abuse? This troubling question should cast doubt on the ability of moral campaigners to attain their objectives, yet "such disappointed expectations tend to act as a spur to greater efforts". Moreover, once the practical problems have been identified, rather than being solved, they themselves tend to become areas of study and the more they are studied, the more complex they become and their solution seems further away than ever.

If, argues King, we are to move beyond moral indignation at the suffering of children, "there has to be some consolidation of these responses around acceptable moral principles ... [and] practical measures have to be devised for changing people's behaviour towards children". At a philosophical level moral campaigns for child protection bring together three concerns: debates about definitions of children's interests, distinctions between children and adults, and the politically sensitive issue of identifying the appropriate division between the family and the public sphere. At the level of practical intervention, the issues are: how to make parents more responsible for their children's welfare? how to improve the intervention by social workers? how to ensure more efficient cooperation between different agencies? In responding to these concerns we encounter the necessity of "passing from the abstract paradigm of vice and virtue to the practical world of harm and benefits".

The purpose of the chapter is not to show how these difficulties may be overcome: rather it is to query the notion of what King calls "disappointed expectations". The problem, he says, lies not in a "faulty world" but in the "unrealistic notions of what is achievable" and, therefore, "these disappointments arise from the insistence on a model of society and its operations which leads inevitably to disappointments". In opposition King proposes a model that rejects seeing "the social world as a factual entity", preferring instead to regard "all claims to make sense of the world as no more than attempts to give meaning to events which have no intrinsic meaning; meanings are possible only when they emerge out of interpretations".

In King's opinion, reformers need to reformulate morality. As it is, they draw on a version of society that ignores complexities: they see the world in terms of "personal responsibility, individual conscience, commitment, sacrifice, guilt, and the like", and they promote these concepts so as to give the impression that institutional, governmental and global bodies "act and think in identical ways to people or that should be seen in such a way as if they consisted only of collections of individuals, whose personal opinions, hopes, fears, attitudes and beliefs lie behind the formulation of decisions and policies". Reformers, he says, use concepts derived from moral philosophy, although the problem is not in making people more moral but in how to "translate moral agendas for children into *effective social action*" (*original* emphasis).

Of course, where children are involved, the process of 'translation' requires that adult society have an appropriate (and just) understanding of children and childhood. Moss and Petrie (Chapter Four), well-known advocates of early childhood education and care, provide a wide-ranging and thought-provoking account of how children are popularly perceived in British society. The chapter illustrates two sociological tendencies. One is the controversial and mainly feminist hermeneutic, so pervasive throughout social policy writing, namely that which is critical of 'the family' (especially the traditional heterosexual family) and of "parent-centredness", in particular what is referred to as the "notion that 'mothering' is the paradigmatic act of caring" (Tronto, 1993, p 109, also quoted in Moss and Petrie). The second tendency derives from the 'new' social studies of childhood, with its emphasis on social construction, children's agency, and children's rights.

This approach is increasingly influential among professionals and academic researchers, if not in government circles.

There is also a third feature of the authors' approach which, although not specifically detailed in their chapter here, informs the book from which it is taken: "the need for some theory" (Moss and Petrie, 2002, pp 17-54). In contrast to the view of a politician speaking about Sure Start (a programme focused on young children and their families in disadvantaged areas) who claimed that the programme was "based on evidence and experience, not on theory and dogma", Moss and Petrie comment:

> We do not believe there is a choice between 'theory' and 'no theory', or indeed between 'theory' and 'practice'. Nor that somehow 'evidence' or 'experience' can be neutrally produced and interpreted, and that actions self-evidently and inevitably follow. Theories … shape our understandings and govern our actions, whether we recognise this or not, through the concepts and explanations they provide us with to make sense of the world and our experience. (Moss and Petrie, 2002, p 17)

The chapter opens with the reminder, since it is often overlooked or not even recognised, that where the nature of children and childhood is concerned, everything we think of and do to children "represent ethical and political choices, made within larger frameworks of ideas, values and rationalities" (for these choices in relation to the broad sweep of current government policies, see Lister, Chapter Twenty-Five; Hendrick, 2003; Fawcett et al, 2004; James and James, 2004). The authors then discuss the "dominant discourse" of childhood in Britain, which portrays the child as: an incomplete adult; as the future; an innocent ("primitive"); and as redemptive. This discourse is said to be increasingly influential within the government for reasons of economic and social efficacy and, in a climate of risk and uncertainty, services for children (for example, early education) are administered instrumentally, under the terms of business ethics, with the intention of producing future workers and citizens suitable for advanced liberal society. In other words, children are regarded as 'human capital' by a government intent on creating a 'social investment state' (on the dominant discourse, see James et al, 1998; Lee, 2001; James and James, 2004; on 'social investment', see Lister, Chapter Twenty-Five).

The services provided for children, which are discussed at length in the chapter (although in practice the 'customers' are adults, very often parents, and the authors avoid asking whether or not young children would choose the 'services' were they free to do so) are increasingly premised upon a key governmental approach: 'what works?', which is evaluated through 'quality control', meaning what brings the greatest economic reward, and this in turn encourages the view that 'services' belong in the marketplace, rather than within the realm of the public good. In a theme that is reiterated in several other chapters in this Reader (see especially Chapters Six, Twelve, Fourteen, Twenty-Five and Twenty-Six), Moss and Petrie conclude that 'modern' (adult) society is unable to understand children as a social group and childhood as an important period in the life course in its own right.

We adults "only recognise and value children in relation to the adults they will become and childhood as an opportunity for shaping a desired adulthood".

With reference to the 'new' sociology of childhood, Ridge (Chapter Five), in her methodologically oriented chapter, argues for a child-centred approach to understanding how the experience of poverty and social exclusion affects children in their everyday lives. It is well known that growing up in poverty has a variety of adverse outcomes for children, but much less is known about how *children themselves* interpret the experience and how it influences their own perceptions of their lives. In order to rectify these omissions, Ridge puts children at the centre of her empirical inquiry, and in so doing confronts the difficulties in using sparse quantitative data. As she says, accessing suitable data is problematic in view of the "almost complete dearth" of statistics that place children at the centre of the analysis, just as they tend to be ignored in social and statistical accounting (Qvortrup, in James and Prout, 1997). Similarly, collectors of qualitative data have paid little attention to children's voices, either in terms of discussing or seeking out their views. Ridge maintains that adopting a more child-centred approach will entail a radical rethink about the adult-centric conceptual frameworks traditionally used by researchers, such as the developmental paradigm, which in its crude form can produce notions of incapacity and incompetence in childhood. Ridge notes, however, that at least within certain areas of the sociological sciences, there is a shift in progress among professionals in seeing children less as 'object' and more as 'subject' (on the methodological issues involved, see Christensen and James, 2000).

This is an important chapter in two respects. First, rather than simply presenting children as passive victims of poverty it alerts us to the experiential reality of 'poor' children and, therefore, helps to humanise them. And, given the scale of child poverty, this should be of major concern to social scientists, the general public and, not least, the government and its agencies. Second, in drawing attention to the paucity of child-centred statistics, it highlights one of the areas of social knowledge where children have been traditionally invisible, or certainly "have not been the primary focus of attention" (Bradshaw, 1990, quoted in Daniel and Ivatts, 1998, p 7; under New Labour, however, official child-centred data has grown). In both senses, if children are to be accepted as social actors with discussant and active participatory rights befitting an emancipatory citizenship, then recognising them as individuals, with specific experiences, will be crucial, as will be the urgent requirement to disaggregate them from adult-centric knowledge bases.

Given the tentative hold children have on public recognition, one of the crucial concepts in contemporary child welfare is the controversial notion of children's rights, which is a major area of research and political discussion (see Franklin, 2002; for a critical view, see Pupavac, 2002). As Lansdown shows (Chapter Six), children in law are rarely granted the right to make decisions on their own behalf (see Piper, Chapter Thirteen). Instead, responsibility for such decisions and for the welfare of children has traditionally been vested with those adults who care for them, on the presumption that not only are adults better placed than children to "exercise responsibility for decision-making, but also that in so doing they will act in children's best interests". However, there are three reasons why this emphasis on 'the welfare approach' has its limitations: adults often abuse their power over children; adults do not always act in children's best interests, even when no deliberate abuse of power is intended; and children's interests are often ignored in public policy in contrast to those of powerful (adult) interest groups (as almost every chapter in this volume confirms; see especially Chapters Twelve, Seventeen to Nineteen, Twenty-One, Twenty-Four, Twenty-Five). According to Lansdown, we should move beyond a welfare perspective to a position where children increasingly are "the subjects of rights rather than merely the recipients of adult protective care" and that these rights should be considered alongside the traditional approach that sees children as simply having needs for love, care and protection. In common with many other voices, Lansdown calls for more attention to be given to listening to children, including small children, and to providing them with opportunities for participation in matters that affect their own welfare.

Nowhere are children's rights more systematically and cruelly ignored than in cases of child abuse. This subject is nowadays an extraordinarily complex issue, involving numerous socio-medico-economic-psychoanalytic-environmental factors (see Parton et al, 1997). In his wide-ranging account of child welfare policy, with particular reference to "the refocusing of children's services", Nigel Parton (Chapter Seven) persuasively argues that "new strategies have emerged which do not have as their central focus either meeting the needs of children or responding to child abuse, but the assessment and management of risk" and, therefore, the pervasiveness of "uncertainty and ambiguity", as being central to policy and practice, is in danger of being overlooked. (For a clear exposition of the concept of 'risk' in contemporary social policy, see Kemshall, 2002.) Given that the key interest for the 1989 Act was the assessment of risk in terms of 'significant harm', and owing to the difficulty in making a proper assessment, which was deemed to be beyond the competence of health and welfare workers, it was left to the courts to make the final decision, based on forensic evidence. Social workers, then, lost much of their counselling role and became managers of risk assessment. Elsewhere, Parton has claimed that the 1989 Act transformed the definition of child abuse from the socio-medical sphere to that of socio-legal expertise (1991). The process of assessment, however, which is based on 'social knowledge' (Parton, 1991, p 146), involves not only protecting children from abuse within the family, but also protecting parents from what might be viewed as unwarrantable state intervention. And yet, at the same time, as a consequence of neo-liberal economic policies, the volume of 'need' from existing and potential clients has grown well beyond the capacity of welfare resources. In this context, even within the realm of child abuse (aside from other areas of child welfare), "Resources and skills are focused on investigating, managing and sifting 'high risk' cases from the rest".

We live in an age of 'advanced liberalism' (meaning here self-governance/self-regulation) in which 'governmentality', the term used to signal the ensemble of technologies deployed by the state in the governing of populations, uses consciousness of 'risk' as a disciplinary procedure since individuals are compelled to take responsibility for their own condition: they are the managers of their own fate (Kemshall, 2002). People identify the risk and take precautions to avoid it. To paraphrase Nikolas Rose, we are the governors of our own souls (Rose, 1990; see also Rose, in Barry et al, 1996). But, says Parton, since all children are potentially imprudent, the principal focus becomes "the situations they are in and the parents or carers ... who have had devolved to them the responsibility for managing and monitoring risk on the child's behalf". The emphasis is then placed on those families who are socially and economically marginalised and excluded.

In the process of managing risk, the nature of child welfare work and the relationships between social workers and their clients is also changed, as is how social workers think of themselves. Together, these changes, within the context of risk assessment and risk management, are an example of government 'at a distance'. Such a governmental style serves to disguise social and economic inequalities: the problem of rising demand for services for children (as a result of increasing social exclusion) set against inadequate resources is portrayed not as an issue of inequality but as one of coming to terms with risk. In such a scenario, 'need' is eliminated (Kemshall, 2002, pp 79-81).

The 'reframing' process might well be described as a feature of the social investment state: focus on the 'needs' of specific groups of children, but underplay structural economic and social class determinants, thereby reframing the matter as one of personal responsibility in the quest to equip oneself to take advantage of 'life's chances' (Giddens, 1998; Esping-Andersen, 2002; Fawcett et al, 2004; see also Lister, Chapter Twenty Five). Furthermore, the target of the 'reframing' is always one that advances the process of investment, rather than one that searches out the fundamental issues of child abuse, such as, for example, the generational distribution of power within families and the cultural priorities which sustain this pattern. Thus the emphasis on risk focuses on social work as identification and procedure (investigations) but tends to gloss over contexts that give rise to risk and, more importantly, over those that give rise to abuse. Preventative work remains at a minimum; it is discretionary (Kemshall, 2002, pp 79-81; Parton et al, 1997). Parton wants us to characterise child welfare and child protection work in terms of "uncertainty" rather than risk, and to see "the notion of ambiguity" as being central to its practice and to the way in which it is experienced by children and their carers.

One response to child abuse of all kinds is to prioritise improving socio-economic circumstances which, as all professionals agree, are crucial both to parenting skills and developmental outcomes for children. Associated with this approach is the concept of 'social capital' (nowadays increasingly influential within the social sciences), which refers to "cultural practices, norms, networks, links, know-how and tradition, through which people conduct informal interactions of all kinds". With regard to child welfare, 'social capital' (which shares some of the same characteristics as the eco-perspective on the prevention of child abuse; see Jack in Foley et al, 2001, pp 185-92) seeks to position it within a social, economic, and environmental universe.

Virginia Morrow (Chapter Eight), however, describes social capital as a nebulous and "elusive concept", subject to various definitions, and as referring to sociability, social networks, social support, reciprocity, trust, community activities and active citizenship. In effect, she says, it can include anything "from how parents interact with their children to how people feel about where they live, to whom they know, how much they use their 'networks', and how much they trust their politicians". Furthermore, it is "gender-blind, ethnocentric", and has been imported from the US without much reference to cross- and inter-cultural differences.

One of Morrow's principal criticisms concerns the use of the concept in discussion of family breakdown in the UK, where, she says, it serves to create a 'pathologising discourse' that generates a perception of children who are damaged through being in the 'wrong' kinds of family, which in turn draws upon the controversial notion of the 'parenting deficit'. Lying behind much of this scepticism as regards the value of social capital in relation to the consequences of family breakdown for children, is the influential and previously mentioned critique of the traditional heterosexual two-parent family as the most stable and nourishing family form (for a conservative response, see Morgan, 1996, 2000). Thus the chapter is at pains to stress the possibilities of creative relationships for children that may (or may not) be found in "the diversity of family structures" and to criticise 'social capital' for undervaluing children's agency. However, the concept is also criticised for playing down "wider socio-cultural influences on children" with respect to the possibilities for autonomy, participation, and decision making, particularly within the education system, and for its failure to consider "environments of risk", such as school buildings and playgrounds, road traffic, and so on.

In much of the debate on social capital, the focus is on 'the poor' who are deemed to live in declining communities with little or no sense of social cohesion and which lack the virtues of self-help, mutual cooperation, and positive inter-personal relationships. This may well be true to a certain extent, but critics argue that encouraging people to believe that they can 'help themselves' can be seen as a feature of what is known as the 'dark side' of social capital, namely that the analysis may deflect attention away from the social structural problems – unemployment, bad housing, ill-health – that lie at the heart of community degeneration (Di Gennavo, 2004, pp 137-40). Yet, in opposition to this view, many researchers have argued in favour of building up social capital in poor communities, claiming that this "is a more effective way of promoting children's welfare than the present emphasis on formal child protection and family support services and efforts to increase parenting skills and responsibilities" (Jack and Jordan, 1999, p 242).

Broadly speaking, it does appear that the concept is "poorly specified as it relates to children and the use of the term is inherently problematic". If, for example, as Morrow claims, research shows that social capital increases for those who are already well integrated into their communities "and who have some sense of self-efficacy" (who are likely to be adults), then she is right to conclude that "The extent to which this is the case for children and young people remains to be established". Since the concept is currently positioned within an adult-focused analysis that prioritises notions of trust and reciprocity between (adult) individuals, it may well be that only when children (especially those in the middle and older age range) are genuinely included in participatory citizenship, will it be possible to link social capital directly to their well-being.

No chapter in this volume covers a more comprehensive topic than that by Nigel Thomas in his overview of the relationship between children, parents and the state (for a philosophical survey, see Archard, 2003; for an authoritative legal account, see Cretney, 2003; see also Fox Harding, 1997; Fawcett et al, 2004; James and James, 2004). The chapter explores "some assumptions about the relationship between children, parents and the state that underlie law and social policy", and examines "their implications for children's involvement in decisions". Thomas considers a number of themes, including:

- the nature of parental authority;
- state interest in enhancing child welfare;
- state intervention in parental conduct;
- state support for parental authority;
- the 1989 Children Act and the position of children;
- 'Gillick principles' (referring to the 'Gillick competent child' – those under 16 who are deemed to have sufficient knowledge and understanding to consent to medical treatment);
- the 'best interests' of the child;
- 'dynamic self-determination' as a means of reconciling 'best interests' with children's rights.

Unsurprisingly, what emerges from this survey is the confusion surrounding the nature of 'family policies' provided by the state, which have been described elsewhere as "implicit and reluctant" (Fawcett et al, 2004, pp 31-50; see also James and James, 2004, pp 189-212; Archard, 2003, pp 65-116). Not only does the state have an ambivalent attitude towards the concept of 'family policy' in relation to the provision of services to support families, often overseeing a mix of approaches from the laissez-faire to the authoritarian (Fox Harding, 1997), it is also multifaceted in its attitude to intervening in parental conduct on behalf of children. This raises the central issue of when, in a liberal society, is it justified for the state to intervene in the private sphere – the so-called 'liberal dilemma' (for helpful discussion of the family and 'justice', see Archard, 2003, pp 103-15). As Thomas and others have noted, although the state actively supports parental authority, notably and controversially the right to use 'reasonable' physical chastisement, the extent of state intervention varies between different social classes and between different socio-economic groups within the working class.

In general, much of the official attitude to parenthood is expressed in the 1989 Children Act, which sees it as a 'partnership' between the state and parents with the latter having a 'responsibility' that cannot be relinquished, although other parties may acquire it for temporary periods. The Act introduced the 'paramountcy principle', not entirely new in itself but given added emphasis, which made the child's welfare the paramount consideration in all court proceedings concerned with care and upbringing. On the other hand, the Act provides for the law to intervene in family disputes only when it is clearly in the interests of the child's welfare to do so and, of course, this is always a matter of judgment, not fact. As a limited gesture towards children's rights, some allowance was made for children, on the basis of their age and competence, to be consulted in decisions about their lives (for adverse legal practice in this respect since 1989, see Roche, Chapter Twelve; Piper, Chapter Thirteen; James and James, 2004, pp 78-108).

The 1989 Act will be supplemented in part (the exact manner and extent is not yet clear) by the forthcoming Children Bill which, following the government Green Paper *Every child matters*, is set to initiate the most comprehensive reform of child welfare services for 30 years. There will be a new Ministry for Children, Young People and Families, which will bring together children's services, family policy and law, policy on teenage pregnancy, and the Sure Start programme for disadvantaged families. There is no doubt that this development marks "a significant shift in British policy and culture away from a society which has traditionally preferred to leave the responsibility of children's care outside of school to their parents" (Williams, 2004, p 407), to one that adopts a much more universal approach to child welfare in virtually all its forms. In other words, we are witnessing further evolution in the exercise of the 'liberal dilemma' in the new and highly orchestrated context of what is being called the 'social investment state' (see the introduction to Part 4 and Lister, Chapter Twenty-Five). It is important, however, to recognise that although the Green Paper acknowledges that reform must involve not just resources, but "an attitude that reflects the value our society places on children and childhood" (p 4), children remain fixed within 'the family'. No wonder, then, that the document is "less forthcoming" on how to create a culture of respect for young people (Williams, 2004, p 411). In effect, the Green Paper is restructuring the relationship between children, the family and the state, without providing for children to be treated as individuals separate from the family. It is as if the child only becomes a person in the familial environment (and to a lesser extent in that of the school), unlike its parents (and other adults) who have social status (and agency) throughout civil society. Although the family may be seen as protective of children, in its current form, it is essentially an educative institution (which is certainly how the government sees it) that emphasises a kind of guardianship *of* childhood in order to rear children *for* adulthood. Thus in the Green Paper, as in so many other contexts of children's lives, the *becoming* features of childhood overwhelm the *being* of children (Williams, 2004, p 412) and, therefore, there is little or no conceptualisation of children as active agents who are able to participate in the negotiation of their own 'best interests' (James and James, 2004, p 199).

The idea of 'best interests', as Thomas informs us, is beset with difficulties, notably those of 'indeterminacy' and of 'culture' (for a helpful discussion of the 'best interest principle', see Archard, 2003, pp 38-53). The former refers to the problem of identifying children's best interests, which are open to numerous interpretations from moral, medical, social, educational and other perspectives. The question of culture is particularly acute since Britain is officially a 'multicultural' society in which 'cultural relativism', is not without influence in social policy and social work (see Owusu-Bampah, Chapter Ten; for a critique, see Barry, 2000). All 'best interests', aside from often being in conflict with 'Rights' (see Roche, Chapter Twelve), are conceived not only by 'Law' (James and James, 2004), but also within particular cultural contexts – national and class specific: for example, there are well-known differences in attitudes to children and particularly to child-rearing between Britain and Sweden (the latter being far more liberal); similarly, there are different approaches to child rearing, education, gender roles and so on within and between the working and middle classes. This, then, must raise the matter of who (and they are always adults), within the culture, decides on what is best for children in such important and emotional matters as circumcision, arranged marriages, adoption and fostering, and discipline and punishment.

Drawing on the writings of John Eekelaar (1994), the legal theorist, Thomas refers critically to his search for a way to reconcile 'best interests principle' with children's rights primarily through what he calls "dynamic self-determinism" (primarily with reference to child custody cases). According to Eekelaar the intention is to put the child in an environment that exposes it to a range of influences on which it can draw as it develops and, therefore, may be said to contribute to the outcome. The process is 'dynamic' because it appreciates that situations change as the child grows up, and self-deterministic to the extent that the child is allowed certain provision to influence final decisions. Thomas suggests that such a course is unlikely to advance the reconciliation very far since the fact that children may be ignorant of their own best self-interest does not necessarily mean that adults are better informed. To make it more meaningful, he says, children, even young children, would need to be given 'substantial weight' in any dialogue concerning their interests (Neale, 1999, pp 455-76; Smart et al, 2001; on participation in general, see special issue of *Children & Society*, 2004; Hallett and Prout, 2003).

Given the enduring complexity of 'children, parents and the state', it is likely to remain a vexed area of social policy if only because it clearly involves three essential sets of interests. But more than merely interests are involved here for the relationships also embrace (or are embraced by) fundamental matters of liberal individualism, distributional justice, notions of equality, paternalist responsibility, citizenship, and democratic justice. We know from our historical understanding that 'the family' has been pivotal to the ongoing evolution of 'the state' or what might be better described as a kind of 'social politics' – the arena in which so many of the tensions inherent in liberal democracy have been exposed and attempts made at reconciliation. In such an environment, the rights (in the loose sense of the word) of children are always at risk. This is partly because with the best will in the world it is often difficult to assess the meaning and appropriateness of such rights in order to measure up 'freedom' with a liberal and caring paternalism. But it is also because at nearly every level of politics there sits 'power' in all its diverse forms. Children are nearly always excluded from Power – they meet it in circumstances not of their own choosing and then they have to work on it accordingly (children's agency, while not explicitly a variable in the technology of Power, is discussed in James et al, 1998; Lee, 2001; Mayall, 2002; James and James, 2004).

There is, however, a crucial lesson that we should learn from history, namely that parents cannot be trusted in all circumstances to do their best for their children. For reasons of incompetence or malevolence, there will be times when children need protection, which must come from all of us in the form of the state, and how the state acts is likely to be controversial. Many contemporary commentators are critical of the way in which New Labour 'uses' the state in pursuit of its own ideological objectives. But it has ever been so. States are no more than what their citizens concede to them. Perhaps not since the end of the 19th century, the period when the relationship between state, family and citizen underwent some profound social and political changes (see Harris, 1993; Hendrick, 1994), has there been such a demand for a way of understanding the ongoing tensions between 'modernity' and 'post-modernity'. In our current age of globalisation, it is fashionable to speak of "reinventing the family" as we go in search of "new lifestyles" (Beck-Gersheim, 2002). Whether such enterprises will resolve the dilemmas involved in reconciling children, parents and the state remains to be seen. And what will happen to children – "young human beings" (Archard, 2003, p 1) – is surely one of the most important ethical questions facing us today.

In a society such as Britain, where racism continues to exist despite our official commitment to multiculturalism, matters of 'culture', particularly those of minority ethnic groups, are bound to be controversial. The term 'anti-racism' covers a variety of political positions, so that is it sometimes hard to know exactly whose voice is speaking, the degree to which it is representative, and with what authority. Kwame Owusu-Bempah (Chapter Ten) adopts a perspective that emphasises the integrity of Black and Asian cultures in Britain, and he is suspicious of interference from welfare professionals who bring 'liberal values' to their work with minority ethnic families, especially in child protection cases (see also Barn et al, 1997; Gibbons et al, 1995). Many of these professionals, according to Owusu-Bempah, use 'race' (a "socially fabricated" concept and a "fallacy") as a frame of reference, even though they may eschew the word itself.

The chapter forcefully asserts that professional intervention should be guided by "cultural beliefs and values" as well as "needs". The particular focus of criticism concerns social workers' responses to child raising and child care within minority ethnic groups. Owusu-Bempah is keen to link child rearing to "the group's culture". He makes much of the so-called "individualistic" culture of Britain, which he sets against minority ethnic "collectivist" cultures in order to locate their child-raising practices within the context of "group loyalties", meaning the family and the community. Thus social workers are berated for failing to appreciate the African adage that "it takes a whole village to raise a child" and for failing to accept that adoption and fostering in the larger community is widely practised throughout sub-Saharan African cultures (among those criticised are Dwivedi and Varma, 1996; for life in a sub-Saharan village, see Rwezaura in Allston, 1994, pp 82-116). Professionals, it is said, "overreact" to or misconstrue minority ethnic practices, which are claimed by Owusu-Bempah to be integral to the relevant 'culture', and these in turn are held to be integral to "one's psychological processes" (on the 'overreaction' of liberal social workers in disciplinary matters, see also Barn, 2002).

However, the adoption of a 'politically correct' approach may well have been one of the factors contributing to the failure of social workers to prevent the tragic and horrific death of eight-year-old Victoria Climbié, killed by her aunt (and guardian) and her partner, after having been sent by her parents from the Ivory Coast to live the good life in England. When the (black) social worker concerned heard of the child having to stand to attention in the presence of her aunt, she "concluded that this type of relationship was one that can be seen in many Afro-Caribbean families because respect and obedience are very important features of the Afro-Caribbean family script". As Ratna Dutt, Director of the Race Equality Unit, commented: "There is some evidence to suggest that one of the consequences of an exclusive focus on 'culture' in work with black children and families, is [that] it leaves black and minority children in potentially dangerous situations..." (The Victoria Climbié Inquiry, Report, 2003, part V, p 16).

Owusu-Bempah takes the view that in many instances, the liberal critique of minority ethnic child care, such as concern about adverse psychological consequences of certain child-raising practices, originates in an implicit assumption that Western culture is superior to all others (Owusu-Bempah and Howitt, 2000, pp 80-112). He links the attitude of practitioners (including many non-white professionals) to the research literature which, in so far as it is critical of African-Caribbean family structure and South Asian families, he says is racially prejudiced. He concludes with the proper reminder that dealing with the needs of black children requires "a recognition of, and solutions to, racism's injurious effects on them". This chapter is important because it raises the question of the place of 'multiculturalism' in a liberal democracy and posits many controversial claims concerning the 'right' of minority cultures to exercise discretion as to how they will rear their children. What is missing, however, is the perspective of the child – so commonplace in the writings of the 'new' social studies of childhood, yet so often absent in other academic contexts of social policy.

If the standpoint of the child ignored, so, too, is an intellectual argument in support of cultural relativism; it is merely assumed to be unproblematic. In claiming that "no group's culture is superior or inferior to that of another", Owusu-Bempah is adopting a normative relativist position, which holds that it is wrong to pass judgement on the values of others (Wong in Singer, 1991, p 442; for a comprehensive critique of 'cultural relativism', see Barry, 2000; for reconciling culture and human rights, see Alston, 1994; for a critical review of multiculturalism, see Goodhart, 2004; for a defence of 'cultural toleration', see Kukathas, in Shapiro and Kymlicka, 1997, pp 69-104). This relativism seems to be almost unassailable, since being rooted in "egalitarianism, in liberalism and in modernism" makes it difficult for liberals to criticize (Freeman, in Fottrell, 2000, p 22). The danger with cultural relativism is that it embeds itself in the view that traditional practices (custom) are necessary for the integrity of a 'culture'. Such an assertion is a dead-end for reasoned argument. Custom cannot determine what is just. Hence the relevance of Mill's famous dictum: the "despotism of custom". We cannot allow Reason to be ignored: "the argument for my practice must be more than that the practice exists" (Freeman, in Fottrell, 2000, p 23).

Many multiculturalists exert a moral pressure on liberals to leave the welfare of children to the good will of their respective culture, except in extreme circumstances. In defence of certain practices, such as circumcision, arranged marriages, or submission to religious beliefs, it is sometimes argued that it may be abusive *not* to make the child live according to custom, since failure to do so will exclude it from its birth culture and, therefore, undermine its psychological, moral and social development (Frosh, in King, 1999, p 207; Owusu-Bempah and Howitt, 2000, p 87). Even if this were true (and as it stands it is much more of a presupposition than a social scientific 'fact'), it would not make the child-rearing practices just and humane. Furthermore, the presentation of 'culture' in this style presupposes that it can be viewed as a single entity. But what of opposition to particular child-raising practices from within the culture? What about the protests of children themselves? What about the absence of consent, surely a, if not *the*, crucial consideration? These questions should not be allowed to go unanswered. We should avoid romanticising 'difference' at the expense of those who have no choice but to suffer its consequences. We must not be intimidated and allow 'fundamentalists', of any kind, to speak "on behalf of those who do not share their views, even though they remain attached in many ways to their culture, community and religious practices" (Frosh, in King, 1999, p 209). We must not reify the idea of 'culture' (Arthur, in La Follette, 2003, p 425).

In describing "principles of good practice" for professionals, Owusu-Bempah has argued elsewhere that they should "go beyond the philosophy of child-centredness", to include "the family (nuclear and extended) and the wider environment". He advocates an eco-system approach as being more appropriate, since it would "understand the structural factors that either facilitate or impede the family's functioning and consequently the child's well-being" (Owusu-Bempah, in Foley et al, 2001, p 48; on the eco-perspective, see Jack and Gordon, 1999, pp 242-56; Jack, in Foley et al, 2001, p 48). But this puts too much emphasis on poverty and inequality, while eliding the equally significant role of 'cultural' practice in child abuse:

> In societies where the physical punishment of children is either rare, or legally prohibited, the child physical abuse rate tends to be significantly lower than in countries where corporal punishment is sanctioned ... societies that place a strong emphasis on children's rights, as citizen ... are likely to experience a much lower level of all kinds of child abuse. (Jack, in Foley et al, 2001, p 189; for details see Belsky, 1993)

In other words, *cultural values* matter. To suggest that professional practice should be guided by "not just humanitarian or liberal principles but by a principle of 'genuine empowerment'" (Owusu-Bempah, in Foley et al, 2001, p 48), would put children at risk. The critical question is, "genuine empowerment" for whom? Furthermore, perhaps we should be careful before subordinating "humanitarianism or liberal principles" to a mere category of "just"; whatever their imperfections, they remain the basis for the promotion of Justice.

One of the themes of this Reader is the nature of the 'moral agendas' that we adults propose for coming to terms with children's welfare, and the problems of turning such agendas into beneficial social policy (for a thoughtful collection of essays, see King, 1999). However, a core problem facing ethicists throughout the social sciences are the multifarious stances on offer in contemporary society. Is there a truth? If not, how shall we assess 'value'? Is it possible to proceed in search of the just action? If truth is still possible, how shall we recognise it? In his chapter, Terry Carney (Chapter Eleven) grapples with certain inherent features of this quandary as he searches for a suitable political model. He considers two main forms: 'social citizenship' and 'active citizenship' (the social democratic solution), and 'contractualism' and the privatisation of state services. Neither solution, he says, is perfect but the emphasis should be on "dissolving the dichotomy between the public and the private spheres of action". With one eye on 'postmodernism' (meaning more open, more local, more responsive settings), Carney proposes two alternative models. One is a "dialogic community" built on relations of "interdependence, which may arise outside the law and the traditional boundaries of the state" (King, in King, 1999, p 18). The second model is communitarianism, which is strong on ethical content but is open to abuse through individualism, commercialism, and intolerance (for intolerance of young people under New Labour, see James and James, Chapter Fifteen; Hendrick, 2003, pp 205-54).

After reading Carney, the conclusion may well be the "impossibility of the political system being taken over by moral values" (King, in King, 1999, p 19). If values do 'enter' the system, it is only in the form of "political communications, that is as policies or political solutions to social problems". Thus "what was once a moral principle is obliged to do business with all those other values and interests that vie for attention within the discourse of politics" (King, in King, 1999, p 19). Of course, this is true. This may explain why, in the last analysis, "Carney moves away from grand political ideas to more modest proposals, such as family group conferences or other popular justice institutions, which may possibly be able to exist at the level of interpersonal communications without having to win political approval" (King, in King, 1999, p 19). On the face of it, this is a depressing conclusion for it appears to be asking us to accept that there is an unbridgeable gulf between moral values and political systems. And yet, one should not abandon optimism quite so readily. The histories of oppressed and marginalised peoples throughout the ages are testimonies to the continual and by no means always unsuccessful struggle to successfully unite principles of justice ('moral agendas') and politics. Postmodernists may not care much for sociological or historical 'grand narratives', but read carefully, they are a helpful guide to the crevices of Power and the deceits of the powerful.

Good intentions into social action

Michael King

Morality

Little in life arouses moral indignation and demands moral judgements and action more than the suffering of children, so let us start [...] with morality and the ways we distinguish between good and evil. Moral discourses take the spectacle of children's suffering and seek out the evil that has caused that suffering. In a powerful symbolic way the suffering of children comes to represent the exploitation of the powerless, the abuse of the defenceless, innocence defiled. The relief of this suffering, the banishment of evil, the restoration of good, becomes a moral campaign for which children symbolise virtue, innocence and powerlessness. Children become symbols of the good which needs to be protected against the powerful, against evil – the abusers, molesters, batterers, exploiters, who treat children in selfish, callous, indifferent, cruel ways. Children must also be protected against the imperfect world that adults have created with its dangers, its pollutants, its inequalities, its injustices. Children's suffering inspires moral campaigns to combat what comes to be seen as 'abuse', to rescue children from it, to protect them from it and prevent it and to punish those who continue to perpetrate it. 'Abuse' itself comes to represent an evil which can eventually be defeated through concerted efforts on the part of the social forces of good, the task becomes one of rooting out the causes of this evil and systematically eliminating them, predicting where the next outbreak will occur, and making anticipatory strikes, identifying victims in advance and moving them metaphorically, and in some cases, literally to safer ground.

Once the evil that causes children's suffering has been renamed 'abuse', the way lies open for different forms of action to expose abuse and combat it and its effects. This action may take a social hygienic form, where abuse is seen as endemic in those parts of society which lack such healthy attributes as community spirit, neighbourliness, a social conscience, parenting skills, self-discipline, religion and education as would immunise them against evils. They may take on the medical form of diagnosing pathologies to be remedied through therapy and treatment of the biological or psychological symptoms or underlying causes of the aberrant behaviour. Recently, they have taken on the form of classifying certain families as 'dysfunctional' and of correcting the malfunctioning through various kinds of remedial treatment. All these campaigns against abuse are founded on the notion of intervention, interfering with the relationship between the abused and the abuser, or changing the conditions that are seen to give rise to the abuse. This intervention is authorised by such powerful moral justifications as 'the needs of the child', 'children's welfare' or 'the interests of the child'. Although, as we shall see, in order to achieve social authority these moral actions have usually to be supported today by medical or scientific evidence.

A very different form that moral campaigns take begins with the spectacle of the vulnerability and powerlessness of children. Here children's suffering is seen as the result of this powerlessness (or the powerlessness of those who wish to protect or rescue them) and the advantage taken of that powerlessness by adults who dominate and exploit them or act in ways that are indifferent to their needs and interests. This moral campaign has taken the form of giving children 'rights', that is, rights of autonomy which oblige adults to regard them as people rather than objects, of arming them with the power to say 'no' and to make known what they want so that other adults may help them to achieve these ends. In this way they, or those authorised to interpret what they want or need, will be better able to defend themselves against the harms perpetrated upon them by adults and the adult world. Rights, therefore, not only represent power in the hands of the rights-holder, but they also force others to treat the rights-holder with respect. As one author wrote [...] of children's rights, "giving rights to children is ... a public and palpable acknowledgement of their status and worth" (Archard, 1993, pp 168-9).

Moral principles into social action

If the immediate responses against child abuse are to move beyond the stage of emotional reactions and serve as a springboard for campaigns to protect and relieve the suffering of children, there has first to be some consolidation of these responses around acceptable moral principles. Second, practical measures have to be devised for changing people's behaviour towards children.

For the first of these requirements, philosophers are at hand to remind us that society's treatment of children is not merely a matter of early intervention, practical reasoning and skilful prediction. There are issues of principles and values at stake, which need to be resolved by society, before policies can be drafted and decisions made. Moral philosophy occupies itself specifically with the analysis of moral tenets – what constitutes virtue and vice and how these distinctions are morally justified. Yet moral philosophers do not confine themselves to the analysis of the values contained in codes for good and evil, morality and immorality. They are also, and perhaps even principally, concerned with showing how these codes can be improved so as to serve as guidelines for 'practical action', for the encouragement of moral behaviour and for the discouragement of immorality. Here moral philosophy often merges with political philosophy in attempting both to set out for society a set of moral objectives, and indicating the ways of achieving these objectives through different forms of social organisation. Much of the theoretical writing on children's rights is of this nature. Political philosophy assists in a general understanding of the ways that moral values may become deployed in society. While they are not directly concerned with practical issues such as the drafting and enforcement of laws, they attempt to analyse political institutions and to propose the kind of political order that would be necessary for moral principles to find expression in practical action. These may be related to such matters as the role of the state, the family, education, the class structure or the deployment of legal and other regulatory measures, such as distributions of wealth and power. At this level of philosophical analysis, the moral campaigns for preventing, and protecting children against, the evil that is child abuse bring together three important concerns: (1) debates about what is and what is not in the interests of children, (2) issues around the distinction between children and adults, and (3) problems relating to the division between private and public and more particularly, between the family and the outside world.

This leads to the second requirement, the need for effective practical action. How can society make parents take more responsibility for their children's well-being? How can social workers better intervene at an early stage in situations of risk? How can greater cooperation between all those social agencies concerned with different aspects of children's lives be achieved, to enable more effective and better-informed decisions to be made or to empower children or those that seek to protect them? Issues such as these are the stock-in-trade of policy formulators and decision makers. In seeking to answer these difficult questions they necessarily pass from the level of abstract principles to that of applying practical knowledge. This does not represent an abandonment of morality, but rather the necessity of passing from the abstract paradigm of vice and virtue to the practical world of harm and benefits. This brings into the arena disciplines, such as paediatrics, psychology and psychiatry, pedagogy and nutrition, which in modern society have the task of identifying the kinds of behaviour and environmental conditions that are good for children and those which are likely to harm children. The last 50 years have seen a massive growth, not only in the number of such experts, but also in the width and depth of their expertise. Harms which were once considered as inevitable or matters of fate are now seen as controllable, and the results of decisions or the failure to make the appropriate decisions.

Disappointed expectations

It is often very difficult to know whether these moral campaigns succeed in achieving their objectives. Of course, where these objectives are very specific, such as raising the level of nutritional intake or the reduction or elimination of certain diseases, success and failure are relatively easy to measure. But here the moral concern has been translatable directly into concern for medical action and the attainment of health targets. Where the target concerns changing social policies towards children, the results are far more difficult to estimate. Some appear to succeed, others not. Some work for a time, but then government policy changes or enthusiasm for them wanes and they stop working so well. Others, which appear to work well, create new problems for children which were not anticipated by the promoters of the campaigns or the policy makers who attempted to convert moral principles into social action.

So is it surprising that, despite our living in a 'golden age' for children's rights, where 187 nations of the world have ratified the United Nations Convention on the Rights of the Child, even in the prosperous countries of the West children are still subjected to so many forms of harmful behaviour? Why should this be so in a world which has pledged itself to promote the welfare of children? Why do millions of children still suffer the most serious deprivations? Why are they still being exploited? Why are they still being damaged and their future blighted by the behaviour of adults?

These are troubling questions which cast serious doubt on the efforts of moral campaigners to eliminate abuse and construct a better world for children. Yet far from deterring these campaigners in their efforts to promote the welfare of children, such disappointed expectations tend to act as a spur to greater efforts. Disappointments will often lead to revigorised attempts to succeed, but this time using new techniques, new modes of analysis which are guaranteed to improve efficiency and effectiveness. Past failures tend to be seen and explained away as the result of 'practical problems'. The original objectives are still seen as achievable but, as always, problems arise when you try to put principled policies into practice, and part of the task is to overcome them. These obstacles to success, these 'practical problems' may be identified as, for example, lack of resources or the lack of will to allocate sufficient resources to fund programmes, national interests which stand in the way of child-centred policies, superstition and irrational beliefs based on religion or tradition. Obstructions to progress may also be seen to come from vested commercial interests in things remaining as they are or the difficulty of providing adequate proof in the courts to convict people who harm children. Once these 'practical problems' have been identified, it would seem to be only a matter of time before the obstacles they present can be overcome and the campaigns for improving children's lives be set back on track. However, it rarely seems to work like that. Instead, the obstacles themselves tend to become major areas for study and analysis and the more they are studied the more complex the situation seems to become and the further we seem to be from the original problems and ways of solving them. Things have moved on to reveal that what was once thought to be the important issue is now seen as peripheral, and problems of which we were previously unaware are now shown to be central to any resolution. Why should this be? How can social action for children be made more effective? How can success be guaranteed? How can obstacles and unintended consequences be anticipated in advance and so overcome?

It would be comforting if this book [from which this chapter is taken – Editor] were able to answer these questions by pointing to some magical formula which would dissolve all impediments to the improvement of children's lives. Instead, what it attempts to do is to question the very notion of 'disappointed expectations'. Yet, this in itself may well be a useful exercise, for, if people's expectations are changed, the deployment of their energies and inventiveness may also take different directions. If this and the succeeding chapters are able to show that the disappointed expectations of moral campaigners are in fact products not of a faulty world, but of their own unrealistic notions of what is achievable and how these achievements may be realised, some benefits may yet emerge. Yet, in one respect, the aim of this book is to go much further than that. What it attempts to do is to demonstrate in the various themes and topics covered that these disappointments arise from the insistence on a model of society and its operations *which leads inevitably to disappointments.* This is not a matter of self-delusion in any simple meaning of the term, but results rather from the insistence on certain beliefs about what society consists of, which in turn lead to policies and courses of action based on those beliefs. What this book argues is that if the policies and the actions do not lead to the desired results, this is not because of 'practical problems', but is a consequence of particular readings of modern society and the way that it operates. What it will suggest is that these readings construct not only what appear to be solutions, failures and disappointed expectations, but also the very problems that give rise to them. To take this line of inquiry and question the way that moral issues concerning children are constructed will not itself led to solutions, but it may lead to interesting reformulations of problems.

What then are the principle characteristics of this model of society which give rise to such hopes for regulation and control of harmful conduct towards children, but also to such disappointments? They can be identified as follows:

- a continuity between consciousness and the social world;
- people as the primary agents for all social events;
- direct input-output relations between social groups and organisations;
- the possibility of identifying definitive causes.

A continuity between consciousness and the social world

This model of society makes no clear distinction between the attitudes, beliefs, ideas and thoughts that pass through the minds of individual people and their communication to others in ways that have meaning for others or make sense to others. It assumes that society is no more or no less than collective consciousnesses made social. It follows, therefore, that to change society one needs only to change the attitudes and beliefs of people. Philosophical ideas, political ideologies, and moral beliefs which may be powerful forces in altering individuals' attitudes towards children and formulating justifications and explanations for their behaviour in relation to them, may, according to this vision of society, also change society in certain preferred directions.

The converse of this view, which I shall be describing later in this chapter, is that consciousness is quite separate from society. While ideas and ideologies may have the power to change people's attitudes, including their way of seeing the world and their own behaviour – in Michel Foucault's term, with 'the care of the self' (Foucault, 1979) – this should not be confused with changing society.

People as the primary agents for all social events

Society is seen, according to this perspective, as the sum of all those people who exist within its boundaries. Neither it nor the social institutions which are regarded as essential to the operation of society, are any different from the people within them. The unity of society, its common purpose and goals, means the unity of its people. It is their conduct and their decisions in their varied social roles which will determine society's future. When, therefore, one talks of law or politics, what one is really referring to are lawyers and politicians. According to this view, social systems such as law, politics and science have no separate identity from the people who operate them. To change society one needs, therefore, to change people, and to improve society, one needs to improve people's behaviour by applying moral programmes, for example, making them less selfish, less violent, less intolerant, and more generous, kind, altruistic, etc. These changes, according to this approach, will automatically improve the operation of social systems, and in the case of children's interests, will cause them to work in ways that promote and protect those interests. This is not to deny that changing the processes and procedures of institutions may also offer a way forward, but since there is no clear distinction between organisations and the people who operate them, the success or failure of such reforms are seen to depend entirely upon their effects on people. Regulation of social organisations, therefore, is no different from the regulation of the people who belong to these organisations. It consists of putting into places of power and responsibility people who are likely to be virtuous, and devising structures to ensure that these right-minded people fill these positions and continue to act in virtuous ways once they have been appointed.

Direct input–output relations

Just as organisations are seen as people, and groups of people relate to one another in direct ways, so the conduct of organisations is no different from the expression of the sum of the people who run them. Relations between the different organisations of society are therefore seen as operating in a relatively simple and direct manner with information passing from one to the other and the decisions of one having a direct effect on the behaviour of the other. This direct input–output relationship may take different forms, according to the perspective of the particular analysis being applied. Society may be seen, for instance, as involving networks of power relationships between people who represent different points of view and/or different interests. More cynical analysts tend, for example, to see politicians, in particular, using their power to make the courts or social workers, universities or scientists, all dance to their tune. Banks and large corporations may be seen as attempting to control the politicians in ways that ensure that their interests are always served. Different interest groups may combine with one another to change society in ways that increase their power and wealth or to combat what they see as being threats to the existing order (which is often identical to their own vested interests). The global scene in this perspective is simply an international version of the same game. The only difference is that people are now representatives of different nations or multinational corporations. One finds here the same conception of action to change things for the better as depending upon strategies, alliances, motivation and rational assessments of gains and losses, and the same notion of a direct relationship between policies and actions. The only difference is that these ways of understanding now take on a global or international dimension.

Other, perhaps more optimistic versions, would see the forces of regulation and control as exercising a restraining and salutary influence on what would otherwise be a chaotic, unjust world, but always in a direct, uncomplex way. The police, judges and lawyers, for example, are portrayed as rooting out corruption and abuses of power in political and financial institutions. Once again, however, the relations are between people who represent (and may be representative of) different social organisations. This is of course the stuff of the culture of films, novels and television dramas, but these fictional representations succeed in attracting a large readership and audience because they rely unquestioningly upon a version of how society works which most people believe, or want to believe, to be true. Furthermore, there is no real difference between these fictional representations and the accounts of national and international events in the news reporting of newspapers and the broadcasting media. Both emphasise the individual, or groups of like-minded individuals, as the prime movers, whether for good or evil, for progress or resistance to progress, in the social world. It is their behaviour which is seen as having a direct impact on history and on the future. Changing organisations is seen as the equivalent of changing people. Organisations are attributed with the same characteristics as people, both good and evil.

The possibility of identifying definitive causes

The assumption that the causes of events in the social world are either self-evident or are out there waiting to be uncovered, is a pre-requisite for this model of society. This does not mean that everyone will agree about causes. On the contrary, several different explanations may exist for the same event. People cause harm to children because they are inherently evil, because they have no sense of responsibility, because of their own childhood experiences, because they have not been properly educated in child care, because of stress in their lives. Each of these causal explanations is capable of producing its own kind of regulatory measures, for instance, imprisonment, counselling, therapy, improved living conditions, help in times of crisis, educational courses, or surveillance by social workers.

Failures in regulation are likely to be interpreted in ways which do not usually disqualify the original explanation for the behaviour, but are more likely to cast doubt on the efficiency of those responsible for carrying out the regulatory measures (Howitt, 1992). In a similar manner, apparent successes of regulatory measures based on one causal account do not necessarily invalidate alternative accounts. The continued belief that it is still possible to identify 'the real causes' of harm to children is essential to the notion that such harms are preventable and controllable – whether they consist of a single action by an individual, such as a blow struck in anger which injures a child, or a collective action such as government policies which create 'an underclass', living in pockets of poverty and deprivation. Even if there is controversy over the causes which analysts identify as valid explanations and even if others analysts prefer different explanations, the belief that the establishment of a true cause or true causes is a possibility is a prerequisite to an assumption that regulatory measures may operate upon people's behaviour and so control or eliminate the causes which analysts have identified. The recognition of causes then allows for the possibility of planning and improvements in control over undesirable behaviour. It also allows for prediction and for decisions to be made on the basis that they are not arbitrary or based on speculation, but depend on the existence of chains of causality which have occurred in the past and are likely to recur in the future.

What happens when the unexpected occurs? What happens, for example, when carefully devised plans to secure a child's future welfare, based on accepted ideas about probable sources of benefits and harms to children, are thwarted by such unanticipated events as serious illness, a traffic accident, winning the lottery, falling in love, becoming pregnant, unexpected redundancy, moving home to another country or another part of the same country, or the sudden death of a family member? Only where the occurrence of the disruptive event and its impact on the child and that child's carers were specifically included in the causal account which formed the basis for the prediction will these plans still be likely to hold good. Yet, in practice, when it comes to decisions about helping and protecting children the possibility of unforeseeable occurrences, however common they may be in practice, are unlikely to be included in the evaluation of what is best for the child, simply because they are unforeseeable. By their very nature these events were unpredictable before the decision to adopt the plan, and after the decision they may continue to be seen as chance happenings, which could not have been anticipated and therefore are not to be included in any future exercise in identifying and preventing causes, which may continue unaffected by them. Alternatively, it may be decided that the occurrence of these events should have been foreseen, in which case there may be demands for more detailed and more inclusive causal accounts, so that by including in future the possibility of these events occurring, the accuracy of prediction will be increased. Yet neither the identification of unforeseen causes nor increases in the complexity and scope of causal accounts are likely to prevent the unexpected occurring in future. The problem is not that the particular causal account failed, but that any model which produces the possibility of a definitive account of causality has insuperable problems.

Regulation and authority within a constructed world

It is easy to be critical of people who over-simplify and attempt to foist upon us solutions based on simplistic and reductionist solutions, but this is not the purpose [...] of the preceding section[...]. An alternative approach is to see reduction and simplification as a necessary precursor to any formulation of problems and thus to any proposed solution to those problems. If we take this view it becomes possible to see moral reformers' version of society as consisting of people, or rather of a collective consciousness, to view social organisations as behaving like people and causes as being identifiable as the results of the behaviour of people, not as mistaken, but as *correct in their own terms*, as inevitable if one starts with the formulation of social problems as moral defects.

In order to make this kind of observation we need to pass from a sociology which sees the social world as a factual entity to one which regards all claims to make sense of the world as no more than attempts to give meaning to events which have no intrinsic meaning; meanings are possible only where they emerge out of interpretations. We need to move from a version of social problem solving which offers the prospect of creating order from a disordered, defective world, to one which observes and attempts to give some meaning to these efforts.

From the perspective of a sociological observer of moral campaigns to improve the defective world, the hopelessness of many such enterprises may appear obvious, but to those engaged in day-to-day problem-solving exercises it may take an appearance similar to that of reassembling the jumbled pieces of a jigsaw puzzle. They may remove each of the pieces from the board to be examined separately from the whole. Then, where pieces are found to be defective, they may perhaps reshape them slightly so as to produce a better fit and put them in their proper place. Once the reformed world is intact, there may be difficulties in keeping the pieces in place, as the social world tends to be shaken about from time to time. But what is needed is social cohesion, to be found perhaps in the law, community spirit, a sense of social responsibility, a willingness to compromise, or good common sense and commitment to progress – which, like super glue, will be guaranteed to keep the pieces in their proper place. Once firmly in place, all the pieces, the elements of the social world, can be relied upon to contribute to the assurance of a secure, happy future.

It was this style of problem solving that led to the United Nations Convention on the Rights of the Child. The problem to be solved here was the suffering and impotence of children throughout the world; the pieces of the jigsaw puzzle were the nations of the world, many of which were seen as pursuing policies and permitting practices that were harmful to children's interests. These defects could be remedied by sensible reshaping. Rules and principles cold be produced which would act as guidelines for all future treatment of children in the world, and the combination of law and public opinion would operate as the glue to keep it all together.

Few contemporary sociologists, one should emphasise, would see the social world or society's problems in this unproblematic way. Rather, contemporary social theories, whether postmodernist or poststructuralist, would be likely to question whether the notion that a thing called 'the social world' or 'society' exists as an object to be dissected, manipulated, shaped and improved. Instead what they would propose is that such concepts only have meaning because they become formulated in people's minds and as part of individual or collective interpretations of external events. Society for them is a construct, the meaning of which depends upon the values, beliefs and interpretations of whoever is attempting to make sense of these events.

Once it becomes necessary to regard society or the social world not as an object, but as a construct, a collective abstraction which helps people to make sense of the past, exist in the present and plan for the future, it follows that there may exist not one but many different notions about what society consists of, what makes it work well or what causes it to malfunction. Furthermore, it becomes inevitable that programmes for reform, whether global, national or institutional, will be dependent upon the acceptance of one particular version of what society is – the version which makes it appear that such reforms are possible.

Similarly, recognition of this constructed nature of society and the existence of multiple versions of social reality changes fundamentally the way that a sociological observer would view moral campaigns for improving the world or guarding against undesirable changes to that world. From their perspective, the task of regulating and controlling the future will no longer be seen simply as one of working to a particular blueprint to mobilise the forces of change or overcome the obstacles to change. In addition, part of that task will also include creating a convincing impression that there is indeed 'a society' that is common to everyone, whether it is called 'society' or 'the community', 'our country', 'our world', 'the common good' or 'our culture', so that this entity, this 'something' which the would-be regulators have constructed, can be seen as capable of control in the ways that they have devised. In relation specifically to children, it may be necessary, in order to avoid, eliminate or reduce the risks in situations which are seen as damaging to children, to make people believe that they are part of the same collectivity – be it 'the extended family', 'the nation' or 'the community', be it Europe, the West or the global village – which has common interests and the common objectives of improving children's well-being and meeting their needs, which are achievable by working together. Once this notion of collectivity, of consensual interests has been established it may, of course, be reinforced by reference, for example, to 'family values' ' the views of society', 'the interests of society' or 'the common interest' in ways that help to reinforce the belief that this unity actually exists as an object and that it is the power of human action that will change it for better or for worse.

A major problem for moral campaigns today is that of establishing authority for their particular view or construction of society, for without such authority there can be little chance of achieving either the concerted action against harm and abuse or the consensus or 'sense of community' on which such collective action depends.

Determining where today's morality resides is the first problem facing such campaigns. There was a time when religion was able to provide the overriding authority both for the existence of society and the code of conduct that was thought necessary to make that society virtuous. Morality at that time consisted of obeying what were accepted as the laws or commands of a deity or deities who existed beyond the reach of human action. People cold affect the behaviour of God or the gods only indirectly, by, for example, making sacrifices or obeying His or their commandments.

Later, when religious authority declined in its effectiveness, moral campaigns were able to rely up to a point upon the authority that resided within individual consciences. Now it was the inner voice which dictated not only personal, but also collective, social responsibility. Virtue or vice in society and the world could be seen as the result of people's adherence to or departure from personal moral codes. Where harm and abuse existed, they were the result of defective individuals or faulty decision making by people working within organisations. It is this type of moral authority which justified the model of society examined earlier which makes no clear distinction between consciousness and society. It is a belief in this moral authority which makes possible a version of society where adherence to moral principles offers the guiding light for the maintenance or improvement of children's well-being and failure to respect those principles result in harm and abuse of children. Discipline and altruism are seen as necessary if 'society' is to progress in ways which are recognised consensually as desirable. An important aspect of effective regulation within this model of society become, therefore, formulating common goals which are capable of uniting people with very different political and religious beliefs, different interests, different ideologies and different life-styles. The idea of rights of children provides one set of goals on which it may well be possible to secure the nominal support of everyone, or almost everyone, at least where this is seen as meaning the reduction of suffering and the creation of a better life for children.

It is a short step from a society constructed upon a belief in the authority of the individual conscience to one which vests that authority in a collective conscience representing a consensus or agreed minimum standards as to what constitutes good and bad behaviour towards children. Society is now seen as operating under the authority of a rule of law. The existence of laws, or law-like instruments, such as rules, regulations and list of accepted practices and guidelines, not only provide the necessary authority for social action; they also convey the impression that behaviour may be effectively regulated through enforcing or encouraging obedience to these 'laws'. This will apply whether the behaviour to be regulated is that occurring between members of families, within organisations or within the boundaries of nation states. The only difference is that the precise legal instrument for authoritative regulation will vary according to the particular level of behaviour that it is intended to regulate. Yet the difficulty with a mode of regulating harmful or potentially harmful behaviour to children which depends on legal authority is that it presupposes a society where law is indeed accepted as the supreme moral authority for what is good or bad for children. Those who wish to give this privileged role to law may well be able to construct such a society for themselves, but [...] there is no guarantee that others will accord the same privileged role to the legal system or to any other form of authority.

A multi-authority society

The fragmentation of authority

The sociological equivalent of the holy grail, or the philosopher's stone, that elusive entity or element that will provide the key to perfection, is some model of society that captures all complexity in the world, some construction which, when subjected to empirical testing will be found to correspond exactly to the world 'as it really is'. Of course, such a model does not and cannot exist, if only because its very construction would change the external world in ways which the model would not be able to predict, so model and external world would be out of phase as soon as this 'super model' of society came into being. As observers of the social world, including all those different versions of society which are able to co-exist, we are in a somewhat better position to deal with at least some of the complexities than those, like moral campaigners, who are obliged by the very task they have set themselves, to commit themselves to one particular source of authority and so to a version of society where it is possible for that authority to operate effectively so as to achieve the campaigners' moral objectives.

A version of modern society which comes rather closer to reflecting some of its complexity is one where not one but several different bodies of knowledge may be used at different times and in different situations to give authority to decisions, understandings, recommendations and other statements. It could be argued that personal beliefs as to what is right and wrong, good or bad, true or false, etc, might represent the sources of such bodies of knowledge, but there are serious problems with a model of society based on this idea. If this were the case, there would be so many different sources of authority that nobody would know which to accept and which to reject. It would be impossible for people even to communicate except in the most trivial ways. Each one would rely on his or her version of truth or justice, right or wrong. They might be able to exchange platitudes about the weather or their health, but it would be quite impossible for them to cooperate on some concerted action or to take any joint decisions. Even if those who shared the same personal beliefs or moral standards were able to get together under the banner of some 'ideology', this would only form an acceptable basis for social authority where there was wide acceptance of that ideology as being right and true. Yet it is quite clear that modern society exists and continues to exist despite enormous differences in people's personal beliefs, whether they be political, religious, moral or whatever. For this to happen, therefore, there must be some other sites of authority which are unrelated to personal beliefs or to the consolidation of personal beliefs into ideologies.

If we turn specifically to the issue of children, how is it possible within modern society to determine what is good and bad for children or even to devise valid ways for deciding this question? It seems an impossible task today because we are supposedly living in a multicultural, pluralist society where different people and different groups of people give expression to different, equally valid values in their upbringing of children. Yet the fact remains that such decisions are being made all the time. Where then does the authority for such decisions come from?

One obvious answer is that the authority comes, not from the personal beliefs of the people who make decisions or recommendations about what is good or bad for children, but from the status that we accord to certain people who hold particular positions. We may see these people as capable of drawing upon specialist bodies of knowledge such as law, economics or science and it is this knowledge which gives their decisions and recommendations the necessary authority. Alternatively or additionally, their authority may derive from the fact that they have been appointed to particular positions through the authoritative products of some institution, such as legislation from parliament, legal decisions from the courts, or the appointment of examiners from education. These institutions are therefore seen as legitimate bodies for vesting authority in such people. The important point here is that these bodies of knowledge or systems of appointment operate quite independently of the particular people who make decisions or who contribute to their development. Those accounts of what is good or bad for children's interests and what will be good or bad for them in the future – such as court welfare reports, psychiatric assessments, scientific findings, judge's decisions, acts of parliament, or policy papers – which carry authority in modern society, do not today take the form of personal beliefs. In order to be recognised as socially authoritative, their decisions must conform, both in the language in which they are written and the reasoning which led the writers to their conclusions, to expectations derived from the particular body that possesses the authority to make such statements. These are likely to be law, politics, science and economics, but could also in some situations include religion and education. The differences between these different versions of authority that these bodies or systems represent do not reflect variations in personal consciousness or individual moral values, but rather denote distinctions between the social functions that each of them fulfils for society and its operations.

Let us look at a rather far-fetched imaginary example. A judge strongly believes that television soap operas are destroying children's imagination and that consequently parents should be actively discouraged from exposing their children to them. In deciding between the competing claims of parents for their six-year-old boy to reside with them, the judge asks each one in turn how much control they intend to exercise over the child's television viewing. Having heard their answers, he then gives residence of the child to the one who he considers is more likely to restrict the boy's exposure to soap operas. Contrary to what one might expect, the result of such a decision will not be for the law automatically to amend the catalogue of factors that it recognises as likely to cause harm to a child, and so justify an order to protect that child. Before the law would be able to adopt this judge's views, his or her beliefs, *as law*, in other words, before such beliefs could be given legal authority, there would first have to be some process of transformation from 'personal views' into grounds or justifications for legal change. Excessive exposure to soap operas would have to be officially recognised by courts not only as a possible cause of harm to children, but also as a valid ground for protective measures towards children. This process may take the political form of legislation, a section in a statute which requires courts to recognise the harm, or, alternatively, a court decision which is confirmed on appeal. Once this recognition has been achieved, the knowledge that excessive watching of soap operas may cause harm to children would be applicable in all future cases, until such time as this knowledge is modified or discarded, again through legal operations, the processes by which the law is changed. It will have achieved the authority of the political and legal systems.

An important additional development to the story is that before arriving at any decision the appeal court judges or a parliamentary committee on legislation would take account of any scientific evidence on the effect of soap operas on children. So law and politics in this particular matter would turn to a different form of knowledge and a different procedure which could be relied upon for determinations of what is good and bad for children. Once again this knowledge exists quite independently of the personal beliefs of the individuals, who in their roles of psychologists and psychiatrists provide such evidence.

Let us pause to take stock of the implications of these events for our model of modern society. Here we have a society which depends for its acceptable accounts of what is good or bad for children on statements which are given an authoritative status because the process by which they were reached conforms with the operations and programmes of a particular social system, which is recognised as a site of authority. Neither of these systems can claim to be dominant, in the sense that the authority of one does not preclude the authority of the others. While each of the systems operates according to its own procedures and its own criteria for determining truth, justice, rightness, these systems are nevertheless dependent the one upon the other for the production of authoritative statements. Law, for instance, will depend upon politics producing legislation for it to interpret and adjudicate upon. It will also depend upon science to produce expert evidence and advice on what is scientifically beneficial or harmful to children. Politics will depend upon law to give its legislative acts the authority of the courts. Science will depend on law and politics for recognition of the truths and falsehoods that it reveals and their transformation into social policies and legal decisions. The nature of the relationship between the systems and the authority they offer is both one of autonomous, simultaneous existence and one of interdependence.

One further matter arising from this case needs to be explored. The fact that the court of appeal decided to call upon scientific evidence did not mean that all existing psychological or psychiatric knowledge relating to children's welfare automatically became law. If that had been the case, we should have been back with the direct input–output model that we described earlier. No doubt there exists a wealth of scientific knowledge about a multitude of factors that might adversely or beneficially affect children's development, but only a small proportion of this knowledge finds its way into legal decisions. There may be several reasons that the courts fail to recognise some and not other items of such knowledge, but these reasons are much more likely to be related to concerns of the law than to the scientific status of such knowledge. The harms that they reveal may, for example, be too difficult to prove in court or they may simply not have been raised as an issue in legal proceedings. Similarly, political bodies may choose to ignore certain scientifically proved harms to children, because it would not be politically expedient to draw attention to them or because it would be far too expensive to tackle them. Legal, political or economic recognition of what is scientifically harmful to children will not, therefore, consist of direct translations from the scientific. Instead, these systems, will select such scientific knowledge as will have meaning within their own programme and will reformulate it in ways which allow such knowledge to exist as part of their own operations. The same will, of course, be true of scientific (including sociological) accounts of law, politics and economics. These accounts would also be selections of such features of those systems as are capable of being formulated within scientific theories and research methods.

Decision making

The selection of explanation

In modern society a multiplicity of explanations exists for the same social event. Where harms to children is concerned, it is no longer possible to point one's finger at one factor or set of factors and say definitively, 'this is the one and only explanation for what happened'. Even the results of official government inquiries, the decisions of courts or scientific research projects, arouse controversy and provoke alternative accounts and explanations drawing upon different attributions of causality. It is not simply that people apply different belief systems in their interpretation of events in the world and, therefore, cannot agree on one version of historical events.

There is not even agreement on what criteria should be applied to determine the truthfulness or validity of different versions. Scientific criteria are not the same as legal proof, which is not the same as political reality. This multiplicity of ways of evaluating possible explanations reflects the fragmentation of functions in modern society and the way in which modern society vests authority simultaneously in several of these systems. The best that society can do today is to produce causes which are recognised as true or probably true, using the interpretative framework of one system, according to that system's own procedures or processes for determining validity.

Where a society is predominantly organised according to the different functional operations that proceed simultaneously alongside one another, as is today's society, the existence of not one but several sites of authority necessarily creates serious problems for social activists who wish to change that society in predetermined directions. These problems arise from the possibility that statements produced using one set of criteria, which society regards as authoritative, may not be able to take into account a whole range of factors which would be recognised as relevant, or even essential, using criteria derived from different sites of authority. As we have seen, a court cannot take into account simultaneously all possible accounts of causality factors. It has to select between them. Any decisions it makes have only to be lawful. It may be blind to political accounts, such as one which identifies the power imbalance between men and women as the crucial factor in child sexual abuse. Its members may also close their eyes to scientific notions of what constitutes truth and validity. Once a legal decision has been made based on this selected version of causality, it remains valid as law, even though the rationale for the decision does not conform with what many people believe to be 'the true explanation' or 'a fair outcome'. The same will be the case in the selection of what constitutes relevant or valid evidence for decisions. Economic decisions, for example, will be based on information selected because it has validity within economics or may be easily translatable into factors for economic programmes. One cannot expect a company making an economic decision to close down an unprofitable factory to take account of the effects on the children of people made redundant as a result of the closure. Social scientists may demonstrate a correlation between unemployment and child malnutrition, and paediatricians may prove the existence of a relationship between child malnutrition and performance on intelligence tests, but, unless these findings are reconstructible as economic factors, the company is likely to be blind to them and, despite the possible adverse consequences for children, the decision it makes is still likely to be regarded as good economics.

The existence of system selectivity, the restricted vision of the external environment, including all possible explanations and versions of causality in that environment, represents at one level a retreat from the overwhelming complexities of the modern world into more reassuring, more certain, more controllable ways of organising the present and predicting the future. Here within the internal, controlled environment of the system, disruptions such as information about gender inequalities or consequences for children's intelligence, are not permitted to penetrate in their original form. They may enter only if the system is able to see them and only after they have been transformed into some form of knowledge or information that can be subjected to that system's operations. This has considerable consequences for the way in which matters of chance and danger enter the system's operations and programmes.

Risks and dangers, chance and foreseeability

In the same way that information from a system's environment may enter a system only upon its transformation into a form that the system is able to recognise, what were once regarded as 'dangers' may come to be perceived as 'risks', if by 'dangers', we refer to 'acts of God', matters of coincidence or chance happenings, and 'risks' is the term used to describe losses which are seen as the result of decisions or the failure to take decisions. By reformulating dangers within the programmes of those systems which society has designated as capable of producing authoritative accounts of causality, these dangers become reconstituted as 'risks'. In relation to the physical abuse of children, what were once, for example seen as the unlikely results of over-zealous disciplining now are seen as being the consequence of the lack of vigilance on the part of social workers. As each system increases the complexity of its own internal programmes to deal with an increasingly complex social world (itself the product of the increased complexity of other systems), so the scope of what is 'knowable' and so seemingly 'controllable' widens and so risk increases. Risks, unlike dangers, create the expectation that avoidance and reduction of losses, such as harms to children, are possible, since decisions are seen as being the causes of these events. This in itself does not make the world a safer or a more dangerous place for children in any absolute way, but it does mean that it becomes a more 'risky place both for children and adults and especially for those whose role is to protect children and promote their welfare. Expectations have been raised of the possibility of control through decision making over a wide range of factors that are seen as dangerous for children's well-being. As more and more knowledge is acquired about those factors which affect outcomes for children, so children's lives become increasingly risky (and also dangerous) and the pressures grow for decisions to be made which avoid or minimise these risks. Yet, as we have seen, what is and is not construed as 'risky' depends on the interpretive framework of the decision makers and those observing the performance of the decision makers.

Within organisations there are always pressures to reduce risks, but the selection of what constitutes risk, and what dangers (not attributable to decisions) will be determined by the internal programmes of the organisation. Child protection teams, for example, may see the physical abuse of a child as a risk attributable to the team's decision, and the child's mother's emotional devastation following the separation from her abusing partner, as a danger. For family therapists, on the other hand, the mother's emotional collapse and the consequent break-up of the family may be seen as a risk that is attributable to their therapeutic decisions, and the recurrence of the abuse of the child as a danger. Risks, therefore, may be perceived as dangers and dangers as risks. While each organisation may attempt to minimise the risk that it recognises within its programmes and so give the appearance of efficiency and control, they will be blind to those risks that they do not recognise, or may see them only as dangers. The more efficient their operations become in reducing risk, the more extensive may become the categories of events that they perceive as dangers and the risks that these dangers create for other organisations.

In the light of what we now know about modern society and its organisation, the distinction between chance factors and 'practical problems', between what events are perceived as controllable and what are accepted as beyond the reach of regulation becomes largely redundant. The designation of 'chance factor' can be applied only to a narrow range of occurrences, such as natural disasters, and even here it is becoming increasingly likely that some blame will be attributed to defects in forecasting or in the technological devices deployed as indicators of impending hurricanes, earthquakes, volcanic eruptions, etc, or the failures of the authorities to clear the area or bring in rescue teams sufficiently quickly. The same is of course the case where disasters to children occur, whether they concern an individual child's death or serious injury or the deaths or suffering of vast numbers of children. What could at one time have been attributed to 'chance factors' are increasingly likely to be seen as 'practical problems'. Campaigns to save, help and protect children are increasingly likely to identify such items as 'human error', 'self-serving attitudes' or 'administrative inefficiencies' as the causes of these events.

Yet the situation may seem very different from the perspective of the decision makers for whom unforeseen occurrences appear to throw off course even the most carefully considered predictions and the best laid plans. Of course, an observer of the decision maker's past performance will always be able to see in retrospect beyond the information that was available at the time the decision was taken. For the observer events were unforeseeable only because of the failure of the minister or the social work team to recognise them as possible future occurrences.

From a safe vantage point an observer will engage in the exercise of identifying those features which distinguish the predictable from the unforeseeable. These are then interpreted as such matters as lack of foresight, defects in the system or misinterpretation of the signs. For the people being observed, however, the demarcation line falls between what can be known and, therefore, possibly brought under control, and what remains unknowable and thus uncontrollable. In their version of reality and causality, in their account of what is knowable, this distinction relates entirely to matters external to the system itself, but occurring in that system's environment. In practice both of these distinctions fail to do justice to the complexity of the situation. Take the example of a decision by a social worker to place a child with long-term foster parents, who appeared from the extensive information collected for the file to have all the positive attributes for promoting that child's future well-being. Yet, shortly after the placement of the child, there was a world economic recession and a collapse of the housing market. As a result both parents lost their jobs, could not pay the accumulated arrears on their mortgage, were eventually evicted and obliged to move to much smaller rented accommodation. They felt unable to continue with the fostering arrangement and returned a by now desolate child to the children's home. How helpful in this situation is the distinction between chance factors and foreseeable problems? Both the recession and the collapse of the housing market were predictable (at least by some economists) but the problem was that what was 'knowable' to social work's programmes did not include economic forecasts. For social workers economic 'risks' were seen as 'dangers'. Yet, the observer of the social work assessment could legitimately argue that, as the result of poor decision making a child was made to suffer the disappointment of a failed fostering – which, according to some psychologists, might affect the child's emotional development for many years to come.

This example raises fundamental questions concerning attempts to plan for the future of children in today's world. If the distinction between chance factors and practical problems can no longer be relied upon to indicate what is and what is not controllable or able to be regulated, being itself a construct of the perspective of the particular observer, how can one believe that it is possible to create a better world for children?

Reformulations of morality

Judging by the multitude of non-governmental organisations that exist and are active throughout the world in promoting the well-being of children in a myriad of different ways, it is clearly still possible to have faith in the creation of a better world. My argument [...] should certainly not be taken as a demand for the abolition or curtailment of the activities of these organisations. It is rather to suggest that they are able to continue in their activities only by presenting to themselves and to the external world a version of society which ignores the complexities, the difficult issues that I have raised in the last few pages. They are able to do so only by remaining at a level of pre-sociological analysis or, using the terminology of systems, to close themselves away within a system which sees the world in terms of personal responsibility, individual conscience, commitment, sacrifice, guilt, and the like. The way that they are able to make these concepts appear to operate at the level of institutional, governmental and global decision making, is to reformulate them in terms which give the impression that such bodies act and think *in identical ways to people* or that should be seen in such a way as if *they consisted only of collections of individuals*, whose personal opinions, hopes, fears, attitudes and beliefs lie behind the formulation of decisions and policies.

Put slightly differently, while the programmes of these child welfare organisations may relate to complex political, legal, economic, educational, scientific and religious issues, the organisations for helping and protecting children are able to make sense of these different spheres of knowledge and activity largely through concepts derived from moral philosophy. Of course, moral philosophy with its codes and principles may also be seen as representing in its own right a distinct system of understanding with its own identity and its own concerns, but, for campaigners for a better world for children, the problem is not, it must be emphasised, how to make people more moral but rather how to translate moral agendas for children into *effective social action*. In attempting such a difficult task society can no longer return to a pre-Marxian epoch where it conceived of itself as collections of individuals or the sum of individual consciousness. In modern society what determines the degree of social effectiveness of decisions and actions based on the prospect of change are not those principles, precepts, ideas and convictions of moral or political philosophers. Rather they are exclusively social events, and social events, as we now know, are quite separate from the factors that motivate, inspire and restrain individuals. Moral principles run up against all those obstacles which were identified as preventing a personal belief from becoming an authoritative communication for modern society – for example, scientific processes and truth criteria, political expediency, economic viability and legal rules of procedures and evidence.

This does not mean that campaigns for the acceptance of moral principles are not recognised or have no effect whatsoever within society. It is rather that they can serve only as 'irritants' to social systems. As such those moral principles which campaigners wish to prevail can enter social systems only in a transformed state, that is, only in forms that allow for their reconstruction within each system, that make sense for the system's programmes and operations.

Furthermore, when it comes to authoritative accounts of social events in the modern world the hermeneutics of moral standards for individuals (or groups of individuals) simply do not have the capacity to reformulate or replace social forms of knowledge. While morality insists on the distinction between good and evil, between morally right and morally wrong, society relies and continues to rely on those other distinctions offered by systems which it regards as authoritative in matters concerning children's welfare. Psychoanalysis, for example, may direct the search towards the experiences of the child and its parents during the formative years of life. Political activists, such as feminists and anti-racists, may look to the power relationships that existed at the time within the family and/or the broader social environment. Economists may investigate correlations between income and property of families and the different forms of parenting behaviour. Judges may refer to the weight of the evidence which favours one side rather than another. Cultural relativists may seek the answers in differences in child-rearing customs and traditions. Geneticists may look for family predispositions. Sociologists may seek the answers in social conditions. Moral campaigners may, of course, reformulate all or any of these methods of obtaining the right answer in terms of good or bad for children, but the problem remains that within the social world, outside the moral discourse what counts is not moral formulations, but social communications – the communications of social systems. [...]

This chapter [edited] was taken from King, M. (ed) (1997) *A better world for children*, London: Routledge. The right of Michael King to be identified as author of this chapter has been asserted by him in accordance with the 1988 Copyright, Designs and Patents Act.

Children – who do we think they are?

Peter Moss and Pat Petrie

[...] Our construction of childhood and our images of the child represent ethical and political choices, made within larger frameworks of ideas, values and rationalities. In this chapter we want to explore what we believe to be a dominant discursive regime about children, a discourse which creates particular linked understandings of childhood in British society, and images of the child to match. Carlina Rinaldi (1992) puts the matter succinctly: "Many images take something away from children, children are seen as weak poor, needy". That, it seems to us, sums up the most powerful images of the child in Britain today. In some other parts of the world, other images are as powerful, or more so; while in yet other places, perhaps particularly in the English-language world, this image of the 'weak, poor and needy' child will resonate. [...]

But before laying out our case, we should make two things very clear, lest the reader misunderstand our case from the start. First, to problematise – question – a dominant image of the child as 'weak, poor, needy' is not to deny that children are, in many respects, at a disadvantage compared to adults; it is not to deny that many children are living in material poverty; it is not to deny that children have needs. Nor are we saying that public provision for children should ignore issues such as child protection or the need of some children for more support than others by reason, for example, of a disability.

Nor, if we suggest that the dominant image emphasises children's dependence on their parents, do we imply that children should be regarded as independent and autonomous. Rather, we would question the dependence/independence dichotomy, with its assumption of the desirability and feasibility of becoming a detached, independent human being. Like Sevenhuijsen (1999b), in her critique of Giddens' book on *The Third Way* (1998), we think there is a "need to deconstruct the normative image of the independent wage-earning citizen which is at the heart of contemporary notions of social participation and citizenship". Like her, too, we would prefer to "acknowledge everybody is dependent on care" and talk instead about our dependences on, and interdependence with, others – both children and adults.

Instead, our questioning is partly about proportionality and perspective. Why, as a society, do we in Britain choose mainly to talk about and portray children in such predominantly negative ways? [...]

Second, to speak of a 'dominant discursive regime' can give the misleading idea that we, as authors, think all people in Britain (or, more broadly, in the Anglo-American world) speak about and act towards children in only one way, share the same image, and that this way is the realisation of some general and coherent philosophy. This is not our position at all. We are not painting some

Orwellian picture of a post-1984 society. We see in Britain a variety of ways of thinking and talking about childhood, and many and various images, not all by any means the image of the weak, poor and needy child. We could give many examples but will confine ourselves to four. At a national level, we can point to the increasing attention being paid in Britain to children's rights (Wales, for example, has appointed a Children's Commissioner), to children's participation, and to what has been called a new sociology of childhood or new childhood studies. Or at the level of a particular provision for children, we began this book with a description of the *Venture* in Wrexham, Wales: this seems to us to provide an example of what we call a 'children's space', a space that was psychologically available for children, and a space that supported social interaction and processes. Many play service providers would share the *Venture's* aims.

Such examples assume very different understandings of the child compared to those found in the dominant discourse, and can support an image of the child as rich, competent and powerful.

Indeed, we would agree with Wyness, when he proposes that there are contradictory developments within policy in Britain: "whilst the trends are still towards strengthening the subordinate roles of children, there is now some recognition that children are socially competent actors" (Wyness, 1999, p 30). Broadly speaking, Wyness argues that educational reform has headed off in one direction, emphasising children's subordinate position to adults and especially parents as consumers of education, subjecting children to a highly centralised curriculum and not treating them as social agents with rights and responsibilities. While social welfare policy has tended to move more in the other direction. The shift in Britain towards responsibility for most policy and provisions for children being located within the education system raises important questions about whether and how this system can adopt new constructions of childhood.

If there is a dominant discourse, as we suggest, it is not the result of applying some grand design or philosophy, nothing so deterministic as this. Rather it emerges from a process of assembling together some ways of thinking, talking and acting, what Rose calls "contingent lash-ups of thought and action" (1999, p 27). This process of assembly is guided, we shall argue later in the chapter, by a mixture of forces: modernity, advanced liberalism and the business values of a neo-liberal market economy. The resulting assemblage – the dominant discourse of childhood – has a certain coherence of logic, a kind of rationality, yet is not without contradictions. We are not describing some monolithic and stylistically coherent structure, constructed in a short space of time to a master plan by a tightly controlled army of workmen, but rather an edifice erected over many years, influenced by different styles and built by many different architects and builders. [...]

The dominant discourse: constructions and images

We can discern three related constructions of the child that carry particular influence in Britain: the child as incomplete adult or futurity; the child as innocent and vulnerable; the child as redemptive vehicle. [...]

The child as incomplete adult or futurity is the child as empty vessel or *tabula rasa*, starting life with nothing, but requiring to be filled with socially sanctioned knowledge and culture, and growing into a predetermined identity. This child is passive, or perhaps pre-programmed, and so the subject of technologies which ensure an efficient process of reproduction or transmission of knowledge, skills and dominant social values which, successfully installed, ensure the best rate of return on the investment made by parents or government. A related idea is the child as nature, an essential being of universal properties and inherent capabilities whose development is viewed as an innate process – biologically determined, following general laws: "the dominant developmental approach to childhood, provided by psychology, is based on the idea of natural growth…. [Childhood therefore is] a biologically determined stage on the path to full human status i.e. adulthood" (Prout and James, 1997, p 10).

What both have in common is the idea of adulthood as a stage of completion, maturity and full human status, epitomised by the economically productive and independent worker (before the inevitable decline from this peak to old age and the dependence of 'second childhood'). The child is in the process of becoming an adult, and represents potential human capital awaiting realisation and exploitation: he or she is that which is yet to be, a 'structured becoming' (Jenks, 1982). This process of becoming entails linear progress, as the child passes through successive, orderly and predicted 'developmental' or 'key' stages. The metaphor is climbing a ladder, or building an edifice on foundations. Each stage of childhood is preparation, or readying, for the next and more important, with early childhood devalued for its immaturity yet recognised as a necessary foundation for successful progress through later life. This child therefore is defined as lacking, deficient, passive, incomplete, under-developed – and the more so the younger the child is. It is in this sense, rather that that of material disadvantage, that we say the image is of the 'poor' child, the 'weak' child, the 'needy' child.

But the child is also *an innocent, in the golden age of life*, even 'primitive', an idea that has been intriguing for many centuries. It is a construction to be found from Rousseau to Golding, which contains both fear of the unknown – the unruly, the uncontrollable – and a form of sentimentalisation, almost a utopian vision, where childhood is seen as a golden age. This image of the child generates in adults a desire to shelter children from the corruption of the world, by finding the means to offer children protection, continuity and security. Yet despite these best efforts, there is the inevitable loss of a quality with which children are born – an innocence, a naivety, an innate goodness.

Where does the child find protection, continuity and security? First and foremost in the immediate family, in particular with parents. Indeed, throughout the dominant discourse, the child's primary relationship is understood to be with her/his parents, especially the mother, and parents are presumed to have the most powerful influence on children. Other relationships may exist, but appear as secondary, even marginal to the parent–child relationship at the centre. This is expressed in the "notion that 'mothering' is the paradigmatic act of caring" (Tronto, 1993, p 109), with its concomitant assumption that caring is dyadic or individualistic.

> Too often, care is described and defined as a necessary relationship between two individuals, most often a mother and child. As others have noted such a dyadic understanding often leads to a romanticizaton of mother and child, so that they become like a romantic couple in contemporary Western discourse. The dyadic understanding also presumes that caring is naturally individualistic, though in fact few societies in the world have ever conceived of child rearing … as the responsibility of the birth mother. (Tronto, 1993, p 103)

There is a binary distinction here between 'hearth and home' and 'the wicked world', the private and the public sphere. Despite the evidence that child abuse is far more likely to happen in the family than outside, the family is still viewed as a haven of caring and warmth, a place of safety, the location of (gendered) care, in contrast to an instrumental, uncaring and often dangerous outside world. Indeed, it is almost as if, in Britain at least, there are no ways of talking about children being located in a network of relationships, stretching both within and outwith the home, a discourse which emphasises connectedness rather than the exclusivity of the parent/mother–child relationship.

These ideas of 'parent-centredness' have been given academic support from many sources. For example "what was called the 'socialisation process', primarily by parents in the family, was seen as a fundamental determinant of the character and personality of children as they grew up" (Prout, 1999, p 2). Socialisation theory not only gave parents centre stage. The other side of this coin constructs a 'poor' child:

> Socialisation theory depicts children as passively being given beliefs, knowledge, norms and attitudes, for example, rather than actively appropriating, selecting, interpreting and transforming them. It sets the process as a one-way transmission, from adults (assumed to be rational and competent) to children (assumed to be irrational and incompetent). (Prout, 1999, p 2)

Unlike the previous understanding, this understanding of the child as innocent assumes some loss in achieving adulthood: it is not a matter of unalloyed progress. Yet it also offers a child who is essentially weak, not only needing protection but also dependent. The child is isolated and decontextualised, except for her position in the family and her relationships with her parents, her relationship with the rest of society uncertain and full of potential danger.

Both understandings merge in the idea of the *child as redemptive vehicle*, the 'Christ child' or the socially engineered child. Here is the child as innocent who can save the world as s/he grows into adulthood – but who, to do so, will need to be shaped or filled or inscribed by adults who are themselves part of the corrupt world. What adults hope to find are effective technologies which, applied to children at early enough ages, can ensure a 'head start' or 'sure' start.

This theme of the redemptive potential of children, and the image of the child as redemptive agent or vehicle goes back a long way. Hatch refers to the rising expectations of science and technology in the 19th century which,

> coupled with a romantic view of the purity and perfectibility of the child, led to the perception that children are appropriate vehicles for solving problems in society. The notion was that if we can somehow intervene in the lives of children, then poverty, racism, crime, drug abuse and any number of social ills can be erased. Children become instruments of society's need to improve itself, and childhood became a time which social problems were either solved or determined to be unsolvable. (Hatch, 1995, p 119)

But it is not just a matter of the child redeeming. The child also needs to be redeemed. There is a recurring theme in education and other children's services of rescuing children from their economic, social and cultural conditions through planned intervention: "the notion of rescuing [combined] religious views of salvation with secular notions about the effects of poverty, class and social/racial discrimination" (Popkewitz, 1998, p 21).

Once again, we have before us a child who is weak, poor and needy – until subject to effective intervention, a sort of process of conversion (to the true path) or inoculation (from the infectious bacilli of the child's social milieu). Popkewitz, writing about the strong 'culture of redemption' in American education, comments that while "the redemptive theme is rhetorically positioned in the name of democratic principles, the concrete strategies are concerned with governing the soul". In other words, if the child is to achieve her mission, then she must be acted upon so as to embody the right or appropriate sort of ideas, values, subjectivities, ambitions and practices. Discourses of redemption and salvation "make the child an individual who is not reasonable, capable and competent but who – with the proper care and nurturing – can be saved" (Popkewitz, 1998, p 25).

These understandings of the child as futurity, as innocent and as redemptive agent are closely linked. It is the incompleteness of the child, the lack of corruption, the ability to inscribe the *tabula rasa* and to govern the soul that makes the child such a promising agent of redemption.

> The child may act as a repository for nostalgic longings for stability and certainty or as a figure of redemptive possibility, but a primary significance of this, I suggest, is that in a world seen as increasingly shifting, complex and uncertain, children, precisely because they are seen as especially unfinished, appear as a good target for controlling the future. (Prout, 2000, p 306)

Constructing 'children's services'

> From a social constructionist perspective [early childhood institutions],
> as well as our images of what a child is, can be and should be, must be
> seen as the social construction of a community of human agents,
> originating through our active interaction with other people and with
> society.... [Early childhood] institutions and pedagogical practices for
> children are constituted by dominant discourses in our society and
> embody thoughts, conceptions and ethics which prevail at a given
> moment in a given society. (Dahlberg et al, 1999, p 62)

Dahlberg makes the connection between our image of the child and our
understanding and image of public provision for children. So too does Carlina
Rinaldi: "the poor image of the child supports an image of pre-schools and social
services". Speaking of Britain, Prout also connects: "despite the recognition of
children as persons in their own right, public policy and practice is marked by an
intensification of control, regulation and surveillance around children" (2000, p
304). He relates this tendency in public policy and practice to a widespread
understanding of the child as futurity and redemptive agent, and an increasingly
intense search for means to control the future through children.

Given this context, how do we understand or construct public provisions for
children in Britain? It seems to us that they are constructed as instruments or
technologies for producing child outputs of outcomes. The child is poor, weak
and needy. She needs to be made less so through becoming the subject of processes
and methods which will regulate, protect, normalise, shape, develop, prevent,
supervise – and which do so to ends that must always be predetermined and
calculable and which entail controlling the present for the sake of determining
the future.

This understanding of public provision we refer to as 'children's services'. Of
course, the word 'services' has many meanings. Some will object to our association
of it with this particular understanding or construction of public provision. 'Service'
can have the sense of offering yourself to the other, the performance of a duty or
obligation, being of service. A 'service ethic' has been an important motivation
for many people working with children, and embodies values that have much in
common with the ethical part of our framework.

Our use of 'services' links to other meanings, in particular dictionary definitions
of 'service' such as 'performance of a function' and "the checking and (if necessary)
repairing and/or replacing of parts ... to ensure efficient operation" (*Chambers
Dictionary*, 1998). It is our contention that the use of the term 'services' is often
(though not invariably) associated with this sense. In any case, by questioning the
term 'children's services', by suggesting it is problematic, we intend to show that
it cannot be taken as neutral nor can its meaning be assumed to be self-evident:
instead, the meaning of 'children's services' is contestable.

One metaphor for this construction of children's services is the factory or processing plant, vividly used by Lilian Katz when she speaks of early childhood provision (in the US) while relating it to the compulsory school system:

> It seems to me that early childhood programmes are increasingly in danger of being modeled on the corporate/industrial or factory model so pervasive in elementary and secondary levels of education.... [F]actories are designed to transform raw material into prespecified products by treating it to a sequence of prespecified standard processes. (Katz, 1992, pp 33-4)

It may be that 'metaphor' is the wrong word, as indeed is 'model'. Another way of viewing 'children's services' and 'factories' is as forms of organisation that both share certain understandings, purposes and practices, and are the product of a particular stage of modernity, what Foucault calls 'disciplinary societies'. We shall return to this theme later in the chapter.

An important component of this construction of children's services is instrumentality. Provision is made for a specified purpose, in the name of which the child is acted upon to produce outcomes, which are both pre-determined and normative. Moreover, the 'customers' for these services are first and foremost adults. Purposes, functions, objectives and outcomes are usually defined by adults, and legitimated in relation to the needs of adults and the state of adulthood, that is, producing the required adult, in particular a competitive and flexible member of the workforce and an autonomous subject who will assume responsibility for his or her own risks; protecting children from risks posed by adults; preventing future problems of adolescence or adulthood, such as delinquency and drug abuse; compensating children for parental difficulties and disadvantages; promoting gender equality between adult women and men; and so on.

Thus, provisions for children understood as children's services are not provided as places for children to live their childhoods, and to develop their culture – although in practice they become such places through the subversive competences of children. Nor do they treat childhood and the technologies applied to children as political, ethical and therefore contestable issues. The important question is 'what works?', ensuring the highest return on investment, not 'what is our image of the child?'. Indeed, as public provisions for children, as well as private provisions (such as childcare services and private schools which offer to sell their product, for example, 'childcare', to adult consumers, for example, 'working parents') are increasingly viewed as businesses, competing to sell services to parents in the market place, to compete successfully brings even stronger demands for a guaranteed product, proven by league tables and other indicators that evidence success.

One consequence of this construction of children's services is a prominence given to [...] business ethics valuing return on investment. Another consequence is a continuous process of atomisation of the child in public policy. A particular need or problem, located in a particular part or facet of the child, is defined, by a particular discipline, profession or branch of government – and a service, with its attendant technologies and particular group of technicians, is then put in place to deal with that need or problem. Or else an existing service is redefined to take on board a new problem which adds a new outcome: for example, early childhood services are now seen as a vehicle for reducing juvenile and adult crime and, as such, brought into programmes intended to prevent future offending. The output of the service is not only pre-determined, but also ever more particular and specialised, produced by specialist staff and specialist techniques.

This process of atomisation – both of the child and 'children's services' – is no accident. It represents a particular way of understanding the world with its roots deep in modernity and modernity's search for order out of complexity. Modern (Newtonian) science, for example, as it emerged in the 17th century, viewed nature as passive, an object to be known, and hence dominated and controlled, and as a mechanism "whose elements can be disassembled and then put together again in the form of laws" (Sousa Santos, 1995, p 13). The factory, an archetypal modern economic organisation, is also based on principles of atomisation, the efficient production of particular outcomes achieved through breaking down the production process into component parts.

Fink makes the connection between modernity, ways of working with children in schools and their similarities with other forms of economic and social organisation:

> When Cartesian rationalism is combined with the Newtonian mechanical school of physics that suggested that we live in an orderly universe that was knowable through rational scientific methods, we have the basis for much of Western thought. Within this intellectual paradigm the world is knowable through logical, linear, cause–effect techniques. If we can just take things apart and then put them together again the object of study, be it the universe, the human body, or the child's learning needs, is knowable.... Our businesses, schools and other social organisations reflect this way of thinking. For example, a pupil who attends virtually any secondary school is looked upon not as a whole living, breathing, feeling person, but in terms of his or her parts – the history part, the science part, the maths part, and so on.... The pupil then progresses in assembly-line fashion from year to year until he or she leaves school. (Fink, 2001, p 229)

The process of atomisation is sustained and reflected by the ever-growing numbers of government departments and other public agencies which find an interest in the child as a means to pursue their particular goals. Currently in England, and confining ourselves to government departments, there are: the Department for Education and Skills; the Department of Health; the Department of Culture, the Media and Sport; the Home Office; the Department for Work and Pensions; the Treasury; the Cabinet Office; the Lord Chancellor's Office; and the Department for Trade and Industry (which has responsibility for maternity and parental leave). Furthermore, within several of these departments there exist a number of units and divisions each with different interests involving the child. Divisions and sub-divisions occur, too, within the workforce, with an ever expanding typology of practitioners – nursery workers, childminders, playgroup workers, teachers of various kinds, residential and field social workers, various youth and play workers and so on.

Because of their functionality and purposiveness, services, together with the practitioners who staff them and the departments who have oversight for them, target certain groups of children, see certain parts of the child, bring certain understandings of the child, want certain outcomes from the child, have certain rationalities which shape how they think about and legitimate intervention with children. To take one example, different services or programmes in England define different age groups as the subject of their particular interventions, for example: three- and four-year-olds for early education; four- to 11-year-olds for primary schooling; 0 to three-year-olds for Sure Start; 0 to 14-year-olds for the National Childcare Strategy; four to 12 for 'On Track', an initiative to prevent crime; and so on. Or to take another example, the process of atomisation has been described in relation to what in Britain are called 'out of school' or 'school-age childcare' services, which in recent years have attracted the attention of an increasing number of government departments:

> These interests in school-age childcare services are, in practice, separate. They are seen by the different departments as means towards their own distinct ends so that, at the level of central government, different stakeholders focus on the child in different ways, each in the light of their different value systems. For each department, a slightly different 'child' comes into the frame: the child who needs protection or, by contrast, the child from whom society needs protection; the child as the customer of leisure and recreation; the child as the offspring of employees, who needs child care in the interests of the employer, the labour market and female equality; the child as a member of society with a claim on its recreational resources. (Petrie, 1994, p 84)

The process of atomisation does not, however, go unremarked: or at least its symptoms are noted. Compartmentalisation and poor inter-departmental or inter-agency coordination are increasingly seen as causes of inefficiency and inadequate outcomes. The response is increasing calls for coordination, partnership and 'joined-up' government, and initiatives to promote these new alignments: bringing the atoms into a new and closer relationship with each other. Yet this presents its own problems. One concerns the intrinsic difficulty of bringing different systems (and those who work within them) into closer working relationships. The term 'social autopoiesis' refers to the way social systems continually refer back to themselves for authority and to make sense of the external world: "each [system] is closed to its external world in the sense that information from the world cannot penetrate the system in a direct manner ... [but] has to be reproduced in the system's own terms" (King, 1997, p 26). In other words each system sees the world through its own lens, each system formulates problems in terms of its own agenda and perceived competence: direct communication between systems is an impossibility since "these systems are able to relate to one another only by attempting to impose their own self-generated evaluation and criteria for success upon the other" (King, 1997, p 205).

This discussion of incoherence, fragmentation and compartmentalisation takes us into difficult territory, with no obvious way out. The road to greater coherence, integration and unity may lead to somewhere worth going [...] a less atomised approach to the child might be produced through a more encompassing theory and practice of work with children, pedagogy, which adopts a more holistic perspective. But as King's analysis suggests, there is no perfect solution since different social systems will always exist within society, even if some degree of reconfiguration takes place over time: pedagogy will not encompass all of the systems involved with children (for example, health, law). To a greater or lesser extent we are fated to live in and with a multiplicity of systems: "this phenomenon of system non-communication provides the language for a description of society which acknowledges the existence of different perspectives, different codes of interpretation, different bodies of knowledge and different criteria for evaluation" (King, 1997, p 207). [...]

Evaluation of children's services

> In truth there is little that is merely measurable.... Drawing analogies from the 'new science', Margaret Wheatley argues that we have been deeply misled by the belief in scientific objectivity and a reduction into parts that obscures our vision of the whole. The challenge, she says, is to see beyond the separate fragments to the whole, stepping back far enough to appreciate how things move and change as a coherent entity. It is hard, especially in a climate obsessed with measurement, to resist our well-trained desire to analyse the parts to death. Possibly there is an inverse relationship between importance and what can be easily measured. The deeper we venture beneath the surface, the more profound the moral and spiritual character of learning and the more elusive of measurement it becomes. (Scottish Council Foundation, 1999, p 12)

In Britain, current research and evaluation of public provision for children, including schools, foregrounds the quantification and measurement of pre-determined outcomes and the workings of particular aspects of the technology: frequent terms used in addition to outcomes are indicators, targets, goals. This approach incorporates a private sector strategy that has been described as a 'compliance model of quality control':

> Compliance models define quality as 'fitness for purpose'. They involve the specification of standards and the institution of formal systems of quality control to ensure that products conform to these standards. Compliance models ... are characterised by routinisation and standardisation. (Gewirtz, 2000, p 354)

This approach to evaluation is clearly related to a particular understanding of public provision for children – the construct of 'children's services' as sites for technologies to produce predetermined results. As the quotation starting this section suggests, it adopts a partial and, once again, atomised approach, focused on the readily quantified and unable to pick up the unexpected and complex. David Boyle develops this theme:

> The problem is not so much trying to measure – sometimes you have to try…. The danger is when people or institutions think they have succeeded. That's when the damage is done and the spirit dies. Every 'bottom line' firmly held, is a generalization that fails to do justice to the individual moment or the individual person…. It is time we looked at those areas of human nature where computers can't follow – the world of the non-measurable, non-calculable. Love, intuition, imagination, creativity…. Over-reliance on numbers sweeps away your intuition along with ideology. It leaves policy-makers staring at screeds of figures, completely flummoxed by them. (Boyle, 2001, p 223)

Evaluation of children's services in this approach also foregrounds objectivity, resisting subjectivity and interpretation. Processes of observation, however, can never be objective and neutral, the observer never being able to stand outside the world in which he or she is situated so as to 'know' what is really going on. Moreover, the insertion of the evaluation process itself influences what is evaluated, the 'tail wagging the dog' phenomenon in which attention is focused on demonstrating attainment of the particular criteria or targets that have been laid down. This problematisation of objectivity is not confined to the social sciences. Modelled as they are on natural sciences, approaches to social scientific evaluation which rely on objectivity and atomisation are brought into question by the crisis in the paradigm of modern natural science and the 'new science' that has accompanied the crisis. Heisenberg and Bohr, for example, in quantum physics "demonstrated that it is not possible to measure or observe our object without interfering with it, without actually changing it in such a way that, after being measured, the object is no longer the same as it was before" (Soursa Santos, 1995, p 18). Or, as the bio-physician Heinz von Foerster puts the matter: "objectivity is a subject's false view that observing can take place without him" (1991).

The inherently political nature of evaluation, denied in the depoliticised and technical discourse of managerialism, also problematises objectivity claims. This is the nub of the discussion by Nikolas Rose of what he terms 'political numbers'. He recognises that numbers are "crucial techniques for modern government … [and] have become indispensable to the complex technologies through which government is exercised". But he does not take them at face value:

> Acts of social quantification are politicised not in the sense that the numbers they use are somehow corrupt – although they may be – but because political judgements are implicit in the choice of what to measure, how to measure it, and how to present and interpret the results…. [W]hilst

numbers are indispensable to politics they also appear to depoliticize whole areas of political judgement. They redraw the boundaries between politics and objectivity by purporting to act as automatic technical mechanisms for making judgements, prioritizing problems and allocating scarce resources…. The apparent objectivity of numbers, and of those who fabricate and manipulate them, helps configure the respective boundaries of the political and the technical. Numbers are part of the techniques of objectivity that establish what it is for a decision to be disinterested. (Rose, 1999, pp 198-9)

Concepts such as 'quality', coming from the business world and now frequently used in the evaluation of children's services, have also come under critical scrutiny. For example, in the early childhood field, an increasing number of writers on 'quality' have understood quality to be a subjective, value-based, relative and dynamic concept, with the possibility of multiple perspectives or understandings of quality. Some have gone further, arguing that the very concept of quality is constructed within modernist values and assumptions, presuming as it does the possibility of identifying stable, objective and rational criteria which can be applied irrespective of time, place or values (for a fuller discussion and critique of the concept of quality, see Dahlberg et al, 1999). Readings has similarly problematised the concept of 'excellence', much beloved in and applied to the university sector: "Measures of excellence raise questions that are philosophical in that they are fundamentally incapable of producing cognitive certainty or definitive answers. Such questions will necessarily give rise to further debate for they are radically at odds with the logic of quantification" (1996, p 24).

These and other critical evaluators have problematised an approach to evaluation that is situated within the modernist project with its epistemology of logical positivism, its belief in stable criteria, its assumption of the objective social scientist and its distaste for philosophy and moral issues. Linked to the increasing dominance of economism and the logic of markets in all spheres of life, with the conversion of ethical and political issues into managerial and technical issues, "what can't be measured and has no easily auditable outcome ceases to exist within certain influential frames of policy making" (Rustin, 1999, p 256). In this context, evaluation becomes focused on methodological concerns, overwhelming ethics.

Why children's services?

What rationalities and forces produce the constructions of childhood and public provisions for children we have just described? It seems to us that three […] themes […] contribute to this assemblage of ideas about children and children's services, and to the taken for granted quality that indicates a dominant discursive regime: modernity and its understanding of the world; the values and needs of a resurgent neo-liberal or free market capitalism; and advanced liberalism. However, we do not claim a comprehensive account. We seek to start, not complete, the exploration of possible linkages between a wider philosophical, social, economic and political frame, and the ways in which we think, talk and act towards children.

The idea of the child as poor and needy, because immature, dependent and incomplete, is part of an Enlightenment narrative which envisaged a state of pure reason as maturity, represented by the autonomous, independent and self-sufficient adult. The child is in a state of nature that must be ordered, indeed "to arrive at reason is to destroy nature, to reach maturity is to forget childhood" (Readings, 1996, p 63). Central to this narrative, and its belief that knowledge would make mankind free and rational, is the role of education, which involves a process of transmission to an empty vessel, to fill or mould the child into the adult ideal: "education, that is, transforms children, who are by definition dependent upon adults, into independent beings, free citizens" (Readings, 1996, p 158). Here we have many elements of the dominant construction: children valued primarily for what they will become, children as wanting, needy and poor, education as the producer of predetermined outcomes.

This narrative is not only about a happy ending, it is also about the way of getting there. For within modernity there is a belief in the possibility of and right to seek dominance and control – be it of nature or nurture. Through control, progress can be achieved, order imposed and the future assured. The child viewed as futurity is the vehicle for progress, order and living happily ever after.

What we have just outlined is an idea with a long historical pedigree. But it retains currency in contemporary British public policy. We can take two examples. The first concerns the high policy priority given by the Labour government (voted into office in 1997, and re-elected in 2001) to developing provisions and programmes for young children and their families. This has included an expansion of 'early education and childcare', and a large-scale intervention – Sure Start – aimed at children under four years of age and their families in areas of disadvantage. The emphasis is, however, very much on the future, of working through young children as the means to long-term goals.

> This investment [Sure Start] will make a difference to families in the short and medium term but above all it is an *investment* in higher school standards and greater social cohesion in *ten* or *fifteen years time*. It is a crucial step towards breaking the cycle of deprivation.... Children's experience in the early years of their life are critical to their *subsequent development*. They have a significant impact on their *future performance* at school and the extent to which they are able to take advantage of opportunities *later in life*. That is why we have invested heavily in early years education. (Department of Education and Employment, 2001, paras 1.13, 2.1; emphases added)

For the second example, we turn to the pledge made by the same Labour government to eradicate child poverty. While welcoming this new concern by government with child poverty, Prout points out that the government's stated rationale for tackling child poverty is mainly concerned with ideas of investment in the future and the reduction of adverse adult outcomes.

The central focus is on the better lives that will, it is predicted, emerge from reducing child poverty. It is not on the better lives that children will lead as children. In pointing this out I do not question the government's sincerity in its attack on child poverty. Nor do I doubt the need to make a collective investment in children.... My point is that on its own a focus on futurity is unbalanced and needs to be accompanied by a concern for the present wellbeing of children, for their participation in social life and for their opportunities for human self-realisation. In trying to understand why such a strong emphasis is placed on the futurity of children it is important to remember that, despite the different local and national shapes that modernity takes, a powerful common dynamic can be seen in the attempt to take control of both society and nature through rational knowledge and planning. It is this project of control, I would suggest, that is rather one-sidedly expressed in the concentration that current UK policy has on children as a means of shaping the societal future. (Prout, 2000, pp 305-6)

Prout argues that 'modernity's project of rational control', in particular via children and through the 'quintessentially modernist idea of prevention', appears to have become more intensive at a time when that project seems to have met its limits. [...] There is a sort of vicious circle in operation. As society becomes more complex and uncertain, and as prevention becomes more difficult to engineer, "the failure of such interventions summons up a renewed commitment to prevention ... [and] children as a primary target of prevention seem caught in a system that can only respond to its failure through ratcheting up control" (Prout, 2000, p 306). In the last five years, Britain has witnessed a flood of social strategies, programmes, plans, targets, indicators and other initiatives, many involving new or reformed 'children's services', intended to address the social ills that have piled up over the preceding 20 years and to prevent fresh outbreaks. The consequence is, as Prout observes, public policy and practice that are marked by "an intensification of control, regulation and surveillance around children".

Burman (2001) points to a similar contrast between "the manifest failure of the project of modernity" and persisting hopes of effecting change through children and their development. Children have been one of the main subjects of modernity's project of social improvement, providing a perceived means to fulfil broader economic and political agendas. We (that is adults) place on children great expectations, to achieve what we could not, and to put right what we made wrong. The result, as Burman poignantly observes, is that "onto the child we heap the thwarted longings of decaying societies and try to figure something better. It's a hard burden for children to carry. Surely they should be their own future, not ours" (Burman, 2001, p 11).

Over and above a response to increasing complexity and uncertainty, why might this project of rational control become more intensive at this time? Why is the instrumental and controlling construction of 'children's services' becoming more dominant in public discourse, in Britain at least? Linked economic and social factors play a part. Changes in the economy and employment, within the context of increasing global competitiveness, bring business and government to the point of needing both more 'services' and services that are more efficient in the production of desired outputs. The need for more women workers and the increasing concentration of employment on women and men in their so-called 'prime working years' (that is, between 25 and 50 years of age, coinciding with parenthood) (Deven et al, 1996) leads to an increasing institutionalisation of childhood, to ensure safe and secure care for children while parents are working. At the same time, there is a growing belief in the importance of early education for later performance both in school and at work. The 'business case' and *raison d'état* coincide:

> As a global economy takes hold, politicians and business leaders – heretofore largely uninterested in young children – are voicing concern and demonstrating readiness for action. Facing an increasingly competitive global economic market, they are worried about economic productivity…. Given this climate, quality early care and education services have been advocated as a cost-effective approach to maintaining a stable, well-prepared workforce today – and preparing such a workforce for the future. (Kagan et al, 1996, p 12)

But economic change also generates other demands for children's services, not just more of them but services guaranteed to produce more effective outputs – including better control. For the economic values espoused by neo-liberal or free market capitalism – flexibility, competition, inequality, individualism – and the practices they produce are a recipe for social dislocation, serving up a long menu of attendant problems which threaten in due course to impede the efficient operation of the market economy. The social consequences of this particular form of capitalism are beginning to be defined and discussed.

Richard Sennett (1998) identifies 'new capitalism' with short-termism, linked to 'flexibility'. He argues that the corrosion of long-term commitment in the workplace – and the trust, loyalty and mutuality that it fosters – is dysfunctional for personal and family life:

> It is the time dimension of the new capitalism, rather than hi-tech data transmission, global stock markets or free trade that most affects people's emotional lives outside the workplace. Transposed to the family realm, 'no long term' means keep moving, don't commit yourself and don't sacrifice….This conflict between family and work poses some questions about adult experience itself. How can long-term purposes be pursued in a short-term society? How can durable social relations be sustained? How can a human being develop a narrative of identity and life history in a society composed of episodes and fragments? (Sennett, 1998, p 27)

Bauman similarly traces a connection between the economic values of 'new' and 'neo-liberal' capitalism and their social consequences. Transparency and flexibility are key concepts for this economic order:

the pressures which they simultaneously reflect and reinforce turn increasingly into the major factors of a new inter-societal and intra-societal polarization. Scope and speed of movement make all the difference between being in control and being controlled; between shaping the conditions of interaction and being shaped by them; between acting 'in order to' and behaving 'because of'; between pursuing goals with near certainty of success or defensive actions undertaken in a situation composed entirely of unknown variables that change without warning....The deepest socio-psychological impact of flexibility consists in making precarious the situation of those affected and keeping it precarious. (Bauman, 1999, pp 27-8)

Furthermore, Bauman argues, a prime victim of neo-liberal theory and practice has been solidarity, defined by him as "the dense network of solidarities, overlapping and criss-crossing, observed in all societies as (however imperfect) a shelter and guarantee of certainty, and thus of trust, self-confidence and the courage without which the exercise of freedom and the willingness to experiment are unthinkable" (Bauman, 1999, p 30). Gray also notes a clear connection between free market (neo-liberal) capitalism and a serious weakening of social cohesion:

It is odd that there are still those who find the association of free markets with social disorder anomalous. Even if it could itself be rendered stable the free market is bound to be destructive of other institutions through which social cohesion is achieved.... By privileging individual choice over any common good it tends to make relationships revocable and provisional. (Gray, 1999, p 37)

Neo-liberalism may extort a high social price, but it appears to deliver the goods economically. It also appears difficult, if not impossible, to control, since capital can seek more congenial surroundings at the first hint of serious trouble. It seems more feasible to adapt society to capital, than expect capital to be responsive to social needs. The consequence of economic deregulation, to create a world fit for the practice of neo-liberal capitalism, has been increased social regulation, a search for more effective methods of control and surveillance. As the nation state loses economic power, the shaping of children as the future labour force becomes an increasingly important role (Prout, 2000), an important contribution to supply side economics, the proper role of the nation state as development agency. The dual aim is to produce a subject suited to new conditions, who embodies the values and assumptions of neo-liberalism (including what Fendler [2001] refers to as the 'flexible soul'), and to deal with the disconcerting consequences of that practice. Neo-liberalism assumes winners and losers in the great game of continuous competition, and a role for services in containing the discontent and repairing the failures of the losers. There remain the same belief and hope as was current in the 19th century: "if we can somehow intervene in the lives of children, then poverty, racism, crime, drug abuse and any number of social skills can be erased".

Thus, 'children's services' as producers of outcomes have received a double and linked boost from economic and social rationales. More services are wanted – but they must be efficient producers, they must offer 'best value', their outcomes must be economically calculable, they must 'deliver' the goods that have been advertised. The instrumental rationality, with its concern to guarantee and maximise predetermined returns on investment, which Bauman refers to as 'business values', is in the driving seat. Under the bonnet, there is a new engine. What are wanted are services that deliver their predetermined outcomes – and what is available, what gives new promise of achievement, is new or revamped technologies which claim to deliver improved performance.

What those technologies are we shall come to shortly. But before that we need to consider the role of advanced liberalism in the construction of provisions for children as 'children's services'. The theory of liberalism speaks of autonomy, freedom and choice, and the limitation of government. John O'Neill writes of "Liberal atomism … [requiring] individuals be considered absolutely independent of their institutional contexts …[so that] the liberal political subject is constituted in total isolation" (1994, p 39). Because liberalism assigns the dependent child to the private sphere, and as the private responsibility of her parents, liberal theory has great difficulty in finding a place for the child in its political discourse, except perhaps as "potential human capital from whom a dividend may be expected" (O'Neill, 1994, p 46). Indeed O'Neill goes so far as to speak of "the *missing* child in liberal theory".

But in practice liberalism does control, it does attempt to govern in the interests of morality and order. The state seeks to govern without governing society, by acting on the choices and self-steering properties of individuals. [...] It does this by working through families, and other institutions such as schools, to create individuals who do not need to be governed by others but will govern themselves. The family has always been understood to be far too important to be actually left to its own devices, and to address this dilemma (the public importance of the private family), "a whole range of technologies were invented that would enable the family to do its public duty without destroying its private authority" (Rose, 1999, p 74; see also Donzelot, 1979). The trick has been to govern through the family without appearing to do so. The account by Rose of the development in Britain of public interventions involving the family and the child provides a critical analysis of this process:

> The modern private family remains intensively governed, it is linked in so many ways with social, economic and political objectives. But government here acts not through mechanisms of social control and social subordination of the will, but through the promotion of subjectivities, the construction of pleasures and ambitions, and the activation of guilt, anxiety, envy and disappointment….The autonomous responsible family stands as the emblem of a new form of government of the soul. (Rose, 1990, p 208)

Yet a continuing problem is that some, even many families, remain unwilling or unable to embody and enact the desired aspirations, objectives and norms, and have had to be the subject of more overt interventions (for a fuller discussion of this history, see Rose, 1990, 1999).

> [The family of the labouring classes was] to be shaped, educated and solicited into a relation with the state if it was to fulfil the role of producing healthy, responsible, adjusted social citizens. The political task was to devise mechanisms that would support the family [of the labouring classes] in its 'normal' functioning and enable it to fulfil its social obligations most effectively without destroying its identity and responsibility. The technical details of the internal regime of the working-class family would become the object of new forms of pedagogy, for example through medical inspection of schoolchildren and the invention of health visitors, to instil norms of personal hygiene and standards of child care. While the mothers of the wealthier classes had been solicited into alliances with medics in the nineteenth century ... one sees a new specification of the role of the working-class mother as one who was to be educated by educationalists, health visitors and doctors into the skills of responsible government of domestic relations. (Rose, 1999, pp 128-9)

This description of developments at the turn of the last century resonates with later interventions. Taking a historical perspective, the Sure Start programme started in Britain in 1998, becomes the latest in a long line of interventions, aimed at instilling norms and skills into a marginalised underclass, so they may be included in liberal society, and at eradicating poverty – which remains stubbornly persistent across the years.

But with the emergence of advance liberalism has come new confidence in the possibilities of intervention: "neo-liberalism does not abandon the 'will to govern': it maintains the view that the failure of government to achieve its objectives is to be overcome by inventing new strategies of government that will succeed" (Rose, 1996, p 53). Cometh the hour, cometh the technology! Central to the aspirations of the Labour government in Britain has been the application of the procedures and techniques of new managerialism. Linked to the application of selected knowledge and research, mostly situated within a positivistic, empirical–analytic paradigm, managerialism promises human technologies able to produce more certain outcomes. It offers rationalism, neutral and objective knowledge and "calculative technologies ... [that] provide a foundation for enacting the new logics of rationing, targeting and priority setting" (Clarke, 1998, p 177). Critical of the *ancien régime* of control – professional, bureaucratic and political forms of rule, all relics of the social state – managerialism "proclaims itself the universally applicable solution to problems of inefficiency, incompetence and chaos" (Clarke, 1998, p 174). It promises rationalised order and certainty, removing politics and ethics and replacing them with techniques of control:

> [Managerialism promises to cope] with the complexities and uncertainties of the modern world – 'the chaos of the new' – through the quasi-

scientific techniques of strategic management and the delivery of fast-paced change and innovation…. The problems which the managerial state is intended to resolve derive from contradictions and conflicts in the political, economic and social realms. But what we have seen is the managerialisation of these contradictions: they are redefined as 'problems to be managed'. Terms such as 'efficiency' and 'effectiveness', 'performance' and 'quality' depoliticise a series of social issues. (Whose efficiency? Effectiveness from whom?) And thus displace real political and policy choices into a series of managerial imperatives. (Clarke, 1998, pp 178, 179)

Parton has described this process in social work with children, how new managerial strategies, consisting of systems, procedures and organisational frameworks, have emerged concerned with 'risk-management'. Replacing notions of "artistic, situated judgement" for intrinsically complex, ambiguous and uncertain situations, these strategies for risk management "operate as if issues were resolvable in any kind of realist scientific or calculative/probabilistic sense" (1998, p 23).

Managerialism is not the only technology underpinning advanced liberalism's newfound belief in the processing qualities of 'children's services'. For example, there are what Rose refers to as the 'psy sciences', which he claims "play a key role in rationalities and techniques of government, with legitimacy claimed by 'engineers of the soul' on the basis they can deal truthfully with the real problems of human existence in the light of a knowledge of the individuals who make it up" (Rose, 1999, p xxii). The role of developmental psychology, one of these sciences, has been the subject of extensive critique (cf Walkerdine, 1984; Burman, 1994, 2000; Morss, 1996; Dahlberg et al, 1999), most recently by Fendler who talks about 'developmentality': "normalization operates through the discourse of developmentality when the generalizations that stipulate normal development are held to be defined and desirable … (and serve) as the norm and the lives of individual children are evaluated with reference to that norm" (2001, p 128).

What managerialism offers, however, is the means to more effectively control, coordinate, deliver and monitor other technologies, some of recent origins, others of long standing. It sits in the control centre of the modern state, targeting, guiding and assessing impact. With the computer, it personifies what Gilles Deleuze (1992) called the 'society of control', in the process of succeeding Foucault's 'disciplinary societies' which themselves emerged in the 18th century and reached their peak in the early 20th century. Disciplinary societies created "vast spaces of enclosure … [and the] individual never ceases passing from one closed environment to another, each having its own laws: first the family; then the school; then the barracks; then the factory; from time to time the hospital; possibly the barracks". But in control society, monitoring is continuous, standards ever changing and the individual is never finished with anything, "controls are a modulation, like a self-deforming cast that will continuously change from one moment to the other … control is of short term and of rapid rates of turnover, but also continuous and without limit, while discipline was of long duration, infinite and discontinuous".

Taking the example of one children's service, the school, Deleuze outlines some consequences of being in a society of control:

> Just as the corporation replaces the factory, perpetual training tends to replace the school and continuous control to replace the examination – which is the surest way of delivering the school over to the corporation.... What counts is that we are at the beginning of something.... For the school system, continuous forms of control and the effect on the school of perpetual training, the corresponding abandonment of all university research, the introduction of the 'corporation' at all levels of schooling. (Deleuze, 1992, pp 4, 6)

The joylessness of children's services

The concept of 'children's services' is both more influential now in policy and practice, confronted by economic and social change and uncertainty, yet more open to question as its values, assumptions and aspirations are caught in a growing scepticism about modernity. With an ever-growing emphasis on the technical and economic aspects of children's services, two lines of questioning open up. One is whether they will work in their own terms. Will they produce the desired outcomes? Will they deliver the flexible and autonomous workers, parents and adult citizens who will enable Britain (or any other country) to be winners in the global free market place – or at least not fall off the juggernaut?

The other line of questioning is about the very terms and conditions of 'children's services'. The more atomised, controlling and deliver-driven they become, the more instrumental and technical their approach, the more triumphal and dominant the discourse of economism and performativity – the more we are drawn to ask whether they have lost all connection with ideas of the good life and of what is truly important and worthwhile about being human. As Sennett (1998) puts is, "operationally, everything is so clear; emotionally so illegible". Michael Fielding poses this issue in relation to education policy in Britain:

> The discourse of performance and the now regrettably familiar 'delivery' is not only offensive, it is dishonest: offensive because it violates both our interpersonal realities and our intellectual self-respect; dishonest because one can no more deliver learning than one can, with integrity, reduce the richness and complexity of vibrant professional practice to the 'effective management of performance'.... [T]here seems no place for either the language or the experience of joy, of spontaneity, of life lived in ways that are vibrant and fulfilling rather than watchfully earnest, focused and productive of economic activity. (Fielding, 2001, pp 8-9)

Joy, spontaneity, complexity, desires, richness, wonder, curiosity, care, vibrant, play, fulfilling, thinking for yourself, love, hospitality, welcome, alterity, emotion, ethics, relationships, responsibility – these are part of a vocabulary which speaks about a different idea of public provision for children, one which addresses questions about the good life, including a good childhood, and starts with ethics and politics. Once again, we need not reject all economic or other instrumental roles for these provisions. The issue though is whether this is the primary role or whether "the vision is one in which economics is the servant of a wider and deeper human flourishing" (Fielding, 2001, p 10). [...]

In this chapter, we have explored some linked understandings and images of the child and of public provisions for children. We have also argued that these constructions do not appear from nowhere, but are the product of certain forces…: particular ways of understanding the world, particular economic forces and particular values and beliefs. Faced by problematic conditions for which they are in part responsible, these forces re-double their efforts to find solutions by governing children: we get more of the same, with ever stronger technologies brought in. One theme that emerges is the very instrumental approach to children and children's services apparent in Britain (and perhaps in other countries too), verging on a mechanistic focus on means and ends, which has led us to talk frequently about technologies, factories, processing plants, and to foreground managerialism as a new technology of control.

Before proceeding we need to make clear what we are and are *not* saying. We are not saying that the ends pursued by 'children's services' are necessarily undesirable; nor that public provision should have no predetermined objectives; nor that managerial technologies have no place. What we are saying is that predetermined objectives, and the instrumental thinking that underlies them, should not be assumed, should not be taken for granted, but should be regarded as contestable propositions and matters of political choice. It is possible to imagine them playing a lesser, even minority, role in a different, less instrumental and controlling understanding of public provision for children, produced from a different understanding of who children are [...] In short, we need to problematise the concept of 'children's services' and the understandings of children that produce and sustain this concept. By 'problematise' we do not mean reject these understandings out of hand, but rather recognise that they are perspectival and contestable, not universal and self-evident. They are choices we can make, not givens we are fated to accept without question.

What we are also saying, or at least arguing, is that modernity, neo-liberal capitalism and advanced liberalism share an inability to understand children as a social group within society, and childhood as an important period of life of value in its own right. Such ideas do not sit well with a discourse which values independence, paid work, privatised family life, markets and consumerism. They can only recognise and value children in relation to the adults they will become and childhood as an opportunity for shaping a desire adulthood.

This chapter [edited] was taken from Moss, P. and Petrie, P. (eds) (2002) *From children's services to children's spaces*, London/New York: RoutledgeFalmer. The right of Peter Moss and Pat Petrie to be identified as authors of this chapter has been asserted by them in accordance with the 1988 Copyright, Designs and Patents Act.

The challenge of child poverty: developing a child-centred approach

Tess Ridge

[...] We know from previous studies (Bradshaw, 1990; Kumar, 1993; Gregg et al, 1999; Bradshaw, 2001a) that growing up in poverty has severely adverse outcomes for many children. What we know far less about is how the experience of poverty and social exclusion impacts on children's own perceptions of their lives. We also have little understanding of how children interpret their experiences of poverty and how those experiences may be mediated through their differences and embedded in a diversity of social and structural environments. [...]

The challenge of childhood poverty

> I will set out our historic aim, that ours is the first generation to end child poverty forever, and it will take a generation. It is a 20-year mission but I believe it can be done. (Blair, 1999, p 7)

Blair's historic pledge in 1999 to end child poverty within 20 years meant that the issue of childhood poverty moved, at last, from the periphery to the centre of the policy agenda. This is a welcome development and in stark contrast to the preceding 20 years, when childhood poverty was marginalised or denied, even though the numbers of children in poverty showed a three-fold rise, from 1.4 million in 1979 to 4.5 million in 1998/99 (DSS, 1996, 2000a). Throughout that 20-year period, this extraordinary increase in child poverty remained largely unacknowledged in either political discourse or public policy (Bradshaw, 1990; Oppenheim and Harker, 1996; Walker and Walker, 1997). Therefore, the Labour government's public commitment to eradicating childhood poverty signalled a new and overdue interest in the lives and well-being of Britain's poorest children. To achieve its aim of eradicating child poverty in 20 years and of halving it in the next decade the government has embarked on a programme of radical welfare reform, which is intended to fundamentally change the systems of support for children in the UK. However, despite the much needed and welcome increase in policy attention and additional resources, ensuring that the needs and concerns of low-income children themselves are acknowledged and addressed presents a significant challenge for policy makers and professionals working with children.

Historically, children in poverty have remained largely absent from poverty discourse and public policy responses. Although policy is increasingly family-focused (Home Office, 1999), it is not necessarily child-centred, and children's interests and needs are easily subsumed and hidden within family interests and needs (Ridge and Millar, 2000; Ruxton, 2001). Anti-poverty measures directed towards children and their families have always been constrained by tensions between the interests of the state and the rights and responsibilities of the parent; in this arena the needs and rights of the child can come a poor third. Yet children are particularly vulnerable to changes in family policies, especially social security policy and the provision and adequacy of benefits. Even in today's policy climate, children have tended to appear in the policy process in complex ways: as burdens on their parents, as adults-to-be, as threats to social order and stability (Ridge and Millar, 2000). They rarely appear simply as children, with their own concerns, their own voices and their own agency.

Government has responded to child poverty in ways that have tended to focus on the futures of children who experience poverty in childhood, a concern for the child as the adult-to-be (DSS, 1999a; HM Treasury, 1999). This echoes traditional concerns about children that focus less on the lived experience of childhood and more on the child as an investment for the future, and this in turn leads to policies taking a particular form. However, the effects of poverty in children's lives need to be understood in both the short term (outcomes in childhood itself) and the long term (outcomes in adulthood) (Millar and Ridge, 2001). An important facet of that process must be an acknowledgement and understanding of the issues that concern children. Without an informed awareness of the economic and social pressures that disadvantaged children experience in the immediacy of their everyday lives, policies directed towards the alleviation of child poverty and social exclusion run the risk of failing to respond adequately to those children's needs.

What do we know about children in poverty?

Although historically childhood poverty has frequently tended to be ignored or obscured [...] there is now a considerable body of statistical knowledge which explores the dynamics and consequences of child poverty using data from a range of social surveys, including the National Child Development Study (NCDS) and the British Household Panel Survey (BHPS). These provide a comprehensive overview of the dynamics of child poverty, including durations and the extent and nature of persistent poverty in the UK (see Hill and Jenkins, 1999; and Jenkins et al, 2001, among others). Concern about the number of children living in poverty has meant that the measurement and monitoring of the economic well-being of children has greatly improved (see DSS, 1999a; Bradshaw, 2001b). We know an increasing amount about the degree to which children are experiencing poverty, and under what circumstances. Research indicates that children are vulnerable to high rates of poverty, and are likely to experience it over long durations and for repeated spells (Hill and Jenkins, 1999). There are strong links with worklessness, ethnicity, lone parenthood, sickness, disability, and long-term reliance on inadequate means-tested benefits (Bradshaw, 1990; Kumar,

1993; Oppenheim and Harker, 1996; Adelman and Bradshaw, 1998; Gordon et al, 2000; Howard et al, 2001 [...]). These and other studies have also provided insights into some of the outcomes of poverty for children, including poor health, poor cognitive development, low self-esteem, poor educational achievement, homelessness, poor housing conditions, and poor environments (Bradshaw, 1990; Kumar, 1993; Hobcraft, 1998; Gregg et al, 1999; Machin, 1999; Bradshaw, 2001a; Ermisch et al, 2001).

Undoubtedly, these studies provide a valuable insight into the possible consequences for children of experiencing poverty in their childhood. However, much of the focus of quantitative studies has been on the impact of childhood poverty on the future adult; a greater understanding of the impact of childhood poverty in childhood itself may be obtained through child-centred research.

Can quantitative data be child-centred?

Accessing data suitable for a child-centred exploration of children's social lives is problematic. There is an almost complete dearth of statistical data that places children at the centre of analysis (Jensen and Saporiti, 1992), and children have tended to be ignored or excluded from social and statistical accounting (Qvortrup, 1997). Where children have appeared it is often as an adjunct to adult data, or in data concerned with the impact of children on adult lives and family economies. Interest in children's lives per se is still relatively rare (Scott et al, 1995). Large-scale surveys that focus on social and material enquiries at the individual and household level have all tended to exclude respondents below the age of 16 years. Increasing acknowledgement that children are not merely passive members of households but have their own views, attitudes and experiences to relate has gone some way towards increasing research with children and young people (see Middleton et al, 1994; Shropshire and Middleton, 1999).

Shropshire and Middleton (1999), using a children's questionnaire, raised concerns about the extent to which children's economic learning, behaviour and aspirations are affected by disadvantage. They found that children in poorer families may be 'learning to be poor', controlling their expectations and reducing their aspirations, in the face of their family's severely constrained economic circumstances. Some insight into why they may be reducing their aspirations and expectations may be gauged from surveys measuring childhood deprivation, using an index of socially perceived necessities. These reveal how deprived children are missing out on a broad range of essential items and activities enjoyed by their peers (Middleton et al, 1997; Gordon et al, 2000). The *Poverty and Social Exclusion* survey of Britain (PSE) shows that one third (34%) of British children go without at least one item or activity deemed as necessary by the majority of the population, and nearly one fifth (18%) go without two or more items or activities (Gordon et al, 2000). Studies such as the *Family fortunes* survey (Middleton et al, 1997) and the *Poverty and Social Exclusion* survey of Britain (Gordon et al, 2000) establish through research with adults (mainly mothers) a list of items and activities that are considered basic necessities for children in Britain today. However, valuable as these are, they all entail adult perceptions of children's needs; there has been little engagement with children themselves about things that they themselves would consider essential for their material and social well-being.

Qualitative research with children

A greater insight into the lives of children living in poverty could be gained from qualitative research, which is inherently more reflexive and responsive. However, when moving from the more quantifiable aspects of childhood poverty to the social and relational impact of poverty and social exclusion in childhood, it is evident that there are considerable gaps in our knowledge. Despite the considerable body of statistical data relating to child poverty, there is a dearth of meaningful qualitative data. Indeed, it is only recently that adults in poverty have had any voice in poverty research, an area traditionally dominated by 'experts' (see Bradshaw and Holmes, 1989; Cohen et al, 1992; Kempson, 1996; Beresford et al, 1999). Although organisations such as the Child Poverty Action Group would appear to have a specifically child-focused perspective, to date little of their research has focused primarily on children themselves. Previous publications such as *Hardship Britain* (Cohen et al, 1992), while giving a rare qualitative insight into the experiences of people in poverty, have had no input from children. *Hard times* (Kempson et al, 1994) provides a valuable account of strategies used by families on a low income to meet their needs. However, although the study explored in detail the lives and experiences of 74 'families', children's voices and experiences in general were absent. *Life on a low income* (Kempson, 1996) is a review of 31 qualitative studies in which people in poverty speak for themselves. Of the 31 studies chosen, however, very few provide an arena for children's and young people's voices to be heard (see Middleton et al, 1994; Anderson and Quilgars, 1995; Jones, 1995; Roaf and Lloyd, 1995). Of these, only *Family fortunes* (Middleton et al, 1994) involved interviews with children rather than with young people who had left their family homes. When children and young people leave the family home and enter the public domain either as 'victims' through homelessness and the care system, or as 'villains' through juvenile crime, they become more visible. Although a relatively recent phenomenon, studies which interview young homeless people, children in care or young care leavers, for example (Butler and Williamson, 1994; Biehal et al, 1995), are at last becoming more common and are an important aid to policy and developing an understanding of young people's lives and experiences. However, in general, as Bradshaw (1990) argued, we know very little about what children themselves think and feel about poverty; and 10 years on we are still in a similar situation.

For some qualitative understanding of the experience of poverty for children and young people, we must turn in the main to three publications, *Family fortunes* (Middleton et al, 1994), and two studies by the Children's Society, *Same scenery, different lifestyle* (Davis and Ridge, 1997), and *Worth more than this* (Roker, 1998). *Family fortunes* explores the economic pressures on parents and children in the UK. Children's involvement in the research was through group discussions and questionnaires, which explored their social lives and aspirations. The sample of children, aged 8-16 years, was drawn from schools and made up of children from diverse socioeconomic backgrounds, so in this case the focus was not primarily on children in poverty. Their responses were divided into two socioeconomic groups for analysis: the 'more affluent' and the 'less affluent'. The interviews explored with children how they spent their time, what possessions they had and what they felt they needed in order to participate in the world around them. They also explored the social pressures that children experience from peers. What emerges is a disturbing picture of how children from low-income families "begin to experience the reality of their 'differentness' at an early age" (Middleton et al, 1994, p 150). These issues are further highlighted by Davis and Ridge (1997) and Roker (1998) in two studies which explored the experiences of children and young people from low-income families from a child-centred perspective. What was particularly apparent using this approach were the social and peer pressures exerted on children; the financial demands of participation and the fears and social costs of exclusion.

What is currently missing in child poverty research?

Developing a more child-centred approach to understanding the experience of poverty and social exclusion in childhood will entail a radical rethink about the conceptual frameworks with which poverty has been traditionally analysed and understood. Much of our analysis of poverty has been framed within an adult discourse of economic distribution and material resources. If we broaden our perspective to include the more relationally dynamic notion of social exclusion, we are still no further enlightened. Although the notion of social exclusion is now an important part of mainstream political rhetoric, it is a poorly understood concept. Our ability to recognise the causes and consequences of social exclusion and our capacity for understanding and acknowledging the processes of social exclusion are still developing. It is also a concept that is open to different social, political and cultural interpretations and bias (see Levitas, 1998). Yet, whatever the values underpinning the different notions of social exclusion, the defining characteristics have always been predominantly adult centric.

Current political rhetoric and policy is directed towards a notion of social exclusion that is primarily concerned with exclusion from the labour market, and although many children are economically active, this approach is focused on adult experiences and needs and has little to tell us of the experience of social exclusion within childhood. When the dangers of social exclusion for children and young people do appear on the policy agenda, it invariably focuses on the child as the 'adult-to-be'. The prioritising of truancy, school exclusions, teenage pregnancies, homelessness and the 'worst estates' by the Social Exclusion Unit (see SEU, 1998a, 1998b, 1998c, 1999), while acknowledging some of the most serious problems facing society at present, also reflects adult concerns of 'youth' as a threat to social order and stability. Alternatively, children have been seen mainly as a future resource, as a form of human capital, to be protected and developed. Yet, while the effects of poverty and social exclusion will undoubtedly reverberate from childhood into adulthood, children experience social exclusion within the immediacy of childhood, among their peers. Therefore, social exclusion for children could signify much more than exclusion from society as conceived by adults. It may also mean exclusion from the norms and customs of children's society. In this respect, childhood needs to be seen as a social experience in itself, where the demands of participation and inclusion may be considerable, and likewise the costs of exclusion (Ridge and Millar, 2000).

Clearly, it will be hard to operationalise a concept of social exclusion relevant to children which is based on adult themes, because children are structurally and institutionally excluded from many of these areas at the outset. Therefore, any conceptual framework must be contextualised within the state of childhood itself. It would need to encompass the discourse, agency and identity of the child, while also recognising the stratifications of power inherent in adult/child social relations; and the social boundaries, constructions and institutions, which shape the experience of being a child.

What is child-centred research?

What does it mean to put the child at the centre of research and analysis? Much previous research involving children has been largely *on* them, rather than *with* them or *for* them (Hood et al, 1996). In the past, the main areas of interest have been the family, health and education. However, in all these fields, children's own perspectives have historically seldom been the central focus. Only recently through initiatives from the Economic and Social Research Council (ESRC) and the Joseph Rowntree Foundation have children been seen as 'social actors' with their own stories to tell. Much research with children has been observational and heavily informed by the developmental paradigm, which confines children to a series of stages towards adulthood (Hood et al, 1996). This poses mature adulthood as the ultimate goal by which children are measured. The consequence of this is to confine children's lives and experiences to an adult agenda, where the effects of early childhood, educational achievement and so on have been studied for their impact on the adult-to-be rather than on the child of the present. This tendency is clearly evident in many studies of childhood poverty. Dominant assumptions about the nature of children and childhood have led to a model of the child as a 'research object' (Hogan and Gilligan, 1998). However, there is a growing recognition that children are social actors in their own right, rather than inadequately socialised future adults (James and Prout, 1997). This means a shift from 'object' to 'subject', and a recognition that children themselves are best informed about their lives and the issues that are meaningful to them. Children have their own set of opinions and judgements, which, while not always the same as those of adults, nevertheless have the same moral legitimacy (Fine and Sandstrom, 1988).

The assumption that children are 'naturally' incompetent and incapable is very socially pervasive and has often resulted in children being viewed as unreliable witnesses about their own lives (Qvortrup, 1994). As a consequence, adult proxies have often been used to speak for children. However, the use of adult proxies – parents, teachers, social workers and so on – raises issues of the reliability and veracity of such accounts. Adults' views of children and children's views of themselves may differ greatly (see Mahon et al, 1996), and issues perceived by adults as relevant to children might not be those articulated by the child (Ennew and Morrow, 1994).

Putting it into practice

Child-centred research practice requires an informed and considered approach at every stage of the research process. This means developing skill and sensitivity not just in the practical methodological techniques of establishing rapport, openness and trust (Butler and Williamson, 1994; Alderson, 1995), but also in acknowledging and addressing ethical considerations and issues of power and control (Morrow and Richards, 1996). Issues of access arise, and the need to ensure that informed consent is sought from children as well as the adults with their care; this is challenging in an environment where adults have the power to refuse consent even when children wish to participate (Thomas and O'Kane, 1998). Parents, teachers and other key adults in children's lives can equally assume children's consent, and the researcher needs to be particularly vigilant to ensure that children and young people are fully involved in the consent process. It can also be particularly hard for children to withdraw from, or discontinue, an arrangement made by key adults who have power in their lives (Hill et al, 1996). Space and privacy for children to talk in confidence will also need to be negotiated (Mauthner, 1997). Children are vulnerable, not only through their inherent weakness and dependence on adults, but also critically through their lack of rights and their lack of political and economic power. This is often overlooked, resulting in an overemphasis on children's physical vulnerability and a lack of focus on their structural vulnerability (Lansdown, 1994). However, although research must be informed by an awareness of children's vulnerability and dependence, it also needs to ensure that they are accorded respect and autonomy within the research process. Only by engaging directly with the child and seeing them as independent actors negotiating a complex social world, with an intricate web of social and familial relationships and loyalties, can a valid account be obtained.

Understanding children's experiences of poverty

The qualitative study

This was a new empirical study using in-depth interviews to explore the lives and experiences of a group of children and young people from low-income families. The fieldwork was carried out in the spring and summer of 1999, in urban areas of Bristol and Bath, and rural areas of Somerset. The children interviewed were drawn from a random sample provided by the Department of Social Security (now the Department for Work and Pensions). They were all living in families in receipt of Income Support, and had been so for more than six months. The sample was divided into lone-parent and two-parent families. Two-parent families were families where an adult or a child was disabled, rather than using the more usual characteristic of unemployment. This enabled a better match between lone-parent families and two-parent families, as both types were likely to experience poverty over a long duration[3]. Children were also grouped according to their location and the sample was divided between rural and urban children. This enabled a comparative exploration of potentially differing experiences. Children and their families were approached on a random basis, within the parameters of family type and location, and interviews were carried out until the required sample size of 40 children was attained.

The final sample of 40 children and young people contained 20 children from each family type, 10 each from rural and urban locations. There were 19 girls interviewed and 21 boys. Ages ranged from 10 to 17[4], with the majority of the sample aged between 10 and 15 years (34), and over half of the sample (22) between 10 and 12 years. All children and young people in the sample were white, which reflects the make up of rural areas for the 20 children in the rural sample. The urban sample was approached on a random basis using inner-city postcodes. However, no families in ethnic minorities were encountered before the sample of 20 children was completed. Wherever children in families had siblings who were within the age category these were also interviewed.

Poverty is in many ways a socially unacceptable word, heavily imbued with stigma and prejudice. Therefore, research which seeks to explore the nature and impact of poverty needs to be conducted with great sensitivity. This is especially so when the research subjects are children and the research agenda requires considerable openness, trust and self-reflection. Previous research with children using a group environment has proved very fruitful (see Burgess, 1984; Middleton et al, 1994; Hill et al, 1996). However, logistically there are few opportunities to get children together, other than in an institutional setting such as a school, where there are inherent difficulties in selecting out children who are from low-income families from others, without reinforcing stigma. Therefore, the study used individual in-depth interviews which made it easier to ensure confidentiality and privacy. It also provided a safer and more intimate environment for disclosure and exploration of sensitive issues such as friendship and self-esteem, issues which could be obscured or leave a child painfully exposed in the shared environment of a group interview.

The interviews explored children's experiences at school, at home and with their families; and it [sic] focused on their economic and material environment, their social relationships and their own understandings of the impact poverty has made on their lives. Because the interviews were designed to be as child-centred as possible, a very flexible and unstructured interview procedure was chosen, which evolved over the fieldwork period, incorporating new areas of interest as they were identified by children. Children are rarely seen as individuals in their own right, and generally subsumed into the family. By interviewing siblings within families it is possible to gain some understanding of how children within families may experience their circumstances very differently.

All the interviews were taped and subsequently transcribed. Analysis of the data was carried out manually using thematic indexing. Themes included those issues initially highlighted in the interview schedule and were broadened out to include issues identified by children themselves. The interviews had been structured in a few areas, for example whether or not children received any pocket money; this allowed some basic comparative work to develop some generalisations and identify differences. A comparative approach was also adopted to identify any key differences between children on the grounds of gender, age, family type, and location (rural or urban). Differences between children and young people who were or were not working were also examined and where siblings had been interviewed, their responses as individuals and as family group members were noted and explored. All children's names have been changed to anonymise the data, and care has been taken at all stages to ensure the primacy of children speaking for themselves.

In addition to interviews with children and young people, interviews were also conducted with 17 parents of the children in the sample. This was a smaller sample and was not intended to mirror the child sample. Interviews with parents were only undertaken when parents were uncertain about the interview process, and wished to be reassured about the process, or when they particularly wanted to have their say about bringing up children on a low income. However, as most parents were happy for their children to be interviewed, the opportunity was taken to interview the child, and where appropriate their siblings, rather than to request an interview with the parent/s. Of the interviews conducted with parents, nine were lone parents and eight were parents from two-parent families. The parents were interviewed separately at the same visit as their children, and all interviews, with children and parents, were completely confidential; each was unaware of any comments the others may have made. All interviews were taped and transcribed. The interviews and analysis focused on adult perceptions of areas already highlighted by children. This ensured that as far as possible it was the children's issues and concerns which set the agenda.

The quantitative study

The quantitative study analysed a cross-section of data from the BHPYS. This is a survey that utilises child-centred research ethics, and is a unique and important source of data relating to children's leisure activities, health, and their attitudes to family, education and work. However, despite its potential, this is a rarely used data set, and previous analysis has tended to focus on children's health and mental well-being (see Brynin and Scott, 1996; Brynin, 1997; Clarke et al, 1999; for a recent exception see Ermisch et al, 2001). Because of the child-centred nature of the collection and generation of the data, and its coverage of social relationships and social attitudes, this was a uniquely suitable data set for the purposes of this study. [...]

The data was used to explore how children and young people experience their school environment. This is one of the most critical areas in children's lives. Current education policy is increasingly driven by demands to improve academic standards. But school also plays a particularly significant role in children's lives as a site of social as well as pedagogical learning. There is also increasing interest in the school as an environment for developing 'soft skills'[5] for future employability. The greater parts of children's social interactions with other children are also contextualised within the school environment. Analysis of the BHPYS data provided an ideal opportunity to explore children's and young people's experiences and perceptions of school life and their relationships with their teachers. Wave 7 (1997 data), the latest issue of data at the time of analysis, was used to explore children's experiences, and analysis was carried out on a cross-sectional sample of 720 children and young people who were aged between 11-15 years. The data compared the responses of children living in families receiving Income Support and/or Jobseeker's Allowance with those of children who were in families that were not receiving these benefits.

Understanding the everyday challenges of a childhood in poverty

[...] Many of the issues that have traditionally been associated with the lives of children in poverty – on the one hand, drugs, drinking, prostitution, school exclusions and truanting, and on the other, violence, neglect and abuse – are of critical concern. But there is also a need to understand and acknowledge some of the other everyday experiences and demands that the majority of children from low-income families face. Normative perceptions of 'poor' children's lives have often been informed through media-induced panics, and stereotypical images that focus mainly on child abuse and neglect, or drug abuse and criminality (Scraton, 1997). The images engendered are of 'poor' children as either villains or victims (Daniel and Ivatts, 1998). Negative stereotypes obscure the everyday realities of such children's lives and impinge on their rights to social justice. These one-dimensional images not only shape and distort social perceptions and understandings of children in poverty, they can also affect the lives of disadvantaged children among their peers, fostering stigma and the potential for difference and exclusion. One of the underpinning aims [...] is to redress the balance somewhat, to facilitate an awareness of child poverty that can incorporate a richer and far more complex understanding than our present perceptions allow, of the everyday challenges faced by children who are 'poor'. [...]

Children's welfare and children's rights

Gerison Lansdown

Children, as minors in law, have neither autonomy nor the right to make choices or decisions on their own behalf. Instead, responsibility for such decisions and for the welfare of children has traditionally been vested with those adults who care for them. It has always been presumed not only that adults are better placed than children to exercise responsibility for decision making, but also that in so doing they will act in children's best interests. In addition this presumption has been established as a legal obligation on the courts, which for many years have been required to give paramountcy to the welfare of the child in making decisions concerning their day-to-day lives (1989 Children Act). This model of adult–child relationships constructs children as the passive recipients of adult protection and good will, lacking the competence to exercise responsibility for their own lives.

In recent years we have begun to question the adequacy of this approach and to re-examine the assumptions on which it has been based: first, that adults can be relied on to act in children's best interests; second, that children lack the competence to act as agents in their own lives; and third, that adults have the monopoly of expertise in determining outcomes in children's lives. There have been a number of factors contributing to this process of change. Certainly, over the past 20 years, we have witnessed a growing body of evidence concerning children's lives that challenges any capacity for complacency about the extent to which children's welfare is being protected by adults.

The limitations of a welfare approach

Adults can abuse their power over children

Adults in positions of power over children can exploit and abuse that power, to the detriment of children's well-being. During the 1970s we first became aware of the extent to which children are vulnerable to physical abuse within their own families. The extent and scale of violence that parents were capable of perpetrating on their own children emerged though the work of Henry Kempe in the USA and was brought home forcefully in this country with the case of Maria Colwell, a young girl who was returned from care to live with her parents, who subsequently beat her to death (Howells, 1974). It was not, however, until the 1980s that the phenomenon of sexual abuse within families, as a day-to-day reality for many thousands of children, hit the public consciousness in this country with the Cleveland scandal into the sexual abuse of children (DHSS, 1988). There was, and probably still is, considerable resistance to the recognition that parents and other adult relatives could and do rape and assault their children. It challenges the very notion of family life that we wish to believe exists for all children – the view that children are safest within their families. It also challenges the legitimacy of the powerful cultural desire for protecting the privacy of family life because it undermines the comfortable assumption that parents can always be relied on to promote the welfare of their children.

It took until the 1990s to uncover the next scandal in the catalogue of failure on the part of responsible adults to protect and promote the welfare of children. In a series of public inquiries it became apparent not only that children in public care in a number of local authorities had been subjected to systematic physical abuse by staff in children's homes, but also that these practices had been surrounded by a culture of collusion, neglect, indifference and silence on the part of the officers and elected members within those authorities. It is now acknowledged that this experience of abuse was not simply the consequence of a few paedophiles entering the public care system (DH/Welsh Office, 1997). Rather, it is an endemic problem, affecting children in authorities across the country and symptomatic of a fundamental failure to provide effective protective care towards vulnerable children.

One of the most forceful lessons to emerge from the series of public inquiries into the abuse of children in public care was the extent to which the children involved were denied any opportunity to challenge what was happening to them (DH/Welsh Office, 2000; Kirkwood, 1993; Levy and Kahan, 1991). They were systematically disbelieved in favour of adult versions of events. They were denied access to any advocacy to help them articulate their concerns. Indeed, if and when they did complain, they risked further abuse. In other words the adults involved, could, with impunity, behave in ways entirely contrary to the children's welfare.

We can, then, no longer disregard the fact that children can be and are both physically and sexually abused by the very adults who are responsible for their care, both within families and in state institutions. And in confronting that reality, it becomes necessary to move beyond the assumption that a simple reliance on adults to promote the well-being of children, because of their biological or professional relationship with the child, is an adequate approach to caring for children.

Adults do not always act in children's best interests

Actions detrimental to the well-being of children do not merely occur when adults deliberately abuse or neglect children. During the course of the 20th century adults with responsibility for children across the professional spectrum have been responsible for decisions, policies and actions that have been inappropriate for, if not actively harmful to, children while claiming to be acting to promote their

welfare. One does not have to look far for the evidence. We separated
from parents in the war evacuations. We excluded mothers from hospita
their children were sick, in pain and frightened. We failed to acknowledg
small babies experience pain and denied them analgesics. We undertook ro
tonsillectomies that were unnecessary and often distressing to children. we
promoted adoption for the babies of unmarried mothers with no possibility of
future contact. We placed children in care and cut them off from their birth
families. We looked after them in large, unloving institutions that stigmatised
them and denied them opportunities for emotional and psychological well-being.
We removed disabled children from their families and placed them in long-term
institutional care. In all these examples, there is now public recognition that
children were more harmed than helped by these practices.

In addition the existence of public policy that serves to act against the best
interests of children is not simply a matter of history. We continue to place disabled
children in special schools on grounds of the 'efficient use of resources' rather
than the promotion of the child's best interests (1996 Education Act, Section
316). In this situation it is the law which condones practice that can operate
against a child's best interests. However, in the field of public care, and despite the
Children Act clearly requiring courts to give paramountcy to the best interests of
children, there is growing evidence from organisations working with looked-
after children that local authorities, when implementing care orders imposed by
the courts, are making placements decisions based on cost rather than best interests
(Children's Rights Office, 1998). Additionally, the curriculum being introduced
by the government prescribing attainment targets for children at ever earlier ages
has the potential of jeopardising the right to play.

Public policy often supports the rights and interests of parents ahead of those
of children, even when the consequences of so doing are detrimental to the
welfare of children. There is, for example, a clear conflict of interest between
children and parents in the field of assisted reproduction, in which both law and
practice favour the interests of the parents. Our present legislation fails to protect
the right of children born through assisted reproduction techniques to access to
knowledge of their biological identity. The law actively prohibits children access
to identifying information about their biological parents, and there is neither an
obligation on the part of nor any encouragement from the relevant professionals
for parents to be open with their children about the origins of their birth (1990
Human Fertilization and Embryology Act). The desire for a pretended normality,
the fear of children not loving the non-biological parent, the fear of a reduced
supply of donors if anonymity were not preserved and the difficulty in confronting
children with the truth all play a part in perpetuating the current collusion
against a commitment to respecting the fundamental right of the child to a
knowledge of his or her identity (Blyth, 1990; Freeman, 1997).

It is evident that it is not children's welfare but rather the directly competing
interests of parents to maintain secrecy and to have a child that is the overriding
factor determining legislation and practice in this field. There is, for example,
ample evidence from the experience of adoption on the importance of honesty
and openness with children about their origin. All adoption agencies would

endorse this approach as fundamental to good practice. Additionally, in the context of our enhanced understanding of genetics, there is a growing need for children to have accurate information about their biological make-up. Furthermore, there is a growing likelihood of individuals undergoing genetic testing at some stage in their lives, when the truth about their true parentage will emerge. How much more painful it would be to discover the reality in adulthood. If the welfare of children were the pre-eminent factor in decision making, there is little doubt that the law would be amended in their favour.

In 2000 the government issued a consultation paper setting out proposals to change the law on the physical punishment of children in order to comply with the findings of the European Court of Human Rights that the law in this country failed to protect a child from inhuman and degrading treatment under Article 3 of the European Convention on Human Rights (ECHR, 1998). The consultation sets out three questions for consideration. Should the defence of 'reasonable chastisement' be removed from certain forms of physical punishment, such as hitting children around the head in ways that might cause brain injury or damage to the eyes and ears? Should the defence cease to be available against a charge of actual bodily harm and should the defence be restricted to those with parental responsibility? (DH, 2000).

However, the consultation document fails to ask the central and most significant question – should parents be allowed to hit their children at all? The absence of this question is not accidental. There was considerable pressure on the government, from an alliance of some 250 organisations, to include in the consultation paper the option to change the law to remove the defence of 'reasonable chastisement' for parents and to give children the same protection from all forms of assault as adults. The government refused to do so. It is clearly recognised under international law that the continued practice of hitting children represents a breach of their human rights. The Committee on the Rights of the Child, the international body established to monitor government progress in implementing the UNCRC, has already criticised the UK government for its failure to introduce legislation to protect children from physical punishment by parents and recommended a review of the law to introduce appropriate protection (CRC, 1995). When the government appears before the committee again in 2002, it will be censored if it has failed to act on this recommendation. The reality is that the government is not willing even to consult on a proposal to end all physical punishment of children because to do so would be seen to interfere with the rights of parents.

There is considerable evidence that the physical punishment of children is not an effective form of discipline, that it can and does cause harm, and that as a form of punishment it can and does escalate (Leach, 1999). In addition almost every professional body working with children is unanimous that we should change the law to protect children better and give parents a positive message that hitting children is both wrong and unnecessary (Barnardos, 1998). It can also be seen from the experience of the eight countries that have banned it that it does not lead to a rise in prosecutions of parents, it does change parental behaviour in favour of more positive forms of discipline and it does not lead to worse-behaved or ill-disciplined children (Durrant, 1999). Again, then, it is not the welfare of children that informs the law and its proposed reform, but the need to assuage adult public opinion.

Children's interests are often disregarded in public policy

Children's interests are frequently disregarded in the public policy sphere in favour of those of more powerful interest groups. It is not necessarily the case that children's welfare is deliberately disregarded but that children, and the impact of public policy on their lives, are not visible in decision-making forums and, accordingly, never reach the top of the political agenda. Just consider, for example, the impact of public policy on children during the 1980s and 1990s. In 1979 one in 10 children were living in poverty. By 1991 the proportion had increased to one in three (DH, 1993b). That alone is a sufficient indictment of our neglect of children. Even more significantly, however, it is children who bore the disproportionate burden of the increase in poverty during that period: no other group in society experienced a growth in poverty on a comparable scale. The consequences of that poverty on children's life chances are profound, impacting on educational attainment, physical and mental health, emotional well-being and employment opportunities. At a collective level then, our society failed to promote and protect the welfare of children over two decades.

There is little analysis of public expenditure to assess whether the proportion spent on children and their well-being reflects either their level of need or their representation within the community. What little we do know indicates that the lack of data is likely to cover very significant inadequacies in spending on children, indicating their weak position in the lobbies that influence public agendas and expenditure. We know, for example, that health authorities spend 5% of their mental health budgets on children and adolescent mental health services, even though this age group represents 25% of the population (Audit Commission, 1999). It is of course likely that services for older people will necessitate a disproportionate claim on these budgets, but no systematic assessment has been made of whether the current balance in any way reflects comparative levels of assessed needs. Also, as long as children lack powerful advocates in the field of health, such discrepancies will not be effectively challenged.

Similarly, in the field of housing, countless estates have been built in which the needs of children have been completely disregarded – no play spaces or facilities, dangerous balconies, and lifts with controls out of the reach of children (Freeman et al, 1999). We have also grown increasingly intolerant of children in the public arena. Far from developing towns and cities that are designed with children in mind, that are child-friendly, as befits a society with the welfare of children at its heart, we now tend to view children as undesirable in streets and shops, particularly when they are in groups. The introduction of powers to impose child curfews, the refusal of many shops to allow children in and the decision by the Millennium Dome to refuse entry to the under-16s if they are not accompanied by an adult are all testimony to a perception of children as threatening, hostile and outside the legitimate bounds of society. Public spaces are seen to be 'owned' by adults, young people's presence in those spaces representing an unwanted intrusion. Yet these are the adults on whom children rely to promote their best interests. These are the adults who are responsible for protecting children's welfare.

Children's competence and contribution

The welfare model of childcare has perpetuated the view that children lack the capacity to contribute to their own well-being or do not have a valid and valuable contribution to make. Yet a failure to involve children in decisions that affect their own lives has been the cause of many of the mistakes and poor judgements exercised by adults when acting on children's behalf. There is now a growing body of evidence that children, both in respect of individual decisions that affect their lives and as a body in the broader public policy arena, have a considerable contribution to make to decision making (Alderson, 1993; John, 1996; Marshall, 1997). Children, even when very young, can act, for example, as peer counsellors, mediators or mentors for other children. Local and health authorities have successfully involved children in the development of new hospitals, anti-poverty strategies and advice services. In other words far from being 'in waiting' until they acquire adult competencies, children can, when empowered to do so, act as a source of expertise, skill and information for adults and contribute towards meeting their own needs.

Moving beyond a welfare perspective

Once it is acknowledged not only that adults are capable of the abuse of children, but also that children's welfare can be undermined by conflicting interests, neglect, indifference and even hostility on the part of adults, it becomes clear that it is not sufficient to rely exclusively on adults to define children's needs and be responsible for meeting them. Indeed, the welfare model has failed children. The traditional perception of children as having needs – for love, care, protection – is now challenged by a recognition that children are subjects of rights, a concept that has gradually developed during the course of the 20th century, culminating in the adoption by the UN General Assembly in 1990 of the UNCRC. The Convention now has almost universal acceptance, having been ratified by 191 countries throughout the world. Only the USA and Somalia have not yet made the commitment under international law to comply with the principles and standards it embodies. The Convention is a comprehensive human rights treaty encompassing social, economic and cultural as well as civil and political rights.

The recognition of children as the subjects of rights rather than merely the recipients of adult protective care introduces a new dimension to adult relationships with children. It does not negate the fact that children have needs but argues that children therefore have rights to have those needs met. The rights contained in the Convention fall into three broad categories, each of which impose different obligations on adults: freedoms to protection from the state, protection by the state to ensure respect for individual rights, and rights to the fulfilment of social and economic needs. The discourse in respect of human rights traditionally centred on the need for boundaries to the abusive exercise of power by the state to protect the civil and political rights and freedoms of individual citizens. While those protections remain important – there is still a need for powers to constrain the intrusion of the state into individual liberties – there has been a growing recognition that rights are not only abused by the state but also perpetrated by individuals against other members of a society. There is thus a need for the state to play an active role in protecting the rights of citizens from violations of their rights by others. This is particularly true of children. Because they lack autonomy, and their lives are substantially circumscribed by the adults who have responsibility for them, there is a clear onus on the state to intervene actively to protect those rights. In addition, children have socio-economic rights that impose obligations on the state to make available the necessary resources to ensure that children's well-being is promoted.

For example, if a child has a right to protection from discrimination, the government has the responsibility to introduce the necessary legislation, backed up by enforcement mechanisms, training and public education. If a child has a right to free full-time education, it is the responsibility of the state at a local and national level, as well as the child's parents, to ensure that education is made available and that the child is able to benefit from it.

Implications of respecting children's human rights

One of the underlying principles of the Convention is that the best interests of the child must be a primary consideration in all actions concerning the child (UNCRC, 1989, Article 3). This principle does not, however, merely take us back to a welfare approach: a commitment to respecting the human rights of children requires an acceptance that promoting children's welfare or best interests requires more than the good will or professional judgement of adults. The Convention injects two fundamental challenges to traditional practices in respect of children.

First, the means by which the best interests of children are assessed must be the extent to which all their human rights are respected in any particular policy, action or legislation. In other words the rights embodied in the Convention must provide a framework with which to analyse the extent to which proposals promote the best interests of children (Hodgkin and Newell, 1998). This approach also extends both to matters affecting the rights of an individual child and to children as a body. In providing child protection services, for example, do interventions that seek to protect the child from abuse also respect the child's right to privacy, to respect for the child's views and evolving capacities, to continuity in family life, to contact with the immediate and extended family? In a proposed local housing development, have the rights of children to adequate play facilities, safe road crossings and leisure services been properly considered? Similarly, one can apply a comparable analysis to decisions taken within families. Many parents currently drive their children to school and justify so doing in terms of the potential dangers of both traffic and abduction or assault to which the children might otherwise be exposed. A rights-based approach would necessitate a broader analysis of the rights of children. What impact does driving children to school have on their right to the best possible health, to freedom of association, to play, to a growing respect for their emerging competence?

In all these examples it can be argued that unless a comprehensive rights-based approach is taken, there is a risk that a decision or intervention is made that responds to one aspect of the child's life and in so doing fails to acknowledge other rights or needs. Indeed, it may inadvertently impact adversely on the child.

Second, if children are subjects of rights, they themselves must have the opportunity to exercise those rights and be afforded the means of seeking redress when their rights are violated. In other words they must have opportunities to be heard. Article 12 of the Convention embodies the principle that children have the right to express their views on matters of concern to them and to have those views taken seriously in accordance with their age and maturity. It is a procedural right that has increasingly been recognised as necessary if children are to move beyond their traditional status as recipients of adult care and protection and become social actors entitled to influence decisions that affect their lives (Lansdown, 1996; Willow, 1997). Children are entitled to be actively involved in those decisions which affect them as individuals – in the family, in schools, in public care, in the courts, and as a body in the development, delivery, monitoring and evaluation of public policy at both local and national levels.

Listening to children and taking them seriously is important because children have a body of experience and views that are relevant to the development of public policy, improving the quality of decision making and rendering it more accountable. Beyond this, it is an essential element in their protection. Children who experience respect for their views and are encouraged to take responsibility for those decisions they are competent to make will acquire the confidence to challenge any abuse of their rights. The active participation of children must also be backed up by clear and accessible complaints and appeals procedures and the availability of independent advocacy if they are to be able to challenge failures to respect their rights.

It is in the field of education that the failure to recognise the importance of listening to children as an essential component of promoting their best interests is perhaps most evident. The current government has placed a considerable emphasis on education whose focus has been almost exclusively the issue of academic attainment. Certainly, the UNCRC includes the rights of children to an education on the basis of equality of opportunity, and the determination of the current government to ensure that high aspirations and opportunities exist for all children is consistent with the fulfilment of that right.

However, unlike children in most other European countries, children in the UK are denied the right to express their views and have them taken seriously within the education system (Davies and Kirkpatrick, 2000). There is no right to establish a school council, and children are expressly excluded from sitting on governing bodies. Children are not consulted over the National Curriculum, teaching methods, school policies or proposed legislation. Children, as opposed to their parents, have no right of appeal against a permanent school exclusion. There are no complaints procedures that can be followed in the event of injustice, discrimination or abuse. There are no regional or national networks of school students to act on behalf of pupils. In other words the government agenda in respect of children perpetuates the view that education is something that adults do to or for children, the child being constructed as the recipient. It fails to recognise the obligation to respect children's human rights within the education system – the right to be listened to, to be respected, to learn through day-to-day experience about the meaning of democracy and human rights. Children's best interests can only be promoted if these rights, alongside the right of access to education, are realised.

Conclusion

There is a continuing resistance to the concept of rights in this country, particularly when applied to children. It is a resistance shared by many parents, politicians, policy makers and the media. It derives, at least in part, from a fear that children represent a threat to stability and order if they are not kept under control. Furthermore, it reflects the strong cultural tradition that children are 'owned' by their parents and that the state should play as minimal a role as possible in their care. Attempts by the state to act to protect children are thus viewed with suspicion and hostility.

But promoting the rights of children is not about giving a licence to children to take compete control of their lives irrespective of their level of competence. It is not about allowing children to ride roughshod over the rights of others, any more than adult rights permit such abuses. It is rather, about moving away from the discredited assumption that adults alone can determine what happens in children's lives without regard for children's own views, experiences and aspirations. It means accepting that children, even very small children, are entitled to be listened to and taken seriously. It means acknowledging that, as children grow older, they can take greater responsibility for exercising their own rights. It involves recognising that the state has explicit obligations towards children, for which it should be held accountable. A commitment to respecting children's rights does not mean abandoning their welfare: it means promoting their welfare by an adherence to the human rights standards defined by international law.

This chapter was taken from Foley, P., Roche, J. and Tucker, S. (eds) (2001) *Children in society*, London: Palgrave/OU. The right of Gerison Lansdown to be identified as author of this chapter has been asserted by her in accordance with the 1988 Copyright, Designs and Patents Act.

Risk, advanced liberalism and child welfare: the need to rediscover uncertainty and ambiguity

Nigel Parton

The purpose of this chapter is to analyse and reflect upon the current state of child welfare policy and practice and how this has changed over recent times. In the process it aims to make a contribution to the current debates on 'the refocusing of children's services'. A central part of the argument is that new strategies have emerged which do not have as their central focus either meeting the needs of children or responding to child abuse, but the assessment and management of risk. In selecting such a focus, such developments are in danger of overlooking a central characteristic of policy and practice in terms of the pervasiveness of uncertainty and ambiguity. Not only do these characteristics need to be reorganised, but they need to be built on in order to take our thinking and practices forward. [...]

Destabilising the present

While Foucault is often regarded as playing the major role in contributing to a range of new departures in the social and human sciences over the last 25 years, perhaps his major contribution is in terms of the conceptual devices and tools which he made available for understanding the contingencies of the systems of power in which we live and which thereby inhabit us today. Concepts are deployed to demonstrate the negotiations, tensions and accidents that have contributed to the fashioning of ourselves and our times. Following Barry et al (1996), two elements can be seen to characterise Foucauldian histories of the present: the general *ethos* of the approach; and the concern with *liberalism*.

Foucault always attempted to introduce an 'untimely' ethos to the present and thereby introduced a sense of its *fragility* and *contingency*, thus demonstrating that it does not necessarily have to be like this. In the process, we can think about the present differently and act in new and creative ways for the benefit of the future (Bell, 1994). The present is seen, not as necessary, inevitable or homogeneous, but as something to be decomposed, problematised, and acted upon. In destabilising and fragmenting the present, a space for the work of *freedom* and *change* is thus opened up (Rose, 1993b). The *ethos* is one of a permanent questioning of the present and a commitment to uncertainty, not to establish the limits of thought but to locate the possible places of their transgression and thereby open up novel ways of thinking and acting – of resistance.

The second characteristic of the Foucauldian approach that I will draw upon is the concern with the vicissitudes of *liberalism* in the shaping of the political contours of the present, and it is here that the notion of governmentality takes on some significance. In the late 1970s, Foucault initiated research on what he called the art of government and he suggested that the possibilities for liberal forms of freedom may not be in conflict with the exercise of discipline but be dependent upon it (Foucault, 1991; Gordon, 1991). He was concerned with linking the analysis of the constitution of freedom with the exercise of rule; with the extent to which freedom has become, in 'free' liberal democratic societies, a resource for and not merely a hindrance to government, and is closely aligned to the emergence of post-enlightenment thinking.

The early 18th-century science of police dreamed of a time when social order could be regulated in very fine detail by a sovereign state via a closely calibrated and centralised series of interrelated economic, social and cultural policies (Pasquino, 1988; Reiner, 1988) which aimed to produce a totally administered society. Liberal government abandoned such an approach for a vision of society where government would be based around the exercise of freedom and where the relationship between liberty and discipline, freedom and rule, while interdependent, was subject to continual re-negotiation and fine balancing. In this respect, then, we can see the tensions and questions which are currently characterising the 'refocusing of children's services' debate as striking at the core of liberal forms of government as they emerged from the early 19th century onwards. How can we devise a legal basis for the power to intervene into the private sphere of the family in order to protect children, but in a way which does not undermine the family and convert all families into clients of a sovereign state? Such a question is posed by the demand to ensure that the family is experienced as autonomous and free and the primary sphere for rearing children, while also recognising that there is a need for intervention in some families where they are seen as failing in this primary task (Parton, 1991). However the way this question is responded to varies in time and place and, as I have already suggested, is currently undergoing significant mutation.

Foucault argued that the idea of governmentality has increasingly dominated politics since the 18th century and it is the regulation of the population which has proved its unending concern. Such an approach does not reduce the exercise of political power to the actions of the reified sovereign state, but draws attention to the range of mechanisms whereby different groups and forms of knowledge regulate, and thereby construct and constitute, the lives of individuals, families and the community. This conception of political power is hence both wider and more complex than analyses which reduce politics to the activities, priorities and decisions of the state. The concept of governmentality both broadens and redirects the analysis of political power. It recognises that the exercise of power takes place via an ever shifting set of alliances between political and non-political authorities (Parton, 1994). Professionals and other 'experts' are crucial to its operation.

Social work and the birth of 'the social'

One of Foucault's central concerns was to provide a critique of the way modern societies regulate and discipline their populations by sanctioning the knowledge-claims and practices of the new human sciences – particularly medicine, psychiatry, psychology, criminology and, to some extent, social work – which provided the opportunity for the emergence of what he called the 'psy' complex (see also Ingleby, 1985, and Rose, 1985) and which instituted a regime of power exercised through disciplinary mechanisms and the stipulation of norms for human behaviour. The normal family, the healthy child, the perfect wife and the proper man both inform ideas about ourselves and are reproduced and legitimated through the practices of the 'psy' complex. According to Foucault, from the late 18th century onwards, these new knowledges increasingly colonised the old powers, to such an extent that the more traditional forms of sovereign law and judicial rights were transformed. No longer were the crucial decisions taken in the courtroom according to the criteria of judicial rights (and wrongs), but in the hospital, the clinic or the welfare office, according to the criteria of 'normalisation' (Foucault, 1977a).

The notion of 'normalcy' has become one of the most powerful metaconcepts in human affairs. However, it only acquired its sense of 'usual' or 'typical' in the 19th century, originally in medical contexts where the opposite was always 'pathological'. While normalcy became measured by statistical means which acted to describe difference, it was also associated with being right and healthy. As a consequence, the abnormal was not merely different but wrong and diseased. Contemporary ideas about normalcy were forged in the medical world of the early 19th century (Hacking, 1990, 1991).

Normalising mechanisms require a knowledge of the whole person in his or her social context, and depend on medico-social expertise and judgements for their operation. They depend on direct supervision and surveillance, and they emphasise the need to effect change in character, attitudes and behaviour in an individualised way. They are concerned with underlying causes and needs, and attempt to contribute to the improvement of those being served as well as to social defence. Because they 'psy' professions have the exclusive insight into the problems, knowledge and techniques required, they require wide discretion to diagnose and treat, and thereby normalise.

The emergence of philanthropy and subsequently social work in the area of child welfare provided a particular set of policies and practices which contributed to what Jacques Donzelot (1980) has referred to as the growth of the 'social'. The emergence of the 'social', and social work in particular, is associated with the transformations that took place from the mid-19th century onwards around an expanding grid of intersecting and interrelated concerns and anxieties about the family and the community more generally. The 'social' discourse developed as a hybrid in the space identified between the private sphere of the household and the public sphere of the state and society. It operated in an intermediary zone. It produced and was reproduced by new relations between the law, administration, medicine, the school and the family. Central to its emergence was the incorporation of a range of philanthropists into the judicial process in respect of children and young people, and the emergence of psychiatry as a specialism which informed not only judicial decisions but the practice of the successors to the philanthropists – social workers – and hence inserted the notion of normalcy into the operation of the 'social'.

The emergence of the 'social' and the practices of social workers, who were its primary technologists, was a positive solution to a major problem posed for liberalism (Hirst, 1981). Namely, how can the state establish the health, development and hence rights of individual family members who are weak and dependent, particularly children, while promoting the family as the 'natural' sphere for caring for those individuals, and thus not intervening in all families which would destroy the autonomy of the private sphere? Philanthropy, and subsequently social work, developed at a midway point between individual initiative and the all-encompassing state. It provided a compromise between the early liberal vision of unhindered private philanthropy and the vision of the all-pervasive and all-encompassing police or socialist state which would take responsibility for everyone's needs and hence undermine the responsibility and role of the family.

Issues in relation to the child exemplify these tensions: for children to develop their full health and sensibilities, they could not be left to the vagaries of the market and the autonomous patriarchal family (Dingwall and Eekelaar, 1988). The emergence of the 'social' was seen as the most appropriate way for the state to maintain its legitimacy while protecting individual children. For liberalism, "the unresolved problem is how child rearing can be made into a matter of public concern and its qualities monitored without destroying the ideal of the family as a counterweight to state power, a domain of voluntary, self-regulating actions" (Dingwall et al, 1983, pp 214-15).

Originally, with the emergence of modern industrial society, this activity was carried out by voluntary philanthropic organisations, and Donzelot (1980) argues that two techniques were of significance in their relationship with families, particularly on behalf of children – what he calls 'moralisation' and 'normalisation'. 'Moralisation' involves the use of financial and material assistance which was used as a leverage to encourage poor families to overcome their moral failure. It was used primarily for the deserving poor who could demonstrate that their problems arose for reasons beyond their control. 'Normalisation' applied to attempts to spread specific norms of living via education, legislation or health, and involved a response to complaints, invariably from women about men, and hence provided a means of entry into the home. In return for this guidance, and moral and minimal material support, philanthropic workers were given an insight into what was happening inside the home and leverage to bring about changes in behaviour and lifestyle. Clearly, however, there were problems if individuals did not cooperate or did not approach the worker in the first place, so that children were left to unbridled parental devices.

In the late 19th and early 20th centuries in Britain, such philanthropic activities were increasingly absorbed into the formal institutions of the state. This process continued through to the early 1970s, with the introduction of local authority social service departments as the 'fifth social service' (Townsend, 1970). While moralisation and normalisation were to be the primary forms of contract, this was increasingly framed in legislation which would also give the possibility for coercive intervention. 'Tutelage', as Donzelot calls it, based on the notion of preventive intervention, would combine a number of elements, although coercive intervention would be used for the exceptional circumstances where the techniques of moralisation and normalisation had failed.

During much of the 20th century, the growth and formalisation of modern child welfare social work, and its absorption by the state, were based on attempts to develop new strategies of preventive penology on behalf of young people who were identified as actual or potential threats. Again, it was concerns about normalisation and preventive penology which were the central concern (Platt, 1977; Garland, 1985). This form of social work was concerned about the growth of crime and delinquency and about the apparent failures of the more traditional judicial and community forms of social regulation that provided the central rationale for the growth of social work (Hall, 1976; Cooper, 1983; Harris and Webb, 1987). It is only since the early 1970s that concerns about child abuse and child protection have again dominated policy and practice (Parton, 1985, 1991).

However, the space occupied by child welfare social work, the 'social', has always been complex. It both interrelates with and is dependent upon a number of other more established discourses, particularly law, health/hygiene, psychiatry and education. While the space which it occupies between the public and the private is a crucial one, a variety of discourses have impinged on and interpenetrated it. It is for this reason that social work in the area of child welfare and child protection is potentially such a contested area and one subject to such diverse and sometimes competing rationales and definitions. Thus, while it is important that social work had a diffuse mandate so that it could be interpreted and operated in a variety of ways, this has left it in an ambiguous position. Perhaps most crucially, the ambiguity arises from social work's sphere of operation itself: between civil society, with its allegiances to individuals and families, and the state, in the guise of the courts and their 'statutory' responsibilities. Child welfare social work has always operated on a terrain which is ambiguous, uncertain and contested.

This ambiguity captures the central, if sometimes submerged, element of social work as it emerged from the late 19th century onwards. Social work essentially occupied the space between the respectable and the deviant or dangerous classes, and between those with access to political and speaking rights and those who were excluded (Philp, 1979). It fulfilled an essentially mediating role between those who were actually or potentially excluded and the mainstream of society. In the process, it mediated not only between the excluded and state agencies, but crucially between other diverse state agencies and discourses, together with a wide range of private, voluntary and other philanthropic agencies, and the diverse overlapping discourses which inform and construct them.

Child welfare and the spread of 'welfarism'

While the spheres of government, from the late 19th century, were increasingly wide-ranging and complex, and social work strategies formed only a small element within them, none the less, they were a crucial part of the process which drew individuals into the sphere of government. Social work provided an important, but ambiguous, strategy to enable 'government at a distance', or indirect methods of social regulation, to take place. This was important if the liberal ideal of maintaining autonomous free individuals who were at the same time governed was to be realised (Miller and Rose, 1988).

For social work to operate quietly and in an uncontested way, it required a supportive social mandate together with an internal professional confidence and coherence. The latter, particularly in the period following the Second World War, was provided primarily by a body of knowledge borrowed from neo-Freudianism and ego-psychology social casework, while the professional aspirations veered towards medicine and psychiatry (Payne, 1992). Similarly, the growth of social work from the late 19th century onwards in Britain ran in parallel with, and was interrelated with, the development of social interventions associated with the establishment of the welfare state in the post-war period – what Rose and Miller (1992) refer to as 'welfarism'.

The key innovations of 'welfarism' lay in the attempts to link the fiscal, calculative and bureaucratic capacities of the apparatus of the state to the government of social life. As a political rationality, 'welfarism' was structured by the wish to encourage national growth and well-being through the promotion of social responsibility and mutuality of social risk, and was premised on notions of social solidarity (Donzelot, 1988).

Post-war welfarism was symbolised by the idea, following William Beveridge, of social insurance. Social insurance fundamentally transformed the mechanisms that integrated the citizen into the social order. Not only were individuals to be protected from the evils of 'Want, Disease, Idleness, Ignorance and Squalor' (Beveridge, 1942), but they would be constituted as citizens bound into a system of solidarity and mutual inter-dependence. Social insurance was seen as a scientific and statistical method of encouraging passive solidarity among its recipients. Everyone would contribute and everyone would benefit, although some would do so more that others. The overall rationale of welfarism was to make the liberal market society and the family more productive, stable and harmonious; and the role of government, while more complex and expansive, would be positive and beneficent.

Not surprisingly, during this period, child welfare social work was imbued with a degree of optimism which believed that measured and significant improvements could be made in the lives of children and families via judicious professional interventions. In the context of the institutional framework of the other universal state welfare services, while social work was constituted as a residual service, it was based on a relatively positive and optimistic view of those it was working with and of what could be achieved. There was a degree of consensus that social work with children and families was a positive development in the context of the development of 'welfarism' (Packman, 1981).

Child welfare and 'advanced liberalism'

However, just at the point when child welfare social work emerged to play an important role in the welfarist project, 'welfarism' itself was experiencing considerable strains in both its political rationality and technological utility. As a consequence, the rationale and activities of social work with children and families became particularly vulnerable to criticism and reconstitution as they could be seen to personify all that was problematic with welfarism.

The problems encompassed both the economic and social spheres, from the mid-1960s onwards. In the economic sphere, they included: a slow-down in economic growth (particularly in Britain compared to its western competitors); increased difficulties in controlling inflation; a gradual increase in unemployment; and a growth in proportional terms of the public sector in comparison to the so-called private productive sectors of society. In the social sphere they included: the rediscovery of poverty and significant areas of continued and growing social deprivation; the growth of violence in terms of crime, and various forms of social indiscipline; a decline in individual responsibility and attachments to the traditional nuclear family; and a failure of the various 'social sciences', and of the various social experts who operated them, to contribute to social well-being (Parton, 1994).

The possibility of supplanting welfarism by a new rationality of government was provided by approaches informed by the New Right, often associated in the UK with Thatcherism (Levitas, 1986; Gamble, 1988), which were increasingly dominant from the mid-1970s onwards. The central element of both the critique and recommendations for change was that not only the political rationalities but also the technologies of government pursued by 'welfarism' were themselves central to the problems and thus required fundamental change. Increasingly, it was argued that 'welfarism', in terms of its moralities, explanations, vocabularies and technologies, needed to be rethought, and that this indicated the need for a new form of government.

However, it would be simplistic to see the criticisms of child welfare policy and practice as arising simply from the anti-welfare New Right, for vocal criticisms were also voiced from the left – feminists, anti-racists, various user groups, and other professional and community interests, as well as from within social work itself (Clarke, 1993). What has happened, however, is that the critiques can be seen to have informed and consolidated a range of new strategies of government which we can term *advanced liberal* and which includes the following key elements: extending market rationalities – contracts, consumers, competition – to domains where social, bureaucratic or professional logic previously reigned; governing at a distance by formally separating the activities of welfare professionals from the apparatuses of the central and local state and the courts; governing them by new systems of audit, devolved budgets, codes of practice and citizens charters; and giving individuals new freedoms by making them responsible for their own present and future welfare and the relations which they have with experts and institutions. No longer is the emphasis on governing through society – the social – but through the calculating choices of individuals (Rose, 1996a). It is in this context that we need to understand the development of new strategies for governing child welfare that came to fruition with the 1989 Children Act (which came into operation in October 1991).

During the 1970s and 1980s, a number of criticisms developed which helped refashion the nature of child welfare work as it had developed in the post-war period. Some of the anxieties emanated from within social work itself and concerned the apparently poor, and even deteriorating, quality of child welfare practice in the newly created local authority social services departments (Parker, 1980). More widely, however, a whole variety of different concerns were developing which became increasingly important and which prompted a fundamental rethink of child welfare policy and practice (Parton, 1991).

First, from the 1960s onwards, with the growth of the women's movement and the recognition of violence in the family, it was recognised that, not only may the family not be the haven of tranquillity it was assumed to be, but that women and children suffer a range of abuses at the hands of men. Much of the early campaigning was directed to improving the position of women and it was only from the mid-1970s, with the growing concerns about sexual abuse, that much of the energy was directed to the position of children (Parton, 1990). Such critiques helped to disaggregate the interests of individual family members and supported the development during the period of the Children's Rights movement (Freeman, 1983; Franklin, 1986, 1995). There was also the growth, from the late 1960s, of a more obviously civil liberties critique which concentrated upon the apparent extent and nature of intervention in people's lives that was allowed, unchallenged, in the name of welfare (see Morris et al, 1980; Taylor et al, 1980; Geach and Szwed, 1983). Increasingly, lawyers drew attention to the way the administration of justice was unfairly and unjustly applied in various areas of childcare, such as the parental rights resolution and the place of safety order, and argued that there was a need for a greater emphasis on individual rights.

However, during the mid-1980s, the parents' lobby gained its most coherent voice with the establishment of Parents Against INjustice (PAIN). PAIN was to prove influential in ensuring that the rights of parents and of children to be left at home, free of state intervention and removal, were placed on the political and professional agendas. As a result, state intervention, via the practices of health and welfare professionals, as well as parental violence, were identified as being actively and potentially abusive.

However, it was child abuse inquiries that provided the major catalyst for venting major criticisms of policy and practice in child welfare and of the competencies of social workers. While these were in evidence from 1973 onwards, following the death of Maria Colwell (Secretary of State for Social Services, 1974; Parton, 1985), they gained a new level of intensity during the mid-1980s via the inquiries into the deaths of Jasmine Beckford (London Borough of Brent, 1985), Kimberley Carlile (London Borough of Greenwich, 1987) and Tyra Henry

(London Borough of Lambeth, 1987). It was child abuse public inquiries which provided the key vehicles for political and professional debate about child welfare policies and practices in a very public way, and in the full glare of the media (Franklin and Parton, 1991; Aldridge, 1994). Not only did they provide detailed accounts of what had gone wrong in the particular cases but, critically, they commented on the current state of policy and practice more generally, and made recommendations as to what should be done (DHSS, 1982; DH, 1991).

Up until the mid-1980s, the 30 plus inquiries had all been concerned with the deaths of children at the hands of their parents or caretakers. All the children had died as a result of physical abuse and neglect, and many had suffered emotional neglect and failure to thrive. The child welfare professionals, particularly social workers, were seen to have failed to protect the children, with horrendous consequences. Rather than the deaths being seen as resulting simply from individual professional incompetencies, they were usually regarded as particular instances of the current state of policy, practice knowledge and skills, and of the way systems operated and inter-related (Hallett and Birchall, 1992).

The emphasis in public inquiry recommendations was to encourage social workers to use their legal mandate to intervene in families to protect children, and to improve practitioners' knowledge of the signs and symptoms of child abuse so that it could be spotted in day-to-day practice.

However, the Cleveland Inquiry (Secretary of State for Social Services, 1988) provided a quite different set of concerns and seemed to provide a different set of interpretations of what was wrong and how we should respond. This time, it seemed, professionals – paediatricians as well as social workers – had failed to recognise the rights of parents and had intervened prematurely into families where there were concerns about sexual abuse. While, again, the reasons for the problems were seen as residing primarily in inter-agency and inter-professional misunderstandings, in poor coordination and communication, and in the legal context and content of child welfare work, the emphasis in this Report was rather different. Now, not only was there a call for the law itself to be changed, but professionals were enjoined to be much more careful and accountable in identifying the evidence, legally framed, for what constituted sexual abuse and child abuse more generally. It was not simply a question of getting the right balance between family autonomy and state intervention, but also getting the right balance between the power, discretion and responsibilities of the various judicial, social and medical experts and agencies (Ashenden, 1996). In this respect, the juridical experts were seen as central. For the law and legal thinking needed to be brought to bear in decision making which had such fundamental consequences for children and parents, and hence for the family, which was seen as being fundamentally undermined by the events in Cleveland.

Thus, while quite different in their social location and their focus of concern, we can see a growing set of constituencies developing, form the late 1970s onwards, which criticised the post-war welfarist consensus in relation to child welfare. These were most forcefully articulated in and via child abuse inquiries. What emerged were arguments for a greater reliance on individual rights, firmly located in a reformed statutory framework where there was a greater emphasis on legalism.

Within this emphasis, the rule of law as ultimately judged by the court has taken priority over those considerations which may be deemed, by the professional experts, as optimally therapeutic or 'in the best interests of the child'.

In many respects, the 1989 Children Act did not seem consistent with other pieces of social legislation that were being introduced at the time, for many of its key principles seemed to be much more consistent with the premises of welfarism. The Act took much of its inspiration from the Short Report (Social Services Committee, 1984), and the Review of Child Care Law (DHSS, 1985). Consequently, the central principles of the legislation encouraged an approach to childcare based on *negotiation* with *families* and involving parents and children in *agreed* plans. The accompanying guidance and regulations encouraged professionals to work in *partnership* with parents and young people. Similarly, the Act strongly encourages the role of the state in *supporting* families with children in need and the keeping of statutory proceedings and emergency interventions to a minimum (Packman and Jordan, 1991).

However, the Act was centrally concerned with trying to construct a new set of balances related to the respective roles of various state agents and of the family in the upbringing of children. While it would be inappropriate to see the legislation as a direct consequence of concerns arising from child abuse inquiries, it was child protection issues that were its central concern (Parton, 1991). Notions of individual rights and of legalism framed the legislation in ways which were not previously evident.

The other key element to emerge in the Act was the criteria to be used for making decisions and, therefore, for the way priorities should be framed. The assessment of high risk had become central (Parton, 1991, Chapters 3 and 5). In the Children Act, high risk is framed in terms of significant harm. The criteria for state intervention under the Children Act is that the child concerned is suffering, or is likely to suffer, significant harm, (Section 31[2]a). For the first time, the criteria for state intervention included a prediction of what might occur or might be likely to occur in the future.

Assessments of actual or potential high risk have become the central concern. However, in a context where the knowledge and research for assessing and identifying high risk are themselves contested, and where the consequences of getting that decision wrong are considerable, it is not seen as appropriate to leave the decision to the health and welfare experts alone. The decisions, and the accountability for making them, are ultimately to be lodged with the court and to be based on forensic evidence. This view has been reinforced by the 1992 Criminal Justice Act and the Home Office Memorandum of Good Practice on video interviewing (Home Office, 1992). As a consequence, the legal gaze, and the identification and weighing of forensic evidence, cast a shadow throughout child abuse work and child welfare more generally, but subjected to a variety of checks and balances set in place by the need to work in partnership with children and families and with a range of other agencies and professionals. Social workers are still central, though not as social caseworkers or counsellors but as case managers or key workers, coordinating and taking central responsibility for assessing and managing 'risk' and for monitoring and evaluating progress. This all takes place in a context where procedures set out the *process* for carrying out the work and thereby, potentially, make policy and practice more explicit and accountable.

Concerns about risk, particularly about child abuse, now lie at the heart of child welfare policy and practice (Parton et al, 1997), and developments in Britain run parallel with similar changes in the USA where the trends and issues are perhaps even more evident (Lindsay, 1994). We can now summarise what the essential factors have been which have contributed to this situation.

First, the problem of child abuse has dominated child welfare policy and practice for nearly 30 years and the term has been officially broadened well beyond the original conception of the 'battered baby syndrome' (Dingwall, 1989; Hacking, 1991). It includes neglect, physical abuse, emotional abuse, sexual abuse and most recently 'organised' abuse (Home Office, 1992). The definitions are broad and all inclusive and, while we do not have a mandatory reporting system as in the USA, health and welfare professionals may be found morally and organisationally culpable if they do not report their concerns to an appropriate investigating agency, essentially social services departments or the police (Parton, 1996b).

Secondly, and directly related to the foregoing, public, professional and political awareness has grown considerably. This was reflected in the 1980s by the tremendous increase in the number of cases placed on child protection registers following a case conference (Parton, 1995). What is of greater significance, however, is the dramatic increase in allegations requiring investigation – now estimated as running at over 160,000 per year (Dartington Social Research Unit, 1995). This is even more evident in North America and Australia where trend statistics on child abuse referrals/allegations are available. In the USA, the numbers of child abuse and neglect reports have increased from 9,563 in 1967 to 1,154,000 in 1980, and to 2,936,00 in 1992; while, in Western Australia, they have increased from fewer than 3,000 in 1989/90 to nearly 8,000 in 1993/94 (see Parton et al, 1997, for a more detailed analysis).

Thirdly, this broadening definition and growth in awareness and allegations has taken place in a context where social workers now have a clear responsibility to ensure not only that children do not suffer in the family, but also that parental responsibility and family autonomy are not undermined. The notion of child protection subsumes within it, not only the protection of child from significant harm, but also the protection of the parents and family privacy from unwarrantable state interventions.

Fourthly, however, these developments have taken place in a changing economic context which has had a direct impact on social services departments and on social work practice with children and families. The amount of need and of potential clients has grown as increasing sections of the population have become marginalised from the mainstream of the economy and as the incidence of poverty, deprivation and social exclusion has increased (Barclay, 1995; Hills, 1995; Oppenheim and Harker, 1996). Not only have other state health and welfare services had insufficient resources for the demands made of them, thus increasing the call upon social services, but social service departments themselves have been subject to continual resource constraint, cut-back, and reorganisation (Schorr, 1992; Association of Directors of Social Services and NCH, 1996; Statham, 1996).

This increased actual and potential demand in the context of reduced resources means that state child welfare agencies are finding it almost impossible to develop the more wide-ranging, preventative, family support strategies encompassed by the 1989 Children Act. Priorities and choices have to be made, not just between the more traditional child welfare responsibilities on the one hand and responding to child abuse on the other, but also in relation to child abuse itself. It is in this respect that the investigation of 'high risk' takes on its particular significance and gets to the heart of what it means to do contemporary child welfare work. The imperative becomes to differentiate the 'high risk' from the rest – so that children can be protected, parental rights and responsibilities can be respected, and scarce resources directed to where they will, in theory, be most effective. Resources and skills are focused on investigating, managing and sifting 'high risk' cases from the rest.

The child protection system has been set up, essentially, to identify actual or significant harm, and this is dominating the provision and priorities of child welfare services more generally. Increasingly, the priorities are framed according to legalistic criteria where the identification of forensic evidence is central, even when the case is not strictly provable. Where cases cannot be so constructed, or where the weight of evidence is not sufficient, the case is quickly filtered out of the system and services are not provided (Gibbons et al, 1995). What the current system does is provide mechanisms and rationales – however administratively and professionally time-consuming – for controlling demand and thereby prioritising work, and it is the notion of risk which lies at its heart.

Risk and contemporary child welfare

This emphasis on risk is indicative of a move towards a logic in which the possibility of incurring misfortune or loss in the future is neither to be left to fate, not to be managed by the providential state. As a consequence, an analysis of risk helps us to understand a number of related features of contemporary child welfare policy and practice (see Rose, 1996b for a similar analysis of the vocation of psychiatry).

The first feature I will consider concerns the way in which the subjects, or consumers, of child welfare services are to be thought about and constrained to act. The notions of partnership, parental responsibility, and the risk of significant harm, rather than being in contradiction, can be seen crucially to frame current thinking. Individuals are increasingly held responsible for their own fate and that of their children, through a kind of calculation about the future consequences of present actions – trying to make the future calculable. Risks are to be identified, assessed, monitored, reduced and insured against by the prudent citizen, effective professional, or efficient organisation (O'Malley, 1992; Alaszewski and Walsh, 1995; Kemshall and Pritchard, 1996). Individuals are constrained to think about their present conduct in terms of risks to be calculated, averted or monitored, so that social workers have become not so much concerned with subjects and their relationships of social existence, but as advisers or managers of personal risk.

Individuals are expected to manage their own risk and to take responsibility for failures to manage it (Rose, 1996b). Risk management thus becomes a technique of the prudent self. In terms of government, a new set of relations is set in place between the technologies for the government of others and the modes in which human beings are to understand and govern themselves.

As a consequence, child welfare policies and practices are now crucially concerned with dividing and sifting the prudent from the imprudent, the self able to manage itself and high risk situations, and those who must be managed. By definition, all children are potentially imprudent, so the key focus becomes the situations they are in and the parents or carers, primarily women, who have had devolved to them the responsibility for managing and monitoring risk on the child's behalf (Parton et al, 1997). This art of the management of risk to children is key to understanding the sphere of operation for child welfare, at the junction of the self-managed world of the affiliated and the twilight world of the socially and economically marginalised and excluded, particularly those sections of the poor who make up the biggest proportion of the 'clients' of child welfare services, such as single-parent households, substance misusers, homeless families and certain ethnic groups. The ordered world of social problems has been displaced by the fragmented world of the excluded. It is this fragmented terrain which becomes the sphere of operation for child welfare workers captured by concerns about risk. In the process, the will to cure or to rehabilitate becomes little more than the refinement of a particular type of relation to the self-prudent in term of: self-management; making and keeping to contracts; setting and achieving recognisable targets; and learning the skills of the management of the 'family'.

However, the new mentalities of risk not only reconstitute the nature and focus of child welfare work and the nature of relationships between social workers and their clients, they are also significant in terms of the way workers think about and organise themselves and are organised – their obligations and the way they are made accountable. As Mary Douglas (1992) has argued, the concept of risk has increasingly become central to politics and public policy because of its uses as a forensic resource. The more culturally individualised a society becomes, the more significant becomes the forensic potential of the idea of risk. Its forensic uses are particularly important in the development of different types of blaming systems, and "the one we are in now is almost ready to treat every death as chargeable to someone's account, every accident as caused by someone's criminal negligence, every sickness a threatened prosecution" (Douglas, 1992, pp 14-16). Risk assessment and risk management – the identification, assessment, elimination or reduction of the possibility or consequence of loss or misfortune – become the essential element of the *raison d'être* of social workers. The government of risk takes place through a transformation of the priority systems, and hence subjectivities, of the professionals themselves.

For, within these new strategies of the government of child welfare, audit becomes one of the key mechanisms for responding to the plurality of expertise and the inherent undecidability of the various truth claims about risk. As Michael Power (1994a, 1994b) has argued, audit in a range of different forms has come to replace the trust once accorded to professionals both by their clients – now users and customers – and the authorities which employ, legitimate and constitute them. Audit responds to failure and insecurity by the managerialisation of risk.

Risk is rendered manageable by new relations of regulation between the political centres of decision making and the front line social worker, via the introduction of a variety of new procedures, forms, devices and systems for making and noting decisions and thereby making them visible. In the process, the entities to be audited – social workers and other professionals – are themselves transformed in order to make them auditable. Where the key concern is risk, the focus becomes, not making the *right* decision, but making a *defensible* decision (Howe, 1992; Dingwall et al, 1995), where the processes and procedures have been followed and where the range of misery and need coming the way of the child welfare agency can be prioritised and contained. In the USA, there has been a proliferation of formalised child protection risk assessment models, now covering over forty states (Berkowitz, 1991). They have arisen as a response to the growing number of cases coming forward and the stagnant resources available to child welfare agencies (English and Pecora, 1994). While neither as advanced nor as formalised, similar systems and technologies are being developed in Britain (Cleaver et al, 1995). As Castel (1991) has suggested, we are approaching a situation in which a general system for risk prediction and risk management of child abnormalities is being refined, and upon which is recorded a range of factors whose connection with abnormalities, whether this be framed in terms of child abuse or children in need, is abstract and statistical – for example, age of mother, previous history, household composition, labour market status – and where a certain combination of such factors results in the allocation of a service or the intervention of child protection agencies. In effect, information gathered from a variety of sources is brought together to consider the nature and significance of risk for the child.

The importance of such developments, therefore, is not only in terms of their implications for children and their carers but for the professionals themselves and for the way in which their policies and practices are judged. Procedures and mechanisms for risk assessment and risk management have the effect of changing the role of professionals who are governed 'at a distance' from the formal political or court apparatus, but who face the prospect of legal or organisational sanctions if they fail to follow the designated steps to ensure that all the risks are investigated and accounted for. In the process, they are made responsible for placing their part in the strategy of risk reduction and harm minimisation – to the child, the family and the organisation – under threat of sanction and blame if things go wrong (Parton, 1996b).

Conclusions: risk, uncertainty and ambiguity

In this [chapter], I have argued that the increasingly central concern with risk in child welfare agencies, in Britain and across the English-speaking Western world, points to important changes, both in the way social workers think about and constitute their practices, and in the way social work is itself thought about and thereby constituted more widely. I have argued that, not only can concerns about risk be seen to characterise contemporary child welfare policies and practices, but also, following Foucault, risk provides a small but significant instance of the important changes in the government of freedom in, and of advanced liberal rule.

In this context, the emphasis in the current debates on refocusing children's services and on the importance of developing preventive services to support families and children in need is of considerable importance. As has been demonstrated in numerous studies of services for children in need following the 1989 Children Act (Aldgate and Tunstill, 1995; Colton et al, 1995), the problems of rising demand set against fixed or diminishing resources, mean that the nature and level of need are increasingly (re)framed or rationed in terms of risk. As Jane Lewis and her colleagues have demonstrated in relation to the community care changes "it seems inevitable that in the main only need defined as high risk will receive service" (Lewis et al, 1995, p 91). Thus, concerns about risk and how it might be reframed lie at the heart of current debates. But, rather than try to refine our current practices further in terms of the technologies of risk assessment and risk management, I wish to contend, in conclusion, that we would be much better prepared if we recognised the central and pervasive concerns related to uncertainty and ambiguity.

The idiom of risk presupposes the ideas of choice, calculation and responsibility, so that whether or not the risk/calculative attitude prevails depends on the degree to which child rearing and child welfare are regarded as fixed, inevitable and influenced by fate, or as subject to human agency and control. The more we have assumed that areas of life have moved from the former category (fixed, inevitable and subject to fate) to the latter (subject to human agency and control), the more we have taken them from the sphere of the natural and God-given and made them the objects of human choice and responsibility. In the process, our contemporary conceptualisations of risk have predominantly assumed that the world can be subjected to prediction and control, and that rational systems of accountability should be constructed in case things go wrong (Lash et al, 1996). Such notions of risk have rationalised and scientised areas of social life which, I would suggest, are much more appropriately conceived of in terms of uncertainty. It is important, in this regard, to distinguish between the predictable and the unpredictable, or more correctly the calculable and the non-calculable forms of indeterminacy. While the former may appropriately be referred to as 'risk' the latter is more appropriately understood as 'uncertainty'. It is my contention that the vast majority of social work, particularly in the area of child welfare and child protection at the individual case level, is much better characterised in terms of uncertainty than of risk, and that the notion of ambiguity is central to its operation and the way it is experienced by the children and carers on the receiving end and by the other professionals with whom we work.

Most of the risks which social workers are expected to assess or manage are 'virtual' in the sense that they can neither be directly sensed (touched, heard, seen or smelt), nor subjected to scientific evaluation in any quantified or probabilistic sense. They only exist (or are constituted) in the theorems, formulae or procedures we draw upon to think about them. As Adams (1995) and Reddy (1996) have suggested, our obsessions with scientised, calculative notions or risk have failed to recognise that much or our experience is better characterised as uncertainty.

As a consequence, systems, procedures and organisational frameworks which operate *as if* issues are resolvable in any kind of realist, scientific or calculative/probabilistic sense are in great danger of missing the point. We are in a situation where notions of artistic, situated judgements should be valued, and where organisations should concentrate on developing notions of mutual trust and be respectful of different points of view.

The rehabilitation of the idea of uncertainty, and the permission to talk about an indeterminacy which is not amenable to or reducible to authoritative definition or measurement, is an important step, I would suggest, for recognising the contemporary complexities of practice. Rather than seeing a commitment to uncertainty as undermining and lying at the margins of practice, I would suggest it lies at the heart, and that its recognition provides an opportunity for valuing practice, practitioners and the people with whom they work. Notions of ambiguity, complexity and uncertainty are the core of social work and should be built upon and not defined out. A commitment to uncertainty opens up creativity and novel ways of thinking which are in danger of being lost in a climate obsessed with concerns about risk, its assessment, monitoring and management. In this respect, the current debates about the refocusing of children's services can ensure this is not the case, but more particularly to recognise that values and politics lie at the heart not just of what we do but of the way we do it. Essentially, I am arguing that a prime focus in current debates and in the way we respond needs to be a recognition of the increasing pervasiveness of uncertainty and insecurity among professionals and those with whom they work. This is not meant to be a message of doom – rather the opposite. Traditionally, social workers have been seen as 'experts' in working with uncertainty and ambiguity. We should try and devise strategies and practices which not only rediscover this perspective but which develop it in the future (Parton and Marshall, 1998). In the process, we need to (re)think the nature of professional judgement and the way in which relationships between users and social workers are (re)framed.

Acknowledgement

This [chapter] has been informed by numerous discussions I have had with practitioners, managers and other academics and researchers. I would particularly like to acknowledge my debt to Nikolas Rose, David Thorpe and Corinne Wattam who have all, in different ways, acted as my mentors in recent years.

---

[1] This [chapter] provided the basis of Nigel Parton's Inaugural Professorial Lecture, of the same title, given at the University of Huddersfield on 13 January 1997. It was taken from the *British Journal of Social Work*, 1998, vol 28. The right of Nigel Parton to be identified as author of this chapter has been asserted by him in accordance with the 1988 Copyright, Designs and Patents Act.

Conceptualising social capital in relation to the well-being of children and young people: a critical review

Virginia Morrow

[...] This [chapter] explores some of the origins, definitions and applications of the notion of social capital as it relates to children[1]. It suggests that social capital is an elusive concept that is currently poorly specified, and that the use of the term is inherently problematic, and needs to be carefully critiqued and empirically grounded before it can be usefully applied in social policy formulations. Given the apparent emphasis on elements of social capital in recent government policy statements, we need to know (a) what it is, and whether or not it is a positive attribute, (b) how or if it can be measured and (c) if it is a positive attribute, how it can be generated. [...]

What is social capital?

The notion of 'social capital' as it related to children was developed most systematically by Coleman in the US (1988, 1990). Coleman was a key social theorist, who was influential in policy making, and much of his later theorising was based on his work published in 1961, *The adolescent society: The social life of the teenager and its impact on education.* This was based on a study of students from 10 high schools in the Chicago area, and Coleman paints a picture of a wide divide between generations. He found that young people were highly likely to be influenced by their peers on a range of issues, including social participation, social leadership and club membership. Further, he found that students were generally anti-intellectual, and tended to see disapproval from friends as more important that disapproval from parents or teachers. Coleman (1988) developed the notion of social capital to explain aspects of this phenomenon, although his definition is rather vague:

> Social capital is defined by its function:... like other forms of capital, social capital is productive, making possible the achievement of certain ends that in its absence would not be possible... A given form of social capital that is valuable in facilitating certain actions may be useless or even harmful for others. Unlike other forms of capital, social capital

inheres in the structure of relations between actors and among actors. (1988, S98)

In other words, social capital appears to be a resource derived from people's social ties. He gives a number of somewhat arbitrary examples to illustrate his definition, one of which is the following:

> A mother of six children, who recently moved with husband and children from suburban Detroit to Jerusalem, described as one reason for doing so the greater freedom her young children had in Jerusalem. She felt safe in letting her eight year old take her six year old across town to school on the bus and felt her children to be safe in playing without supervision in a city park, neither of which she felt about to do where she lived before. (1988, S99-100)

In his explanation of the above example, he suggests that "The reason for this difference can be described as a difference in social capital available in Jerusalem and suburban Detroit" (1988, S99-100). Normative structures within the community inhibit crime, and these norms constitute a "powerful, though sometimes fragile, form of social capital" (1988, S104).

Coleman distinguishes between social capital within the family and outside the family. Social capital within the family is "the relations between children and parents (and, when families include other members' relationships with them as well)" (1988, S110):

> Social capital within the family that gives the child access to the adult's human capital depends both on the physical presence of adults in the family and on the attention given by the adults to the child. The physical absence of adults may be described as a structural deficiency in family social capital. (1988, S111)

For Coleman, single-parent and dual earner families are lacking in social capital because parents simply do not have enough time to given their children enough attention: too large a family (ie too many siblings) can also reduce the social capital of individual children. Social capital outside the family is found in the community "consisting of the social relationships that exist among parents, in the closure exhibited by this structure of relations, and in the parents' relations with the institutions of the community" (1988, S113). Coleman's particular conception of social capital, focusing as it does on the quality of relations between and among families and communities, has underpinned the communitarian debate. He saw working mothers and lone parenthood as two of the main causes of declining social capital and loss of community cohesion, and these ideas have been picked upon by communitarian writers like Etzioni (1993) (see Frazer and Lacey, 1993 for a critique). In a later discussion of youth unemployment, Coleman (1994a) identifies the problem of youth unemployment as residing in the declining motivation on the part of young people and recommends local business investment in education as the solution: he proposes "a 'bounty' on the head of each child in the system, a bounty collectable by whatever actor undertook to develop the child in a way that would reduce the costs and increase the benefits" (1994a, p 49), although quite how this solves the problem of lack of motivation is by no means clear.

Several North American studies have taken up Coleman's concept of social capital and attempted to test it empirically by taking a number of crude and somewhat arbitrary measures (such as number of parents, number of siblings, and church attendance; see, for example, Runyan et al, 1998) and attempt to confirm cause-and-effect hypotheses about family structure, levels of social capital, and outcomes in adulthood; see also Bianchi and Robinson (1997), Boisjoly, Duncan and Hofferth (1995), Parcel and Menaghan (1994), Teachman, Paasch and Carver (1996); see Fine (1998) for a critique. However, Furstenberg and Hughes (1995), in a study of 'at risk young' (in this case, the adolescent children of teenage mothers), suggest that "Coleman's notion of social capital is attractive because it provides a conceptual link between the attributes of individual actors and their immediate social contexts, most notably the household, school, and neighbourhood". It also has the potential to link "the overly narrow purview of psychology and the overly broad purview of sociology" and can help to identify ways in which "parental investment is enhanced or undermined by the presence or absence of community resources" (1995, p 582). They suggest there is no unitary relationship: rather, it is more useful to examine how "different types of social capital (parents' resources inside the family, the social network, and their embeddedness in the community) might be related to various arenas of success in early adulthood" (1995, p 590). They emphasise the multidimensional nature of social capital and the effects on academic success, on conventional behaviour and psychological well-being (and one could include health behaviour). They conclude that we "need to clarify the concept and probably recognise the problems of thinking that social capital is a common set" (1995, p 590).

Following Coleman, Robert Putnam, in an influential work (1993) and a number of papers (eg 1995), has redefined social capital as a key characteristic of communities, rather than of individuals. For Putnam, social capital consists of the following components. Firstly, networks, which together constitute the civic community (institutions, facilities and relationships) in the voluntary, state and personal spheres; and the density of the networking between these three spheres. Secondly, people's sense of 'belonging' to the civic community, together with a sense of solidarity and equality with other community members. Thirdly, norms of cooperation, reciprocity and trust which govern the functions of networks (this links with Coleman's formulation, and Fukuyama, 1996). Fourthly, social capital consists of positive attitudes to the institutions, associated facilities and relationships constituting the civic community, as well as civic engagement, which involves participation in the process of sustaining and/or using such voluntary, state and interpersonal networks. For Putnam, levels of social capital are a causative factor in explaining economic growth (or decline). His conceptualisaton of social capital has been taken further to explore how economic development impacts upon the level of health in communities (see Campbell, 1997), the premise being that people's sense of self-efficacy in relation to their social networks, neighbourhoods and local or national civic structures (their 'social capital') will have some effects on health and well-being.

Problems with social capital

As these examples show, 'social capital' is a rather nebulous concept that can include anything from how parents interact with their children to how people feel about where they live, to whom they know, how much they use their 'networks', and how much they trust their politicians. In Coleman's case in particular, it is not adequately contextualised in socio-economic history; in both Coleman's and Putnam's formulations, it is gender-blind, ethnocentric, and arguably a concept imported from the USA without due attention to cross- and inter-cultural differences.

A number of specific criticisms can be made of Coleman and Putnam's formulations. Firstly, Coleman does not contextualise his argument, in terms of social and economic history: in areas of socio-economic disadvantage, there may be no effective long-term rewards for school achievement, and young people may be well aware of this – their responses (dropping out, turning to crime) might be reasonable and logical, given their circumstances. Further, as Portes and Landolt (1996, pp 20-1) note (for USA):

> In poor areas, many people rely on their social and family ties for economic survival.... There is considerable social capital in ghetto areas, but the assets obtainable through it seldom allow participants to rise above their poverty. For all their negative connotations, inner-city youth gangs are also social networks that provide access to resources and enforce conformity.... For a ghetto teenager, membership in a gang may be the only way to obtain self-respect and material goods. In the long run, however, the pressures from these groups may hold him down rather than raise him....

Thus some groups or communities make demands upon individual members in ways that might compromise their personal social mobility.

Coleman's theorising also tends to be ahistorical (Elder et al, 1993): his 1961 study, on which he bases his notion of social capital, paid no attention to historical context; most of the young people in his study were born in the Second World War and this must have had some effect on their lives (eg stress of adjustment on father's return after three years absence). His more recent claims (and indeed those of Putnam, 1995) about the erosion of 'community' in the US communities are also ahistorical and hark back to a romanticised 'glorious past' (Levi, 1996). Hall and Wellman (1984) writing about social support and health are implicitly critical of the "loss of community argument":

> These concerns that community had been lost have not stood up well to the systematic data-gathering techniques of the 1970s and 1980s.... It is clear that if social scientists actually search for ties they will find them. They will also find that such relationships provide supportive resources. Not only do such ties help people to stay healthy, they also play an important role in helping people deal with the pressures, opportunities, and contingencies emanating from large-scale social systems. (1984, p 24)

Elsewhere, Pahl has noted that "bemoaning the lack of social cohesion of contemporary times in comparison with some putative golden age a couple of generations before, has a history of at least 2,000 years" (Pahl, 1997, p 89). However, as Campbell (in press) notes, if people's subjective accounts of their communities reflect this, we need to pay attention to it because it is likely to have important consequences for their sense of belonging and self efficacy.

Secondly, Coleman and Putnam ignore the effects of gender, except to portray the consequences of women's employment as negative, both for community cohesion and for their individual children (Putnam, 1995; see Frazer and Lacey, 1993). This should alert us to the invisibility of women's work in creating or sustaining social networks and hence social capital. Thirdly, it is not clear that we can transpose these arguments from the US to the UK in a straightforward manner (Rustin, 1997). Bourdieu has warned of "persistent and serious misunderstandings in the international circulation of ideas" (1991, p 382). There are many obvious cultural differences between and within these two States, ranging from levels of violent crime in the US (which undoubtedly have an effect on 'social capital' and how people feel about where they live) to different levels of (and norms about) business involvement in community activities and fundamentally different notions of citizenship, civic participation and local democracy. The history and nature of race politics are also radically different (Wilson, 1996a). Whether or not it is possible to transpose policies from market-driven systems to those in welfare states needs careful examination (see Heinz, 1994 in relation to youth unemployment).

Further, as noted, the US research derived from Coleman has largely focused on 'family structure effect' rather than community-effects (or indeed wider structural effects) utilising the notion of social capital (although there is a good deal of research on social networks/support and health eg Cohen and Syme, 1984). The research cited above has tended to take a top-down view of the effect of parents on children, and the focus has been on parents' ability to invest in their children's well-being or future. A more 'active' conceptualisation of children, drawing on the sociology of childhood (James and Prout, 1990a) would explore how children themselves actively generate, draw on, or negotiate their own social capital, or indeed make links for their parents, or even provide active support for parents (eg Becker et al, 1998; Morrow, 1996; Song, 1996; Nestmann and Niepel, 1994). In other words, children's agency, constrained though it may be, is downplayed in US research and children appear as passive burdens on adults' time (although this possibility also reflects the dominance of developmental psychological accounts of childhood in US sociology in general).

Further, much of the US work is based on large-scale quantitative analysis of big national datasets not specifically designed to measure 'social capital', and the focus is on the 'quantity' of social capital, not the quality. I would argue that the extent to which families mediate children's social capital needs to be established rather than assumed. As noted, Coleman (and others) use the number of siblings as an indication of a lack of social capital, because the more children in a family, the more dilute the amount of adult attention to the individual child, which produces weaker educational outcomes. This ignores how siblings may interact to support each other. Many of the studies which measure social capital seem to assume that individual children are only influenced by family structure and school. They do not give an account of the broader social context, such as friends, social networks, out-of-school activities such as paid work, and children's activities in their communities. Nor do they pay much attention to structural constraints and how these impact on social capital, and these constraints may be differentiated according to gender, ethnicity and location. Thus, in Coleman's account, youth unemployment is ultimately due to individual failings, rather that external labour market processes. This seems an obvious criticism to make, but a similar approach can be identified in UK policy responses to youth unemployment, for example, when training schemes appear to be based on the presumption that work opportunities follow skills wherever they are available.

The ideas developed in the (mainly European) empirical research on children's networks and peer groups do not appear to have been incorporated into the social capital debates in the US. Coleman's conceptualisation is generally undynamic and woolly, a 'catch-all' to describe rather than explain the effects of inequality (it cannot explain change, or social mobility) and ultimately individualistic. Finally, it is premised on a model of the nuclear family norm and narrow definitions of family that ignore wider kin relations.

Incorporating 'social capital' into policy and rhetoric

In the UK context, a powerful political and popular rhetoric has been generated about the harmful effects of family breakdown on children, and the social capital literature both draws on this and feeds into it. While the reasons for the development of this rhetoric are undoubtedly partly economic and political (lone parents cost the State more), the pathologising discourse has the effect of generating an image of children in the 'wrong' kinds of family as being damaged. The concept of social capital (in Coleman's sense) has been uncritically used by Maclean and Eekelaar (1997, p 48) in a UK study based on the family structures of 250 children whose parents were divorced or separated. Here we have (yet another) definition of social capital, as

> comprising mainly the set of relationships of commitment and trust on which the child can call from the time of its birth, though we would

include the material resources which tend to be associated with access to those relationships. When, therefore, children's parents live apart, their value as a resource for children may be damaged, or at least altered in some way.

This relates to the concept of the 'parenting deficit' (Etzioni, 1993; see also Perri 6, 1997, who uncritically takes these views on board; rarely are children who are separated from their parents and raised in institutions discussed in these accounts). While parental conflict undoubtedly has a deleterious effect on children's well-being, there may be benefits from living in complex family forms that are rarely explored. Amato (1995, p 41) argues for a social network/resources perspective to explain why children in single-parent households are disadvantaged (socially rather than economically), and points out that "we know very little about the consequences for children of being raised in large extended families or in communes in which multiple adults provide child care". He points out that peers may provide children with resources and compensate for a lack of support from adults, although this needs to be established. He also suggests that while "conflict between parents 'squanders' the structural advantage of a two-parent household ... other adults co-residing or in frequent contact with children can compensate to a large degree for a non-residential parent". Similarly, non-nuclear family structures may expand the potential for sources of social support and thus enhance social capital (Dunne, 1999). Further, assumptions about 'the family' are ethnocentric, and no account is taken of the diversity of family structures and kinship obligations that exist in different minority ethnic groups in the UK. This is a real pitfall for the concept of social capital, and the exception among the advocates of social capital appears to be the Australian sociologist, Cox (1995, p 32), who suggests that

> We need families to continue as the first level of custodianship of the child. But rearing children into socially competent adults require more skills and resources than most families can offer. Parenthood is often seen as the rights of parents to choose what they want for their children, as if they owned them. This view is different from a concept of custodianship where parents or carers are presumed to be responsible to the broader community for the welfare of the child, as in Aboriginal customary law.

To this one could add different conceptualisations of parenthood from a range of other cultures and evidence from social anthropology (see Ennew, 1992). "Shared family management systems" such as those of the Abaluyia of Kenya are "sociocentric, requiring the children to seek and offer assistance in the context of a large hierarchical network of siblings and adults, who are doing joint tasks" (Weisner, 1989, p 172). Concepts of 'social parenting', and ideas that 'children are for sharing', and 'it takes a whole village to raise a child', are in marked contrast to Anglo-Saxon notions of children as the possessions of their parents. Brannen and Edwards (1996, p 6) in a review of research on children and parenting, stress the historical focus on parenting, and suggest that "the broad thrust of public policy with respect to young children in the UK is with targeting 'deficient' parents or problem families rather than families more broadly, and with children as their parents' rather than a social responsibility". This 'familialisation' of children (Brannen and O'Brien, 1995) has been reinforced in recent government rhetoric (see Home Office, 1998) and is in contrast to conceptualisations of childhood in, for example, Scandinavian countries. Bradley (1990) notes Sweden's appreciation of children's rights and the promotion of the idea that children should be treated as individuals. The widespread provision of state-funded child care and a strong commitment to gender equality in the labour market can arguably be seen as one step towards collectivising child rearing, and while there is an explicit awareness that 'two-parents-are-better-than-one' in Sweden (Bradley, 1990) there is no comparable rhetoric against lone parents (usually mothers) as is pervasive in the UK and the USA.

Other versions of 'capital': broadening the perspective

North American definitions and applications of the concept of 'social capital' are in marked contrast to those found in European sociology and anthropology, stemming from the work of Bourdieu (1984, 1986, 1993). Bourdieu's is a more complex and contextualised account of different forms of capital: he distinguishes between cultural capital and social capital. Cultural capital can exist in various forms: institutional cultural capital (that is, academic qualifications); embodies cultural capital (particular styles, modes of presentation, including use of language, forms of social etiquette and competence, as well as a degree of confidence and self-assurance); and objectified cultural capital (material goods such as writings, paintings, and so on; see Shilling, 1993 who refers to some aspects of this as 'physical capital'). Social capital for Bourdieu consists of social networks and connections: "contacts and group memberships which, through the accumulation of exchanges, obligations and shared identities, provide actual or potential support and access to valued resources" (1993, p 143) and sociability, in other words, how networks are sustained, which requires necessary skill and disposition. For Bourdieu, "economic capital is at the root of all other types of capital" (1986, p 252) and he is primarily concerned with how economic capital underpins these other forms, and how forms of capital interact with wider structures to reproduce social inequalities (see also Jenkins, 1992; Willis, 1977). Bourdieu posits men and women, at least, as agents: as does Giddens, who has argued that the day-to-day activities of social actors draw upon and reproduce structural features of wider social systems (1984; see Reay, 1998 who uses this approach in exploring social class in relation to mothers' discourses about choice of primary school). While neither Giddens nor Bourdieu attempt to see children as actors, it seems likely that the social context of children's everyday lives, whether at home, at school, in their neighbourhoods or localities, will have important consequences for their well-being.

However, there are some limitations to Bourdieu's analysis. First, as Nowotny

(1991) speculates, there may be different rules for the conversion of capital for men and women, which relate to women's (historical) concentration in the private sphere. She develops the notion of 'emotional capital': "knowledge, contacts, and relations as well as emotionally valued skills and assets, which hold within any social network characterised at least partly by affective ties" (1991, p 148). This is also likely to have relevance for differences between girls and boys, especially in relation to self-identity, experiences of puberty, and body-image, which appear to be so critical during middle to late childhood. Secondly, Bourdieu's understanding of social capital has been criticised for being implicitly elitist, although this may be a misunderstanding, because the concept can (and should) be expanded to include working class as well as middle class children. However, as Jenkins (1992, p 141) suggests, despite limitations, Bourdieu is 'good to think with', because he is concerned with

> the manner in which the routine practices of individual actors are determined, at least in large part, by the history and objective structure of their existing social world, and how... those practices contribute – without this being their intention – to the maintenance of its existing hierarchical structure.

An example of UK research using Bourdieu's conceptualisations of different forms of capital is Allatt's (1993, 1996) study of three middle-class English families. Allatt found that parents encouraged a range of qualities in their children, including "responsibility, individualism, hard work, effort and pleasure in achievement, social competence and access to critical social networks" (1993, p 157); they also used their social networks on behalf of their children – in other words, they taught their children both how to use social capital and how to create their own social capital. She concluded "This is a critical transfer, since such aspects of social capital have to be recreated with each new generation" (1993, p 143). Further, she showed that parents try to develop their children's agency and indeed saw this as an aim and outcome of their parental investment.

Interestingly, in contrast to Coleman and Putnam, neither Bourdieu nor Allatt focus on 'community' in their formulations of social capital, and the networks described by Allatt are what others might call 'weak ties', which are much wider and looser than local family or community-based 'strong ties' (which incidentally may inhibit economic success and social mobility) (eg Perri 6, 1997, based on Granovetter, 1973). Different interpretations of the concept of social capital arise not least from the fact that these writers intend different things by the term. The US formulations have their roots in De Tocqueville's ideas about the forms of horizontal associations being a cause and an effect of US citizens' 'civicness'. Thus, people's involvement outside the political and economic spheres in activities such as sport and other recreations may have an effect on how they behave not only in political spheres, but also economic and social spheres. This is a different vantage point from the more structural approach of European sociology, which aims to understand how different forms of social interactions underpin and explain class and other phenomena of modern capitalism (Renata Serra, personal communication).

Overall, the social capital research has not yet moved beyond adult-centred perspectives and preoccupations and explored how children as social actors shape and influence their own environments. As Portes and Landolt (1996, p 22) suggest, there is a danger that the concept of social capital produces a series of "tautologies, truisms and stereotypes" – especially when "social capital and the benefits from it are confused, the term merely says that the successful succeed". However, it is important not to throw the baby out with the bathwater. The basic premise, that people's sense of self-efficacy in relation to their social networks, neighbourhoods and local or national civic structures, and corresponding feelings of alienation/ powerlessness or engagement/effectiveness, will have some health-related effects seems plausible and worthy of further investigation. We can move forward, I suggest, by coupling Bourdieu's original formulation of social capital as in relation with other forms of capital and as rooted in the practices of everyday life, with a view of children as having agency (albeit constrained); thus linking micro-social and macro-social structural factors. This usage of social capital contrasts with the static and circular models of social capital developed by Coleman and Putnam, and sees 'social capital' as a tool or heuristic device for exploring processes and practices that are related to the acquisition of other forms of capital.

Social capital and well-being: what are the links?

The [chapter] now turns to a discussion of how social capital and well-being (or health) might be linked. In medical sociology, Wadsworth (1996, p 160) proposes the notion of health capital, by which he means the health legacy of early development, that is, "from mother in the form of prenatal development, from both parents in the form of genetic endowment and postnatal care, and from the social and physical environment in all its aspects in the early years of life". Wadsworth notes how high levels of unemployment and relative poverty have "a damaging effect on mental and physical health of adults" and are also highly likely

> to affect the health and social capital of a new generation of children through the reduction in family income, the hopelessness of parents, and the pressures on children to begin earning early to increase family income or to leave home in order to reduce expenditure, with consequent loss of opportunity for further and higher education. (1996, p 163)

The problem with this is that it is again based on parents' ability to invest in their children rather than developing any notion of children's agency.

In a recent study for the HEA, Campbell (in press) has used Putnam's formulation of social capital to explore whether there is a link between social capital and health for adults. Campbell (1997, p 15) suggests that "we need to explore the extent and nature of the role played by peers in shaping and constraining behaviour". This is likely to be highly relevant for children. Like Furstenberg and Hughes (1995) cited above, Campbell argues that, "concepts such as social capital and civic community represents an important intermediary stage between the micro-social individual and the macro-social levels favoured in such polarisations". She also notes that "health education approaches whose basis was derived uncritically from social psychology and epidemiology, and which aimed to change individual lifestyles, ignores the wider community, environmental and socio-economic factors shaping health". The basic argument, then, is that the extent to which people are embedded within their family relationships, social networks, and communities, and their sense of belonging and civic identity, constitutes 'social capital'. This stock of 'social capital' in turn has an impact on health and well-being.

Further, as many writers in the field of health promotion now acknowledge, "Most behaviour, either conducive or detrimental to health, is influenced as much or more by the routine organisation of everyday settings and activities as by the personal decisions of individuals" (Mechanic, 1990, p 16). In other words, it is not the *nature* of health behaviours, but the *contexts* in which they take place (where, when, and with whom), that need to be analysed. It seems likely that the relationships between structure and agency have important consequences (positive or negative) for children's health behaviours. The following section takes, as a brief example, the institution of school as one of the key everyday contexts of children's and young people's lives, and explores some possible implications of children's experience of school for 'social capital'.

The everyday context of children's lives: school

The focus on family-effects in previous research may have inadvertently played down school-related issues, which obviously impact on children's self-esteem, self-efficacy, and the extent to which they feel they have some control over their lives. In the UK, the place that children from the age of four years spend a significant proportion of their time is at school. The effect of this on their health and well-being is rarely considered. Mayall et al (1996, p 212), in a study of children's health in UK primary schools concluded that:

> Children faced certain contradictions within the formal and informal agendas and conditions of school.... Some children were faced with lavatories and wash-basins which failed to measure up to hygiene messages, and were almost certainly below the standards they lived with at home. And, notably, food provided at school was likely to include unhealthy components, judged by health education messages, and by family standards.

Further, it seems likely that children's self-esteem will be influenced by the current climate of pressures in education of test results, grades and rewards for achievement. Presumably this will exacerbate pressure on fitness-related activities like sport, as well as expressive subjects like music, drama, and art, which may enhance children's self-esteem. It seems possible that the place that children spend most of their time (school) may enhance their 'institutional cultural capital' but not their emotional well-being, and may not even do that if they are not doing well academically. Others, for example West (1997), suggest that pressures at school may have direct or indirect health consequences for children in secondary schools, and this has been recognised cross-culturally. For example, a cross-national survey carried out for WHO on the health behaviour of school children aged 11, 13 and 15 also concludes that the

> challenge to most educational systems is to create a positive school
> environment and provide a more positive experience for young people
> ... as young people progress through school they become more alienated
> from their schools and ... students who have a negative school experience
> are particularly likely to engage in health damaging behaviours. (King
> et al, 1996, pp 184-5; see also Maggs et al, 1997; Coggan et al 1997)

On the other hand, schools may already have, or be building, important links with local communities by involving children in voluntary work, the value of which may be missed in school league tables. Similarly, schools may be the main places where children interact with their friends, and this may be important for their social support systems. However, the effects of the interface of family, school, and neighbourhood, from children's perspectives, is ill-understood, and the concept of social capital may be useful in exploring this interrelationship.

Conclusions

In conclusion, this [chapter] has suggested that Coleman's and Putnam's definitions of social capital and the corresponding attempts of (US) researchers to 'measure' social capital are problematic. As Levi notes, "We need a more complete theory of the origins, maintenance, transformation, and effects of social capital" (1996, p 52). The paper suggested that the concept remains a descriptive construct rather than an explanatory model; at this stage it is perhaps best construed as a useful heuristic device, a tool with which to examine social processes and practices.

More worryingly, the concept of social capital is being expected to carry a heavy burden as a theoretical basis upon which to develop social policy responses to economic and health-related deprivation. There is a danger that 'social capital' will become part of what might be termed 'deficit theory syndrome', yet another 'thing' or 'resource' that unsuccessful individuals, families, communities and neighbourhoods lack. This is why Bourdieu's notion of capital is a useful way forward, because it is essentially a theory of privilege rather than a theory of inadequacy. If we are going to develop the concept of social capital theoretically, and explore its relationship to health, then we need a more contextualised and empirically grounded account than Coleman can offer, and we need to divest it of Putnam's romanticism. The pitfall of the notion of social capital as previously used in relation to children and young people (particularly in US research) is that it plays down children's lives. It also plays down wider socio-structural influences on children, especially the middle and older age range, in terms of the possibilities for autonomy, participation and decision making in the environments and institutions in which they are situated, particularly within the education system which is, after all, where children spend a large proportion of their time. Finally, it ignores wider structural factors which create environments of risk which are completely beyond the control of individual actors, particularly children – such as the physical school environment, traffic on roads, and so on. As Modell (1994, p 51) notes, "any meaningful notion of social capital must be situated in a larger set of social and cultural relations that surround the way children grow up in any given society".

The objectives of Putnam's argument are essentially to explain the notion 'civicness', trust in institutions, and interest in public affairs, while the objectives of European social science are to explore the functions of social and personal networks for individual or group well-being. The latter formulation is likely to be more relevant to children and young people, given their exclusion from civic participation at the macro-level. One way forward may be to integrate Bourdieu's formulations into health research (see Williams, 1995); this seems highly relevant for children and young people. However, as noted, we need to be wary of reading Bourdieu as implying that cultural capital and related social capital is something that middle classes possess in abundance. Including a sense of belong and integration into local communities and a sense of self-efficacy allows for understandings which cross class and which could be used in empirically based work which attempts to counter pathologising discourses of, for example, social exclusion and inclusion.

Theoretically, then, the concept of social capital in the context of health-related research has the potential to be useful because it links micro-social individual behaviour and macro-social structural factors, it contextualises these within social relationships, social interactions and social networks, and it enables the incorporation of community and neighbourhood factors. Health behaviours and practices may superficially appear to be a private matter for the individual, but in reality health practices take place in a range of social contexts, and we need to recognise that there is an interplay between choice/freedom and constraint, between structure and agency (Williams, 1995). For children, choice and freedom are constrained by everyday contexts, which will vary from school/institution, family, and peer group; and a range of community, environmental, and socio-economic factors are all likely to play some part. This is where a model of social capital might usefully be developed. As the social network/social support research shows (for adults) social capital increases for those individuals who are well-integrated into their communities and who have some sense of self-efficacy. The extent to which this is the case for children and young people remains to be established.

Acknowledgements

The author would like to thank Pat Allatt, Gill Dunne, Eva Gamarnikov, Nina Hallowell, Angie Hart, Wendy Luttrell, Renata Serra and Rachael Wood, and other colleagues at the LSE Gender Institute, together with two referees for *The Sociological Review*, for their helpful comments on earlier versions of this [chapter]. Grateful thanks are also extended to the Health Education Authority and the Eleanor Rathbone Trust.

Note

[1] For the purposes of this [chapter] I am following the definition in the UN Convention on the Rights of the Child and will refer to all children and young people under the age of 18 as 'children'.

Children, parents and the state

Nigel Thomas

My intention in this chapter is to explore some assumptions about relationships between children, parents and the state that underlie law and social policy, and to examine their implications for children's involvement in decisions. This means looking at the nature of parental rights and responsibilities, the obligations of the state to provide services to children and families, the rules governing state intervention in family life, and the ways in which disputes about children are adjudicated. I also consider the impact of the 1989 Children Act and of recent court judgements in England and Wales, and review some problems with the concept of 'the child's best interest'. Finally I suggest some principles for including children in decisions when both their families and the state are involved, against which actual practice in decision making may be tested.

All the negative or limiting assumptions about children and childhood found in some of the accounts reviewed earlier [...] – whether those accounts are sociological, psychological, historical, philosophical or lay – recur in the fields of family law and social policy. Children are silent or muted. They are seen as incompetent, as unable to judge what is best for them. Their interests are identified with those of their parents, or are seen in terms of a future and not a present orientation. Finally, they are identified as a separate kind of being from adults, with their own distinct, and disabling, status.

The nature of parental authority

Most legal and philosophical accounts of parental rights accept that the position of parents is a social construction. The view that parental authority is a natural right is no longer tenable; if nothing else, the evidence of cultural variation has seen to that. There is less agreement about what kind of social construction it is. One view is that children are the *property* of their parents. Barton and Douglas (1995) suggest that this is not as untenable as some philosophers have argued, although they do object that it "feels uncomfortable" (p 22)[1]. This is weak; a more substantial objection is that it is clearly not the case in most contemporary societies that parents can dispose of their children as they see fit. In general we are free to do whatever we want with our property, including giving it away, selling it, or destroying it, so long as we do not contravene another law or rule. Even a domestic pet we can sell or give away as we please, although we may be prevented from treating it cruelly. Our children, however, are not ours to dispose of, and there are many limitations on how we may behave as parents. It was not always so; and perhaps the view of children as property has more relevance to ancient or medieval societies than it does now.

Another view is that children are in *trust*. According to Barton and Douglas this implies that parents hold rights on the presumption that they are best placed to bring up their children, and only to enable them to carry out their responsibilities. They suggest that this view of parenthood "may be incoherent" because the situation does not readily fit the legal forms required and because many parents continue to exercise their role despite evidence that others might do it better (Barton and Douglas, 1995, p 25)[2]. Barton and Douglas imply that the position of parents may best be characterised as a combination of ownership and trusteeship, holding together the view that having children is a private undertaking and parents have the right to bring up their children in the way that seems fit to them, and the view that we all have a collective interest in the upbringing of future citizens and in ensuring that children are treated decently.

However, it is arguable that trust is becoming more valid than property as an account of the rights of parents. Children were more like parental property in the past than they are now – the objections made in the late 19th century to the first legal intervention to prevent parental ill-treatment of children illustrate this. The shift from one view to another is still continuing, although unevenly. In the USA Ruddick observes that "the language of the law still reflects the older view of children as their parents' chattels" (1979, p 127). Ruddick suggests that the 'trust' analogy does work; from contract theory he derives the idea that parents make an implicit commitment to care for a child in ways that ensure its future, and not to do it harm; this is a commitment *to the child* rather than to the state, on the model of a two-party trust. He argues that this allows for parental latitude in decision-making, which serves children's interest in having parents who are committed to the task. "Parents free from intervention take more pride in, and hence more responsibility for, their children and treat them more consistently" (Ruddick, 1979, pp 127–8).

Blustein (1979) focuses on parental duties rather than rights, but many of his arguments are similar. Procreation cannot provide sufficient basis for parental duties, and ultimately the source of child-rearing duties can only lie in social practices, which vary quite widely. In ancient Sparta and in Nazi Germany natural parents often had a very limited or non-existent role in the upbringing of children – the extreme case of 'children of the state'. Blustein suggests that every social practice is an attempt to accommodate the interests of children, parents and society as a whole, and that those interests are interdependent: "mutual adjustment of interests, not their ranking or aggregation, is required" (p 120). Dingwall and Eekelaar (1984) argue that parents are 'agents' or 'trustees' who exercise their parental rights on an implied licence from the community[3]. This makes them entitled to help and support as well as to regulatory control. However, they also suggest that "all children have an equal *prima facie* claim against the present adult world, for optimal conditions of upbringing compatible with society's fundamental economic and ideological structure" (p 25).

The state's interest in children's welfare

Providing such conditions may be one of the objects of 'family policy', but states differ in the extent to which they openly adopt such policy. Kamerman and Kahn (1978) distinguish between *explicit* and *implicit* family policy, between purposes which may be 'manifest' or 'latent', and between consequences which may be "intended or unintended, direct or indirect, mutually consistent or inconsistent". They suggest that some countries have family policies that are explicit and comprehensive, in that there are relatively clear over-arching goals which those policies are designed to achieve. Other states accept the existence of family policy as a field and therefore evaluate policies to some extent in terms of their impact on families. A third group only have 'implicit and reluctant' family policies; these include the United Kingdom and the United States[4].

Land and Parker (1978) agree that the UK has resisted an explicit family policy. However, within a range of policies there are assumptions about how families should operate which may amount to a 'hidden agenda' of policy making. They suggest that

> what is being protected are particular patterns of responsibilities and dependencies within the family and a long-established division of labour between the sexes and between generations. By presenting these as 'natural' or 'normal' the state can support and sustain them without appearing intrusive, thus preserving the illusion that the family is a private domain. At the same time, such strategies deny that there is an ideological dimension either to family life or to the policies themselves. Great care is taken in the delivery of services and benefits to the family not to upset the pattern of power and dependency within it. (p 332)[5]

[...] [O]ne problem with promoting children's involvement in decisions when they are in state care may be that it represents a challenge to conventional power relationships in families; and this is something the state is generally reluctant to do.

Fox Harding (1996) also suggests that "Britain is ... very far from a *laissez-faire* model which does not attempt to mould family life at all" (p 186). She argues that the British approach includes both *laissez-faire* and authoritarian elements. Of course the last century has seen a much greater level of intervention by the state in children's lives: in protecting them from abuse and neglect; in providing basic health care and education; and also in making and enforcing rules about what they can and cannot do.

Donzelot (1980) has claimed that in fact the primary purpose of intervention is to control, not just the children and families who are directly subject to intervention, but all members of working-class families. He argues that there was a fundamental change in the relationship between the state and the family between the society of the *ancien regime* characterised by a patriarchal alliance between the state and the head of the family, and the modern apparatus where the state is represented by 'experts' who make alliance with the mother through which the family is brought under surveillance – the *tutelary complex*. This development, he argues, was the state's response to the challenge of controlling the working-class family and dealing with poverty without encouraging destitution or fomenting rebellion; or, implicitly, by redistributing power and wealth. Assistance to families is linked inextricably with surveillance, so that a family's own need is used to bind them into the power system.

Donzelot has been criticised for supporting patriarchy (Barrett and McIntosh, 1982), and there are problems with his analysis. He does not explain why, if the purpose of the tutelary complex is to control working class families, the penetration of parental advice seems much greater among the educated middle class; and his focus is entirely on relationships between adults. As in much writing on family policy, children only appear as problems for adults to deal with, never as subjects in themselves[6] Parton (1991) puts the question differently: "how can the state establish the rights of individual children while promoting the family as the natural sphere for raising children and hence not intervening in all families and thus reducing its autonomy?"

There is an assumption that the state has a legitimate interest in the welfare of all children; that they do not simply belong to their parents. In Tudor England, as Pinchbeck and Hewitt (1969) show, destitute children were sometimes regarded as 'children of the state' and a potential asset, but there seems to have been a clear difference between them and children maintained by their families. The modern concern with the welfare of all children, rather than simply the destitute, may be linked to the twin developments of political democracy and mass armies at the end of the 19th and beginning of the 20th century. Political democracy produced concern with the development of children's minds; the demands of warfare with their bodies. As a result it became important for the state to concern itself with what went into both: with education on the one hand, and health and nutrition on the other. It could be argued that the State's concern with the welfare of children is at bottom no more than a concern with maintaining order; but this would be to discount the much more varied motivation of the philanthropists, trade unionists, doctors, teachers and social workers who struggled to improve child welfare services. A culmination of this concern with the welfare of all 'the nation's children' was probably the period immediately after the Second World War, when optimism about democracy and solidaristic social organisation were at their highest. Steedman (1986) has written movingly of how state welfare provision in the 1950s was able to give a sense of being valued and having 'a right to exist' to a child whose own family failed to give her that message: "I think I would be a very different person now if orange juice and milk and dinners at school hadn't told me, in a covert way, that I had a right to exist, was worth something" (p 122)[7].

The state's intervention in parental conduct

If one of the central questions of family policy is about what services are provided to support families, the other is about when the state should intervene to regulate the conduct of parents. In modern societies the autonomy of all parents is significantly reduced by compulsory education and universal health surveillance. However, there are circumstances in which it is seen as legitimate for the state to intrude further into individual families and regulate, modify or even replace their parenting. What is the ideological justification for this? Dingwall (1994) argues that

> The family is a site where the moral conditions for liberalism are reproduced. If its internal regime is unjust, then not only are the freedoms of some members diminished, but public life is also threatened because of the impairment of members' capacities to participate in the institutions of liberal democracy. It is here that the argument for intervention rests, that no group can be permitted to disable those under its control for participation in civic life. (p 64)

Of course the extent of state intrusion into parental autonomy is not the same for all social groups. Others besides Donzelot and Parton have argued that surveillance and intervention fall more extensively and heavily on the working class or the poor (Jenkins, 1975; Holman, 1988; Frost and Stein, 1989; Jordan, 1990; see also Stedman Jones, 1971). This is partly because some reasons for intervention are more likely to apply to families with fewer resources or more sources of stress, and also because the network of surveillance is often combined with the provision of services used by these groups. The state of course is not the same as society, and the wider family and community have an interest in the quality of care given to children (community sanctions may have been more important in the past when the state's role was less). However, to the extent that outside intervention in how families care for children is undertaken by agencies of the local or national state, it is likely to be experienced as 'other' by most social groups, but especially by those who are more excluded, marginalised or distanced from the prevailing culture: for instance the long-term unemployed, ethnic minorities, homosexuals, or people with disabilities[8].

There is disagreement both in academic writing and in real life about the proper boundary between the authority of parents and the power of the state to intervene. There is disagreement about when the state may intervene – whenever a child's best interests are not being promoted; or when certain specified minimum standards are not met; or only when children are being flagrantly ill-treated; or only when normal care arrangements have broken down. There is disagreement about whether the state's primary duty is to children, and to some conception of their best interests aside from their families, or whether it is first to families as social units that include children. Some years ago Fox (1982) established that these different perspectives, which she characterised as 'kinship defender' and 'society-as-parent protagonist', were actually held by different professionals and academics specialising in child welfare. She later developed her analysis to incorporate four distinct value positions: *laissez-faire*, state paternalism, parents' rights and children's rights (Fox Harding, 1991).

Fox Harding characterises the *laissez-faire* position in terms of "a belief in the benefits for society of a minimum state" and "a complementary belief in the value to all, including children, of undisturbed family life". This tends to support existing power relationships within families between men and women and between parents and children: "Parents' and children's interests are, largely, identified, and by implication the interests of the two separate parents are also identified; the family as a whole has a life as a unit whose boundaries the rest of the community should respect" (pp 15-16). *State paternalism*, on the other hand, is distinguished by "a strong sense of identification with the suffering child ... the child is seen as essentially dependent, vulnerable, and with needs which are different from those of the adult". Parents' duties rather than rights are emphasised, and

> much greater faith is placed in the value of beneficent state action to protect children's welfare. The state not only has the *duty* to intervene where there is inadequate care or suspicion of it, but also the *capacity* to provide something better for the child. The state decision makers – courts and social workers – are seen as able to make sound and valid assessments of what would be best for the child. (pp 60-1)

The *parents' rights* perspective

> favours extensive state intervention but not of the coercive kind. Birth families should be supported in their caring role; children should not enter substitute care except as a last resort or on a 'shared care' basis; having entered care, most of them should be kept in touch with their original family and should wherever possible return to it. (p 107)

As with the first perspective, this approach tends to emphasise the identity of interests between parents and children, rather than the difference. In the *children's rights* perspective, in contrast,

> the emphasis is on the *child's* own viewpoint, feelings, wishes, definitions, freedoms and choices, rather than the attribution by adults of what is best for the child – and therefore, it might be inferred, the very existence of a child care 'system', with the function of making *decisions about* children, is called into question. (p 155)

Fox Harding argues that this perspective is fundamentally different from the other three, but in some ways more marginal to child care policy and practice, at least at present.

This typology is helpful as a framework for interpreting the relationship between children, parents and the state. Fox Harding suggests that all four strands were significant in British policy making in the 1980s, with the result an 'uneasy synthesis' in which the dominant elements were parental rights and state paternalism.

The state's support of parental authority

A challenging version of the *laissez-faire* position is that taken by Goldstein, Freud and Solnit (1973). They argue forcefully that parental autonomy is actually in children's interests; to focus on their 'best interests' is to encourage over-interference, and in reality it is not possible to do the job of parenting well without having nearly total authority[9]. (They even propose that courts should not make orders governing contact between a child and a separated parent, on the grounds that the custodial parent must have complete discretion as to whether or not to allow such contact.) Fundamental to their argument is the concept of the 'psychological parent' of which a child can only have one, or one set. Without much evidence beyond their combined wisdom, and in fact against much psychological evidence, they assert that a child is incapable of forming attachments to more than one set of parent figures. The work of the 'psychological parent' is essential to the child's healthy development, and should not be impeded except in cases of gross failure.

Richards (1986) has dismantled Goldstein et al's argument: psychological evidence shows that children *can* relate to separate adults; the courts do have a role in setting expectations of appropriate conduct; and the argument is based on an idealised fantasy of a particular type of family.

Goldstein et al's conclusion is that parents' authority should not be intruded upon except in narrowly defined situations where there is a major and demonstrable threat to the child's well-being. In such cases, parental responsibility should normally be taken from the offending parent and transferred to another. Their definition of situations in which parental freedom may be intruded upon is not in fact very different from that contained in much contemporary legislation, for instance the 1989 Children Act in England and Wales. However, their account of the forms that intrusion may take is rather different. Not for them the notion of 'partnership' or 'shared care'; for Goldstein et al parenting is all or nothing. Rather than parenthood as ownership, this is parenthood as sovereignty. As Owen (1992) puts it, "the sovereignty argument allows the family to be treated as a benevolent dictatorship, which can be justifiably swept away and replaced by another dictatorship if it becomes corrupt" (p 128)[10].

In all these discussions children tend to be regarded as objects – of parental duty, of state intervention – and not as subjects. What seems often to be taken for granted is that children will do as they are told by whichever adult is assumed to have authority over them. An exception is Blustein (1979), who devotes some attention to considering whether children owe duties to their parents. He concludes that they have a responsibility to facilitate their parents' exercise of their functions when they are young, and that they have obligations to their parents when they are grown up[11]. Seymour (1992) explores children's and parents' rights with the example of a 15-year-old who decides to leave home. He asks not only whether she has the right to leave home, but whether her parents have the right to stop her. They certainly do not have the right to do so by direct action, he suggests. They can invoke the law, but a law designed "to provide procedures for children thought to be at risk because of their unruly behaviour" and "to establish mechanisms by which the state can control troublesome juveniles and so protect itself from the threat which they pose. Thus the fact that Mary's parents may request the police or welfare authorities to invoke these laws does not mean that they have personal rights which the law will enforce" (p 103). Seymour is writing against a background of Australian law, and his comments would also apply in the British context. In the USA, on the other hand, parents do have some power to call on the state to enforce their parental authority, although the end result of such action is again likely to be separation. There appears to be no equivalent in the modern world for the *lettres de cachet* for which Donzelot (1980) appears nostalgic[12].

Ultimately the justification for expecting children to obey authority seems to depend on one of two assumptions. One is that children are developmentally immature and need to be dependent and have their lives directed until they are ready to take charge. The other is that children are a potential source of disorder, a threat to social stability or established interests[13]. Hendrick (1994) has suggested that throughout the development of modern welfare services children have been viewed simultaneously as threats as well as victims: "children who were victims posed a variety of *threats* to public health, social stability, family cohesion, and educational progress" (p 13). But ordinary children may also be seen as representing a threat, because of their unfamiliarity with or disregard of conventional rules of social interaction, because of their spontaneity which produces embarrassment and their vulnerability which produces danger, or simply because they are seen as holding the future both for their parents and for society as a whole.

The Children Act 1989 and the position of children

The web of powers and responsibilities that extends between children, their parents and the state is complex, ambiguous and contested. There is no dominant view of the relationship that is officially prescribed or generally supported, and there are contradictions in most of the positions taken. The central tensions come from the state's wish to support families without undermining their 'independence', and the desire to ensure that children are brought up 'properly' without interfering officiously in family life or parental autonomy; delegating responsibility to welfare professionals is one way to distance the state from head-on collision with families. To the extent that children's rights to participation and autonomy have become part of official policy, the same ambiguities apply. If it is difficult for the state to overcome its reluctance to intrude in order to protect children from physical or sexual abuse, it is even harder to do so in order to defend a child's right to an opinion. Article 12 of the United Nations Convention does not apply to decision making within families, and few countries have begun to establish rights for children to be consulted in such decisions. Where possible, for instance in decisions about education, the assumption that parents represent their children's wishes and interests continues to be made.

All these ambiguities are contained within the 1989 Children Act; its brilliance as a piece of legislation lies in its ability to contain such contradictions whilst appearing to be based on clear and strong principles. The Act takes a position on all the questions considered in this chapter. It locates parental rights within 'parental responsibility', which parents do not relinquish although others may from time to time acquire it. It provides that other family members, and children themselves, may intervene in matters of children's upbringing. It defines the duty of local authorities to provide services in terms of children's need to achieve a reasonable level of health and development. It sets a criterion for compulsory intervention based on significant harm to the child caused by inadequate parental care. It provides that the law should intervene in private disputes only if it is in the child's interest to do so, and on the presumption that it will normally be in the child's interests to remain in contact with parents and other significant figures. Finally it provides for children to be consulted and to have a voice in decisions about their lives, taking account of their age and understanding.

The Act has reframed legal interventions into children's lives in order to reflect these principles. Custody and access orders, with their emphasis on parents' rights and powers, are replaced by residence and contact orders made only if the child's interests demand it, with shared parental responsibility and a presumption of reasonable contact. Local authority accommodation of children is redefined as one of a range of services to be provided to children in need, rather than a last resort in cases of failure. Compulsory intervention is based on grounds of harm or likely harm to the child rather than on a range of parental inadequacies. Throughout the Act there is an emphasis on working with the grain of children's family networks and on planning in consultation with people of significance to the child. Stress is laid on establishing and taking into account the wishes and feelings of the child, parents and other family members or people whose views are likely to be of importance. Courts are expressly directed to discover and take account of these views, as are social work agencies. Guardians *ad litem* now have to be appointed in virtually all public law cases, with a duty to advise the court as to the child's best interests and to ensure that the welfare principles are adhered to. Above all the Act provides a framework in which competing accounts of children's welfare, parents' rights and the state's obligations can be contested.

'Gillick principles'

Another major change in the legal position of children has come from the decision of the House of Lords in *Gillick versus West Norfolk and Wisbech Area Health Authority*, usually referred to as 'the Gillick judgment'. This had an impact on children's rights within families, in that it appeared to establish an increasing right of children to determine their lives provided that they understand the implications of their decisions. Scarman's judgment held that "the parental right to determine whether or not their minor child below the age of 16 will have medical treatment terminates if and when the child achieves a sufficient understanding and intelligence to enable him or her to understand fully what is proposed" (1986 1 Family Law Report 224).

It became clear in subsequent cases that the implications of the judgment were not as far-reaching as had originally been thought, at least when interpreted by judges (see Freeman, 1987; Lyon and Parton, 1995; Roche, 1996a). For instance, Donaldson ruled in 1991 that parents could still consent to treatment on behalf of a 'Gillick-competent' child who was refusing it, and that the court had even wider powers to override the wishes of the child. This was confirmed by subsequent judgments of Donaldson and of Sir Stephen Brown, President of the Family Division. It has been argued that the original judgment represented merely a transfer of authority from one group of adults to another – parents to doctors. On the other hand Coleman (1993) suggests that

> For at least two reasons ... the Gillick case has made the position of the under 16s worse rather than better. First, the complexity of the case, and the legal wrangles surrounding it, have left teenagers confused and uncertain where they stand. Second, the publicity accorded to Mrs Gillick, as well as the tightening up of definitions, has left doctors with less room to manoeuvre and has caused almost all medical practitioners to exercise greater caution than before.

Nevertheless Scarman's original statement has commanded wide assent among those dealing with children in the courts; particularly when echoed by the principle in the 1989 Children Act that a child's wishes should be given due consideration having regard to his or her 'age and understanding'. The Children's Legal Centre (1988), considering investigations of abuse, proposes a right of all children to be consulted and, if of sufficient understanding, to decide what should happen. They quote the Official Solicitor's evidence to the Cleveland inquiry: "children should be regarded as having increasing rights to consultation and control which should be accorded due respect even before they have reached an understanding and intelligence which is judged to entitle them to make a decision".

The question arises of how a child's level of understanding is to be established. Seymour (1992) wonders if the Gillick judgment has

> opened the way for case-by-case decisions in a range of situations whenever children are old enough to argue that they have the capacity to make informed assessments. If this view is accepted, it might be seen as establishing a new right for older children, one which could be defined as: *an entitlement, in all disputes, to have their actual capacities determined, rather than being subject to presumptions based on their ages*. (pp 100-1)

He argues that if accepted this presents a challenge to our concept of childhood, but suggests that in practice the effect is likely to be minimal because the decision as to whether a child has the requisite capacity will depend on whether her proposed course of action is seen as being in her best interests; in other words "the suggested right will be read down and will not mean what it says" (p 101).
[...]

The best interests of the child

There is an underlying assumption that, when the state becomes involved in making decisions about individual children, those decisions will be based on consideration of the child's welfare. In the past the criteria might have been to do with social order, moral propriety or the inheritance of property. Since 1948, however, the law in England and Wales has held that decisions by agencies providing care must be based on the child's welfare except where the safety of others takes priority. The 1989 Children Act made the child's welfare the *paramount* consideration in all court proceedings about the care or upbringing of children, and reaffirmed the duty of an agency providing care or accommodation to promote the welfare of the child and to consider the child's interests when making decisions. At the centre of our child welfare law, then, is a concept of the best interests of the child as something that can be determined objectively[14].

The notion of 'best interests' has inherent problems, which may be described as the *problem of indeterminacy* and the *problem of culture*. The problem of indeterminacy is that we cannot know incontrovertibly what is in a child's best interests, nor always agree on what values are important. Mnookin (1983) argues that "what is best for any child or even children in general is often indeterminate and speculative, and requires a highly individualised choice between alternatives" (p 8). He points to the uncertainty of predictions about children's development. A longitudinal study at Berkeley, California (McFarlane, 1964) "attempted to relate personality development to specific variables and to show that these variables have the same effects on different children. In this respect it was unsuccessful. Many instances of what looked like severe pathology to the researchers were put to constructive use by the subjects" (Mnookin, 1983, p 10). Mnookin quotes Skolnick (1973): "the researchers experienced shock after shock [as] it turned out that the predictions they had made about subjects were wrong in about two-thirds of the cases"[15]. Mnookin also refers to research by Phillips et al (1971) who discovered that professionals of similar background and experience, studying files, frequently made different decisions as to which children should be removed from home and which should be supported at home. In the 50 per cent of cases in which they agreed, their reasons for their decisions were usually different.

Elsewhere Mnookin (1976) has argued that we can be more sure in some situations than others, and that we need legal and administrative standards which limit interventions to those situations where we have a reasonable level of certainty that we can at least choose the 'least detrimental alternative'[16]. He proposes that difficult and complex decisions about state intervention in family life should be governed by 'determinate rules' rather than 'indeterminate standards'. The rules are to be based on three principles: a high value accorded to family autonomy; an assumption that continuity and stability in relationships are important, especially for younger children; and a principle that "legal rules ... should not contradict deeply held and widely shared social values" (p 265). He does not favour giving children a determinative role but suggests that as children grow older more weight should be given to their views, and that for adolescents this weight might be predominant. This solution to the problem of indeterminacy has elements in common with that proposed by Eekelaar, which is considered in more detail below.

The problem of culture is first that standards of best interests only exist in a cultural framework, and one culture's version may simply not be accepted by another; second, that children have an interest in being an accepted part of their inherited culture which may have to be balanced against their other interests[17]. Both problems in practice involve questions of social and political values. In arguing for modesty in asserting children's best interests Mnookin, like Goldstein et al, is also arguing for families to be protected against too much state intervention; it could be argued that this represents a demand for respect for cultural difference no less than defences of corporal punishment or clitoridectomy. The often-quoted letter from Susannah Wesley to her son is an illustration of how a sincere regard for what are believed to be a child's best interests can lead to treatment which would be seen by others as highly abusive[18].

However, my main concern is less with these inherent problems and more with what happens at the point where the best interests principle meets the principle of considering the child's wishes and feelings. The conflict is not simply one between children's rights and adult duties. If we take as a starting point the accounts of children's rights and adult duties contained in the UN Convention and in the 1989 Children Act, we can distinguish:

1. a child's right to participation
2. a child's right to protection
3. an adult duty to promote the child's best interests
4. an adult duty to listen and consider the child's wishes and feelings.

It is apparent that there is potential for conflict within children's rights and within adults' duties, as well as between the two. It is this conflict that Eekelaar (1994) explicitly addresses in developing the concept of 'dynamic self-determinism'.

'Dynamic self-determinism'

Eekelaar argues that there is a need to reconcile the 'best interests principle' with children's rights, not simply because the implementation of the United Nations Convention demands it, but because the best interests principle is suspect without a framework of children's rights[19]. He argues that "an acceptable conception of the status of minority in modern conditions can only be achieved through a reconciliation between the 'principle' and children's rights" (pp 44-5)[20]. His solution is to reconstruct the principle in terms of (a) 'objectivization' and (b) 'dynamic self-determinism'. 'Objectivization' echoes Goldstein et al and Mnookin, in replacing discretion where possible with general rules of disposal[21]. Dynamic self-determinism provides the flexibility which would be missing from a totally 'objectivised' determination. The aim is to place the child in an environment which is reasonably secure, but which exposes it to a wide range of influences. As the child develops, it is encouraged to draw on these influences in such a way that the child itself contributes to the outcome. The very fact that the outcome has been, at least partly, determined by the child is taken to demonstrate that the outcome is in the child's best interests. The process is dynamic because it appreciates that the optimal course for a child cannot always be mapped out at the time of decision, and may need to be revised as the child grows up. It involves self-determinism because the child itself is given scope to influence the outcomes. (Eekelaar, 1994, pp 47-8)

Although Eekelaar's principle is developed with custody determinations in mind, it is consistent with arguments for 'open' adoption or for shared care with contact, as he partly acknowledges. Although Eekelaar does not mention it, the idea has a lot in common with Feinberg's (1980) 'right to an open future'. He does link it with the ideas of 'self-realisation' in humanistic psychology and with forms of political liberalism – particularly the ideas of Raz (1986) about the value of autonomy and the ability to choose one's life-goals.

Eekelaar explains that 'dynamic self-determinism' does not mean giving way to licence, impulsiveness or self-destruction. Nor does it mean delegating decision-making to children, for two reasons. First, "the method does not primarily seek to elicit *decisions* from children. Nor does it primarily seek the child's *views*, in so far as this implies a balanced evaluation of the whole situation, though if the child wishes to offer such an opinion, it should surely be listened to". He allows that "the child's wishes, if articulated, are likely to be a significant factor in the adults' decision", but only when elicited in "an environment in which the child's competence and personality can be assessed" – and this is a professional task: "Applying dynamic self-determinism, this assessment should include [the professional's] interpretation of the child's expressed wishes (if any), their stability and their consistency with the process of self-realisation occurring within the child" (Eekelaar, 1994, p 54).

Second, he asserts that "unless the child is competent ... there can be no question of the child's opinion being determinative". *Competence* he bases on Scarman's "sufficient understanding and intelligence to enable [the child] to understand fully what is proposed" and further on Raz's notion of an autonomous decision as "one wherein the desires chosen to be followed are consistent with (and intentionally so, not by accident) the individual's ultimate goals ... [and] achievable within attainable social forms" (Eekelaar, 1994, p 55). The first part of this notion has something in common with Palmeri's (1980) concept of a *rational life plan*, which she uses to argue that children should have much greater autonomy and rights of participation in decisions. The final qualification, on the other hand, Eekelaar sees as "helpful in constructing a concept of legal competence for children", because children do not always have the cognitive ability to predict the behaviour of others and so assess whether their goals are realistic. He adds the qualification that even a competent child may be prevented from taking a decision which is contrary to his or her most basic self-interest "narrowly defined ... in terms of physical or mental well-being or integrity" (Eekelaar, 1994, p 57).

In principle 'dynamic self-determinism' seems to provide a basis for reconciling children's rights with the 'best interests' principle. However, as outlined by Eekelaar it takes us less far than at first it promises. As Cohen (1980) put it, "a child's ignorance of his or her own self-interest does not improve the adult's knowledge of that child's best interest" (p 11). In fact there is some evidence that children may be better and more consistent judges of what is important in their lives than are adults (Yamamoto et al, 1987). For these reasons a version of 'dynamic self-determinism' that gives substantial weight to the part to be played by children of any age in dialogue about their interests is likely to be a better solution to the problem of indeterminacy, and to the problem of culture, than the non-interventionism advanced by Mnookin and by Goldstein et al – which in effect usually leaves decisions with existing carers, for good or ill. It is surprising that Eekelaar does not place more emphasis on the child's right to participate in the decision by actually expressing a view and having that view heard. He also has little to say about the process of dialogue between children and adults over the child's situation and options for the future. [...]

Principles for including children in decisions

The idea that children's participation in decisions ought to increase with age, understanding and competence is a common one, as we have seen. Perhaps in 'democratic' families this is what happens: that all children are listened to attentively, but that as they get older one moves from an assumption that parents will listen and decide, to an assumption that the young person's wishes will have force unless this will result in harm. It is arguable that the task of professionals in planning and decision making is to support this process in the families where it happens naturally, and to model it where it does not.

Eekelaar and Dingwall (1990) take the view that this is not enough, and that legislation should specify precisely when a child's wishes should determine the outcome. They suggest that the Children Act 'virtually ignores' questions of children's degree of autonomy: "it does specify that, in certain contexts, courts or welfare authorities must give particular attention to the wishes and feelings of the children with whom they are dealing and special provisions have been enacted permitting children in some circumstances to refuse to undergo medical examination. But, apart from that, it seems that the decision-maker's views will normally take priority over those of the child if there is a disagreement. The Act has nothing to say about what happens when an ordinary person with parental responsibility has a difference of opinion with a child over how that responsibility ought to be exercised" (pp 23-4). Lyon and Parton (1995) concede that the Act does extend children's rights of autonomy but suggest that this, "rather than constituting children and young persons as subjects, has provided a new set of strategies and mechanisms for using the voices of children as elements in the newly constituted government of families" (p 53).

The 1989 Act is certainly far from being a comprehensive charter of children's rights, and it is true that it says nothing directly about decision making within families. It does, however, open to children the possibility of legal challenge to the arrangements made by their parents for their care, a fact which has caused some consternation both among the public and among professionals[22]. It is equally true that the obligation on courts and welfare authorities to consider the voice of the child does not make clear how the child's wishes and feelings are to be balanced against the views of parents and others when they differ. The magazine *Childright* (1990) has even suggested that the Act has weakened the rights of children in care or accommodation, taking a 'backward step' in adding to the duty to consider the wishes and feelings of the child, which had been in Section 18 of the 1980 Child Care Act and before that the 1975 Children Act, a duty to consider the wishes and feelings of a parent or person with parental responsibility and of anyone else whose views the local authority consider relevant.

> No primacy is given to the child's wishes, even a child who is old enough to understand the implications of the decision.... For the last 15 years Section 18's provisions about the wishes and feelings has [*sic*] on numberless occasions prevented social workers from infringing the rights of children in care. Let us hope that the much diluted duty does not enable social workers in future to tell the child: 'Well you think this, but others whose views are legally just as important think otherwise'.

The law does not, then, offer a path through these dilemmas about whose views should prevail. It may be, however, that it at least points the direction in which the path should go. The repeated emphasis on first ascertaining the wishes and feelings of the child, and then on giving them due consideration having regard to the child's age and understanding, clearly opens the way for principles to begin to be established that will give children an *increasing* influence on the outcome of decision making. [...] In the case of young children, up to say seven years, it seems clear that most important decisions will need to be made by adults, whether parents or professionals, but that children should be given the opportunity to reflect on what is proposed and express their wishes and feelings in whatever way is most suitable for them. In the case of adolescents, from about age thirteen, many would agree that the 'default' position should be the opposite: that unless there are strong reasons to impose an adult view of what is in a young person's interests, his or her own wishes and feelings should prevail.

In the case of children of middle years the balance is more even. For the purpose of this research it seems useful to set out in advance certain principles regarding what might constitute effective and appropriate participation by children of this age in important decisions about their lives. The principles which I offer are:

1. that the child should have an acknowledged right to take a full part in the discussion which leads up to the decision (without being obliged to do so if they do not wish);

2. that the choices to be made and their implications should be clearly explained to the child;
3. that the child's views should be carefully attended to by all those responsible for making the decision;
4. that the decision should then be made by the responsible adults on the basis of what is considered to be in the balance of the child's interests (including the child's interest in having her or his views taken into account);
5. that the plan should be explained and recorded with explicit reference to the part which the child's views played in determining it; and
6. that if the child's wishes are not to be acceded to, the reasons for this should be explained to the child and to anyone else who has a legitimate interest.

Notes

[1] Earlier they write: "In many ways, the presumption of ownership, or at least of possession, is at the core of the liberal conception of the family and of parenthood. Imagine that a child is born in a hospital and is abducted from the nursery. When, a few hours, or days later, the child is found and returned to the parents, this is because he or she is regarded as 'their' child. The baby is not the child of the 'state', to be placed in a community nursery until the genitors, or perhaps others who might make better parents, are entrusted with caring for him or her. The baby is regarded as *belonging* to the parents" (p 20). They contrast this conventional view of the position of biological parents with the status of adoptive parents who are subject to vetting; but the position of adoptive parents, once they have adopted, is precisely the same.

[2] Lawyers tend to expect these concepts to fit a legal form, which may account for some mutual incomprehension between them and philosophers.

[3] A similar view is expressed by the Department of Health in its introduction to the 1989 Children Act: "The Act uses the phrase 'parental responsibility' to sum up the collection of duties, rights and authority which a parent has in respect of his [sic] child. That choice of words emphasises that the duty to care for the child and to raise him to moral, physical and emotional health is the fundamental task of parenthood and the only justification for the authority it confers" (DH, 1989, p 1).

[4] Papadopoulos (1996) has shown how in Greece a strong cultural belief in the importance of 'the family' can coexist with minimal support for actual children in families.

[5] The (often adverse) comparison of assumptions about state support for families in the UK and US with those in much of continental Europe is an abiding theme in discussions of family policy. Cannan (1992) looked at the development of family centres in Britain and how a service targeted at families who are not coping, and provided only as long as they are not coping, has grown at the expense of – even on the ruins of – more general day care provision. In France, on the other hand, there appears to be an acceptance that ordinary families will need and expect a range of provision including day care in order to

enable them to live normally. In Britain, she suggests, "there is a long tradition of British individualism which opposes the family and the state, and limits state intervention to families with pathologies" (p 142). She opposes this to European ideas of social *integration* which have the support of the Christian Democratic tradition as well as of the left, and gives as an example the shift whereby "in most European countries the former welfare emphasis in daycare has given way to more open access since the 1970s" (p 148).

[6] For example, a recent comprehensive overview of policies toward children and families, numbering twenty contributors and four hundred pages, fails to mention children's rights, children's views, or anything that recognises children's subjectivity; Zigler, Kagan and Hall (1996). The comment in the Cleveland report that "the child is a person and not an object of concern" (Butler-Sloss, 1988) is often quoted, deservedly.

[7] Since the 1970s there has been a discernible shift away from a universalist approach to child welfare. Cannan (1992) suggests that "the relationship between the family and the state which was drawn in the late 1940s establishment of the welfare state may have been a strange interlude in the development of British social policy" (p 144). Since then policy has reverted to a selective approach, with all that that means in terms of stigmatised service provision. As we shall see when we come to look at the 1989 Children Act, it is possible to see some recent legislation as an attempt to hang on to elements of a universalist approach against all the odds.

[8] Frost (1990) points out that 'rolling back the state' actually increases the need for intervention to protect children. In effect, he says, non-intervention and intervention are two sides of the same policy coin: "the government, which has made a virtue of rolling back state support and coterminously boosting the independence of 'the family', has also presided over the largest number of place of safety orders ever taken" (p 38).

[9] See also Ukviller (1979) who is firmly committed to parental autonomy in the face of arguments based on children's best interests.

[10] None the less the argument that 'best interest' alone should not be a doorway for state intervention in families without some additional threshold is widely accepted. In England and Wales the Review of Child Care Law noted that "taken to its logical conclusion, a simple 'best interests' test would permit the state to intervene whenever it could show that the alternative arrangements proposed would serve the children's welfare better than those proposed by their parents … it is important in a free society to maintain the rich diversity of lifestyles which is secured by permitting families a large measure of autonomy in the way in which they bring up their children" (quoted in Parker, 1994).

[11] Elshtain (1989) questions whether there is a conflict between authority and obedience in the family and a democratic society. (Since Locke it has often been assumed that there is no connection between the two frameworks, but this seems too convenient.) Elshtain initially puts forward a strong case for parental authority: "Family relations could not exist

without family authority, and these relations remain the best basis we know for creating human beings with a developed capacity to give authoritative allegiance to the background presumptions and principles of democratic society as adults" (1989, p 63). However, she finds this position unsatisfactory because it contains a number of arbitrary elements – the recognition of only certain kinds of family, a valuing of obedience that begs the question. She attempts to modify the model to take account of ambiguities, but with only limited success.

[12] On the other hand Carney (1992) takes issue with Seymour and argues for a broader view of the state's responsibilities based on social rights of citizenship.

[13] The concept of socialisation appears to contain both of these assumptions in some measure, and one of the many things which that concept obscures is the need to pick the two assumptions apart in order to understand them more fully.

[14] Where reference is made to the views of children, parents or significant others it is in this context. There is an interesting contrast between Section 1 of the 1989 Act, which makes the child's welfare the paramount consideration in court proceedings, and Section 22, which directs a local authority to promote the welfare of a child looked after by it. In Section 1 the court is instructed to make use of a checklist of factors to be considered in determining what is in a child's interests. The first item mentioned on the list is "the wishes and feelings of the child". The clear intention is that the child's wishes and feelings are to be regarded as evidence of what is in the child's interests, whether directly – in that the child's wish may straightforwardly indicate the disposal to be preferred; or indirectly – in that, for instance, the fact that a child has certain feelings may point to ways in which his or her needs are or are not being met by the current situation. In Section 22 the local authority is required to ascertain the child's wishes and feelings and to give them due consideration having regard to the child's understanding. It is not clear from the context whether the intention is that this should inform consideration of what is best for the child's welfare, on the lines of Section 1, or whether it is required because it is assumed to be positively in a child's interests to have notice taken of his or her wishes and feelings. The distinction is subtle, but may be important.

[15] This is Mnookin's account of the research. Macfarlane's own account also refers to particular categories of deficit which did predictably produce poor long-term outcomes, such as "the loss of the warm, supporting parent during the preschool years, with no adequate substitute," or "homes of unequivocal pathology where irrational pressures made integrations impossible" (McFarlane, 1964, p 122). However, these examples do not vitiate Mnookin's argument.

[16] Mnookin uses 'least detrimental' and 'best interests' as alternative standards appropriate to different legal settings, but argues that both are subject to uncertainty both as to predictions and as to values.

[17] For an illuminating discussion of the areas of conflict between universal standards of 'best interests' and different cultural formations, see the contributions collected by Alston (1994). Roche (1995) also makes a useful contribution to this debate.

[18] See Newson and Newson (1974, p 328).

[19] See Wolf (1992).

[20] Eekelaar also shows how the origins of parental responsibility lie in parental interests. Referring to Graveson's 1953 monograph *Status in the common law*, he relates: "Graveson, it seems, conceived the status of infancy as (apparently always) grounded in the law's special solicitude for the wellbeing of children. How quickly we forget! In 1765 Blackstone explained the legal disabilities of married women as being 'for the most part intended for her protection and benefit. So great a favourite is the female sex of the laws of England'" (Eekelaar, 1994, p 44). The point, of course, is that legal protections are often erected to compensate for legally constructed disabilities.

[21] See Goldstein, Freud and Solnit (1973, 1980), Mnookin (1976, 1983). Eekelaar's suggested rules are more extensive, because he allows more knowledge about the benefits and hazards of particular disposals for children's welfare.

[22] Donegan (1993) quotes a leading representative of directors of social services as suggesting that "the pendulum has swung too far in favour of the rights of the child".

This chapter was taken from Thomas, N. (2002) *Children, family and the state*, Bristol: The Policy Press [pbk edn]. The right of Nigel Thomas to be identified as author of this chapter has been asserted by him in accordance with the 1988 Copyright, Designs and Patents Act.

Race, culture and the child

Kwame Owusu-Bempah

Introduction

> To be born into an ethnic minority in Britain – particularly ... whose origins are in Bangladesh, the Caribbean or Pakistan – is to face a higher risk of leading a life marked by low income, repeated unemployment, poor health and housing ... than someone who is white. (Amin and Oppenheim, 1992, p 63)

That British society is both racially and culturally heterogeneous is publicly acknowledged, as a fact enshrined in a variety of legislation (1976 Race Relations Act, 1989 Children Act, and 1990 NHS and Community Care Act). The challenge in the approaching century is how we build on that acknowledgement; whether we are prepared to formulate policies and design procedures to ensure the provision of services appropriate to such a society; whether we are prepared to ensure that, regardless of race or ethnicity, all children have an equal chance of achieving their potential.

Britain has historically been a multicultural nation, originally Welsh, Scottish, Irish and English cultures, European (Western and Eastern) cultures, and regional and class cultures. The issue now, therefore, is not culture or ethnicity *per se*, but rather the cultures or cultural practices of groups who are perceived by the majority group to be racially different – people who are not white Caucasian. The following discussion highlights some of the important issues about race and culture, and their implications for policy and practice with ethnic minority children in today's (and tomorrow's) Britain, children of racial and/or cultural backgrounds perceived by the national majority as different.

Race

What, then, is race? Many, including policy makers and practitioners, now recognise race as socially fabricated; they accept that race is a social and political entity with no scientific basis, a fallacy. Not only does race lack a scientific basis, but even the artificial divisions between the so-called racial groups are nebulous and unstable, shifting according to the prevailing social or political wind (Davis, 1991; Dummitt, 1984; Howitt and Owusu-Bempah, 1997). Nevertheless, the quest for the notion of race and its meaning continues. This is mainly because race is a social construction that best serves the interests of those who designed it (Howitt, 1991). It provides a rationale or justification for policies and practices which advantage some and disadvantage others; it enables its inventors to justify their control over others, to rationalise their monopoly over power and resources. In short, it enables the acceptance of the otherwise unacceptable. As Appiah (1985) adroitly puts it, it is because "there is nothing [else] in the world that can do all we ask 'race' to do for us" (pp 35-6). He points out, however, that "What we miss through our obsession with [race] ... is, simply, reality" (pp 35-6).

Reality in the present context, the reality facing us, is that race implies more than anatomy; it has acquired social significance beyond anything imaginable. Race implies not just a superior–inferior dichotomy (as many believe), but rather a 'trichotomy', distinctions between socially superior, not-so-superior and inferior groups. It serves as a cue to more significant attributes of a group, including its culture, whereby one group's culture is presumed to be superior (or not-so-inferior) to those of others. The discourse and rhetoric employed to identify and describe different racial groups and their worth have changed substantially over time; but the notion of race as a vital social reality endures. In other words, we seem to have difficulty in abandoning our belief in race because it is fabricated specifically to justify, or assuage our conscience about, our differential and unfair treatment of groups on the grounds of their skin colour.

The idea that racial classification determines the perception and treatment of people is an idea that spans several centuries, and one for which there is more than ample historical and contemporary evidence for both real and artificial groups (Esmail and Everington, 1993; Howitt and Owusu-Bempah, 1990; Owusu-Bempah, 1994; Richards, 1995). Owusu-Bempah (1994) and Richards (1995), for example, provide empirical demonstration of the continuing influence of the myth of race on the thinking and practice of professionals, such as social workers and nurses. Such research evidence is unsurprising, given that a profession's guiding principles, values and practice are largely influenced by prevailing societal values, beliefs, myths and folklore. Racial myths and stereotypes still pervade British society. In other words, in their dealings with ethnic minority children and families, for example, professionals have a long tradition of using race as a frame of reference. Thus, practitioners' perceptions, assessments and treatment of black or ethnic minority clients have been adversely affected or clouded by (mis)conceptions of race.

There is contemporary evidence indicating that professionals have a repertoire of beliefs and assumptions about ethnic minorities and their cultural practices, especially their child-rearing practices, which adversely affect their work with ethnic minority children (eg, Owusu-Bempah, 1994; Richards, 1995). This is in spite of the fact that many professionals today avoid the term 'race'. Although they try to distance themselves from 'race', they still use it as a mutable concept, a concept which alters, fluctuates and adapts to the prevailing sociopolitical environment. For instance, the term 'culture' or 'ethnicity' is often employed euphemistically by politically correct professionals to signify the more contentious term 'race' or 'racial', to denote 'black' (with all its negative or, at best, exotic connotations). For example, Maitra (1996) has noted that, the children of immigrants from Western and Eastern European countries quickly tend to lose their ethnic or cultural minority status, while second- or even third-generation South Asians, Africans and African-Caribbeans remain ethnic minorities. They are perceived by professionals as out-groups and expected to be like 'us' in order to receive appropriate services, be they education, health care or even justice.

Culture

Any meaningful professional intervention should be guided not only by clients' needs, but also by their cultural beliefs and values. The 1989 Children Act actively encourages workers to "include the wider family and friends in situations where shared care of children is the cultural 'norm'". Besides, many recognise that attention to the cultural context of children's environment and experiences (including their child-rearing experiences) is necessary in order to provide appropriate services (Boushel, 1994). Yet social workers still fail to appreciate, for example, the African adage 'It takes a whole village to raise a child'. They fail to accept the fact that adoption and fostering within the extended family or the larger community is a characteristic of sub-Saharan African cultures. This failure or reluctance continues to cause difficulties for both workers and their African clients, especially regarding private/informal fostering among students. Similarly, Maitra (1996) has observed that with ethnic minority children, professionals often require parenting assessments when the cause of the conflict appears to be parental authority, the parents' insistence on traditional practice. Professionals tend to disregard the fact that such family conflict is a common feature of all families, irrespective of culture. That is, family conflict assumes greater salience or significance for professionals when it involves ethnic minority families.

The tendency of many professionals to overreact to or misconstrue ethnic minority cultural practices may be due to a lack of understanding or respect for ethnic minority cultures. Culture, in its true sense, is more or less a composite structure of beliefs, mythology, religion, ideas, sentiments, institutions and objects internalised in varying degrees by its members, and which guides and regulates their thoughts and conduct. The culture of a given group is the sum of the shared ways of thought, reactions, rituals, customs, habits and behaviour acquired directly or vicariously by its members. It includes child-rearing practices, kinship patterns, marriage rites, diet, dress, music and art. Except for artefacts, most of the elements of a culture are intangible. They are things which its members carry in their minds and as such are a potent or motivational force in moulding and shaping their dreams, aspirations and conduct – their personality. In short, one's cultural background is inseparable from one's psychological processes.

Culture and the child

In terms of child-rearing practices or child care, we derive our meaning and understanding of childhood from our culture. Thus, how a group perceives childhood and, hence, brings up its children is determined by the group's culture. This evidently gives rise to cultural variations in the meaning of childhood and child-rearing practices. For example, in 'individualistic' cultures, such as Britain's, a high premium is placed upon loyalties to the 'self' (oneself), so that children in these societies are brought up to be individualistic. In these cultures, children are taught to see themselves as autonomous, distinct agents, immune from situational or environmental control; the child is socialised to conceive the 'self' as all-important and relatively omnipotent. By contrast, many other societies are collectivistic, in that they place a great emphasis upon group loyalties. Children are, therefore, socialised to see themselves in terms of their relation to both the physical and the social environments, to relate interdependently or coexist with their environment (Landrine, 1992; Marsella et al, 1985; Owusu-Bempah, 1998; Owusu-Bempah and Howitt, 1995, 1997; Triandis, 1986). Members of these cultures feel psychologically empty or incomplete without a sense of belonging to the family and the community. This characteristic is manifest even in second-generation members of these cultures living in countries whose societies are characterised by individualism, such as Britain (van den Heuvel et al, 1992; Marsella et al, 1985; Owusu-Bempah, 1998).

For example, a study carried out on behalf of the Joseph Rowntree Foundation (Hyton, 1997) suggests that ethnic minority (or collectivistic) individuals who develop values which oppose the materialism and individualism of the UK majority community cope better with most social and personal problems. In this study, it was found that ethnic minority families preferred solving problems for themselves to voluntary agency or statutory solutions. Indeed, most of the ethnic minority respondents expressed concern about the actions of professionals, such as school teachers and social workers. They saw them as interfering in and undermining parental authority. It was also found that a majority of the ethnic minority women interviewed were adapting to life in the UK, but preferred to stay within their own cultural traditions. These findings reinforce the call by many (eg, Owusu-Bempah, 1998; Silavwe, 1995) for caution in the application of Western principles and values in cross-cultural social work with children and families.

It must be emphasised that even though most of Britain's ethnic minority communities may be described as collectivistic, each has identifying characteristics. Culturally, they differ in many important features, including child-rearing practices. These variations, in turn, differ from the majority culture, which is often placed above that of the ethnic minorities. Consequently, professionals tend to misinterpret and pathologise minority cultural beliefs and habits, including their meanings of childhood and child-rearing practices. For example, South Asian children, especially girls are typically viewed by professionals as overprotected, overcontrolled or oppressed by their families and their socialisation process as a whole. The obverse is believed about African-Caribbean children, that their families have no control over them, resulting in their "delinquency – drug-taking, promiscuity, education underachievement and criminality". Paralogistically, these very same professionals seem to recommend the practices of each group for the other. They advise South Asian families to be lax in their socialisation of children: "the social worker I had ... prior to my son was taken into care ... said the child should not be taught, he should be allowed to go out and play and that's how they learn" (Howitt, 1992, p 165). African-Caribbean families, on the other hand, are advised to restrict and control their children.

Psychologically, much of the (unconscious) professional urge to influence ethnic minority children and families to toe the majority cultural line stems from the assumption that they would be 'better off' if they experienced themselves and the world as Westerners, as the professionals themselves do. There seems to be a long tradition of this urge among those concerned with child welfare. For example, Wagner (1979) remarked of Dr Barnardo: "he was fighting to retain custody, not principally to prevent children returning to cruel parents, but to prevent their being brought up as Roman Catholics" (quoted by Forsythe, 1995, p 7).

This is not to suggest that negative aspects of an ethnic minority family should be accepted as normal and used as an excuse for a non-intervention stance when a child desperately needs intervention and protection. Simple adherence to banal 'ethno-sensitivity' (sensitivity to ethnic minority cultures) may assume, for example, that abuse (seen as such even by members) is acceptable in the child's culture. The consequences of such oversensitivity may be no less harmful than insensitivity.

In essence, no group's culture is superior or inferior to that of another (Montagu, 1974). The differences observed between cultural groups are due to the simple fact that each group lives in a different physical and/or social environment:

> Thus, although the caretakers of young children do have goals that are universal (eg, protection, socialisation), there are societal differences in the behaviours of caretakers that are related to the community's ecology, basic economy, social organisation, and value systems. (Whiting and Edwards, 1988, p 89)

This means that there is no justification for professional concern about the adverse psychological effects of another cultural group's child-rearing practices. A recent British study (Hackett and Hackett, 1994) supports this view. The study was conducted in Manchester, and involved 100 Gujarati mothers and 100 indigenous white mothers. It examined the differences in child-rearing practices between the two groups. Specific areas of interest were discipline, feeding, sleeping arrangements and toilet training. The investigators found marked differences in all these areas. In the area of discipline, for example, they found similarities in the use of smacking and withholding privileges. However, the Gujarati mothers, compared to their white counterparts, preferred emotional methods of discipline, such as threats to send the child away (for misbehaviour), to withdraw love and affection from the child, or to bring in an outside authority-figure, for example a teacher, doctor, social worker or police officer.

The Gujarati mothers' tactics of child discipline may be at odds with Western received wisdom. That is, many child care professionals, such as social workers trained in the Rogerian, Bowlbian or Ericksonian tradition, are likely to disapprove of these methods. However, it must be noted that the Gujarati children involved in the study were found to be emotionally better adjusted than their white counterparts. Hackett and Hackett's study clearly cautions against ethnocentrism, or 'professionocentrism', the belief or assumption that, in the professional–client encounter, professional values are the only values; the belief that there is only one opinion, professional opinion; the assumption that the professional text is the sacred text (or the only knowledge-base); in short, the professional arrogance that the practitioner always knows best what is in the client's interest.

To be fair, it must be acknowledged that in recent years, partly as a result of pressures from ethnic minority communities, social workers and other professionals have made efforts to 'understand' Britain's ethnic minority cultures. Nevertheless, this by itself is not sufficient to enable them to meet the needs of ethnic minority children. To achieve this, they need also to respect their cultural backgrounds. Additionally, they must expand their knowledge of the social, political and economic causes of their clients' problems, while appreciating the role that they can play in helping or worsening those problems. The aim is to develop effective strategies to overcome the barriers to providing appropriate services to ethnic minority children and families.

The role of the research literature

Very often, discussions of this type tend to concentrate solely on practice and practitioners; usually, little is said about the source(s) of practitioners' knowledge-base regarding race and culture or ethnic minorities generally. Since practitioners derive their knowledge, including ideas about race, culture and ethnicity, largely from the academic and professional literature, we must discuss the role that writers and educators play in the creation and maintenance of the beliefs and assumptions held by practitioners and policy makers about ethnic minority communities and their cultures and family structures. (See Howitt and Owusu-Bempah, 1994; Owusu-Bempah and Howitt, 1997, for detailed discussion.) To aid this discussion, we may use the portrayal of African-Caribbean children and families in the literature to typify some of the ways in which writers often present distorted and unfavourable images of ethnic minority children to practitioners, policy makers, and the public at large.

Following a report published in the 1960s (Moynihan, 1965) concerning African-American families in the US (which purported to reveal 'a tangle of pathology') writers have continued to encourage practitioners, policy makers and the public to see the African-Caribbean family structure – the keystone of any culture – as defective and problem-ridden. This picture has influenced all and sundry to construe African-Caribbean families as degenerate and dysfunctional, and to treat them accordingly. In Britain, examples of the objectification of the 'tangle of pathology' notion and its influence on social policy, and professional thinking and practice are to be found in the works even of those who should know better. These include such writers as Lobo (1978), Brian and Martin (1983), Dwivedi and Varma (1996) and Coleman (1994). For example, Lobo, a paediatrician of Indian origin, described African-Caribbean child-rearing practices in ways very similar to Moynihan's; for example, "The curiously cold and unmotherly relationship between many West Indian mothers and their children has been noticed... There is a distinct lack of warm, intimate, continuous relationship between the children and their mothers" (Lobo, 1978, p 36). Perhaps because Lobo expected readers to accept these damaging claims about African-Caribbean child-rearing practices as self-evident, he deemed it unnecessary to provide any empirical evidence to support them. Instead, he presented them as social facts warranting further unsubstantiated assertions: "these poor child-rearing practices are known to be able to cripple a child's development" (p 37). He went further in providing professional child care workers with the *coup de grâce* for the African-Caribbean family, although in a seemingly understanding and sympathetic way, by describing the problems facing African-Caribbean children and families as a legacy of slavery times:

> The father in the West Indian culture is not the central, stable, providing person that he is in the Asian or European cultures. The loss of African child-rearing practices and their inadequate replacement by European practices are ascribed by most observers to the destructive effect of slavery.
> (p 37)

Contained within this passage is a clear stereotype of the African-Caribbean father as irresponsible, absent or, missing, or where present, as someone who spends his welfare money on booze, drugs and gambling, while the best his neglected children can hope for is not to be beaten or abused in other ways. Furthermore, African-Caribbean mothers are held not to meet the standards of their European and Asian counterparts. Lobo's view is that the effects of the paucity of African-Caribbean parenting skills, and the African-Caribbean family as a whole, warrant only one comparison: "the 'maternal deprivation' effects of the West Indian child *living at home* is matched only by other children brought up in old-fashioned orphanage-institutions" (p 37; emphasis added).

In the 1970s and early 1980s, this comparison would have hit a grating chord. At the time, child care professionals were increasingly anxious to de-institutionalise the care of children. Also, concerns about the problems of inner-city living had encouraged initiatives to provide alternative learning environments for pre-school children. Moreover, simple mother–infant physical contact (deemed essential for the healthy development of even monkeys) and continuity in a parent–child relationship, deemed vital by the then influential psychiatrist Bowlby (1951, 1969), are missing in the African-Caribbean family, according to Lobo's account. The consequences of such deprivation for the child's well-being were (and still are) believed to be detrimental: "When deprived of maternal care, the child's development is almost always retarded – physically, intellectually and socially – and symptoms of physical and mental ill-health may appear" (Bowlby, 1951, p 15). Thus, at the time, it would have been impossible to imagine a much worse environment for a child than Lobo's portrait of African-Caribbean families. It is impossible to assess the extent to which this picture of the African-Caribbean family has influenced, and continues to influence, the decisions of child care professionals (health visitors, teachers, social workers, school psychologists, child psychiatrists and therapists) concerning African-Caribbean families and children.

Could the sentiments so clearly enunciated by Lobo be responsible, at least partly, for the often reported over-representation of black children in the public child care system? Lobo's views must not be seen as history. They are still being reproduced, in textbooks in one form or another and at the very end of the 20th century, one still comes across them in students' written work. Students tend to accept them unquestioningly, owing mainly to the pseudo-scientific aura surrounding them.

Assertions of black family pathology are victim-blaming and serve only to convey the message that there is little, if anything, that can be done by policy makers and professionals to improve the lot of African-Caribbean children and their families.

The web of influence of such writers as Lobo on the race thinking of professionals involved with black children is too complex to trace completely; one can only speculate. Nevertheless, there are numerous examples of its direct and indirect influence from research built on the assumptions of the 'black family pathology' thesis (Howitt, 1991; Owusu-Bempah, 1994, 1997). A further example of the ways in which writers reinforce the belief in the 'black family pathology' concerns an influential textbook for nursery nurses (Brian and Martin, 1983). Its authors, a teacher and a health visitor, chose to discuss black children specifically under the heading 'children with special needs'. They discuss the following categories of children under the same heading: premature babies, children with handicaps (whom they define as children "whose development is impaired by disease or injury", p 232), deprived and disadvantaged children, materially, environmentally and socially deprived children, and intellectually, culturally and educationally deprived and disadvantaged children.

Brian and Marin (1983) resort to myths about African-Caribbean families and their cultural practices, especially their child-rearing practices, when recommending ways of 'helping' their children. They draw special attention to the 'problems' of a lack of educational encouragement at home, and disciplinary problems presented by African-Caribbean children as a consequence of their upbringing. Regarding educational encouragement, they write, "[West Indian] children may need special guidance in handling and caring for play materials or books, as these are often lacking in their homes" (p 246). When dealing with problems of discipline, Brian and Martin again resort to stereotypes concerning the children's lack of self-control' and 'sense of rhythm':

> They find a great deal of choice bewildering, as they are not encouraged to be self-regulating at home. Strict discipline and ... corporal punishment at home can mean that softly-spoken restraints and explanations about behaviour limitations go unheeded at nursery... Their responsiveness to music makes it almost impossible for them to remain still when music is being played. (pp 246-7)

Contrast this with the textbook's account of Chinese families and their children:

> Young Chinese children may be involved in the family business ... because
> this is their culture – that *all* contribute to the family income ... business
> ... hours may not be compatible with ideal children's bedtimes, and in
> the nursery hours the children may appear fatigued ... [Chinese] children
> are encouraged in the home to be docile and hard-working. Education
> is rated very highly. (p 247; emphasis in the original)

The sympathetic understanding communicated to readers about the circumstances of Chinese families contrasts markedly with the way in which African-Caribbean families are accused of physical abuse of their children, and blamed also for the children's presumed inferior intellectual make-up, emotionality and lack of discipline. That Chinese children to nursery age supposedly 'contribute to the family income' seems to raise no concern for the authors.

At the very least, such textbook pronouncements do nothing to counter and challenge the racist attitudes, assumptions and stereotypes of the readers. Worse still, they may well cultivate and reinforce ideas hostile to the well-being of black children in the minds of students and practitioners dealing with ethnic minority children. Put crudely, the authors' message to nursery staff and school teachers is: be firm with African-Caribbean children; occupy them in a corner of the nursery or classroom with music; don't waste time and valuable resources trying to engage them intellectually. Brian and Martin encourage other practitioners to assume child physical abuse or neglect in African-Caribbean families, but, at the same time, encourage them to ignore the same behaviour (in the form of child labour) in Chinese families. The first edition of this textbook was published in 1980, the third appeared in 1989. Its long-term influence on child care professionals must be of concern to anyone involved in the care of ethnic minority children.

As a result of the proliferation of such writing and research, social workers, teachers, health workers and other professionals working with ethnic minority children can readily find (pseudo) evidence to support the view that these youngsters and their families are a problem, and to treat them accordingly. Some writers tend to encourage professionals and policy makers to ignore the structural problems facing these children and their families, to seek the causes of their difficulties in their culture, especially their family structure.

Dwivedi and Varma (1996) continue to encourage child care professionals to do that. Writing in 1996, they give the following description of African-Caribbean families, and their children's developmental needs: "West Indians [in Britain] tend to be unaware of the emotional needs of the growing child.... Many West Indian children now attending secondary schools are grossly retarded educationally" (pp 43-4). Readers may judge for themselves whether it is ethically and professionally responsible to publish such material in a volume aimed at child care professionals of the next century. The same authors deliver a *coup de grâce* to the educational aspirations of African-Caribbean children in the following recommendation:

> We ... need to think in terms of planning, for the children ... the type
> of curriculum which would aim at exploiting their particular interests,

with emphasis on … woodwork, metalwork, handicraft, art…. For this group particularly we would need a reorganization of the traditional remedial class within the school, if we hope to sustain their interest in class, and reduce the degree of difficult behaviour seen at school. (Dwivedi and Varma, 1996, p 47)

Coleman (1994) offers a new version of the 'black family pathology' thesis in which parenting skills are claimed to be harmed by parental migration. She argues that emigrant parents from the Caribbean temporarily left their children with grandparents. This hardly applies to the circumstances of most of the children she describes – young children of 'mixed-race' parentage, born in Britain. Nevertheless, according to her, this engendered resentment in the children towards their mother in particular. She also stresses the adverse inter-generational effects of this form of parental 'neglect': "this, in turn, may inhibit healthy parenting on the part of the mother to her own child. A pattern of ambivalent and inconsistent parenting can therefore be established" (p 5). The basis of this assertion is uncertain. Also noteworthy is the exclusion of the father in this scenario. Like other writers, Coleman reinforces the popular stereotype of the absent-father African-Caribbean family. She adds a further pillar to the black family pathology propaganda by highlighting informal adoption as yet another compounding factor in the difficulties facing black children in Britain.

The arguments put forward by the above authors all present versions of the Moynihan problem-approach to the study and understanding of black families – the stereotypic view that black families are intrinsically degenerative and pathologise their offspring. They disregard and encourage others to ignore other perspectives to the understanding of African-Caribbean and other ethnic minority families, and the difficult circumstances in which they live. Sadly, such literature, reinforced by the media and political propaganda, is seen by many as an authoritative confirmation of the popular belief that black families have problems which they can deal with only with the help of white professionals. Father absence, lone-parent mothers, matriarchal family structures, divorce, lackadaisical discipline and so forth are believed to typify the African-Caribbean family. The list for South Asian families is different, but equally long: overcrowded households, oppressive males and over-protection (or suffocation) of their children are a few of the 'pathological' features typically ascribed to them.

Black family strength

There are, of course, other perspectives to the study and understanding of ethnic minority families. Unlike the problem-family approach, these perspectives regard the structures of ethnic minority families as a means of dealing with a hostile social and economic environment. The structural-functional model, for example, stresses the positive, resilient and adaptive features of black and other ethnic minority families. This perspective sees the involvement of the extended family and the community, including informal fostering and adoption as a means of coping with poverty or establishing social networks (eg McAdoo, 1988; Littlejohn-Blake and Darling, 1993; Hyton, 1997).

In the US, Littlejohn-Blake and Darling (1993) reviewed studies concerning the strengths of the black American family. They suggest, among other things, that:

1. There is a religious and spiritual commitment in some black families which provides a purpose and orientation in life and faith that things will improve.
2. Black families are more capable of absorbing other people into the household. This is one of the mechanisms by which economic and moral assistance can be provided; informal adoption may provide a community social service in times of difficulty or in difficult circumstances. The informal network provides strength, stability and guidance within the community.
3. Black parents are ambitious for the economic and educational advancement of their children.
4. Children in black families develop pride and a strong sense of self- or personal identity including self-esteem as well as ethnic awareness.

The recent British study (Hyton, 1997) described previously reported similar findings.

As we have already seen, even helping professionals – for instance, social workers and nurses – problematise ethnic minority families and relate to them in ways which adversely affect them and their communities. This happens in many areas of their work with the ethnic communities, including child protection. That ethnic minority families are inadequate families which fail or oppress their children frequently and dramatically is a dominant theme in the activities and beliefs of child care professionals. The commonly held assumptions that African-Caribbean youngsters manifest 'behavioural difficulties' or 'intellectual deficits', or that South Asian children, especially girls, are pathologically submissive owing to their 'oppressive' upbringing, mean that public provision for these children has been tailored accordingly, but catastrophically, for their welfare. Such views must be rejected when addressing the needs of ethnic minority children and their families.

Black professionals

As I have indicated already, even those whom one would expect to be more understanding or sympathetic toward ethnic minority children and families' circumstances sometimes propagate ideas or perspectives damaging to their well-being. This raises the pertinent question as to whether the recruitment of more ethnic minority professionals by itself will improve the situation for ethnic minority clients. Both British and North American studies suggest that this is not necessarily the case (eg Barth, 1997; Courtney et al, 1996; O'Brian, 1990; Owusu-Bempah, 1989, 1990, 1994, 1997). Thus in the area of fostering and adoption, for example, Barth (1997) suggests (on the basis of research evidence) that the power of the ethnic matching preferences be reduced in the interests of the children: "distasteful as this may be to many adoption specialists of all ethnic backgrounds, reducing the emphasis on racial matching must be a component of any serious plan to provide equal rights to a family for African-American children" (p 302). Such views as this seriously question the usefulness of the notion of 'black perspectives', for instance in social work. Its utility is further questioned by its proponents' (eg Ahmad, 1990; Robinson, 1995) failure to define it. No group of workers, including social workers, can claim a professional status on the basis of ideas which cannot be defined. It appears, therefore, that this notion serves only to muddy the waters. To borrow Wakefield's (1996) suggestion in relation to ecosystems, 'black perspectives' proponents confuse the field's intellectual discourse by trying to force their ideological agenda on the profession. In practical terms, one cannot guarantee the effectiveness of a practice based upon fuzzy ideas, so that the claim that social workers need 'black perspectives' in order to ensure their effectiveness appears to be baseless. Indeed, Owusu-Bempah (1994, 1997) has argued that the only utility of such untested ideas as 'black perspectives', 'black culture', 'black identity', all of which derive from the notion of race (itself unfounded), is in further disadvantaging ethnic minority children (and adults) in the provision of services and facilities.

This is *by no means* to suggest that ethnic minority members have no part of play in the child welfare professions. The argument here is that, as far as helping ethnic minority children and families is concerned, their most valuable contribution would appear to be one of helping other colleagues to develop an understanding of, and respect for, ethnic minority cultures and cultural practices. Individually, they cannot claim expertise in all matters cultural. Many (eg Owusu-Bempah, 1990; Owusu-Bempah and Howitt, 1999; Stevenson, 1998) have warned against the temptation to use ethnic minority professionals to 'ghettoise' services to ethnic minority communities and their children.

Conclusion

It goes without saying that provision for ethnic minority children must vary according to the child's individual requirements. No standard package is available which could be expected to meet the needs of all children. However, as a group, these children have a shared pool of needs or experiences which are distinct from those of children from the dominant culture. Their experiences of racism are among the most salient of these. Being on the receiving end of racial prejudice, abuse and discrimination is inevitably influential in ways which simply do not apply to other groups of children. Furthermore, research (Brown, 1984; Modood, 1997; Skellington and Morris, 1992) shows that racism is experienced by the significant people in their lives – parents, siblings, uncles, aunts and grandparents – in virtually every important sector of society.

The racial injustice experienced by their significant others is directly and vicariously experienced by children. It is quite easy to see how the inter-generational effects of racial disadvantage operate. For example, parents who were discriminated against in education are more likely to transmit negative feelings about schooling to their offspring; bad child care decisions made by professionals may cause both the parents and the children to suffer a sense of injustice; a child whose mother received inadequate or inappropriate antenatal care owing to racism within the health care system may carry the effects for life; parents who have been allocated poor housing on racial grounds have little choice but to live in deleterious circumstances with their children. The list is endless. Dummett (1984) has described the process by which racism takes its toll as being a pattern rather than a simple accumulation of experiences: "each instance of discrimination against you increases the likelihood of discrimination working against you in some other instance" (p 134).

Addressing fully the needs of black children requires a recognition of, and solutions to, racism's injurious effects on them. Such solutions, however, will not be found without a genuine desire and a concerted political will to change. Furthermore, the necessary changes can be effected only if child care professionals and policy makers have accurate information about ethnic minority children upon which to base decisions and practice. Racially and culturally unbiased messages in which there is no room for myths, assumptions, stereotypes and conjecture are crucial to this important task. None of this is outside our collective will or individual power: "None is totally without power; all groups have … and, therefore, the capacity to veto business as usual" (Willie, 1993, p 454). The issue, then, is whether we are prepared to exercise our power in ways which will benefit ethnic minority children.

Obviously, the necessary changes require a new approach not only to practice and policy, but, more importantly, to professional education. In other words, to enable practitioners to be effective, and policy makers to formulate the right policies, their education and training, including the literature which they are assigned, should be empowering. Their education should equip them with "the means to critically appropriate knowledge existing outside their immediate experience in order to broaden their understanding of themselves, the world, and the possibilities for transforming the taken-for-granted assumptions about the way we live" (Spring, 1994, p 27). In other words, as Spring suggests, practitioners are empowered to empower the powerless when those practitioners change their way of thinking, when they become aware that they can exercise political power to bring about changes in their social and economic conditions and those of their clients. In short, at the core of an empowering child care practice should be an untiring quest and burning desire to eliminate racial injustice, to promote the well-being of all children, regardless of their race, culture, ethnicity, creed, gender or class.

This chapter was taken from Tunstill, J. (ed) (1999) *Children and the state*, London: Cassell. The right of Kwame Owusu-Bempah to be identified as author of this chapter has been asserted by him in accordance with the 1988 Copyright, Designs and Patents Act.

Liberalism or distributional justice? The morality of child welfare laws

Terry Carney

Introduction

Child welfare is a subset of national welfare policies. As with the welfare state, it has taken many turnings as social, economic and political values and priorities have altered. Childhood is a social construct, a product of the culture of the time (James and Jenks, 1996, pp 17-18). Not only has it changed over time, but various groups of professionals may interpret (or 'read') childhood and children's needs differently at given times (King, 1981), or according to different cultural values and national perspectives (comparative international examples of laws and systems of administration may differ radically from British experience, for example). This chapter [...] locates itself more in political theory than may be comfortable for some historians, philosophers, or lawyers. [...] It reflects the cultural forces which, it is argued, have shaped thinking about our subject matter of children, law, morality and distributional justice. Each of which terms is notoriously slippery. All are 'fat' words: they conceal many (sometimes even incompatible) shades of meaning[1]. [...]

Changing conceptions of the (welfare) state

Child welfare and 'citizenship' concepts

Citizenship concepts theorised by political scientists and social policy analysts (among many others) have provided a powerful tool not only for conceptualising the welfare state, but also for drawing out distinctions both between 'active' and passive forms of state action, and between individual and collective expressions of welfare[2]. 'Social' citizenship, as portrayed by T.H. Marshall in a famous and much republished lecture first delivered in the late 1940s, was conceived as one of three interlocking sets of rights. The trilogy comprised both the previously recognised categories of 'civil' (legal process) and 'political process' rights (such as franchise) which were successively consolidated during the 18th and 19th centuries in Britain. This was complemented by the set of 'social' rights emblematic of the 20th-century welfare state[3]. Social citizenship, then, was the principal new 'good' conferred by the welfare state. This social right to full participation in society was elevated to equal importance with guarantees of political rights such as universal suffrage, or civil rights such as equality before the law[4]. If those rights are extended unconditionally, they constitute a 'status' or passive entitlement akin to the liberal institution of property (indeed, in North America, claims to welfare were conceptualised as 'new property' rights: Reich, 1964)[5]. This analysis has been applied to child welfare too. Thus, even a rights sceptic such as O'Neill concedes the validity of *some* negative rights for children (1992, p 32)[6].

However, social rights of citizenship can also be conceived as the ingredients necessary to found the 'activity' of social participation[7], or in terms of what people *do* as distinct from what they *get* (Davidson, 1997). This overcomes the objection that when welfare is conceived of merely as a passive 'status' (see Moon, 1993), it fails to guarantee more than the basic necessities of life, leaving people at risk of social isolation in two ways: by ignoring their necessary social relationships, and by leaving them with a level of provision which fosters 'outsider' status. This critique, and the wider vision of active citizenship, may be applied to young people too[8]. This wider conception of social rights builds on two important elements of a traditional analysis of the welfare state – first, the recognition of the moral duty of the state to protect vulnerable people irrespective of fault; and second, compliance with the principle of the rule of law (that entitlements should not be at the whim of the state or be subject to arbitrary change). However, the active version of citizenship is not unproblematic, and may be too vague and woolly an idea to take us very far (Goodin and Le Grande, 1987, p 12).

In the first place, it does not immunise against moral panic reactions. One of the most disturbing reactions to extreme and atypical situations such as the Bulger case, is that politicians may succumb to populist pressure to 'throw away the key', as the Home Secretary arguably did in this instance by fixing a 15-year non-release term[9]. Even in routine cases, ideas of active citizenship for the young must also be leavened by a realistic understanding of the challenges of the transition to adulthood, and of the role of culture and economic circumstances in defining its speed. Otherwise expectations of the young will be set at unrealistic levels.

Nor is this the only rub. Active citizenship may be code for opening the door to "the visible hand of rulers who tell people what to do" (Dahrendorf, 1994, p 13). It may go hand in hand with state withdrawal of responsibility for welfare provision, leaving vulnerable young people to the vagaries of the market, their 'family', and more personally accountable for their fate (Harris, 1993, p 206). This is particularly so under 'citizenship of contribution' formulations popularised by Conservative administrations in Britain[10]. Australian and American experience with 'work for the dole' initiatives is another indication of that trend. Australian government reforms removing unemployment benefits for young people (under 21) not in full-time education or training, is yet another.

Active citizenship, then, is an imperfect benchmark. But it is notable for its endorsement of a state responsibility to foster the interests of (young) citizens in participating in the life of the community; a duty which *can* ground positive rights to such things as income support, housing, employment and training measures, but one which may not *necessarily* lead down a legal pathway which will guarantee such rights. Indeed, there is of course a respectable argument that law is entirely irrelevant, that it is a mistake to attempt to incorporate other dialogues into law, since law mangles and reconstitutes relationships in ways which alter original meanings[11].

Short of this, there is a strong case for at least recognising that, as contained in international instruments (such as the UN Convention) welfare 'rights' are expressed much more loosely, and are hedged with many more qualifiers, than are traditional civil rights (like freedom from torture). They serve more as rhetorical claims, sounding in the sphere of politics, than as rights statements awaiting easy conversion into legally secured entitlements[12]. As a consequence, traditional forms of 'prescriptive' legislation, and redress by way of judicial (or even administrative tribunal) adjudication may not be an ideal vehicle for their realisation.

Yet it does not necessarily follow that law cannot express such entitlements in other, more 'relational' forms[13], or that such entitlements cannot be adequately protected under more flexible, informal and mediated forms of review[14]. Tribunals (with lawyers in the minority) have been found to out-perform courts when dealing with substitute decision making for instance (Carney and Tait, 1997). The positive entitlements envisioned by active citizenship participation need not remain mere weasel words whose realisation lies outside the province of law. Rather it is the contraction of the state which may be the more significant inhibiting factor.

Child welfare in the 'contractualist' welfare state

Just as debate about social citizenship rights became a shorthand way of describing the rise of the postwar *bureaucratic* welfare state, so reflections on 'contractualism' may be seen as emblematic of its decline, and its transformation. Contractualism is a word which resonates with a return to individualism, both in greater reliance on individual provision than on state services or regulation, and in the return of contractual relations. This rise of 'contractualism', with its individualisation of social relationships, is a feature of contemporary social policy[15]. Contractualism, as the term implies, injects ideas of private contract into the way the state relates to citizens (such as contracting out delivery of mental health or other services)[16], or as a precondition to gaining access to public benefits and services or to income security (which is also moving from 'status' to 'contract')[17].

It reflects a deliberate policy of withdrawing the state from its (Keynesian) regulatory oversight of such things as credit, trade and wage relations[18], and is said to better accommodate new (so-called post-Fordist) forms of industrial production, the rise of globalisation, and the more pluralist postmodern culture[19]. It permits the state to manifest itself in a greater variety of forms (it does not just make laws and deliver services) and in a greater variety of settings than it previously did (private entrepreneurs may take over state responsibilities for aged care, or the family may become an agent of state regulation). Commentators speak of this as the state becoming more 'differentiated'. In its contemporary form the state is now characterised by greater fragmentation, flexibility and sensitivity to markets[20]. The hallmarks of this situation include disaggregation, localisation and variation in patterns of service provision[21]. Individual contractual agreements are becoming a prime way of achieving this within welfare. Privatisation is also on the march in the related field of family law (Singer, 1992). This is a trend which has both negative and positive features.

On its more arid side is its association with a form of classical liberalism, where individual choice is a zone of 'negative' liberty from interference; moral responsibility is attributed to all actions; and state engineering distributional equality is not a valid goal. Contractualism necessarily dilutes the influence of rules or standards set by parliament, and expands the space for the exercise of either private discretion (as in much family law reform) or, in the case of welfare services, for the exercise of administrative discretion by public servants (or private contractors doing the bureaucrats' traditional work). This carries the potential of magnifying inequalities of power. Relationships are often expressed in loose, subjective language, and they are no longer transparent to public debate. Negotiation and compliance may be left to the parties, or private sector agencies (or to mediating agents). Any state oversight is unlikely to continue to follow Weberian ideas of objectivity, neutrality and arm's-length administration. Private brokerage replaces governance by parliamentary rules and standards. Review by courts or tribunals may be withdrawn or rendered ineffective[22].

In more positive vein, contractualism may bring benefits. In family law in recent times in Australia, Canada and America, state regulation (public ordering) has been open to the charge that its operation has often been sexist (implicitly stereotyping male and female roles), reinforcing of (male) hierarchy, and riven with dubious value assumptions such as female dependency (Singer, 1992, pp 1532-3). Contractualism has also been advocated as a device to promote social participation by providing access to a wider range of social good or entitlements (such as work: Pixley, 1993, pp 11, 31); to replenish the mutuality of reciprocal relations between citizens and the state (Wilson, 1994, p 53); and to inject greater flexibility and accountability (Nelken, 1987, pp 209-12). One of these claimed benefits is the emphasis on tailoring the formation of 'self-regulated' social relationships (Yeatman, 1995, p 132).

Contractualism, with its dismantling of public law in place of expansion in the spaces within private ordering may take place, poses a particular difficulty for children, however. It is problematic enough for adults, but at least there is general acceptance of their capacity for autonomous action, and of the legal right to express that autonomy (unless contrary to the public interest or private welfare). As Yeatman observes, this leaves room to inject a feminist critique as a way of moderating the application of contractualism for adults. Adults can agree among themselves to adopt a 'combined ethic of care and empowerment' in place of contractualism's rampant individualism. This is a plausible gloss on contractualism as a policy for adults but it is not open as a way of moderating its application to children. This is because children's development of moral and decisional capacity is progressive (Morgan, 1986, pp 181-95) and, traditionally, the law has been reluctant to attribute autonomy to the child (Morgan, 1986, pp 163-74).

A solution for those unable to choose for themselves might be thought to lie in giving this mediating role to parents or other substitute decision makers acting as 'trustees' of the interests of the child. Yeatman remains unconvinced by this. She argues that in practice the fidelity of the trust reposed in such parental or other 'carers' will be measured against sexist and individual-centred standards such as those of 'good' mothering (Yeatman, 1995, p 135). Instead of injecting a counter-balancing ethic of care, grounded in a web of relationships negotiated between adult equals, contractualism as it applies to children will remain a private, individual space, one dominated by 'mothering' ideas which tend to reinforce the inferior status and power of women. In short, children and their (female) parental carers will continue to be disempowered by contactualism. While the traditional welfare role of public agencies of the state (eg child protection laws) is equally open to criticism that its vaunted 'best interests of the child' test is nothing more than an 'empty vessel' into which 'adult prejudices and perceptions' are poured (Rodham, 1973), at least this operates as a *public* space. Because it is a public space it has the attraction of being more contestable than is the privatised space implicit in contractualist policies for children.

The critical aspect of contractualism as it applies to children, then, is that there are damaging implications of the policy precisely because it *shifts* responsibilities from the public to the private (family) sectors without replicating the limited protections offered by public welfare, and without challenging the validity of that public/private divide (Woodhouse, 1993). In the case of adults, we have seen that it is conceivable that a more communal ethos can be agreed between individual citizens as a way of ameliorating contractualism without requiring its outright rejection. In the case of children, however, it is not possible to avoid the need to reconcile three sets of interests: those of the child, those of the family and those of the 'public'. Since children (and families) are not always self-sufficient, striking a balance between individualism and communitarianism necessarily raises questions about whether the answer is to be found by saying that support "ought to come from family members, binding the individual", or whether it ought to come "from the state, liberating the individual but binding the community" (Woodhouse, 1993, p 512)[23]. This is a tricky conundrum for contactualism. On the current evidence it is difficult to avoid the conclusion that more attention needs to be paid to finding ways of further *dissolving* the dichotomy between public and private spheres of action, such as by seeking creative ways of adapting the existing role and function of *public* agencies and services. This is the question to which we will now turn.

Postmodernism?

Various writers claim that contemporary social conditions call for more localised, open-textured, and 'responsive' settings for the application of policy. This is especially prominent in countries which have witnessed high levels of immigration, leading to much more heterogeneous (or 'multicultural') populations, with consequential changes to the public polity (Davidson, 1997). While mainly driven by other influences (globalisation, technology, etc) this has led countries such as America, Canada and Australia to give earlier attention to the implications of these global trends than may be the case in Britain or parts of Europe.

One possible response is to introduce a system giving much more scope for discretion (Simon, 1983). Under that scheme, social expectations (or 'values', p 1224) would be very lightly sketched by the legislature as 'standards' (not rules) and their real content then supplied later by way of "collegiate processes of professional officers and decentralised enforcement proceedings in which citizens participate" (Simon, 1983, p 1242). Enforcing the adherence of administration to those expectations would rest with their ethical standards and professional culture[24]. This approach is less radical than it seems at first blush. The contraction of state child protection laws, from their wider 'preventive welfare' mandate to concentrate instead on tangible and immediate harms, certainly led to the vacation of ground previously occupied by public welfare agencies and services, leaving it free to be occupied in new ways – by the family; by voluntary self-help groups; or by professional social workers operating in the non-government sector. And it has been argued that England's experience with a wider 'welfare' role, such as through reliance on postnatal and health visitors, also depended on the forging of tacit understanding between the (professional and semi-professional) agents of the state and the families they worked with (Dingwall et al, 1984). Given the shifts in juvenile justice policy, there have been significant changes in the proportionate reliance on family responsibility, philanthropic and non-government services, professional discretion and state agency regulatory interventions (such as through the children's court).

The interest in placing much greater reliance on such new approaches than has been the case in the past stems from a couple of sources. First it recognises that there may be some force in the iconoclasm characteristic of so-called 'postmodern' scholarship, a scholarship which questions the validity of traditional categories and boundaries[25]. Second, it re-engages philosophic (and socio-political) questions about liberty. It revisits what Erich Fromm, in this book *Fear of freedom*, described as the distinction between freedom *from*, and freedom *to*; or as Berlin (1969) put it, the difference between negative and positive liberty (see Ferry, 1994, p 294). As we have seen, positive liberty often rests in collective action that is expressed either by the state (in child protection or welfare services) or informally through 'community'. As the state has contracted (or been transformed), renewed interest has been generated in how positive liberty might be realised either outside the state (and law) or at least in its 'shadow'[26].

One way in which this might be realised is by fostering what Handler (1988) calls a 'dialogic community'. This expression of interdependence may arise naturally outside the law (and traditional boundaries of the state), or it may arise in areas where discretions are provided: "[i]t asks: in these spaces, what are the conditions necessary for community?" (Handler, 1988, p 1001). In either setting, it is plain that these conditions must include adequate guarantees against oppression from inequalities of power and subjection to hierarchy. Within child protection it must also deal with latent (or express) coercion, and the vulnerabilities which expose some children and some families to a need to engage with these services or agencies. As Foucault (1973) recognises, these are the features which allow the state to extend its reach into apparently private spheres.

However, in situations of caring for the frail or vulnerable, the participatory 'dialogic community' only very rarely emerges, instead, succumbing to forms of 'legal-bureaucratic' relationships. This may be attributed to over-dominance of the negative conceptions of rights enshrined by 'liberal legalism' (Handler, 1988, p 1018). Additionally, the state may be overreaching itself or chasing the wrong (substantive) objectives when it would be better to focus on creating suitable processes (dialogic spaces)[27], or, as Teubner argues (1983), on recognising that the areas of interest may be self-governing and self-contained 'domains' with their own internal logic[28].

These are important debates, but where do ethics and morality fit in? Populist stereotyping may inappropriately demonise children by stripping away the facade of 'innocence', or by seeking to correct their immorality[29]. Certainly it can be argued that it is right to resist repeating the errors of legislating such moral standards under the mounting pressure of public campaigns which have echoes of the 'moral crusades' of the late 19th century. [...] We can sympathise too with Archard's plea to confine the definition of abuse justifying state intervention to serious breaches of 'core' values about which there is little disagreement, ensuring that in law it serves as a genuine 'boo-word' (Archard, in King, 1999, p 76).

However, postmodern interpretations of law would argue that law is heavily value laden (and historically contingent) in any event. Moreover, might it not be *more* damaging that populist morality finds expression in the extra-legal 'dialogic spaces' lying in the community domain? Is community scapegoating more or less intensive than that practised by the legislature, or by its courts, tribunals or local authorities? Irrespective of its scope and intensity, what about the lack of transparency (and procedural protections) in community settings? Was Simon right to prefer 'professionalisation' over 'proletarianisation' (participation or democracy)?

Communitarianism?

Communitarian scholars in North America tend to argue that a sound ethical base *will* emerge if there is space for "extended, uncoerced, open conversation", which allows the Aristotelian idea of a consensus of "[p]hronesis, or practical knowledge" to emerge (Handler, 1988, pp 1063-4). The French perspective developed by Ferry ('methodological communitarianism') baulks at adopting the cultural relativism embedded in the idea of phronesis, preferring a methodology which transcends context and permits universal ethical principles to be derived and applied (Ferry, 1994, pp 299-300). One key to achieving this is addressing the structural 'limitations' of communication; in other words, cultivating the political institutions and cultural conventions of a genuinely pluralist and 'open society' (Ferry, 1994, pp 302-3). But Ferry ends with an argument for incorporation of 'non- or irrational' views as well (Ferry, 1994, p 306), perhaps raising doubts about whether communitarianism is able to resist the irrationalism of any incoming tide of community fear and loathing.

Handler's endorsement of dialogic community ideas is reassuring on these points, spelling out in great detail both the magnitude and complexity of the task of creating genuine dialogic spaces either within the bureaucracy (his main focus) or externally (as many continental theorists prefer). Notions of "understanding *and* cooperation" are seen as central moral values (Handler, 1985, p 107; emphasis added). Relationships of trust must be built in place of mere mechanical contractual dealings (p 1078)[30], and community movements must be mobilised (particularly for dependent clients: pp 1108, 1112). Nor does Handler under-estimate the powerful contrary forces at work, including under-resourcing, power imbalances and unprofessional behaviour.

Certainly, the dialogic community, and the communitarian ethic it reflects (cf MacIntyre, 1981),is a fragile alternative to legal liberalism and the associated legal-bureaucratic pattern characteristic of the postwar welfare state. Yet, as the Weberian model of law and administration crumbles and shrinks, it reinstates the reliance on the voluntarism, community support and private provision emblematic of 19th-century welfare and community organisation[31]. Alternatives such as the dialogic community call for ever closer scrutiny – however fragile or contingent they may prove to be. As Fraser and Gordon (1994) point out, citizenship theory does not resonate in North America, accustomed as it is to a simple dichotomy between charity and 'contract'. In substance, however, this reading of communitarianism equates with what is elsewhere termed 'neo-republican' citizenship[32]. Whatever its label, it may be an idea whose time has come.

Conclusion

What we have seen in this chapter is that there are at least two ways in which these citizenship rights and entitlements of children may be expressed: first in terms of protecting against *negation* of those entitlements; and second, in terms of positively *securing* that access[33].

The traditional late 19th-century welfare state sought to achieve its (limited) social policy objectives through a scheme of protective interventions (and associated institutional or other services), which were grounded in the moral innocence or perfectibility of children, and whose philosophic rationale was paternalism. It was an 'active' form of state mandate in child protection, but by the 1960s its force was spent, undone by the evidence of lack of success in achieving its idealistic goals, and by clear indications of the heavy price paid in terms of incursions into the liberty of action of children and young people alike.

For a time, the 'rights movement' wrought a transformation of policy, splitting it into two arms. Protective intervention for its part reverted to a harms-based rationale during the late 1960s, a rationale more respectful of the due process (or civil citizenship) 'status' of children and families. Liberalism was revived. Services for children and families were altered too. The legacy of mainly 'institutional-based' services initially formed part of the passive citizenship of the 1940s welfare state. These too were reconceptualised as a more universal, non-stigmatising expression of state obligations to assist and support citizens (children and their families) while they continue to live in the wider community, thus maximising their potential for social participation. Briefly, the basic interests of children began to be recognised as an 'active' form of social citizenship rights.

Another way of expressing this is as a rebalancing of four main kinds of rights: (1) protective rights; (2) choice rights; (3) developmental rights; and (4) capacity rights (Sampford, 1986, pp 32-3). What we have witnessed is that in place of policies grounded mainly in a 'protective' rationale, laws were rewritten to put more weight on negative (or 'choice') rights, while services became more reflective of 'positive' (or 'developmental') rights and the allied 'psychological' capacities required if citizens are meaningfully to exercise those rights. The latter are pivotal. This chapter has found classical liberalism wanting in its failure to recognise the 'connectedness' of human life[34]. Social citizenship rights are founded in social *relations*; it is not simply a question of the state providing a new entitlement (what the person *gets*) by making utilarian policy calculations about what is or is not in the interests of the greatest good for the greatest number. It involves constructing *active* opportunities for the citizen to realise citizenship through what the person *does* (Davidson, 1997).

The question is whether law has a role to play in fostering environments where 'positive' or 'developmental' or more simply 'social' rights may flourish. Such rights rest in the application of the 'equality principle'[35], which is why their realisation has been so dependent on the distributive arm of the welfare state over much of the course of the 20th century. If they are not to be trumped by competing policy considerations, they must be expressed as 'ranking interests' in their own right; they cannot simply be derived from parental (and societal) interests in shaping future adults. Social reciprocity is the nub of this thesis: that citizen and state owe mutually responsible duties to each other; welfare is not simply a 'good' owed unconditionally to the citizen on preordained terms.

It is this reciprocity between citizens which builds the case for equivalent rights for adults in the aftermath of the transformation of the welfare state into the 'bargaining' or contractualist state spawned by contemporary values and trends, which seems likely to dominate at least the early states of the 21st century. It is argued here that children of all ages are vulnerable to an erosion of their (few) public sector rights on two main fronts. They are vulnerable in a world tempted to demonise or otherwise scapegoat the young in response to societal insecurity stemming from economic change. And they are vulnerable to the rise of centrifugal moral forces associated with the rise of pluralism (often emblematic of that diverse body of scholarship travelling under the banner of 'postmodernism'). Plainly, privatisation risks accentuating those dangers.

This threatens distributional justice for children. Diagnosis is comparatively easy. What is problematic is finding a convincing foundation for a new approach. The reciprocity characteristic of communitarian or genuinely contractual models make sense only for older (Gillick-competent [...]) adolescents. For younger children the 'ethic of care and connection' is difficult to operationalise without compounding the impact of historical ideas such as 'good mothering'. Creative solutions may be needed if we are to bridge the public/private divide.

Some quite radical ideas give expression to this, such as New Zealand's use of 'family group conferences' to deal with the vast bulk of both delinquency and child protection matters, or North American 'sentencing circles'[36]. If properly designed, these certainly open the private spaces to incorporation of wider family and local community engagement[37]. However, they are vulnerable on another score: that minimum protections of justice and fairness may be jettisoned[38]. Less radical measures, such as tribunals or other 'popular' justice institutions may instead hold the key[39].

Notes

[1] The looseness and ambiguity of language invites closer analysis to clarify meanings, but in cultural terms preservation of this ambiguity may be highly functional because it fosters dialogue essential to formation of common value positions.

[2] These debates within citizenship theory are well summarised by writers such as Stewart (1995), Rees (1995) and Moon (1993).

[3] Marshall's original essay is republished in Marshall (1973, pp 67-127). For an accessible contemporary discussion, see Kymlicka and Norman (1994, pp 352-81).

[4] For an extended discussion of these ideas, see Harris (1987).

[5] Simon (1986) pointed out that resort to concepts of property rather impedes redistributive goals.

[6] Her main argument is that positive (or welfare) entitlements to things such as 'kindness', development of talents, 'involvement' or 'good feeling' are imperfect obligations (not owed to every child like freedom from sexual abuse) and not an incident of a *particular* relationship (such as carers or teachers). Moreover, rights analysis is said to be of most political power in correcting inappropriate repressive abuses of power, whereas children are *legitimately* in need of dependent nurture (pp 39-40). For a critique see Coady (1992, pp 49-50).

[7] Further, Oldfield (1990), Leisink and Coenen (1993, pp 5-6).

[8] Thus Harris (1993, p 185) endorsed an integrative 'citizenship of entitlement' analysis in which the extension of civil and social rights are the basis for participation by disadvantaged young people in the social and economic life of the community.

[9] For details of this sage, see Aldridge (1994) and Palmer (1996) The term set by the minister was almost double the eight years envisaged by the trial judge or the ten years contemplated by the Lord Chief Justice. Two adverse rulings by the European Court of Human Rights ultimately led to the restoration of some elements of due process and respect for the rule of law with regard to release and recall procedures applied to children convicted of murder.

[10] Finlayson (1994, pp 9, 13-16).

[11] This argument is elaborate and critiqued by writers such as Handler (1988, pp 1043-4).

[12] This argument is set out more fully in Carney (1991a).

[13] These ideas are developed in Carney (1991b) and (1993).

[14] See further, Carney (1994) and (1996). Conciliation or mediation of complex relational disputes appears to be superior to classical 'adjudication' of them (Carney, 1998).

[15] Yeatman (1995) provides a good review of the elements and implications of contractualism.

[16] See, for instance, the discussions by Hollingsworth (1996) and Prager (1992).

[17] Weatherley (1994). Also Carney (1998).

[18] Kosonen (1995, p 820).

[19] See Walby (1995) for an accessible treatment of this argument.

[20] Clarke and Newman (1993, p 47).

[21] Latham (1996, p 6).

[22] This is elaborated elsewhere; see Carney (1996).

[23] James and Jenks (1996) likewise muse over the implications of these trends in postmodern society, querying whether childhood is being reconstructed to amplify forms of state control (or Foucault's 'social policing'), while at the same time social insecurity may be leading people to invest ever more heavily in the myth of innocence, resolving the contradiction by demonising extremes of childhood violence.

[24] Simon argued that in choosing the 'professionalising' route ahead of its more democratic (or 'market' oriented) 'proletarianising' alternative, his solution at least had the attraction of "[P]romis[ing] to overcome some of the deficiencies of Weberian bureaucracy as an instrument of control and, by extending the reformer's own mode of life and work, to create valuable allies for her". However

> [t]he disadvantages are, first, that if the strategy fails to inculcate the reformer's perspective, organisational autonomy may be used in ways that will frustrate her ends; and, second, that the expansion of professional status dilutes the exclusivity of the positions and perhaps the privileges of the reformer and her present allies. (Simon, 1983, p 1262)

[25] See, for example, Mnookin (1985).

[26] Such a reconciliation of liberal and communitarian principles was foreshadowed by Freeman (1992, p 54, n 11).

[27] A body of mainly US scholarship argues a more modest case, suggesting that substantive objectives of the law are appropriate, but should be recast to promote 'therapeutic' goals where this is not inconsistent with other values. See generally D. Wexler (ed) *Therapeutic jurisprudence: The law as a therapeutic agent*, Durham NC: Carolina Academic Press, 1990; M.A. Levine, 'A therapeutic jurisprudence analysis of mandated reporting of child maltreatment by psychotherapists', *New York Law School Journal of Human Rights*, vol 10, p 11, 1993; M. Perlin, 'What is therapeutic jurisprudence?', *New York Law School Journal of Human Rights*, vol 10, p 623, 1993.

[28] Further, Handler (1988, p 1047).

[29] As was once done on the 'uncontrollable' child or 'exposure to moral danger' grounds for taking children into care; see Carney (1985).

[30] Simon's decentralised professionalism may be a partial guarantor here. See Simon (1983, pp 1195, 1199).

[31] This is eloquently expounded in Finlayson (1994).

[32] See, for example, Van Gunsteren (1994, p 45).

[33] Just over a decade ago Eekelaar spoke of a need to recognise 'basic interests' of children. These were said to encompass entitlements to "general physical, emotional or intellectual care [which is] within the social capabilities of [the] immediate caregiver", see Eekelaar (1986, p 170).

[34] Further, Campbell (1992).

[35] Dingwall and Eekelaar (1984, p 106).

[36] These models are reviewed and described by writers such as Morris and Maxwell (1995), La Prairie (1995) and O'Connor (1997, pp 280-8).

[37] Poorly designed programmes fail to engage the community, while, however, giving the appearance of doing so. For a recent critique of programmes allegedly sensitive to indigenous communities, see, C. Cunneen, 'Community conferencing and the fiction of indigenous control', *Australian and New Zealand Journal of Criminology*, vol 30, pp 292-311, 1997.

[38] See for example Bargen (1995).

[39] Such as continental multidisciplinary children's courts or Australia's experiment with tribunals to decide adult guardianship questions: see Carney and Tait (1997).

This chapter was taken from King, M. (1999) *Moral agendas for children's welfare*, London/New York: Routledge. The right of Terry Carney to be identified as author of this chapter has been asserted by him in accordance with the 1988 Copyright, Designs and Patents Act.

Part 3: Policies, trends, contexts and ramifications

> Nothing you do for children is ever wasted. They seem not to notice us, hovering, averting our eyes, and they seldom offer thanks, but what we do for them is never wasted. (Garrison Keillor)

The focus in this part of the Reader is on a critical examination of a selection of policies or policy areas, which address not only 'child welfare' in the narrow sense of the term with reference to content and objective, but also consider their ramifications in relation to moral agendas, social investment strategies, rights, concepts of childhood, and the ever-changing relationship between children, parents and the state. The chapters, when considered together, explore the 'joined-up' nature of a number of policies, not so much as a feature of New Labour's commitment to 'joined-up government' (Newman, 2001), but rather as they criss-cross one another in their goals and in their impact on children's lives.

There is little doubt that 'holistic' government in pursuit of 'social investment' has gradually displaced the older notion of welfare associated with the post-war 'classic' welfare state whose emphasis was on universalism and comprehensive benefits. Nowadays, 'social welfare' is subordinated to economic and political policies of a nature and to a degree that is quite unlike anything to be found previously, and represents a major reinterpretation of 'values' as espoused by New Labour through its Third Way programme. Notwithstanding the change of priorities and objectives, this being a 'critical' Reader, many of the chapters adopt an oppositional stance, as they refuse to chant the government mantra of 'no rights without responsibilities', preferring instead to emphasise 'interconnectedness' of a more traditional kind, inspired by ideals of justice and equality and focused on structural economic and social inequalities (see, for example, Chapters Fourteen to Twenty-Three).

Since 'rights' are such a crucial feature of all the debates on the emancipation of children, it is appropriate to open with Jeremy Roche's discussion (Chapter Twelve) of the 1989 Children Act, which many children's advocates feel has not fulfilled its promise. He begins by conceding that the Act may be seen as providing a framework for advancing rights, but maintains that "it cannot bring this about by itself". The important distinction, he says, is between welfare and liberty rights. The former are enshrined in the legislation through the endorsement of what is called 'the paramountcy principle', the 'welfare checklist' and the 'no order' principle. There is also a 'threshold criterion', which attempts to limit the extent of state intervention (local authority social workers) into family life (although whether this extends the rights of children is not always evident). Indeed, it is the case that to a certain extent the welfare rights tend to be wrapped up in the changed relations between local authorities and parents, as well as in the reshaping of a number of legal responsibilities. Welfare rights, although obviously crucial to human dignity, are not inherently problematic since they do not challenge 'adultist' assumptions about children (see Moss and Petrie, Chapter Four).

Liberty rights, on the other hand, raise controversial issues concerning power and authority. According to Roche, the Act is supportive of these rights in four respects: children are allowed to apply to the court for certain categories of 'order'; children may have unmediated access (that is, without an adult intermediary) to a range of legal services and to the courts; in certain circumstances 'competent' children have the right to refuse medical attention; and there is the right to complain about specific aspects of a local authority's responsibilities for children in need and those who are 'looked-after'. Thus, the Act "moved towards a recognition of the child as a legal subject".

In practice, however, the liberty rights of children have not been enhanced in any substantial manner. Judges, solicitors and court welfare officers have proved very reluctant to see children as *competent* actors in their own interests where three contentious issues are involved: children as litigants, children in court (in proceedings regarding care and custody), and with respect to their right to refuse medical treatment (Sawyer, 1995, 1997, 1999). Children in "law talk", says Roche, are "idealised and demonised" and this leaves little opportunity for "a more honest conversation about children, family and social justice" (see also Thomas, Chapter Nine and Piper, Chapter Thirteen). One concern, rarely openly admitted but felt by different groups of adults (for example, feminists in relation to mothers' power; teachers in relation to school discipline; disability activists in relation to the rights of young carers; and conservatives and religious fundamentalists in relation to parental authority) is that "rights claims challenge existing hierarchies by making the community hear different voices". Ultimately, children's rights are about "rethinking and redefining adult–child relations", and this is a cultural (as well as an ethical) project (see Moss and Petrie, Chapter Four and Prout, Chapter Twenty-Six), although Roche warns that it does not automatically lead to a change in the law. Such a shift in adult attitudes is crucial, however, if present power relationships involving children and adults are to be challenged and held to account.

The seminal role of the law in child welfare is further discussed by Christine Piper (Chapter Thirteen), who focuses on the different 'assumptions' about children's 'best interests' in the family justice system and the juvenile justice system (see also Goldson, Chapter Fourteen and James and James, Chapter Fifteen). As Piper shows, the assumptions are said to be based on scientific knowledge, which is assumed to embody the authority of science and law and, therefore, escapes critical scrutiny as it enters into the realm of common sense. On the one hand there are the assumptions of the family justice system with its 'judicial ideas' about the best interests of children in line with the 'paramountcy principle' enshrined in the 1989 Children Act, which are derived from social and medical research (the child as vulnerable and often incompetent, and in need of a stable and secure environment, particularly involving both parents; see Lee, 2001; James and James, 2004, pp 10-28). These assumptions are geared to an 'abstract' child, making it difficult for the individualised child's voice to be heard. On the other hand, in contrast to the family justice system, the basic assumption of the youth justice system, where there is little concern for the possibly damaging consequences of bringing minors to court, is that children (aged 10-13) and young people (aged 14-17) are sufficiently mature and capable to take responsibility for their actions and wishes. The different assumptions are not the result of 'non-law knowledge' about children in the justice system, since much of this knowledge points to a similarity of factors between both groups of children: the vulnerable and the rational child are not two distinct beings. So, how can the different assumptions be explained?

Piper argues that 'law' is one 'system' among many in modern society, and that, as with every other system, it is continually adjusting itself to inputs from other 'systems' (for example, medicine, politics, psychology; see King, Chapter Three). It is difficult for law to adapt itself to all external knowledge when that knowledge conflicts with law's operations. Such knowledge, however, cannot be ignored (this would undermine law) and, therefore, it is absorbed via a sub-system procedure in accordance with the social and legal functions of regulating the family and dealing with offending children. Thus children are subjected to two different sets of legal responses that imprison them in two different paradigms: of family law and of criminal law. In the former the child's welfare is legally 'paramount'; in the latter the court has only to 'have regard to' the welfare of the child. This means that non-legal knowledge is not as important in criminal cases as it is in the family court where 'child welfare science' informs its quest to serve the child's best interests. Both sets of assumptions carry within them what Piper terms "political messages" concerning individual and parental responsibility: "The resulting political norm currently functions to reduce expenditure on social welfare and legal aid, and to secure social stability though stable families and healthy, well-behaved children".

The assumptions of the law in the service of political objectives are nowhere more evident than in the governmental rhetoric surrounding the 'anti-social' child as considered by Goldson (Chapter Fourteen), James and James (Chapter Fifteen) and, in a medical context, by Coppock (Chapter Sixteen). This image has rarely been more self-consciously deployed than under New Labour with its raft of documents and legislative Acts. In his telling critique of what he calls "the punitive turn", Barry Goldson charts the evolution of the "institutionalised intolerance" (Muncie, 1999), shown in policies for 'anti-social', 'disorderly' and/ or 'offending' children and young adolescents, to the point where "children's civil liberties and human rights are increasingly threatened with compromise, if not violation". In order to contextualise much of the oppressive legislation that has been enacted since the mid-1990s, Goldson first identifies and discusses the process of demonisation, whereby particular children often appear as "totemic symbols of deep social crisis", and the decline of the concept of "universal welfare", which has been replaced by the notion of "individual responsibility", resulting in "targeted intervention" at those children deemed to be "*posing risk*" (emphasis in the original; for the concept of 'risk' in contemporary social theory, see Beck, 1992; for 'risk' in social policy, see Kemshall, 2002).

Goldson then turns to consider the nine pieces of relevant legislation passed since 1994 (eight of which are New Labour Acts passed since 1998). Four main themes are identified: "an actuarial emphasis"; crude notions of restorative justice;

"unsophisticated rehabilitative ideals"; and "an overtly punitive orientation ... through processes of re-penalisation and child incarceration". The chapter focuses on the first and the fourth, with the former taking liberties at the "shallow end" and the latter taking liberties at the "deep end". The "shallow end" refers to policies of early intervention, the cornerstone practice in youth justice policy, which in emphasising *risk* rather than *guilt* tends towards authoritarianism while also undermining traditional principles of criminal justice. Indeed, the favoured community response of preventive action at the "shallow end" is likely to lead to greater emphasis being placed on incarceration at the "deep end". Where incarceration of young people is concerned, the number of custodial sentences imposed on children and young adolescents rose from 4,000 per annum in 1992 to 7,600 in 2001, and during the same period, the child remand population grew by 142%. Moreover, the average length of sentence served grew longer and the number of children under 15 so sentenced increased from 100 in 1992 to 800 in 2001.

In general, this chapter shows that the developments outlined here signify a profound shift in emphasis away from the classic justice model of the 1980s and early 1990s, to a "curious – even paradoxical – hybridity", comprising notions of risk, restorative and victim perspectives, rehabilitative ideals, and an overtly punitive orientation. There is a strong and compelling message that crucial to this change of emphasis has been the obfuscation of the complex relationship between social justice, material context and individual responsibility on the one hand, and the "insidious conflation of crime, disorder and anti-social behaviour" on the other. (One of the means by which this has been accomplished is through what has been described as a conscious and manipulative use of language by New Labour in order to control public perception; see Fairclough, 2000.) The current approach to juvenile justice by the government may be seen as a depressing testimony to the sentiment that has often been expressed by a variety of social and political philosophers, but which is regularly ignored by politicians courting popular favour: "The attitude that a society takes to children, especially to children who see out their childhoods within the most formidable personal circumstances and adverse social-structural contexts, is an important indicator of its core values and principles". If, Goldson concludes sadly, "we hold a mirror to contemporary policy responses to children in trouble ... it returns a particularly ugly image".

A similar focus on New Labour's suspicion of children and adolescents is to be found in James and James (Chapter Fifteen; see also James and James, 2004), which shows that while adults generally welcome the government's emphasis on involving 'communities' in areas of local policy in order to revitalise civil society, the outcome for children and adolescents has subjected them to greater surveillance and other forms of control. This has had the effect of limiting their agency and restricting rights, rather than increasing their participation as citizens. Moreover, it has also served to legitimise 'zero tolerance' of childish misbehaviour, and to justify ignoring the psychosocial factors that cause so much of the troubled and troublesome behaviour that brings young people into conflict with the authorities. Thus, despite the official commitment of Britain to the UN Convention on the Rights of the Child (1989), children continue to be marginalised in a variety of contexts. In focusing on the community, schooling, youth justice, and divorce, and in revealing the ways in which they impinge on children's lives, the authors persuasively portray these areas of policy practice as evidence of a "seldom acknowledged social control agenda", which may well be indicative of "a deep ambivalence about the place of children in contemporary British society".

For instance, although much of New Labour's rhetoric regarding a contractual society (between the individual and the community) abounds with references to young people's participation (what might be termed 'active citizenship'), in practice schemes for 'listening' to young people have been relatively scarce and to date there has been little real attention given to translating young people's views into policy (see Hallett and Prout, 2003, and special issue on 'Participation', in *Children & Society*, April 2004). More often than not, the participation process is about "selective empowerment" of certain groups of adults and the *extension* of control over children and adolescents (see Anti-Social Behaviour Orders mentioned below, and increasing use of curfew orders for under-16s).

The chapter ends with a quotation from Etzioni (one of the intellectual forces behind Blairite communitarianism) to the effect that communities resemble a cyclist who, forever on a changing terrain, must continually correct tendencies to veer to one extreme or the other. Perhaps, suggest James and James, through marginalising children (young citizens), we (adults) are in danger of losing our balance. Or perhaps not, since that would suggest being out of control. Perhaps something quite the contrary is developing: the conscious construction of a new type of citizenry for a 'post-modern' society, in which (adult) communities are given widespread discretionary powers to determine the nature of their relationship with children, while the children themselves – popularly perceived as both unstable and unfinished – will continue to be denied liberty rights in deference to their 'best interests'?

One example of the gross infringement of children's civil liberties are Anti-Social Behaviour Orders (ASBOs), which can be publicly (the child subjects may have their photographs in the newspapers and on flybills) applied to any aspect of a child's behaviour, and are granted to local authorities in the civil court where complaints can be made anonymously and judgement is given on the basis of 'balance of probability', not as in the criminal court where guilt has to be established 'beyond reasonable doubt'. Failure to comply with an Order is a criminal offence carrying a sentence of up to five years. Aside from the violation of children's human rights, these Orders are also an assault on an important principle of criminal justice. Of course, the targeting of young people in this respect is not an isolated example of governmental authoritarianism, rather it is part of a much wider strategy that begins with the motto "no rights without responsibilities" (Giddens, 1998, p 65) and ends with the revising by New Labour of traditional concepts of justice, equality, and citizenship as part of its modernising project. In fact, the Prime Minister recently announced "the end to the 1960s liberal consensus on law and order" (Quoted in *The Guardian*, 19 July 2004; see also Lister, Chapter Twenty-Five; Newman, 2001; and Hendrick, 2003).

A clue to government thinking in the future was given in a newspaper interview by the New Labour local authority official in Manchester responsible for pushing

ASBOs to their legislative limit. With reference to the young people involved, he is reported as saying:

> We could prosecute all these yobbos in a criminal court if we liked.... But because we're a caring council, we want to give everyone an opportunity to change. We're not about criminalising people, we're about getting them to change their behaviour, and this is a warning system.... Yes, we used to bang on doors when we were young.... But there used to be badger-baiting once, too. It's different now isn't it? Things are moving on; people want to live differently. It's right that people should have high expectations for themselves. It's about respect.... We don't want people [children] running in our gardens. It's unacceptable. We have moved on; we want more. (Aitkenhead, *The_Guardian*, 24 July 2004)

This is a crucial feature of what New Labour means by modernisation: opportunity, change, intolerance, reform, punishment, risk, and no rights without duties. What this schema elides, aside from such traditional liberal concerns as justice, is the notion of difference: of different values, of different ways of living, of different social capacities. It seems that the families caught up in ABSOs are seen "only as problems. But what of their problems?" (Aitkenhead, *The Guardian*, 24 July 2004).

The theme of demonisation, surveillance and control of young people is continued in Vicki Coppock's chapter (Sixteen), which has three principal concerns: medical definitions of normal/abnormal in relation to child and adolescent mental health; the implications of such definitions for the rights of these young people; and the alleged deterioration of mental health among this social group in recent years (see also Fawcett et al, 2004, pp 130-45). Coppock begins by informing us that the current understanding(s) of "disturbed" and "disturbing" are the products of theoretical paradigms that have long historical antecedents. First, there occurred the emergence in the late-Victorian period of 'individual' psychology and psychiatry as representatives of positivist 'scientific' inquiry, with its emphasis on observing, weighing and measuring children. Second, during the same period, psychology and psychiatry in presenting their data, including intelligence tests for the measurement of IQ, managed to turn themselves into the arbiters of 'normality' and 'abnormality'. Third, the tendency at the time within the psycho-medical discourse to fuse the 'mental' with the 'moral', as when the 'feeble-minded' were perceived by many commentators to be a physical, moral, mental, and political threat to the reproduction of a healthy British race, gave a moralising dimension to psycho-medicine (see also Jackson, 2002, and Gijswijt-Hofstra and Marland, 2003; Thomson, 1998; for psycho-medical attitudes to 'adolescents' in the late Victorian and Edwardian period, see Hendrick, 1990).

In considering influential theoretical models of human behaviour, Coppock notes that while psychological and psychiatric research admits to fundamental disagreements within the professions over definitions and treatments, the 'medical model' ("symptom, syndrome, diagnosis, aetiology, pathology, therapy and cure"), which is dominant, serves to conceal doubt and confusion. It also tends to discourage looking for other reasons to explain disturbing behaviour (Fawcett et al, 2004, p 137-9). The issue quickly becomes not one of whether or not there *is* an 'illness', but "*which* treatment should be given, *when* and *where*". (Moreover, the model acts as if it were produced in a social vacuum, whereas it is widely accepted that discourses of race and gender – and social class – influence constructions of 'acceptable' and 'unacceptable' behaviour.) Where 'conduct disorders' are concerned, the normal diagnostic labels allow for a wide variety of behaviours to be included – from lying and disobedience to self-harm. And since conduct problems are the common presenting problem among young people, such 'problems' may well be seen as "statistically" normal. Much of the behaviour may be nothing more than "non-conformity".

While never denying that many young people do experience mental illness, Coppock reiterates the claim made elsewhere that the process of definition and identification "has as much to do with the feelings and behaviour of other people, and with social customs and routines, as with anything happening inside their heads" (Malek, 1991, p 44; see also Coppock in Franklin, 2000, pp 139-54, and Hill and Tidsall, Chapter Seventeen of this volume). For instance, how young people are labelled often depends on the 'system' to which they are first referred – education, health, social services, criminal justice – with each one having its own form of diagnosis and labelling. Thus a child may be given the parental label of "*emotionally and behaviourally difficult* (education – special needs), *beyond parental control* (social services), *conduct disordered* (health – psychiatry) or *young offender* (criminal justice)". Not only does this reveal the arbitrariness of the labelling process, but equally worrying, how the label "is contingent upon the first point of contact, identification and referral".

In common with other contributors to this volume, Coppock is concerned with children's rights, which are especially problematic in the contentious area of mental health. Rights critiques have been widespread with reference to adults, and are increasingly so with respect to young people (see Fawcett et al, 2004, pp 141-3). Children usually become involved in the mental health system for a variety of reasons. Once in the system, however, 'control' becomes overtly medical and, as 'young people', they find themselves at risk from oppressive treatments defined as "therapy": behaviour modification, solitary confinement, and drugs, each of which raises matters relating to civil liberties. Furthermore, since the majority of young patients are held as 'informal' patients, there is no legal framework to safeguard their rights (unlike 'formal' patients who are protected under the 1983 Mental Health Act). Similarly, the issue of 'informed consent' has aroused great controversy. Despite attempts to make professional practice more responsive to the concept of 'rights', the failure of the courts to allow children to refuse consent to medical treatment, an inherently paternalistic attitude, has seriously undermined the principle of the 'Gillick-competent' child (see James and James, 2004, pp 156-61).

The third concern of this chapter is what is known as the current so-called 'crisis' of childhood. Since the mid-1990s an increasing number of children and adolescents have found themselves caught within the web of the mental health complex with one in 10 children under the age of 11 being diagnosed with a mental health condition (see Coleman, 2000, pp 230-42; Fawcett et al, 2004, p

131). This worrying trend is illustrated by the rising number of people being diagnosed with Attention Deficit (Hyperactivity) Disorder (ADHD) who are being treated with drugs, despite disquiet among many professionals about the uncertainty of the evidence for the 'disorder'. (Mental health services in general, however, continue to be described as "under resourced, inadequately staffed, fragmented and ill-equipped" to meet the needs of children; Kurtz, 2003; see also Fawcett et al, 2004, pp 131-45; James and James, 2004, pp 161-2.) As Coppock observes, the dramatic rise in concern, and the alleged increase in, mental disorders among young people of different ages, has to be seen in relation to the "childhood in crisis" theory, popular among politicians, the media and some professionals, that has been in evidence since the end of the 1980s and which was given momentum by the killing of a two-year-old by two eleven-year-old boys in 1993. As Goldson (Chapter Fourteen) and James and James (Chapter Fifteen) show, a continuing suspicion of young people has been evident in the approach of New Labour since it came to power in 1997, particularly in its punitive programme for dealing with troublesome/troubled children (see Goldson, Chapter Fourteen and James and James, Chapter Fifteen and 2004, pp 167-88). It would be hard to deny that now, just as in the past, definitions and demarcations of health and ill-health, normal and abnormal, are "riddled with social and political meanings". However, this does not mean that such demarcations are entirely and always nothing more than 'social constructions'. For instance, a forthcoming study, 'Time trends in adolescent mental health' does seem to show that the mental health of teenagers in Britain has declined during the last 25 years (*The Guardian*, 13 September 2004). Even so, Coppock is surely correct in maintaining that if children are to be treated in a more democratic manner in the future, we shall need to resolve the contradictions inherent in adult–child relationships for only then can "adultism be deconstructed and the human rights of children and young people respected".

One of the most important of all social contexts for the lived experience is that of 'health'. The inverted commas are meant to alert readers to the fact that health is a classic example of a socially constructed concept, which is particularly relevant where children are concerned since their understanding of good health is not always the same as that of the adults around them (Mayall, 1996). Malcolm Hill and Kay Tidsall, in their chapter (Sixteen), rather than focusing on particular policies, provide a comprehensive survey of understandings of, and connections between, "children and health". After a brief consideration of what is meant by 'health', the authors discuss the following topics: perceptions of health, understanding illness, risk in relation to health, accidents, behaviour, and risk taking, health differences and inequalities, responsibilities and rights, and children's health services.

The prevailing view of positive health as that which includes mental or psychological well-being, as well as physical health, although laudable in some respects, does make it difficult to distinguish 'health' factors from relationships between "the body, the mind, emotions, lifestyles, cultures and social structures". The medicalisation of the totality of life, as the chapter recognises, may easily serve to deflect social and political critiques into matters of medical management, technology and service provision. This is evident in the authors' discussion of 'risk' in a variety of contexts, which they relate to the wider risk discourse as presented in the work of Ulrich Beck (1992), the influential German social scientist.

Within this discourse, risk is related to 'accident', which can be tracked as a pattern and as something predictable. The result is that the victim can be blamed for not taking greater care, for not foreseeing what was likely to happen. In other words, "health promotion" as risk is individualised, "as a new form of social control and state regulation", rather than being, as the discussion of health differences and inequalities shows, the product of levels of income and social class. Life is no longer to be "lived healthily, but virtuously" (Fitzpatrick, 2001, p 8, quoted in James and James, 2004, p 140). And, as Coppock argues with respect to mental health, children and adolescents are increasingly the target for health scares of one sort or another: obesity, stress, alcoholism, anorexia nervosa, teenage pregnancies, smoking, and brain damage from use of mobile phones. Such an emphasis, with its accompanying statistics, fails to observe that, for example, 80% of children are not overweight and that 75% of children do not suffer from stress (James and James, 2004, pp 140-1). However, as Hill and Tisdall make clear, this is not to deny that many children, especially those from underprivileged backgrounds, do face a number of health risks: for example, those relating to respiratory illnesses, traffic accidents, deaths from fire, dental deterioration, and birth weight (see also Daniel and Ivatts, 1998; British Medical Association, 'Growing up in Britain', 1999).

The authors conclude that while childhood is a period of relative good health, compared with later life stages, policy has tended to concentrate on "surveillance, curative medicine and health education", rather than, say, poverty and the local environment. On the other hand, the government's major policies on reducing unemployment and social exclusion, together with its commitment to eradicate child poverty, will undoubtedly lead to further improvements in health, although as one leading researcher has warned, "the assessment of changes in health status is difficult and mostly relies on proxy measures" (Kurtz, 2003, p 173). A recent comprehensive study on the state of child well-being shows that there has been some improvement in reducing child poverty; infant and child mortality; encouraging breast feeding; survival rates for cancer and cystic fibrosis; injury death rates; suicides and teenage pregnancy rates. There has, however, been a deterioration in terms of obesity; immunisation from measles; diabetes; asthma; HIV/AIDS; smoking, alcohol and drug use; and parental reporting of long-standing illness. The same study also noted that data for monitoring child well-being was inadequate (Bradshaw, 2002). What still requires urgent consideration is the involvement of children in the management of their own health needs, rather than as is usually the practice of perceiving 'needs' in terms of "the prospects they hold out for a healthy adult life in the future", which tends to marginalise children as healthcare consumers (James and James, 2004, p 157; Mayall, 1996). The government, however, is currently unveiling its long-awaited 'National Service Framework for Children, Young People and Maternity Services', which is claimed will make the health service more child-centred.

Some of the important issues concerned with 'health' and its sociological meaning are also raised by John Davis et al (Chapter Eighteen), who provide a critical assessment of the recent change in the way that disabled children and young people are characterised in social policy. The chapter charts the shift from the medical model of disability that presented children as passive, vulnerable and in need, to a social model, emphasising social inclusion, that sees disabled children as rights holders, active citizens and requiring full inclusion in educational and recreational activities. The authors claim that this shift in perception and practice, which was underpinned by 'social structural discourses', is problematic: they say that the social model and social inclusion perspectives tend to homogenise disabled children, thereby ignoring their differences and complexities.

On the basis of ethnographic data, and in accordance with the prevailing emphasis on consultation and participation, Davis et al maintain that if an effective policy framework is to be created, "social policy must take as its point of departure the accounts of disabled children". The requirement is for a multilayered approach, central to which "are strategies that help develop dialogue, empowerment and interdependency between children, young people, parents, policy makers, practitioners and peer group". At present, it appears that there is too much emphasis on the nature of the impairment and associated services for care and support, which leads to children with special needs being generalised within a pathological model of childhood. When asked about their own needs: "disabled children's aspirations about future employment and family life seem to reflect those of non-disabled children, and are more a reflection of their gender and socio-economic backgrounds than their status as children with disabilities" (Priestley, 1998, p 217, quoted in James and James, 2004, p 165). What these children want is "respect": "It's like you want help, but you don't want charity" (quoted in Davis et al, in this volume).

Anne Skevik's chapter (Nineteen) provides a timely reminder that while feminist social policy has developed new concepts for analysing welfare state provision and variation, 'children and social policy' remains a neglected topic, particularly the study of the differences in policies for children. Indeed, Skevik is blunt: "Social policy is not for children". And this is not as exaggerated as might appear since current concerns, within the context of the government's social investment strategy, focus on one or more of the following: children in their futurity role, in relation to adults through social inclusion, as hindrances to mothers' labour market participation (through expansion of childcare provision), and as reluctant participants in the creation of a new code of civic responsibility (Fawcett et al, 2004). Skevik seeks to explore social security from the child's perspective (see also Ridge, Chapter Five), and in so doing shows that an explicit emphasis on children in policy analysis reveals aspects of welfare states that are hidden in adult-centric studies (for the invisibility of children in comparative European social policy, see Fink in Fink et al, 2001, pp 172-6; see also Ridge, Chapter Five this volume).

The chapter is a comparative study of social security policies for children living with one parent and the development of universal child benefits in Britain and Norway. Two features in particular are identified: "the separation of parenting and partnering for the purpose of social benefits, and the extent to which the 'worthiness' of the parents determine transfers to children". Unsurprisingly, the evidence suggests that the UK is much closer to the 'organic' view of the family: what is good for 'the family' is good for everyone in it. Consequently, in the UK children are seen as primarily the responsibility of their parents: "the state deals with parents, and parents deal with children". Norway is much more individualist in its approach, seeing "a man, a woman, and a child who are linked to each other by biological and legal ties".

In the organic conception of the family, women and children tend to be background figures in relation to the husband and father:

> If the man in the house dies, the adult woman is elevated to the status as head of the household, while the orphaned child remains in the shadow. The widow may be awarded some social benefits to help her cope ... [which] may include additions for dependent children, but the child has no independent rights as an orphan. This implies that the benefits are lost to the family if the widow remarries or starts cohabiting. As soon as there is a new man in the household, the family unit is seen as reconstituted. There is no separation of the roles as partner/spouse and parent. A second point is that ... families who do not correspond to the uniform ideal are often branded as inferior ... divorce, cohabitation and unmarried motherhood are to be discouraged ... irresponsible and unfortunate behaviour must not give easy access to state money.

The child, however, remains out of view behind the parent.

The 'individual' family provides for more direct contact between children and welfare:

> When a man dies, he leaves both a widow and an orphan ... the child can have claims on the state even if the mother does not. Even if the mother does not qualify for widow's pensions, or she ceases to qualify through remarriage, the orphan may still qualify. Parenting is distinctly separated from partnering.

Such a view encourages a lack of discrimination between widows and orphans and one-parent families in the sense that whatever reservations there may be about family form, "the child cannot be blamed or punished for the sins of the mother". The most striking difference between Norway and the UK, says Skevik, is that the former has a policy towards parents and children, while the latter has a policy towards families (Fawcett et al, 2004, pp 31-50), which is clearly visible in benefit policies and in arrangements for child maintenance.

Lucinda Platt (Chapter Twenty), in her detailed analysis of administrative data on benefit receipt for the city of Birmingham, continues the theme of how the social security system penalises certain groups of children. She begins by noting the commitment of the present government to eliminate poverty within a generation and its attempt to improve racial equality with the 2000 Race Relations Amendment Act. Platt's study, however, reveals a disproportionate impact of poverty on children from particular ethnic groups since, aside from racial discrimination and structural disadvantage, "even an equitably administered benefit system can systematically disadvantage certain minority groups by the way the rules are established", and Britain has one of, if not the most, complicated benefit systems of any welfare state. Platt highlights a number of specific impacts not revealed in global studies. For instance, in focusing on children in non-working families receiving either Income Support or income-based Jobseeker's Allowance, she shows that the severity of poverty can vary within the population of those who claim means-tested benefits. This in turn reveals the inequalities of the benefit system, as it relates to children's ethnicity.

With an emphasis on the importance of a child-centred approach to children's needs, particularly in relation to benefit payments, Platt focuses on the proportion of children in each minority ethnic group, and is able to demonstrate that "very little of children's poverty can truly be considered transient and without impact". She finds high proportions of Bangladeshi children living in "chronic poverty, with 43% living in families with a chronic shortfall", followed by slightly smaller proportions of Pakistani and Indian children living in poverty. A slightly higher proportion of Black Caribbean children than White UK children live in families with a chronic shortfall. Bangladeshi and Pakistani children in particular, owing to the greater prevalence of large families in their communities, have "higher shortfalls of income relative to needs" than do children from other ethnic groups. And children in large families are at greater risk because the system tends to favour those living in the modal family of one or two children. One reason why benefits impact in this way is that rather than *children's* needs (in large families) being the first priority (see Chapter Nineteen), the main concern is to keep benefit incomes below wage levels in order to minimise disincentives to labour market participation, which leads to a payment scheme that "relatively favours the first or only child". According to Platt, the results of her study imply that the structure of the benefit system "is not consistent with the government's commitment to both the elimination of child poverty and overcoming discrimination".

Both Skevik and Platt's chapters are relevant to Paul Daniel and John Ivatts' account of 'Housing policy and children' (Chapter Twenty-One), since all three testify to how easily children are either ignored or subordinated in the policy process, which is usually primarily concerned with adults in their individual roles, rather than as being responsible for children. This wide-ranging and informative chapter is divided into two main sections: the consequences for children of post-1979 housing policies and homelessness. Under the first heading a number of topics are discussed: increased home ownership, negative equity and repossessions, the residualisation of social housing, the sale of council houses, less affluent households, single parents, minority ethnic children, poor families, the geographical segregation of the poor, and poor families in rural areas. Homelessness is examined primarily with reference to developmental retardation, psychological effects, physical well-being, and education.

The chapter opens with a reminder of how critical proper housing is for the development of children, and the younger the child, "the more important is the quality of the physical shelter and of the immediate environment". Nor is it merely a question of 'homelessness' or not, for the nature of accommodation produces indirect effects: overcrowding, dilapidated conditions and lack of space can make good parenting difficult, just as warmth, security, gardens, and other facilities can help to promote effective parenting. Furthermore, adults in sub-standard accommodation can seek out alternative (mainly recreational) circumstances; young children and their mothers have far few such opportunities and, therefore, good housing is particularly critical for them. In the sense that it represents 'home', housing is more than just a physical context; it embodies a variety of psychosocial needs which, through human interaction, help us to shape 'feelings', and these in turn are crucial to understandings of self and identity on the one hand, and, on the other, to the meanings we ascribe to, for example, 'family', 'haven', 'security' and 'warmth' (Mallett, 2004).

In several respects, children have undoubtedly benefited form housing policies since over half of British houses have been built since 1945 and a number of amenities have enriched their lives beyond the dreams of earlier generations. But, of course, large numbers of children have been among the worst affected in those areas with remaining housing problems. The authors are damning in their condemnation of politicians as they charge that in no other area of government has so little heed been taken of the consequences of policies for children. Both the New Right and New Labour have sacrificed children's welfare in this respect to their ideological goals as low priority is given to social housing, and council dwellings are being sold off at the rate of 50,000 annually. Other influences, such as the pressure to be a 'two-income family', longer working hours, and extra time spent commuting – all in pursuit of being able to afford ever more expensive private housing, are "insidiously detracting from the quality of child rearing, or at least making life more stressful for many parents and potential parents". And yet, time and time again, the child's experience of living in, as well as the longer-term consequences of, poor accommodation is simply ignored. If we listen, Skevik's (Chapter Nineteen) statement repeats itself: "Social policy is not for children" (see also Chapters Twenty-Five and Twenty-Six). No wonder Daniel and Ivatts conclude pointedly:

> Children's lives are demeaned and distorted – sometimes perhaps beyond repair – by bad housing conditions; and often their health may be seriously undermined and their educational opportunities unnecessarily restricted and impoverished. There is therefore a strong case for arguing that any measures to improve the housing circumstances of less well-off families would achieve more for children's welfare than any other social policy reforms.

The relative invisibility of the hardship of so many groups of children has, until recently, been widespread, and even now the degree and extent is often disputed. The emotive and analytic power of 'the family' (and of 'parents'), as several chapters have shown, is difficult to bypass in search of the child as an individual. Housing and social security benefits are obvious examples. Less easily identifiable are 'young carers' (of disabled parents), who continue to struggle for an identity separate from their parents. It was not until the 1990s that the existence of 'young carers' (under 18), of which there are about 50,000, was recognised and their significance appreciated, thanks largely to the pioneering research of Aldridge and Becker at Loughborough University (Aldridge and Becker, in Franklin, 2002, pp 208-15). During the course of the decade there was, and continues to be, as is shown below, criticism from within the adult social model disability movement as to the identification of young carers as a welfare category and as being in need of 'rights'.

In their chapter (Twenty-Two), Bibby and Becker trace the government response to the recognition of young carers, the course of implementing accompanying legislation, the development of 'young carers' projects', children's rights and disability rights, and the move towards a family-centred approach. Legislation in 1995 and the publication in 1999 of the government's National Strategy for Carers, covering nine different areas, were important landmarks in official recognition. The implementation of the legislation, however, was not always successful since the important 'assessment of a carers' needs' occurs only if requested by the young carer and the take-up rate is low. On the other hand, the development of 'young carers' projects', funded from statutory sources and by the voluntary sector, in support of young people, was more successful.

Young carers pose an interesting dilemma for our perceptions and expectations of children in that they exhibit a dual status: they are children (and adolescents) in need of support as children, but they also have a separate set of needs as carers:

> Young caring transgresses the social construct of 'children' as a group occupying distinctly the realm of 'childhood', where they have the right to physical and emotional sustenance, protection from harm, and where they are allowed to make the gradual transition to 'adulthood'. Indeed, when children undertake caring at what might be deemed an inappropriate age, they occupy a distinctly 'adult' realm simply on account of what they do. (Aldridge and Becker, in Franklin, 2002, p 211; for the adult 'social model' critique of the value of 'young carers', see Olsen and Clarke, 2003, especially pp 69-102)

However, the call by young carers' advocates during the 1990s for a rights-based framework not only revealed the ambiguous status of the carers, it also proved to be controversial within the adult disability community.

Adult disability activists alleged that research into young carers, together with the rise of a young carer literature, further silenced the voice of the (adult) cared for, especially those who were parents (Olsen and Clarke, 2003). The critics claimed that the rights of young carers were being given precedence over those of the people for whom they cared. Rather than see resources going to young carers, the preference, they argued, should be to put resources "into integrated living schemes and personal assistance, which would render dependence upon young carers unnecessary" (Shakespeare, in Lewis et al, 2000, p 58; Keith and Morris, 1994/95). This may be sensible in the long term, but it ignored the possible negative and restrictive impact in the here and now that 'caring' may have on children's development (Fawcett et al, 2004, p 151). Another criticism levelled at the young carer approach was that it involved giving 'rights' to children that non-disabled parents would find undermining of their role as parents. This was interpreted as disempowering disabled adults, many of whom were suffering from low income and transportation and support problems (Keith and Morris, 1995, pp 36-57; Olsen, 1996, pp 41-54; Aldridge and Becker, in Franklin, 2002, pp 216-18).

What emerged from the debate in 1998 was a 'family perspective' that incorporated a children's rights framework within the social model of disability (Becker et al, 1998). This perspective emphasised support for the whole family: the focus was on helping disabled parents to be *parents* and, therefore, possibly to avoid the need for their children to act as carers in any unusual capacity. At the same time, the perspective emphasises on behalf of young carers, "the importance of the right to assessment and to support, advocacy, information and counselling services ... [and] ... to be included in family discussions about needs, assessments, service provision and the rehabilitative programmes for their parents" (Fawcett et al, 2004, p 153). But there are dangers here for young people. The emphasis on the family "can fail to differentiate between different wants, expectations and support needs, and can gloss over the context of an individual's life and the full interplay of family relationships, especially power relationships" (Fawcett et al, 2004, p 155). To see children either solely or mainly as in the context of the family, as the 'new' sociology of childhood has shown, is inherently restrictive, since children also have meaningful lives in the external world (James and James, 2004).

In her critique of 'education and the economy', Sally Tomlinson (Chapter Twenty-Three) focuses on a particular aspect of what she refers to as "education in a post-welfare society", that is, a society in which the needs of global capitalism are a major influence on national economies and, therefore, on government policies. The environment in which the alleged demands of globalisation are met is 'the social investment state' (see Lister, Chapter Twenty-Five), where the concept of 'human capital' is drawn on in order to promote the work ethic and to create a skilled and adaptable workforce, which can effectively participate in a competitive (national and international) labour market. The reasoning is succinctly expressed in a government pamphlet: "Investment in learning in the 21st Century is the equivalent of investment in the machinery and technical innovation that was essential to the first industrial revolution. Then it was capital, now it is human capital" (DfEE, 1996, quoted in Tomlinson, 2001, p 4; see also Hendrick, 2003, pp 216-24). The counterview that there is little in the way of evidence showing a direct correlation between school performance and national economic competitiveness was, and is, largely ignored; nor are variables such as class, gender and race given much consideration (Tomlinson, 2001, pp 4, 154; Wolf, 2002). Education is also deemed to be important because it is regarded as connecting children to a comprehensive strategy for reducing social exclusion (which emphasises individual failings), with all its attendant social, economic and behavioural problems. So, on coming to power in 1997, the New Labour government identified the centrepiece of its domestic policy as: 'Education, education, education'. In the words of Tony Blair, the Prime Minister: "[I]t is great for the individual, it is right for society and it is also economically essential" (Blair, in *TES*, 5 July 2002). The fundamental assumption governing this policy is that of classical liberal economics: "education is an investment which lifts individuals out of poverty by increasing their returns in the labour market" (Woodward, 1997, p 2, quoted in Tomlinson, 2001, p 154).

After providing a brief account of the recent history of education policy, and discussing the evolution of the labour market in the 1990s, Tomlinson queries the extent to which the much hyped 'new economy' is indeed that new or that extensive. One of her key themes, however, is the nature of the relationship of the global economy to education. The term 'globalisation', refers to "processes of trade and financial flows, information and communications technologies, movement and migration of people and their labour, and cultural convergences between countries exemplified by ... music, jeans and MacDonald's". In such a world, the fit between education and employment, especially between highly skilled workers and national economic competitiveness, remains 'problematic'. Furthermore, exactly how education affects 'the poor' is another area of uncertainty. Tomlinson maintains that "qualifications and skills and lifelong learning will be of use to individuals only if there are economic and political policies which aim for a secure and productive life for all members of a society". At present, she says, existing policies help to legitimise inequality and the exclusion of the socially weak.

In the conclusion to her study, which is the second part of the chapter included here, Tomlinson views education as having passed since the mid-1970s "from being a key pillar of the welfare state to being a prop for a global market economy". Since the 1990s there has been a decided move away from 'welfare' as a social right to it being conceived primarily as a functional means to 'work'. In the Third Way politics of New Labour, the welfare state has evolved into more of a social investment state, which is to operate in the context of the 'positive welfare society' where "the contract between individual and government shifts, since autonomy and the development of the self – the medium of expanding individual responsibility – become the prime focus" (Giddens, 1998, p 128, and Lister, Chapter Twenty-Five). In other words, personal responsibility is to be exercised in pursuit of employment. Unsurprisingly, in such an environment, nowadays education has little to do with reducing social inequalities; its economic significance overshadows everything else. Of course, the economic content of education has always been important, and rightly so. What is new is the exclusivity of this aspect of education in opposition to the traditional humanist claims made on its behalf, such as developing the potential of the individual.

Other commentators have similarly argued that viewing education simply as a branch of economic and social discipline has at least three undesirable consequences: "It severely limits the exercise of informed professional judgement by teachers; it seriously undervalues the arts and humanities ... and it does not fully or properly take account of the implications of poverty, deprivation, and social change ..." (Tomlinson et al, 2000, p 244). We need to remember that 'education' is more than the ability to be able to read and write and to count (however indispensable these skills are in themselves); it should involve "the inner life of the young" who must be given "the tools of personal autonomy and relationship". After all, preparation for life "demands investigation and exploitation of resources of the human psyche, of imagination and the creativity of the human spirit" (Tomlinson et al, 2000, p 252). However, the government's continued efforts to create what it calls a 'world class' education system, through the market mechanism (inherited from the Conservatives), has certainly benefited the middle class and aspirant groups (although whether it benefited the children as *children* is open to debate). On the other hand, as Tomlinson claims, 'education markets' did not "encourage social balance in schools, equalise opportunities or help the socially excluded, and social segregation in education worked against the possibility of preparing good citizens who care about each other". When, then, the government refers to 'world class' education, the question is 'Whose world?'.

The critical and controversial chapter on daycare (Chapter Twenty-Four) is included here as an antidote to the numerous publications emanating from Higher Education social policy departments (and those of the government), advocating institutional daycare for young children. Penelope Leach, a psychologist, and a prominent advocate of children's welfare and rights, and author of several best-selling childcare books, argues against the current trend towards providing universal and comprehensive daycare provision for parents (in practice, more often than not, mothers) of young children. In the publications of academic social policy, the majority of which appear to assume that it is a 'good thing', Leach's critical work seems rarely to be cited, if ever, as her position in emphasising the importance of 'mothercare' for very young children, is regarded as 'traditional' and 'conservative' (also rarely cited is Morgan, 1996, and the leading academic critic, Belsky, for example, 2001, 2002; Moss and Petrie, 2002, are critical of some forms of daycare, such as where the intention is *simply* to facilitate greater employment opportunities for mothers, but not of the principle itself; see also Brannen and Moss, 2003, especially pp 36-41). Feminists object to what they see as the 'mothering persona' advocated by Leach (even though she hedges it with qualifications), since it is said to specifically obstruct gender equality in the labour market, and generally to undermine the feminist project to distance women from childcare, the home, housewifery, and the 'private' (female) as opposed to the 'public' (male) spheres of civil society.

This chapter is openly 'ideological' in that it does not conceal its normative programme behind a facade of a purportedly objective social scientific style of presentation. The argument is not expressed in terms of a sociological paradigm, a theory of early education, a critique of current social constructions of childhood, but simply as one of the ways in which society (adults) could do more to make life better for children today, not least by acknowledging our *moral* responsibilities ('obligations') *to* small children (O'Neill, in Alston et al, 1992, pp 24-42; see also Hendrick, 2002, pp 280-1). Leach goes to the heart of contemporary debate in identifying the driving forces behind the current campaign to expand daycare as being "about big issues like the economy, the labour market and women's votes; it is not about the small people whose care IS the issue". As she says, "The truth is that institutional daycare offers advantages to adults that have nothing to do with infants' safety or happiness". Leach is one of the very few writers on the subject to speak of children's *happiness*. The noun refers to a feeling of pleasure or contentment, which is presumably a desirable end of adult relationships, but it never seems to figure as a factor in the writings of advocates of Early Childhood Education and Care (ECEC).

In issuing her direct challenge to the ethical priorities of those who favour the huge expansion of daycare now under way, with further expansion promised for the future, Leach is by no means a solitary voice – although, as mentioned above, it is one that is rarely heard in academic circles. (However, for a thoughtful feminist analysis see Ribbens et al, in Carling et al, 2002, pp 110-28 and 199-217.) The implicit censorship concerning public debate on the matter, was graphically illustrated by the furore surrounding an article in *The Guardian* (8 July 2004) which, drawing on the disputed findings of a large research project, reported that the government may be rethinking its advocacy of day nurseries for children under the age of two in the face of mounting evidence that nursery care can lead to aggression and antisocial behaviour. The author of the article (Madeleine Bunting) was assailed by the daycare lobby and by feminist journalists, who accused her of leading an 'anti-feminist backlash' (for feminist responses, see Polly Toynbee who obscured the issue by fusing it with anti-abortionism, religious fundamentalism, and the 'aggressive' fathers' rights movement in order to claim: "Women have no choice now but to halt this backlash", *The Guardian*, 14 July 2004; see also the dismissive Leader in *The Observer*, which ridiculed the research report as a "scare story", 11 July 2004; for a similar response from the creator of the Sure Start programme, see Benjamin, *The Guardian*, 14 July 2004). Bunting countered the numerous attacks with the warning that if we cannot debate how we care for babies "we're sunk", and went on to observe: "It's an extraordinary paradox that, just as we're discovering the importance of that early parental care, we've – and this applies just as much to you, Dad – never been so quick to hand it over to someone else" (*The Guardian*, 19 July 2004; on the importance of parental care for babies, see Abrams, *The Guardian*, 17 July 2004, and the acclaimed synthesis of the latest findings in neuro-science in relation to why love is essential to brain development in the early years of life, by Gerhardt, 2003).

The daycare issue is usually presented in two main forms. First, it is claimed that greater public childcare provision will provide opportunities for mothers (especially poor, lone mothers) to become wage earners and, therefore, lift themselves and their children out of poverty and its multifarious disadvantages. Second, it is also claimed that daycare in a proper 'educational' sense helps to promote social and cognitive development in young children. But there is much more to the matter than these claims admit. The objective of many, perhaps the majority, in the ECEC lobby, certainly those who are feminists, is to redefine the meaning of parental 'care' and the idea of 'motherhood' and, indeed, of what is always referred to – critically – as the heterosexual two-parent family as a social institution. Sonya Michel, a prominent American feminist welfare historian has written that feminists who are "seeking to *transform* the way in which young children are reared" can do "more good if they remain in the shadows while other social actors lobby for child care on behalf of interests that are not explicitly feminist.... The terms of such alliances may require feminists to cloak their own support for child care in the rhetoric of another interest group" (emphasis added). Consequently, "child care advocates have most frequently made common cause with early childhood educators, whose goals tend to appear more benign to wary publics ... *educators have helped overcome objections to placing small children in childcare by emphasizing the social emotional, and cognitive benefits in group situations*" (Michel, 2002, pp 333-4; emphasis added; see also Randall, 1996, 2000).

The lobbyists are much influenced by feminist (and postmodernist?) 'ethics of care', particularly as expressed in the writings of the American political scientist, Joan Tronto (1993) and the Dutch political scientist, Selma Sevenhuijsen (1999). For example, Peter Moss, Professor of Early Childhood Provision at the prestigious Thomas Coram Research Unit, University of London, and one of the leading ECEC advocates, refers critically to understandings of the "care" of young children as centring on a "dyadic adult–child relationship" before quoting approvingly from Tronto:

> Too often, care is described and defined as a necessary relationship between two individuals, most often a mother and child. As others have noted such a dyadic relationship often leads to a romanticization of mother and child, so that they become like a romantic couple in contemporary Western discourse. The dyadic understanding also presumes that caring is naturally individualistic, though in fact few societies in the world have ever conceived of child rearing ... as the responsibility of the birth mother. (1993, p 103, quoted in Brannen and Moss, 2003, p 36)

Of course, what is missing here is the view of the children, since they have not been asked for their opinion. No doubt children would have difficulty in grasping the coded message encased in Tronto's prose. Probably they just want to be happy wherever they are (for a glimpse of the less than satisfactory reality of nursery care, provided by a nursery manager, see Steele, *The Guardian*, 14 August 2004). Whatever our view on this controversial matter, the way that it is connected to governmental social and economic strategies, the professional ambitions of the ECEC lobby (both academic and organisational), and the ideological goals of feminism, shows it to be a classic example of the political deployment of concepts of 'child' and 'childhood', primarily for the benefit of adult interests.

The 1989 Children Act and children's rights: a critical reassessment

Jeremy Roche

In this chapter I consider the background to the 1989 Children Act and outline those provisions of the legislation that can be seen as promoting the welfare and liberty rights of children. I then examine some of the case law on the Children Act and, using recent research findings, attempt a critical reassessment of the legislation. I argue that what the promotion of children's rights requires is not so much amendments to the Children Act, although some useful amendments could be made, but a shift in adult thinking and practice concerning children. The demand for children's rights is a social and political project and while the 1989 Children Act can be seen as providing a framework for significant change it cannot bring this about by itself.

The demand for reform

The origins of the 1989 Children Act are complex. On one level the legislation was informed by a series of official reports including the Department of Health and Social Security review of childcare law (DHSS, 1985) and the Law Commission report on guardianship and custody (Law Commission, 1988). The message of these reviews was that the current law was unclear, unnecessarily complicated and characterised by procedural and substantive injustice. The government White Paper described its purpose in bringing forward proposals for change in the law relating to childcare and family services as the achievement of "greater clarity and consistency" to help "parents and children who may be affected by the law and those who work professionally within it" (DHSS/Home Office, 1987, para 4).

Running alongside these institutional reviews of the legal framework were the child abuse scandals of the 1980s, which centred on local authority social services practice (see generally Reder et al, 1993). The inquiry into the death of Jasmine Beckford found, among other things, that the social workers involved treated the parents as the client rather than the child: "Jasmine's fate illustrates all too clearly the disastrous consequences of the misguided attitude of the social workers having treated Morris Beckford and Beverley Lorrington as the clients first and foremost" (London Borough of Brent, 1985, p 294).

Further, the social workers were found to have "had no idea what the legal implications of a care order were" (p 207); failings of professional practice were a major cause of the "inevitable disaster" of Jasmine Beckford's death. The media response to this event was one of condemnation of the social workers involved for their failure to take timely action to protect the child.

In contrast the Butler-Sloss report into the Cleveland case criticised those involved (paediatricians, police and social workers) for their over-zealous approach to protecting the children believed to be at risk of sexual abuse. However, here the "villains" were the consultant paediatricians, not the social workers. In the words of the report:

> By reaching a firm conclusion on the basis of physical signs and acting as they would for non-accidental injury or physical abuse; by separating children from their parents and by admitting most of the children to hospital [Dr Higgs and Dr Wyatt] compromised the work of the social workers and the police. (Butler-Sloss, 1988, p 243)

Nonetheless, Cleveland was seen as an instance of the local authority over-reaching itself even though it took the actions it did on the basis of the diagnoses of the two doctors. Earlier the report had noted that for some children the child protection process itself was experienced as abusive – as Butler-Sloss observed, "the voices of the children were not heard".

Also in the mid-1980s the House of Lords gave its famous decision in the Gillick case. This case was concerned with whether the DHSS could lawfully issue a notice to the effect that while it was desirable to consult the parents of a person under 16 years of age who sought contraceptive advice and treatment, in some circumstances the doctor, exercising their clinical judgement, retained the right to provide such advice and treatment without informing the parents. Mrs Gillick sought a declaration from the High Court that this notice was unlawful. The case reached the House of Lords and in his oft-quoted judgement Lord Scarman held that: "The underlying principle of the law ... is that parental right yields to the child's right to make his own decision when he reaches a sufficient understanding and intelligence to be capable of making his own mind up on the matter in question" (*Gillick v West Norfolk and Wisbech AHA* [1985] 3 WLR 830 at 855)[1].

So, prior to the 1989 Children Act the law was seen as ineffective in promoting appropriate child protection practice and preventive work with families and as failing to involve parents and children sufficiently in decision making. It was also seen as being too complex and as failing to strike the right balance between family privacy and the power of the state to intervene to protect children.

The 1989 Children Act

In the words of the Lord Chancellor the legislation was the "most far reaching reform of childcare law ... in living memory"[2]. Section 1 of the Act laid down three key decision-making principles. Under the Children Act the welfare of the child was the paramount consideration[3], unnecessary delay was seen as prejudicial to the child's welfare and to be avoided, and the so-called no order principle required the court not to make an order unless it considered that "doing so would be better for the child than making no order at all". In addition the Act provided a "welfare checklist", ie a list of factors the court was required to take into account when hearing any contested application for a section 8 order and applications for orders under part IV of the Act[4]. With two exceptions the checklist was derived from existing case law. First, under section 1(3)(a) the court had to have regard to the "ascertainable wishes and feelings of the child concerned (considered in the light of his age and understanding)". While this was within the spirit of the Gillick decision it was both less and more than that decision[5]. It was less in the sense that on one reading of Lord Scarman's judgement the common law was recognising the decision-making autonomy of children – under the Act the court merely has to take the child's wishes and feelings into account. The court's view of the child's welfare will prevail. It is more in that the court has to consider the child's wishes and feelings as a matter of routine. Second, under section 1(3)(g) the court was required to have regard to the range of powers available to it in the proceedings in question. This provision allowed the court to make an order different from the order applied for and thus underlines the courts' new decision-making flexibility[6].

The Act introduced the concept of parental responsibility. This concept can be seen as promoting a new model of parenthood – once a parent always a parent[7]. For example, in the field of private law under the Act, parental responsibility for the child survived the making of an order for divorce. In the area of public law, even when a child was being 'looked after' by the local authority under a care order the child's parents 'shared' parental responsibility with the local authority. This was of symbolic and practical importance. Symbolically it served to reinforce the idea that you were always a parent – you still had the responsibility, even though in certain circumstances it could be circumscribed. Practically the concept was important because it linked either with other provisions in the Act or developments outside the legislation[8]. The intended net effect of the concept was to reduce the likelihood of matrimonial disputes over children and to promote partnership between the local authority and the parents of children in need and 'looked after' children.

Children and parents acquired new procedural and substantive rights under the Act. Parents whose children had been taken from the home under an emergency protection order could challenge the order after 72 hours. There was a presumption of contact between children and their parents both when the child was the subject of an emergency protection order (EPO) and when in care; children and parents had the right to take disputes about contact to court. Local authorities could not acquire compulsory powers over a child without the approval of the court[9].

The Act also envisaged a different kind of relationship between local authorities and families experiencing difficulties in bringing up their children[10]. Under section 17 of the Children Act the local authority was under a general duty to "safeguard and promote the welfare of children within their area who are in need" and "so far as is consistent with that duty to promote the upbringing of such children by their families, by providing a range of services appropriate to those children's needs". Under Part III of the Act the local authority was thus under a duty to provide support to families with children in need thereby safeguarding and promoting their welfare and avoiding the need for more coercive forms of intervention later. Such support was to be arranged on the basis of partnership between the local authority and the family (Thoburn, 1995). When children did end up in care, parents still had a right to be involved, section 22 imposing a duty on the local authority to consult with the child and the child's parents before making any decision in respect of the child.

Furthermore section 22(5) of the Act imposed a duty on the local authority to give due consideration to "the child's religious persuasion, racial origin and cultural and linguistic background" in making any decision about a child they were looking after. There were other provisions in the Act aimed at fostering respect for such identity rights of the child[11].

Finally, the Act repositioned the court, in some instances making it the key decision-making forum[12], in others withdrawing judicial scrutiny[13]. In the public law field the role and powers of the guardian *ad litem* (GAL) were redrawn in order to secure for the court the availability of a report from an independent welfare professional that was thorough and based on access to all the relevant information[14].

Children's rights

So in what ways can the 1989 Children Act be said to have advanced children's rights? The Act can be said to have advanced the 'welfare rights' of children through its endorsement of the paramountcy principle, the provision of the 'welfare checklist' and the no order principle[16]. The threshold criteria[17] can be seen as an attempt to limit state intervention into family life by requiring a minimum threshold of harm to be established before any compulsory powers over a family can be acquired by the local authority. Lord Mackay argued:

> It is not proper to intervene on any level of harm. The fundamental point is that State intervention in families in the shape of the local authority should not be justified unless there is some level – 'significant' is a good word for it – at which significant harm is suffered or is likely to be suffered. (cited in Allen, 1992, p 125)

Such a 'threshold' could be argued to promote the welfare rights of children by limiting the discretion of the local authority to intervene in the name of the welfare of the child – a concept that has been used and can be used to legitimate a very wide range of actions. Many of these, with the benefit of hindsight and from a more critical vantage point, appear to have undermined the welfare of the children involved (Robertson and Robertson, 1989). Even when a child did end up being 'looked after' by a local authority under a care order this did not severe the parent–child link. The local authority acquires 'parental responsibility' under the provisions of the Act but not such as to extinguish the parental responsibility of the parents in its entirety. The Act, also through its emphasis on the local authority providing supportive services to families with children 'in need', promoted children's welfare rights. Children are best looked after in their own families and the role of the local authority should be to support families in bringing up their children. Children are thus spared the trauma of having to leave their home with all the resultant damaging consequences for their education, self-esteem and identity. However, 'welfare rights' while important are not the only concern of the modern children's rights movement – such rights do not in any way challenge 'adultist'[18] assumptions about what children are like[19]. The liberty rights of children[20] raise very different issues.

There are four aspects of the legislation that can be seen as supportive of children's liberty rights. First, the Act allowed for the possibility that children themselves may want to make applications for one of the new section 8 orders[21]. Section 10 specifically provided for the eventuality in which a child applied to the court for permission to make an application for a section 8 order. The court can only grant the child leave to apply if "it is satisfied that he has sufficient understanding to make the proposed application". Nonetheless, the Act in its contemplation of the possibility of the child become a litigant could be seen as advancing and extending the child's autonomy.

Second, and linked to the above, is the departure from the settled rule that a child could not bring or defend an action except via a guardian ad litem or 'next friend', ie via an adult intermediary. Rule 9.2A of the Family Proceedings Rules 1991[22] provided that a child could prosecute or defend proceedings without a 'next friend' in two situations: where the proceedings are not "specified proceedings" and the child has the leave of the court and where a solicitor has accepted instructions from the child having considered in the light of the child's understanding that the child is able to give instructions[23]. These two provisions opened up the possibility for the first time of the child having unmediated access to legal services and the courts.

Third, a number of provisions of the Act gave the child, if he or she was of sufficient understanding to make an informed decision, the right to refuse to submit to a medical or psychiatric examination or assessment[24]. Thus section 44(7) provides that even where a court has directed that the child undergo a medical or psychiatric examination or other assessment the "child may, if he is of sufficient understanding to make an informed decision, refuse to submit to the examination or other assessment"[25].

Finally, under section 26 of the Act the child was given the right to complain about the local authority's discharge of their functions under part III of the Act. This applied to children in need as well as children who were being 'looked after'. Prior to the Act there had been no legal requirement on local authorities to set up complaints procedures. Local authorities were now required to set up such procedures and they had to have an independent element[26].

So while the Act can be said to have been concerned with the welfare of children, with much of the change focused on altering the power relations between local authority and parents and recasting the responsibilities of courts and local authorities, it also moved towards a recognition of the child as a legal subject. How does this assessment measure up in the light of subsequent events?

Ten years on: a critical assessment

Since 14 October 1991 when the Act was brought fully into force there have been a number of developments. Research has shown that some of the positive hopes for the Act have failed to materialise. Later I will consider whether this is due to shortcomings in the Act's framework or whether the roots of the 'failure' lie in the practices and attitudes of adults and professionals. But first I want to provide a brief summary of some of the research findings on the operation of the Act as a whole before exploring some of the case law and the research which examines how children fare when engaged with the law and legal processes.

Under section 17 of the Act, families with children in need should have had access to support services from the local authority; the provision of such services was seen as key to the safeguarding and promoting of children's 'welfare rights'. However, support on the basis of partnership for families with children in need as envisaged by section 17 has been undermined by wide variations among local authorities in their interpretation of children in need. Instead local authority practice concentrated on children 'at risk' – a resource-hungry strategy that was singularly unsuccessful as a preventative strategy[27]. Aldgate and Statham in their review of the research observe: "Several of the studies on family support services show clearly that in some cases that had been 'closed' by social services the children could be identified as 'in need' within the Children Act definition" (2001, p 22).

The Framework for Assessment provided an estimate of the numbers of children in need. It estimates that there are over four million children "living in families with less than half the average household income" (DH, 2000, para 1.1). Of these four million 'vulnerable children' there are between 300,000 to 400,000 children in need (para 1.6). The research by Thoburn et al (2000) into family support revealed that 98% of families whose children were at risk of suffering emotional maltreatment and neglect were characterised by the "extreme poverty of their material environment". Nonetheless, according to Brandon et al (1999) it is child protection concerns that constitute the gateway to support services. This is despite the wording of the guidance to the Act, which stated that the definition of children in need was deliberately wide to emphasise "preventive support and services to families"[28]. Clearly, in a context of substantial child poverty, the variations in the definition of children in need and the failure on the part of local authorities to comply with their statutory duties under section 17 has resulted in a lottery as far as support services for children in need are concerned[29].

In relation to the liberty rights of children there are three issues that capture the direction of the judicial wind in the interpretation of the Act; these are child litigants, children in court and the child's right to refuse medical treatment.

Early on there was anxiety about the so-called 'children divorce their parents' scenario. The social unease over the child litigant is neatly captured in an *Observer* article in 1993 by Polly Ghazi:

> Parents who turn up their noses when their children bury themselves in
> Viz, Smash Hits or Just 17 may be making a big mistake. The magazines

may soon contain advertisements for a booklet entitled Your Say in Court, which could have a significant effect on family relationships. Aimed at 10-to-16 year-olds it provides a step-by-step guide on how to 'divorce' parents. (*The Observer*, 25 July 1993)

There was also judicial unease about such child litigants. As a result, in 1993 the High Court issued a practice direction, which states that all applications for leave to apply for a section 8 order should be heard by the High Court (Practice Direction [1993] 1 FLR 668). The High Court has also decided that in considering such applications the court will have regard to three issues; what is in the child's best interests, if leave is granted is the child's application for a section 8 order likely to be successful, and the jurisdiction to allow child applications should be cautiously applied and only exercised when matters of importance are raised. In *Re S* [1993] 2 FLR 437 Sir Thomas Bingham MR, referring to the Act requiring a balance to be struck between two principles, observed:

> First is the principle to be honoured and respected, that children are human beings in their own right.… A child's wishes are not to be discounted or dismissed simply because he is a child. He should be free to express them and decision-makers should listen. Second is the fact that a child is, after all, a child. The reason why the law is particularly solicitous in protecting the interests of children is because they are liable to be vulnerable and impressionable.

So the judiciary have imported further requirements, which had to be satisfied before the High Court would give leave to a child to apply for a section 8 order; they did so on the basis of the child's vulnerability. This high threshold seems to conflict with the spirit and the letter of the Gillick decision.

Linked with this anxiety about the child as a legal subject is a concern with the child who is a party to proceedings being visible, being in court. Section 95(1) of the Act provides that when hearing any proceedings under parts IV and V of the Act the court has the discretion to decide whether or not the child should attend the hearing or a specified part of the hearing. The 1991 Rule 16(2) of the Family Proceedings Courts (1989 Children Act) Rules provides that the proceedings can take place in the absence of a child who is a party if the court "considers it in the interest of the child, having regard to the matters to be discussed or the evidence likely to be given" and the child is represented by a GAL or solicitor. Rule 11(4) states that the GAL must advise the court on a number of matters including the child's wishes regarding attendance at court. In *Re C* [1993] the GAL supported the 13-year-old girl's wish to attend the care proceedings; she was present throughout the proceedings before the family proceedings court. When this case went to the High Court on appeal, even though no party objected to the presence of the child, Waite J. ruled that "young children should be discouraged from attending High Court appeals from the justices in family proceedings". He urged GALs to give very careful thought beforehand to whether children should be present and that they should be prepared to explain their reasons to the judge. The more recent case of *Re H (Residence Order: Child's Application for Leave)* [2001] 1 FLR 780 reinforces this image of the absent/silent child object. In this case a 12-year-old boy wanted to intervene in his parents' divorce proceedings in order to ensure that he ended up living with his father. The High Court refused his application for leave to apply for a residence order on the ground that as father and son were of one mind on this matter there was no argument that might be put to the court on behalf of S which would not be advanced on behalf of the father. In the course of his judgement Johnson J. stated (p 783):

> I would wish to assure S that the judge ultimately deciding where he shall live will take full and, indeed, generous account of his wishes, but I see no advantage to the court in making that difficult decision or advantage to S himself in his being legally represented. Whether or not he would be allowed to be in court is a matter that would be decided by the judge hearing the final issue, although, speaking for myself, I would doubt that the judge would allow S to be in court[30].

The paradoxical message is clear; the child who is the very reason for the court sitting need not necessarily be heard or seen directly. The advice given to GALs and the extra barriers put in the way of children applying for leave to apply for a section 8 order testify to the judicial disquiet with the idea of the visible participating child. In their own interests children should not be witness to the resolution of the conflict in which they are central.

The case law on the seemingly clear-cut right given to children by the Children Act to refuse to submit to a medical examination or assessment provides further proof of the difficulty judges experience when faced with the imagery of the autonomous child. As noted above, under the Act children were given the right to refuse to submit to a medical or psychiatric examination and assessment, and in so doing the Act was merely putting on a statutory footing the House of Lords decision in Gillick[31]. However, in *South Glamorgan County Council v W and B* [1993] 1 FLR 574 the High Court gave leave to the local authority under section 100(3) of the Act to bring proceedings to invoke the High Court's inherent jurisdiction in the event of the 15-year-old girl's refusal to submit to the psychiatric assessment ordered under an interim care order (see section 38(6) of the Act). She did not consent and the High Court exercised its inherent jurisdiction to order that the assessment proceed and therefore by-passed the 'right' given to mature minors under the Act. Brown J. stated: "In my judgement, the court can, in an appropriate case ... when other remedies within the Children Act have been used and found not to bring the desired result, can resort to other remedies". So the 'mature minor' enjoys the right under the Children Act to refuse to submit to a court-ordered assessment but this right can be 'trumped' in 'appropriate cases' by the High Court's exercise of its inherent jurisdiction[32].

Perhaps we are asking too much of the judiciary. Required as they are to give paramount consideration to the welfare of the child, it is perhaps not surprising that they err on the side of caution[33]. In addition to the judicial caution evidenced by such cases the research into the operation of the Act paints a picture in which it is not just courts but professionals who are uneasy and struggle with notions of children's rights once they extend beyond the right to welfare.

The Act gave to children the contingent right to instruct a solicitor. Research has revealed how fragile this right is. Sawyer (1995) in her research into the way solicitors assess the competence of children to participate in family proceedings found that they varied in their approach. The process of assessing competence was seen as neither simple nor clear-cut, for instance age was one factor but not the only one. Sawyer found that lawyers went beyond what was demanded of them in their legal role when it came to assessing the competence of the child with welfare considerations regularly intruding, especially in private law cases (1995, pp 95-96)[34]. In considering the question of the separate representation of children in family proceedings she notes that two concerns are raised. First "there is the question of whether having a right to state 'wrong' opinion is so good in itself that it necessarily outweighs the risks inherent in the advocation of a view of the child's welfare which may be incorrect" (1995, p 168). In the public law context this concern is resolved by the involvement of the GAL – who can put a 'better view'. There is also the issue of "whether having the right to speak out and be heard … gives rise to any risks in the child's position outside the proceedings, including his or her own individual family relationships" (1995, p 168). In the private law context this is the familiar 'children should not have the burden/responsibility put on them' argument[35]. According to Sawyer the idea of Gillick competence "cut little ice" with the practitioners in the context of private family proceedings (Sawyer, 1997, p 20). Sawyer observed (1995, p 169)

> Few believed that even a competent child's view should always be followed; even the interviewees committed in principle to 'children's rights' appeared to proceed with considerable paternalist – or parentalist – assumptions in practice, albeit they used different formulations to justify the exercise of the function[36].

In Sawyer's more recent research (1999) into the role and work of the court welfare officer (CWO) in the context of private law disputes she confirms earlier work that depicts their role as one of promoting parental agreement wherever possible in order to avoid a formal trial of matters relating to the children (see also Piper, 1993). Only where this is not possible will they report to the court on the child's welfare. While they saw contact as the 'child's right' and believed in principle in seeing the child, very few actually did so. Further, "Some CWOs would only see children if effectively forced to do so in the final stages of preparing a welfare report for a contested hearing; this was then done in order to avoid criticism or re-referral by the court" (Sawyer, 1999, p 262). Sawyer also writes that (1999, p 261):

> The idea of involving the children as an active participant in the process was not on the everyday agenda at all. Even when an older child was seen and listened to this was often unwillingly and for the practical

reason that some older children are capable of disrupting arrangements parents have been helped by CWOs to make.

Lyon et al (1999) explored the support needs of children when their parents break up. In their examination of the way in which the present system supported children they found a number of serious shortcomings. Children were given little information about the process or their rights. Some of the young people involved in the research were angry "that they were being denied access to a crucial service of information concerning the issue of parental relationship breakdown and the potential impact of divorce proceedings on children and young people" (para 2.06)[37]. There was no information available informing young people of their rights in relation to divorce and its aftermath, in particular their right to make an application to vary the post-relationship breakdown arrangements that did not meet their self-defined needs. One respondent said:

> Looking back, I think that we should have been given much more information. We didn't have a clue as to what was going on and the whole thing was just a muddle in my head. I think that I should have had someone to talk to, and maybe have some influence on the custody arrangements.

Children might want to be included in some way and to have access to proper information about the divorce or separation process, to know where they stand in relation to this and what their rights are in such situations. On occasion they might want separate representation and the services of a lawyer – although, as Sawyer concludes, much will depend on the lawyer they approach (Sawyer, 1997, p 21). However, perhaps a key stumbling block to seeing children as legitimate legal actors lies in the idea of family privacy. Feminists have already radically altered our understanding of the idea of family privacy, asking among other things 'whose privacy?' Okin argues (1989, p 184):

> the family in which each of us grows up has a deeply formative influence on us. ... This is one of the reasons why one cannot reasonably leave the family out of the "basic structure of society", to which the principles of justice are to apply.

She goes on to observe that if we properly address the question of justice within the family it will be a "better place for children to develop a sense of justice". However, while Okin is concerned first and foremost with gender, considerations of children rights should prompt a rethink on two issues. First, that it should no longer be assumed that women's interests are always coincident with those of children. Second, children may have their own view on a host of issues associated with family life and their life within the family. Beck alerts us to the democratisation of family life and argues that "equality of rights for the child certainly collides with the protection of the family and requires or allows the deprivatisation of privacy to a certain extent" (1997, p 162).

In the public law context, Masson and Winn Oakley in their research into the representation of children in care proceedings found that "neither children's interests nor their wishes are strenuously advocated by their representatives" in every case (1999, p 136). They found that despite having party status in care proceedings children were not on "an equal footing" with the other parties (1999, p 14). They write:

> Representation of children and young people in these proceedings is largely based on shielding them from the process rather than assisting them to participate ... their party status does not help to make the proceedings real for them[38].

The unsatisfactory aspect of this situation in both the private and public law fields is expressed by Sawyer in her rehearsal of the arguments in favour of children having access to legal services. She writes:

> The essential advantage of involving the legal process, from the participants' point of view, may be seen as ensuring that people have a chance to speak on matters which concern them so that everyone may be satisfied that justice is done. (1995, p 163)

Perhaps what is at stake here is the idea of actually listening to children and treating them with the same equality of concern and respect you would adults. The practical and symbolic issues raised by this are particularly awkward and controversial when it is the child who wants to make a public issue out of a private trouble[39].

These findings should not surprise us. In the widespread distrust of welfare professionals so fashionable since the 1980s perhaps we have lost sight of the sociology and socio-legal literature of the 1960s and 1970s, which explored the myriad ways in which clients were routinely vulnerable to professionals working to their own agendas. In the midst of the concern about the abuse of power by welfare processionals, lawyers and courts were elevated to the only guarantors of procedural and substantive justice. No longer was law a 'con game' (Blumberg, 1969), it was the only process whereby the decisions of welfare professionals could be held accountable. If adults are vulnerable to the imposition of agendas by professionals, how much more so are children. What the above discussion of professional practice on the part of some lawyers and court welfare officers reveals is a paternalistic disregard. Too often children do not count – and certainly not enough to displace the systemic inducements to do other than fully advocate for one's client.

Smart and Neale (2000) in their research into children's perspectives on post-divorce parenting refer to a "newer debate" as to whether professionals working in the family justice system are adequately "ascertaining the wishes and feelings of the child". They observe in the context of recent research and policy debates that the shift away from seeing the child as an inevitable victim whose welfare must be safeguarded, towards a framework within which the child is seen as a potentially active participant in his or her own family's progress is probably only slight, yet it is potentially important.

Smart and Neale found that children wanted to share in a certain amount of information, but they did not necessarily want to carry the burden of adult responsibilities. "They wanted to be respected as children and young people, not as if they were adults" (2000, p 165). Later they observed that the children in their research distinguished between participation and choice although where "children were frightened of, or disliked a particular parent, they were often much more forceful in insisting that a child should decide on his own who he should live with." They conclude that the invitation to participate (not as yet extended to children) might "oblige us to start to approach the whole issue of ascertaining the wishes and feelings of the child in a different way".

Conclusion

What underpins much 'law talk' about children is a concern to protect them (from others, themselves and their own choices) and an anxiety about them. Children are idealised and demonised (Griffin, 1993), there is little space in between for a more honest conversation about children, family life and social justice. The suspicion that surrounds children is undermining of the UNCRC but is also being resisted and challenged. The demand for inclusion, for the right to participate, is central and integral to the project of imagining different kinds of adult–child relations – although the form such conversations might take is uncertain, especially in professional settings. Children's rights are about rethinking and redefining adult–child relations and are a means "with which to articulate challenge and hold to account relationships of power". As Federle argues (1994, pp 355-6):

> ... rights claims challenge existing hierarchies by making the community hear different voices. Community and claiming are part of a slow historical process that will invigorate the debate about children's rights and will, someday, lead to a better life for children through the articulation of ideal relationships between children and adults in the larger community.

There is debate as to whether the 1989 Children Act still provides an acceptable framework for children's rights[40]. Some changes have been argued for and legislation introduced. For example, the 2000 Care Leavers Act seeks to improve on the Children Act by imposing more carefully defined duties towards care leavers on local authorities. There have been calls for the role of GALs to be extended to private as well as public law matters[41]. This looks as if it has been superseded by the plans to establish the Children and Family Court Advisory and Support Service[42]. The 'Children are unbeatable' campaign has argued for the end of the parental right to chastise their children. Given that the UN

Committee on the Rights of the Child recommended in its response to the UK government's first report to the Committee that the UK tackle the question of the parental right to chastise, it is perhaps time that a provision was enacted bringing this right to an end[43]. However, the direction of change seems to be quite different. Two recent consultation papers reveal the government's concern to emphasise notions of parental right rather than children's rights. First, in *Protecting children, supporting parents* (DH, 2000) the government in response to the decision of the European Court of Human Rights in *A v UK* [1999] 27 EHRR 611 asks where the line should be drawn in law as to the acceptable physical punishment of children. The consultation paper ruled out outright abolition of this parental right on the grounds that public opinion[44] was against such a ban, it would be contrary to 'common sense', it would bring the law into disrepute and fails to see that smacking has an educative role[45]. As if this was not bad enough the government more recently has issued a consultation pack on National Standards for the Regulation and Inspection of Day Care and Childminding. In this it is suggested that childminders subject to parental agreement should be able to smack a child in their care and smoke. Both proposals have been condemned (Haynes, 2000) and taken together can be seen as reinforcing notions of children as the property of their parents. How else is one to understand the proposal about smoking, which contradicts the government's own campaigning on the subject.

I am left with two observations: the way in which we think about children and children's rights has to shift and in that process adult practices including professional practice centering on children will shift. Continued reliance on the language of children's rights is part of this shifting process but one that does not necessarily lead to direct change in the law. The rhetoric of rights is as much about shifting our imagination as it is about specific demands for legal change. We might all benefit from taking children and their rights more seriously. Masson and Winn Oakley suggest (1999, p 144) that "greater opportunities to participate, where they wished to do so, might encourage some children to engage with the proceedings". This would necessitate "changes in court practice, such as clearer use of language, shorter hearing and more attention to the needs of ordinary people" – this would also benefit parents, relatives and carers. Perhaps the law reduces 'us' all to children. We also need to follow through the implications of Smart and Neal's observation that "the subtleties of family relationships may not be captured by such a brief and alien intervention in which children may apparently be quizzed on their views for the first and only time in their childhood" (2000, p 168)[46].

Finally, these shifts in thinking about children will be uneven, contested and championed in different ways, in different places and in this sense the 'politics of childhood' (and 'children's rights') will intensify. Increasingly children themselves are challenging and resisting adult constructions of incompetence (see Anderson, 2000). If we do not grapple with the negative ideas associated with children, and their imprisonment between innocence and threat, to socially include children in public and private spaces they will remain distrustful of irregular and sporadic adult invitations to participate, on adult terms, for adult purposes and within adult agendas. The children's rights project involves both the law and agitation around the law and legal processes. Some of the disappointing jurisprudential and policy developments since the 1989 Children Act came into force testify to the fragility of the children's rights project[47]. They serve to underscore the idea that it is also a cultural project, which necessarily straddles the public and private sphere and requires adults to rethink their attitudes towards children and childhood.

Notes

[1] One concrete consequence of the House of Lords judgement was that those who worked in family planning settings were now reassured that they would not be acting unlawfully in providing such advice and treatment – this was of practical significance for many young women – see 'Victory for Mrs Gillick is a tragedy for thousands of young people', *Guardian* 30 January 1985.

[2] It has also influenced childcare legislation in a number of jurisdictions, eg Malta, Ghana.

[3] Under the previous legislative framework the welfare of the child had been the 'first and paramount' consideration.

[4] These were applications for care and supervision orders and education supervision orders.

[5] Lord Mackay said in Committee: "This Bill does nothing to change the underlying Gillick principle, which has to be taken into account by all who exercise parental responsibility over a child mature and intelligent enough to take decisions for himself" (*Hansard*, House of Lords, vol 502, col 1351).

[6] The Act also blurred the boundary between public and private law in part through the ability of the court to make any order, not just the order applied for, in family proceedings.

[7] I am indebted to Katherine Gieve for using this phrase in an interview with me on the Children Act conducted in 1990.

[8] For instance, changes to divorce procedure whereby there is less judicial scrutiny of post divorce arrangements relating to the children and the development of mediation services both link with the concept; as the Booth Committee commented on conciliation: "It is of the essence of conciliation that responsibility remains at all times with the parties themselves" (1985, para 3.10)

[9] The local authority is still the gatekeeper to the system. In *Nottinghamshire County Council* v *P* [1993] 2 All ER 815 the Court of Appeal stated that the court cannot force a local authority to apply for a care order even though, as in this case, the local authority had applied for a prohibited steps order.

[10] The White Paper referred to the provision of services by a local authority as a "positive response" and not as a mark of failure either on the part of the family or the professional involved. "An essential characteristic of this service should be its voluntary character, that is it should be based clearly on continuing parental agreement and operate as far as possible on a basis of partnership and co-operation" (White Paper, para 21).

[11] For example, section 74(6) provides that in considering the needs of any child for the purposes of deciding whether the care provided by a child minder is "seriously inadequate" the local authority must have regard "to the child's religious persuasion, racial origin and cultural and linguistic background".

[12] With the ability to control its own proceedings.

[13] For example, the retreat from divorce. See Bainham (1990) and Roche (1991).

[14] Under section 42 the GAL was given extensive rights of access to records held by the local authority and the NSPCC.

[15] By welfare rights I am referring to the child's right to basic provisions such as shelter, food and clothing as well as the care and protection of children.

[16] Although the welfare principle has been subject to substantial criticism – see, for example, Reece (1996).

[17] Section 31(2) of the Act provides that a court may only make a care or supervision order if "it is satisfied – (a) that the child concerned is suffering, or likely to suffer, significant harm; and (b) that the harm, or likelihood of harm, is attributable to – (i) the care given to the child, or likely to be given to him if the order were not made, not being what it would be reasonable to expect a parent to give to him; or (ii) the child's being beyond parental control".

[18] See Dalrymple and Burke (1995).

[19] See, for example, Kohm and Lawrence (1997-98, p 369) who see Articles 12 and 14 of the UNCRC as blurring the line between adulthood and childhood.

[20] By liberty rights I am referring to those rights associated with the child's autonomy interest, e.g. the right to make their own decisions on matters that concern them.

[21] These are contact orders, prohibited steps orders, residence orders and specific issue orders. These orders are very flexible and the court can make a section 8 order on its own motion as well as on application.

[22] This came about as a result of amendments to the Family Proceedings Rules in April 1992. At the time the change was not seen as particularly important (see Thorpe, 1994).

[23] The solicitor is under a duty to take instructions directly from the child where the child is in conflict with the GAL. In *Re H (A Minor) (Care Proceedings: Child's Wishes)* [1993] 1 FLR 440 the court referred to the solicitor's failure to take instructions exclusively from the child when there was clearly a conflict between the child and the GAL as constituting "a fundamental forfeiture of the child's right".

[24] For example, under an interim care or supervision order – section 38(6).

[25] This is again consistent with the Gillick decision.

[26] The 1991 Representations Procedure (Children) Regulations laid down minimum standards with which local authorities had to comply.

[27] Another consequence of such an approach was the failure to invest in innovative preventive support work with families.

[28] The Guidance continued (DH, 1990, vol 2, para 2.4): "It would not be acceptable for an authority to exclude any of [the three categories of children in need] – for example, by confining services to children at risk of significant harm which attracts the duty to investigate under section 47."

[29] Other aspects of the legislation's emphasis on partnership have also failed to materialise. The Act required the local authority to have regard to the racial, cultural, religious and linguistic background of any child they are looking after. However, social work as a profession is not immune from the institutional racism that pervades many social institutions. Dutt (2000) and Dutt and Phillips (2000) analyse the problem of racism within social work practice. See also Barn et al (1997)

[30] The court had accepted that he had sufficient understanding to make the application for leave. Later Johnson J. refers to the "spectre" of the "mother being faced across a courtroom by solicitor or counsel acting on behalf of the child she bore". Clearly such an image is more compelling than that of a child rendered silent and invisible by judicial practice – of course justified on the basis of the child's welfare – although this is far from self-evident.

[31] The courts had started the retreat from Gillick before the 1989 Children Act came into force (see *Re R* [1991] 3 WLR 592 (see, generally, Roche, 1996a). More recent cases on medical treatment and the rights of the mature minor include *Re L (Medical Treatment: Gillick Competence)* [1998] 2 FLR 810 and *Re M (Medical Treatment: Consent)* [1999] 2 FLR 1097.

[32] In contrast the 1995 Children (Scotland) Act inserted into the 1991 Age of Legal Capacity (Scotland) Act the following provision:

A person under the age of sixteen years shall have legal capacity to consent on his own behalf to any surgical, medical or dental procedure or treatment where, in the opinion of a qualified medical practitioner attending him, he is capable of understanding the nature and possible consequences of the procedure or treatment. (section 2(4) of the Age of Legal Capacity (Scotland) Act)

[33] O'Donovan (1993, p 95) reminds us of the ways in which the law denies children's subjectivity. It does so by seeing only those aged 18 years and over as full legal subjects, by seeing children as lacking those attributes that are the prerequisite of legal subjectivity, e.g. capacity, and by dealing with children via a paternalistic discourse. O'Donovan also comments on the double-edged quality of the welfare principle, noting that welfare itself is often a good reason for ignoring what the child says.

[34] Again the Scottish legislation provides a nice contrast. The 1991 Age of Legal Capacity (Scotland) Act as amended by the 1995 Children (Scotland) Act provides (section 2[4A]) that "a person under the age of sixteen shall have legal capacity to instruct a solicitor, in connection with any civil matter, where that person has a general understanding of what it means to do so". Later it states the presumption that children aged 12 years or over have such understanding.

[35] However, children might not welcome 'enforced intimacy' in whatever professional/ formal setting it takes place. The meaning and feel of professional intervention may be very different for child and professional. For many children having some control over both agendas and outcomes is what matters – hence the appeal of Childline, whose success is based on offering a confidential service. Research carried out by Childline confirms that it is this confidentiality that is so important to children who phone about all kinds of issues, including relationship breakdown. It is of note that children who make use of their service often just want a totally safe place to talk about a matter that concerns them and often children are able after such a confidential conversation to decide for themselves what they will do.

[36] See also Diduck (2000) who writes of lawyers' support for limiting children's involvement in divorce disputes.

[37] This echoes Lyon and Parton's (1995) question "how do children find out about their rights to use Section 8 orders?".

[38] Piper (1999a) argues that the 'good' family lawyer sees him- or herself, as among other things, being involved in 'client-handling'. See also Smart and Neale (1999, chapters 8 and 9) for an analysis of the changing role of family lawyers.

[39] Where the family is together and it is the child who is seeking to bring an issue before the courts, the anxiety raised is understandable – but I would argue this is not a good enough reason for denying children a right of access to legal advice and representation (Roche, 1999, and Lim and Roche, 2000). Where the parents are separating this privacy argument gives way to a paternalistic concern to protect the child from full knowledge of all that is involved in the period of transition and redefinition.

[40] For example, the Mostyn Report (1996) argued that change to the law was needed in order to make a more positive contribution to the prevention of child abuse. It also recommended that legislation based on the UNCRC should be introduced in order to secure the rights and needs of children.

[41] In *Guarding children's interests* (The Children's Society, 2000) the children interviewed in the research made it clear that they valued the role of the GAL and saw the ideal GAL as someone who listened to them and explained the legal process. However, some children did have a negative experience – e.g. one child thought that confidentiality had been breached.

[42] At this early stage it is hard to state whether this move will be of any benefit to children. There is a suspicion that the changes are driven by cost-cutting considerations rather than the desire to refine the mechanisms whereby the child's voice can be heard in the legal process.

[43] This would both signal and be a sign that there had been a shift in the way children are viewed although the 'success' of such a move would be dependent on other initiatives centering on children. See, for example, Durrant and Olsen's (1997) interesting analysis of the Swedish experience.

[44] They did not include children in this.

[45] For a useful review and summary, see Roberts (2000).

[46] This links with ongoing debates about what is happening to the family. See Beck (1997) and Roche (1999). Note also the different direction taken in Scotland. The 1995 Children (Scotland) Act departed radically from the legislation in England and Wales and was influenced by the provisions of the UNCRC. Section 6 of the Act imposes a duty on parents to consult with their child on any major decision. The Scottish Law Commission had consulted on this matter. It stated (1992, paras 2.62-64):

> The question as we saw it was whether a parent or other person exercising parental rights should be under a similar obligation to ascertain and have regard to the child's wishes and feelings as a local authority was in relation to a child in its care.... There are great attractions in such an approach. It emphasises that the child is a person in his or her own right and that his or her views are entitled to respect and consideration.... On consultation there was majority support for a provision requiring parents in reaching any major decision relating to a child, to ascertain the child's wishes and feelings so far as practicable and give due consideration to them having regard to their age and understanding.... Many respondents clearly regarded such a provision as an important declaration of principle.

The Act also provides that children aged 12 or over are presumed to be capable of forming a view.

[47] But not all; the current war on child poverty is a good example of a positive development that might provide space for other children's rights initiatives, e.g. enhanced participation in their local communities.

This chapter was taken from Franklin, B. (ed) (2002) *The new handbook of children's rights*, London/New York: Routledge. The right of Jeremy Roche to be identified as author of this chapter has been asserted by him in accordance with the 1988 Copyright, Designs and Patents Act.

Assumptions about children's best interests: the risks in making assumptions about harm to children[1]

Christine Piper

In the family justice system, despite past judicial protestations that there are no 'rules of thumb' and that each case is decided on its merits (see, for example, *Pountney and Morris* [1984] 4 FLR 381; see also Hayes and Williams, 1999, pp 264-7), there operate judicial ideas about what is generally believed to be good and bad for children. Family law lecturers have produced, discussed and amended lists of such 'non-rules' over the years, explaining to undergraduates the 'principles' on which courts apparently make decisions about the residence and upbringing of children. These 'considerations' (see Bromley and Lowe, 1992, pp 384-94), whether relating to maternal preference, the status quo, parent–child contact, blood ties (see Weyland, 1997), have similarities (assumed or made explicit) with the findings of social and medical research and, in that sense, have been based on what might loosely be termed 'child welfare science' (King and Piper, 1995, chapter 3). The resulting generalisations, made by professionals working in the family justice system, are theoretically rebuttable in individual cases because they are only generalisations about what is best for children.

In relation to private proceedings in the family justice system, the most influential assumptions can be grouped into two clusters: the first set coalesce around the idea that children need, above all, two parents who cooperate with each other and who both keep in contact with their children. The second set concerns the vulnerability of children in the context of decision making within the legal system. The last few years have seen the production of a growing body of converging social science research results showing how these assumptions operate in practice and the potentially deleterious effects if applied inappropriately.

Children need parents to be reasonable

Several empirical research projects in the mid-1990s focused on the practice of family law solicitors. Solicitors interviewed believed that 'getting parents to act sensibly' was their main aim: "It's a question of working out what's reasonable and sensible' and getting over to parents how important it is for 'children [to] continue to have a relationship with both parents and [to] see that, as far as they're concerned, the parents can communicate and talk about them" (King,

1999a, p 261; see also Neale and Smart, 1997). The assumptions underpinning this approach are that parental conflict (and particularly conflict played out in court) is very bad for children and that contact with both (biological) parents should be ensured. As Kaganas (1999) has pointed out, these pro-contact and cooperation assumptions have become stronger since the early 1980s, and judges and the Law Commission have referred, generally and specifically, to empirical research. So influential are such assumptions now, that solicitors acting for 'opposing' clients may at times appear to be "acting in concert in the face of one (or two) difficult parents" (Bailey Harris et al, 1998, p 29). Indeed, solicitors must ensure they do cause parents to act sensibly if they themselves are to be deemed sensible by judges (Bailey Harris et al, 1998, p 29) and 'good' lawyers by their colleagues (Neale and Smart, 1997, pp 337-8).

If family justice professionals start with the strong assumption that contact is beneficial then, very easily, parental opposition to what is perceived so clearly as a 'good' is 'explained' away as implacable (unreasonable) hostility. Similarly, a child's reluctance to stay overnight with a non-residential father 'must' be the result of deliberate alienation by the other parent. Davis and Pearce, for example, note a particular instance where a "district judge lambasted a resident mother who had dared to assert, in the course of a directions appointment, that her daughter (aged five) did not want to see her father" (Davis and Pearce, 1999a, p 238; see also Sanders, 1999). The professional pressure to deliver a parentally agreed outcome may inhibit the questioning of parents in case issues emerge that would work against that outcome. Some practitioners have expressed views almost akin to the adage that one should let sleeping dogs lie in order not to jeopardise parental cooperation or contact (Hester et al, 1997, pp 17, 40). While subsequent initiatives in guidance and training may have altered practice substantially, as recently as 1995 court welfare officers and mediators expressed views against screening for domestic violence on the basis that it might encourage allegations, as did speakers in the parliamentary debates on the Family Law Bill (Kaganas and Piper, 1999, pp 185, 196). Humphreys has referred to a 'judicial alienation syndrome' to describe a similar judicial blindness about the domestic violence context in contact disputes (1999), although there are now exceptions, notably the approach of Hale J (now LJ) in *ReD (Contact: Reasons for Refusal)*, where she stated that "'implacably hostile' should not be used to describe mothers whose fears 'are genuine and rationally held'" (*Hale, LJ [1997] 2 FLR 48 at 53*; see also In *Re L (a child) (Contact: Domestic Violence) and others*, CA, *The Times*, 21 June 2000.)

Furthermore, if parents do not agree about contact they are perceived as not acting sensibly and are deemed to have nothing to say which is 'sensible'.

Cantwell et al (1999, p 230) found parents who felt "disempowered, disrespected and defeated" and, who faced "an uphill battle to get their view of their son's needs heard". Davies and Pearce (1999a, p 239) similarly report instances of judges making "condemnatory" and "dismissive" remarks to such parents, who often "faced an additional difficulty in that their own solicitor might be advising them that resistance was pointless".

Without these corollaries, practitioners and judges might more often hear about and respond appropriately to domestic abuse. There are still professionals who believe abused partners will always tell them about abuse (Piper and Kaganas, 1997) and who may, therefore, refer parents to joint meetings that pose a risk to their safety – a concern currently being expressed in relation to parent education classes in the US (Fuhrmann et al, 1999). Furthermore, professionals might discover that the father has insufficient parenting skills to look after and play with a child, or has no suitable accommodation in which to care for a child, or that contact might be so disruptive to the care-giver that the quality of care for the child is affected (Cantwell et al, 1999, pp 227-30). Looking at the situation of the family concerned (or listening to those involved) might make more visible those factors, relating to the individuals concerned but, also, to socioeconomic inequalities, which ought to be fed into the development of family-related policies.

Courts and answering questions are harmful

Another strong assumption in the family justice system is that children are harmed by the 'burden' of saying what they want (Cantwell and Scott, 1995) and particularly harmed if they take part in court proceedings. Professionals may consequently encourage agreement by portraying the law as "a very heavy handed thing" for family matters and by commenting to parents that, "the real answer to it is that those issues are dealt with by the responsible parents and not by the courts" (Piper, 1993, pp 146-7). Professionals, perceiving children as vulnerable victims of circumstances and of their parents, may also be reluctant to question children – directly or indirectly – about the outcome they would prefer (Fortin, 1998, pp 168-72). Judges similarly take a protective stance in relation to children being made parties to proceedings and to their presence in court (Fortin, 1998, pp 173-82).

There is, however, growing evidence that some children are not helped by their lack of involvement. For instance, ongoing research (the KIDS Project) with 8- to 14-year old children (of recently divorced parents) shows that some of that age group are concerned that the court welfare officer did not report their views and feelings accurately (Perry and Scanlon, 1999). Another study, using questionnaires completed by 14- to 21-year-olds, shows that a majority of them thought there should be an information or consultation service specifically for children and young people whose parents are separating, with individual respondents expressing the distress they had felt at not being heard (Lyons et al, 1999, pp 49, 197):

> My brother and I needed help ... but there didn't seem to be anyone to help us out in telling what we wanted and things just became awful. I tried to work everything out so it would be fair to everyone.... But no one listened to me and everything afterwards was just such a mess.

The power of assumptions

The widely accepted reading of what occurs in the family justice system is that parents, local authorities and others bring to the courts disputes and concerns about the upbringing of children and that courts, governed by the paramountcy principle in relation to the welfare of the child, seek to discover the best interests of the children before them. Where the evidence presented by the parties does not make that sufficiently clear, the court welfare officer is asked to see the parties and their children and prepare a report for the court, providing factual material about the family and outlining what outcome would most likely promote the child's best interests. The assumption that this apparently objective and empirically based assessment will occur where there are contested views about the child's best interests has been challenged by recent developments. The settlement culture (Neale and Smart, 1997; Bailey Harris et al, 1998; King, 1999), the use of mediation (Home Office, 1994a, chapter 3), the practice of non-privileged discussions with the parties at and before directions appointments (Home Office, 1994a, chapter 2) and, the development of methods other than traditional investigative interviews of parents separately for preparing reports (Home Office, 1994a, para 4.12) have modified the extent and nature of such assessment (James, 1995; Trinder, 1997; Davis and Pearce 1999a, p 240).

Furthermore, the legal precedents incorporating assumptions about children's welfare, as Davis and Pearce (1999a, p 238) point out, carry more weight when used – in the vast majority of cases successfully – to motivate agreement and to avoid adjudication than they do during judicial adjudication. The point at which the assumptions may receive scrutiny – in court proceedings – is, then, the point that is rarely reached because unchallenged assumptions promoted a parentally agreed settlement.

It is probable that assumptions carry less weight in public law proceedings where the individualised assessment of the child plays a greater part (see, for example, Hunt and Macleod, 1998; Brophy and Bates, 1999) but the empirical research on the family justice system discussed above would suggest that assumptions have become increasingly influential in the daily operation of the family justice system in relation to private proceedings, which are the focus of this [chapter]. The research also suggests that strong assumptions can result in discussion about the best interests of the child who is the focus of dispute becoming dominated by talk about an 'abstract' child and solicitors and judges in particular may respond to increased pressures on their time by referring to assumptions about the best interests of the abstract child as a substitute for further inquiry about the wishes and needs of the child in question (Neale and Smart, 1997; Bailey Harris et al, 1998; Piper, 1999a). The professional imperative to see what a particular child is like is, thereby, considerably reduced, and parental views about the welfare of that child may struggle to be heard if they conflict with assumptions, as indeed may the views of those professionals who wish to challenge assumptions. This is not to deny that particular presumptions about the welfare of children generally may be supported by the conclusions of research studies but, rather, that evidence as to whether they apply to the particular child whose upbringing is in question may not be sought.

That abstract assumptions should hold such sway over individuals working within the family justice system is clearly a product of our so-called scientific age. The academic critique of 'science', from within science and from the sociology of science (for an early text see Knorr et al, 1981), has undermined the uniqueness and authority of the scientific method itself but has not yet affected 'popular' conceptions of science and medicine: presumptions assumed to be based on scientific research are, for most of us, 'true' – they become facts. In contrast, religious 'truths' about the reincarnation or resurrection, for example, are no longer generally held to be true as they were in previous centuries.

Despite a popular and professional belief in the utility and authority of child welfare science, however, once ideas based on scientific research have been transferred to the discursive context of law, they become largely immune to scientific 'testing'. Those of us who have listened to our children complaining that their experiment at school or university has 'gone wrong', that it has not proved what it was 'supposed' to prove, might see an analogy here. The validity of the rule itself is not tested or challenged: the process and ingredients are. For the student scientist this may be a sensible course but, its benefits in relation to ascertaining the child's best interests are not so obvious because strongly held assumptions can preclude a search for explanations other than those which 'fit' the presumptions made. Alan Bennett's comments about his mother in a hotel lobby describe a not so dissimilar process:

> You see that woman over there? I think she's the owner of the hotel, and that fellow with her must be her nephew'. And when the woman came in next day by herself she'd say, 'Oh I see the owner's here. She must have quarrelled with her nephew', forgetting it was all invention in the first place. (Bennett, 1997, pp 48-9)

Of course, assumptions – rules of thumb – are needed to make professional life 'workable': reductionist tendencies are apparent in any pressured and complex area of activity. Moody and Tombs (1982, chapter 3) for example, showed how such working rules of thumb emerge in practice in the context of the work of the Scottish Procurator Fiscal. Given current financial constraints and the acceptance of child welfare specialists that, whatever the form of the enquiry, there can be no surety of a 'right' answer, it would be pointless to argue for a full-scale investigation in all child cases. Furthermore, assumptions do not always preclude investigation – they may, rather, trigger an investigation using section 37 of the 1989 Children Act (as revealed, for example, in the case of *Re M (Official Solicitor's Role)* [1998] 2 FLR 815 CA). Nevertheless, an awareness of how and why particular sets of assumptions have become so powerful is of more than academic interest: professional practice is affected by assumptions about the strength and provenance of assumptions. A clear indicator of the fact that the body of assumptions used within the legal system does not equate to unproblematic simplifications of the whole range of knowledge about children can be found by focusing on the assumptions that are powerful within that part of the system that deals with children who offend.

Assumptions in the youth justice system

The assumptions about what should and should not happen to children and young people are very different in the youth justice system. Where it is deemed that the seriousness of the offending warrants it, children aged 10 to 13 years and young people aged 14 to 17 years are prosecuted (see Code for Crown Prosecutors, 1995; Home Office, 1994b) and there is little concern about having minors in court. Indeed, *No more excuses* proposes training for magistrates so that they can talk directly to children (Home Office, 1997, para 9.6). Children must be there – and in certain circumstances can be named (Dodd, 1999) – and they must take responsibility for their wishes and actions, a responsibility that underpins the provisions in the 1999 Youth Justice and Criminal Evidence Act. This provides (sections 1-3) that, on a young offender's first appearance at a youth court, a referral order will normally be made on a finding of guilt. The young person, referred to a youth offender panel (sections 6 and 7) established by one of the local authority youth offending teams set up under section 39 of the 1998 Crime and Disorder Act, will then be involved in negotiating a contract (sections 8 and 9) about the activities in which they will engage in the referral period and about the expectations of outcome. These contacts may have serious consequences if the agreement is not kept by the offender (Schedule 1). Well-developed abilities to negotiate with adults, to act responsibly and to be held accountable for actions will be expected of the child or young person.

Similar assumptions about capability and maturity are evident in recent provisions for reprimands and warnings (1998 Crime and Disorder Act, sections 65 and 66). The latter – the second 'caution' – will also be accompanied by referral to a youth offending team, which will negotiate with the offending child or young person a preventative activity – a process that already occurs in the areas that have similar 'cautioning plus' schemes (see Audit Commission, 1996). In relation to all these new provisions, there are no assumptions made about the potential harm to the child of putting on them the burden of being involved in decision making and being at least partly responsible for outcomes that will affect their life.

These recent provisions are a culmination of policy trends apparent in the early 1990s. While they evidence a changed balance in regards to prosecution and diversion – apparent in the different wording of the two most recent Codes for Crown Prosecutors in relation to young offenders (Crown Prosecution Service, 1988, pp 64-5, 1994, paras 6.1-6.9) – and a greater stress on the responsibility of the child or young person, they are not in essence out of line with earlier juvenile justice policies. Throughout the 20th century, there were tensions between welfare and justice approaches, and policy never unambiguously enshrined an idea of the child as a vulnerable victim (Fionda, 1999). This different assumption in youth justice about the ability of children to be held responsible is not explained by non-law knowledge about the children who come into contact with the youth justice system. The research evidence about the abusive and conflictive family background of a large proportion of children who offend, particularly persistent offenders (Hagell and Newburn, 1994, chapter 7), those sentenced under section 53 of the 1933 Children and Young Persons Act for murder or grave crimes (Boswell, 1991) and those 12- to 14-year-old offenders eligible for secure training orders (Crowley, 1998), suggests that children who offend are not a watertight category, distinct in their characteristics from those dealt with in private or public law family proceedings. It might also suggest that intra-familial conflict is a relevant factor in many criminal as well as family proceedings. In addition, research about the educational level and general background of adult prisoners, for example, would suggest that those who commit (or continue to commit) offences are less, rather than more, likely to be capable of coping with the intellectual and psychological requirements of a criminal process (Morgan, 1994, pp 910-12).

'Scientifically', then, there is little basis to sustain the existence of two very different sets of assumptions within the one legal system – about the vulnerability and needs of children who come to the attention of the family justice system and, the capacity for rational wrongdoing of those who find themselves in the youth justice system. If that is so, it brings into question the authority of the assumptions that so influence professional practice.

How has this come about?

King has argued that, "What distinguishes modern society from past eras is ... the dependence for its stability upon the constant readjustment of highly differentiated systems for observing and making sense of the world" (1999b, p 8). Law is one such system in this 'multi-authority society' (King, 1997, p 15), which must continually adjust to changing ideas emerging from other systems in its environment. As a self-referential system (King, 1997, pp 26-8), however, law can only organise a readjustment within its own procedures, so that what emerges are new or revised legal communications. It is, then, legitimate to view law as 'enslaving' messages from child welfare science and, at the same time, to acknowledge law's dependent status. For, if law does not reconstruct authoritative external knowledge and could not, therefore, 'know' it or 'think' about it, its functional role of regulating issues and disputes arising in other social systems would be diminished. In that sense, the authority of law is 'challenged' when the external world produces reality constructions that are difficult for law to reconstruct and, thereby, absorb into its 'thinking'. Law has faced such difficulties in relation to dealing with family disputes and juvenile offending. What has resulted are two different selections of reconstructed external knowledge stemming from the requirements of the specific legal operations and social functions of these two sub-systems of law.

Law's capacity to regulate the family

Much of child welfare science has presented no difficulty for law. It could, for example, reconstruct attachment theory and 'know' it as a 'maternal preference' principle in case law. It could also use the legal notion of expert evidence to introduce and reconstruct other medical and psychological knowledge (see King, 1991; King and Kaganas, 1998). Law's functioning could have been undermined by one particular 'truth' generated by several scientific disciplines – that the legal process itself is bad for children in so far as conflict, dispute and the generation of polarised positions are intrinsic to it (King and Piper, 1995, pp 83-7). Instead, law's response to this, and to those political and scientific communications upholding the importance of the father's involvement (Kaganas, 1999), was the individualised, simplified and selective reconstruction into legal communications of non-legal ideas about contact and parental cooperation, which could then be used to encourage private settlement and mediation and to discourage applications to court and hearings in court.

Particular scientific notions have thus become 'legal' principles and precedents, assumed as 'true' and quoted as 'law' by divorce court welfare officers and by judges (Davis and Pearce, 1999b). The 'being said' of these principles within legal communications is what matters (Davis and Pearce, 1999b, p 146): what no longer matters – once science has become law – is empirical assessment of the consequences of legal decisions made. Such an assessment may then be made by, for example, psychological research. Those findings will be disseminated generally (Kaltenborn and Lempp, 1998) and may, potentially, be reconstructed by law again but will not affect a decision already made. Law's authority is intact and law no longer engages with a particular scientific notion except as its own legal communication.

Law's capacity to deal with offending children

In the 1970s and 1980s, the development, within the sociology of deviance, of theories that explained a career of offending as a product of the 'labelling' by justice agencies of someone as an offender, also constructed involvement with the law as bad for children. Other criminological studies, revealing structural, rather than personal, explanations for offending, produced constructions of reality that law could not easily 'know', given its central function of delineating culpability. Those working with these knowledges external to law organised diversionary processes and institutions – with their roots in social work, criminology and child welfare science. In Scotland, courts gave way to children's hearings. The scope of law's authority and workload in relation to decisions about such children and young people was apparently diminished. However, this meant that, in England and Wales at least, law's communications remained largely unreconstructed in relation to those children with whom the criminal law continued to deal – those convicted of the most serious offending. In addition, those very diversionary institutions that were the response to non-legal knowledge about offending subsequently developed law-like offence-focused criteria for decision making and used a 'tariff' approach to outcome (King and Piper, 1995, chapter 6). Recent initiatives in restorative justice, such as reparation and restorative cautioning, provide further examples of the (potential) reconstruction within law of ideas whose origins are external to law (Dignan, 1999, pp 53-9) to fit other objectives (Goldson, 1999) and to operate as legal communications.

The result of these two separate sets of responses by law was the consolidation of very different images of children – 'semantic artefacts' in autopoietic theory – in family and criminal law. That occurred, not so much because of the new knowledge 'out there' but because of the different functions of law in these two areas. Criminal law adjudicates on culpability and punishes in relation to the weight of that culpability: the accused child is potentially culpable and responsible and must be present in court to face their accusers. The requirements on children in the youth justice system are essentially the same as those on adults and the only other available response to knowledge about the capacities of children has come in the form of setting age limits of particular forms of legal process and outcome, notably in setting a minimum age where the child is presumed to be criminally liable. These rigid age boundaries (even more rigid now that the rebuttable presumption that the child of 10 to 13 years is *doli incapax* has been removed by section 34 of the 1998 Crime and Disorder Act) are themselves a reconstruction of scientific knowledge (by politics as well as law) and are, for example, contrary to developmental theories (Brannen, 1999, pp 145-7).

The use of reconstructions of child welfare science by the youth justice system has, therefore, been largely peripheral to the central function of the criminal law. Science incorporated via the provision of pre-sentence reports by social workers or probation officers affects the choice of outcome but does not influence the fundamental legal decision on culpability.

Furthermore, criminal law can function without 'knowing' very much of the external knowledge about children because Parliament imposed a lesser welfare test than the paramountcy test for use in the youth criminal jurisdiction (England and Wales): 'have regard to' the welfare of the child. The child's best interests are not the focus of criminal law's role and, consequently, the youth justice system does not have to make decisions about the child on the basis of 'non-legal' knowledge. Legal rules of thumb that are reconstitutions of child welfare science are not therefore central to the adjudicatory task of the criminal court. By contrast, without reconstructed external knowledge, the family justice system could rarely function to delineate norms and adjudicate 'best' outcomes for families and children, given the statutory framework with which it must operate. Furthermore, as the selection and reconstitution of ideas in both systems is determined by the needs of the system, it cannot, therefore, be taken for granted that prevailing assumptions incorporate current and comprehensive non-law perspectives on childhood.

Political messages

It is not, however, sufficient to conclude that the assumptions that constrain practice in the family justice system are simply inadequate and distorted representations of the range and complexity of scientific and medical knowledge about children and families. Such a conclusion ignores the fact that the assumptions may also be reconstructed political communications, notably communications about individual and parental responsibility. The specialist family lawyer is 'on message' if they convey the values promoted in government policy documents about the responsibility of parents (Eekelaar, 1999; Piper, 1999a). Magistrates, social and youth justice workers involved in putting into operation the new parenting orders will similarly be conveying the political importance of parents taking responsibility for their children's offending. This is not surprising: a piece of legislation, although written to fit into existing substantive law and practice, is a document that incorporates policy that law must reconstitute. Furthermore, where legislation is internally inconsistent, law cannot avoid a role in a political project whereby law is used "to give the appearance of having created shared values" (Dewar, 1998, p 484).

The currently important political message that individuals must take responsibility for their lives, their children and their actions is not a novel message: the giving of priority to the exercise of parental responsibility, if necessary over other aspects of the child's well-being, has a very long history (Piper, 1999b). What has a much shorter history is the development of a social and political willingness to blame parents for a variety of family and social ills, the turning point in this development being the passage of the 'Cruelty Act' (1889 Act for the Prevention of Cruelty to and Better Protection of Children). However, both law and politics have since reconstructed science to give priority to particular notions of parental harm which support functional objectives. As we have seen, law has reconstructed the message that harm is imposed on children by parents separating and being in conflict to encourage the two parents to make their own arrangements, to agree and to be cooperative, so aiding settlement and avoiding adjudication. Politics has also reconstructed that notion, based on the premise that "how families behave affects us all" (Home Office, 1998, p 5; see also Lord Chancellor's Department, 1993, p 16). The resulting political norm currently functions to reduce expenditure on social welfare and on legal aid, and to secure social stability through stable families and healthy, well-behaved children. Within law, we can see such ideas reconstructed as the goals of dispute minimisation and enhancement of parental authority and control.

Conclusion: the importance of theory

Law, then, responds to legislation that is, inter alia, an incorporation of political objectives and operates with case law, which is, inter alia, a selective reconstruction of child welfare science. This theoretical approach to analysing why particular assumptions about children's best interests have such authority and influence within that family justice system allows us to make a distinction between the people who work within that system and law as a system of communications. This is useful because, in practice, there has been a fudging of the lines between professional activities and boundaries in line with a professional discourse that stresses the benefits of inter-disciplinarity and multi-disciplinary working (Piper and Day Sclater, 1999). These often undefined terms either reflect an idea that benefits automatically ensue when professionals gain an understanding of how other disciplines and professions approach and solve problems (Murch and Hooper, 1992; Wall, 1997) or they appear to envisage the creation of a new hybrid: "a multi-faceted discipline" (Wall, 1995, p 52).

Whatever the focus, I would argue that multi-disciplinary working is not beneficial without some theoretical understanding of what multi- or inter-disciplinarity means. The current, untheorised approach to 'systemic' family justice has led to an uncritical over-reliance on assumptions about the child's best interests, not just by legal professionals but also by 'welfare' professionals operating within the family and youth justice systems. It has also obscured the fact that once a legal principle is formulated from external knowledge it remains law – whatever the developments in non-legal disciplines – until law can and does readjust to significant changes in its environment (King, 1997, p 20). Furthermore, professional confusion has ensued: it is not surprising that lawyers might sometimes reflect that what they are saying to clients may not really be 'true' (Piper, 1999a, pp 105, 108). Criticism of the unquestioning use of particular assumptions is now occurring but, without a clearer understanding of the nature of how different systems can and cannot operate alongside each other, there is a danger that 'ruling' assumptions will simply be replaced by their converse or by similarly over-simplified notions, newly reconstituted from scientific and political ideas. In that case, confusion and frustration among the providers and the customers of family justice will continue.

Note

[1] This [chapter] arose out of papers given at a conference organised by the National Council for Family Proceedings, entitled 'Assumptions and Presumptions in Family Justice Thinking' (The Tavistock Centre, 9 December 1998), and a seminar entitled 'Children, Parents and the Family Justice System' at Leeds University (22 April 1999). I am grateful to Michael King for his constructive comments on an earlier version of this article and, also, to the anonymous referees whose comments, in their different ways, were challenging and helpful.

This chapter was taken from the *Journal of Social Welfare and Family Law*, 2000, vol 22, no 3. The right of Christine Piper to be identified as author of this chapter has been asserted by her in accordance with the 1988 Copyright, Designs and Patents Act.

Taking liberties: policy and the punitive turn[1]

Barry Goldson

Introduction

Hewlett (1993, p 2) observes that "an anti-child spirit is loose in these lands". This is no aberration. A certain ambivalence to children, particularly working-class children, has characterised British social policy since the 1800s, perhaps especially so in England (Hendrick, 1994, 2003; Goldson, 2004a). This said, in recent years 'anti-child spirit' or, to put it another way, 'institutionalised intolerance' (Muncie, 1999a), has assumed a peculiarly conspicuous presence in respect of policies targeted towards children cast as 'anti-social', 'disorderly' and/or 'offending'. Indeed, for children who are seen to transgress prescribed behavioural codes and boundaries (whether civil or criminal), policy has taken a discernibly punitive turn and children's civil liberties and human rights are increasingly threatened with compromise, if not violation. This chapter will critically analyse this phenomenon by examining contemporary policy responses to 'troublesome' children in England and Wales. Before we turn to this, however, three broader points are worthy of mention in order to set some contextual bearings.

Contextual bearings

Public perceptions and delusional fears

The related public perceptions that children are increasingly inclined to behave 'anti-socially', disturb civil order and/or commit criminal offences, together with the sense that 'modern' forms of 'delinquent' behaviour are more serious than was previously the case, are not uncommon (Allen, 2002). Furthermore, such negative perceptions have claimed significant purchase over the processes of contemporary policy formation (Pitts, 2000; Hancock, 2004). In other words, there is a clear relation between the consolidation of public anxieties on the one hand, and policy makers' determination to 'get tough' on the other (for recent examples, see Home Office 2004a; Office for Criminal Justice Reform, 2004). The apparent relation of fear and appeasement through 'toughness' raises a fundamental question, however. Is public anxiety the *source* of, or the *product* of, the new 'toughness'? While this question probably needs to be framed rather less deterministically, the relation itself is important in terms of policy analysis, not least because the fears and anxieties that characterise public perceptions rest on decidedly shaky foundations.

Indeed, seemingly contrary to widely held perceptions, children are *not* responsible for the majority of recorded and detected crimes. In 2001 for example, almost 88% of detected crime in England was committed by adults (Nacro, 2003a). Perhaps more significantly, the incidence of youth crime appears to be in decline when measured over the last decade or so. Thus official data indicate that between 1992 and 2001, the number of 10- to 17-year-olds cautioned or convicted of indictable offences fell by 21% from 143,600 to 113,800 (Home Office, 2002). It is also clear that such decline is not simply attributable to demographic changes (that is, fewer children in the overall population), as it is also expressed in proportionate terms. In other words, the number of children per 100,000 of the population cautioned, reprimanded, warned or convicted of an indictable offence, fell from 2,673 in 1992 to 1,927 in 2001 (Nacro, 2003a).

Furthermore, in the same way that the incidence of youth crime tends to be 'amplified' within the realm of public perception, so too does its gravity and seriousness. The typical perception of violent offences against the person is misleading. Most offences committed by children are directed against property, and the categories of offences generally regarded as the least serious, that is, theft and handling stolen goods, comprised almost half of all recorded crime attributable to children in 2001 (Home Office, 2002). In actual fact, violent offences against the person account for less than 14%, and robbery – for which we can generally read 'taking mobile telephones' (Harrington and Mayhew, 2001) – for only 2.4%, of all offences for which children were held to be responsible (for a fuller discussion see Goldson, 2004b).

While it is necessary to exercise care and caution in reading, analysing and interpreting 'official' sources of youth crime data (Muncie, 2004a, pp 15-19), the dissonance between public perceptions and recorded 'realities' is striking. On the basis of the available evidence it would appear that the fears and anxieties that apparently pervade the public realm are actually delusional. If such concern is only tenuously rooted in reality therefore, where does it derive and how is it nourished?

Demonisation, conceptual conflation and extended system reach

Jewkes (2004) has observed that the manner in which crime is presented in the media, both factual and fictional, distorts and manipulates public perceptions and fuels fear and anxiety. This certainly applies to juvenile crime and child 'offenders'. Shape (a consortium of children's charities and a national crime reduction agency) recently surveyed articles in eight national newspapers (four tabloids and four broadsheets) over a three-month period, subjecting them to intensive content analysis (Shape, 2004). The consortium found that terms such as 'thug', 'yob' and 'lout' featured consistently while in "some of the more sensational reports young people were described as 'brutes' or 'monsters' [...] 'scum' or 'menace' [... and] in a number of articles the terms of reference used [... served] to de-humanise them in order to portray the young people involved as somehow from another world and not children or young people at all" (Shape, 2004, para 3.2). Such 'othering' or 'demonising' processes, whereby the identities ascribed to a targeted constituency of children serve to separate them from 'normal' childhood, stoke fear and anxiety and ultimately instil contempt (Davis and Bourhill, 1997; Goldson, 1997). In this way, particular children are presented as totemic symbols of deep social crisis (Scraton, 1997). Such processes have traversed the boundaries of symbolic expression and media representation, however; they have penetrated the institutionalised realm of policy discourse itself (Goldson, 2001).

Indeed, within a context in which "the ideological whiff of child hate" (Haydon and Scraton, 2000, p 447) lingers, major strategic policy documents comprise platforms on which the most senior ministers draw stark distinctions between "decent law abiding citizens" and "offenders" (Blair, 2004a, p 5), while others pledge that government will "protect the innocent" and "pursue the guilty" (Blunkett et al, 2004, p 7). The mission "across the country", we are told, is to protect "decent families and communities" in their "struggle against thugs and vandals who make their lives a misery" (Blair, 2004b, p 5). Furthermore, the government has recently restated its determination to 'tackle' what it terms "some of the most fundamental challenges of our time" in order to "secure the freedoms we enjoy in the face of terrorists and criminals who seek to exploit them" (Home Office, 2004b, p 1). The implied association of global 'terrorism' and domestic 'crime' is extraordinary. Such vulgar essentialism and juxtaposition accompanies a broader and longer-established process of conceptual blurring whereby 'crime', 'disorder' and 'anti-social behaviour' are crudely conflated. On face value, as we have already noted, all of this is intended to appease fears and anxieties but paradoxically it bolsters them; by insinuating notions of epidemic moral breakdown and the permanent presence of danger and threat. Moreover, it provides the 'legitimacy' on which the state and its agencies *take liberties*, by extending the reach of correctional intervention and ultimately consolidating the power to punish. Thus the 1998 Crime and Disorder Act (the statutory linchpin of the contemporary youth justice system), is simultaneously directed at the 'criminal' *and* the 'non-criminal', and the 2003 Anti-Social Behaviour Act provides for a range of new powers, interventions and restrictions targeted particularly, although not exclusively, at children in both criminal *and* civil proceedings (see below).

From universal welfare to individual responsibility

The children who are most acutely targeted by such correctional interventions and authoritarian incursions are invariably drawn from the most damaged, distressed, neglected (and correlatively sometimes neglectful) families, neighbourhoods and communities. This is not to suggest that *all* poor children are troublesome, or that *only* poor children are refractory, but the intersections of poverty, child crime and state intervention are undeniable. Indeed, poverty is the unifying social characteristic of the majority of child 'offenders', and such adversity has deepened and widened in recent times. In 1979/80 for example, 10% (1.4

million) of all children in the UK were living in poverty (defined as below 50% of mean income after housing costs), but by 1999/2000 the corresponding figures had risen to 34% or 4.3 million children. In other words, three times as many children were impoverished in 2000 than was the case 20 years earlier and as the 21st century dawned, babies in Britain faced a one in three chance of being born into income poverty (Dornan, 2004a, p 1).

The lived experience of child poverty is inadequately expressed by the above statistics, however. It is perhaps only by translating such measures, and applying them to the everyday realities of poor children, that we begin to appreciate their real meaning. In this way Piachaud (2001) reminds us that 50,000 children aged 8 to 10 have nothing to eat or drink before going to school in the morning and that their parents routinely make personal sacrifices in order to provide 'basic items' for them (see also Adelman et al, 2003). Novak (2002) has charted the negative impact of poverty on children's health and education (see also DH, 2002; Department of Education and Science, 2002). Holterman's (1996) excellent analysis of public expenditure on children refers to the deleterious effect that poverty can have on general child development (see also McCulloch and Joshi, 1999). In short, poverty damages and disfigures children's entire experience of childhood and, with depressing predictability, such adversity imposes a disproportionate purchase over the lives of black children (Goldson and Chigwada-Bailey, 1999; DWP, 2003). As Dornan (2004b, p 1) has noted: "growing up in Britain in 2004 is tough, on the one hand our society expects compliance from its young [...] yet on the other hand it continues to expose them to an unacceptable risk of child poverty with all that entails".

While it would not be true to say that contemporary youth justice policy completely overlooks such antagonistic material conditions, its gaze is primarily fixed at the level of individual and/or familial circumstance. To put it another way, the perceived remedy for 'anti-social behaviour', 'disorder' and 'crime' is increasingly harnessed to notions of moral restoration and individual responsibility, as distinct from wider social–structural relations. Thus *individually targeted intervention*, as distinct from *universal welfare*, tends to be the favoured 'modern' approach, and this marks a fundamental departure from the principles that have guided (however inadequately) child welfare and youth justice services since the inception of the welfare state. Indeed, the concepts of universal welfare and broad-based family support delivered at the point of need, have receded in modern times. There can be no doubt that statutory services (especially personal social services) are now more sharply focused and narrowly targeted than was previously the case (Jones, 2002). Eligibility criteria have been consistently cranked up, support services are ever more remote and, in many respects, statutory intervention is now rationed and residualised; reserved for children perceived to be *facing risk* (which is normally code for those at the sharpest end of the child protection system), or *posing risk* (potential or actual 'offenders'), children increasingly displaced from mainstream child welfare services, and instead drawn into the correctional realm of the steadily expanding youth justice nexus.

For the purposes here, it is policy responses to children who are thought to pose risk that are of interest. Linking back to the notion of individual responsibility, for such children (and their families) 'risk' is increasingly associated with pathological constructions of wilful irresponsibility and individual failure (Goldson and Jamieson, 2002). The passport to services, therefore, is defined along purely negative lines. In order to 'qualify', in order to be offered a service, or perhaps more accurately to be 'targeted' by an 'intervention', children and families must be seen to have 'failed' or be 'failing', to be 'posing risk', to be 'threatening' (either actually or potentially). In this way, conceptualisations of universality and welfare for *all* children 'in need', retreat into a context of classification, control and correction where interventions are targeted at the 'criminal', the 'near criminal', the 'possibly criminal', the 'sub-criminal', the 'anti-social', the 'disorderly' or the 'potentially problematic' in some way or another.

To sum up thus far. In England and Wales we are witnessing (as we have been for the last decade or so) the emergence and consolidation of an increasingly authoritarian process that has introduced new modes of punitive correctionalism targeted especially, although not exclusively, at identifiable groups of children. We have referred to three broad contextual dimensions. First, public perceptions that tend to distort and exaggerate the extent and nature of juvenile crime and in so doing harbour fear and anxiety. Second, media representations that serve to perpetuate demonic constructions of 'otherness', and the institutionalisation of such processes through political rhetoric, policy statements and the conflation of 'anti-social behaviour', 'disorder' and 'crime'. Third, an increasing tendency to 'individualise' complex social–structural relations; to 'responsibilise' children and their families; and to rely on an expanding control apparatus to settle the contradictions of socio-economic formations, poverty and multiple disadvantage. This has given rise to a 'new punitiveness' (Goldson, 2002a), a "blizzard of initiatives, crackdowns and targets" (Neather, 2004, p 11), a "toughening up [of] every aspect of the criminal justice system" (Blair, 2004b, p 6), introduced via innumerable policy statements and ultimately implemented through statute.

The punitive turn

Nacro (2004a, p 1) observes that "the pace of reform within the youth justice system in recent years has made it difficult for many [...] to keep abreast of changes". Indeed, the sheer volume of policy that has been ground out over the last decade in general, and since the election of the first New Labour government in 1997 in particular, is unprecedented. In many respects it is the punitive tone and tenor of such developments in law and policy that is more significant, however. In a chapter such as this it is not practical to undertake a comprehensive policy analysis, but it is desirable to review some of the key milestones.

1994 Criminal Justice and Public Order Act

This Act was introduced by the Conservative Party. Section 1 created a new custodial sentence, a Secure Training Order, providing for the incarceration of children between the ages of 12 and 14 years in privately run 'secure training centres'. This effectively reversed a decacerative trend in youth justice policy, in respect of children of this age, that dated back to the 1908 Children Act (Rutherford, 1995). New Labour, while opposing various aspects of the Criminal Justice and Public Order Bill in its committee stages, abstained during the final vote (Howard League, 1995, p 3), effectively acceding to the introduction of the new child jails.

1998 Crime and Disorder Act

This Act provided that the 'statutory aim' of the youth justice system is the prevention of offending (section 39) and it served to radically reform, and extend the reach of, intervention and sentencing by introducing a range of new disposals available to the police and courts including: Anti-Social Behaviour Orders (section 1); Parenting Orders (section 8); Local child curfew schemes (section 14); reprimands and warnings (sections 65 and 66); Reparation Orders (section 67); Action Plan Orders (section 69); and the Detention and Training Order, a new custodial sentence (section 73) (Bell, 1999). The Act further abolished the principle of *doli incapax* that had previously served to provide legal safeguards in respect of children aged 10 to 13 years (Bandalli, 2000).

1999 Youth Justice and Criminal Evidence Act

Most notably, this Act introduced a new interventionist sentence, the Referral Order (section 1) for almost all children and young people on first conviction, effectively making it a mandatory sentence. The Referral Order exposes children, most of whom are convicted of minor offences, to potentially wide-ranging and intensive modes of correctional intervention (Wonnacott, 1999; Goldson, 2000; Haines, 2000).

2000 Criminal Justice and Court Services Act

This Act served to implement the Final Warning Scheme (section 56), a further interventionist initiative (Bateman, 2003), and it increased the penalties available to courts for imposing on parents of children who do not attend school regularly (section 72) (Goldson and Jamieson, 2002).

2000 Powers of the Criminal Courts (Sentencing) Act

This Act (sections 90 and 91) provided for the sentencing of children convicted of grave crimes and, according to Bateman (2002), when combined with specific sections of the 1998 Crime and Disorder Act, it comprises a 'recipe for injustice'.

The legislation also made provision for the electronic monitoring and surveillance of children (Nacro, 2003b).

2001 Criminal Justice and Police Act

This Act extended both the application of child curfew schemes (section 48) and powers in respect of those eligible to impose child curfew schemes (section 49) (Walsh, 2002). It also extended the powers of the courts to send children to prison and other locked institutions while on remand (Section 130) (Goldson, 2002b), and it further applied the electronic surveillance of children (Nacro, 2003b).

2002 Police Reform Act

This Act extended the range of people eligible to apply for Anti-Social Behaviour Orders and introduced interim Anti-Social Behaviour Orders that can be imposed prior to a full court hearing (sections 61-6) (Stone, 2004).

2003 Anti-Social Behaviour Act

This Act was implemented following the publication in March 2003 of a White Paper entitled *Respect and responsibility: Taking a stand against anti-social behaviour*. The White Paper (Home Office, 2003, pp 1-2) set out a nakedly authoritarian vision of a "something for something society" where rights are reserved for the "responsible [...] decent law abiding majority", while the so-called "out of control minority" face a raft of new punishments and sanctions. Children are especially targeted by the provisions of the legislation that received Royal Assent on 20 November 2003. Among an extended menu of punitive measures that focus on the young, the police are granted further powers to remove under-16-year-olds from public places if they "believe" that a member of the public "might be" "intimidated, harassed, alarmed or distressed", and if two or more young people, together in a public place, fail to disperse under the instruction of a police officer, they commit a criminal offence and face the prospect of custodial detention (Walsh, 2003). The 2003 Anti-Social Behaviour Act also made the parents of children regarded as "disorderly", "anti-social" or "criminally inclined", eligible targets for formal statutory orders (Nacro, 2004b).

2003 Criminal Justice Act

This Act, which also received Royal Assent on 20 November 2003, extended drug-testing provisions (previously restricted to adults) to children, thus exposing them to "highly intrusive and demanding" interventions (Nacro, 2004c, p 8). The legislation further extended parenting orders to be used in conjunction with the Referral Order (as provided by the 1999 Youth Justice and Criminal Evidence Act, see above) (schedule 34). Perhaps more significantly, these and other provisions of the Act open up the "potential to exacerbate already high levels of custody and increase the use of restrictive community sentences for those who might otherwise have received a lesser penalty" (Nacro, 2004a, p 7).

It is difficult to encapsulate the core themes that underpin such a wide-ranging corpus of law and policy. This said, four key elements are discernible. First, an actuarial emphasis, underpinned by notions of 'risk factors' and a calculus of variations. This serves to legitimise early (often quite intensive) forms of intervention, framed within a context of responsibilisation and criminalisation. Second, rather crude constructions of restorative justice paradoxically set within a system that remains overtly adversarial and retributive. Third, unsophisticated rehabilitative ideals and specious notions of individual restoration, seemingly derived from an expectation that 'programmes' of intervention can somehow 'fix' or 'correct' the child 'offender', while essentially disregarding the wider social structural contexts and aetiological complexities that we considered earlier. Fourth, and arguably most problematic of all, in the final analysis an overtly punitive orientation, most explicitly expressed through processes of re-penalisation and child incarceration. For the remainder of this chapter, emphasis will be placed on the first and fourth of these elements: the question of early intervention at the 'shallow end' of the youth justice process, and the practices of child incarceration at the 'deeper end' of the same process. By focusing more sharply on the polar ends of the 'new correctional continuum' (Goldson, 2002c), we might gauge the extent to which recent developments in youth justice law and policy are literally taking liberties from children.

Taking liberties at the 'shallow end'

Early intervention

Early intervention is a cornerstone of contemporary youth justice policy (Goldson, 2000). A broad range of measures has been introduced, aimed at children who paddle at the shallow end of 'anti-social behaviour', 'disorder' and/or juvenile crime or, alternatively, to 'target' children who are perceived to be 'at risk' of offending. There is a seductive commonsensical logic to such developments and they are frequently packaged within benign discourses of child welfare. 'Assessments' of children are premised on the rationale that early identification of those at 'greatest risk' of perpetuating 'anti-social', 'disorderly' or 'offending' behaviour allows for pre-emptive and preventive intervention. In this sense it is difficult to quarrel with policy and practice initiatives that claim to divert vulnerable children from problematic behaviours. However, it is important to look beyond what Wright (1978) once termed the 'level of appearances', and in so doing the very same initiatives assume a fundamentally different guise.

In the first instance, 'risk factor' discourses essentially serve to 'scientise' and sanitise indices of poverty and multiple disadvantage. In this way, the emphasis shifts from adverse social–structural conditions to individualised 'failings', as we discussed earlier. Neither is there any substantial evidence that 'risk factor' assessments can predict, with any degree of accuracy, the child offenders of the future. Thus Sutton et al (2004, p 5), paradoxically among the keenest and most prominent advocates of the early intervention 'risk factor' paradigm, counsel the need for 'caution':

> In particular, any notion that better screening can enable policy makers to identify young children destined to join the 5 per cent of offenders responsible for 50-60 per cent of crime is fanciful. Even if there were no ethical objections to putting 'potential delinquent' labels round the necks of young children, there would continue to be statistical barriers. Research into the continuity of anti-social behaviour shows substantial flows out of – as well as in to – the pool of children who develop chronic conduct problems. This demonstrates the dangers of assuming that anti-social five year olds are the criminals or drug abusers of tomorrow....

It follows that there are grounds for questioning the rationales that underpin recent policy and practice initiatives, such as Youth Inclusion and Support Panels (YISPs) that seek to 'identify' the "most *at risk* 7- to 13-year-olds" in 92 local authority areas of England and Wales and engage them in 'programmes' (Home Office, 2004a, p 41; emphasis added). Furthermore, the general principle of coercive "early intervention to address *criminal-type* anti-social behaviour in *children under ten* (the age of criminal responsibility) where a voluntary approach has not worked" (Home Office, 2004a, p 42; emphasis added), can only be seen as a criminalising mechanism that undermines fundamental principles of justice, exposes the youngest children to ever greater levels of surveillance and regulation and, in the final analysis, violates their civil liberties and human rights.

Criminalisation, 'guilt' and the erosion of justice

The ideologies and 'domain assumptions' (Gouldner, 1970) that underpin 'risk'-based early intervention are both intrinsically authoritarian and antithetical to long-established principles of criminal justice. *Guilt* is no longer the founding principle. Intervention can be triggered without an 'offence' being committed, premised instead on a 'condition', a 'character' or a 'mode of life' that is adjudged to be 'failing' or posing 'risk'. The conventional applications of youth justice require first, publicly specified offences, and second, proven guilt and responsibility, proven, that is, according to strict and transparent codes of evidence, fact and law. They involve an open trial in a court of law, clearly defined safeguards in the form of defence and professional representation/advocacy, and the availability of review and appeal procedures. In contrast to established youth justice processes, the new modes of risk classification and early intervention are unencumbered by such legal principles as 'the burden of proof', 'beyond reasonable doubt' and 'due legal process'. Instead, intervention is triggered by assessment, discretion and the spurious logic of prediction and actuarialism. On this basis, intervention becomes less a matter of transparent justice and more a question of opaque administrative and professional process. Children face judgement, and are exposed to intervention, not only on the basis of what they *have done*, but what they *might do*, who *they are* or who they are *thought to be*.

Moreover, the behaviour of others – siblings, parents, relatives, peers and friends – is also factored into the equation, children thus becoming 'guilty' by association. This inverts the long-established legal principle of 'innocent until proven guilty'. In the final analysis, "criminal-type anti-social behaviour" (Home Office, 2004a, p 42) is not crime, and terms such as 'potential offender', 'at risk', 'pre-delinquent' and 'crime-prone' all amount to the same thing within conventional applications of youth justice and criminal law: they actually mean innocent! It is this, the right to be considered and treated as innocent, that is being seriously compromised by criminalising constructions of 'risk' and technologies of early intervention.

Surveillance and regulation

According to Rose (1990, p 121), "childhood is the most intensively governed sector of personal existence" (see also McGillivray, 1997; Muncie and Hughes, 2002). Furthermore, the governance of children, or at least identifiable constituencies of working-class children, has intensified in recent times. James and James (2001a) observe that children are increasingly exposed to diversifying modes of social control and, more recently, Garrett (2004) has traced an emerging pattern of 'surveillant practices' within statutory welfare services for children. Whether this is conceptualised within the context of the 'dispersal of control' (Cohen, 1985), the 'disciplinary society' (Foucault, 1991), the 'surveillance society' (Lyon, 2001) or the 'surveillance state' (Jameson, 2002), it is clear that 'suspect populations' are increasingly falling under the gaze of the metaphorical 'electronic eye' (Garrett, 2004). This particularly applies to children who are thought to be 'at risk' of offending and/or those who have been convicted of criminal transgression, where the processes of gathering and sharing personal data, often by using increasingly sophisticated electronic technology, is becoming a commonplace feature of policy and practice.

Not unlike 'risk assessment' and early intervention, processes of information exchange can assume benign presentations; as a means of encouraging interagency cooperation and improving 'outcomes' for children 'at risk'. Consistent with such conceptualisation, Clause 8 of the 2004 Children Bill provides for the removal of all legal barriers that prevent professional agencies from sharing information about children, without the prior consent of the child's parent or the child her/himself. But such practice can just as readily be interpreted as an affront to civil liberties, human rights and the child's claim to confidentiality, particularly when located within the overarching punitive context of youth justice law and policy. For example, recently published guidance from the Youth Justice Board for England

and Wales (YJB) and the Association of Chief Police Officers (ACPO) (2003), in respect of children '*at risk of* offending' states that:

> By following this guidance it should be clear that agencies are able to share personal data, even *without the consent of the data subject* [that is, the child and/or the child's parent/s]. [...] Exchanging personal and sensitive information amongst agencies without the consent of the subject is seen as difficult and is often used as *an excuse* by many not to share and exchange relevant information.... (paras 1.1 and 1.2; emphasis added)

Such developments have to be understood within a wider context in which the free-flow of 'confidential' information is located on a continuum of surveillance and regulation with increasingly authoritarian overtones. In this respect, echoes of benign presentation are barely audible; instead the emphasis shifts to "better intelligence and information sharing [...] to *track offenders down*" (Office for Criminal Justice Reform, 2004, p 42; emphasis added). Ultimately, as Rose has warned, information exchange aids intelligence gathering that can be put to various uses quite different to those that might originally have been anticipated:

> ... by structured risk assessments, risk schedules, forms and pro formas, database fields, into indicators of risk, risk classification, and the like that are communicated to other professionals, to law enforcement agencies, to the courts, to other decision makers, with consequences far removed from those surrounding the initial consultation, encounter, or occasion which led to the information in the first place. (cited in Garrett, 2004, p 67)

Taking liberties at the 'deep end': re-penalisation and child incarceration

The punitive turn in contemporary youth justice policy in England and Wales is perhaps most starkly expressed through the practices of re-penalisation and child incarceration (Goldson, 2002a). The number of custodial sentences imposed on children rose from approximately 4,000 per annum in 1992 to 7,600 in 2001, a 90% increase (Nacro, 2003a). During the same period the child remand population grew by 142% (Goldson, 2002b). Within this general pattern of penal expansion, five sub-patterns are particularly noteworthy.

First, in addition to substantially more children being locked up, periods of custodial detention have also increased. The average length of sentence for 15- to 17-year-old boys convicted of indictable offences for example, rose from 9.2 months in 1992 to 10.8 months in 2001 (Nacro, 2003a). Second, as we have discussed, legislative reform, most notably the 1994 Criminal Justice and Public Order Act and the 1998 Crime and Disorder Act, has provided for the detention of younger children. In 1992 approximately 100 children under the age of 15 were sentenced to custody; in 2001, however, 800 children under the age of 15 were similarly sentenced, an increase of 800% (Home Office, 2002). Third, more girls are being locked up, and the rate of growth is proportionately higher than that which relates to boys. Although the baseline comprises relatively small numbers, the use of custody in relation to girls over the last decade has increased by 400% (Nacro, 2003a). This is set against data that indicates that girls have not become more criminally inclined over precisely the same period (Worrall, 1999; Nacro, 2004c). Fourth, the substantial over-representation of black children and young people continues to prevail at every discrete stage of the youth justice system from pre-arrest to post-sentence (Goldson and Chigwada-Bailey, 1999), and this is particularly evident in relation to penal detention (Wilson, 2004). Meanwhile, research suggests that there are no significant differences in the self-reported patterns of offending between white and black children and young people (Graham and Bowling, 1995; Goldson and Chigwada-Bailey, 1999). Fifth, the most recent figures are particularly worrying. Following what appears to be a temporary and short-lived dip in the number of child prisoners in the latter half of 2003, the chairperson of the YJB has recently reported that the first four months of 2004 have been marked by a 10% increase (Morgan, 2004).

Prisons and other locked correctional institutions fail to comprise either a suitable environment for children or an effective means of addressing their offending. Such institutions are filled (and frequently over-filled) with:

> Children whose lives have been damaged and disfigured by disadvantage, neglect and abuse.... These are the children for whom the fabric of life invariably stretches across poverty; family discord; public care; drug and alcohol misuse; mental distress; ill-health; emotional, physical and sexual abuse; self-harm; homelessness; isolation; loneliness; circumscribed educational and employment opportunities; and the most pressing sense of distress and alienation. (Goldson, 2002b, p 51)

Such children are, in many important respects, "discarded" (HM Chief Inspector of Prisons, 1999, p 23) and "treated like rubbish" (Lyon et al, 2000, p 29). The corrosive and damaging experience of penal confinement invariably means that on release the same children become more troubled, distressed, angry and troublesome. Re-conviction rates are consistently high and many released child prisoners are soon sent back to prison; a clear reminder, if ever one was needed, of the 'revolving penal door' phenomenon (SEU, 2002). As, Foucault (1991, p 232) astutely observed, "prison is dangerous when it is not useless".

Conclusion

The attitude that a society takes to children, especially to children who see out their childhoods within the most formidable personal circumstances and adverse social–structural contexts, is an important indicator of its core values and principles. If we hold a mirror to contemporary policy responses to children in trouble in England and Wales it returns a particularly ugly image. The punitive turn that takes liberties and violates rights is underpinned by an intolerance and contempt for troubled, even if troublesome, children. Such policy has attracted critical attention from the most authoritative sources (see, for example, SSI et al, 2002; UN Committee on the Rights of the Child, 2002; House of Lords/House of Commons Joint Committee on Human Rights, 2003), and leading academics advise that there is "no evidence whatsoever that punishment works" (McGuire, 2004) when measured in terms of reducing crime. The current trajectory of youth justice policy is simply unsustainable in a modern state that lays claim to civility and rationality. The 'time for change' (Monaghan et al, 2004) has surely arrived?

Note

[1] This chapter comprises a substantially revised version of a paper entitled 'Tough on children ... tough on justice' that I first presented at the international conference 'Tough on crime ... tough on freedoms? From community to global interventions', convened by the European Group for the Study of Deviance and Social Control, Chester, England, 22-24 April 2003.

Tightening the net: children, community and control

Adrian James and Allison James

Introduction

In recent years children have become increasingly the subjects of both overt and covert regulation, an indication of what Wyness (2000) and Scraton (1997) term the perceived crisis of childhood. This 'crisis', reflected across a variety of social, legal and political arenas, is one in which children are depicted as spiralling out of control. As Scraton (1997, p vii) notes, throughout the 1990s

> a litany of deviants has been constructed providing evidence that the social and moral fabric of British society is collapsing, infected at its childhood foundations. The streets, it is argued, are inhabited by drug users, runaways, joyriders and persistent young offenders. Schools suffer the excesses of bullies, truants and disruptive pupils. Families have become 'dismembered', replaced by lone mothers, characterised by absent fathers.

Although, as Wyness and Scraton both observe, it is debatable whether or not such a 'crisis' *is* actually taking place, there has, nonetheless, been an increased concern to monitor and regulate children's lives, with the consequence that the opportunities children and young people have to be relatively free from adult control have been greatly reduced (Valentine, 1996). Contemporary moral discourses that construe society as being 'at risk' from children or, conversely, children as 'at risk' from society (Scott et al, 1998) are continuing to tighten the net of social control on children's lives. Such a development is, however, highly intriguing in the light of the 1989 Children Act since, by implicitly acknowledging children's agency, the Act ostensibly offers children the possibility of *more*, rather than less, rights of participation and consultation.

This [chapter] suggests, therefore, that recent strands in social policy reflect a deep ambivalence about the place of children in contemporary British society for, although espousing a communitarian ideological agenda (Johnson, 1999, p 91) and claiming to combat social exclusion, the New Labour government appears to be working to exclude, rather than include, children as citizens (Archard, 1993). The [chapter] argues, then, that recent developments in social policy may be impinging on children's everyday lives at school, in the community, and at home in ways that, although on the face of it appear to be benign and empowering, might have rather different consequences for children themselves. This situation needs to be urgently addressed for it is precisely through such political and policy mechanisms that the future generational and conceptual space of childhood is socially constructed (James and Prout, 1990a; James et al, 1998; James and James, 2001b).

The Third Way, communitarism and the community

Communitarianism represents, in large part, a backlash against the political ideologies of the past. As Driver and Martell (1997) argue, for New Labour,

> ... community will create social cohesion out of the market culture of self-interest. If communitarianism is New Labour's answer to Thatchersim, so too is it Tony Blair's rebuff to Old Labour. Community will restore the moral balance to society by setting our moral duties as well as rights. (1997, pp 27-8)

With its emphasis on duties and responsibilities rather than rights, the communitarian perspective of the present government involves the reinvention of social democracy through the defining of a third way in politics. Giddens, one of its major proponents, argues strongly that "[t]he fostering of an active civic society is a basic part of the politics of the third way ... [t]he theme of community is fundamental to the new politics, but not just as an abstract slogan" (1998, pp 78-9). According to Giddens, of particular significance in the Third Way is its diagnosis of the cause of so many political and social ills. These are located in the civic decline that is evidenced in "the weakening sense of solidarity in some local communities and urban neighbourhoods, high levels of crime, and the break-up of marriages and families" (Giddens, 1998, p 787)[1].

For Giddens, the solution to such a decline is clear. Investment in education and training will lead to the growth of a more flexible, cosmopolitan labour force through the development of common educational practices and standards. In addition, it will foster "the development of cognitive and emotional competence" (1998, p 125), which, by implication, will ensure that the values espoused by the government are more readily accepted by the public. In relation to crime policies, Giddens argues that "the police should work closely with citizens to improve local community standards and civil behaviour, using education, persuasion and counselling instead of arraignment" and urges that "a renewed emphasis upon crime prevention rather than law enforcement can go hand in hand with the reintegration of policing with the community" (1998, pp 87-8). And in relation to the family, he argues for its democratisation, through the promotion of "quality, mutual respect, autonomy, decision-making through communication and freedom from violence" (1998, p 93). In sum, for Giddens,

> ... [e]quality and individual freedom may conflict. Third Way politics looks for a new relationship between the individual and the community, a redefinition of rights and obligations.

> One might suggest as a prime motto for the new politics, no rights without responsibilities. A second precept, in today's society, should be no authority without democracy. (1998, pp 65-6)

Although not directly acknowledged, Giddens' thinking echoes the communitarian perspectives developed by Etzioni, who seeks inter alia also to address the tricky question of "how to maintain both social order and personal autonomy in one and the same society" (Etzioni, 1996, p 1). He argues that this can only be achieved in communities that respond to the needs of their members and that

> If the values the community fosters and the form of its structure (allocation of assets, application of power, shapes of institutions, and mechanisms of socialization) do not reflect its members' needs, or reflect only the needs of some, the community's order will be ipso facto imposed rather than truly supported. (1996, pp 1-2)

This focus on communities as relatively undifferentiated social entities, however, obscures the significant fault lines and social diversities that fracture their structure and work to exclude certain sections of the population from community participation. As we suggest here, alongside class, gender, ethnicity and health status, age and generation can also work to exclude rather than include people from belonging to the community (O'Neill, 1994). To what extent, for example, are children currently defined and constructed as members of the community? Are children being expected to be responsible, without being given any substantive rights? How far are adults being encouraged to continue to exercise authority over children without any overall increase in the rule of democracy? In sum: to what extent are children recognised as citizens and as active members of the community who can be included within, rather than excluded from, the communitarian agenda of the present government?

A major consideration in determining answers to these questions must be, we suggest, the extent to which the rhetoric of the UN Convention and the 1989 Children Act about children's autonomy and agency is being – or, indeed can be – put into practice through the communitarian-based policies of New Labour. For example, according to Etzioni the notion of community is exemplified by "a commitment to a set of shared values, norms and meanings, and a shared history and identity – in short, a shared culture" (1996, p 5). This latter characteristic is immediately problematic. In the context of a pluralistic multi-cultural society, a hegemonic consensus actively works to exclude certain sections of the population from participation for, as O'Neill notes, the risk of liberal theory is that it becomes "difficult to think of class, race, sexism and ageism except as slight obstacles in the path of individuals" (1994, p 42). And in relation to children this risk is exacerbated: we "imagine equality as the initial state of children and freedom as the state of children and youth before they assume the burden of institutions in later life" (O'Neill, 1994, p 44). Such a 'naturalising' of the concept of childhood (James et al, 1999, p 196; Gittens, 1998), however, masks the extent to which there are plural childhoods, shaped and differentiated by the inequalities of class, gender and ethnicity (but see Qvortrup, 1994, p 5).

In his exposition of communitarian ideology, Etzioni notes that "there is a fundamental contradiction between the society's needs for order and the individual's quest for autonomy", a contradiction that can place obstacles in the path of realising a communitarian agenda (1996, p 3). In the particular case of children, this difficulty is compounded since communities also have a responsibility to provide socialising structures that will foster both children's autonomy and their ability to conform. Part of the 'problem' of children is precisely that they are still in the process of acquiring values, norms, meanings and identities. By definition of their youth, they do not, as yet, have a fully shared history and therefore cannot be assumed to be acquiescent to the values of the community. Children have therefore to be encouraged to explore their agency, their difference, and their individuality, but only within the broader, common societal framework (James, 1993).

It is clear, therefore, that childhood constitutes a prime site for managing the tensions between conformity and autonomy, and thus also for identifying and working out the internal contradictions of communitarianism. But in doing so this may give rise to censure for, as Etzioni himself points out, community censure represents "a major way that communities uphold members' commitments to shared values and service to the common good – community order. And indeed, community censure reduces the reliance on the state as a source of order" (1996, p 5). Perhaps it is no wonder, then, that the net of social control has increasingly tightened around childhood during the 1990s. As we shall show, the control of children's behaviour is increasingly a focus for policy initiatives under New Labour for it is through shaping the form that 'childhood' takes that the socialisation of children can be most effectively regulated. And it is through the regulation and control of children in the present that a particular kind of future, adult community can be produced (James and Prout, 1990b). It could be argued, then, that the state's current interest in childhood is, in this sense, very much self-interest.

The rights of children, as articulated in the UN Convention and the 1989 Children Act, would seem to suggest that children's status as citizens is unequivocal. However, as Etzioni argues, citizen's rights have historically been endangered "not when the community demanded that those who have rights also live up to their responsibilities, but when this was *not* done" (1996, p 8; emphasis in original). Thus, as we shall show, a significant feature of much recent government rhetoric is the emphasis that is placed on the failure of some citizens to live up to their responsibilities and the importance of communities demanding that they should. For children, however, who have relatively few rights, demands that they live up to their responsibilities as members of the community, that they observe and conform to dominant adult norms and expectations, are inherently problematic in the absence of any necessary or taken-for-granted commitment by children to the adult value consensus.

These theoretical considerations have thus illuminated a number of key issues with regard to the citizenship[2] of children under New Labour and to children as participative members in the new social democracy. For children themselves, these considerations are, however, not simply theoretical. They have been made real in terms of a number of important recent social policy developments and initiatives that have already begun to or will shortly impinge on their everyday lives, reducing further their spheres of autonomous social action.

Schools and education

One indication of the tightening of the net of social control around children and childhood can be seen in the variety of mechanisms, established in recent years, which reflect explicit educational objectives while concealing some more implicit ones of regulation and surveillance. For example, the introduction of the National Curriculum and the accompanying standard attainment targets (SATS) have provided the basis for school league tables. These are designed to promote broader collectively held values about the importance of excellence in education and, through transparency, to increase parent power and choice in relation to their children's schooling.

In addition to the fact that such mechanisms emphasise parental rights and choices, rather than the rights of children themselves to receive high quality education, the market framework within which league tables are embedded also creates means of disciplining (and excluding) children: those who under-perform at primary schools may have a limited chance of being offered a place at the better secondary schools; children who are deemed disruptive may be excluded from schools rather than, as previously, their problems being addressed within the school; or schools may protect their position within the leagues tables by not entering less able children for public examinations. The continuation of school league tables under New Labour has thus broadened the control that the state has over the future of childhood, masking subtle forms of social exclusion under the guise of a new social democracy and the public good.

These implicit forms of social control are penetrating more deeply, too, into *all* children's lives. The age-related SATS tests, have led, for example, to a reduction of the freedom of children in terms of what they learn and the ways in which they learn at school. Recent research (Christensen and James, 2001) demonstrates, for example, that although maths is traditionally a topic that many children are apprehensive about, considerably more time is now spent on maths and less on more popular subjects such as art, music and drama. This has had the effect of substantially changing the quality and nature of school experience for staff, as well as for pupils (see also Pollard et al, 1994). That this, in itself, works as an insidious form of social control can be seen in John Major's approving commentary on the National Curriculum:

> Children don't go to school for 'an experience'. They go to learn the basic skills that they are going to need in later life – being able to read and write and do sums. (Major, 1994, cited in Pollard and Filer, 1996)

Under New Labour, such regulation of the curriculum has intensified with the introduction of literacy and numeracy hours in schools and a range of other mechanisms designed to narrow the gap and the 'control discontinuities' between school and the home/family, viz: the introduction of contracts between schools and parents; the proposed introduction of the use of community volunteers to monitor and follow up school absences; and the introduction of older people as reading mentors (who could also act as role models, share life experiences, etc). Increased powers have also been given to the police to stop children who are outside school during school hours and return them to school or any other place designated by the local authority (1998 Crime and Disorder Act, section 16).

As part of this process of narrowing the gap between 'home' and 'school' as institutional sites of childhood, political pronouncements have also been made about the adequacy of some parents – criticism has been made of their failure to get their children out of bed in the morning, to ensure their children get to and stay at school, to ensure they do their homework, etc. As the Audit Commission argued, "successful approaches to tackling truancy and disruptive behaviour often involve parents, who may condone absence from school" (1996, para 34). Parent–school contracts, which emphasise parental responsibilities rather than children's rights, are part of a strategy for dealing with such issues. Simultaneously the government is placing increasing pressure on parents to give children more help with their homework, to the extent of providing a magazine, leaflets, and a website (www.parents.dfee.gov.uk) that will give guidance on how to make use of everyday family activities such as shopping for educational purposes (*The Independent*, 7 December 1999).

Such examples reflect what Wyness describes as the incorporation of parents into the "broader project of educating children" by making parents more responsible for what their children do (2000, p 44). That children are seen as valuable human capital as part of the communitarian agenda is made explicit in the White Paper, *Excellence in schools* (1997). This encourages "parents and local communities [to be more] effectively involved in the education of children" (cited in Wyness, 2000, p 44). But in reasserting that parents and communities are responsible for children, it may be that children are being denied autonomous agency and the opportunity to develop responsibility for themselves.

The introduction of school councils might be seen as a counterweight to these tendencies through their potential to give children some say about their school experiences. Recent research raises some doubts, however, about their nature and functioning (Alderson, 1999). The explicitly stated purpose of school councils is to provide a forum for dealing with student complaints and encouraging student participation as part of school governance. It must be acknowledged, however, that they also have the potential to act as a further mechanism of social control. Designed to deal with dissident students, under the guise of an apparently democratic and participative process, school councils may work as a forum in which complaints can be 'managed' by the school without major compromise or disruption. They might also be seen as providing an 'education' that encourages children to adopt preferred styles of citizenship through rewarding some behaviours and discouraging others. As the Audit Commission comments, "the role of schools in crime prevention is mainly through general education and socialisation, connecting young people with society and teaching them how to use information, obey rules and learn the link between effort and reward" (Audit Commission 1998, para 83).

Such developments should be seen in the context of a government that has established a National Advisory Group on Education for Citizenship and the Teaching of Democracy in Schools (DH, 1999, para 9.12.7) in order to spread good practice to all schools in England and Wales. The government is also seeking to link personal, social and health education with citizenship education because "it is important for young people to have a clear statutory *entitlement* to learning about their duties, responsibilities and rights as citizens, the nature of democratic government and the skills needed to play an active part in their school, neighbourhood, communities and society" (DH, 1999, para 9.12.7; emphasis added). That this is framed in terms of an entitlement clearly reflects the rhetoric of communitarianism and citizenship, while ignoring the reality that, for children, much recent policy is having precisely the opposite effect and is denying their agency. It is perhaps indicative of current thinking about children's status as citizens, then, that in this list of entitlements rights appear last, after duties and responsibilities (see Roche, 1996).

Of perhaps even greater significance is the recently formulated inter-departmental Connexions Strategy (DfEE, 2000), which "establishes a learning framework for the whole of the teenage years" (para 4.2). It aims to create a new service that will "ensure that more and more young people ... make a successful transition from adolescence to adulthood and working life" (Foreword). Indeed, the strategy even proposes the creation of a new profession since it "will be delivered primarily through a network of Personal Advisers" (para 6.1) who will "continue the work begun in schools on education for citizenship and teaching of democracy to enable young people to play a full and active role in their local communities" (para 3.9). Considerable stress is placed on the importance of consulting, involving and taking account of the views of young people. However, the strategy also aims to ensure that young people do not fall through this net and in order to ensure that no young person becomes "lost to the Connexions Service" (para 8.9) it proposes the establishment of "a database to track their progress through their teenage years" (para 8.9). The network of personal advisers will be used to "maintain contact with all the young people in its area [which] ... will allow monitoring of the help provided to those not in learning or at risk of becoming disconnected from their current learning or work" (para 8.90).

This is not to suggest, however, that such developments are necessarily unwelcome to parents or, even perhaps, to children themselves. A recent review of relevant research (Dyson and Robson, 1999) concludes that initiatives such as home-school reading schemes and other school-based projects aimed at developing links with parents can, indeed, enhance children's attainments and are often welcomed and supported by parents. But as Dyson and Robson (1999) note, a warning needs to be sounded, which, in important respects, represents a major challenge to such policy expressions of communitarian thinking. First,

> The model of parent–child relations and of family values embedded in
> the parental involvement movement may well devalue the practices and
> values of families who may already be somewhat marginalized. The net
> effect may simply be to alienate those families and disadvantage their
> children further.

Such policy effects are thus unlikely to strengthen civic society but, rather, weaken
it further.

Second, such parent–school partnerships often take place on terms that are
very much dictated by the latter, with the consequent marginalisation of parents
and, more importantly for our purposes, of children. This issue "may be particularly
important where parents belong to social groups (such as some minority groups,
for instance) that already experience marginalisation" (Dyson and Robson, 1999).
Such developments seem unlikely, therefore, to foster in them and their children
the "commitment to a set of shared values, norms and meanings, and a shared
history and identity – in short, a shared culture" as envisaged by the communitarian
perspective.

Crime, youth justice and the community

As a result of growing concern about the apparently increasing lawlessness of
children, and following the remarks of the judge in the Bulger trial, James and
Jenks argued that "the government's response to the growing moral panic about
the nation's children has been to establish a set of controls upon children's activities"
(1996a, p 327). The lead set by the Conservatives in this regard seems to have
been eagerly taken up by New Labour for, as Crawford observes,

> ... crime, as a compelling symbol of lost community, has a particularly
> salient place in communitarianism. The perceived decline of a 'sense of
> community' and the fracturing of actual communal institutions in the
> late twentieth century, are associated in the minds of communitarians
> with a crisis of social regulation. (1999, p 194)

Youth crime is an increasingly prominent political issue and has been addressed
most recently by the provisions of the 1998 Crime and Disorder Act where a
clear link is established between youth crime, education and parenting. As the
Home Office guidance on the Act makes clear, "tackling youth crime is likely to
require action to deal with some of the underlying causes of youth offending,
such as truancy and school exclusions" (Home Office, 1998, para 2.13). The
provisions of the 1998 Crime and Disorder Act – for example, the anti-social
behaviour order (section 1), parenting programmes made available through
parenting orders (section 8), or voluntary attendance on such programmes as
part of a less formal mechanism used by youth offending teams for dealing with
offending behaviour – provide clear evidence of an extension of explicit control
over children. But they also represent less benign instances of the drive to reassert

parental responsibility for and authority over children. Although parenting orders and parenting programmes appear to offer a means of resocialising dysfunctional or inadequate parenting behaviour, how this is to be defined and by whom is far from clear. Even less certain is how such programmes might address possible links between behaviour and structural factors, such as unemployment and poverty, as opposed to cognitive or behavioural shortcomings.

The shift of emphasis in terms of ministerial responsibility in relation to such issues – away from the Department of Health, which has hitherto had the primary responsibility for children's issues, toward the Home Office – may also not be without significance, both in practical and symbolic terms. For example, the Ministerial Group on the Family – which produced the Green Paper, *Supporting families* (Ministerial Group on the Family, 1999) and in which considerable prominence was given to the provisions of the 1998 Crime and Disorder Act – was chaired by the Home Secretary. And, in 1999, it was the Home Office that allocated over £1 million out of its Family Support Grant, established in 1998, to target services and projects that help parents cope with their teenagers.

The Home Office was also instrumental in the recent establishment of the National Family and Parenting Institute which, in its intention towards establishing what it calls the 'millennial family', speaks volumes about the government's communitarism vision. With its implied overtones of future prosperity, happiness and good governance, it is through better parenting and the reconstruction of 'the family' that the future of children, and by implication 'proper' childhood, can be ensured. As Jenks notes:

> ... the modern family enabled the modern State to invest in 'futures'. The ideology of care both lubricated and legitimized the investment of economic and cultural capital in the 'promise' of childhood. Childhood is transformed into a form of human capital which through modernity has been dedicated to futures. (1996, p 15)

The Institute will be working closely with, among others, the Trust for the Study of Adolescents. This Trust, which currently has an active research programme within secondary schools, is also providing advice and support for those responsible for developing parenting programmes in response to the requirements of the 1998 Crime and Disorder Act. The development of the latter is being supported to the tune of over £3.9 million of grants from the Development Fund of the Youth Justice Board to "encourage the development of programmes for parents of children at risk of offending and parents of young offenders, so that parents will be involved in helping their children towards a crime-free life" (Home Office Press Release 323/99, 15 October 1999). Any consideration of children's own views, responses and contribution to the parenting relationship is noticeably absent from these initiatives (James, 1999).

A more obvious social control mechanism is the introduction of local child curfew schemes (1998 Crime and Disorder Act, section 14), which can be aimed at children younger than 10 who are not under the supervision of a 'responsible adult' between 9pm and 6am. Such schemes have a distinctively communitarian flavour. They are to be introduced only after discussion with the police and the local community, this support being regarded as essential to the success of such schemes. Although at the time of writing no local authority has yet introduced a local child curfew, and very few anti-social behaviour orders have yet been made [since 2001 a number of child curfews have been imposed and hundreds of ASBOs have been made – Editor], it is their availability that is significant: first, it registers an increase in the breadth and depth of the surveillance of childhood or, more correctly, particular types of childhood; second, it reflects the extension of a pseudo-parental responsibility to the community as a whole, outwith the family; and third, it works to deny children's autonomy and their right to be responsible and govern their own behaviour.

The Act also represents a sea-change in terms of the links that have been created between the police and local authorities in relation to community safety. As Innes has argued in a recent review of the development of zero tolerance policing in Britain and the US:

> ... the fundamental flaw with making policing overly accountable to community demands, is that it can all too easily become a tool for the expression of the 'tyranny of the majority', where policing strategies are used to target stigmatised, unpopular minority groups. (Innes, 1999, p 407)

Through such devices then, it might be suggested that a wedge is being driven between those children inhabiting 'correct' as opposed to 'incorrect' childhoods (see Ennew, 1986, p 22).

Other schemes, such as the use of volunteer mentors (predominantly white females), drawn from the community, to change problem behaviour in primary school children (Roberts and Singh, 1999) also cross the school–community divide. Recommended by the Audit Commission (1996, para 37), such schemes aim to target selected children in order to have the maximum impact on reducing the likelihood of subsequent criminal behaviour. It is worth noting in passing that the Connexions Strategy (see above) envisages a major expansion of the use of the National Mentoring Network (DfEE, 2000, para 2.7) since mentors will have an important role within the new service.

The funding role of the Home Office in such developments is also not without significance. As the Audit Commission, in its review of youth justice, recommended, "all public services should co-operate with institutions that socialize young people – such as families, schools, religious institutions and community organizations – to ensure that children have the opportunity to become responsible and capable citizens" (1996, para 45). It also identified local government as providing the necessary structure in which such a coordinated policy could be delivered.

The increasing emphasis on consultation also reflects the government's agenda for reforming local democracy and its desire that all sections of the community should be involved in such consultations including, inter alia, "[r]elevant hard-to reach groups [such as] young men [and] children" (Home Office, 1998, para 3.52). Indeed, the Home Office argued that "it will be essential to involve young people as part of the solution to local crime and disorder issues, not just part of the problem" (Home Office, 1998, Executive Summary). Such consultation is part of a wider process "whose ultimate aim is to maximise community control and to involve the community in the delivery of community safety" (Nacro, 1990a, p 8; emphasis added). However, recent evidence suggests that with one or two exceptions, such as the Hastings Young Person's Council (Nacro, 1990a, p 5) and a small number of school-based schemes (Home Office, 1998), "[e]fforts to engage young people as part of the community rather than as a problem to be dealt with by the community were less in evidence" (Nacro, 1999b, p 6).

Central to these ideas is the intention that all such initiatives should be targeted on deprived communities with high crime rates. As Crawford argues, "the need to restore a 'sense of community' around issues of crime and its control therefore, implies an assumption that high crime areas lack sufficient 'community'" (1999, p 199). It is important to note in addition that, to the extent that the focus is on the prevention of offending and not just *re*offending, the focus for this communitarian initiative is on children and young people as an *entire* social category, and not just young offenders. Such a policy targets young people as a threat that must be controlled and yet tries to encourage them to accept their responsibilities to the community while not necessarily acknowledging their rights (Scraton, 1997). As James and Jenks observe, "such public accountability for children represents a revival of the concepts of 'the child' as public property taking us back to the pragmatic origins of mass education, the economic policy of 'human capital' and the educational ideology of vocationalism" (1996a, pp 327-8).

Such reactions and concepts are not easy to reconcile with a political philosophy that espouses the need to link responsibilities with rights, authority with democracy unless, of course, it is the case that children and young people are not seen as being members of the community and therefore as having only responsibilities and no rights, and only the need to conform and to obey authority, rather than to participate democratically (Roche, 1996b).

Families and divorce

In the areas of education and crime policies, we have identified mechanisms that are active and proactive forms of social control aimed at children through, largely the reassertion of 'family' values. Such forms of social control are clearly visible but, in addition to these, there are other less obvious but equally important *passive* mechanisms at play. As we shall show, these also hinder the development of a culture in which children's agency and, by implication, their citizenship, is acknowledged.

A significant development in recent years has been the growing interest in the development and application of mediation for the resolution of a range of community-based disputes, be these between employers and employees, victims and offenders, neighbours, or parents. This provides a mechanism whereby the community, rather than the state through the courts, resolves conflict. While undoubtedly cheaper mediation is at least as, if not more, effective than recourse to law and also, significantly, chimes with the main tenets of communitarianism to foster an active civic society. Of particular interest here is the recent emphasis on the use of mediation as a means of resolving disputes between parents over children when marriages and other parenting partnerships break down. This, we would contend, provides a clear example of a passive control mechanism for the regulation of children. It is dominated by an emphasis on the responsibility of adults to resolve such disputes and to make decisions about the future arrangements for children.

It is, of course, the case that the 1989 Children Act *did* place much greater emphasis than hitherto on the importance of taking account of the wishes and feelings of children. Children's involvement in child protection proceedings, for example, was considerably enhanced as a consequence of the Act. Similarly, in other areas of childcare policy, such as the Quality Protects initiative for children in local authority care, greater emphasis is now being given to consulting and responding to the views of children In contrast, however, in spite of the rhetoric accompanying the Act, in family breakdown and divorce the evidence is that the legal and social welfare practices engendered by the legislative framework deny children an effective voice. As we have argued elsewhere in relation to the working of the 1989 Children Act:

> Under the present law, in spite of a child-orientated rhetoric, it is adults
> – judges, magistrates, parents and welfare professionals – rather than
> children who remain in control when it comes to divorce and separation
> and thus, in relation to divorce, the Act can be said to be fostering a
> particular model of 'the child' in which ideas of agency are underplayed
> and those of structure fore-grounded. (James and James, 1999, p 198)

The child welfare rhetoric of the 1996 Family Law Act is equally powerful and yet mediation, which lies at the heart of the Act, is an adult-dominated process, designed to help adults, and not children, to reach decisions. It has become synonymous with securing the welfare of children in divorce, however, by virtue of the argument that it also serves to reduce the conflict between parents that can be so detrimental to children's welfare (James, 1995). Since there is no requirement to involve children directly in mediation,

> A major consequence of this arguably, then, is that even the currently
> limited child welfare safeguards of the formal legal process may be being
> further weakened and a particular model of the passive, dependent child
> increasingly endorsed. (James and James, 1999, p 199)

Conclusion: politics, policies and ideology

Running through our analysis of recent political initiatives with regard to children and the regulation of childhood is, therefore, the worrying prospect that these might represent a dark side of communitarian thinking and that 'the Third Way', while in principle seemingly having much to commend it and much that is socially positive, also has a deeply embedded ad seldom acknowledged social control agenda. It is also arguable that both the rhetoric of and the mechanisms for encouraging community involvement that we have elaborated, represent a post-modern version of the social contract. In contrast with the Hobbesian version that defined the relationship between the individual and the state, the Third Way defines the relationship between the individual and the community. This is achieved by a reordering of the relationship between the community and the state and the transfer of significant social control functions, together with the creation of new control mechanisms, to the community. However, as we have indicated, although they abound with the rhetoric of participation, such mechanisms are essentially about the selective empowerment of (some) adults only and of more widespread control over children as a group, and delinquent children in particular.

Thus, for example, while the *Supporting families* Green Paper offers many tempting morsels to those who would wish to see the development of some form of family policy, closer examination suggests that it has a strong social control agenda embedded within the rhetoric: for example the early years initiative, greater use of grandparents, the role of health visitors in terms of policing families for child abuse, and so on. The production of the 'millennial' family, and presumably 'millennial children' is its thrust. It is arguable, therefore, that the communitarian philosophies of New Labour are having the effect, at least in part, of incorporating the family and the community into the social control mechanisms of the state.

Such developments should also be viewed in the context of the increasing emphasis on the rights of children internationally, which is evident in the UN Convention on the Rights of the Child (UNCRC). As James and Richards have argued, there is currently a growing recognition that:

> ... children are important social actors and, as the UN and some nation states are beginning to recognize, they have rights, The challenge to sociologists, psychologists and policy makers is to identify what these *are* and *should be*, and to frame legislation which takes full account of these alongside the rights of parents. (1999, pp 36-7)

Reflecting such concerns, in its response to the first UK report on the UNCRC, the UN Committee suggested, inter alia, that the UK should give greater priority to:

> ... the child's right to make their views known and to have these views given due weight, in the legislative and administrative measures and in policies undertaken to implement the rights of the child. It is suggested that the State party consider the possibility of establishing further mechanisms to facilitate the participation of children in decisions affecting them, including within the family and the community. (DH, 1999, Appendix A, para 27)

Progress to date in the UK leaves much to be desired, however. Although the government has responded to some of the recommendations of the UN Committee in relation to the first report, this is often qualified in such a way that any additional rights given to children remain in the gift of adults. Thus, for example, although panels considering the exclusion of children from school should now allow the pupil to attend and "speak on his or her behalf, if he/she *and* his/her parents request" (DH, 1999, para 9.25.1; emphasis added), they may refuse to allow this if they believe there is 'good reason' for doing so.

Similarly, in spite of a recommendation by the UN Committee that "serious consideration" should be given to raising the age of criminal responsibility throughout the UK (DH, 1999, Appendix A, para 36), the 1998 Crime and Disorder Act went in the opposite direction. Perversely, it ended the limited protection that the long-established presumption of *doli incapax* gave to children between the ages of 10 and 14 by requiring the prosecution to prove that a child being prosecuted knew what they were doing was wrong. This thereby effectively reduced the age of criminal responsibility to the age of 10. Similarly, in relation to the field of divorce and family law, the government argues that the provisions of the 1996 Family Law Act (DH, 1999, para 7.19) enhance the rights of children and yet, as we have argued above, it provides few effective means for their wishes and feelings to be heard.

Beneath the rhetoric of the second report, the reality of change is limited. Our examination of many of the recent initiatives with regard to children and young people has revealed areas of concern in relation to the status of children as citizens, as members of the community, and of the community's attitudes towards them. In spite of the UN Convention, therefore, and all of the political rhetoric about children and their rights to be heard, it can be argued that this may, in effect, amount to little more than an artifice that conceals the real nature of the way in which mechanisms for retaining and increasing the control over children are being sustained and even extended. It would appear that the net of social control has an increasingly fine mesh and is permeating more areas of more children's lives than ever before. As Freeman has pointedly observed, "we have also to appreciate that ours is a culture that does not particularly like children. The adage that 'children should be seen and not heard' has an authentically English ring about it" (1998, p 342).

It is evident that communitarian principles that underpin the broad-based political agenda of New Labour will result in a significant extension of control over children and one that, in terms of the government's response to the UN Committee, is largely covert and concealed beneath the rhetoric of the *extension* of children's rights. The question is how far this process can, or should be allowed to, go. As Goldson observes:

> Children are not only future members *of* society they are active participants *within* society, and as such the temporal and spatial institutional arrangements intrinsic to familial and state forms of socialization require critical scrutiny. (1997, p 27)

Etzioni acknowledges that:

> ... for a community to maintain an overarching pattern, to be metastable, [it] must respond like a person riding a bicycle; it must continually correct tendencies to lean too far in one direction or the other, as it moves forward over a changing terrain. (Etzioni, 1996, p 9).

The question we seek to raise, therefore, is whether current trends in social policy reflect the possibility that this particular political cyclist might be in danger of losing its balance by marginalising and limiting the freedom of an important but relatively powerless group of citizens – children.

Notes

[1] Such a depiction recalls the so-called 'crisis' in childhood identified above and might, we would suggest, be worthy of similar deconstruction as a discourse of fear.

[2] For example, Beiner (1995); Oliver and Heater (1994); Twine (1994).

This chapter was taken from the *British Journal of Sociology*, 2001, vol 52, no 2. The right of Adrian James and Allison Janes to be identified as authors of this chapter has been asserted by them in accordance with the 1988 Copyright, Designs and Patents Act.

'Mad', 'bad' or misunderstood?

Vicki Coppock

Children's behaviour, its definition, assessment and regulation, is rarely out of the news. It remains the focus of both professional and popular discourses, constantly labelled and regularly invoking calls for greater intervention. Within the ensuing debates the 'mad', 'bad' or 'sad' child is publicly defined and rarely consulted. Invariably, the public and professional debates turn on the conflated issues of 'acceptable' behaviour and 'normality'. The process of defining, identifying, explaining and responding to deviant or 'abnormal' behaviour becomes the vital reference point against which normality is itself defined. What has emerged is a process, in both professional and popular discourse, based on binary opposition. Yet it is an arbitrary process that sets boundaries around normality without reflecting on historical, cultural, ideological, socioeconomic and political contingencies. What follows is a critique of this process as it relates to children and young people whose behaviour is defined as 'disturbed' or 'disturbing'.

While clinical studies have attempted to give scientific rigour to judgements about disturbed or disturbing behaviour in children and young people, they rely heavily on adults – parents and professionals – to make initial judgements that determine particular behaviours as problematic. Thus, "we have to see clinicians in their social role as authoritative interpreters of disturbance, adding a further layer to the commonsense definitions used by parents" (Grimshaw and Berridge, 1994, p 8). As Steinberg states:

> The process by which adolescents become psychiatric patients has as much to do with the feelings and behaviour of other people, and with social customs and routines, as with anything happening inside their heads. (cited in Malek, 1991, p 44)

This is not to deny that many children and young people experience mental distress. Nor is it suggested that parents and professionals are engaged in a conspiracy of ill-will. However, the medical model of mental health, which dominates the theory and practice of child and adolescent mental health, requires scrutiny in terms of its reliability and validity as an indicator of that distress. Such scrutiny is essential given the extent to which the medical model is utilised in professional interventions that impact significantly on the lives and opportunities of children and young people. Central to the dynamics of professional knowledge and practice is what Hood-Williams (1990) refers to as 'age patriarchy' – the way in which a range of elements including, theoretical knowledge, institutional sites, legal codifications and professional practices, structure the experiences of children and young people.

From an initial historical and theoretical contextualisation of constructions of the mental health of children and young people, this chapter explores the problematics of the defining process, and its consequences, in the form of inconsistent institutional responses. The implications of differential interventions for the rights of children and young people are important issues here. Contemporary debates concerning the perceived deterioration in the mental health of children and young people are critically examined, along with policy developments in child and adolescent mental health service provision. Finally, it is necessary to consider fundamental changes in adult–child power relations as the basis for creative and appropriate future policies and professional responses.

Historical and theoretical contexts

It is not possible to comprehend the significance of contemporary understandings of 'disturbed' and 'disturbing' behaviour in children and young people without reference to individual and, in particular, developmental psychology as the key framework of explanation. Theoretical knowledge and professional discourse emanating from psychology and psychiatry have stood as arbiters of normality and abnormality since the latter half of the 19th century. Individual psychology emerged in the context of late Victorian 'scientific' inquiry. Scholars of evolutionary theory, anthropology and philosophy, obsessed with numbers, measurement and quantification, searched for social laws to explain human behaviour. As part of this positivist tradition, child study – observing, weighing and measuring children, documenting their interests and activities – reflected the increasing importance of science. Not only did this tradition provide a set of procedures for conducting research, but also a set of practices associated with the modern state (Burman, 1994). Rose (1985) highlights the centrality of individual psychology in the role of classification and surveillance. Gradually, commonsense assumptions were translated into scientific truths, creating the context for, and giving legitimacy to, increasing practices of social regulation and reform. The emergence of individual psychology, at least in part, formed a response to wider social and political concerns of the late 19th century (Rose, 1979, 1985, 1989, 1990; Foucault, 1977a; Donzelot, 1980). The consequences of early capitalist production, rapid industrialisation and urbanisation produced unprecedented social upheaval, human squalor and misery. Fear of civil unrest was a real concern to the upper and middle classes, given the precedent set by the French Revolution. Fuelled by the 'scientific' rhetoric of Social Darwinism, attention focused on the physical and mental/ moral 'quality' of the general population. Having discovered the principles of inheritance, there followed the possibility of the degeneration of the population through bloodlines and the 'over-breeding' of the poor, criminals, the physically and mentally disabled (Sapsford, cited in Clarke, 1993). The fusion of the 'mental' and the 'moral' was crucial, "to the extent that the object of political anxiety and scientific intervention became the 'feeble-minded', who came to signify physical, moral, mental and political disintegration" (Burman, 1994, p 13). The stage was set for psychology to offer the 'tools' necessary for the identification, classification, control and regulation of those identified as threatening the social order. The establishment of compulsory schooling provided the psychologists with living laboratories in which they could observe large numbers of children (Rose, 1990). A mass of data was collected, standardised and analysed to construct norms for childhood growth and development. Mental testing provided an instrument through which 'normal' or 'abnormal' mental health and/or ability could be assessed and established. Yet, as Burman observes:

> The normal child, the ideal type ... is a fiction or myth. No individual or real child lies at its basis. It is an abstraction, a fantasy ... a production of the testing apparatus that incorporates, that constructs the child, by virtue of its gaze. (Burman, 1994, p 16)

Moreover, the practice of scientific research was dominated by the preoccupations and priorities of white, middle-class men, so that what became known about children and childhood carried assumptions implicit in patriarchy, colonialism and capitalism. Walkerdine (1984, p 173) comments that the coincidence of interest between the emerging profession of individual/developmental psychology and the wider political context cannot be reduced to some causal determination but "each should be taken as mutually implicated, making and remaking each other possible, intertwining to produce a discursive and political nexus".

For James and Prout (1990a) three themes underpinned the construction of the 'normal' child – rationality, naturalness and universality. Rationality is taken as the hallmark of adulthood, reinforced by a false ideology of childhood irrationality and incompetence. Just as femininity cannot be conceived outside its subjugation to masculinity, so childhood has been constructed as an inferior binary opposite to adulthood. Such assumptions have confirmed and legitimated the powerlessness of children by asserting their incapacity. 'Naturalness' and 'universality' provide the key ideological feature of inevitability, leaving little or no room for contradiction or conflict. The 'normal' child takes on an eternal, timeless quality, so embedded in the general consciousness that it becomes impenetrable. Consequently the premises on which it is based – white, western, middle class, male – have seldom been exposed, let alone challenged. Ultimately, such conceptions fail to acknowledge a variety of social relations and determining contexts within which children and young people are located.

A range of theoretical models of human behaviour has emerged from the late 19th century onwards. They co-exist and compete with each other, tending to polarise around the nature versus nurture debate. The search for the 'x' factor, that which distinguishes 'normal' people from 'abnormal' people, has embraced such diverse issues as poor parenting (that is, mothering), faulty social learning, biochemical imbalance and genetic structure. What they each have in common, however, is a focus on individual, familial and/or social pathology, and the overarching application of the 'medical model'. As Hargreaves (cited in Ford et al, 1982, p 35) explains, the medical model approach adopts "the whole conceptual apparatus of symptom, syndrome, diagnosis, aetiology, pathology, therapy and cure". While research has demonstrated a wide discrepancy between the criteria used for the identification of 'problem behaviour' and the assessment of individual cases, thus confirming "fundamental disagreements between the professions over issues as basic as the definition of a disorder or the concept of treatment" (Hersov, cited in Kurtz et al, 1994, p 3), the medical model conveniently disguises these disparities. It is in the acceptance of a specific behaviour as a 'problem', an 'illness' to be treated, that the power of professional hegemony is located. Once agreement has been reached, the only point of professional debate is *which* treatment should be given, *when* and *where* (Ford et al, 1982).

The medical model generates a polarised understanding of mental health rather than one that recognises human behaviour as richly diverse and fluid, better represented as a continuum. It also fails to acknowledge that knowledge is not produced, nor do professionals practice, in a vacuum. Race and gender characteristics, for example, clearly demonstrate the operation of subjective assessments in this field (Fernando, 1991; Russell, 1995). Discourses around femininity and masculinity have produced gendered constructions of 'acceptable' and 'unacceptable' behaviour for girls/women and boys/men. While "for boys, aggression, assertion and delinquent behaviour are deemed natural, part of their progressive development ... [for girls] ... any deviance has been viewed as a 'perversion' or the result of individual pathology which rejects passive, naturally feminine behaviour" (Coppock et al, 1995, pp 29-30). Similarly, an examination of the history of psychology and psychiatry illustrates the way in which ethnocentric and racist thought and practice has permeated these disciplines (Fernando, 1995). Negative stereotypes of black and minority ethnic children and families in Britain have been incorporated into the knowledge base and practices of professionals, constructing them as 'pathological' and 'deviant' (Dominelli, 1997).

The role of the state in relation to child health, welfare and education has been well-established through a mushrooming network of institutions and academic/professional disciplines – medicine, psychology, psychiatry, health visiting, teaching and social work. Although each profession has developed within its own distinct institutional framework, professional practices have 'converged' at the site of discourse and 'knowledge' derived from within 'the psychology complex' (Foucault, 1977a; Rose, 1985). While it has been acknowledged that services for children and young people have been far from unified, evolving unevenly and without coordination, a professional hegemony can be identified within which the lives of *all* children and young people have been constructed through the dominant discourses of development and socialisation.

The problematics of the defining process

While theoretical developments and changes in practice imply a journey of innovation and progress in this field, critical research reveals this to be a misleading assumption. The historical vagaries concerning definitions of 'disturbed' and 'disturbing' behaviour in children and young people, when set alongside structural inconsistencies in service development, clearly expose the scope for significant professional discretion and autonomy in decision-making processes. Although constructions of 'normality' and 'abnormality' have been firmly institutionalised in the state's response to children and young people, the catch-all nature of the formal diagnostic labels used allows for a wide interpretation of 'disturbance', from lying and disobedience to attempted self-harm (Jaffa and Deszery, 1989). For example, the *International Classification of Mental and Behavioural Disorders* (ICD-10 WHO, 1992) states:

> Disorder is not an exact term, but it is used here to imply the existence of a clinically recognizable set of symptoms or behaviour associated in most cases with interference with personal functions. Social deviance or conflict alone, without personal dysfunction, should not be included in mental disorder. (cited in NHS Health Advisory Service, 1995, p 17)

Yet the diagnostic classification of *conduct disorders* persists in child and adolescent mental health practice (see Kurtz, 1992; NHS Health Advisory Service, 1995; Royal College of Psychiatrists, 2002). Clinical features cited include stealing, lying, disobedience, verbal or physical aggressiveness, truanting from school, staying out late, smoking, drinking and drug-taking. Moreover, it is widely acknowledged that conduct or behaviour problems are the most common presenting problem of childhood and adolescence, to the extent that it is feasible to argue that such 'problems' are statistically normal. For example, the Elton Report (DES, 1989) *Discipline in schools* noted that 97% of primary and secondary teachers reported 'disruptive' behaviour in their classrooms (that is, talking out of turn and hindering other pupils, making silly noises, work avoidance, not being punctual, getting out of seat without permission). Similarly, the 1986 NHS Health Advisory Service Report (cited in Malek, 1991, p 8) notes that "many of these behaviours might be regarded as an extension of normal adolescent behaviour but had been unacceptable....". Significantly, Rutter (1977), one of the most prolific writers and researchers into child and adolescent mental health, has stated that non-conformity can never be used as an indicator of psychiatric disorder and that psychiatric treatment has little to offer in cases involving 'disorders of conduct'. This brings into question the validity of diagnostic labels and the reasons behind the ongoing 'treatment' of substantial numbers of children and young people under these classifications. The circularity of definition is exemplified in a study by Wallace et al (cited in DH and DfE, 1995) where mental ill-health in children and young people is defined as "a disturbance of function in one area of relationships, mood, behaviour or development of sufficient severity to require professional intervention". Within the medical model, therefore, the presence of certain behaviours is simultaneously taken to signify the existence of, being also the consequence of, some abnormality.

The claim to specialist knowledge is central as it underpins the professionals' claim to be qualified to 'know better' than clients, to be trusted by the public and to be given rewards and prestige, with significant powers of intervention (Williams, 1993). 'Expert' control distances parents and children through the use of technical jargon, a vocabulary that confuses and often predetermines outcomes through a subscription to categories or disease models. For parents the model has attractions in that they can feel relief at receiving an explanation for their child's behaviour that absolves them of the charge of 'bad parent'. For professionals the model allows them to be 'caring' while also repressing deviance, through the provision of help or treatment. In both cases the constraints of the model allow adult definitions of 'acceptable' and 'unacceptable' behaviour to prevail, leaving little room for any alternative understanding of the behaviour as an appropriate or reasonable response to stressful relationships between adult(s) and child/young person. For this is a relationship rooted in wider structural relations.

Research examining agency intervention in the lives of children and young people classified disturbed or disturbing (Malek, 1991) identifies the involvement of four main systems – education, social services, health and criminal justice. Moreover, it is recognised that each of these systems broadly deals with the *same* types of behaviours (NHS Health Advisory Service, 1986; Malek, 1991; Audit Commission, 1999b). As Malek states:

> Many of the characteristics of young people which are perceived as making a significant contribution to their admission to psychiatric care are similar to those presented by young people who come to the attention of legal, educational, or social services authorities. This is particularly true of those who are admitted primarily for behavioural and/or emotional problems. (Malek, 1991, p 41)

Each system, however, assigns its own diagnostic label or definition derived from the historical vagaries and precedents of its particular professional knowledge base/discourse. Consequently a child or young person could be given the label of *emotionally and behaviourally difficult* (education – special needs), *beyond parental control* (social services), *conduct disordered* (health – psychiatry) or *young offender* (criminal justice). This reveals not only the arbitrariness of the processes through which 'disturbed' and 'disturbing' behaviour in children and young people is defined by parents and professionals, but also how the diagnostic label and its application is contingent upon the first point of contact, identification and referral. Thus, the defining process is as much a cause of concern as the definitions employed.

The process is usually set into motion following parental complaints concerning a child's or young person's intolerable behaviour. Typically, this includes disobedience, lying, staying out late, running away, truancy, theft, verbal and/or physical violence (see Steinberg, 1981; Jaffa and Dezery, 1989; Grimshaw and Berridge, 1994). Where help is sought invariably determines the route to provision. If pursued through the family doctor or health visitor, the 'problem' is diagnosed within a medical framework, most likely following the route to child and adolescent psychiatry. If pursued through school, it is given an educational focus and is referred to an educational psychologist. Within social services, it is likely to be defined as a social/legal problem, depending on whether or not the child or young person has committed an offence. In Malek's (1991) research, professionals revealed that diagnoses often are made for administrative and bureaucratic reasons and do not always give a realistic indication of a child or young person's situation. Certainly, it does not follow that routes to provision are the result of rational assessment and planning as implied by the medical model. Moreover, within each system and at each stage of the defining process, assessments of behaviour operate within the determining contexts of race and gender, producing fundamentally different patterns and outcomes for girls and boys, and for black and white children and young people (see Campbell, 1981; Hudson, 1983; Harris and Webb, 1987; Cain, 1989; Harris and Timms, 1993; Children's Legal Centre, 1994; Grimshaw and Berridge, 1994).

Once 'the problem' acquires the status of requiring 'expert' intervention, things can be done to children and young people that otherwise would not be possible. Thus, for example, the 1981, 1993 and 1996 Education Acts allow for formal assessment and statementing and for the removal of children and young people from home for residential 'special' education. The 1989 Children Act, the 1991 and 1993 Criminal Justice Acts; the 1994 Criminal Justice and Public Order Act and the 1998 Crime and Disorder Act also allow for their removal from home to be looked after, remanded or to serve a sentence in the care of the local authority. Finally, they can be treated by a child and adolescent psychiatrist in the community or admitted to a residential psychiatric facility simply with parental consent, or under the provisions of the 1983 Mental Health Act. Not only is the process governing the system through which children and young people are processed arbitrary, but also the implications of differential treatment between systems are far-reaching as each system offers them different legal rights (Daly and Hamilton, 2002). While general concerns have been expressed about safeguards guaranteeing the protection of rights, especially as a wide range of institutional and personal abuses have been identified in all settings, research has revealed how the mental health system offers children and young people the least protection from such abuses (see Children's Legal Centre, 1991, 1993, 1995; Malek, 1991; Hodgkin, 1993, 1994; Daly and Hamilton, 2002).

The rights of children and young people in the mental health system

Rights critiques have been strongly articulated in the field of adult mental health research, policy and practice but are relatively underdeveloped in the child and adolescent mental health arena. Nevertheless, since the early 1990s concerns have been expressed about rights and abuses have increasingly become the focus of critical researchers in child and adolescent mental health settings. Interventions in the lives of children and young people because of their perceived 'disturbed' or 'disturbing' behaviour can escalate into a spiral of increasing restriction. Many children and young people can find themselves in the mental health system either because of a lack of resources within one of the other local authority systems (Malek, 1991) or because one of the other systems considers them too disturbed for their intervention (Ivory, 1991). Once in this system, measures of control take on an overtly medical focus.

Critical analysis within psychology and psychiatry has acknowledged and shown the ease with which oppressive control can be redefined as 'therapy' (Edelman, 1977). This is particularly poignant for children and young people defined as 'disturbed' or 'disturbing', given the predominantly paternalistic framework that governs child welfare interventions. Prominent cases have highlighted the thin line between methods used to control children and young people and the rhetoric of therapeutic intervention in their 'best interests' (Children's Legal Centre, 1991, 1993; Ivory, 1991; Ogden, 1991; Fennell, 1992). In addition to the routine practices of behaviour modification, seclusion or solitary confinement, psychiatry utilises an even more powerful method, that of drug therapy. From this evidence it has become clear that the treatments directed towards 'difficult' or 'disturbing' behaviour within the mental health system often have grave consequences for the civil liberties of children and young people.

In principle, the United Nations Convention on the Rights of the Child (UNCRC) and the 1989 Children Act provide the apparatus for protecting the rights of children and young people in the mental health system. However, a range of practice issues and legal anomalies has been exposed that casts doubt as to whether the language of rights and the mechanisms of convention and law provide a sufficient challenge to the oppressive structures of mainstream child and adolescent mental health research, policy and practice.

Although children and young people receiving mental health care can be afforded protection under the 1983 Mental Health Act if they are 'formal' patients, the majority are admitted 'informally' by their parents or the local authority 'looking after' them. Often the term 'informal' is incorrectly substituted by the term 'voluntary', constituting a serious misnomer. As Stewart and Tutt argue:

> ... there is a sense in which all children in mental hospitals are hidden in custody because they are not allowed to discharge themselves without their parents' consent and nearly always it was their parents, or occasionally care authority, who originally requested admission. (cited in Malek, 1991, p 5)

In these settings there is no legal framework within which the rights of children and young people can be safeguarded, particularly in relation to the restriction of liberty, consent to treatment or complaints procedures. There is no access to Mental Health Review Tribunals, nor do they come within the scope of the Mental Health Act Commission. The Commission has expressed considerable concern about the lack of safeguards and has requested that its remit be extended to cover informal patients. Consequently, in 1990 the Department of Health issued a New Code of Practice in relation to the 1983 Mental Health Act. This was revised in 1993 to bring it in line with the 1989 Children Act. The purpose of the Code was to supplement the Act, offering practical guidelines and guiding principles around admission, consent to treatment and complaints procedures. However, there is no statutory duty attached to the Code. It applies to all patients, including those under 18. In relation to this age group the Code states that practice should be guided by the following principles:

- Young people should be kept as fully informed as possible about their care and treatment; their views and wishes must always be taken into account.
- Unless statute specifically overrides, young people should be regarded as having the right to make their own decisions (and in particular, treatment decisions) when they have sufficient 'understanding and intelligence'.
- Any intervention in the life of a young person, considered necessary by reason of their mental disorder, should be the least restrictive possible and result in the least possible segregation from family, friends, community and school (Children's Legal Centre, 1993, p 7).

Accumulated evidence (Children's Legal Centre, 1991, 1993; Hodgkin, 1993, 1994; Audit Commission, 1999b; Daly and Hamilton, 2002) demonstrates that professional practice does not reflect the spirit of the Code, including:

- lack of knowledge and implementation of legal rights concerning consent to medical treatment, and a general lack of rights to self-determination;
- ongoing segregation outside mainstream institutions and schools, away from family, community and friends;
- 16- and 17-year-olds placed and treated on adult wards;
- discriminatory practices leading to unjustifiable intervention and detention on the grounds of class, race, ethnicity, gender, sexuality, disability and so on;
- unnecessary restriction of liberty, use of restraint, locked rooms, seclusion, time-out and so on;
- inadequate assessment and, thereby, lack of care;
- indiscriminate use of drugs to control rather than treat;
- inappropriate and degrading behaviour modification techniques – deprivation of sleep, food, clothing and family contact;
- ongoing placement of children and young people in adult psychiatric facilities;
- lack of rights to confidentiality and privacy;
- use of peer pressure/bullying to maintain discipline.

In particular, the issue of informed consent is deeply controversial. Since the 1969 Family Law Reform Act, 16- and 17-year-olds have had a statutory right to consent to medical treatment, and since the landmark ruling in *Gillick v West Norfolk and Wisbech Area Health Authority* ([1986] A C 112), those under 16 have had a statutory right to consent to treatment (without parental knowledge or consent) provided they have 'sufficient understanding and intelligence'. This ruling was thought to have marked a new era in relation to children's rights as it dismissed the idea that parents had absolute authority over their children until they reach 18. The Gillick Principle was evident in the 1989 Children Act, bolstered by the UNCRC in the same year. A series of high profile cases, however, has cast doubt on the scope of the Gillick decision in relation to the right of a child or young person to *refuse* consent to treatment (Lawson, 1991; Masson, 1991; Fennell, 1992; Freeman, 1993; Bates, 1994). It had been assumed that a 'Gillick competent' child was entitled to give and to refuse consent to treatment. Yet the Court of Appeal decided that any person with parental responsibility, or the High Court with its inherent jurisdiction, in certain situations, is able to override a child or young person's right to refuse treatment.

The cases of *Re R, Re W* and *Re H* (cited in Fennell, 1991; Lawson, 1991; Masson, 1991; Freeman, 1993; Bates, 1994; Children's Legal Centre, 1995) each involved consideration of the compulsory treatment of 'disturbed' children and young people. In each case the right to refuse medical treatment was overridden. Moreover, their refusal to consent to treatment was taken as indicative of their 'Gillick incompetence'. Fennell suggests that this is problematic:

> What is not acceptable is the automatic assumption that refusal is irrational and can be overridden whether or not the patient is competent. This is the very assumption which underlies Lord Donaldson's guidance – that children under 16 are never competent, even if they are *Gillick* competent, to refuse treatment as long as someone else with a concurrent power of consent agrees to it. (Fennell, 1992, pp 327-8)

Adults are presumed to be competent unless there is evidence to the contrary. Thus, it is the severity of the test for 'Gillick competence' that "provides the basis for decisions in individual cases which ignore the child's wishes" (Masson, 1991, p 529). From this, Masson deduces that it is virtually impossible to envisage a situation where a child or young person with a negative mental health label could ever refuse treatment. She challenges the paternalism inherent in the Court of Appeal decisions that allows adult views to dominate and suggests that this stems from "the belief that paternalism is better than self-determination where decisions relating to children are concerned" (Masson, 1991, p 529).

In matters to do with the fundamental right to bodily integrity the adult patient's autonomy is considered more or less inviolable. By contrast, children and young people have little option but to submit to medical treatment considered in their best interests, and as such they have no veto over what happens to their bodies. As Roberts (1999, p 15) states: "meaningful consent implies the possibility of saying 'no' and having this refusal respected". Both the 1989 Children Act and the UNCRC clearly place a duty on health professionals to seek the views of children and young people 'in accordance with their age and maturity'. This means that they should be consulted over all forms of treatment, including any potentially negative effects, or possible alternatives. There is no valid excuse for a child or young person to be excluded from actively participating in this decision-making process. To ensure that a child or young person has sufficient understanding and intelligence to make an informed decision about their treatment requires that adults allow them the information and opportunities for discussion they require (British Association for Community Child Health, 1995).

In July 2001, the Department of Health published *Consent – what you have a right to expect: A guide for children and young people* (DH, 2001). However, this guide fails to acknowledge the hidden processes of professional power and authority bearing down on children and young people in these situations. Several commentators have argued that it is the reliance on common law and discretionary guidance and the reluctance of professionals to *formally* detain children and young people under the 1983 Mental Health Act that leaves them exposed and vulnerable to human rights abuses (Masson, 1991; Fennell, 1992; Bates, 1994). It is a reluctance derived in the 1957 Percy Commission, which stated that children and young people should be admitted "by the exercise of normal parental authority" (in Bates, 1994, p 133). In June 2002, the government unveiled its draft Mental Health Bill for consultation. It is anticipated that new provisions would be made to accord greater rights to refuse treatment to young people aged between 16 and 18 years, and access to Mental Health Tribunals for those under 16. While the process of review represents an opportunity for the current unsatisfactory situation facing children and young people in the mental health system to be brought more fully into the open for critical debate, it remains the case that the proposed legislation does not resolve many of the issues raised above (Daly and Hamilton, 2002).

The current 'crisis'

It is clear that the situation has become a legal minefield in which the debate is conducted exclusively by adults, leaving children and young people without a voice. Those small advances made towards their involvement in decisions about their lives, respecting their views and enabling them to take greater responsibility, have been negated or exposed as rhetoric. This is of particular concern given that statistical evidence since the mid-1990s indicates that increasing numbers of children and young people are being diagnosed with, and treated for, mental health problems (NHS Health Advisory Service, 1995; Mental Health Foundation, 1998, 1999; *Community Care*, 2000; ONS, 2000; *Community Care*, Mental Health Foundation and Young Minds, 2002). Moreover, significantly more children and young people are experiencing the overtly medical, psychiatric system with all this implies for their civil liberties.

This trend is most forcefully illustrated through an analysis of the increase in numbers of children and young people in Britain being diagnosed with Attention Deficit (Hyperactivity) Disorder (ADHD) and treated with stimulant medication such as methylphenidate (Ritalin). ADHD is a diagnostic category of the *Diagnostic and Statistical Manual of Mental Disorders* (DSM IV) of the American Psychiatric Association (1994). As such it is conceptualised as a mental illness. Children and young people are diagnosed with ADHD if they demonstrate particular behavioural characteristics (such as inattention, fidgeting, being easily distracted, disliking schoolwork, talking excessively and interrupting) to such a degree and so persistently as to indicate the presence of 'disorder'. Nevertheless, ADHD remains a heavily contested diagnostic category with many child and adolescent psychiatrists conceding the 'shakiness' of the 'evidence' for the existence of such a 'disorder':

> At present there is no biological marker that clearly identifies affected children. Furthermore it is unclear whether the disorder is unique or

merely one end of the continuum of age appropriate behaviour. (Guevara and Stein, 2001, p 1232)

The above statement makes an analysis of the statistical data on prescribing rates for Ritalin over the last decade all the more remarkable (DH, 2004). From just 2,000 prescriptions dispensed in the community in 1991, the figure had risen to 14,700 by 1995; to 47,900 by 1996; to 158,000 by 1999 and by 2003 it had reached a staggering 314,500. These figures do not include prescriptions from private practice, nor do they take account of prescriptions for other psychoactive medications used in the treatment of ADHD such as Dexadrine and Clonadine. British children as young as four have been prescribed Ritalin even though the drug is contraindicated below the age of six years by its manufacturer, Novartis. Concerns worldwide have prompted the United Nations to call on governments to seek out over-diagnosis of ADHD and over-prescription of medication. Clearly, the rapidly expanding diagnosis and pharmacological treatment of ADHD is a worrying indication of the increasing social control of children and young people through medication, amounting to a breach of their human rights (Breggin,1998; Coppock, 2002).

Such a dramatic statistical trend warrants closer examination and an understanding of the context of change. Over the last decade there has been extensive political and professional debate focusing on a perceived 'crisis' in the psychological health of children and young people, fuelled by intense media coverage of 'problem' behaviour (Jackson and Scott, 1999; Muncie, 1999; West, 1999; Buckingham, 2000; Franklin, 2002). It is suggested that society is witnessing unprecedented levels of 'disturbed' and 'disturbing' behaviour in children and young people. Moreover, this alleged deterioration is repeatedly connected to notions of increased violence and lawlessness (Haydon and Scraton, 2000; Goldson, 2002d; Muncie, 2004b). This is derived not only in the media and from the outbursts of politicians, but also in the statements of professionals who claim to work in the interests of children and young people. For example, Peter Wilson, Director of Young Minds, stated that:

> Most of us in the field agree that the degree of distress in young people is much more extreme now. They are exhibiting more extreme behaviour and are given to finding more violent solutions to their problems. (cited in Sone, 1994, p 16)

Similarly, Sue Bailey, consultant adolescent forensic psychiatrist, claimed to be dealing with "slightly more psychotic children than two years ago" (cited in Sone, 1994, p 16).

The intertwining of the 'mental' and the 'moral', so evident in the Victorian understanding of deviance, has gained a new lease of life. Politicians across the political spectrum, social commentators and professional 'experts' have been busy with television, radio, and newspaper specials devoted to the subject of whether children and young people are 'madder' and/or 'badder' than in previous generations. Genetic predisposition, chemical imbalances, religious/moral degeneracy, attachment failure, maternal deprivation, paternal deprivation, ill-discipline, bad teachers, broken homes, single mothers, video nasties, the list is almost endless in the search for explanation, as illustrated by the following quotes:

> I believe that human nature spurts out freaks. I believe these two are freaks and they just found each other. (Detective Sergeant Phil Roberts, Interviewing Officer, Bulger Investigation, *Public Eye*, 24 November 1993)

> Evil can creep up on children. (John Patten MP, *Newsnight*, 24 November 1993)

> By the age of ten a child should have developed a conscience. By the age of ten some children's experience of life has left them without a conscience at all. (Mark Easton, Reporter, *Newsnight*, 24 November 1993)

> Unmet emotional needs lead to inadequate parenting and damaged children. (Doreen Goodman, 'What About the Children?', *Guardian*, 22 February 1993)

> I've seen a growth in violent behaviour by boys who were brought up with no male figure. They feel close, dangerously close to their mothers and are frightened of it. (Valerie Sinason, child psychotherapist, *The Sunday Times*, 21 February 1993)

Whether the 'problem' is located within the individual child or seen as a consequence of a deteriorating society, there is a shared assumption of pathology and the need for *more*, not *less*, professional intervention to normalise and readjust their behaviour. At no point is the oppositional behaviour of children and young people interpreted as a legitimate expression of their anger, frustration and distress directed at a society in which they are at best tolerated (Mental Health Foundation, 1998). Instead of finding better ways of meeting the needs of all children, those who most openly express their distress are pathologised, medicalised or criminalised, and in too many cases drugged.

The professional and political interest in the subject of child and adolescent mental health services has intensified in the wake of the perceived crisis. A series of policy initiatives has emerged over the last decade aimed at overhauling service provision. In 1995 a major review by the NHS Advisory Service, *Together we stand*, reported that "child and adolescent mental health services are essentially unplanned and historically determined; that their distribution is patchy; that the work being done is variable in quality and composition; that the work they do seems unrelated in strength or diversity to systematically considered local need" (1995, p 3). It recommended that service provision be restructured to reflect "a coordinated, tiered, strategic approach to the commissioning and delivery of child and adolescent mental health services". Three years later, the government made child and adolescent mental health services one of the national priorities for health and social services. It provided a new modernisation fund for the service – £84 million over three years – which came on top of some £150 million in 1998/99. £2 million in specific grants for innovative pilot projects was also made available. However, in 1999 the Audit Commission report, *Children in mind*, disclosed that child and adolescent mental health services were still in a mess.

In 2001 a children's taskforce was established by the Department of Health to draw up a Children's National Service Framework (DH, 2003) and set standards for a wide range of health and social care services. In the process the rhetoric of quality assurance and service user involvement has dominated official discourse. With regard to child and adolescent mental health, it has been acknowledged that, "children, young people and families must all feel that a service has enabled them to present their own perspective on the problems that they bring and that they have been listened to.... Such communication is ... a potent test of a service's quality" (NHS Health Advisory Service, 1995, pp 82-3). Nevertheless, adult, professionally-driven approaches continue to dominate the field of child and adolescent mental health research, policy and practice. This is exemplified in the constitution and activities of the Mental Health and Psychological Well Being of Children and Young People External Working Group, one of six groups set up to develop the Children's National Service Framework. The main group membership consists of 21 senior professionals from psychiatry, psychology, health and education. Seven of the nine sub-groups consist of up to nine adults of similar senior professional status. The 'user participation' sub-group consists of just two individuals, both experts at the Department of Health. There is no direct representation of children and young people themselves. While some user consultation research has been commissioned (Baruch and James, 2003), it is the adult voice that dominates the activities of this group. While such imbalances persist it is unlikely that anything will change and the Audit Commission's observation that, "what had been learnt from consultation with users and carers had not actually been used to inform service development" (cited in National Children's Bureau, 1999, p 2), will continue to hold true.

Challenging professional discourses and classifications

Throughout the 20th and now extending into the 21st century, concerns have been expressed about the behaviour of children and young people, eliciting persistent responses from the state via a range of professional interventions. Yet, there is a sense in which the contemporary 'crisis' reflects an intensification of a much wider moral panic around childhood. This implies that it is adults' fear of the loss of their control, the loss of their power over children and young people, which is at the heart of the much-proclaimed 'crisis'. Psychological and psychiatric 'expertise' has inspired panic in adults about childhood, predicting catastrophe from the slightest parental 'mistake'. It has cultivated a belief in the ability to know, understand and predict the course that 'normal childhood' should take. It is this claim that has been found wanting, understandably leaving lay adults bewildered. Through critical research and analysis the hegemony of professional discourses around mental health that underpin and legitimate adult power over children and young people has been exposed as at best spurious and at worst overtly oppressive. The definition and demarcation of mental 'health' and mental 'ill-health', of 'normal' and 'abnormal' 'childhood(s)' are riddled with social and political meanings.

The rhetoric–reality divide between rights in discourse and rights in practice is indicative of the failure to acknowledge the persistence of those structures of power that lie at the heart of adult–child relations in child and adolescent mental health. Speaking of rights-based strategies in adult mental health, Rose (1986, p 177) argues that, "while rights strategies have won significant victories ... there are fundamental limitations to such rights strategies for mental health reform. They disguise problematic political objectives and depoliticise debate over the organisation of psychiatry". In other words, rather than empowering mental health service users, rights-based strategies may merely reorganise relations. That is, oppressive systems are capable of skilfully hijacking the language of rights to convey a powerful illusion of inclusivity, participation and empowerment. Rights-based strategies do not, of themselves, transform the relations of dominance between professionals and those subject to them. Power structures must be brought into the open.

Rose's critique can clearly be applied to the position of children and young people in mental health settings. Notwithstanding the importance of an articulation of children's rights in convention and statute, critics have argued that while there are no meaningful penalties for breaches the value of such rights is merely symbolic. This is evidenced in the UK government's repeated failure to fully implement the UNCRC and to comply with the recommendations of the UNCRC (1995, 2002). Although successive UK governments have produced a mountain of documentation and research initiatives that talk up the issues of inclusion and participation, the Committee has judged them guilty of paying little more than lip service to children and young people's rights. The established political or professional rhetoric cannot disguise the fact that the UK government's commitment to the holistic well-being of all children and young people is inadequate, fragmented and under-resourced (Calouste Gulbenkian Foundation, 1993; Children's Rights Development Unit, 1994; Hearn 1995; UNCRC, 1995, 2002). In this, the position of children and young people in the mental health system remains unchanged. Despite the potential challenge of rights discourses to the dominance of medical authority, clinical research and practice still tends to exclude the views of children and young people in the mental health system and treat them as passive objects. Indeed, contemporary developments in child and adolescent mental health service provision have consolidated professional hegemony, contributing to the long history of policy, legislation and practice in this field, which has served to strengthen adult control.

There remains a desperate need to construct new ways of responding to children and young people in distress. Critical research points to the lack of 'ordinary' people and places to whom they can turn for help and support (Laws, 1998; Laws et al, 1999; Mental Health Foundation, 1999; Smith and Leon, 2001; Youth Access, 2001; White, undated). The messages from children and young people in these studies pose a fundamental challenge to mainstream child and adolescent mental health research, policy and practice. They reveal that:

- Children and young people want accessible, informal, 'ordinary', flexible sources of help.
- They want a greater range of options in services.
- They want services to be responsive to *their* definitions of mental distress, not just professional, medical definitions.
- They do not want access to help and services to be contingent upon the application of a pathologising, stigmatising formal diagnosis.
- They want more say about their own treatment.
- They want less reliance on drug treatments.
- They would value more peer support mechanisms – befriending, advising and supporting.
- They want to be listened to.
- They want to have their competence recognised, particularly their ability to articulate their needs/views and to create solutions to their own distress.
- They want to be understood, respected, acknowledged and supported.

Sadly, research such as this is overwhelmingly funded and commissioned through non-governmmental organisations and therefore tends to remain outside of the mainstream, 'subordinate' to mainstream medical research and therefore marginalised.

It is clear that a positive approach to the mental health needs of children and young people can be achieved only in the context of a wider change in adult–child power relationships. This demands that children are respected as people first, that they are listened to and that they have the right to make informed decisions about their lives, free from adult judgements concerning their competence to do so. Practitioners need to acknowledge that while their practice is grounded in the traditions of the medical model of mental health they will fundamentally fail children and young people. They must retreat from institutionalised 'age patriarchy', which involves the abuse of knowledge and power. Moving on means dealing with the messy contradictions inherent in adult–child relationships. It means asking questions, recognising inadequacies and challenging oppressive structures. Only then can adultism be deconstructed and the human rights of children and young people respected.

This chapter [revised] was taken from Scraton, P. (ed) (1997) *Childhood in crisis?*, London: UCL Press. The right of Vicki Coppock to be identified as author of this chapter has been asserted by her in accordance with the 1988 Copyright, Designs and Patents Act.

Children and health

Malcolm Hill and Kay Tisdall

Introduction

According to Ariès (1973) the progress of hygiene and public health measures were a defining feature of the creation of modern 'childhood' alongside the development of schooling. For much of history, and still today in many parts of the world, children have faced a hazardous journey towards adulthood, with many having their lives cut very short. Debilitating diseases and malnutrition affect millions of children in developing countries. Only in modern times has it become the normal expectation that nearly all children will not only survive, but experience predominantly healthy lives. "Our forefathers would have been astonished at the elimination or control of common fevers, which they regarded as one of the inescapable burdens of childhood" (Court and Alberman, 1988, p 9). Notions of health and youth are commonly associated in people's minds and children are the healthiest group in the population, although as we shall see below a considerable proportion of young people do report longstanding illnesses. Since childhood is now widely presumed to be a healthy state, those who are seriously or chronically ill or disabled tend to evoke heightened anxieties and are vulnerable to greater social disapproval or marginalisation.

A significant consequence of changed health patterns is the present perception that behaviour is a major contributor to health and hence the key target of health policy. Vaccination, hygiene and other measures have to a considerable degree countered 'external', non-human health threats to children, so that eating, drinking, smoking, drug-taking, lack of exercise and sexual activity have emerged as defining areas for health improvement. Since many 'unhealthy activities' are pleasurable, scientific pronouncements readily blur with moral prescriptions, as 'healthy' comes to be identified with 'good' and 'unhealthy' as reprehensible (Backett, 1992). Childhood is a key site for attempts to influence behaviour, since this is the time when it is thought many habits are formed that have far-reaching health consequences. Hence health promotion strategies directed at children often have as goals the prevention of poor health in adulthood.

There has always been a tension between society's legitimate interest in public health and the rights of individuals and families to behave in private as they wish, but the centrality in modern health policies and campaigns of everyday activates sharpens the issue. [...] [F]rom a Foucaultian point of view, health professionals have been portrayed as major actors in the establishment of state social control over behaviour within families. The so-called psy-complex – a set of understandings derived from medicine, psychology and psychoanalysis – is conveyed by health and allied professionals mainly to parents but also to children in order to promote healthier child-rearing (Mayall, 1996). Increasingly children themselves have been the subjects of both general health education and specific campaigns (eg about dental care). Such social control need not be malign in intent or impact, but does raise questions about power, choice and autonomy. Children's weak position to challenge or resist adult influences makes them especially vulnerable. Moreover, the history of child health advice and treatment indicates frequent contradictions and changes, exemplified by volte-faces about the desirability of breast-feeding (Hardyment, 1983; Meadows, 1988; Gottlieb, 1993). Hence it is reasonable to doubt whether all current 'truths' will still be accepted as such in future years.

This chapter begins with considerations of the meaning of health – first to adults, then to children. Next, issues of health risk are examined, followed by responsibilities and rights with respect to healthcare. Finally, the nature and relevance of health services for children are briefly reviewed.

What is health?

Traditionally health has been seen as the absence of illness, but nowadays that is seen as an overly negative standpoint. The prevailing professional view is that health should be viewed more widely to include positive health and to embrace mental or psychological as well as physical health. The oft-quoted definition of the World Health Organisation refers to health as a "state of complete physical, mental and social well-being and not merely the absence of disease or infirmity" (Downie et al, 1990).

In many ways it is laudable that health policies and professionals adopt a broad view of illness and health, recognising the close interrelationships between the body, the mind, emotions, lifestyles, cultures and social structures. On the other hand, it can become difficult to identify what distinguishes a person's 'health' from the totality of their lives. Emotional and social issues become medicalised. The "assimilation of social movements and cultural influences into the health agenda" may deflect "social protest into technologies for their management and administration" (O'Brien, 1995, p 195), although many health professionals themselves recognise the importance of social and environmental conditions for health.

Where mental health is concerned, there is little consensus about the meaning of the term (Tudor, 1992; MacDonald, 1993). The main image of the 'mentally healthy person' portrays an autonomous, self-actualising individual, although such qualities are not perceived as normal or desirable qualities in all communities and cultures (Sartorius, 1992; Harris, 1992). The conventional medical view maintains a sharp distinction between normal children and those with a psychiatric disorder. Emotional difficulties and behaviours unacceptable to adults, which in other contexts are regarded as social problems, educational issues or special needs (see Chazan et al, 1994) become perceived as symptoms of mental or psychiatric disorder (Rutter and Rutter, 1993). Whether or not children come to be regarded as in need of psychiatric help depends to a considerable degree on the professionals and organisations they happen to be referred to. Consultation with a general practitioner (family doctor) is more likely to lead to a medical response, whereas concerns arising at school may lead on to special educational measures. Moreover, shortage of social services facilities has resulted in an overspill into the comparatively better resourced health sector. Yet children in psychiatric institutions are particularly vulnerable to abuses of their civil liberties, including the use of drugs to control them rather than providing positive treatment (Malek, 1991; Coppock, 1996).

The relationship between disability and health is a complex and contentious one. The example of pregnancy shows that it is not necessary to be ill to be able to benefit from medical care, but equally 'medialisation' may have drawbacks and be resented as subverting or sidelining other kinds of social and emotional care and control (Oakley, 1980). Children with some kinds of disability benefit from medical treatment. For example, medication can control the frequency and severity of fits for children who have epilepsy. For other disabled children, and especially those with learning difficulties, the need is much more for a range of educational and social inclusion measures [...]. For many years, significant numbers of so-called 'mentally handicapped' children were kept in long-stay hospitals, largely cut off from the outside world. This is no longer seen as appropriate or acceptable. In recent years it has been possible for many children with cognitive impairments to stay in or move to family settings, partly as a result of changed perceptions of their needs and capacities. Such arrangements are more in keeping with Article 23 of the United Nations Convention on the Rights of the Child, which states that a disabled child should live "in conditions which ensure dignity, promote self-reliance, and facilitate the child's active participation in the community".

Children's perceptions of health

Evidence suggests that British children share with health educators a view that health is primarily to do with diet and certain kinds of behaviour. This is not a coincidence, given the dissemination of such messages in schools. When asked to talk or draw about the main elements or requirements for their health, primary school children mostly focus on three main issues (Williams et al, 1989; Mayall, 1994c; Oakley et al, 1995):

- food and nutrition
- exercise
- dental hygiene.

For example:

> We brush our teeth and ... we ... I drink lots of milk to keep my teeth nice and white. (Rita, aged five, quoted in Mayall, 1996, p 92)

Indeed some young people with health problems or disabilities regret the lack of attention in schools to the understanding of childhood illnesses and conditions, as this young person with epilepsy illustrated:

> You talk about smoking and things, and you could [discuss epilepsy] then. I think we should do things about diseases. (quoted in Laybourn and Cutting, 1996, p 36)

Like adults, children often acknowledge or show discrepancies between the views they express about what they should do to be healthy and what they actually do. Most children seem to be quite well informed about the negative effects of eating too much food with high sugar, fat and salt contents. They also describe fresh salads and fruit as desirable, although not necessarily desired (Backett, 1990; Morrison, 1995). Nevertheless, for the majority of secondary school children, health considerations rate far below taste, appearance and price as factors in food choice (Brannen et al, 1994). As many as half of 15- and 16-year-olds in one study admitted to eating junk food daily (Oakley et al, 1995). Young children too deploy a range of strategies in order to gain access to 'unhealthy' foods like sweets and crisps. Trading the contents of packed lunches is one way of subverting parents' dietary intentions (Prout, 1996).

When asked, children affirm that physical activity promotes fitness and deem sedentary activities like watching TV as 'unhealthy', but they also report TV watching as a favourite pastime. Judgements and stereotypes about whether other children are healthy or unhealthy are mostly based on appearance (slim or fat), eating habits (especially the volume of sweets consumed) and athletic prowess (Backett and Alexander, 1991; James, 1993).

Particularly in adolescence, gender-based expectations about appearance and health impinge significantly on eating patterns (Brannen et al, 1994). For girls and young women, slimness is perceived as a vital social asset and restricted eating the main way of achieving this:

> I tend to sort of worry about how I look ... I just watch what I eat and weigh myself every now and then to make sure I'm still around that weight.

> I think boys don't really care what they eat, they'll just eat anything they want. Whereas girls sort of think about it and think 'Oh, should I be eating this, will it make me fat?' (Both quoted in Morrison, 1995, pp 251, 255)

Some females question cultural stereotypes regarding body image and the desirability of dieting, however:

> I've see 'Home and Away' and there's this girl Shannon and she thought she was too fat. And she was doing exercises and not eating her food and she was getting skinnier and skinnier and she wouldn't eat. And I thought

it wasn't good to do that cos it doesn't matter what size you are. (Girl, aged eight, quoted in Borland et al, 1996)

Children recognise smoking as a significant threat to health (Oakley et al, 1995). In one study involving primary aged children, key facts were widely known – that nicotine is an addictive substance, causes a number of types of cancer, affects the respiratory system and can kill (Borland et al, 1996). Yet the level of regular smoking remains significant among children in their mid-teens – about one in five (Power, 1995).

Children's understanding of illness

Research in this area has been of two kinds:

- asking mainly healthy children about illnesses in general;
- asking children about specific illness that they (or a sibling) have.

Very young children often find it hard to specify the precise location of pain and discomfort. American studies revealed that children often describe illness in terms of behaviours of the sick person and others (Eiser et al, 1983), for example:

- want to lie down
- irritable
- don't go to school
- my mother gives me medicine
- doctor gives me a shot (quoted in Campbell, 1975).

The range of children's definitions did not vary greatly by age and was not dissimilar to the definitions of mothers. However, older children mentioned more specific symptoms and diagnoses. They also showed greater awareness of social aspects of illness. In comparison with their often detailed knowledge about health promoting behaviour noted in the last section, children nowadays are often confused or lacking in their knowledge of the symptoms of even relatively common illnesses and of the role of injections (Eiser et al, 1983; Oakley et al, 1995). This may well be true of many adults, too.

Pre-teen children tend to see illnesses as having four main types of cause (Vaskilampi et al, 1996):

- contagion (microbes, viruses)
- association with dirt and pollution
- overeating and poor diet
- being outdoors with inadequate clothing.

Young children often explain illness through contagion from nearby objects or people, although the precise mechanism for this can be vague:

> If I have an illness and go near someone, they might catch it.
>
> Someone has it first, then it goes to someone else. (Quoted in Wilkinson 1988, p 122)

The explanations of illness given by well children have often been interpreted within a standard-stage framework based on Piaget [...]. Broadly a three-fold progression was identified (Bibace and Walsh, 1980; Eiser et al, 1983; Wilkinson, 1988):

1. Under age seven – ideas that illnesses have 'magical' causes (eg the sun, trees, God in the sky), or is a form of punishment for wrongdoing.
2. Seven- to 11-year-olds – vague mechanical explanations are offered for illnesses, with many children thinking that nearly all are caused by germs.
3. Teen years – greater recognition of the interaction between body, mind and environment; more specific connections made between particular conditions and body parts.

The stage-based pattern implies inherent limitations of children's thinking, but some elements can be regarded alternatively as reasonable conclusions drawn by children about their social worlds. Certain young children's 'misunderstandings' about illness as punishment can be seen as logical inferences from adult warnings about the dangers of breaking social rules (such as "eating food too quickly", quoted in Wilkinson, 1988, p 151). A more fundamental problem with stage frameworks is that several studies have revealed little difference according to age in children's perceptions. The results seemed to depend more on the type of sample and the way questions were framed (Eiser, 1989). Further, children with direct experience of an individual illness are much better informed about its nature, causes and prognosis than the average adult. It may be inferred that exposure to details is at least as important as any age-related differences in cognitive ability. Most children know much more about lung cancer than any other kind of cancer, because health education has devoted so much attention to the link with smoking (Oakley et al, 1995).

This debate has important practical implications. If young children are incapable of understanding illnesses in similar ways to adults then there is a justification for not attempting to explain or for offering special kinds of explanation (eg comparing invisible processes to concrete daily events in children's lives). On the other hand, if children's understandings are more affected by experience, information or observation, then straightforward communication not only respects children's abilities, but avoids dangers of children drawing possibly false inferences from adults' behaviour or being confused by the use of complex analogies (Eiser, 1989; Yoos, 1994).

The knowledge and understanding of children who are seriously ill – or with a sibling who is ill

Even more than with adults, it is commonly presumed that children with serious of life-threatening conditions should not be kept informed of the nature and course of their illnesses, either because they will not understand or because they will be unduly distressed. Consequently, "children are often so poorly informed that they are unable to make as many decisions regarding their own health as is considered desirable" (Eiser, 1989, p 94). However, sensitive research carried out with children dying of cancer found that they were much more knowledgeable than adults assumed, often drawing conclusions about their status from detailed observations of behavioural changes in doctors and nurses (Bluebond-Langner, 1978). Although comprehension tends to increase with age, it is affected even more by access to information and the care taken to communicate effectively, eg using lay terms and giving concrete examples (Ireland and Holloway, 1996).

Studies have shown that children with serious illnesses feel less stressed when they gain an understanding of the diagnosis, prognosis and treatment. Conversely, children are not protected from distress when adults try to keep secret the seriousness of their condition (Claflin and Barbarin, 1991). Information and experience can demystify and give a greater sense of mastery over events:

> It's much better now that I know what is going on. (Eight-year-old)

> I like to sort of feel like I have some control over a decision.... I like to know what is going on. It's my life. (10-year-old, quoted in Hockenberry-Eaton and Minick, 1994, p 1028)

Children with cancer reported gaining support from relatives and staff, but also took coping action themselves, particularly by pursuing their positive interests (Hockenberry-Eaton and Minick, 1994). Typically the young people with cancer aimed to maintain as normal an appearance and lifestyle as possible:

> I just decided to go on with life and forget about what I looked like and do the best I can and people will forget. (quoted in Rechner, 1990, p 14)

Similarly, children are able to recognise how calmness and relaxation may reduce asthmatic symptoms (Ireland and Holloway, 1996). Besides behavioural coping, children also use cognitive strategies, such as reminding themselves that painful treatment will soon be over and identifying strengths in themselves, their families and friends (Claflin and Barbarin, 1991).

As with other potentially shameful phenomena, many children prefer not to tell other people about serious illnesses, apart from close friends and relatives (Hockenberry-Eaton and Minick, 1994). Visible signs of ill-health threaten secrecy, and challenge personal and social identity:

> Losing my hair was a hard thing to put up with. I looked at myself and thought 'Wow! There is something' and everyone else looked at me and said 'Yes, there is something seriously wrong with him'. (16-year-old, quoted in Cadranel, 1991)

Appearing 'imperfect' can be acutely distressing in a society that places so much value on health and good looks, as defined according to cultural norms.

Bluebond-Langner (1991) investigated the perspectives of well children on their siblings with cystic fibrosis. This is a degenerative illness – "the most common fatal inherited disorder in childhood" (Cadranel, 1991, p 240). They too reported how the salience of the disease reduced markedly as care tasks, hospital visits and treatment became a regular part of everyday life:

> Most of the time I forget she has it 'cause the things become quite routine. Like, you know, we're having therapy in the morning is, like, I don't even think about it anymore. (14-year-old, quoted in Bluebond-Langner, 1991, p 137)

In the early stages of the illness, they invested effort in thinking about their brother or sister as being 'like everyone else' and presenting this image to peers and others. Not only did this minimise feelings of difference and stigma by association, but "well siblings felt justified in making demands for attention, privileges and special foods like the patient gets" (Bluebond-Langner, 1991, p 139). Typical sibling concern about favouritism arose:

> Since he's come along, it's like we don't even exist. (14-year-old)

> You can't let him get away with everything just 'cause he's sick. (12-year -old, quoted in Bluebond-Langner, 1991, p 1340)

As the disease became progressively disabling, its impact on family life became increasingly pervasive and the attempts at normalcy harder to sustain:

> It's in your thoughts all the time. (16-year-old, quoted in Bluebond-Langner, 1991, p 1340)

Even when able to acknowledge that the illness is terminal for children in general, several clung to hopes of a miracle recovery for their own sibling.

Risks to health

We turn now from the subjective meanings of health and illness to considerations of children's differential exposure to health hazards. Illness and injury have been increasingly referred to as risks to health, thus forming part of a wider risk discourse that characterises much of present-day life (Beck, 1992 [...]). Children's health risks include:

- dying in childhood;
- falling ill;
- being involved in an accident;
- premature death in later life as a result of illness or behaviour starting in childhood.

About 10,000 children die in the UK each year, rather more than half of them aged under one year (Woodroffe et al, 1993). The infant mortality rate is often cited as an index of national health levels. Although the UK rate is very low compared with 100 years ago, it is significantly higher than in much of western Europe (Kurtz and Tomlinson, 1991). The most common causes of children's death in England and Wales in 1991 were sudden infant death syndrome for infants and injuries/poisoning for older children, with congenital abnormalities and neoplasms significant at all ages (Botting and Crawley, 1995).

Suicide is rare below the age of 12, but significant numbers of teenagers kill themselves, accounting for one tenth of all deaths in that age group. Four times as many males as females kill themselves each year and the number has risen sharply since the 1970s – thought to be due to increases in youth unemployment and parental divorce rates (Woodroffe et al, 1993).

Fortunately, life-threatening conditions and actions are rare in childhood, but ill-health is more widespread than many people think. Half of a sample of over 500 12-year-olds expressed concerns about their health, especially their diet and body shape (Brannen and Storey, 1996). In another large-scale survey, one in five children in their early teens reported that they had a long-standing illness (Ecob et al, 1993; Sweeting and West, 1996). Just under one in ten were affected by a condition that they said limited their activities. The most common conditions reported were allergies, headaches, skin complaints, chest problems and asthma. If various emotional/psychological problems are also taken into account as 'mental health' issues, then the number of young people who are not in good health becomes considerable. Referring to teenagers, Bennett (1985, p 11) spoke of "the widespread but misguided belief that they are a fit and healthy group".

The most common reasons recorded for children visiting their general practitioners are respiratory conditions (including asthma and bronchitis), which account for about half of consultations for children under five (Botting and Crawley, 1995). Several studies indicate that the increase in recorded consultations and hospital admissions for asthma represents a real spread of the illness and is not simply a matter of changed diagnostic practices. Since the prevalence of asthma is quite evenly distributed across the child population, it is likely that the cause of the increase is environmental, although the commonly quoted suggestion of air pollution is just one of several possible factors under investigation (Anderson et al, 1995).

About one child in 600 develops cancer, of which the most common forms are leukaemias and brain tumours. The past 25 years have witnessed a sharp improvement in survival rates. Although infections are a frequent cause of minor ill-health, they now rarely cause serious illness or death (Botting and Crawley, 1995). High rates of vaccination have contributed to large falls in the incidence of several infectious diseases (eg diphtheria and measles) and of related deaths. However, AIDS is "a new disease to which children are at risk through infection transmitted during pregnancy, delivery or breast feeding by an infected mother" (McCormick and Hall, 1995, p 168). Slightly more than half of the children known to be HIV-positive have become so as a result of blood transfusion or other blood-related transmission.

Accidents and risk

Accidents are the most common cause of hospital admissions for children (Jarvis et al, 1995). Accidental injuries and poisoning account for 24% of deaths of children aged one to four years, rising to 60% for 14- to 19-year-olds (Woodroffe et al, 1993). The most common types of fatal accidents are caused by road traffic, fire and drowning. Two thirds of child pedestrians who die in road accidents are boys and even higher percentages of cyclists killed are male (Polnay and Hull, 1993). This is partly linked to the greater freedom of movement afforded to boys than to girls [...].

Large numbers of children are admitted to hospital each year as a result of less serious injuries. Accident statistics indicate that exposure and vulnerability are affected by age, gender, environment and social class (Woodroff et al, 1993). Falls account for half of all accidental injuries inside the home. Accidents outside the home become more common as children grow older and typically spend more time apart from adults.

The great majority of injuries to children are deemed accidental. The term 'accident' implies randomness and lack of responsibility, but within the discourse of risk analysis "the accident becomes patterned and predictable" (Green, 1995, p 117). It then becomes possible to identify the circumstances in which accidents are more likely to occur and alter them. It is also a short step to saying that the victim should have predicted the accident and taken avoiding action. Children have learned that one way to stop accidents happening is to:

> Be very, very careful. (Amelia, aged eight, quoted in Green, 1995, p 129)

Yet they recognise that most accidents result from an interaction between a person and the physical world that has an unexpected outcome:

> We was sliding down the stairs and I was on her lap and then suddenly I fell down and she fell on top of me. (Maria, aged eight, quoted in Green, 1995, p 127)

Differing ideas about the causes of health needs affect the kinds of solution suggested. A study in a deprived area of Glasgow revealed that health professionals tended to think that children's exposure to accidents was largely due to faulty parental guidance, which they therefore tried to modify with advice about teaching children 'safe' behaviour. Parents, on the other hand, saw the risks as stemming mainly from poor housing and environmental design (eg unsafe wiring, balconies or roads). Their proposals were to make the environment safer and restrict traffic (Roberts et al, 1995). Preventive measures at societal level can be effective, as illustrated by the reduction in burns following regulations about flame-resistant nightclothes and the decline in poisoning associated with the introduction of medicine containers with more secure lids (Golding et al, 1988; Woodroffe et al, 1993). Sweden initiated a national policy for accident prevention in the 1950s, with the material environment as prime target of intervention (Court and Alberman, 1988). It was recognised that children's understanding of their environment can be very good, but before the age of about 10 they have difficulties in assessing traffic distance, speed and direction and in adapting safely. Rather than make children responsible for hazards from adult-driven vehicles, it was acknowledged that they had a need and right to protection, eg through better separation of traffic (Garling and Valsiner, 1985).

Behavioural health risks

Several of the most significant health and death risks for children do not derive from illnesses, but are related to behaviour and 'lifestyle' (for example, smoking or drug-taking). The main targets with respect to children of the *Health of a nation* White Paper and the report *Scotland's health* in the early 1990s had little to do with childhood illnesses, but concerned accidental death, smoking, drug and alcohol misuse, dental health and teenage conceptions.

Very few young people suffer immediate or short-term negative consequences from consumption of cigarettes, alcohol or drugs, but professionals are concerned that habits formed in youth carry significant risks of ill-health in later life (Smith et al, 1996). In several of these respects children's health risks have increased over the last decade (eg drug-taking). Self-reports about behaviour known to evoke adult disapprobation are open to doubts about accuracy, even when given anonymously. Such information suggests that about one quarter of 15-year-olds smoke regularly and about one in three have an alcoholic drink at least weekly (Woodroffe et al, 1993; Power, 1995). Despite the decline in the number of adults who smoke cigarettes, the proportion of school children who smoke regularly has remained stable (Roker, 1996). Far fewer children of Asian backgrounds smoke and consume alcohol, compared with white people and African Caribbeans (Brannen et al, 1994). Cannabis use is common among secondary school children (Barnard et al, 1996). It seems that *average* levels of physical activity by school children have declined, while sugar and fat intakes have remained static (Jackson, 1995). Over half of young people have had sexual intercourse by the age of 19 and it appears that as many as half did not use a contraceptive on the first occasion (Millstein and Litt, 1990; Brannen et al, 1994).

The health of children is also affected by actions of their parents. Parental heavy drinking heightens the likelihood of violence within the home and of car accidents. Smoking by parents not only exposes children to the effects of passive inhaling, but also increases the chances that the children will acquire the smoking habit (Woodroffe et al, 1993). Conflict within the family also has a number of adverse health or welfare consequences for children (Sweeting and West, 1995).

Risk-taking

Risk refers to the probability of something happening – in this context a negative health event. 'Risk-taking' denotes more active processes of engaging in activities that have high risk for negative outcomes, such as drug-taking or 'joy riding'. Young people are often depicted as risk-takers par excellence, although many are in fact cautious or anxious about many risks (Plant and Plant, 1992). Some young people perceive themselves as 'invulnerable' to the risk under consideration and may also feel overconfident about their knowledge (eg of contraception or drug risk). However, this is not necessarily a feature of their age group, but may reflect social circumstances or personality (Millstein and Litt, 1990). Peer pressure is often cited as encouraging risky behaviour, although generalised images and expectations may be as significant as direct incitement (Mitchell and West, 1996; Roker, 1996). Sometimes peer influences discourage 'risky' behaviour. For example, having close friends who are reliable contraceptive users is associated with "more responsible sexual attitudes and behaviours for both adolescent men and women" (Milburn, 1996, p 10).

One public health strategy aimed at reducing risk-taking has been to ensure people are aware of the risks. Usually increased knowledge proves to have little or no effect on behaviour (eg in relation to unprotected sex, drugs and smoking). For example, extensive knowledge about AIDS and the use of condoms does not necessarily lead to young people practising safe sex. Reluctance to use condoms is affected by power and self-image, as young men's sensitivity about their masculinity and young women's wish not to appear like a 'whore' can prevent open communication about safe sex (Henggeler et al, 1992). Young people are often well aware of the risks they take – indeed that can be part of the attraction. Actions that adults may perceive as health-threatening can appear pleasurable or stress-reducing to young people (Hurrelmann and Losel, 1990). They perceive any risks as small, not applicable to themselves or so far in the future as not worth worrying about (Furnham and Gunter, 1989; Smith et al, 1996). Often the short-term risk for any individual is low, while rational choice may be submerged by social and emotional considerations (Plant and Plant, 1992).

Health differences: health inequalities

Health risks are not evenly distributed. Many forms of ill-health in childhood are markedly over-represented in families with low incomes, especially those living in inner-city areas (Kurtz and Tomlinson, 1991). "A child in the lowest (unskilled manual) social class is twice as likely to die before age 15 years as a child in the highest (professional) social class" (Woodroffe and Glickman, 1993, p 193). Many features of childhood mortality, morbidity and development have been shown to be closely and negatively related to income and social class (Townsend et al, 1992; Woodroffe et al, 1993; Long, 1995). These include:

• perinatal and post-neonatal mortality rates;
• birth weight;
• height;
• dental health;
• respiratory illnesses;
• traffic accidents;
• deaths from fire.

Since the appearance of the Black Report in 1980, which documented marked socioeconomic differences in health (Smith et al, 1990; Townsend et al, 1992), debate has raged on the extent to which this results from statistical artefact, health selection (people in poor health being less able to obtain good jobs and high incomes) or social causation (poverty leads to ill-health). The evidence is complex, but there is support for the argument that deprivation directly or indirectly is a major contributor to ill-health. For example, a clear link has been established between damp housing and bronchitic symptoms (Woodroffe and Glickman, 1993). Lack of money is the main reason parents in poor households give for buying little fresh, healthy food (Dobson et al, 1994; Dowler and Calvert, 1995; Ward, 1995 [...]). Certain parental behaviours like smoking impact on children's health and these in turn are related to indices of social class and are often a means of coping with stress (Spencer, 1990; Graham, 1996). Children whose parents are unskilled are least likely to be taken for immunisations and other health services (Townsend et al, 1992).

The poverty–health correlation is strongest in the pre-teen years and emerges again in early adulthood, but class differentials are negligible during youth (Macintyre et al, 1989). Sweeting and West (1995) found only a minor influence of material deprivation on self-assessed health and self-esteem for Glasgow young people aged 15 and 18. This is the period when immediate health risks are smallest, so that family and lifestyle patterns seem to be much more influential in accounting for variations. However, certain specific conditions and impairments, as well as deaths from accidents, do show social class gradients at these ages (Townsend et al, 1992).

Gender influences the pattern of some illnesses and health-related behaviour. For example, anorexia nervosa is 12 times more common among females than males, which is clearly connected to cultural expectations about eating referred to earlier. Twice as many boys as girls aged 11 to 18 take exercise or engage in sport (Woodroffe et al, 1993). These are 'healthy' pursuits, although they carry risks of injury and strain. Whereas more boys experience chronic illnesses in early life (including asthma and migraine, the two most common), by mid-adolescence the pattern has reversed (Sweeting, 1995). Significantly more young women than men report having health difficulties and worries. Use of prescribed medicines is also higher (Brannen et al, 1994; Triseliotis et al, 1995).

Some specific problems (eg sudden infant death syndrome) are less common among children from minority ethnic backgrounds. Others (eg tuberculosis) occur more frequently, although incidence depends on the specific population grouping (Black, 1985; Woodroffe et al, 1993; Raleigh and Balajaran, 1995). Cultural explanations such as 'Asian diet' have sometimes been used inappropriately to explain ethnic variations in ill-health. In a few instances, there is a genetic component (eg sickle cell disorders). More often, material deprivation plays a significant part, as it did for white Britons earlier in the century (Mason, 1995).

Whereas health 'differences' may be seen as acceptable, application of the term 'inequality' implies social concern and an impetus for policy action. Significant health inequalities are not just unfortunate for the individuals concerned. They also have societal consequences, such as health service costs, reduced employment prospects and hence economic contributions, and public health consequences (Vagaro, 1995). This implies need for action at the societal level (for example, to reduce poverty, or alter attitudes to the female physique). Townsend et al (1992) called for the abolition of poverty to be adopted as a national goal, but government responses have instead taken the form of declaring poverty to exist, rather than practical action to deal with deprivation. The strategies embodied in the *Health of a nation* White Paper (DH, 1992) mainly focused on behavioural change (eg in relation to childhood accidents and teenage pregnancies) and failed "to recognise the role of poverty and social disadvantage" (Spencer, 1996a, b, p 150).

Responsibilities and rights in relation to children's health

Responsibilities for health

Generally, mothers assume the primary role as physical and psychological carer, cook, cleaner and so on, which lays the foundation for a child's health status (Mayall, 1986). They are usually the first to notice or be told that a child may be ill, drawing on culturally shaped knowledge about what is normal or deviant to differentiate substantial from passing or spurious health concerns. Mothers are also much more likely than fathers to notice and recall symptoms, provide basic care when a child is sick and organise contacts with health services (Mayall, 1994c; Brannen et al, 1994). Approaches to general practitioners are not made lightly, since mothers are concerned not "to bother busy doctors, nor to be seen as neurotic or overacting" (Cunningham-Burley and McLean, 1991, p 38). Children's sicknesses are often treated by means of domestic remedies like rest or hot drinks, perhaps abetted by non-prescribed drugs (Ahonnen et al, 1996).

Even at the age of 16, young people often seek advice from their mothers about whether to go to the doctor or not. Mothers are more likely to accompany teenage daughters than sons to the surgery, while fathers rarely go with either (Brannen et al, 1994). Children are more likely to attend the dentist if their mother goes on a regular basis. Several studies have shown that mothers are also children's main sources of information about health and related behaviour (Farrell, 1978; Sex Education Forum, 1994; Sharpe et al, 1996). Other relatives like a sister or an aunt can also serve as role models or sources of advice about diet and exercise (Borland et al, 1996).

As children grow older they accept more responsibility themselves, although parents retain a role to check and supervise:

> We're keeping ourselves healthy by doing things ourselves. It's my body, so it's my job. (Tim, aged nine, quoted in Mayall, 1996, p 94)

> If you just go and sit around and do nothing, that's not going to improve your health. So it's up to you. (quoted in Mayall, 1994c, p 47)

Children perceive themselves as having a role in the prevention and treatment of minor illnesses, eg by resting, taking an aspirin, and being careful in food choice (Bush et al, 1996). Children with disabilities or chronic conditions can take responsibility for self-care and medication (eg proper use of an inhaler for asthma, using appropriate creams for eczema or tablets for hay fever) and for monitoring (eg fits chart and sugar level) (Lindon, 1996). In general, the more serious the illness, the less scope there is for children to influence what happens in the face of adult–child and medical–lay power hierarchies. Most also have a high level of awareness that use of pharmaceuticals is a matter for doctors to prescribe and (usually) mothers to supervise (Prout and Christensen, 1996).

Friends have an important role in discussing health care, supporting a child after an accident or referring to adult help (Mayall, 1996). They can be important helpers for children with conditions like diabetes or epilepsy – especially when they have been warned what to do when unusual behaviours or a fit occurs:

> Dan starts doing stupid things – not like him at all. Or else he just stops in the middle of the road. So we get him out of any kind of trouble, then we make him eat something. He's told us what to do. (16-year old, quoted in Lindon, 1996, p 122)

Disclosure and explanations by young people themselves help friends to be less anxious and offer appropriate help:

> It doesn't worry my friends now because they know what to do ... I had to tell them what to do, like cos you're unconscious, so you have to put them in the recovery position and things like that.

> They're a lot calmer now [during a seizure]. Some friends were hysterical and crying and stuff, but now they just basically know what to do and they are really calm about it. (Quoted in Laybourn and Cutting, 1996, p 16)

One class of nine-year-olds stated that the main locales which enable them to keep healthy are the home and neighbourhood (sports centres, parks), with formal health services having a secondary role, while school barely figured at all (Mayall, 1994b). However, school does influence children's experience and knowledge. Teachers and school secretaries act as gatekeepers to parental or medical attention if children report felling unwell. Teachers are often concerned to discourage attention to what they regard as low-level or false claims to be ill. These are interpreted as 'fussing' or excuses to evade educational requirements (Prout, 1986; Mayall, 1996). There is clearly scope for misjudgement, although some children do indeed feign illness by changing their behaviour or appearance. Then legitimation may be needed when they feel really ill:

> I told them I was ill, but sometimes we say it to get out of school. So I was taken to the GP's and he said I had gastric flu. (quoted in Brannen et al, 1994, p 91)

On the other hand, some children are reluctant to tell teachers they feel unwell. When a classmate is ill or has an accident, other children often take on roles of messenger, supporter in help-seeking, comforter and protector of space or activities which the sick child has to leave (Christensen, 1993; Mayall, 1994b; Hill et al, 1995).

Schools also purvey deliberate and unintended health messages. Children can become aware of practices that contradict health education advice promoted in the formal curriculum, both as regards appropriate healthy behaviour and notions that children should take responsibility. In one study children "regarded school as detrimental to health.... It provided poor food and placed restrictions on eating and drinking and exercise" (Mayall, 1996, p 107). In secondary schools, pupils value choice but also recognise that the quality of food available in canteens and especially from machines is often 'unhealthy' (Morrison, 1995). In many cases, little account is taken of vegetarian requirements or of needs and wishes of children with non-British traditions:

> They don't do any Indian cooking or any other sort of cultural meals. (quoted in Morrison, 1995, p 256)

Most children recall coverage in class of topics like dental hygiene, smoking and diet. Nervertheless some are critical of the extent of the input:

> Sometimes teachers tell you when you've got to keep healthy but I think they should explain it more and what you should do. Sometimes they are just too busy with other things. (Girl, aged 11, quoted in Borland et al, 1996)

Surveys of schoolchildren indicate that their priorities for health and social education are often very different from adults' preoccupation with drugs, sex and abduction. For instance, primary schoolchildren show much concern for pets, issues of separation and of bereavement. Fitness and physical activity are of particular importance for boys as is preparation for parenthood for girls (Regis, 1996).

The media, especially soaps, influence children's ideas considerably. Oakley et al (1995) found these provided the main source of information. Children can absorb a range of health messages in this way:

> Some soaps tell you a lot about alcohol. Like I watch Coronation Street and this guy called Jack, he was drunk and everything – he was pure mental. I thought 'What if that was my Dad?'. So it made me more aware of the dangers. (Girl, aged 11, quoted in Borland et al, 1996)

Children's rights in relation to medical treatment and health records

As with education, health policy and services have usually accorded parents authority in relation to their children's health. Discussion of children's ability and legal autonomy to consent to medical treatment usually begins with the Gillick case, which – perhaps unhelpfully – also involved attitudes about sexuality, since it concerned access to contraceptive advice and provision (Archard, 1993). The 'Gillick' principle enunciated in this case established in English and Welsh common law that children under the age of 16 should be able to make a decision about such matters as medical treatment or contraception, without parents needing to know, once they are judged to have 'sufficient understanding' (Children's Rights Office, 1996; Lansdown, 1996). This still leaves adults the discretion to decide when a child's level of understanding is sufficient, but the onus is there to accept the child's choice whenever possible. However, subsequent cases modified this support of self-determination. While it was accepted that a 'Gillick competent' child can give consent (ie opt in), later judgements held that if a child refuses to agree to a course of action (ie opt out) this can be overridden by the consent of anyone with parental responsibility. Such paternalism may make it impossible that "a child or young person with a mental health label could ever refuse treatment" (Coppock, 1996, p 59).

The Gillick principle has not been incorporated in English statute, but the 1991 Age of Legal Capacity (Scotland) Act specified that "a person under the age of 16 shall have the legal capacity to consent on their own behalf to any surgical, medical or dental procedure or treatment where in the opinion of a qualified medical practitioner attending him, is capable of understanding the nature and possible consequences of the procedure or treatment" (Section 2(4)). (Scottish law retains the anachronistic practice of subsuming females within 'he' and 'him'.) Whether a child's refusal can override consent by someone with parental responsibilities has not been tested by any Scottish cases to date.

Silverman (1987) argued that age and presumed rationality do affect doctors' willingness to perceive children as decision makers, but this also depends on the nature of the issue. Although previous research had suggested that even older children were often "cast as incompetent and subordinate" in medical consultations (p 187), doctors in a cleft-palate clinic were at pains to ensure that teenagers were central in decisions about corrective surgery.

Alderson (1990) found that young people had definite views about when they would or could not give consent to surgery and when they preferred to delegate this decision to parents. For children with life-threatening illnesses or undergoing painful treatments, access to information and involvement in decisions seems to help them bear the suffering and, if necessary, prepare for dying (Bluebond-Langner, 1978; Mayall, 1995).

In recent years, medical services have increasingly encouraged families to hold the health records of children. This is partly influenced by consumer rights considerations, but health education is also part of the motivation. The parent-held Personal Child Health Record has become the main health record for every child under five. Studies have shown parent-held records to be popular and well-maintained, at least in the early stages with babies when motivation is likely to be highest (Polnay and Roberts, 1989; Cobbett, 1993).

Some areas have arranged for older children to keep their health records. A 'health fax' was introduced for school medical records in a number of south London secondary schools in 1993. The majority of children liked the fax, but some felt it was aimed at children younger than themselves, while others found it difficult to understand. Many wanted further details included (McAleer, 1994).

Health services and children

Nowadays governments to varying degrees accept responsibility (with parents) for monitoring and promoting children's health. Article 24 of the United Nations Convention is concerned with health and health services. It concentrates on rights to survival and provision, although the general participatory right of Article 12 covers children's entitlement to express opinions on health matters affecting them. Article 24 requires governments to make available medical services, with an emphasis on prevention and primary care. Stress is also placed on informing parents and children about "child health and nutrition, the advantages of breast-feeding, hygiene and environmental sanitation and the prevention of accidents".

Some of the earliest developments in the British welfare state were concerned with the health needs of pregnant women and young children. Midwives, health visitors (specially trained community nurses), community paediatricians, health clinics and school health services make up an impressive system of universal preventive measures in relation to child health. Yet for some time "children have not been a focus of policy" (Kurtz and Tomlinson, 1991, p 211), in part because of the shifts in demography and public concern towards the other end of the age spectrum. Official health policy (as expressed in the White Paper *The health of a nation*) does assert the need for action in all policy areas and with respect to developing healthy surroundings. On the other hand, policies affecting housing, income, roads, alcohol and the tobacco industry often appear to run counter to the health needs of children (and adults) (Smith et al, 1996). The Department of Health has recommended reduced sugar and fat intakes for children, yet the 1980

Education Act ended the universal availability of school meals, abolished nutritional standards and restricted access to free school meals.

The holistic views of health discussed at the beginning of the chapter are at variance with the fragmentation of health services. In policy and organisation, education, pre-school and health services have been largely separate (Mayall, 1996). Moreover, within the health service, the provisions and medical specialities for those who become ill tend to be distinct from those which seek to promoted the health of the whole population (MacFarlane and Mitchell, 1988; Polnay and Hull, 1992). To these long-term fissions within health provision were added the market reforms of the 1980s, which led to the creation of more differentiated and complex systems, including GP fundholding and hospital trusts. The closure of some local hospitals has resulted in increased travel time for children and their parents to attend appointments or to visit during hospitalisations, especially in rural areas (Hawthorne-Kirk and Part, 1995).

By and large the delicate advisory/surveillance role of health visitors when they give advice is welcomed by mothers, although a minority resent their intrusiveness (Mayall, 1996). The goal of school health services have "been largely defect-spotting, with children referred on to a curative service if necessary" (Mayall, 1996, p 23). In primary schools contacts with nurses and, even more so, doctors are infrequent. They mainly provide "a quick inspection service at fairly rare intervals, it is not geared to listening to children's concerns" (Mayall, 1996, p 29). In other countries, children are more able to take the initiative to refer themselves to the school nurse or dental service – or not (Wilkinson, 1988).

Schoolchildren have the lowest rates of hospital admission and GP consultation of all age groups (Kurtz and Tomlinson, 1991). There have been significant changes in children's experiences of hospital over the last 50 years. Rather later than in other spheres, it has come to be seen as desirable for children not to be placed with adults, although this still happens (Belson, 1993). It is now routine for parents to remain with young children who stay overnight and for visiting to be 'unrestricted' (Rutter and Rutter, 1993). Play provision is common and play specialists are employed not simply for recreational purposes but to prepare and support children in relation to treatment procedures. The National Association for the Welfare of Children in Hospital drew up a charter of rights which has been incorporated in policy by many health authorities. These include rights to information and respect, to have personal clothing and possessions, and to be cared for with other children (Belson, 1993).

Hospital admissions for surgery have been much reduced by the ending of routine tonsil and adenoid operations, so that "long-term in-patient care for children is now unusual" (Levitt et al, 1992, p 151). This does not apply to some children with serious illnesses. For them, the pain of treatment is the worst part of their experience (Claflin and Barbarin, 1991). This may become almost intolerable. Here a 14-year-old recounts her response to chemotherapy for cancer two years previously:

> When that vile yellow tube was linked to my arm I could make myself
> sick by just watching it ooze down the tube and into my body ... if I

could have stood up I would have killed myself. The feeling of utter hopelessness, frustration and boredom led to a desperation I never, ever want to experience again. (Anonymous, 1990)

Over the years, medical education and practice has placed increasing emphasis on understanding 'the whole person' – taking account of the patients' views and context. In relation to child patients, though, there has been a tendency to rely on parents to act as substitutes, at least pre-teens (Bernheimer, 1986: Silverman, 1987). Children are often given little opportunity to contribute to medical consultations in which they are the primary focus. A Swedish study in relation to children aged five to 15 revealed that, on average, the child contributed 8% of the conversation, compared with 58% for the hospital doctor and 34% for the parent(s) (Aronsson and Rundstrom, 1988). Much of what children did say was elaborated or mediated by parents. When doctors engaged directly with children they sometimes used a joking style which reduced the seriousness and status of the communication. In a UK survey, hardly any children aged 12 saw a doctor alone and 25% reported that the doctor spoke mainly to the accompanying adult (Brannen and Storey, 1996).

In one study, about two thirds of the sample of 16-year-olds reported satisfaction with their GP about a quarter were dissatisfied or unsure and the rest claimed never to use their GP. Long experience of being spoken about or down to made it difficult for many to express themselves (Brannen et al, 1994). This may be particularly so for those with learning difficulties. Young people have reported concerns about confidentiality and doctors not understanding (Mayall, 1995).

Conclusions

Compared with later life stages, childhood in the UK is a period of relative good health, yet a primary target for health education and promotion about behaviour with longer-term health risks. Thus health strategies have concentrated as much on future as current health needs. The focus has been on behaviours which predispose to wellness or ill-health in later life, such as diet, exercise, smoking and alcohol consumption. On the whole, children are reasonably well informed about official health messages about diet, exercise, smoking and drugs, but this has had only a limited impact on their actual behaviour. Health education conveys comparatively little information about common illnesses or conditions affecting children currently. Even increasingly widespread conditions like asthma are not prominent in the national health strategy, yet children themselves want more information on common physical ailments such as asthma, acne, migraine and diabetes (Jowett, 1995). Enlightenment about physical impairments could not only help the children directly affected, but enlighten their peers.

Implicit in health education programmes is an image of children as important and autonomous actors in relation to their own health, yet only recently have attempts been made to make these messages relevant to the concerns and constraints experienced by children. A health strategy devised by children might include quite different priorities, such as the provision of more recreational areas, protection from stray dogs and drunks, safe road crossings (Kalnins et al, 1991). Whereas education targets children directly, in individual and family consultations with health professionals, parents are often seen as the main mediators and guardians of children's health. Hence, the formal and informal rights of children to information relevant to themselves and to participate in decisions are weakly acknowledged in many instances.

Child health policy has concentrated on surveillance, curative medicine and health education. Yet poverty and local environment still have a major impact on children's health and life chances. This is only likely to reduce when there is concerted action and advocacy across a range of policy areas to tackle material conditions and commercial interests, as well as the behaviour of children and their parents (Spencer, 1996a). [...]

This chapter [edited] was taken from Hill, M. and Tisdall, K. (eds) (1997) *Children and society*, London/New York: Longman. The right of Malcolm Hill and Kay Tisdall to be identified as authors of this chapter has been asserted by them in accordance with the 1988 Copyright, Designs and Patents Act.

Reconstructing disability, childhood and social policy in the UK

John Davis, Nick Watson, Mairian Corker
and Tom Shakespeare

Introduction

This chapter examines the medical and social 'models' that have underpinned social policy aimed at disabled children. It suggests that both 'models' are premised on notions of deficit and dependency. By drawing on ethnographic data, this chapter challenges some of the 'taken-for-granted' assumptions that inform policy approaches to disability and childhood. We want to suggest that what pertains is not natural, or obvious, or automatic, but rests on a particular cultural approach to disability as a 'problem'. By showing that there is nothing inevitable about disabled children's lives, we want to suggest that we can change the ways that we understand and deal with disability in social policy. This chapter will demonstrate the 'need' for policy makers to respond to the complex and fluid nature of disabled children's lives. It will conclude that in order for an effective policy framework to be developed, policy makers must do more than simply carry out consultation with disabled young people. They should not only develop sustained and ongoing dialogue with disabled children but should also act to enable them to alter the service provision that they encounter.

Medical model and social policy

Social policy during the 1970s to the 1990s was regularly attacked for being dominated by medical notions of disability. Dominant approaches to the issue of disability within social policy and medical sociology individualised the issue of disability. This approach, labelled 'the medical model', was criticised by writers in the disability studies tradition, who located the problem of disability in social relations and structural exclusion, rather than in personal deficits of body or mind (Oliver, 1990).

In her research with disabled children in care, Jenny Morris criticised the 'medical model' for failing to look at the context of children's lives:

> There is no room here for recognising that the inability of a 15 year old, who has speech difficulties as a result of cerebral palsy, to be part of the

local teenage sub-culture is created by the pre-judicial attitudes and inaccessible environments which restrict his or her activities, rather than cerebral palsy or speech difficulties in themselves. (Morris, 1997, p 243)

She argued that the medical model reduced children's experiences to biological explanations. In do doing, she believed it ignored the possibility that the social or emotional problems of disabled children may result from a lack of stimulation, interaction, security and love that all children need, and to which children in care may not have access. She states:

To assume that all communication, mobility and behavioural difficulties are solely caused by impairment is further to disable those children by failing to recognise their actual experiences. (Morris, 1997, p 244)

Ideas within disability studies developed by writers such as Morris paralleled work within social gerontology on the structured dependency of old age (Townsend, 1981). For example, Estes argues:

The needs of older persons are reconceptualised as deficiencies by the professionals charged with treating them, regardless of whether the origins of these needs lie in social conditions over which the individual has little or no control in the failings of the individual, or in some policy-makers decision that a need exists. (Estes, 1979, p 235)

From a disability studies perspective medical model discourses that surround disabled children are based on a number of assumptions: that being a disabled child involves a life of suffering; that disabled children are inevitably dependent on others; and that the state will ultimately have to bear the cost of supporting disabled children. Disability studies writers didn't have to look far for evidence of such assumptions; for example, during the 1988 parliamentary debate about abortion, comments such as the following were common:

The private financial burden of caring for a severely handicapped child has been estimated by the courts as £500,000. If one takes into account the cost to the state of statutory provision, the cost could well be another £500,000.... Why should the House consider forcing people to accept such a burden if they do not want it? (*Hansard*, 22 January 1988, in Bailey, 1996, p 162)

Medically influenced discourses tended to pathologise the physical experience of impairment. The problem of disability was defined as that of the person with impairment. Disability was individualised and abstracted from the social context. Consequently, the disabled child or adult was seen as a tragic victim and an unfortunate burden on others (Shakespeare and Watson, 1998). The fact that life involves mutual aid and that everyone is in some measure dependent on others was ignored. In the case of families and relationships, it was assumed that there was a polar dichotomy between families with disabled members, and other, 'normal' families. One set of relationships was perceived to be normal and benign, and the other was viewed as problematic and pathological. It was argued that the problem inhered in the individual with impairment, not in the wider social context in which the whole family found itself (Shakespeare, 2000).

Literature on disabled children was based on a range of normative assumptions about the effects that having a child with impairment had on the parental relationships or family dynamics. For example, having a disabled child meant that family relationships would break down, or that siblings would suffer. The assumption was that typical loving parental relationships were replaced by a relationship of caring and physical support based around the performance of certain tasks (Shakespeare, 2000). Service provision for families with disabled children reflected this assumption. Considerable stress was placed on the need for respite care, for example, on the basis that the intolerable responsibilities of having a child with impairment typically necessitate a break, or a rest (Shakespeare and Watson, 1998). Very little consideration was given as to whether children needed a break from the pressures of being judged as in deficit and of having their bodies and behaviours stereotyped as 'abnormal' and as in need of 'fixing'. By constituting disabled children as passive and 'vulnerable', these discourses failed to explore fully the cultural context within which the experience of social isolation, segregation, and poor self-image are lived. The focus on disabled children's and families' 'service needs' served to perpetuate an image of disabled children as inevitably being in need of 'care' (Robinson and Stalker, 1998). The diverse views of disabled children tended not to be recognised within this focus. They were often presented as a homogeneous grouping; little attempt was made to recognise complexity and difference in their lives. Many policies placed emphasis on the needs and wishes of parents and siblings; it was rare that disabled children themselves were asked for their views (Priestley, 1998).

Medical discourses have not simply disappeared. For example, public health writers such as Nicholas Wald make explicit the ways in which screening programmes are presently evaluated on the basis of cost-benefit analysis regarding the avoidance of the 'burden' of disabled children (Wald, 1992). However, over time alternative constructions of disability emerged that redefined disabled people's life problems as the consequence of the social. These constructions became known as the 'social model of disability' (Oliver, 1990). In the next section we compare this model to recent policy developments in the area of childhood.

Social model of disability and childhood policy

The changing policy context, with an increased emphasis on rights and inclusion, demanded that academics and policy makers recognise the social construction of disability and the importance of disabled people's own views (Oliver, 1990). The 'social model' was founded on the assumption that people are disabled by society, not by their bodies. The finger of blame for disabled people's negative life experience was pointed at the social and environmental barriers, prejudicial attitudes and other processes that served to exclude people with impairments from the mainstream.

In terms of social policy, this shift in thinking brought about the concept of independent living, developed by the Independent Living Movement. The ILM has its roots in the USA and the Physically Disabled Students Program (PDSP) at the University of California, Berkeley, in the early 1960s. Four assumptions underlie the practice of the ILM:

> All human life is of value.
> Anyone, whatever their impairment, is capable of exerting choices.
> People are disabled by society not by their bodies.
> Disabled people have a right to participate fully in society.
> (Morris, 1993, p 21)

The ILM gives prominence to issues such as the right to form personal and sexual relationships (Shakespeare et al, 1996); the right to be a parent (Wates, 1997); the right of equal access to a range of settings (Swain et al, 1993). While the movement endeavours to promote the full range of human and civil rights of disabled people, the promotion of personal assistance as the key strategy in breaking the link between disability and dependency in everyday life has traditionally been its key focus (Morris, 1993).

The provision of personal assistants has been central to the development of ILM in the UK. The cost of this provision is met through direct payments. The 1997 Community Care Direct Payments Act enabled disabled people to manage their own support requirements. This resulted in many disabled people casing to be dependent on local service provision. Independent living has mainly been associated with adult services. There is very little recognition of the experiences of disabled children within 'social model' writing on disability. However, moves towards independent living have been mirrored by the emergence of a children's rights agenda within the UK.

Recent political developments in the UK have recognised the lack of children's involvement in service provision. The 1990s saw the development of a rights-based approach to social policy in childhood. For example, the 1995 Children (Scotland) Act enshrined the right of children in Scotland to have their views heard about services they used. Attempts were made to move to a more communitarian approach to supporting children. MacMurray (1932) argued that a sense of community is reliant on the quality of local personal relationships, economic interdependence and material equality. Central to his work was the perspective that communities are built on mutual relationships established on the basis of trust, respect, reciprocal rights, obligations and support. In the UK this idea has become associated with the concept of integrated services and the 'war' on poverty and injustice (Levitas, 1998). In Scotland, New Community Schools had been one of a number of policy initiatives that have emerged with the aim of challenging the effects of poverty and social exclusion on childhood.

Since devolution in Scotland, New Community Schools have been developed from the concept of Full Service Schools in the USA (Scottish Executive, 1999, 2000). Just as in the USA the New Community Schools vary in size, structure and the new and established initiatives they incorporate. The first phase of 37 projects began in March 1999 and included 150 schools (primary and secondary), nurseries and family centres. Their aim is to work with parents and families to break the destructive cycle of underachievement and address barriers to children's learning to ensure that every child has the fullest possible opportunity to maximise his or her potential (Scottish Executive, 1999). This aim is underpinned by a commitment to integrated services. Children, parents, other community members, teachers, childcare professionals, social workers, and health personnel are expected to work together to adopt strategies that meet each child's developmental, educational, emotional, health and social needs.

New Community Schools aim to make the inclusion of disabled children the 'norm'. Following the passing of the 2000 Standards in Schools etc Act, in Scotland there is a presumption that disabled children will be educated alongside their peers. In England the Children's Fund initiative has similar aims. For example, The Liverpool Children's Fund Plan 'Realising dreams and ambitions' (June 2001) sets a number of aims with regards to disabled children. These are to:

• Engage with disabled children to improve participation, inclusion and access to services.
• Empower children as users of services and to increase their participation in service planning.
• Support improved coordination of services and access to information.
• Achieve a shift in the culture of play, youth and leisure services towards greater inclusion.

Both the New Community Schools and The Children's Fund initiatives place major importance on the inclusion of disabled children in everyday educational and cultural activities. It appears that there has been a major shift in social policy that aims to influence the social and political context of disabled children's lives. In this chapter we explore the philosophical basis for this change and examine the value of the above objectives in the light of disabled children's experiences.

The study

The data in this chapter is drawn from an ESRC Children 5-16 Programme Project: 'Life as a Disabled Child'. The study used a range of qualitative methods, including participant observation and interviewing. However, particular attention was paid to employing informal techniques to develop good working relationships that enabled us to engage with young people on their own terms. The research was carried out in three 'special' schools and three 'mainstream' schools in Scotland and four 'special' schools and four 'mainstream' schools in England. After observing more than 300 children and young people aged 12-19 in their schools, we continued to work with around half in a more in-depth way in their homes and neighbourhood. This included informal individual, paired or group interviews, as well as the compilation of written and visual accounts.

The data used here is from both Scotland and England and includes the views of children who had experienced special and mainstream schools. In the interest of confidentiality we do not want to say too much about the specific young people, their ages, the types of schools they attended and their impairments because this information may be enough for others to uncover their identity. The project has resulted in a number of publications concerning research methods, children's rights, inclusive education, theories of disability and geographies of play. In the discussion that accompanies the data we draw from these papers to add further context to the text.

Structural exclusion, parents and independent living

In our study issues of financial resources dominated discussions with parents. Although not all the families presented their child as in 'need' of service provision, some were compelled to plead special cases for material and legal provision from central and local government:

> *Parent:* We are seen as a financial burden and in terms of our needs we have to fight for everything and only really get things from social work and education which are cheap or easy to provide. I once drew a tree of people Eddie meets and he had over 40 professionals involved in his life.

A lack of resources at local authority level very often meant that services for disabled children were provided on a 'block' basis (eg all children with the same impairment were offered similar services until the money ran out). Often parents had to overemphasise their children's impairments in order to access resources such as after-school care. They were forced by social policy agendas to reproduce the very medical discourses that disabled people find disempowering. This finding reinforced that of other studies that suggested services were very rarely tailored to children's individual requirements and that resources are disproportionately allocated to a minority of disabled children (Fairbairn and Fairbairn, 1992). In order to receive support many disabled children had to go through an inordinate amount of testing and their parents had to shuttle them from 'pillar to post' between different service providers. Many of the families were in constant conflict with different directorates within their local authorities. The long-term consequences of this for the health and well-being of family members can only be guessed at.

We do not mean to insinuate that these families were somehow uniquely 'worse off'. As Beresford (1994) points out, many of the experiences of families with disabled children do not differ qualitatively from those of families with non-disabled children, many of which are 'isolated' and 'impoverished'. Many parents argued that the solution to the problems of service provision lay in the development of key workers to liaise between agencies and the provision of direct payments to disabled children and parents. There is no doubt that many families with non-disabled children would benefit from having a 'key worker' who could seek out access to scarce resources but they would also gain from the reorganising of the way material resources are distributed in society.

The benefits of having direct access to financial resources can be seen in the next example. Bruce received a very large award from a lawsuit at the age of 12. It meant that he could afford two personal assistants, his own transport (van and power chair) and a number of changes to his home to make it more accessible. Bruce was in a position to make choices about his life, deciding what he wanted to do with his 'free' time. In this case Bruce's personal assistant tells the story. Bruce did not use spoken words but confirmed his agreement by use of eye movements:

> *PA*: He gets in about quarter to 4. What he'll do is he'll come in and sit and watch his TV and wait for either myself or [the other PA] to come in … he's waiting until I come in about quarter past and sit with him for about 10/15 minutes. Have a quick drink of coffee and then when the weather has gone off and what night it is. 'Cause on a Tuesday and Wednesday night he goes for a video, 'cause they're only a pound. So that's something he likes doing on a Tuesday and Wednesday. And obviously if it's raining he'll just give it a skip or we'll take it along in the van. And now with … being summer time he's out. But as the dark nights are drawing in. The nights are fairly drawing in. On a Friday and Saturday he's off out on his own either with myself or [the other PA]. We go to the pictures or we go bowling or we go into town.

Bruce's eyes lit up when his assistant talked about the social activities he did. Bruce experienced an element of social freedom because he had access to financial resources. His experiences contrasted with those of children and young people who had to lobby for access to power chairs or rely on voluntary and 'charitable' organisations for the opportunity to attend social events.

This example reinforces social structural characterisations of disability. It emphasises the 'social model' perspective that disability is caused by the unequal distribution of material resources. It also demonstrates the potential importance of direct payments for children and young people. Bruce and his family no longer had to wait for social services to provide him with support, he and his family could directly employ assistants and purchase equipment to meet his requirements. Traditionally in the UK direct payments have not been available to children. Bruce's example suggests that disabled children could benefit from the concept of independent living being applied to them.

Many authors have criticised the 'social model' of disability because it emphasises structural explanations of disabled people's lives at the expense of investigating the cultural context of those lives (Corker and French, 1999). In addition to this criticism, we believe that the implications of social model approaches are that the agency of disabled children is downplayed because their lives can only be analysed in terms of isolation, access to service provision and the acquisition of material support (Davis and Watson, 2002). The problem with this type of characterisation is that it is similar to the medical characterisations of disabled children discussed earlier because it represents these young people as passive victims who require adults to take action to 'fix' their problems.

We also believe that there is a danger that social structural explanations of disability and 'social model' responses to disability enable service providers to ignore deep-seated discrimination that exists in families, schools, hospitals, leisure/community centres, youth clubs and other social settings that children and young people attend. That is, they enable professionals to reduce disabled children's experiences to a technical rational agenda. This results in the concept of social inclusion being reduced to a concept of integration.

Bruce experienced integration because he was able to attend the same social locations as his peers. He did not experience inclusion because he was unable to interact with his peers during this experience. He attended a 'special' school and very rarely interacted with children his own age who were not disabled. His financial status allowed him some form of independence from his family but he spent much of his time with his adult PAs. His PAs had become friends as well as employees. Bruce's financial independence did not mean he had social independence. A more meaningful approach requires the development of an understanding of disability based on a greater examination of its cultural context.

The variability of disability

Many disabled children suggested that their lives varied, depending on the other people they encountered in a specific social context. For example, two Deaf children explained the variability of their family relationships and friendships:

> *Imran:* With my sister, I feel we're the same we can fingerspell and we help each other. We might play football or watch TV and that's OK. With my mum though, if she is trying to explain about a friend of ours who will visit, she will gesture as best she can and that helps me understand. My dad usually initialised everything and that's OK. My mom initialises too and that's OK and I can't communicate with my brother.

Imran tells us that he gets on well with his sister because she can sign but he can't communicate with his brother. He experiences different forms of inclusion within the same family setting. Zoebia's family did not sign and she does not have any close friends; however, she taught her cousin to sign:

> M: Yeah ...
> Z: In terms of friends I don't have any best friends – only people I know.
> M: Mm, would you like to have a best friend?
> Z: I do have one best friend in ... [signs name] ... [to cousin] they live next door.

M: Your cousin seems able to sign very well …

M: Your cousin seem very fluent, how did you learn to sign?

C: [indistinct]

M: From Z. [to Z] So you taught her?

Z: [Nods]

M: [to cousin] You are very fluent and when I walked in I wondered if you were deaf.

Z: No, she is hearing.

For many years a discourse existed within social policy circles that suggested that 'Asian' families reject children who have impairments (Ahmad et al, 2000). Zoebia's relationship with her family may be problematic because they do not communicate 'well' with her. But this may be the same for children in other families who are not Muslim and are not Deaf. These examples force us to question the influence of different categories such as family, ethnic group, 'deaf'. They also warn us not to essentialise these categories or privilege one over the other as causes of service 'need' (Corker and Davis, 2000). In the above case, Zoebia's family had not had the opportunity to learn sign in a form that took account of their multilingual culture or that enabled issues of different cultures ('Asian' and 'Deaf') to be discussed. There is a hint of a suggestion that different family members may have been more or less willing to engage in this learning process. It is tempting to reduce this example to a technical rational discussion of the provision of local sign language training. This would only serve to reinforce the 'hearing' versus 'Deaf' divide. By teaching her cousin to sign Zoebia addresses some of her 'isolation' from peer group and family. She demonstrates the importance of child-centred solutions and establishes her ability to bridge the 'Deaf' versus 'hearing' divide. This ability raises issues for how we analyse ethnicity and disability.

A number of authors have argued that ethnicity is overlooked in care and educational settings (Ali et al, 2001; Ahmad et al, 2000), that disabled children from different ethnic backgrounds believe they are discriminated against in educational settings (Bignall and Butt, 2000; Vernon, 1996), and that these children encounter 'eurocentric' service provision (Begum et al, 1994). The stereotyping of 'Asian' families as rejecting disabled children is questioned by a number of authors (Ali et al, 2001; Ahmad et al, 2000; Corker and Davis, 2000). Ahmad et al (2000) argue that South Asian families are generally supportive of deaf children and that it is social services and education departments that more generally fail disabled children from a variety of ethnic backgrounds because they discount issues of ethnicity.

Although we witnessed such failure – for example, in one area children with Down's syndrome were expected to use facilities in a school on an estate with a history of racial violence (Watson et al, 2000) – we would be wary of essentialising the separation between groups who use services and the people who provide them. Indeed, dualisms such as 'good' and 'bad', 'mind' and 'body', 'deafness' and 'blindness', 'black' and 'white' tend to obscure more than they reveal (Corker, 2002; Corker and French, 1999). They tend to iron out the complexity of people's identities, as Zoebia points out:

> *Zoebia:* Well yeah they [the school] wanted me to change into trousers
> and I didn't want to, I'm Asian (second-generation Pakistani Muslim]
> and I enjoy wearing Asian clothes like the ones I'm wearing now. Like
> this, there are a lot of Asian girls who do wear trousers, I don't. All that
> changing all the time ... There is a boy in year 9 everyone in his family
> are Muslim but his Mother chooses to wear trousers sometimes and not
> Muslim clothes like I'm wearing. It seems strange that she is Muslim
> but doesn't always wear Muslim clothes. I suppose my Mother compared
> to his is more [Zoebia begins to sign 'strict' and only executes half of the
> sign].... His parents are Muslim and sometimes his mother will wear
> clothes like yours and sometimes clothes like mine. My family only
> wear clothes like this and never like them ... it's strange ... I have asked
> him whether his family are Muslim and he says yes and when I asked
> why his family wear English clothes he said that he didn't know.... It's
> strange ... because I thought that all Muslims wore similar clothes but
> Wasim doesn't and that's different and so I thought that he may be Sikh
> but he's not he is Muslim.

We should not assume that all disabled children from South Asian backgrounds
have the same experiences. Children are aware that culture is not fixed and try to
make sense of cultural differences within their own cultural groupings (in this
example 'Asian' and Muslim). It is important to note here that the difficulty of
understanding cultural difference encountered by Zoebia is a difficulty that
disability studies has been slow to recognise. Indeed, the social model of disability
that emphasises the structural nature of disability has been criticised for ignoring
the view of disabled people of different ethnic backgrounds (Begum et al, 1994;
Vernon, 1996). At the centre of this criticism is the wish that writers on disability
take more account of culture.

Overcoming essentialism, understanding our differences

We promote a fluid idea of culture. We believe that processes of social interaction
are contingent on the varied identities of social actors and the variety of
relationships that people forge on a daily basis – for example, power relations,
relations of negotiation, relations of generation (Davis and Corker, 2001). This
definition of culture causes problems for service providers. For example, in Zoebia's
case how can they know when being Muslim is important and when it is not?
The answer surely is to ask the children. However, the institutional and power
arrangements of childhood do not lend themselves to promote the speedy
facilitation of such cultural exchange.

Policy decisions rarely take account of disabled children's opinions because
professional practices can get in the way of asking, and the personal prejudices
and vested interests of service providers are promoted before those of children.
For example, school rules can be applied in an overprotective way to disabled
children because they are also used to protect adults against the fear of litigation:

Dibly: The people here are too protected. I can do a lot more things than they give me credit for. For example, a few months ago I got a pass to go to the back shops and the access person and I agreed that I can go through there, that I've got the confidence to do it. But for the first few times they kept on checking up on me, following me, and they still check up. But I'm very confident about it. I can do it. I can't understand why they want to check up on me, but they do and they keep on doing it. You get this awful feeling, you're over protected. At home I negotiate my way round the local town OK. I'm capable of doing lots. My mother never had any quibbles about it. I just do what I can do, and I just wish here they wouldn't be so over protective. (Davis and Watson, 2001, p 683)

Many of the professionals that worked with Dibly said that they engaged in defensive practice because they feared that their colleagues or senior staff would not respect them or that they would get into trouble if 'something' happened to the children. This demonstrates another tension within social policy. Adults who make decisions about provision for disabled children very often are influenced by legislation that seeks to protect children and their rights. This legislation – for example, 1995 Children (Scotland) Act – guides adults both to ensure that children have choices and that they are protected from harm. This means that adults have to strike a balance between rights and safety. Some service providers resort to rigid policies that protect adult staff more than they take account of the wishes of children (Davis and Watson, 2001). This especially occurs where adults use 'rules' and 'guidelines' unreflexively to deny children choices (Davis et al, 2000).

As Maria indicates there can often be a separation between adults and children:

Maria: He thinks we are all thick anyway. He once asked us all what 'as well' means. We all know what 'as well' means!

Alan: Yeah, he thinks that we don't understand ...

MC: ... OK

Alan: ... he thinks we don't know what 'turn up' means and we do. He thinks we're thick. He made us write down what it meant. So then we had to write longer and longer lists of what words meant. It's such a waste of time. (Corker, 2003)

These Deaf children believe they are not being stretched at school and feel insulted by the teacher. They set up a 'him' and 'us' discourse that reinforces the adult versus child divide. This separation can also be found in the language of the staff in schools, the language of academics who write about 'special' and 'inclusive' 'education', and the texts of writers in childhood studies who make too much of the separation between adult and children's rights (Davis and Watson, 2000, 2001).

For example, in one form of childhood studies children are viewed as a universal minority group who are in opposition to adults (James et al, 1998).

These divisions also occur between children of different ethnic backgrounds and disabled and non-disabled children. In the next examples Imran does not want to go to a mixed ethnicity youth club (his ideal friendship are with deaf 'Asian' children) and Chick wants to go to school with people like him:

> M: Do you go to the Deaf Club?
>
> I: No ... only on a Monday when it is the deaf Asian group.
>
> M: Do all of the deaf Asian kids go, all?
>
> I: Yeah ... oh no some don't, one Indian doesn't come. So, yeah, all but one does and that's a shame because it means that they are at home alone....
>
> M: ... I wondered if any of your friends talked about the [non-Asian] club?
>
> I: I don't know about that. I think that there can be trouble there, [white] people fighting and bad behaviour. I'm not sure about that so I don't go anyway. I think they can be a bit wild and bully people and I don't want to be involved with that. I'd rather go on a Saturday when the people there are a little more sensible, that's when I go.

> *Chick:* Yeah. I'm closer to the people I met there [at the Special Olympics], who have the same condition as me, than I've ever been to anybody. Which is why I might like to go the school there ... I think my greatest friends are down south and abroad not here but far away. I was only with these people for ten days and I got really close. So am waiting to hear about the new school there's a meeting on Friday probably of education, social work and health in the council and it will come down to money. They will probably say no to start with and we'll have to fight because that's what usually happens. We'll probably have to appeal.... No, I mean what can we do. I mean what am going to say at the meeting is that you wouldn't stick an able-bodied boy in a special school and expect them to be OK, by the end of the week they'd want out. I don't want to be the one boy to conquer everything, the school or the world. Well, I would like it because a probably get loads of money but I don't think a can do that and I don't believe people want to do that. I can't do the fighting all the time. I can't wait for the day I say bye-bye to this school.

We do not want to down play these children's experiences. There are many reasons why these children emphasise their differences from other children. For example, a lot of children had experienced bullying (Watson et al, 2000). However, the difficulty with their position is that it reinforces their own isolation from mainstream experience. In the short term this may have benefits but in the long term, on leaving school, they will be confronted with the same conditions once again.

The status quo in writing on 'special education' involves writers blaming a lack of inclusion on a number of structural barriers – for example, class sizes, league tables, political intrusion on the management of schools, teachers' attitudes to change (Davis and Watson, 2001). The examples above suggest a deeper cultural division. Inclusion in both 'mainstream' and 'special' schools is interrelated with adult's and children's notions of difference and normality. Many disabled children are put under pressure in educational settings to demonstrate that they are 'different' (in order to justify special provision) and yet 'normal' (in order to obtain social acceptance). The mistreatment of disabled children in educational settings relates as much to the unreflexive imposition of discourses of difference and normality as to the financial restrictions experienced by schools.

'Real' educational inclusion is not only dependent on structural change but is also reliant on a fusion of a number of factors (eg equal access to educational opportunities, the development of equitable group dynamics and the presence of strong-willed individual pupils, parents and staff). At the heart of good practice is the need to recognise that disabled children are both the same as and different from other children. Irene explains that she mostly wants to be treated the same as other children, yet occasionally will want her different requirements to be understood:

> *Irene:* Yeah. It gets a bit annoying. And like 'cause they're teachers you can't just say, like you've got to be polite or whatever. You just have to, you can't just say, 'I'm not having trouble with this' ... cause in primary, like em, it seemed like em, like everyone like goes quite close in primary and stuff like the boys and girls and stuff like that. And then like if I fell over everyone would be like, 'Oh, Irene are you alright, you alright?' And like if someone else fell over it would be, 'Oh, are you OK?' And like maybe it was because I don't know my character or whatever I dunno. Or maybe it's my visual impairment, but everyone seemed really protective.... It's like they don't make you feel independent. Like they want to do stuff for you. It's like you want help, but you don't want like charity ... Like the best judge of what you can do and what you can't do is yourself, for anyone, not just if you're disabled.

> *Irene:* It wasn't the same for both of us. It was the copying. It was the copying that Maxine couldn't do. I couldn't see it (when the writing was small or the style difficult to read). And he tries to make it bigger but he doesn't understand that she can't copy it....

Irene wants the children to treat her the same and to stop being over-protective, yet she also want specific support in the classroom setting. Irene does not want teachers and pupils to stereotype or stigmatise her. She points out that not all children with visual impairments are the same and that she has different wishes at different times.

Often service providers find it difficult to accommodate the perspectives of children like Irene. We believe that the vast majority of service provision for disabled children in the UK still starts from the position that services are what adults and the 'able-bodied' provide for disabled children. Despite the change in language surrounding inclusion there is little evidence that disabled children are working in partnership with service providers to develop their own solutions to their life problems. There is even less evidence that service provider 'consultation' has resulted in disabled children's own perspectives on their lives being put at the centre of service development. Social policy concerning disabled children rarely recognises the problem-solving skills of disabled children. For the most part it imposes adult solutions that are based on professional and personal prejudice that relate to essentialist notions of disability (Priestley, 1998). Very little time is spent allowing disabled children to identify and solve their own life problems.

The solution to this situation does not lie in blaming adults/non-disabled children and idolising disabled children. The solution lies in developing social policy that promotes negotiation between adults and children and recognises the ability of children, families and service providers to develop their own localised solutions to their everyday life problems (Davis and Watson, 2000). Despite the generally bleak analysis outlined above, disabled children do encounter professionals who are receptive to their ideas and also treat them and their parents with respect (Davis and Watson, 2000, 2001; Davis et al, 2000). During the course of our work we met many professionals who were not involved in defensive practice. They either felt secure as individuals or had the support of other staff and children. These people somehow managed to resist the structural pressures that their colleagues experienced. Not all adults and children are the same, and it is important that we examine the different cultures and identities of service providers as much as the different wishes of disabled children. It is from the professionals and children who do not adopt stereotypical practices that social policy can learn a lot.

Conclusion

Social policy, like law, is traditionally reactive (see Corker, 2003). Yet social policy, unlike law, has the potential to be proactive – to set in place a series of principles that define a just and inclusive society and practical but flexible ways of implementing them. We have argued that the social model of disability, although having many virtues, does not form as strong a basis for social policy as was first hoped. This is mainly because, like the medical model of disability, it does not easily recognise the abilities of disabled children.

In a multi-layered approach we need to:

- Change the structures of social and educational settings and address the cultures of discrimination within.
- Work more closely with children, parents and practitioners to bring forth their own local solution.
- Include the peer group and their solutions.
- Put in more resources to resolve technical rational issues that create barriers to inclusion.

- Put in more resources to enable children, parents and practitioners to engage in more meaningful discussions concerning the variability of disabled children's lives.

Many of these aims are already present in social policy guidelines; however, they are prevented from being meaningfully enacted because some professionals at different levels of seniority within specific service directorates lack the will or ability to put them into practice. Yet, at the same time many children and adults find their own ways to overcome this barrier and promote their own brand of meaningful inclusion. It is important that we, as academics, highlight these pockets of good practice so that they can form the basis for more solid and sustainable action.

Finally, many children told us that, as much as anything else, what they wanted was respect. As Anna told us: "It's like you want help, but you don't want charity." If an appropriate social policy response to the problems faced by disabled children is to be developed then the voices of the children themselves must be listened to and solutions to their life problems must be stimulated by family members, service providers and the children themselves. This will require open dialogue and the recognition that difference and disagreement can be the stimulus for fruitful negotiation.

This chapter [edited] was taken from Hallett, C. and Prout, A. (eds) (2003) *Hearing the voices of children*, London/New York: RoutledgeFalmer. The right of John Davis, Nick Watson, Mairian Corker and Tom Shakespeare to be identified as authors of this chapter has been asserted by them in accordance with the 1988 Copyright, Designs and Patents Act.

Children of the welfare state: Individuals with entitlements or hidden in the family?

Anne Skevik

Introduction

Social policy is not for children. Both political and academic debates circle around the rights and duties of adults. Families, mothers (and sometimes fathers) and childcare/child welfare institutions are made targets for social transfers, but children occur in the debates as objects rather than as subjects of social policy. This is the case even after decades of analysing social policy through the lenses of previously neglected groups, including women, ethnic and sexual minorities, and people with disabilities (see for instance Williams, 1989 for an introduction). This is also highly relevant to the ongoing debate on welfare state variation and welfare state regimes (Esping-Andersen, 1990), as a number of contributions have shown that placing women at the centre of the analysis brings out aspects of welfare state variation that less gender-sensitive analyses have neglected (for example, Langan and Ostner, 1991; Lewis, 1992, 1993, 1997; Sainsbury, 1994, 1996; O'Connor et al, 1999). The question asked in this [chapter] is, can an analysis of social security from children's point of view do the same? More specifically, can a child-centred analysis bring new insights to gender-sensitive social policy debates, in the same way that feminist analyses brought new insights to mainstream debates?

Children are increasingly recognised in the literature as social actors and as potential carriers of social rights (Brannen and O'Brien, 1996). In a global context, the 1989 UN Convention on the Rights of the Child marked an important milestone in the recognition of children's rights. This has also influenced the social policy literature, where there is a growing interest in children's rights and the meaning of citizenship for children (for example, Archard, 1993; Therborn, 1993; Cockburn, 1998; Roche, 1999; Bojer, 2000). There is also a growing empirical literature that emphasises how institutions and policies affect children (for example, Daniel and Ivatts, 1998; Hill and Tisdall, 1997; Pringle, 1998), most typically in terms of child poverty and marginalisation (for example, Vleminckx and Smeeding, 2000; Bradbury et al, 2001). While these developments provide part of the background for this [chapter], the question of children's rights is not the crucial issue here. Rather, the [chapter] aims at showing how the recognition – or not – of children has shaped social policy over time in two countries. Thus it addresses the debate on welfare state variation more directly than it addresses the debate on children's rights. The approach chosen is a comparative study, rich in institutional detail, following developments in two countries over a period of about 30 years. The analysis will focus mainly on what has been called the 'golden age' of the welfare state, that is, 1945 to the 1970s.

The two countries chosen are Norway and the UK. These two countries are placed in different clusters in studies following the 'power-resource' -hypothesis (Esping-Andersen, 1990), yet scholars with a gender-sensitive analytical framework tend to emphasise the similarities rather than the differences between the two countries. For instance, Jane Lewis writes, in her much-quoted article from 1992, that, "The Norwegian system, which has continued to treat women primarily as wives and mothers, is closer in many respects to that of Britain than it is to Sweden" (Lewis, 1992, p 162; see also Leira, 1992; Sainsbury, 1999). To the extent the aim is to develop child-sensitive analysis as a corrective to gender-sensitive analysis, therefore, it makes sense to study countries that gender-sensitive studies have (tentatively) bracketed together. Despite the arguably slow departure from male breadwinner assumptions in both countries, it is a well-known fact that the two countries differ both in terms of outcomes for children (eg UNICEF, 2000) and in terms of institutional arrangements (for example, Millar and Warman, 1996). Studying the ways in which children and families are approached in policies may help us understand these differences.

Children in families and policies

When children are normally invisible in social policy debates, it is often because the family is seen as the relevant unit. The family is pictured as harmonic and unified – what is good for the family is good for everyone within it. Further, the family is seen as a central building block in society, so that anything that is good for the family is good for society. Investing in the family therefore ensures happy citizens and a good society. This 'organic' image is in no way unique to social policy; rather, it is a view of the family with deep historical and philosophical roots. It is also an idea that has been strongly challenged by feminists (for example, Pateman, 1989; Moller Okin, 1989), who have pointed out that the family is also in many cases a site for power, oppression and violence. Moreover, feminists and others have argued, 'the family' is a myth: families come in many different shapes and sizes. The alternative to viewing the family as a uniform and harmonic unit, is to deconstruct the family into individuals and their (legal/biological) relationships. With this starting point, the state no longer relates to a unit with a head of household and his dependants; rather, it relates to a man, a woman and a child who are linked to each other by biological and legal ties. This we may call the 'individual' view of the family.

Each of these two images of the family has important implications for the position of children. When the family is seen as one, and that one is the paterfamilias, both women and children disappear from view. They are hidden in the shadow of the husband and father. If the man in the house dies, the adult woman is elevated to the status as the head of household, while the orphaned child remains in the shadow. The widow may be awarded some social benefits to help her cope with her new circumstance, and these benefits may include additions for dependent children, but the child has no independent rights as an orphan. This implies that the benefits are lost to the family if the widow remarries or starts cohabiting. As soon as there is a new man in the household, the family unit is seen as reconstituted. There is no separation of the roles as partner/spouse and parent. A second point is that the image of the family as a stable unit has a downside: families who do not correspond to the uniform ideal are often branded as inferior. 'Non-standard' family practices, such as divorce, cohabitation and unmarried motherhood, are to be discouraged. This discouraging may very well include the absence of social benefits, even in situations of need. The tension between securing need on the one hand and regulating behaviour on the other may often lead to a victory for the latter concern: irresponsible and unfortunate behaviour must not give easy access to state money. The parent's behaviour is in the spotlight, and the child is hidden behind the parent. Yet proponents of this policy will vigorously deny that they are insensitive to the needs of children: when the stable two-parent family is promoted, they will argue, it is precisely because this family form is most beneficial for children.

The individual view, which conceptualises the family as a set of individuals and relationships, establishes a more direct contact between children and the welfare state. Children occur as individuals – albeit underage – with certain potential claims of their own. Responsible adults may have to act as their guardians or trustees, but this does not undermine the recognition of children. From this viewpoint it is acknowledged that when a man with a family dies, he leaves both a widow and an orphan. These are two different situations, which may imply that the child can have claims on the state even if the mother does not. Even if the mother does not qualify for widow's pensions, or she ceases to qualify through remarriage, the orphan may still qualify. Parenting is distinctly separated from partnering. The wish to encourage the traditional two-parent family will logically be weaker from this point of view, which may imply that widows and orphans are not privileged over other one-parent families. The familiar dilemma between needs fulfilment and behavioural implications is given a twist: sure one may have reservations against the choices of the parent, but the child cannot be blamed or punished for the sins of the mother. One may wish to influence the behaviour of one person without compromising the welfare of another. This may justify a more generous policy toward people living in 'non-standard' families.

When the individual conception family is taken as a starting point, children occur in policies as persons in their own right. How are children approached in political debates if they are not included as individuals? Daniel and Ivatts (1998, pp 11ff) have suggested three central images of children: children as a threat, children as victims and children as investments. The image of children as a social *threat* holds long traditions, relating in particular to children raised by vagrant, criminal or otherwise deviant parents. Such children, it is feared, grow up to become uncivilised little monsters and may pose a threat to other children as well as to their communities. Social policy responses tend to be coined in terms of protection of society rather than children's rights – it becomes a matter of protection *from* children rather than protection *of* children (cf Dingwall et al, 1983, p 214). Conversely, children occur in the social political debate as *victims* when the topic is child neglect and abuse, and sometimes in discussions about poor housing and other misfortunes in which the family may find itself. This conception may recognise the child's need for a minimum protection, but nevertheless tends to inspire compassion rather than actual political measures. Children are portrayed as *investments* when the focus of the debate is on the future of the welfare state and/or the nation: clearly, there is no way of securing the future of either without investing in children. What matters from this perspective is not the children of today, but the adults of tomorrow. All these notions focus on what children are or can become to society, more than they see children as individuals with varying *actual* needs and potential claims on the state.

Having outlined these simplified ideal types of social political approaches to children and families, I will now move on to the discussion of actual policy developments in the two countries chosen. I will limit the discussion to two types of arrangements for children and families with children: universal family allowances/child benefit, and benefits to children in one specific risk situation, that is, children living with only one parent. The discussion encompasses both the existing arrangements, and the arguments that were used for getting these arrangements in place.

The UK: children in the shadows

William Beveridge: children as investment

The Beveridge report (Cmd 6404 [1942]) is undoubtedly the most important document laying down the foundations for the modern British welfare state. So what was William Beveridge's view on children? Overall, Beveridge has been criticised for giving primacy to the male breadwinner (Pascall, 1986; Lister, 1994). Still, he did propose the introduction of children's allowances as one key element in the social security framework. Without children's allowances, Beveridge firmly held, his proposals would not be sustainable. Benefits to children were at the heart of the new system. Shall we interpret this emphasis on children's allowances as a break away from the overall focus of the plan to support breadwinners, and a genuine recognition of children as claimants?

Beveridge's main ambition was to develop a scheme that would abolish 'want', without destroying the work incentives for adult providers. These two aims could pose a dilemma – a dilemma that children's allowances could solve (Cmd 6404 [1942], para 410-12). He was convinced, not least after reading the second Rowntree report (Rowntree, 1941), that having a large family was an important factor in causing want – therefore, to abolish want, large families had to be compensated. The needs of larger families could not be met through the wage system, since wages had to relate to the productivity of the worker rather than to the size of his family. It would be unreasonable to guarantee a sufficient income for the disabled and unemployed, if a similar guarantee could not be made for families with an employed provider. Through children's allowances, however, large families could be guaranteed a reasonable standard regardless of the employment status of the provider. Children's allowances, for Beveridge, were a means to alleviate problems in the adult world – they were a way to overcome the needs/incentive dilemma. Children's allowances should be paid to families not because children had a right to benefit, but because children implied expenses to the family.

These were the main arguments in favour of children's allowances. In addition, Beveridge presented arguments which were of a different nature: "arguments arising from considerations of the numbers of population and care for children" (Cmd 6404 [1942], para 413). His worries about the low birth rate in the UK were reflected in his thinking around children's allowances as well as in his concerns for women as mothers:

> with its present rate of reproduction, the British race cannot continue ...
> children's allowances can help to restore the birth rate, both by making
> it possible for parents who desire more children to bring them into the
> world without damaging the chances of those already born, and as a
> signal of the national interest in children. (para 413)

In addition to increasing the *number* of future British citizens, children's allowances could also help to increase the 'quality': "the small families of today make it necessary that every child should receive the best care that can be given to it. The foundations of a healthy life must be laid in childhood" (Cmd 6404 [1942], para 413). The arguments in this paragraph mirrors Beveridge's concern for children as an investment in the future. Britain must foster many children, and these children must be given the opportunity to live a healthy life. That his interest was not in the rights of children as individual, present citizens of the nation is evident in the way he presented the final argument. It was 'the small families of today' which made it imperative that 'every child should receive the best care' – not that children had an intrinsic right to be cared for in the best way the family and society could possibly manage.

Children's allowances should be paid to families in respect of children. It should not be paid to the first child in families with a working provider. Beveridge argued that this would not be necessary, since almost all full-time working adult men brought home a wage sufficient to provide for two adults and one child. The exclusion of the first child in each family, however, had the effect that most unmarried mothers were excluded from the scheme. This, however, appears to have been relatively uncontroversial. Children's allowances were first of all a way of channelling money into larger families. It was the family's expenses, not the child's social rights, which provided the main justification for the scheme.

Beveridge wanted the children's allowance to be paid at such a level that it covered the actual costs of raising a child. When it was introduced under the name family allowances, it was paid at a lower level than Beveridge had proposed, and was unable to abolish the 'want' experienced by families with many children and one-parent families. It was supplemented by dependant's additions introduced in a number of other National Insurance benefits. For the purposes of the discussion here, the most important of these was the children's addition to the widowed mother's allowance.

Orphans or dependants of widows?

Widow's benefits were established by the National Insurance Act in 1946. They were payable to the widow, with additions for dependent children. Ten years after they were introduced, in 1956, they were subjected to an extensive review by the National Insurance Advisory Committee (NIAC). The committee's report (Cmd 9684 [1956]) contained rudiments of a policy targeted directly at orphans. The report made a tentative attempt to introduce a partial separation between benefits payable to widows and benefits payable to the children of widow's (children's additions). One proposal was to increase the child's addition in the widowed mother's allowance above the rate of increase for dependant's additions in other benefits. This represented the first clear recognition of the argument that widow's children had greater needs than children of other claimants; mainly because widowhood was a permanent state and not a temporary break in earnings. Even more significantly, the NIAC uncoupled the widow's and the child's elements for children older than 16, and proposed that in certain circumstances these might be paid independently of each other. The widow's element should be payable until the child turned 18, provided that the child resided with the widow. The child's element should be payable only if the child was in full-time education or apprenticeship. This was a minor change; nevertheless it opened the door to a more flexible approach to the question of widows and orphans. Over time, it could have provided the rudiments for a separate orphans pension. But this did not happen, and an orphan's pension has never been introduced in the UK.

Child poverty once again

In 1965, following a report from the London School of Economics (Abel–Smith and Townsend, 1965), child poverty made headlines in the UK for the first time since the Second World War. The findings in the new report sparked off a debate between politicians about how best to meet the child poverty problem. Labour was in government at the time, having been elected in 1964 on a programme strongly committed to social political improvements (Glennerster, 1995, p 96). The Labour government was, however, deeply sceptical of means-tested benefits, and opted to counter poverty among children by increasing family allowances. On a very small scale, this was done in October 1967 by a small sum payable in respect of the fourth and subsequent children. A larger increase in family allowances was implemented under the 1967 Family Allowance and National Insurance Act, only a few months later. However, this did not help recipients of the means-tested supplementary benefit as the increased family allowance was taken into account for benefit purposes. Even after these two increases family allowances were lower in real value than they had been 20 years earlier, in 1948 (Brown, 1989). British Labour politicians tried to reach children in poor families by increasing the incomes of all families, but this was a strategy with modest effects.

The second important thing the Labour government did following the Abel-Smith and Townsend report, was to appoint a committee with a mandate to chart the situation of one-parent families. This was known as the Finer committee, after the chairman Morris Finer. The report of the Finer Committee (Cmnd 5629 [1974]) was unquestionably the most thorough and important document in the history of UK dealings with lone parents in the 1960s and 1970s. With regard to children, however, the committee had surprisingly little to say. In this respect, the committee followed in the tradition from Beveridge: it recognised children as a financial burden, but not as individuals with potential claims. The main brain-child of the committee was the Guaranteed Maintenance Allowance (GMA). This was to be payable with one element for the parent and one for each child. However, when the parent no longer qualified – if he/she remarried or started cohabiting – the right to the parent's allowance as well as the child's addition was lost to the family. The Finer Committee did not propose the child should be a claimant in its own right, or see the child's situation – living away from one biological parent – as one that could give rise to social rights. In line with the treatment of children who had lost their father, who were also treated as the widow's dependants, the Committee did not discuss the possibility of seeing the child as an insured person.

The Finer Committee did, however, devote the final section of its report to discuss 'parents and children' and their 'day-to-day family and social life'. In this section, the situation of the child was considered in the light of the evidence the Committee had received and the studies it had examined.

> [The evidence] concerned the sense of loss and suffering, the social isolation, the burden of coping alone with the emotional and material needs of children and with unfamiliar household tasks; and, for the child, the risk of suffering the reciprocal effect of these same burdens in the shape of a lonely and depressed mother and father, grief at the loss of the other parent and a sense of being different from other children. The result for some children may be poor performance at school or disturbed and delinquent behaviour. (Finer, 1974, para 9.2)

Children of lone parents were seen as victims of the situation, and pictured as children under considerable stress. The Committee saw their situation as worrying, and urged more research into the effects on children of living in a one-parent family (para 9.23, p 188). The other recommendations in this section are all concerned with social work services, child care and education. Children, when seen by the Finer Committee, were victims in need of care rather than potential claimants. This perspective was also adopted when the Finer Report was discussed in the House of Commons in 1975. Children were mentioned often, but only as victims of the sad circumstances in which their family lived. The concern for child poverty, which provided the background for the appointment of the Finer Committee in the first place, still prevailed in the 1975 debate. There was, however, no talk of the independent rights of children in any respect, and very little mention of children's needs *as children*. Finer's recommendation of a separate children's element in the GMA, which was not to be affected by the parent's earnings and thereby resembled a children's benefit, got no further mention – and the GMA was rejected on the background of the country's difficult financial circumstances. The emphasis was on *the family*, the one-parent family, with the clear assumption that aid to the family would benefit the child as well as the parent. The children were pitied, but not entitled (cf Gordon, 1994).

Child benefit was introduced in the UK in 1977. The child benefit interim (CBI), which was payable to lone parents only (and that later changed its name to one-parent benefit), preceded the child benefit by one year. Although the child welfare arguments were still vividly remembered, this measure was also strongly linked to the proposed tax credit scheme, which in turn must be seen in the context of the general tax policy (Glennerster, 1995). Unlike the 1946 family allowances, child benefit would be payable to the mother in two-parent families, and it would be paid to families with only one child. In some ways, therefore, the benefit resembled the mother's endowment for which the women's movement in the UK had campaigned since the 1920s (Pedersen, 1993).

Child benefit is still the only benefit in the UK that is payable in respect of all children, regardless of their parent's income and labour market status. In Norway, a more complex system of children's benefits has been developed, particularly in respect of children living with only one parent. This is the topic of the next section.

Norway: childhood as situation of need

Mother's endowment, with recognition of children in need

During the inter-war years in Norway, family support was more or less continuously debated. Three main strategies were discussed: mother's endowments, paying a family wage to the male breadwinner, or giving families benefits in kind (Seip, 1994, pp 180f). A committee reporting in 1934 had outlined a child benefit arrangement. Some of the ideas of this committee were taken up by the war administration led by Vidkun Quisling, and a rudimentary child benefit scheme was introduced in 1944. After the war, this scheme was discontinued – partly because of its strong association with the Quisling government, and partly because it excluded large sections of the population (Bjørnson and Haavet, 1994, p 203). The Norwegian government had spent the war years in London, and therefore was familiar with the Beveridge scheme and the proposed family allowances in the UK (Seip, 1994, p 186). The child benefit scheme that was eventually introduced in 1946 therefore had a long and complex history. Nevertheless, it was universally welcomed and passed through the parliament without debate.

The 1946 scheme was the first benefit payable to all families with children in Norway. However, it was not paid to married couples for the first child. Only unmarried mothers and people on disability benefit would receive child benefit for the first child. The most important argument in favour of the new benefit was to secure children a decent starting point in life, and it was recognised that children without a provider had greater needs than other children (cf Bjørnson and Haavet, 1994, p 203). During the 1920s, the child benefit had been presented as a mother's endowment and had been a rallying point for the feminist movement. By 1946, this emphasis had mainly disappeared but the benefit would still be paid to the mother in couples as recognition of her work (Seip, 1994, p 188). The Norwegian child benefit scheme strongly resembled the British family allowances, with the important exception of the treatment of lone parents with only one child.

The risk of losing a parent

Apart from this extra entitlement, provisions for lone-parent families were meagre in Norway in the immediate post-war period. Local authorities provided some limited means to unmarried mothers around the time of delivery, and the state was responsible for making fathers pay child maintenance (Skevik, 2001, pp 248ff), but no more comprehensive benefits existed. This changed in 1957, when two Acts were introduced determining social security provisions as a matter of right for children living with only one parent. The two acts were the Provider's Benefit Act and the Forwarded Maintenance Act. *Provider's benefit* should be payable to children who had lost either parent by death, and children whose paternity was not established. These were the cases in which reclaiming money from a liable parent was not possible. For all other children living in one-parent families, *forwarded maintenance* would be paid. This provision was intended as a buffer between the liable parent and the child. Despite the public claims procedure, the parent might not pay on time, or he might pay too little or not at all – in any case, his shortcomings would harm the child. The forwarded maintenance would put an end to this. Together, the twin acts from 1957 ensured all children of lone parents received a minimum payment as a matter of right.

The two acts developed from two different sources: the 1948 White Paper *On National Insurance* (St meld no 58 [1948]), and the 1951 report of the Child Welfare Committee. The 1948 White Paper represented the first attempt to create a blue-print for the future all-encompassing welfare state – in ambition, if not in influence, it was a Norwegian Beveridge report. It proposed an entirely new system of benefits, among them a set of family benefits: provider's benefit, child benefit and widow's benefit. These were benefits designed to cover a set of family risks, to complete a framework otherwise oriented towards covering labour market risks. Provider's benefit should be payable in respect of *all* children living with only one parent, to address the increased vulnerability of children in such families. This benefit, just like the other proposed family benefits, was assumed to be a public benefit where there should be no question of reclaiming money from private sources.

In Norway, child maintenance is determined by the Children Acts. The working group on child welfare services that was appointed in 1947 therefore dealt both with reforms in the Children Acts, and with maintenance forwarding and reclaiming. Following the committee's reports from 1951, four important new acts were passed in the mid-1950s: the Maintenance Reclaiming Act in 1955, the Non-Marital Children Act and the Parents and Marital Children Act in 1956, and the Forwarded Maintenance Act in 1957. With regard to forwarded maintenance, the committee argued:

> The maintenance payments the mother and child are entitled to must in almost every case be regarded as a subsistence minimum. When the collection misfires, the consequence is that the mother and child either suffers destitution, or must rely on poor relief (*forsorgsvesenet*). That is both harmful and insulting to the sense of justice. (Child welfare working group report No V, 1951, p 8)

When the Labour government turned to benefits for children in one-parent families in 1957, it thus drew two strings together: the anti-poverty aim of the 1948 Green Paper, and the child welfare concern of the 1951 Committee Report. Children in one-parent families were seen as vulnerable to poverty as well as other forms of stress, and therefore as a category that had to be protected within the emerging welfare state. This happened before any social benefits as of right had been introduced for the parents themselves – not even widow's benefit existed on a national scale in 1957. Provider's benefit (*forsørgertrygd*) and forwarded maintenance (*bidragsforskott*) were introduced simultaneously, with extensive cross-reference between the two White Papers.

Provider's benefit was a benefit for children. The Ministry for Social Affairs made that point explicitly:

> The Ministry adopts the view that the provider's benefit should be limited to be a benefit for children. The question of a benefit for mothers may be discussed as a separate issue later, after one has some experience with how the proposed arrangement will work. (Ot prp no 41 [1957], p 4)

Provider's benefit should be paid to children who had lost one or both parents, and children whose paternity was not known. This differed from the stance taken in the 1948 Green Paper, where it was assumed this should be payable to children of all lone mothers. This narrowing down of the group of recipients was possible because other children living with one parent would receive forwarded maintenance. The distinction between recipients of each benefit should be, the Ministry maintained in the White Papers, that forwarded maintenance should be paid in cases where the money in principle could be recovered. One group of children provided a difficult border-line case: the children born by Norwegian women between 1940 and 1945/46, whose fathers were German soldiers. These men's names might be known, but it was not seen as realistic to recover maintenance from them. The Ministry emphasised that these children would receive provider's benefit as if the fathers had been unknown, and thus that higher expenses should be expected in the first years until all these children had turned 18.

One interesting feature of the 1957 arrangements was that no distinctions were made between different groups of lone parents. The distinction was based on the possibility of reclaiming money; any other characteristic of the parent was irrelevant. This followed from the emphasis on children, as expressed in this quote from the 1948 White Paper:

> the provider's benefit incorporates partly support to lone mothers, partly to others who take on the responsibility for orphaned children. The lone mothers are either widows, or divorced, separated, abandoned or unmarried mothers. The Ministry is of the opinion that all these groups should be treated equally . . . the introduction of such a benefit [is] motivated by the wish that as many orphaned children as possible shall grow up in homes which have the resources required to take care of their upbringing. (St meld no 58 [1948], p 56)

If the new benefits helped the adults in the family, this was a welcome side-effect, but it was children who were in focus in the 1957 White Papers. By the dual laws on forwarded maintenance and provider's benefit, all children not living with both parents were guaranteed a minimum monthly payment. Concerns for incentives effects for adults, as well as the question of whether or not the parent was deserving, were put aside. The treatment of the children of German occupation soldiers is a particularly strong illustration of this. These children, as well as their mothers, were social outcasts after the end of the occupation. That the Ministry not only included these children in the provider's benefit, but openly discussed how this would incur some temporary extra costs on the scheme, indicates a strong commitment to the recognition of children independent of their parents.

The main dividing line in 1957 between recipients of provider's benefit and forwarded maintenance was whether or not maintenance could be reclaimed from the liable parent. Together, the two acts were assumed to cover all children in one-parent families. However, one gap was soon discovered: children whose paternity was known, but whose fathers were not liable to pay or were paying less than the forwarded amount. The Forwarded Maintenance Act was changed in 1963 to include children in such situations. But this amendment in effect altered the basic premise of the Act: it had been introduced as a pure forwarding arrangement. After 1963, it was payable to children for whom reclaiming was not possible, or very little could be reclaimed. The forwarding arrangement thus began very quickly to take on the form of a social benefit.

Orphan' claims: Children's pensions

The 1966 National Insurance Act suspended the provider's benefit, and introduced a new system of provisions for children. *Children's pension*, under the new act, was payable to children under 18 who had lost one or both parents by death. If one of the parents was dead, a pension equal to 40% of the National Insurance base amount would be calculated for the oldest child, while each subsequent child would be awarded an amount equal to 25%. The pension for all siblings were added up and divided equally between the children. If both parents were dead, the pension for the oldest child should equal the pension the parent with the highest claim for bereaved person's pension (formerly widow's pension) would have received. The second child should be awarded 40% of the base amount, and each subsequent child should have 25%. Again, the total amount should be split equally between the siblings. Importantly, the right to children's pension was independent of whether or not the surviving parent remarried or started cohabiting. Only if the parent's new partner adopted the child was the right to children's pension lost.

Excepting a few changes, this has remained the basic outline of the children's pension to this day. Suspending the provider's benefit and creating a new pension for orphans, however, implied that one group of children lost their protection: the children whose paternity was not established. Later in 1966, these children were included in the forwarded maintenance arrangement. Since paternity was not established there could be no question of reclaiming the forwarded maintenance – just as it could not for children whose father was known but not liable to pay (the 1963-reform). This further emphasised that forwarded maintenance was becoming a social benefit more than a mere forwarding arrangement.

If the 1948 White Paper can be seen as a Norwegian parallel to the Beveridge report, the Finer Committee had its parallel in a working group appointed in 1973, led by Aksel Hatland. The working group had been asked to review the entire benefit system for lone-parent families, and approached this issue with a strong emphasis on children. The first report (NOU, 1975, p 18) outlined the distinct situations of need that should give rise to benefit entitlements. In this discussion, parents and children were discussed separately. Children with potential claims were identified as (1) orphans, (2) children who had lost one parent, and (3) children whose parents lived in separate households. Adults in need were (a) lone persons who provided for children, and (b) persons of working age who had lost their provider. Children were therefore legitimate claimants in their own right, as was the parent. This was the Committee's starting point, and it also neatly summed up the existing logic of the Norwegian family benefits.

The committee proposed a separate children's benefit (*barnestønad*), to replace the children's pensions from 1966. This would be paid to children who had lost one parent by death, or whose parents did not live together. In the latter case, the benefit should be coordinated with payments from the non-resident parent, and be withdrawn if the payments from the parent were regular and at a level similar to the pension. This benefit would replace both children's pension and forwarded maintenance. As such, it recognised the individual claims of children living with only one parent, and – as would be the case with adults – it would not ask why the child was in this situation. The committee discussed if a private maintenance agreement should be required before children's benefit could be paid (implying that fathers would have to be named), but rejected the idea of refusing benefit on this basis since that would be harmful to some of the most vulnerable children. Children's benefit should continue to be paid if the parent remarried or started cohabiting, and would not be tested against the parent's income. The level of the benefit should be 30% of the base amount – similar to the forwarded maintenance, lower than children's pension paid to the first child, but higher than the pension paid to second and subsequent children. It would be payable until the child turned 18.

Like the GMA proposed by Finer in the UK, the children's benefit proposed by the Hatland Committee was never taken up by the Ministry. The arrangement introduced in 1966 therefore remains more or less unaltered: children's pension is paid to orphans, while forwarded maintenance is paid to children of other lone parents if the custodial parent applies for it. The committee report is nevertheless interesting because it sums up the way of thinking around family support among chief public officials at the time. The idea had clearly settled in Norway: that children had claims on the welfare state in their own right, and that these claims were separate from those of their parents.

Children in families and welfare states

The most striking difference between the two countries is not in the details but in the overall picture: Norway has a policy towards parents and children; the UK has a policy towards families. This difference is visible in benefit policy as well as in child maintenance arrangements (Skevik, 1998, 2001). The lack of attention paid to children in the British welfare state has also been highlighted by other scholars, such as Paul Daniel and John Ivatts:

> We would suggest that no other factor is as significant in explaining British social policy towards children as the nature of the relationship between the family and the state. This claim is more than a simple recognition that most children spend most of their childhood within families: it is based on the view that children are virtually 'invisible' within the family unit, and they have almost no separate social policy identity. (Daniel and Ivatts, 1998, pp 6-7)

This contrasts with the situation in Norway, where the broad historical accounts of the welfare state (Seip, 1984, 1994; Bjørnson and Haavet, 1994) typically highlight the increased societal responsibility for children as one of the dimensions along which the development of the Norwegian welfare state must be understood[1].

A striking feature of the Norwegian benefit system for lone parents and their children is the commitment to treating children in similar situations equally.

There were few, if any, attempts to draw a distinction between orphaned children and children who live with only one parent for other reasons. Thus when the child benefit was introduced in 1946, it was made payable from the first child for all lone parents. Children of unmarried mothers got their entitlement to provider's benefit (if the father was unknown) or forwarded maintenance (in other cases) in 1957. Provider's benefit was payable in cases where the money could not be recovered from the other parent. For this reason it came to encompass both orphans and children whose paternity was unknown: the group of children traditionally met with most benevolence together with the children traditionally most scorned. The benefit also included the children met with most mockery in the prevailing climate – children who were the results of their mother's involvement with enemy soldiers.

In the UK, orphans were clearly privileged over children whose parents were unmarried, separated or divorced. Unmarried mothers and their children had practically no social rights – they were even excluded from the 1946 family allowances in most cases since most unmarried mothers had only one child. Beveridge viewed children as an investment, but perhaps not all children were equally worth investing in. The disadvantage experienced by children born to unmarried mothers was not compensated for. Only when the CBI was introduced in 1976 did unmarried mothers (along with other lone parents) get a benefit as of right. This was payable in the mother's name, but it was nevertheless the closest British children of lone parents have been to a benefit on their own. Child benefit was introduced in the wake of the renewed emphasis on child poverty, in a political climate where children were pitied as victims of unfortunate circumstance. Avoiding child poverty was seen as equivalent with strengthening the parent's claims, whether in the form of tax relief or a new child benefit. This was evident even in the Finer Report, which discussed children merely as victims of the circumstances under which they lived.

This relatively harsh treatment of children of unmarried mothers (and of unmarried mothers themselves) reflects a strongly held assumption in British policy, namely that children are the responsibility of their parents. The state deals with the parents, and the parents deal with the children – the state's responsibility for children is very limited. Child-centred arguments, such as the argument that reduced benefits for lone parents would harm their children, could be rejected on the account that the parents should never have placed their children in this situation in the first place. The good family form, the stable two-parent unit, was to be encouraged. Parents who chose to break away from this norm, who perhaps even threatened it through their deviant behaviour, could not push their children in front of them in the hope that the state would rescue them from the consequences of their choices. The message from the British state was, 'you've made your bed, now you and your children must lie in it'. In Norway, children were not hidden behind their parents to the same extent. It was clear in Norwegian policy that benefit entitlements were not to be determined by the sins or virtues of the mothers.

Another striking difference between the two countries regards the extent to which claims bases for social rights are separated. This is illustrated here by the treatment of widows and orphans. When a married man with children dies, his wife has lost a husband and the children have lost a father. She is a widow and the children are fatherless. British social policy has treated families like this as incomplete families – still a unit, but a unit lacking one piece. The mother's status changes from 'dependant' to 'head of household', while the children's status remains unchanged. They are still dependants. In Norway, the status of all members of this family changes. The widow acquires a right to widow's benefits, while the children get the right to children's pension. The different risks of losing a spouse and losing a parent are recognised. The differential claims situation is even better illustrated in the cases where the widowed mother remarries. When this happens, UK policies consider the family unit to be complete once again and withdraw all benefit entitlements. There is no distinction between the status as a parent or a spouse; the man (or woman) who marries the lone parent is automatically assumed to take on full responsibility for the child. In Norway in this situation, the right to widow's pension ceases. The husband is replaced. But the father is not – the biological parent is gone forever. Therefore the right to children's pension is unaffected by the presence of a new man in the household. Only by adoption is a parent considered to be 'replaced' in Norwegian legislation.

Conclusion

So, has this discussion of children's social rights made a contribution to the debate on welfare state variation? The empirical discussion suggests that the UK traditionally has been closer to the ideal–typical organic view of the family outlined in the introduction, while Norway has been closer to the individual view. This is a difference that has not been highlighted in previous research comparing these and other countries. Through the examination of the empirical material, two new dimensions of variation have come to the fore:

* the separation of parenting and partnering for the purposes of social benefits, and
* the extent to which the sins or virtues of the parents determine transfers to children.

The first dimension is most obviously illustrated by the rules for widow's and orphan's pensions, while the latter dimension is best illustrated by the similarities and differences between the treatment of orphans on the one hand, and children of other lone parents on the other. Both these dimensions have the potential to strongly influence distribution between families with children, as well as the legitimacy of the benefits. Still, these aspects have been under-communicated in previous research on the welfare state. An explicit emphasis on the treatment of children therefore illuminates features of welfare states that have remained invisible in 'adult-centred' studies.

Acknowledgements

This [chapter] [was] based on research undertaken as part of my doctoral project, funded by the Norwegian Ministry of Social Affairs and NOVA – Norwegian Social Research, and draws on material presented in Chapter 7 of my dissertation (Skevik, 2001). An earlier version was presented at the Society for the Advancement of Socio-Economics (SASE) 13th Annual Meeting at the University of Amsterdam, Amsterdam, the Netherlands, 28 June-1 July 2001. I thank participants at this seminar, the NOVA Social Security Group and two anonymous referees for their comments on earlier drafts.

Note

[1] None of this implies that the concept of children's rights is alien to British politics. This has been an ongoing debate, like in other western countries, with the 1989 Children Act commonly seen as a major milestone. However, the concern for children's rights tends to be much stronger in private law than in public law. The relationship between the 'private' 1989 Children Act and the 'public' 1991 Child Support Act provides a good illustration. For discussion, see Eekelaar (1991), Leigh (1992), Fox Harding (1994), Skevik (1998).

This chapter was taken from the *Journal of Social Policy*, 2003, vol 32, no 3.

Fair but unequal? Children, ethnicity and the welfare state

Lucinda Platt

Introduction, argument and sources

The current British government famously asserted at the beginning of its first term in office its intention to eliminate child poverty within a generation and halve it within a decade (DSS, 1999). It also demonstrated its commitment to strengthening racial equality by enacting the first race relations legislation since 1976, the 2000 Race Relations Amendment Act which reinforced the provisions against indirect discrimination of the earlier Act. In this analysis of child poverty I explore the disproportionate impact of poverty on children from certain ethnic groups.

While it has been demonstrated that around 800,000 children were lifted out of poverty between 1997 and 2001, those who remained in jobless households dependent on means-tested benefits remained below standard poverty lines despite increases in benefit (Piachaud and Sutherland, 2001). At the same time, in Britain, as elsewhere, children from minority ethnic groups tend to be over-represented in this residual population (Adelman and Bradshaw, 1999; DSS, 2000a, b). This [chapter], however, goes beyond the issue of prevalence to examine how the severity of poverty can vary *within* the population of those supported by means-tested benefits. In doing this it reveals systematic inequities within the structure of the benefit system itself, which are associated with the ethnicity of the child.

The [chapter's] findings are derived from analysis of administrative record data on benefit receipt for the city of Birmingham, combined with budget-standard estimates of children's needs that differ by age and family circumstances. From comparisons of children's needs with the benefit amounts allowed for children, I calculate income shortfalls and examine how these differ across children from different ethnic groups. I show that Bangladeshi and Pakistani children in particular have higher shortfalls of income relative to needs than do children from other ethnic groups, a result that can be traced back to the markedly higher prevalence of large families among Bangladeshis and Pakistanis.

The findings are robust to whether income shortfalls are assessed using cross-sectional (point-in-time) or longitudinal measures. The longer-term perspective offered by longitudinal measures takes account of the chronic nature of low income and thence its cumulative impact, and its broader implications for child welfare (Jarvis and Jenkins, 1996; Ashworth et al, 1992; Walker, with Ashworth, 1992; Bradbury et al, 2001). As Walker and Ashworth stress, "without taking time into account it is impossible fully to appreciate the nature and experience of poverty or truly to understand the level of suffering involved" (Walker, with Ashworth, 1992, p 1).

Minority ethnic groups in Britain have diverse and particular histories as well as different experiences of discrimination and disadvantage (Coleman and Salt, 1996; Peach, 1996; Ratcliffe, 1997; Karn, 1997; Modood and others, 1997). The particularity and distinct history of the British welfare state has also been much commented upon (eg McKay and Rowlingson, 1999; Fraser, 1984). The intersection of these two areas therefore provides a unique set of findings that cannot easily be generalised to other contexts. Nevertheless, there are a number of reasons why the findings have a wider import. First, they reveal the distortions that can arise in benefit payments to families with children as a result of the tension between providing adequate support to children and minimising their parents' disincentives to work. This tension is not unique to Britain but is a feature of most 'liberal' welfare state regimes (Esping-Andersen, 1990). Second, they illustrate a child-centred approach to welfare dynamics that removes the focus from exit from benefit or 'benefit dependency' and instead concentrates on the implications of those dynamics for children. This approach contrasts with extant work on welfare dynamics (Bane and Ellwood, 1994; Pavetti, 1993; Noble et al, 1998; Ashworth et al, 1997; McKay et al, 1997). Third, they illuminate the point that, setting discrimination and the causes of structural disadvantage to one side, even an equitably administered benefit system can systematically disadvantage certain minority groups by the way the rules are established.

Britain has possibly the most complicated benefits system of any welfare state. It comprises universal benefits such as Child Benefit, payable on behalf of any child; National Insurance benefits, such as the Old Age Pension and unemployment benefit (now called Contributions-based Jobseeker's Allowance), which are dependent on work record and the number of contributions paid; and means-tested benefits, such as Income Support, which are restricted to those whose incomes (and savings) fall beneath a certain threshold. Means-tested benefits are complex to assess and stigmatising to their recipients. The benefits system is also extending a particular type of means-tested benefit through tax credits which supplement the incomes of those in work but on low earnings who become eligible for a form of reverse taxation. Tax credits also feature complex assessment procedures, but they tend to be more generous and less stigmatising than traditional 'safety net' means-tested benefits.

This [chapter] concentrates on children in non-working families receiving either Income Support (where the parent(s) are not seeking work) or Income-based Jobseeker's Allowance (where the claimant is expected to be actively seeking work). These benefits are designed for those who have no other source of income or whose income is not deemed sufficient to support them. They are paid at nationally determined rates. The rates and applicable amounts of Income Support and Income-based Jobseeker's Allowance are the same and so the two benefits are treated together here. For brevity and simplicity I refer to both benefits as IS.

The population of children supported by IS considered in this [chapter] is identified through the Birmingham Housing Benefit and Council Tax Benefit database – so it covers children who are in families receiving both IS and Housing or Council Tax Benefits. As IS payments are not intended to cover housing costs, receipt of IS renders the claimant automatically eligible for housing costs: Housing Benefit if they pay rent, and/or Council Tax Benefit if they are liable for Council Tax, within the constraints of the accommodation being an appropriate size and the rent being comparable to local 'reference rents'. Thus the vast majority of all children in Birmingham who are supported by IS appear on this local authority data set[1].

Birmingham is the second largest city in Britain and the largest single administrative local authority. Birmingham has a population of about one million inhabitants, of whom roughly a quarter belong to a minority ethnic group. Its industrial decline took place later than that of the old mill towns of the north of England, but between 1978 and 1983 the metropolitan county lost a third of its manufacturing jobs (Walker et al, 1991), and Birmingham continues to have higher than average rates of unemployment. It is a city of contrasts, with the Sutton area to the north of the city containing some of the most advantaged wards in the country; while extreme levels of disadvantage can be found in the inner ring of the city. Birmingham, then, is a city whose size, variety and extensive minority ethnic group population render it a particularly profitable place in which to study the experience of child poverty and ethnicity. While the findings reported later relate to only a single city, they are relevant to the experience of large numbers of children. In addition, given that benefit payments follow nationally determined rules, the issues that my findings raise can be seen as relevant to the whole of Britain.

The analysis reported here used seven quarterly data extracts from the Housing and Council Tax Benefit records from January 1998 to June 1999[2]. Quarterly extracts are sufficiently frequent to maximise the opportunities for observing genuine movement in and out of benefit over time, and they are widely enough spaced to minimise any distortion from false exits and re-entries caused by administrative error or initial shortage of information, known as 'churning'. Anonymised data were supplied at individual level with unique individual and benefit unit (family) identifiers. I linked the records across the seven extracts at the levels of both the benefit unit and the individual child using these unique identifiers, to enable both cross-sectional and longitudinal analysis over the period. At any one of the seven snapshots there were between 66,000 and 72,000 children supported by both Housing Benefit and IS; and over the 17-month period, a total of 106,561 children were so supported.

Analysing ethnicity

While there have been ethnic minorities in Britain for centuries, the sharp increase in numbers occurred in the post-war period when active labour recruitment, initially in the Caribbean and India as well as Eastern and Southern Europe, took place. Due to increasingly stringent controls, starting with the 1962 Commonwealth Immigrants Act, the growth of most minority groups – where it has occurred – has been predominantly through reproduction rather than primary immigration or family re-unification since the 1970s. The vast majority of all minority ethnic group children were born in Britain; while the total numbers of those from the main minority groups who immigrated into Britain since 1945 are small, with very low annual rates since the 1960s.

According to the 1991 Census, minority groups made up 5.5% of the population of Britain. The classification of minority groups in the Census counted seven ethnic groups (including 'white'), and three 'other' categories. Overall these ten minority groups made up nearly 22% of Birmingham's population in 1991.

For this [chapter] I analyse the experience of children from just five ethnic groups. Black Caribbeans[3], Indians, Pakistanis and those classified as White UK[4] make up the four largest ethnic groups in both Birmingham and the UK. The fifth group, Bangladeshis, who made up 0.3% of the British and 1.3% of the Birmingham population in 1991 is included because this study provides the opportunity to distinguish between the Bangladeshi experience and the Pakistani experience. This is rare in British studies of ethnic group disadvantage due to small numbers and is in itself is an important contribution to knowledge in this area.

Patterns of immigration and settlement have varied across these minority groups and I briefly outline some of their key features. Black Caribbean immigration predominantly took place in the earliest phase of post-war immigration in the 1950s and beginning of the 1960s and also concluded the earliest. The vast majority of Black Caribbeans are thus British-born. This group has a more youthful demographic profile that the British population as a whole, but less so than the other principal minority groups. Much Indian immigration also took place in the immediate post-war period, with family re-unification extending the period of immigration beyond that of the Black Caribbeans and into the 1960s. The expulsion of East African Asians from Uganda and Kenya in the late 1960s and early 1970s resulted in further period of primary immigration, of predominantly highly qualified Indians with business and entrepreneurial backgrounds. Indians form the single largest minority ethnic group in Britain and tend to be advantaged relative to other minority groups, although they are still disadvantaged relative to the white population in, for example, unemployment rates.

Pakistani primary immigration took place largely in the 1950s and peaked in 1961, prior to the implementation of restrictions. Thereafter, there was an extended period of family re-unification, extended partly through the increasingly restrictive immigration controls on family entry that were introduced. The Pakistani population in Birmingham forms the single largest concentration of Pakistanis in Britain, a consequence in part of the recruitment of Pakistanis into manual industrial jobs and the relatively late industrial decline in Birmingham. The Pakistani age profile is very young and heavily dominated by children as a result of both migration patterns and high fertility among Pakistani women. Pakistanis form one of the most economically disadvantaged minority groups in Britain, although not as disadvantaged as the final group considered, the Bangladeshis.

Bangladeshi immigration is more recent than the bulk of Pakistani and Indian immigration. While it is difficult accurately to measure migration patterns prior to the secession and subsequent recognition of Bangladesh in 1972, it is clear that Bangladeshi migration followed a distinct trajectory, both in terms of timing, residential location and of the industries entered (Eade et al, 1996). Primary immigration took place during the 1960s and 1970s, and total immigration peaked in the 1980s due to family reunification, often delayed through the obstacles imposed by the immigration rules. The group also expanded quickly as children were born in this country. Bangladeshis formed the smallest minority group in Britain in 1991, although the population has continued to expand since then. The Bangladeshi population in Britain is the most concentrated of the minority groups, with nearly a quarter of the total British Bangladeshi population living in the London Borough of Tower Hamlets. Outside London, the biggest concentration can be found in Birmingham. The Bangladeshis, like the Pakistanis have a very young profile with a dominance of children.

It is well known that high poverty risks for children are associated with living in a large family or in a lone-parent family, and family circumstances differ by ethnic group. Thus there is a close association between ethnic group differences in family type and ethnic group differences in poverty. Differences in demographic characteristics across ethnic groups include high fertility among Bangladeshis and Pakistanis and a predominance of lone-parent Black Caribbean families relative to couple-parent families. Over half of Caribbean families with children were headed by a lone parent in 1991 compared to under a fifth of families overall being lone-parent families. But the differential family structure also influences the profile of the benefit population when broken down by ethnic group. While lone-parent families make up a higher proportion of poor families than they do of all families, children in Bangladeshi benefit-recipient families are still more likely to be living in couple-parent than lone-parent families. And while large families from all groups are more likely to be poor, the average number of children in benefit-recipient Black Caribbean and White UK families is lower than that in other groups. It is these demographic characteristics which drive the analysis that follows.

Assessing children's needs

The empirical foundation of this study is a comparison of the amount of benefits received on account of a child with the amount of income that that child needs. In this [chapter] I use budget standard measures of needs, derived in a manner that I shall now explain.

The estimation of subsistence-based budget standards has a long history, going back to Rowntree's first survey of York in 1899 (Rowntree, 1902). Since then numerous social statisticians have attempted to calculate the fundamental costs of living to produce a poverty standard, such as that employed in the US, or to provide a point of comparison with benefit amounts which are assumed to cover the basic costs of existence. Piachaud, in his seminal study of 1979, created costings solely for children, and compared them with the rates of Supplementary Benefit (the predecessor of IS), thus demonstrating the insufficiency of Supplementary Benefit relative to what children actually cost. More recently costings were produced by a budget study directed by Jonathan Bradshaw; and it is these budgets and in particular the estimates purely for children extracted by Nina Oldfield that I use here as the basis for my estimate of the costs of children (Bradshaw, 1993; Oldfield, 1992, 1993). These budgets are in line with their predecessors in estimating different costs for children of different ages. Specifically, they estimate the costs of younger children as being lower than those of older children, both at a basic level of food costs and for more 'convention'-driven aspects of the budget such as clothing (including school uniform) and transport. The IS scale also rates younger children as being less expensive than older children. However, as my comparisons show, the differences between the budgets and the IS scale vary at different ages, with the IS scale, being based on pragmatism and precedent rather than actual estimations of costs, undervaluing younger children rather more than older children.

Fortunately for my purpose the least generalisable (because most variable) aspect of this budget, housing costs, is not an issue, as I am examining the IS income of families whose housing costs are already covered. I have therefore taken Oldfield's rates excluding housing and childcare costs, have generalised them from the specific ages of 4, 10 and 16 to the surrounding ranges of 0-7, 8-13 and 14+, and have updated them to January 1998 prices using the Retail Price Index excluding housing. The result is an estimate of the cost of the children in each of the IS recipient families at the date of the January 1998 data extract.

Estimates of point-in-time and longitudinal shortfalls of income from needs, and how these vary by ethnic group are presented in the next section. Such comparisons constitute a heuristic device intended as an exploration of ways in which we might think about the welfare of children, rather than conclusive evidence of actual hardship. Nevertheless, I consider the evidence it presents about inequities inherent in the benefit system to be powerful.

Benefit deficits and differences by ethnic group

The point-in-time perspective

The first part of my analysis considers the adequacy of means-tested benefits to support children when compared with a separate costing of children's needs. It does this by considering a single cross-section at January 1998. It therefore examines the extent to which the allocations for children within means-tested benefits are sufficient for their purpose and whether, in practice, the characteristics of children's families mean that some children experience a greater income-to-needs shortfall than others. It has been recognised that there is an arbitrary element to decisions about benefit allocations and that receipt of the same benefit does not ensure an equal economic outcome. As Parker trenchantly put it: "Despite much talk of improved 'targeting', a careful look at [IS rates] suggests that targeting by the Department of Social Security is either carried out blindfold or is based on criteria other than need" (Parker, 1998, p 3).

IS rates allocate amounts to eligible claimants and their families based on rules which incorporate underlying assumptions about economies of scale and age. These assumptions are complicated by the existence of a family premium payable on the presence of children in the family and regardless of number or age of children. Until 1998, this premium took two forms, one for couple-parent families and a more generous variant for lone-parent families. From 1998 the lone-parent variant was abolished for new claimants, although it remains payable for continuously claiming lone parents who were eligible prior to the change in rules.

IS rates thus made some allowance for both intra-familial economies of scale and, at the time of the study, the needs of different ages. The age ranges are quite broad, however, and the economy of scale implied by the family premium is somewhat large at between two thirds and a third of the age-based child rates. IS rates acknowledge the high relative costs of children compared to adults at the lower end of the income scale when compared with the McClements equivalence scale that is used to adjust incomes in the derivation of official poverty statistics (DSS, 2000b). However, IS payments are relatively disadvantageous to large families and relatively advantageous to small families, even though this is at no point a stated intention of the benefit design. I would argue that this feature of IS has come about through a misguided emphasis on maximising payments to families with children, rather than focusing on the implications for all children. It is relatively straightforward to boost the incomes of all families through an enhancement of the family premium; and as the most common number of children in families on benefit is one, and the majority of *families* have one or two children it is an easy way to direct resources towards children living in the modal family. However, the majority of *children* living in benefit-recipient families do *not* live in one or two child families. In my data, while only a third of families have three or more children in them, over half of the children live in families with three or more children. To consider the children rather than the family, however, can raise concerns as to whether benefit incomes remain below wage levels. The concern to minimise disincentives to participate in paid work promotes a pattern of benefit payment that relatively favours the first or only child[5].

Total needs for children can be compared with the IS allowed for children, including the lone or couple parent premium as appropriate. The income shortfall is calculated by subtracting the total IS amounts payable from the assessment of the 'true' costs of children estimated according to Oldfield's rates. This provides a shortfall per family at January 1998, and the numbers of children living in families with different ranges of shortfalls can then be calculated. According to these calculations, Bangladeshi families have the highest average shortfall and White UK families the lowest.

The amount of the shortfall is a measure of the severity of the poverty the families experience. I therefore ranked the shortfalls into three levels (high, medium and low) so that a third of all *families* in each rank. According to such a ranking, 54% of *children* were living in the 'high' rank, thus illustrating that larger families were more susceptible to income shortfalls[6]. This rose, however, to 80% of Bangladeshi children. Thus, looking at a single point in time, Bangladeshi children are liable to have least available funds for their needs, even compared to other children on IS.

The longitudinal perspective

I now consider the impact of time on the experience of benefit receipt among children; and whether variations in the experience according to ethnic group can be detected when a dynamic perspective is taken. Hill and Jenkins (2001) consider two ways of assessing the seriousness of poverty over time. One is whether the person or child is consistently below the poverty line (in this case indicated by receipt of IS over all seven extracts in my study); the other is according to the depth of poverty averaged out over time. I label the first approach persistent poverty.

I have used logistic regression to model the probability of being in persistent poverty (ie being observed to be supported by IS at all seven extracts) using ethnic group as an explanatory variable and controlling for other factors. I have estimated two models, first estimating simply the effect of ethnicity, and taking additional explanatory variables into account in the second model. The results are displayed in Table 1.

Model 1 of Table 1 illustrates that of all those children ever supported by IS, those from all the minority groups are less likely to be continuously in receipt of IS than their White UK counterparts. The difference is most pronounced for Indian children, but is substantial for all groups. Children in White UK families, therefore, once they fall into poverty are most likely to remain there persistently. Controlling for family type and tenure (Model 2) renders the effects of ethnicity non-significant for Pakistani, Indian and Bangladeshi children, suggesting that the differences observed in Model 1 can be explained by the different family structure and housing position of the groups. The greater numbers of poor Bangladeshi, Indian and Pakistani children in couple-parent families and in owner-occupation and privately rented housing means that their poverty is less likely to be persistent than that of White UK children. The lower probability of persistent poverty for Black Caribbean children compared to White UK children remains, however, in Model 2. Having a lone parent would therefore seem to have a different, and less critical, impact on a poor Black Caribbean child than on a White UK child.

Given that there are higher proportions of minority group children in poverty, and far higher proportions of Bangladeshi and Pakistani children, this is an

Table 1: Logistic regression of the effect of ethnic group on continuous receipt of IS (n=80,549)

| | Parameter estimates (SE) | |
	Model 1	Model 2
Ethnic group		
Baseline=White UK		
Bangladeshi	−0.31 (0.041)***	NS
Black Caribbean	−0.28 (0.032)***	−0.36 (0.033)***
Indian	−0.45 (0.046)***	NS
Pakistani	−0.34 (0.023)***	NS
Family type		
Baseline=couple parent		
Lone parent		0.60 (0.016)***
Tenure		
Baseline=Private Tenancy		
Social housing		0.31 (0.017)***
Owner-occupation		NS
Chi square (df)	2,162.1 (11)	4,206 (14)

Note: *p<0.05; **p<0.01; ***p<0.001; NS = statistically not significant.

interesting finding that tends to suggest a more polarised distinction between the poor and the non-poor among White UK children. By contrast, among children from minority ethnic groups greater prevalence in poverty is also accompanied by more movement in and out of benefit support.

I now go on to look at severity in terms of the longitudinally averaged shortfalls. To do this I repeat over all seven extracts the calculations made for a single extract in the previous section, where I compared IS amounts payable for the support of children with the costs of children, estimated using budget standards. The shortfall per family at each extract is then averaged over the seven extracts. If a child is not supported by IS at any extract the shortfall is equal to zero. The weekly shortfall per family averaged across all extracts is thus a product of the amount of the cross-sectional shortfalls and the extent of the persistence on benefit[7].

Looking at how such shortfalls over time average out, the average shortfall for Bangladeshi families was the largest at each extract, at between £75.70 and £84.20 per week (January 1998 prices), and remained the largest when the shortfall per family across all seven extracts is averaged. This shortfall across the entire period stands at over £56 per week: a deficit of more than £20 than the average for all families. The Pakistani and Indian shortfalls follow a similar pattern, but at shortfalls of roughly £10 and £20 per family less, respectively, across the extracts, and of £5 and £10 less respectively for the period average. The shortfalls for Black Caribbean families are similar to those for White UK families in the £46-£50 region for each extract, but they are little more severe by £1 or £2 over most extracts. The average across all extracts for the Black Caribbean families is lower (at £35.10) than that for any other group (including White UK) and for all groups, demonstrating the greater benefit mobility of this group compared to their White UK counterparts which counteracts the slightly greater cross-sectional average shortfalls.

To look in more detail at the ranges of family poverty experience by ethnic group I have rated the shortfalls per family averaged over the seven time points and have defined a family as experiencing chronic poverty when its average is more than twice the average for all families. While this is a somewhat arbitrary level, it reflects a value (greater than £71 per week) at which additional income from times out of poverty would be hard to compensate for over this short period of 17 months. I have further determined that a family is experiencing peripheral poverty if its shortfall averaged across all time points is less than £10, as this seems a value that above benefit-level incomes could be expected to compensate for during periods out of poverty.

Such a process reveals substantial levels of poverty across benefit-recipient families, even when time, and therefore times off benefit, is taken into account. The extent of movement in and out of poverty does not therefore imply that we should be less concerned about those in poverty at a single time-point. Rather, it illustrates that substantial mobility in and out of benefit cannot compensate for the cumulative disadvantage experienced by those living on the margins of benefit levels. It also emphasises the very high proportion of Bangladeshi families having a chronic income-to-needs shortfall, and that Black Caribbean families are the least severely affected, reflecting greater turnover in the benefit recipients from this group.

As my main interest is in the proportion of children, rather than families, experiencing each situation, I have considered the proportion of *children* from each group living in families which fall into the different positions of severity. Such analysis emphasises the importance of taking a child-based approach to children's needs and to benefit payments in particular and demonstrates that very little of children's poverty can truly be considered transient and without impact. There are very high proportions of Bangladeshi children living in chronic poverty, with 43% living in families with a chronic shortfall. They are followed by slightly smaller proportions of Pakistani and then Indian children living in chronic poverty. Black Caribbean and White UK children appear in very similar proportions with a slightly higher proportion of Black Caribbean children than White UK children living in families with a chronic shortfall, at the same time as a slightly higher proportion are also living in families with a peripheral shortfall. This suggests some variation within the experience of Caribbean lone-parent families: while they are more likely to be on a low income in the first place than couple-parent families, their greater risks are accompanied by also a substantial degree of movement away from IS support.

Conclusions

We already know from other sources that Bangladeshi and to a lesser extent Pakistani children are more likely to be growing up in families supported by IS. This [chapter] demonstrates that they are further disadvantaged in the relative adequacy of the benefit compared to those from other ethnic groups who are also supported by IS.

On the other hand, although the prevalence of benefit receipt and poverty may be lower among children from White UK families, this investigation has revealed that once they start being supported by IS they are more likely to remain on benefit support. The picture that emerges is of a certain polarisation in the experience of children from White UK families between those who are supported by benefit and those who are not.

By contrast, the experience of children from minority groups would seem to place far more of them close to benefit levels of income. Their greater mobility in and out of benefit could then be argued to be, in part, a reflection of the greater prevalence of low incomes. There are clear differences among the different minority groups, however. Greater mobility among Indian children is also accompanied by lower poverty prevalence, which suggests that they may be moving away from the relative disadvantage they have experienced in the past and consolidating their position as the most advantaged minority group. For children in Black Caribbean families, being brought up in a lone-parent family does not seem to decrease benefit mobility as it does for all the other groups. The majority of Bangladeshi children would seem to be tied to levels of income close to the IS cut-off level and where IS is therefore a recurrent experience. Children in Pakistani families show a pattern similar to that of Bangladeshis, but less extreme and with more mobility. It could be speculated that in time Pakistani children will develop patterns of poverty experience closer to those of Indian children.

Despite their persistent poverty, the predominant family characteristics of White UK children on benefit (principally smaller family size, but also a tendency to older children among benefit recipients) ensure that they do not end up with such severe poverty gaps as some other groups. Bangladeshi children who ever receive IS experience greater mobility in and out of benefit support, but nevertheless experience far greater cumulative income shortfalls. This is also the case but less extreme for Pakistani and Indian children. For Black Caribbean children, greater mobility and smaller families translate into smaller income shortfalls for those who come in contact with IS.

The results imply that the structure of Britain's benefit system is not consistent with the government's commitment to both the elimination of child poverty and overcoming discrimination. While the latest adjustment to the structure of IS – equalising the allowances for children under 11 with those up to age 16 – will have a substantial impact on the differential nature of the benefit experience, it is unlikely to eliminate the differences altogether; and another substantial increase in the family premium in the benefit year 2000-01 will enhance them. Moreover, whatever changes in benefit amount or demographic patterns the future may bring, this [chapter] has demonstrated the importance of questioning the underlying rationale of benefit payments and analysing the sensitivity of policy to ethnic variations. Even well-intentioned policy cannot be assumed to be ethnically neutral, any more than it can be assumed that it will meet needs without attempting to define or cost such needs. The implied logic of benefits and their differential impact on different types of family needs to be recognised if the support of children is truly to become a priority and the elimination of child poverty in the next generation a reality. The impact of the current benefit structure on the most disadvantaged minority groups also needs to be recognised if indirect discrimination and the perpetuation of disadvantage across generations are to be avoided.

Notes

[1] This source is discussed further in Platt and Noble (1999).

[2] The first period, January 1998 to March 1998 covers just two months rather than three because the (preferred) December 1998 extract could not be accessed by the time of the analysis.

[3] This group combines the categories of Black Caribbean (Black Afro-Caribbean in the Birmingham classification) and Black Other, since those who designate themselves Black Other are predominantly the British-born descendants of those who designate themselves Black (Afro-) Caribbean.

[4] The category of White UK is derived from the Birmingham classification and is narrower than the national Census category of 'White' since Birmingham also recognises White Irish and White Other groups.

[5] Atkinson (1995) has discussed the different ways that countries can and do structure their payments for children to favour older or younger, firstborn or later born children. While the additional boost to a first child is paralleled in Child Benefit payments in Britain, this pattern only occurred from 1991 onwards; and from the introduction of its predecessor, Family Allowance, in 1945 until 1971, first children had been excluded from the assessment of eligible amounts of the benefit.

[6] This meant that in January 1998, over 37 000 children in Birmingham were living with a family shortfall of income to child needs of over £58 (at January 1998 prices).

[7] This shortfall across all seven extracts is not simply the average of the cross-sectional extracts since they do not take account of any families off the data set at that time point. By contrast the average over time calculates the average for every family ever on the data set over the seven extracts with including a shortfall of zero for those time points where the family was not present.

This is a version of an article that appeared in the *Journal of Comparative Family Studies*, 2003, vol 34, no 3, pp 357-77 under the title 'Ethnicity and inequality: British children's experience of means-tested benefits'. The right of Lucinda Platt to be identified as author of this chapter has been asserted by her in accordance with the 1988 Copyright, Designs and Patents Act.

Housing policy and children

Paul Daniel and John Ivatts

> We will base all our work on the belief that all children and young people are entitled to a good start in life, to be protected, to have somewhere to live, to have enough money to live on, to be treated fairly and to be listened to. (The Children's Society, 1996)

Introduction

Housing for children is critical, and the younger the child, the more important the quality of the physical shelter and of the immediate environment generally. An infant's proper growth and development will partly depend on satisfactory housing. A family's home is, for example, the principal determinant of children's essential play opportunities throughout childhood. Children do not choose their housing conditions, and until a child goes to school the home provides the main, or only, physical setting for that child's development and for all his or her early relationships and social interactions.

Furthermore, housing conditions also affect children indirectly since a family's housing has a powerful effect on the well-being of a child's parents. Security, comfort, ease of management and warmth are important factors for facilitating effective parenting; conversely, overcrowding, poor conditions – indeed homelessness – are all circumstances that are likely to lessen the ability of parents to care for their children, and to threaten the stability of family life. Most adults can escape from the limitations of their living conditions by resorting, for example, to the pub or to the local public library. Mothers and children, however, necessarily spend a far greater proportion of time at home than the majority of adolescents and other adults; and mothers and young children generally have far fewer choices as to where to spend their time.

Housing policy differs in important respects from the other main areas of social policy. There is no universal right to housing except for some categories of carefully filtered homeless people (see below). Nor is there a nationally administered and provided housing service as with health and social security.

State housing policy throughout the 20th century has consisted of a complicated pattern of interventions in the housing market in the form of controls, taxation policies and subsidies. As a consequence, housing policy has always been subjected to sharp changes of direction according to the fortunes of the wider economy and regardless of people's housing needs. However, the election in 1979 of the Conservative government led by Margaret Thatcher presaged a radical shift in attitudes towards the public sector in general; and this was to have particular long-term significance for housing policy.

So how well have children been served by housing policy since 1979, and how satisfactorily are their housing needs being met at the beginning of the 21st century? We examine these questions in the following sections.

The consequences for children of post-1979 housing policies

Increased home ownership: a decent home within reach of every family?

Owner-occupation in Britain in 1993 accounted for 66% of tenure, compared to 54% in 1978. This tenure is composed of 9.7 million households with a mortgage and 5.7 million households who are outright owners (mainly among older age groups). Approximately half this increase of 12 percentage points since 1979 has been due to the 'Right to Buy' policy introduced in the 1980 Housing Act; and the other half to private sector construction and sales.

The growth of owner-occupation since 1979 has had two major consequences: first there has been a decline in choice between renting and owning; and second, a related increase has occurred in the number of households with relatively marginal incomes for sustaining the fluctuating costs of house purchase over the medium to long term, but who nonetheless have been persuaded into home ownership. With the shrinking availability of affordable good-quality public rented dwellings, together with the deregulation of the lending institutions and the penalty of higher rents, it was no wonder that so many people found themselves during the 1980s with little choice other than to buy. In any case by the mid-1980s two thirds of all British dwellings were only available on the basis of purchase so inevitably, the pressures to own have intensified. In this context it is all too easy to comprehend the extent to which many households entered into unsustainable financial commitments in order to get their feet on the first rung of the home ownership ladder. This raises the question of whether policies to promote owner-occupation have not resulted in many young families living in poorer-quality accommodation in the owner-occupied sector, especially in maisonettes, flats and cramped two-bedroomed terraced houses, than would hitherto have been allocated to less well-off households in the public sector.

Recent house purchase, moreover, has increasingly been based on two household incomes. For families this means mothers have either to delay starting a family or to continue working shortly after a child's birth; and hence, of course, the frantic search by many parents for some reliable form of elusive child care. Either way, many parents, given also the current insecurities of the job market, are denied any real choice of how exactly they wish to care for their children at the early years stage because of the financial demands of home purchase.

What this also means of course is that those who were unlucky enough to have bought their homes in the latter half of the 1980s committed themselves to heavy repayments even though house prices were subsequently to fall in the early 1990s. If these households consisted of young couples they were also, in the latter half of the 1990s, those most likely to contain young children. There is therefore a strong prima facie case that those households who were worst affected by the hyperinflation of the housing market in the 1980s and its subsequent collapse in the 1990s, were composed disproportionately of families with young children.

Negative equity and repossessions

This conclusion is supported by the accumulated evidence from the 1990s of the extent of financial difficulties experienced by many households in meeting their housing costs. In 1991 house prices began to fall and continued to fall until 1994 since when they remained 'flat' until 1997-98. The result of falling prices was that many of those who bought their homes towards the peak of the boom found them often worth considerably less than the amount they had originally borrowed – a shortfall referred to as 'negative equity'. This, in turn, left a large number of owner-occupiers trapped in their homes. Thus in early 1996 according to a survey by the Nationwide Building Society reported in *The Independent* (31 January 1996), up to 1.7 million households were in negative equity.

Compared to many other recent house purchasers, however, those households locked into negative equity could be considered among the more fortunate. Many tens of thousands who bought their homes during the 1980s found in the recessionary 1990s that with reduced incomes they could no longer continue to pay their mortgages. Thus a further symptom of crisis in the housing market was a rising tide of 'mortgage arrears' and house 'repossessions'. In the peak year of 1991 as many as 75,500 properties were 'taken into possession'; and the number of annual repossessions averaged some 50,000 homes until the late 1990s. This means that for the six years from 1990 to 1995 a total of 350,000 households, or well over three quarters of a million people, many of them children, lost their homes (CSO, 1995a, p 181).

Research findings published by the Department of the Environment in 1995 reveal that all occupational groups were affected by the crisis in owner-occupation. "Repossession", the report emphasises, "primarily hits families with young children". Indeed, "two-thirds of households that lost their homes", the authors note, "contained at least one dependent child under 16 or younger, with almost three out of ten of them containing three or more dependent children" (Ford and Kempson, 1995, p 30). Significantly, four out of ten repossessed households end up in rented social housing, with a further 37% renting privately. Only 8% return to owner-occupation. Most damagingly, however, for children, the Department of the Environment study shows that "the majority of cases moved into temporary accommodation immediately following the loss of their home. Often the location and/or facilities were problematic and in some cases there was overcrowding. Consequently, one in five of them had moved three or more times in less than two years, moving from one address to another" (Ford and Kempson, 1995, p 33).

By the mid-1990s it appears that the sheer overcrowding and physical housing deficiencies of an earlier era had merely been replaced for many families by those housing problems caused by the acute financial strains and anxieties in which a growing number now found themselves. And it is especially children who are being exposed to these new forms of housing stress. Undoubtedly, this situation has been brought about, at least in part, by an undue policy emphasis on owner-occupation regardless of other considerations.

With hindsight, it is now apparent that the 1990s depression in the British housing market bottomed-out in 1996-97, since when average house prices have risen inexorably, actually doubling between 1999 and 2004. This turnaround can be attributed to three main factors: first, the improved employment prospects and rising real incomes under 'New Labour' since their landslide election victory in May 1997; second, historically low interest rates; and third, the continuing failure of the housing market to produce sufficient new homes to meet the manifest demand.

Rising house prices – although with significant regional and district variations – do not mean, however, that the financial difficulties of the 1990s have miraculously evaporated in the heat of the current house price boom that has followed. No doubt, the pressures on many households will have eased, depending, of course, on where they are located. And certainly, those individuals who have bought and sold their home since the mid-1990s are unlikely to have been affected by 'negative equity'. (There were, in fact, 16,202 court orders for mortgage repossession in 2002 [*Roof*, May/June 2004], compared to the annual average of 50,000 that pertained during the previous decade.) However, for the very large number of people who lost their homes in this way in the 1990s and who succumbed, in one way or another, to their debts in the depression of that decade, their present housing circumstances and future prospects will have been permanently blighted. By the same token, the effects of these, often acute housing problems, on the lives of children cannot be simply forgotten or erased.

Children in public sector housing

The term 'social housing' is now used officially to identify public sector housing allocated at 'affordable' rents on a basis of need, and not solely according to the price mechanism. The sector consists of dwellings provided by local authorities, housing associations and cooperatives; and it is expected to provide homes for those households, as Clare Ungerson suggests, "still unable to move into owner occupation" (1994, p 192).

Local authority housing in Britain which in 1978 represented 32% of tenure had fallen by 1993 to 20%, with the total council dwellings stocks falling from 6.5 million dwellings to 4.7 million. Housing association properties have, conversely, increased numerically from approximately 450,000 units to 874,000 (4% of tenure); and since 1990 their construction figures have substantially exceeded local authority building programmes – 34,492 compared to 1,768 respectively for 1993, which reflects the assumption by the housing associations of the main provider role for social housing. Increased building by housing associations has, however, only marginally offset the overall decline in the availability of affordable rented housing. Since 1979, in fact, there has been a net loss of 1.4 million units of social housing, so that together council housing and housing association dwellings now accommodate no more than 24% of households, compared to 34% in 1979 (Newton, 1994).

The residualisation of social housing

Since 1979 this social sector generally has clearly become a more restricted and, as some might argue, an inferior form of tenure, so that a number of commentators speak of the 'residualisation' of council housing. However, this term needs to be used with some caution because local authorities still administer by far the largest stock of affordable rented housing, and as landlords they have an impressive record for the most effective use of this stock.

Nonetheless, public sector housing has become a more 'marginalised' or 'residualised' tenure because it has shrunk significantly in size since 1979 so that the choice of type of accommodation now available has become more restricted, and because the tenants concentrated in 'social housing' are increasingly the poor and socially disadvantaged. It is further argued that recent policies to promote owner-occupation and downgrade the traditional role of the local authorities have only served to create an image of "a second-class sector of second-class people" (Balchin, 1995, p 189).

The composition of the public sector housing stock has changed gradually since the early 1980s. Thus whereas 36% of council dwellings were semi-detached houses in 1979, only 28% were in 1991, and, more significantly from the point of view of children, the proportions of smaller terraced houses and purpose-built flats had correspondingly increased. By 1991, the proportion of housing association properties provided in the form of either purpose-built flats or converted flats or rooms, had also grown – to nearly two thirds of their homes. So with 35% of council homes also being comprised of flats, clearly social housing has increasingly become a tenure of flats, which now represent some 40% overall of the total stock in this sector.

In the same way that choice in social housing has narrowed, so too has the social profile of the tenants become less diverse. The income gap between those households dependent on social housing and other households has widened (see Page, 1993, p 31). Typically, moreover, social housing tenants are 'economically inactive', many being pensioners, single mothers or unemployed. Thus by 1990, 61% of heads of household with council tenancies were inactive compared to 42% in 1981; while of new tenants moving into housing association properties as many as 75% were not in any kind of work. The average weekly total household income, including that of a partner, of council tenants was £86.40 (at 1990 prices) in 1992, compared to an average income of £336.60 for home-owning households with a mortgage (Newton, 1994, p 88).

The sale of council houses

The changing composition of the stock and of the tenants of local authority housing is mirrored in the patterns of sales. Of course the sale of council houses is acknowledged as "perhaps the most notable piece of policy" and one of which Conservative politicians are particularly proud because of the degree of electoral popularity attributed to it" (Williams, 1992, p 159). However, any analysis of the housing needs of children, and of how policy might best serve their interests, immediately raises serious doubts and criticisms concerning the long-term consequences of the Right to Buy policy, enshrined in the 1980 Housing Act.

A striking feature of sales has been the remarkable consistency since the 1950s "in terms of who buys and what properties have been sold". Thus, according to Kerr (1989):

> ... purchasers were predominantly middle-aged, often with a grown-up family and including more than one wage earner. Manual skilled workers were over-represented amongst buyers and so, too, were white collar workers. (Quoted in Malpass and Murie, 1994, p 301)

The purchase of semi-detached, three-bedroomed houses has been particularly popular, and flats correspondingly unpopular. Analysis of the pattern of sales, not surprisingly, indicates that former council houses have added importantly to the good quality housing stock available in the owner-occupied sector; this seems to have been especially the case in the South of England and in rural areas (Malpass and Murie, 1994, p 302). But such houses have, in consequence, been removed from the public sector stock and are no longer available to families with children who are excluded from home ownership because of lack of means.

The consequences for children of a depleted public sector

The loss since 1980 of a substantial proportion of the most spacious family homes in the public sector since 1980 means that poorer families now have a much more restricted choice and may never obtain a house at all. The Right to Buy policy has thus affected a significant shift of housing resources towards older and better-off former council tenants and away from less-privileged households, who often have young children. For many households this has clearly resulted in an inversion of the relationship between housing need and the homes such households with children are actually occupying. Research conducted by Barnardos, for example, on a Bristol council housing estate, found a major problem of "inadequate and inappropriate housing". The majority of the children were cooped up in "walk-up flats", although almost all their mothers had been brought up in houses with gardens and were in many cases desperate to move to a house. Yet, while many of the former council houses on the estate were found to be owned by middle-aged owners, many mothers with young children were living in flats (Gill, 1992, p 12).

This study well illustrates the problems of bringing up children in inappropriate accommodation within a depleted public sector. With a fifth of Bristol's council houses having been sold by 1989, fewer families were able to find an adequate home. Sadly, although many parents wanted to get away from the estate, in reality they were trapped, with no real prospects of improving their accommodation. So, as one mother forlornly commented: "Considering the children are a lot older now, their need for a garden is gone ... we needed a garden when they were babies" (Gill, 1992, p 26).

The housing problems of less-affluent households

The depletion of the social housing stock and generally increased housing costs in all tenures has widened housing inequalities between the majority who can afford to buy their own homes and those on lower incomes. Inevitably lower-income groups have found access to good quality housing becoming more difficult.

Sub-standard housing

By any yardstick there have been notable improvements in the overall quality of British housing since the 1960s. Measures of unfitness, lack of 'amenities', and of overcrowding were all shown by the 1991 English House Condition Survey to have fallen to an all-time low; and currently 84% of English houses are now centrally heated, compared with only 57% in 1981. However, problems do remain: there are still, for example, 1.5 million 'unfit' dwellings in Britain (7.6% of the total stock) and an estimated £15 billion is required for urgent repairs; additionally, 20% of houses have damp problems (one in three of Scottish homes), and 6% of households in Britain are living at a density of one or more people per room. There is also a shortfall of 400,000 dwellings required to match the number of households requiring separate accommodation (Holtermann, 1995, p 61).

The question thus arises as to how far children are affected by these continuing housing deficiencies and shortages. Evidence, unfortunately, does indicate that certain groups of children experience disproportionately bad housing conditions. We examine the housing plight of some of these groups below.

Single parents and housing

The allocation of housing according to ability to pay clearly disadvantages women, whose incomes generally – from whatever source – are on average substantially below those of men. But women are – with or without male partners – the principal carers of children. Thus at the heart of current policies there is a major contradiction: while women are at a financial disadvantage within a market-orientated housing system, more women are living independent lives and, in the case of 1.3 million single mothers, are carrying the prime responsibility for children.

Large numbers of children have, therefore, through no fault of their own, been correspondingly disadvantaged by growing housing inequalities.

The extent of poverty among single mothers has been well documented (Daniel and Ivatts, 1998, ch 3). If we relate these circumstances to an increasingly market-orientated housing system within which there is a diminishing resource of social housing, it is obvious that lone parents are likely to have serious housing difficulties. Thus, the analysis of households' housing circumstances as revealed in the 1991 Census, concluded that: "Of all the household types distinguished by the census, it is the children of lone parent families who have seen the biggest deterioration in their housing situation" (Dorling, 1993).

Ethnic minority children

Children from minority ethnic backgrounds share with one-parent families many of the worst housing privations in contemporary Britain. Moreover, besides the similar high incidences of low incomes, benefit dependency and unemployment that they share with single parents, there are three additional circumstances that considerably aggravate the housing problems of black minority groups. First, these communities are concentrated geographically in inner-city neighbourhoods, which often contain much of the poorest and least-preferred housing; second, there has been a continuing history of racial prejudice and discrimination which has handicapped access for black minority groups to better quality housing in all sectors; and third, the rather different demographic family structures of certain ethnic groups has contributed – partly because of the changed composition of the social housing stock – to additional housing stress within particular communities.

About half of the British black population live in London (see Daniel and Ivatts, 1998, ch 2). However, with higher house prices than in any other region, owner-occupation is an impossibility for most black households, the majority of whom are dependent on social housing (and much of this in the form of high-rise flats), or on private rented accommodation. London also has an older housing stock that is on aggregate in worse condition than elsewhere. Thus inner London has a higher proportion of unfit dwellings (16%) than anywhere else in the UK, and the lowest proportion of 'good' housing (21%). The 1992 London Housing Survey furthermore reported that the sales of council houses since 1980 has meant that the shrinking public housing sector was becoming "less and less able to meet the needs of families", for the principal reason that one in three of local authority three-bedroomed homes and nearly four out of ten of those with four or more bedrooms, had been sold under the Right to Buy policy.

Not surprisingly, the London Housing Survey found that a third of all children living in social housing in London are living in overcrowded conditions; and that as many as 150,000 children in all housing sectors are affected by overcrowding. Asian and Afro-Caribbean children, however, are twice as likely as White European children to be living in overcrowded conditions (NCH Action for Children, 1995, p 76).

At a national level children from the Bangladeshi and Pakistani communities are particularly badly affected, with 31% of all households in these communities being one or more units below 'the bedroom standard', as against 12% for all minority ethnic households and 3% for white households (CSO, 1995a, p 178).

The housing problems of all poor families

Many of the problems of single mothers and minority ethnic groups are shared by all poor families, which besides these two groups include the unemployed, refugee and Traveller families, and families with members who are disabled or chronically sick. It is these groups, and especially those associated with social classes IV and V, who are generally among the poorest in the population and who are concentrated in the least satisfactory housing or in a depleted public sector. Households with children, in particular, are thus more likely to experience overcrowding, the sharing of amenities in 'temporary' or multi-occupied accommodation, damp and cold, the absence of play space, and childhoods impoverished by the insecurities and limitations of their physical environment, than nearly all other types of household in contemporary Britain.

Some evidence even suggests that while housing conditions have been improving for the majority of the population, for some categories of children – such as those of lone mothers – they have actually been deteriorating (see Kumar, 1993, p 130). The 1991 Census has subsequently revealed that 1.3 million children "still live in households with more than one person per room, while 43,000 children under 16 live in households which lack exclusive access to a bath, shower or inside lavatory". There remains also a substantial minority of sharing or 'hidden households', which in total contain 285,000 children – an increase of 9.4% since 1981; and at the same time there has been an increase of 17% in the number of households living in 'non-permanent accommodation' (such as mobile homes and caravans), so that 95,000 households containing 25,000 children under 16 now reside in this type of accommodation (Dorling, 1993).

The geographical segregation of the poor

Since the early 1970s we have been aware of problem estates and 'hard-to-let' properties – often flats. Many of the most notorious for their social problems have always contained unduly high proportions of children and young people. However, since the early 1980s local authorities have lost many of their better-off tenants and many of their best houses. Thus a conjunction of growing family poverty and the consequences of government housing policies have conspired to produce growing ghettos of poor households in many of the most disadvantaged neighbourhoods.

Department of the Environment surveys undertaken during the 1980s indicated that there were over 300,000 council dwellings on 'difficult-to-let' estates. Four fifths of these were found in cities, with over a quarter (28%) in inner London alone. Reasons for the unpopularity of the estates included poor design, vandalism and crime, social stigma, their size, and the consequent anonymity and loss of social control. Specific social factors which appeared to contribute to the general malaise of such neighbourhoods were the concentrations of 'families with problems', 'high child density', and 'lack of play facilities'. Some of the surveyed estates contained double the proportions of children compared to the national average (45% and 22%, respectively), with an average child population for the surveyed estates of 33%. The paradox of the vitality of children and the social difficulties on problem estates is eloquently stated by Anne Power:

> The estate, as a separated but unintegrated community, as a vast uncontrolled but boring no man's land, the estate as an environment often hostile to family living and to children's love of the outdoors and thirst for adventure, caused the loss of confidence by adults in their own community of children. Children became both the perpetrators and the victims. (Power, 1987, p 155)

Since the mid-1980s there have been important government initiatives to improve the worst estates. However, the failure to replace the sold-off council houses and to build affordable new homes in anything like the numbers required has meant that the spatial concentration of the poorest households has continued inexorably. The ghettoisation of many children and adolescents into housing developments characterised by high unemployment and widespread poverty is threatening to extend into the newer housing association estates. These are now building by far the largest share of social housing and, as David Page's (1993) report has shown, these new estates appear very much at risk of becoming the problem neighbourhoods of the future.

Poor families in the countryside

The sale of council housing has also had a similarly damaging, although different, impact on rural communities. The Archbishops' Commission on Rural Areas drew attention in 1990 to some of the social consequences of the sales policy in rural areas: "In every large village many council houses are now sold, while in many small villages virtually all the stock has ceased to be available as rented accommodation..... We feel strongly that there has not been proper recognition by the Government of the real value of council houses in rural areas as the major source of homes to rent for less well-off households" (Archbishops of Canterbury and York, 1990, p 104).

Other reports on rural areas have also found that the loss of public housing since 1980 has contributed significantly to the slow disintegration of rural society in many parts of Britain. Far from the fantasy of maiden aunts cycling along country lanes and local worthies sipping real ale and watching cricket on the village green, rural reality is one of low-income families forced away to the council housing estates of the towns, and of village schools, post offices, churches and local bus services ceasing to function. Thus one commentator writes of "The new rural clearances", and quotes a country vicar with a parish in rural Warwickshire as admitting that, "every couple he had married in the last 15 years had been forced to leave the villages where they were brought up because of the shortage of affordable housing" (Platt, 1987, p 24). Analysis of the sale of council homes in rural areas of Scotland similarly concludes: "Many low income rural households may suffer as a result of this policy" (MacGregor et al, 1987, p 84).

Homelessness

'Homelessness' is a particularly difficult condition to define with any exactness. There are, in fact, degrees or states of homelessness, from the 'rooflessness' of the 'street homeless' to those who have accommodation that is so deficient that it fails to constitute a home as popularly conceived. Some commentators, to overcome such conceptual difficulties, have suggested that, "Homelessness in Britain is a manifestation of housing need in its most extreme form", an inclusive definition which would accommodate a broad spectrum of acute housing needs (Greve, 1990, p 13). The crux of the matter is what constitutes a 'home'.

How many homeless persons are there?

Homelessness has occurred throughout the post-war period. However, the numbers of households accepted by local authorities as being homeless rose most dramatically during the 1980s, from 58,000 in 1978 to 117,900 in 1986 and peaking at 170,500 in 1991. Numbers averaged 150,000 for the years 1993-95 (British figures from *Social Trends*, 1995 and 1996 editions). In total, therefore, since the early 1980s some 3.5 million people – half of them children – have become homeless.

The true number of homeless people is unknown. What the official figures do tell us is the number of households who *have applied* to their local councils, and the number of these who are subsequently accepted as homeless. Approximately half of all homeless applicants are, in fact, turned away by their local authority as not meeting the required criteria. So of 339,400 households who applied to their local councils during 1993, only 160,800 were accepted (CSO, 1995a, p 184).

Half of those who lose their homes are children, and between 70 and 80% of all households accepted as homeless each year consist either of families with dependent children (60-65%) or pregnant women (12-14%). Thus, with an average of nearly 200,000 children a year since 1990 experiencing the loss of their home, homelessness has become a deplorably common experience for children. Moreover, contrary to the popular myths exploited by some politicians, analysis of these figures lends little support to the accusation that homeless families are using the legislation to jump up the housing waiting lists, or that those accepted as homeless consist disproportionately of young women who have purposely become pregnant in order to obtain comfortable accommodation provided at public expense. In fact, the majority of homeless families (59%) housed by their local councils are already on council waiting lists; and while single mothers do represent a disproportionate number of the homeless – 40% of all acceptances – the Department of the Environment's own reports show that the majority of these have experienced the breakdown of a marriage or other partnership, are in their mid-to-late twenties, and that only a very small proportion are unmarried teenage girls (Greve, 1990, p 9).

Placing the blame for homelessness on the irresponsible behaviour of the homeless themselves, to escape any moral responsibility for doing something about this problem, is in any case irrelevant in view of the fact that those who are in many respects the most vulnerable to harm from the experience of homelessness are children.

The unofficial homeless

Many people in grossly unsatisfactory housing conditions, including many young people, simply do not apply to be rehoused; or, if they do apply, they are turned down by their local authorities. Unofficial estimates of the 'hidden homeless' – often women – and of 'hidden households', that is, those sharing with another household who would prefer not to be, and of all those in a variety of hostels, lodgings, or other forms of temporary and insecure accommodation, indicate that the true figure may be well over 1.5 million households in the late 1990s (Burrows and Walentowicz, 1992, p 8).

The effects of homelessness on children

All adverse housing conditions are harmful in varying degrees to children. However, the experience of homelessness is especially damaging to children in four important respects: developmental retardation; psychological effects; the effects on children's physical health; and the educational consequences.

Developmental retardation

A repetitive theme in all the literature about the ways in which bad housing conditions affect children concerns the impact on children's normal development. Parents talk of lost potential, endless frustration, a denial of space for play – in short, the absence of a secure environment within which a child's normal developmental processes can proceed; indeed, the kind of environment which well-housed parents take forgranted for their children. Over prolonged periods of housing deprivation, serious retardation is clearly probable, and damage may be done to a child's innate intellectual potentialities, to its speech patterns, its normal physical development and the acquisition of physical skills and competencies, and to its emotional development, from which the child may never recover. The worst situation is undoubtedly bed and breakfast accommodation, although other forms of temporary housing may scarcely represent any noteworthy improvement. The following account of the work of a Barnardos project in South London among families in temporary accommodation vividly describes the problems:

> In that small room, all their possessions are piled up around the beds. Floor space is minimal to the point of being non-existent. With dangerous corridors, no outdoor garden space and no money, parents find themselves stuck in their room for weeks with small children who crave movement and exploration. The scenario is painful, desperate and potentially explosive. (*Nursery World*, 7 March 1996)

We simply do not know what human potential continues to be lost day in, day out, by our inability to ensure a better housing environment than this for all our children.

Psychological effects

Any psychological effects on children are intimately connected with the above developmental factors. But the worst housing conditions may also be a cause of much psychological disturbance. Again, we simply do not know the quantitative effects of high levels of parental stress, or perhaps the prolonged frustration, on normal developmental patterns. What is clear, of course, is that housing stresses, from whatever source, are conducive to temporary (and often permanent) relationship breakdown. The effects of parental tensions and conflicts, perhaps lived out within the confines of overcrowded hostels, are of course not fully known. But in the extreme case of domestic violence the disturbing psychological effects on children of any age are clearly likely to be very serious. It is not surprising, therefore, that a 1986 survey of children living in Bayswater hotels found that 40% had possible behavioural problems (Stearn, 1986). Another London-based survey of inner-city residents revealed that 45% of the homeless sample exhibited 'significant mental morbidity', compared with 18-20% of the non-homeless. Reviewing this research, the Royal College of Physicians concluded that: "The high prevalence of mental morbidity amongst people in temporary accommodation may be related to uncertainty about the future, poor housing conditions and overcrowding.... The increased mental morbidity of parents is likely to have an adverse effect on their children's development" (RCP, 1994, p 43).

A study completed in 1996 by the Department of Psychiatry of Birmingham University, of 194 children aged from two to 16 living in hostels for homeless families, similarly found that nearly a third of the children (30%) displayed signs of "mental health problems of sufficient severity to require referral for treatment" (Vostanis et al, 1996, p 15). Only 3% of the children in the sample were, however, in contact with the mental health services "despite the high rates of mental disorders among this group" (Vostanis et al, 1996, p 19).

The effects on children's physical health

The most enduring case for good housing is the ill-health effects of bad housing. To be homeless exposes children to severe health risks. For example, the unsuitable temporary housing in which many homeless families are lodged is associated with a high rate of serious accidents to children – falls, burns and scalds in particular. A lack of proper cooking facilities is also a major cause of the very poor diets on which a number of reports have shown homeless families to subsist (see Stearn, 1986; and Conway, 1988).

Bed and breakfast accommodation has a particularly deleterious effect on children's health. A joint report by the British Medical Association and the Health Visitors Association, for instance, noted that homeless children showed "a high incidence of depression, disturbed sleep, poor eating, overactivity, bedwetting and soiling, toilet training problems, temper tantrums and aggression" (HVA and GMSC, 1989, p 12).

Respiratory illness is greatly aggravated by cold and damp, especially that caused by condensation. Temporary accommodation of all kinds is often poorly heated and damp, as of course are also many flats and multi-occupied houses, thus housing-related respiratory illness is widely prevalent among children living in bad housing conditions.

Homeless families' health needs may be great but access to health care facilities for them is often very difficult. The take-up of immunisation, for example, is low, and many families find it difficult to register with local GPs, so that they are forced to make frequent use of local hospital casualty departments. Summing up the situation, the Royal College of Physicians (1994) concluded that: "There is evidence of increased mental, physical and obstetric ill health compared with housed populations, and there are many clinical reports of increased ill health and behavioural problems, especially among the children" (p 39).

The educational consequences

A strong association between bad housing and educational difficulties has been known to exist for some time. The longitudinal studies, for example, of J.W.B. Douglas (1964) and of Ronald Davie and his colleagues (1972), found that children living in overcrowded and defective housing conditions gained lower test scores, were severely retarded in reading, and displayed bad social adjustment. Generally, of course educational achievement is linked to developmental maturation, so that in the light of the restricted development of many children growing up in poor housing conditions, some parallel educational handicap is highly predictable. The educational effects of homelessness should therefore be viewed not as the only, but rather as the worst of the educational disadvantages caused by bad housing.

The ill effects of homelessness on children's education, however, is beginning to be more widely recognised. Thus a survey by the schools' inspectorate (HMI) of children living in temporary accommodation carried out in 1989 in 28 primary and secondary schools in London, Manchester, Blackpool and Great Yarmouth revealed a considerable range of difficulties faced not only by pupils but by the schools and their staff. Lack of sleep, for example, made children "tired, listless and unable to concentrate"; homeless children were also found to be "irregular attenders", and more likely to be late; and because of poor diets they were reported as having an increased risk of illness (DES, 1990).

A more extensive survey undertaken by the Health and Education Research Unit of the Institute of Education of London University on behalf of Shelter has since confirmed and extended many of these findings. If anything, in fact, in the new competitive climate in schools resulting from the 1988 Education Reform Act (see Daniel and Ivatts, 1998, ch 7), the situation is now worse in a number of respects (Power et al, 1995).

With the delegation of expenditure budgets to individual schools, the local education authorities (LEAs) have lost control over the greater part of their educational expenditure. Thus LEAs are reported as finding it difficult to make any additional provision for coping with the problems presented by large numbers of homeless children, who inevitably incur additional administrative costs because of the frequent transfers involved. The schools too face a range of serious problems. Some schools lose income, for example, because of unpredictable fluctuations in the numbers of homeless children enrolled. Again, some LEAs were reported to have entered into lengthy dispute over who should fund the education of homeless children who had been moved across LEA boundaries – a common occurrence in London especially following the abolition of the Inner London Educational Authority (ILEA). Indeed, the report cites instances of 'special needs' children in fact excluded from school because the LEAs involved could not agree as to who should fund the place (Power et al, 1995, p 43).

The survey also revealed that the policy of open enrolment disadvantaged homeless children. Thus, because their families were often moved into a neighbourhood only temporarily, the popular schools were often full; and alternatives could involve complicated (and expensive) travelling arrangements that in most cases LEAs were unwilling or unable to finance. There is some suggestion, too, that with schools' reputations being increasingly dependent on their pupils' test results, many schools are reluctant to accept homeless children, who are likely to perform badly in tests. Not surprisingly, many homeless children were found to miss school altogether for weeks or months on end while in temporary accommodation. And even where parents can find schools willing to accept their children, the same school may not have places in each of the particular year groups and may not therefore be willing to accept all the children in a family. In these circumstances, any idea of parental choice must be meaningless for homeless parents.

The research also demonstrated the many practical problems facing homeless children – the loss of friendships; the difficulties of constantly having to readjust to new schools and of maintaining continuity in the curriculum; and the difficulties of completing assignments and doing homework with nowhere to do it other than in a shared room. Homeless children, moreover, even when they have found a school willing to accept them, still find it difficult to participate fully in school life. They tend to be stigmatised and treated as 'outsiders', so their relationships with their peers and with teachers are often difficult.

Small wonder then, given these disadvantages, that the survey found that of the 71 headteachers involved in the survey, 86% "reported that homelessness had an impact upon pupils' academic progress", and three quarters of the sample reported that both attendance rates and pupil behaviour were affected (Power et al, 1995, p 47).

Conclusion

So how well have children been served by post-war housing policies? The record, of course, is mixed. There is no doubt that great improvements have been achieved: over half of British homes have been built since 1945, and the majority of families have enjoyed housing amenities, home comforts and security which many of their parents and grandparents would have thought inconceivable before the Second World War. At the same time, however, it is also clear that British housing problems have not been wholly solved, and considerable numbers of children remain among the worst affected.

For the first 30 years after 1945 the state assumed responsibility for the assessment of national housing needs and for the satisfaction of these in so far as economic and other circumstances allowed. However, housing policy since 1979 has involved a growing reliance on the market as the best means of meeting housing needs. Allied to this has been an unflagging commitment to the expansion of home ownership as the normal and preferred tenure. This dual policy emphasis has entailed the abandonment of the earlier post-war social priorities that underlay the broad policy consensus of the period. We have moved, as Clare Ungerson argues, from a housing politics focused on 'need' to one dominated by 'ownership' (1994, p 213).

Unfortunately, faith in market forces and in the advantages of home ownership has not solved Britain's continuing housing problems. In place of the early post-war emphasis on investment in housing, government policy since 1979 has increasingly left supply to the market; but at the same time the state has become entangled in complicated strategies for the promotion of owner-occupation. However, construction levels since 1979 have fluctuated at levels substantially below those achieved in the previous 30 years. In addition, the owner-occupied market has become highly volatile and has only recently emerged from crisis, while the incidence of homelessness has reached epidemic proportions since the mid-1980s.

In no other policy area can recent governments have paid so little heed to the consequences of their policy decisions for children. The interests of the young would appear to have been sacrificed to the New Right ideology of the market. And the sacrifice seems all set to continue in the present low production but highly inflationary housing market that has prevailed since 1997. This, together with the low priority afforded to social housing by the Blair government, and with some 50,000 council dwellings still being sold annually, means that in the first decade of the new millennium it is highly improbable that shortages of affordable housing will ease, or that widening housing inequalities will decrease in the foreseeable future.

The continuing volatility and fragility of the British housing market is now creating other problems. So, for example, there is a growing difficulty of access for many potential new households, especially in London and the South East. The shortage of 'key workers' in high house price regions like these has been growing steadily, not least a lack of the personnel necessary to fulfil Labour government policies for improving the health and education services. But the difficulties of moving for skilled workers, and the growing commuting distances for many – with all the attendant transport problems – are all the pressing symptoms of an inflated housing market. We appear, in effect, to be witnessing a creeping sclerosis of the labour market, whereby, for example, a nurse cannot reasonably hope to enter into home ownership anywhere south of Leicester.

Any assessment of the consequences of these developments for children and their parents, must at this stage be somewhat speculative. Thus, for example, we just don't know how many children are simply not being born because their would-be parents are either excluded from, or face long delayed access to independent housing. The pressures for two incomes, the extra hours worked, and the lengthening hours spent commuting by one or both parents, must also be factors which are insidiously detracting from the quality of childrearing, or at least making life more stressful for many parents and potential parents.

Since the election of the Blair government in 1997, conditions affecting the housing market have changed considerably. However, we can only conclude that the structure and operation of the housing market, as it has evolved since 1979, created during the 1990s, and is continuing to manifest, in the first decade of the new millennium, a range of problems for many categories of parents; and these remain detrimental, in various ways, to the rearing of a healthy future generation.

Children's lives are demeaned and distorted – sometimes perhaps beyond repair – by bad housing conditions; and often their health may be seriously undermined and their educational opportunities unnecessarily restricted and impoverished. There is therefore a strong case for arguing that any measures to improve the housing circumstances of less well-off families would achieve more for children's welfare than any other social policy reforms.

This is an edited version of Chapter 5 of 'Children and social policy', which was published in 1998. For this edition, the section covering early post-war housing policy (1945-79) has been omitted, as have those related sections discussing 'new towns', 'high-rise' housing, and changing house design. Students interested in these aspects of British housing policy will need to refer to the original text. For this present publication, we have added some short paragraphs at the end of particular sections, and we have revised the original conclusion in the light of post-1998 developments. The right of Paul Daniel and John Ivatts to be identified as authors of this chapter has been asserted by them in accordance with the 1988 Copyright, Designs and Patents Act.

Young carers and public policy

Andrew Bibby and Saul Becker

The General Assembly of the United Nations adopted its Convention on the Rights of the Child on 20 November 1989. The wording of the Convention which was agreed on that occasion had taken 10 years to draft, and the working group charged with the task was itself building on earlier work which the League of Nations had begun when a declaration on children's rights was adopted back in 1924.

The UN Convention on the Rights of the Child does not occupy a very prominent place in the popular consciousness in Britain. Nevertheless the Convention is the nearest thing there is to a commonly agreed statement by the world community on its obligations to its children and young people. It runs to a total of 54 articles. Several of these are directly relevant to the position of young carers. Article 31, for example, recognises the right of children 'to rest and leisure' and to engage in play and recreational activities appropriate to their age. Articles 28 and 29 lay down the right of the child to education towards "the development of the child's personality, talents and mental and physical abilities to their fullest potential". Article 24 is about the child's right to the highest attainable standard of health. Article 16 sets out a child's right to privacy. Article 12 stresses the right of children to have their own views taken into account. Other Articles cover such areas as family life, responsibilities of parents, children's right to information and much else. This chapter, however, will be concerned with the implications of Article 4.

Article 4 describes the responsibility which rests on each state under the Convention. States are instructed to "undertake all appropriate legislative, administrative, and other measures" to ensure that the children's rights identified in the Convention are protected. States are told that, when it comes to children's economic, social and cultural rights, they should "undertake such measures to the maximum extent of their available resources".

So how does the government in Britain, which ratified the Convention on the Rights of the Child in 1991, measure up when it comes to protecting the rights of the country's young carers? What changes to public policy might be needed to improve the present situation?

Young carers in the UK: the government response

The government's publication in 1999 of its National Strategy for Carers marked something of a landmark in official recognition of the important role played in society by those who care for others. For young carers, the National Strategy was particularly significant, since the needs of these children and young people was considered important enough to merit separate consideration. One chapter of the National Strategy looks specifically at the issues facing young carers.

The National Strategy identifies nine frequent effects on children and young people providing care. These are:

- Problems at school, with completing homework and in getting qualifications.
- Isolation from other children of the same age and from other family members.
- Lack of time for play, sport or leisure activities.
- Conflict between the needs of the person they are helping and their own needs, leading to feelings of guilt and resentment.
- Feeling that there is nobody there for them, that professionals do not listen to them and are working only with the adult.
- Lack of recognition, praise, or respect for their contribution.
- Feeling that they are different from other children and unable to be part of a group.
- Feeling that no one else understands their experience.
- Problems moving into adulthood, especially with finding work, their own home, and establishing relationships.

The government goes on in its National Strategy to pledge improved support for young carers, and offers a number of concrete proposals with implications for local authority social services departments, the education service and the health service. We will look in more detail at these in a moment. [...]

The start of the 1990s saw a major reform in the way in which the state intervened in the lives of disabled, infirm and chronically ill people. The guidelines for what became known as 'care in the community' were laid in the influential Griffiths report of 1988, which was followed by legislation two years later, in the NHS and Community Care Act. The community care reforms actually came fully into effect by 1993 (legislation referred to in this chapter applies specifically to England and Wales; the position of young carers under Scottish law is different. Scotland has parallel legislation to England and Wales).

These changes put family carers at the centre of the 'care in the community' approach. This strategy involved an attempt to move away from the institutionalising of ill and disabled people, which could be welcomed by, among others, disabled people themselves, especially those who had increasingly been articulating an agenda based on a disability rights perspective. But conveniently the new approach also satisfied the New Right thinking of the Thatcher and Major administrations, to the extent that it represented a reduction in state provision of services and an opportunity to save on government expenditure on social care and welfare.

Under the new regime, local authority social services departments maintain a regulatory and financing responsibility, but are less involved in service delivery, which may be undertaken by private and voluntary sector organisations. The key event in this process is the assessment of needs of the person for whom community care is required, which social services departments undertake. Following this, in theory at least, an individual care plan is drawn up, setting out how those needs will be met. The major aim is to enable people to continue living in their own homes within the community.

Where does this leave the carer, on whom much of the unpaid caring work is likely to fall? In theory, under the NHS and Community Care legislation, carers were supposed to be consulted and involved in the process of needs assessment and care plan development. In practice, many carers have argued that, certainly in the first few years of the implementation of community care, this involvement did not take place. Too many social services departments remained locked in a traditional service-led culture.

More substantively, carers and their organisations criticised the NHS and Community Care legislation for failing adequately to meet their own needs. But if this was true for adult carers, for young carers the position was even less satisfactory. Their interests and needs were not covered or protected at all under the legislation, which was intended specifically for adults.

This omission is perhaps understandable, since at the stage when the Act was passed there was little recognition of the existence and role of young carers in society. As awareness of young carers grew in the 1990s, some social care professionals looked instead to another important piece of legislation, the 1989 Children Act, to see if this could be used to offer support for children and young people who were taking on caring responsibilities.

The Children Act framework gave local authorities a duty to "safeguard and promote the welfare of children within their areas who are in need". Could young carers be categorised in this way? A small number of authorities (11 out of 71 surveyed, according to a Department of Health study in 1996) did adopt this approach, which had the advantage of enabling social services departments to offer a range of services to the young carers and their families. But while in theory this approach offered professional recognition to young carers for the work they were undertaking at home, in practice the 'children in need' tag was problematic. Families may – sometimes justifiably – fear that social services intervention can lead to the children being taken into care.

A better way forward seemed to arrive with the passing of the 1995 Carers (Recognition and Services) Act. Since this Act applied to all carers regardless of age, for the first time effective official recognition was given to young carers. For the first time young carers' own needs could be formally taken into account.

In essence, the Carers Act entitles carers providing (or about to provide) a substantial amount of caring on a regular basis to have their own needs assessed at the time when the person they are caring for is having their own formal needs assessment. The result of the carer's needs assessment has to be taken into account when social services draw up the care plan of services to be made available.

Young carers' specific needs were also considered in the Department of Health Practice Guide which accompanied the Act and which was circulated to social services departments. These guidelines pointed out that the denial of proper educational and social opportunities to young carers could have harmful consequences, and went on to state that "the provision of community care services should ensure that young carers are not expected to carry inappropriate levels of caring responsibilities".

Implementing the legislation

Legislation is important, both because it gives public bodies access to financial resources and because it provides an overall official framework for approaching an issue. But there is of course a world of difference between the passing by Parliament of an Act and its implementation at the grassroots. We therefore need to consider what the effect of this legislation has actually been for young carers.

One problem is that the Carers Act has a major limitation: the assessment of a carer's needs takes place only if carers themselves request that it happens. This means that carers have to know their rights and entitlements under the Act, and understand that it is potentially in their interests to take up this particular entitlement.

Surveys of *adult* carers have identified the low take-up of needs assessments. A 1997 survey of 1,600 carers undertaken by the Carers National Association, for example, revealed that only 18% had requested an assessment.

It is not surprising, therefore, if the evidence points to very few young carers having had formal needs assessments. The 1997 survey undertaken by members of the Young Carers Research Group (YCRG) [...] (published in 1998 in *Young carers in the UK*) found that only 249 of the 2,303 young carers surveyed were in this position. As the authors pointed out, this figure was low considering that the survey was of young carers already known to young carers projects:

> Given the relatively low age of the young carers in contact with projects (the average age is just 12), and that many are involved in intimate and other caring tasks or responsibilities (indicative of substantial or regular care), and that many children seem to be experiencing negative effects on their own development or transition to adulthood, then we might have expected a far greater incidence of assessments than is the case.

There is another potential weakness in the way that the 1995 Carers Act is working. While the Act imposes on local authorities the procedure for undertaking if requested a needs assessment of a young carer, it does *not* oblige the authority actually to provide any of the services which the needs assessment may show to be necessary. In other words, if the budget is not there to supply these services, young carers' needs may continue to be neglected.

In practice, in the minority of the cases where needs assessments of young carers have taken place, the evidence seems to show that the outcome is usually positive. As *Young carers in the UK* shows, services were either introduced or increased after an assessment, and most children and their families were satisfied with the outcome.

The issue of needs assessment remains vital, therefore, when considering public policy towards young carers. The 1999 National Strategy for Carers made the following comment:

> Under the Carers (Recognition and Services) Act 1995, young carers can ask for an assessment of their needs. But many are not aware that this is possible. Some local authorities are reluctant to advertise this fact because of their concern about raising expectations. With the help of the voluntary sector, the statutory services should ensure that young carers are not expected to carry inappropriate levels of caring responsibility. To achieve this, disabled or ill parents need support to maintain their independence and to carry out their parenting responsibilities....

The encounter between the young carer, their family and the social services professional can still be an uneasy one but at least the development of a legislative framework for community care in recent years should mean that a social worker or social care professional has some understanding of the nature of the young carer's experience.

In 2000 the government, through the Department of Health, introduced a new framework for assessing all children who become known to social services for whatever reason. This framework requires those assessing children, especially children in need, to consider three 'domains' – the child's developmental needs, the ability of the parent(s) to provide adequate parenting, and family and environmental factors. Future assessments of young carers should taken into account their needs, their development, the needs and capacities of their ill or disabled parents, and environmental factors such as poverty or poor housing. This should, in due course, result in better assessments of existing young carers, the prevention of some children taking on heavy caring responsibilities, and support for the wider family. It is an excellent step in the right direction.

Such improvements are less in evidence, however, in the case of other professionals who deal with young carers, such as teachers or healthcare workers. In particular, there may be a lack of close cross-agency links.

The National Strategy for Carers looked particularly at the situation regarding schools. [...] According to the National Strategy, "the person could benefit from getting to know others who can help young carers and what services are available in the area to meet their needs".

The government has also attempted to brief head teachers and education welfare officers on the particular needs of young carers, in a guidance note circulated for consultation early in 1999. There is official recognition, however, that more could be done. The National Strategy pledges to "promote awareness of young carers in schools through ensuring that teaching on Personal, Social and Health Education includes references to young carers", and it also promises to improve awareness about young carers during teachers' initial training and subsequently after qualification.

This is all commendable, although cynics may argue that schools are currently struggling under a heavy workload imposed by central government which is likely to mean that most head teachers and governors have their minds on other matters. Furthermore, most academic research and writing on young carers has emerged from social policy departments rather than from education departments, so that there has not been the same level of debate in educational circles.

To a large extent, many of the same comments apply also to the health service. GPs, community nurses and other primary health care workers need to be better briefed on the issues raised by young carers. Here the National Strategy for Carers is disappointingly brief, simply pledging – as it did in the case of teachers – to 'improve awareness training'.

The young carers projects

The message from the National Strategy for Carers is that more can, and should, be done for young carers. One very concrete achievement has, however, already come from the work of the pioneer researchers and campaigners on the issue. This is the creation of a network of more than 100 young carers projects and groups.

The development of young carers has been striking. Less than 10 years ago, only two such groups were operating. By 1998, when a detailed handbook of projects was published, 110 could be listed, with a geographical spread from Kirkcaldy to Truro, Ballymena to Thetford.

These young carers projects inevitably differ from town to town, but share many characteristics. They are normally funded from statutory sources but run by the voluntary sector. Major national charities such as Barnardos, NCH Action for Children, the Children's Society, Crossroads and the Princess Royal Trust for Carers are among the organisations involved. The projects also tend to be generic in their approach, offering help and support for all young carers in their area of operation. However, a project specifically for black young carers has operated in Manchester and another for Asian children and young people has been run in London, while in Leeds a young carers project was set up specifically for children caring for people with mental health problems.

What do the young carers projects hope to achieve? Saul Becker, Jo Aldridge and Chris Dearden in their 1998 book *Young carers and their families* put it like this:

> Although working with families is an important aspect of the work of these projects, their primary focus is on supporting children as carers. In this respect most projects offer counselling, advocacy and befriending services specifically for young carers. Some of this counselling and befriending work is provided on an informal basis (someone to talk to, a confidante) although some projects provide or arrange more formal services where applicable. Advocacy is considered an essential service by many projects since many young carers – indeed many children – are unaware of their rights. Project workers can therefore work with them or act on their behalf to try and secure their rights under existing legislation....

> Around 80% of projects arrange leisure activities for young carers. Indeed,
> in many cases these are the services that young carers value most....

For children and young people facing major responsibilities at home, the opportunity to come together for indoor activities, or go out for a group trip, is highly prized – a "thumbs up night", in the words of one young carer, who was reporting on a Christmas meal out at Pizzaland.

The authors of *Young carers and their families* conclude with this assessment:

> Mixing with other young carers can serve to validate the young caring
> experience and reassure children that they are not alone. Although project
> workers stress the fact that young carers rarely sit around discussing
> their experiences or home life, during interviews many young carers
> have said that it can be comforting to know that, among other young
> carers, there is no need to explain their circumstances and their feelings
> will be understood.

The National Strategy for Carers makes a very similar point in its own positive assessment of the role of young carers projects: "These projects can provide relief from the isolation faced by children who are carers. They are places where the young can go for advice, information and support or leisure activities and can share experiences with other young carers".

Notwithstanding the growth of the past few years, there are some major towns and cities in Britain which do not yet provide young carers projects. Any strategy for improving the experience of children and young people undertaking caring responsibilities would need to address – or so it would seem – the current gaps in the network. However, despite the vitally important work which many young carers projects clearly do, a question mark hangs over the future of the concept.

There are two reasons for this. Firstly, there is the issue of funding. Many young carers initiatives have been financed on a project basis, typically for a set period of years, rather than having their costs met from core funding budgets. Project funding is a familiar, and often convenient, way of piloting new ideas and initiatives, but it does raise the problem of what happens when the initial project funding runs out. As early as 1997, this was already beginning to worry several young carers groups.

The funding for young carers projects has in practice come from a variety of sources. The situation in 1997 was reviewed by the authors of *Young carers and their families*:

> Approximately 40% of projects received part of their core funding from
> joint finance (a mixture of social services and health authority funding),
> more than 40% from social services alone and slightly less than one-
> fifth from health authorities. Approximately one-fifth received some
> core funding from charities or voluntary organisations while only four
> projects received part of their core funding from education. In Britain
> the introduction of the National Lottery has provided an additional

> potential source of funding, with nine projects receiving core funding.
> Corporate funding has been low....

The same report went on to comment that fewer than half of the 106 established projects in 1997 considered future funding to be 'likely' or 'very likely' and that 52 were unsure about their financial futures. In fact, although a number of groups have disappeared, it is clear three years on that there has been no major collapse in the funding of young carers projects – at least not yet. Nevertheless, the constant worry about future funding drains staff morale, and also means that resources which should be directed at the key work of engaging with young carers gets diverted into fundraising tasks.

If finance is one concern, the future of the young carers project network faces another challenge, this time from a much less obvious direction. Some people, including those who would argue passionately that society needs to give more resources to help people who are chronically ill or have disabilities, feel that the emphasis on young carers groups has been a mistake. We should be looking in another direction entirely.

Children's rights, disability rights

[...] The critique of the traditional view of disability which has been developed over the past 20 or 30 years by disabled people and their supporters has had both social and political consequences of some importance. It has involved a sharp attack on what could be conveniently described as the 'does he take sugar?' approach to disability. Such an approach, the disability rights movement has pointed out, not only demeans but also disempowers those people in our society who have disabilities.

The power and vitality of the disability movement was there for all to see in the streets protests that followed the initial unsuccessful attempts to introduce a disability bill in Parliament. London police, it was clear, were inexperienced in the appropriate way of removing wheelchair-using demonstrators from under the front wheels of London buses. But while the eventual successful passing into law of the Disability Discrimination Act in 1995 could be seen to mark a watershed for disability rights in Britain, disability campaigners would argue that the battles are by no means over. Some of the tensions of recent years in long-established and powerful establishment charities such as the Royal National Institute for the Blind and the Royal National Institute for Deaf People focus exactly on this issue – are charities like these there to be run *for* disabled people, or *by* them? Empowerment, or continued patronage?

Given this background, it is not surprising if some disability rights activists looked at what was happening with young carers, and decided that they were not very happy with what they saw. Richard Olsen of the University of Leicester has described it like this:

> If the trend in policy and practice was perceived as one emphasising 'caring for the carers' rather than addressing the barriers that disabled people face, then this sudden interest in labelling the children of some disabled parents 'young carers' was bound to engender hostility.... If some disabled people were angry at seeing resources directed at supporting carers rather than, as they saw it, at promoting independence and control on the part of disabled people themselves, then the suggestion that their children should be supported as their carers in this way was always likely to be inflammatory....

As Richard Olsen goes on to point out, the young carer approach "involved giving the kind of rights to children (to consultation about a parental condition, to information about parental treatment, to a separate assessment of need, to property such as washing machines, and so on) that most non-disabled parents would find at the very least undermining of their parental role if granted to their own children".

In other words, perhaps with the best of motives the emphasis on young carers' rights was once again leading to the familiar situation where the disabled person found themselves disempowered, belittled and discriminated against.

Opposition to the notion that the rights of young carers should take precedence over the rights of disabled people developed during the later 1990s and was not confined to the academic sphere. Rick Howell, who had been project manager of the young carers project in Macclesfield for three years until the funding ran out in 1998, contributed a thoughtful piece to the *Journal of Young Carers Work* reflecting on his experiences. He described how one of his social care colleagues had challenged the work that his project, and other young carers projects, had been trying to do:

> He said that young carers projects had created a myth, that to respond to young carers you needed to have a project and be experts.... Young carers projects were perpetuating the idea that children who were carers are a new welfare category and somehow different from other young people. He contended that this was dangerous, because at best it undermined the idea of mainstreaming responses and at worst further alienates and stigmatises parents affected by ill health and disabilities. He suggested that at the centre of many *families'* difficulties were issues such as low income, transport problems and inflexible support.

Rick Howell went on to make his own assessment of the role of his, and other, young carers projects:

> The issue of young carers is 'moving on' and while projects still have a role in the future there is a need to look at new directions.... Do projects make a difference? I would say yeas, a big yes they do make a difference to the lives of many families *and* provide an essential focus when trying to build recognition and services. *But*, are they sustainable or acceptable

as service providers in their current form? Are they the best way to make a long-term difference? These questions are less easy to answer....

Underlying the dispute between the disability rights and young carer perspectives it was possible to see two theoretical approaches and belief systems chafing against each other. The background to the disability rights perspective has been set out above. On the other side was an approach which came from an emphasis on children's rights, and which could offer its own powerful critique, of the disempowerment of children in an adult-dominated and controlled world.

But the dispute was never quite so clear-cut as this might imply. Looked at from the outside, the two positions appear to have a lot in common with each other and would seem to be natural allies, particularly against other, more conservative, philosophies and practices. And, in reality, the arguments advanced by many of those researching and working with young carers, even in the early years of the 1990s, were considerably more subtle than an exclusive belief in the rights of young carers.

Towards a family-centred approach

By 1998, members of the YCRG (in their book *Young carers and their families*) were announcing the arrival of what they hoped would be a new way forward, a new paradigm which would replace the old medicalised view of disability and which could transcend the disability rights and young carer approaches:

> A fourth paradigm, a family perspective, has emerged as a direct consequence of the debate between the rights of disabled people and the rights of children who care, and is congruent with the principle of the government's refocusing strategy which emphasises prevention in a family context as opposed to protection.

This 'whole family' approach argues that offering support either to the young carer or the family member who is ill or disabled is not sufficient: support for the whole family is essential.

The recent YCRG report *Growing up caring* elaborates the arguments further:

> Young carers' independence cannot be separated from their parent's independence. It is not possible to have true independence for one without independence for the other. Ill and disabled parents need to be supported as parents as well as disabled people, so that they can achieve personal independence and control over their own lives and provide the kind and quality of parenting to their children that they wish for. This will enable many families to prevent children from having to take on caring responsibilities in the first place, especially in the absence of any alternatives.

Two interesting points emerge from this extract. First, there is an emphasis, which was not present in earlier writings, on helping disabled or ill parents fulfil their role as *parents*. This was one of the issues that Richard Olsen raised in the extract quoted above. The argument is that disabled or ill parents should have the right to state support not only to enable them to meet their own needs but also to meet their parental responsibilities towards their children – otherwise they are implicitly being patronised and demeaned.

To summarise the argument, the 'whole family' approach looks to replace the one-sided caring which many young carers currently undertake with a more natural, two-way process, where parents (whether disabled or ill, or not) are also enabled to care for their children. In other words, the desired aim is to reach towards the sort of natural exchange of help and affection which reinforces family relationships and which should be a mark of a successfully functioning family.

The second, related, argument raised in the passage above is that – if this parenting support is provided – it will help to prevent children and young people from being forced into a caring relationship in the first place.

The question of the extent to which young carers should be caring at all underlies much research and writing on young carers, and it is clearly a difficult one. On the one hand, young carers have made it clear when interviewed that they would not necessarily welcome professional intervention if the result was a break-up of the family or the enforced hospitalisation of the person they are caring for. Any move to remove existing caring responsibilities from young people could itself be construed as patronising, forcing them back into a childhood role which they have left behind.

On the other hand, nobody would argue that children or young people should undertake some of the things which are revealed in interviews with young carers and the literature written about them – including some extracts in this [chapter]. Whatever the issues at the 'softer' end of caring, there is a clear and straightforward consensus when it come to the 'harder' end – particularly the sort of intimate personal care which some young carers undertake for their parents.

The 'whole family' approach was already being recommended by the government in 1996. A letter from the Department of Health to directors of social services departments states: "Where the disabled person is a parent, it is essential that the community care assessment focuses on the family and considers how to support the parent and recognise the needs of any young carers". The letter was accompanied by an action checklist, with nine points:

- Start with the needs of the family/disabled or ill parent, and see what needs remain for the child.
- Work with the child as part of the family unit.
- Acknowledge the rights of the child including the right to information, to be listened to and to stop physically caring.
- Recognise that poverty and disabling environments, services and attitudes can limit adults' ability to parent.
- Acknowledge the distinction between *parenting* and *parental activity.*

- Recognise that time spent in counselling, talking and therapeutic work can prevent inappropriate and expensive crisis responses.
- Focus more on support for children in need rather than on protection of children at risk.
- Acknowledge young carers' legitimate concerns about professionals' attitudes and insensitivity and their fear of professional intervention.
- Remember 'families do their best'. Start with the family's solution and work with any dilemmas and contradictions.

This remarkably enlightened checklist, if properly adopted and funded, would do much to remove many of the problems and concerns which have emerged in relation to young carers and their caring responsibilities.

If a family-centred approach is to be adopted, however, it will mean re-examining a number of aspects of current work with young carers. Indeed the YCRG report *Growing up caring* issues a clarion call for "a fundamental change to the existing structures for young carers services".

Some young carers projects are already beginning to ponder the way forward and are redefining themselves as projects for families. Mavis Crawforth, for example, is project manager for Choices for Families in Hull, which grew out of work in the city undertaken with young carers. Writing in the *Journal of Young Carers Work* in 1999, she described the work of the new project:

> Disabled parents whose children used the project felt disillusioned and isolated and were surprised to hear from their children that they were meeting other young people living in similar circumstances. At the request of the parents a meeting was facilitated by the project to enable parents to meet others. Those parents who were able to attend quickly established a lot of common ground. By the end of what had been planned as a social event the embryo of a new movement had emerged....

> At that first meeting parents had shared with each other how most of what little energies they had was spent on fighting the system in order to (a) gain a better quality of life for themselves and (b) to have their status as a parent recognised and respected. They were all able to share anecdotal evidence of how they felt their parenting role was or had been undermined....

To sum up, as the YCRG authors of *Growing up caring* state:

> Policies and services which identify and respond to the needs of all family members, but in particular those which support ill or disabled parents to enable them to prevent inappropriate caring roles from developing, will offer the best way forward. This challenges us all to think critically about how services to ill and disabled parents, and to existing young carers, should be structured, what they should do, and how they should fit together.

In conclusion

What have we learned about the lives and experiences of young carers, and what responses are appropriate?

Firstly, there are in our midst children and young people – perhaps about 50,000, perhaps more – making sometimes substantial efforts to care for members of their families. The work which adult carers do can too often be forgotten or ignored. The work which *young* carers do is even more likely to be hidden from sight. It is an achievement of all those who have worked over the past 10 years and more to highlight the issue that the existence of young carers, and the needs they have, are now much more widely recognised in society.

Young carers perform a spectrum of caring work, including domestic work, emotional support and personal care work. Many young carers really are young – primary school children are involved as often as teenagers. Around one in five is undertaking intimate personal care.

Young carers are receiving a poor deal from schools. Many are missing a worryingly large amount of school, and often education service responses are either inadequately heavy-handed or inadequately lax. Teachers need much greater understanding of the young carer experience. Bullying by other children can also be a problem.

Health professionals too need to be better informed. GPs in particular may be treating the individual ill or disabled patient without pausing to consider the family situation they are in. Young carers' own health can be affected by their caring role.

Young carers and their families are, almost by definition, burdened also by poverty. Inevitably social services budgets are under pressure, so that assessed needs cannot always be met. But too many young carers are in any case not receiving their own needs assessment, which is their entitlement under the Carers Act. In addition, the state benefits system does not recognise the particular needs of ill or disabled parents with teenage children.

Young carers have a right to be given the information they need. They suffer from a double disadvantage when relating to professionals: as children dealing with adults, and as lay individuals dealing with those who have authority and power.

Young carers develop skills and competencies from their caring work which are not appreciated or recognised. As a consequence many young carers have unnecessarily limited career choices in later life.

The network of young carers groups have performed sterling work at local level, in supporting individual young carers and enabling them to come together collectively. There are, however, still large areas with no young carers groups or projects. Funding is a problem for many existing groups. But young carers groups also need to develop their practice, to take on board the move to a 'whole family' approach.

More generally, social care professionals and others should consider the needs of young carers at the same time as they consider the needs of their parents. Parents have the right to receive support to help them fulfil their role as *parents*.

The aim should be to have support in place so that children and young people need no longer cope with the kinds of situation which they describe in the second part of this [chapter]. Equally importantly, they deserve to be heard, recognised and respected.

Young carers in their own words

Rah, 13

I think social workers are stupid because I had my first one when I was about seven. They didn't come round to see me! I never saw them! The next thing I knew I was in a strange house with total strangers.

My Mum went frequently into hospital since then, me and my brother went to stay with close friends. Again I never saw them (social workers). I lost trust in them and felt alone.

We than moved house and I think social services just forgot about me and my brothers. I didn't see them for about two years. We then had to move up to [name of town]. We lived in a strange place. She went into hospital again. Caroline came round to speak to me and I started coming to Share the Care. My Mum went in hospital soon after. I met my social worker at the hospital. He said he would come and see me next week. I didn't see him for about two months. My Mum rang up and explained what happened. They said they would sort it out and said they would see us next week. They didn't come. My Mum ended up going to their offices, but of course they said the same thing again.

Now I never see them. My social worker has now left! So now they should know what is happening.

SO PLEASE TAKE NOTICE!

Abigale, 11

Read this to all teachers.

Some people can't get their homework done because they are under lots of pressure and stress, so don't say they are lazy because you don't understand.

You should listen to them.

Instead of saying they're lazy you should give them their word so just let them say what they want to say and don't Butt In!!

PLEASE LISTEN!!!!!!

You have to go to school to learn and some people might think you have to have a break.

That is why you go to school.

When you go to school it makes me mad when people make fun of the disabled people and when it comes to homework.

You say why you have not done your work and you tell them what you have done.

They say You Told Me That Last Week. You Are Lying To Me.

Samantha, 14

When I was about ten years old my dad found out he had depression. My mum didn't tell me straight away because I was still quite young to understand. When I was told I was very scared because I didn't know anything about depression.

A couple of months went by after my mum told me and I suddenly realised I was doing things I had never done before eg cooking, cleaning and paying bills. I also started falling behind with my schoolwork and getting into lots of trouble for falling asleep in class. My mum contacted the school and told them what I was going through. They were very understanding.

Helping out in the house doesn't bother me anymore. It is just like a routine now and it's good to help because then I know I am doing something for my dad, who I love very much. It does make me very tired at times but my mum always makes sure I get a rest. I also have a little sister and a big brother who help me and my mum very much.

Katie, 12

Dear Mum

I wish that you and me could spend some time together sometimes.

I feel really sad and left out.

You make me feel like a pair of hands, just there to help, instead of your daughter and although I am doing things that you tell me to I get really fed up.

We never have any personal time together because you never see me in the morning because you're asleep.

When I get home you send me to the shop or doctor's to fetch things and when I get back you go to sleep and I have to look after myself and my brothers and sisters. Then I make tea and when you wake up you send us to bed and it is like that every day and I really feel as though I am not there, **so please spend some time with me.**

What it's really like	**What I wish**
Lonely	Friends allowed home
No friends allowed home	Allowed to answer the phone and door
Not allowed to answer the phone or door	Can go and talk to family
Family always fall out	Can find it OK to go to school
Nowhere to turn	Not worried when I go out
Upsetting	Not to be tired all the time
Worrying	Not to lie anymore
Hard to go to school	To be a normal child
Tiring	Not to be treated like a 4 year old
Lying	
Treated like a 4 year old	

Claire, 9

I look after my mum. She has a disease called Myasthenia Gravis. She can go into hospital any time when her muscles go weak. It affects her muscles, breathing, walking, speech etc. When my mum's ill I ring the ambulance. She tells me not to but I know it's for her own good!

When my mum's ill I go in a home with my sister. (My brother goes by his self.) When my mum comes out of hospital you can tell the difference but not for long. I help tidy up, undress her, help her in the bath, hoover, etc. After I've helped my mum there's a feeling inside of me which makes me happy.

My mum sees a lot of social workers and helpers. I get on with them fine, except one lady who takes me to school. At school most people understand especially my old year 3 teacher. If I get problems she helps me.

Margaret, 11

When I am working at school I am always worried about my Dad but when I am in the playground with my friends I just totally forget about him and have a good time.

When my Dad is having an operation I am always wondering if anything has happened to him.

Sometimes when I am running all around the house for him I get fed up with it.

When I am doing things for my Dad and my Tamagotchi is bleeping I just want to chuck it out of my bedroom window.

When I am cleaning up the house and my older brother wants me to do something for him I just want to magic him away 'cause he's getting on my nerves.

When my brother and sister are arguing they come running up to me and say nasty things about each other and I have enough to worry about, my Dad. I end up falling out with both of them, but in a way, when I think about it, I really like my brother and sister.

Jasmine, 10

On Monday my Mum went into hospital. I had to stay at a friend's house for a while and I visited Mum on Friday and Saturday. I bought her some flowers and some chocolates, I had a lot of dreams and woke up crying. I was okay when I saw her. I started to feel happy.

On the Saturday I didn't find Mum in bed, that's when I started to worry but one of the nurses came and said 'Are you looking for your Mum?' I didn't say anything, I was so upset when we found Mum, we caught her smoking in the garden. When I was telling her off I sounded like the mother. I was saying things like, 'Get back to bed. Do you want to kill yourself smoking? Give me your cigarette or put it out.'

In the morning I get up and if Mum's getting up I help her out of bed, if not I get ready for school and get her up when she's awake. When I arrive at school I'm fine until 11.00 am. Sometimes I'm okay and I just go to play but if I'm not I go to my head teacher and ask if I can phone my Mum. When I'm coming home I just go straight home unless my Mum asks me to go to the shop. When I get home I help do dinner if it needs doing and watch television, eat dinner, wash up, watch television some more and by 8.45 pm I get ready for bed, kiss Mum goodnight and I'm in bed by 9.00 pm. I read a book for 15 minutes and then it's another day in the morning.

Sean, 12

I care for my brother and I get fed up
I really want to give him away but I cannot
I wish that people could understand how hard it is for me
I have a guilty feeling in my tummy

Lucylee, 13

My mum suffers from manic depression and she has a curved spine. She often needs a walking stick and sometimes can't even get out of bed. My parents are divorced. They split up when I was five just before my mum became ill. She said that's what started it off but I don't really know.

My mum re-married about two years later to a man named David. He is very loving and caring and I have accepted him as my new dad. Myself and my brother Tim both look after my mum while my dad is at work. He is a police officer and works long shifts which can be hard for us when mum is really ill.

My mum has to take lots of tablets. Sometimes they don't work and mum becomes very ill. One time she had to change pills and became so sick she fainted. I had to call the doctor and my dad who was at work When the doctor came he checked my mum and went to get an injection. While he was gone I cried because I was scared but when I heard him come back I stopped. I didn't want him to see me upset so I tried to keep a brave face.

My mum has good days and bad days, it seems most of them are bad but it's nice to see her smile now and again. Tim and I do a lot of the housework and I sometimes have to cook as well as do my homework. It can get difficult but it's good afterwards knowing I've helped my mum. I enjoy helping my mum, I only wish it could be a bit easier.

Michelle, 10

My mum has epilepsy and MS. My mum is aged 38.

My mum has to take 84 tablets a week. She has to take five in the morning, five at teatime, two at night. Every day of the week. My mum's tablets are called: Lamictal, Carbamazepine, Diazepam.

My mum found out she has MS when she was 25 years old and she found out she had epilepsy when she was 31 years old.

Epilepsy means men/women/boys/girls could start to; stare, shake, and start to bite their clothes, punch, and kick, and sometimes their eyes roll to the back of the head.

Sometimes little children might cry just like I did when I first saw my mum in an epileptic fit, but now I am used to it. My older brother knows what to do and so does my younger brother, they help me a lot.

My brothers have jobs to do: my younger brother has to get the pillows and get my Nan or uncle. And my older brother has to get everyone out of the house when my mum is in a fit and make a sweet cup of tea.

My younger brother always cries when he sees my mum in a fit. Because he is young my older brother just laughs, he thinks it's funny.

One day my mum had a fit in my school playground and in my school. She had to go to hospital. Sometimes me and my brothers had to wait till Nan came home or my auntie came up for us.

My younger brother always gets scared and he has to go to hospital with my mum. We all get scared.

This chapter was taken from Bibby, A. and Becker, S. (2000) *Young carers in their own words*, London: Calouste Gulbenkian Foundation. The right of Andrew Bibby to be identified as author of this chapter has been asserted by him in accordance with the 1988 Copyright, Designs and Patents Act.

Education and the economy

Sally Tomlinson

...A post-welfare society [is] defined as one where a work ethic and competition in education and the labour market dominate. It is also a society in which there is a restructuring or removal of welfare benefits on the grounds that excessive welfare provision leads to economic inefficiency. Individuals in post-welfare societies are instructed to 'learn to compete' (DfEE, 1996a) in education and the job market, both for their own economic futures and also to improve the competitiveness of the national economy. While these goals may seem self-evident, in particular the benefits to individuals who undertake more education and training, both propositions are debatable. Neither national government, employers nor individuals can be clear about what sort of education and skill acquisition will be needed in a globalised economy and by 2000 it was clear that even high levels of education were no guarantee of permanent employment. Education and employment limits and possibilities continued to be affected by social class, gender, race, migration and disability. The impact of more education and training on the wider economy was even less clear (Robinson, 1997). The classical liberal economic assumptions that "education is an investment which lifts individuals out of poverty by increasing their returns in the labour market" (Woodward, 1997, p 2) was fast become too simplistic an assumption where labour markets were disappearing, and education had become a rationed positional good, effectively designed to exclude many potential competitors (Brown and Lauder, 1996). This chapter reviews links between education and employment as work became more 'knowledge intensive' and affected by global economic factors, and looks at the prospects for the poor in a society increasingly divided by income and wealth and by the "ability to consume" (Townsend, 1993, P 73).

Recent history

Education policy in the post-war welfare state gradually recognised a clear relationship between education and the economy, once the chronic shortage of labour was addressed. The influence of academic economists [...] convinced government that education expansion and recognition of new technologies was needed for the UK to compete in world markets (Vaizey, 1958). Halsey and his colleagues wrote in 1961 that

> Education is a crucial type of investment for the exploitation of modern technology. In advanced industrial societies it is inevitable that the education system should come into a closer relationship with the

> economy ... as the proportion of the labour force engaged in manual
> work declines and the demand for white-collar, professional and
> managerial worker rises. (Halsey et al, 1961, pp 1-2)

Although policy makers routinely paid lip-service to the importance of education
for social, cultural and personal reasons, in the post-welfare state the economic
imperative came to dominate the political and educational agenda. Successive
governments from the 1970s imposed economic priorities on education, accepting
the received wisdom that formal education was fundamental to success and progress
in a world dominated by free market economics (see Porter, 1999).

The right-wing Thatcher governments during the 1980s turned education
into a quasi-market, in which choice and competition, intended to make consumers
select schools and courses which would maximise qualifications and job prospects,
and drive uneconomical schools out of business, in fact succeeded in polarising
the school system by social class and thus by employment possibilities at levels
not seen since the 1950s. Overt and covert selective mechanisms advantaged
middle class and aspirant groups and created more schools attended only by
disadvantaged children, who continued to experience more difficulty in moving
on to a higher level education or training. Market reforms in education did
indeed leave "a large majority of the working population without the human
resources to flourish in the global economy" (Brown and Lauder, 1996, p 8).

The centre-left 'modernisers', exemplified by the New Labour government
elected in 1997, claimed to pursue both economic efficiency and social justice
(Commission on Social Justice, 1994), arguing that a better educated and trained
workforce was the key to an economy which would induce investment and
create more jobs. However, Labour's retention of the Conservative market
principles in education plus an espousal of the long-held right-wing desire to
return to selective policies, resulted in even more social class polarisation and a
reduction in the chances of many students in disadvantaged areas even to begin
to join in what had become an intensive human capital competition. The well-
intentioned palliative policies of Sure Starts, EAZs and New Deals appeared
unlikely to affect class divisions in education and the labour market and create
high skill 'employability' for all. In addition, as Brown and Lauder (1996, p 12)
pointed out, although the belief that in the global auction for jobs, western
nations would dominate the market for highly paid and skilled jobs presented a
"comforting picture of the global economy", the picture was in fact an imperialist
throw-back. Developing countries, especially those with expanded higher
education systems, were creating an educated workforce which would be attractive
to multinational companies.

The Labour government's education policy from the early 1990s was driven
by a micro-economic ideology which included the beliefs that a centrally
prescribed curriculum from pre-school to higher education, an escalation of
credentials, and a commitment to lifelong re-skilling, would solve macro-economic
problems. While global economic changes, especially the influence of multinational
companies and financial organisations, were reducing the ability of national
governments to control their own economies, Tory and Labour governments

embraced the "attractively simple explanation" (McCulloch, 1998a, p 203) that the British education system was at fault, and not designed to promote high economic performance. Post-1997 the New Labour government became a passionate advocate of the view that economic success depended on tight central control of education, meeting education and training targets, and persuading people to obtain more qualifications and skills. The assumption was that the more people invested in themselves as human capital, the more schools overcame their shortcomings in preparing pupils for economic success, the more competitive the economy would become. "We cannot run a first-rate economy on the basis of a second-rate education system", as Gordon Brown, Chancellor of the Exchequer, observed in a 1997 speech in London's Guildhall. While this was unjust to an education system, which for 20 years had been constantly 'reformed' by successive central government dictates, it also oversimplified the complex relationship between education and the economy.

The plethora of training schemes and new qualifications, reorganisation of post-16 education, the rise and demise of quangos, had not, by the turn of the century, had much effect on most parts of the British economy[1]. Economic successes were largely the result of financial and capital movement, and as Australian academic Marginson (1999, p 29) pointed out, "Education cannot in itself generate capital movements or create wealth". The inevitable economic 'failure' of education associated with credentialism may well contribute to a recurring cycle of disillusion, blame and search for scapegoats. Ostensible meritocratic selective education policies, despite turn of the century concerns over elitism in higher education (Ahmed et al, 2000, p 2), continued in Britain to ensure a familiar social-class based system, divided between high-status academic routes leading to professional, managerial and more secure jobs, the lower status vocational routes leading to less secure futures.

The labour market in the 1990s

By the late 1990s the British public was constantly assured that the economy was doing well, but the job market was characterised by insecurity and uncertainty. Although more people were employed than ever before in the UK, some 26 million, more people who could have been 'economically active' – over 4 million according to a Treasury report in 1998 – were without work (see *Social Trends 30*, 2000, p 66; Turok, 2000, p 59). A major change from the 1970s had been the entry of more women into the labour market, albeit mainly in part-time work and for lower pay than males. In 1997 72% of working-age women were in the workforce, half in part-time work. The educational successes of girls in education, while opening up new opportunities, did not translate into high-level well-paid jobs for more than a few. Middle-class women preferred to take professional rather than managerial jobs, a move that Crompton (1995) argued allowed them to reconcile family and work demands. For both middle-class men and women, the status of university attended appeared more important to their level of occupation than school, but those working in the private sector were likely to earn more than those in public sector jobs (Power, 2000). New Labour social policies post-1997 did encourage women, including single mothers, to find work, more young people stayed in education and training, and fewer older men were employed, including those classed as professional and managerial.

There were significant differences in the kinds of work available to ethnic minorities, who incurred an 'ethnic penalty' (Heath and McMahon, 1997, p 646) which meant that they fared less well in the labour market than similarly qualified whites. Minorities were also more likely to live in cities, where jobs disappeared faster than in other areas. Between 1981 and 1996 1.6 million jobs in manufacturing were lost in cities, which affected jobs in business, sales and other services. A direct effect of this was that more children of unemployed parents were attending city schools. Between 1980 and 1999 the proportion of people living in poor households doubled to nearly one fifth of all households, income inequalities widened and one third of all children were defined as living in low-income households (*Social Trends 30*, 2000, p 93). Disabled people were more likely to be unemployed or in low-level insecure employment, and were particular targets for welfare reform with reductions in eligibility for state support (Hyde, 2000).

There continued to be large regional differences in employment possibilities. The concentration of jobs, even for those with low or no qualification, in the south-east of the UK, became more intense during the 1990s. In 1999 over 70% of poorly qualified people age 24-35 had jobs in the south-east. In the Merseyside region the proportion was 43% (Erdem and Glyn, 2000). Encouraging people in depressed areas to train or retrain and persuading the unemployed and inactive to look for work do not guarantee more employment if jobs do not exist. Measures to help regional employment include getting firms to relocate, relocating public sector activity and improving regional infrastructure, all of which are as important in ensuring employment as education and training (Erdem and Glyn, 2000, p 17).

Jobs and education

When the actual structure of the economy and where jobs have been lost and gained are analysed, the levels of education and qualifications needed or demanded by employers can be better reviewed. Employers in the 1990s were increasingly demanding higher level qualifications for jobs not previously needing them, leading to the situation Dore (1976) described in developing countries as a 'Diploma disease'. A prevailing government and business view was that the economy was structured around knowledge-intensive work, as website designers and ICT consultants took over from coal-miners and steelworkers, and that education should prepare people for a 'knowledge economy'. Although a 1998 White Paper addressed the role of government in *Our competitive future: Building a knowledge-based economy* (DTI, 1998) there continued to be debate over how many would actually be employed in the new knowledge-based economy and how far the occupational structure had actually changed (see Keep and Mayhew, 1999; Gray and Flores, 2000).

A Labour Force Survey in 1998 showed an increase in professional, managerial and technical jobs – up to 36% of the workforce. This made it worthwhile for the middle and aspirant classes to adopt the strategies described [...] and urge their children into higher education, although the increase in managers did include managing fast-food outlets. Clerical, sales, personal and secretarial jobs increased in the 1990s to 34% of the workforce in 1997, some of which needed new-style qualifications (*Labour Force Survey*, 1998). Hutton (2000) calculated that the number of hairdressing shops had risen from 15,000 in 1992 to 70,000 in 1999 – a possible 'hairdressing overkill', but which had the merit of increasing the numbers of self-employed. Other fast growth areas were in telephone sales jobs, drivers' mates and nursery assistants (Hutton, 2000, p 31), where requirements were for personal qualities as much as for qualifications. Manufacturing employment continued to fall as governments failed to invest in either high or low-technical areas and multinational firms moved their factories where labour was cheapest, and also employed 'knowledge workers' from countries with lower wage structures (Lind, 1995)[2].

By the 1990s the terms knowledge economy and knowledge-intensive work had become 'buzzwords' for politicians, although these were seldom defined. Robinson (2000) suggested that knowledge-intensive work was a form of employment requiring more intellectual capital – "the use of conceptual and analytical skills by individuals so that they can sift and arrange information to construct an argument or solve a problem" (Robinson, 2000). This was not a new concept: workers by brain, as clause 4 of the Labour Manifesto of 1918 put it, had always relied on intellectual capital, but the shift from manufacturing to business, financial and professional jobs did mean that more people were likely to be employed using these skills, plus new communication skills.

But for the majority of workers, the relationship between education, skills and jobs remained problematic. Keep and Mayhew (2000) pointed out the risks of conflating the production of high-tech goods such as computers and IT equipment with a workforce of highly skilled knowledge workers. Employees may need a high level of manual dexterity to assemble circuit boards, but they do not need degrees or diplomas to do the work (Keep and Mayhew, 2000). Other writers pointed out that although there might be a skills shortage in the new high-tech areas, most employees in the UK at the end of the 1990s were still performing repetitive, closely supervised tasks (Thompson and Warhurst, 1998). In addition, employers, especially in the service sector, were increasingly using personal characteristics – dress, appearance and accent – as proxy for 'skills' for employment.

A new economy?

Despite the claims that radical shifts were taking place in the national economy in the 1990s, the new economy and occupational structures turned out, at the end of the 1990s, to incorporate much continuity with the old economy. An

IPPR economist noted in 2000 that "although there have been significant shifts the labour market has not been transformed in the last ten years. The new economy still leaves the vast majority of us doing jobs that have been around for years" (Nick Burkitt, quoted in Denny, 2000, p 17). The relationship between an individual's qualifications and their chances of finding work followed the trend since the 1960s, those with higher qualifications having better job prospects, and academic rather than vocational qualifications continuing to have a higher pay-off. In the UK, unlike other European countries, government pushed for 'starred A-levels and world-class tests' rather than raising the status and resourcing of vocational qualifications. Evidence accumulated that the low-cost, poorly targeted training programmes adopted by governments over the previous 20 years had a poor record of helping individuals find jobs. The high expectations that the TECs created at the beginning of the 1990s, abolished at the end, would improve training, were disappointed, as funding policies had encouraged a concentration on low-level, cheap programmes (Jones, 1999).

Although much research had attempted to identify links between education and training levels and global competitiveness, usually defined as growth in the economy, such links had proved difficult to establish. Politicians and sections of the media persistently attempted to make simplistic connections between pupil performance in international comparative studies in maths and science and growth per capita in GDP, but it was all mostly guesswork. Robinson (1997) pointed out that pupils in Bulgaria and the Slovak Republic did well in such tests but their economies did not exactly prosper, while the USA, low down in maths tests scores, had the world's most successful economy. Ashton and Green (1996, p 63) commented that if the link between education and economic growth was strong "one would expect education's effects to shine through the empirical fog. It does not".

The views of young people on the relationship between jobs, education and the economy were seldom sought, but Killeen et al (1999), questioning students at two southern schools in the late 1990s, found that the young people adopted a thoroughly instrumental view of education. They believed strongly that qualifications were a paper currency that could be exchanged for work opportunities. They were also realistic about the lower status of vocational courses. The content of education was irrelevant and "almost any kind of degree course seemed preferred to post-19 education and training rouges" (Killeen et al, 1999, p 113). For employers, education had fast become a potential screening device, and also a means of 'warehousing' potential employees until they could be selected for employment (Killeen et al, 1999, p 114).

At the local level, the disappearance of manufacturing and associated jobs did appear to affect the prospects and attitudes of young people. The threatened sale and closure of the Rover car plant in Birmingham by German owners BMW early in 2000 had immediate repercussions for children at the main secondary school in the area. The head teacher reported that "the atmosphere from Rover is definitely affecting them. You can see the older children thinking – what's the point? A lot of year 11 children have been dropping out, feeling, if jobs can disappear that easily, why bother?" (Mathew Brown, 2000, p 2). The threatened closure of the Rover plant, although reversed by the new management and government funding, provided a good illustration of the difficulties for national governments in responding to the actions of multinational firms, and the insecure relationship between skills and employment at the local level.

The global economy and education

Definitions, debate and critique of 'globalisation' entered business, political and academic thinking in the 1990s but public awareness of the meaning of a global economy and global communication remained low. Giddens, in a BBC Reith Lecture early in 1999, pointed out that "every business guru talks about it [globalisation], no political speech is complete without it, yet ten years ago the term was hardly used" (Giddens 1999a, p 31). The term largely refers to processes of trade and financial flows, information and communications technologies, movement and migration of people and their labour, and cultural convergences between countries exemplified by, for example, music, jeans and McDonald's. It also signifies ways in which multinational businesses, and expanded capabilities for instant financial transactions, have reduced the power of governments in nation-states to control their economies. Communication technologies have encouraged the translation of 'knowledge' into a saleable commodity (see Reich, 1991; Marginson, 1999; see also 'The threat to globalism', special issue of *Race and Class*, vol 40, nos 2/3, 1999), and instant relationships can be conducted across continents. In a global economy, employers are no longer dependent on local, regional or even national labour. When capital and investment can move so easily, it will tend to move to countries where workers have the lowest wages (Gray, 1998; Sivanandan, 1999).

Although the role of national governments in planning their education system and regulating and intervening in the economy remained important (Green, 1997), globalisation meant that relationships between education and employment continued, into the 21st century, to become more uncertain, and the relationship between a highly skilled workforce and national 'economic competitiveness' remained problematic. Lind (1995) pointed out that the world contained not only billions of unskilled workers, but also millions of scientists, architects, engineers and other professionals willing to do world class work for a fraction of the payment that professionals in developed countries expect. If there is high-skill, low-wage competition from abroad, there can be no guarantees that even highly educated people in developed countries will find permanent work (Lind, 1995, p 203). Arguably the notion of a 'safe career' for many educated middle-class people could disappear (Gray and Flores, 2000).

However, the emerging reality resulting from a global economy appears to encourage the creation of a global social class structure, which mimics national social structures. There are highly educated and qualified global elites, often educated internationally, whose background and privileges guarantee them permanent employment, income and wealth. There are well-qualified groups dependent on their own efforts who are increasingly employed on contracts and

411

in short-term jobs. There are qualified groups employed in service and routine jobs, and there are large groups with few or no skills whose chances of employment depend on international, national and regional capital flows and government policies as much as on their own efforts to gain more education and training.

While there is an expanding literature attempting to explain the likely consequence of globalisation, the most influential analysis in the 1990s was that provided by Reich (1991)3, who was concerned that global economic forces would "bestow even greater wealth on the most skilled and insightful, consigning the less skilled to a declining standard of living" (Reich, 1991, p 3). He described three categories of work emerging as that done by symbolic analysts, highly educated people who trade in the manipulation of symbols – from biotechnology engineers to financial consultants, in-person service workers, from waiters to security guards, and routine production workers. His major concern was that the rich and rewarded would withdraw into private enclaves, and questioned what happens in societies where people "no longer inhabit the same economy" and where cosmopolitan elites could "jettison the obligations of national citizenship" (Reich, 1991, p 303).

Prospects for the poor

The employment prospects for the poor both in developed and developing countries continued to be analysed and theorised about in pessimistic detail into the 21st century. In Britain, Hutton (1995) in his best selling *The state we're in* described what he considered to be a divisive and destructive labour market, in which only around 40% of the workforce enjoyed full-time employment or self-employment, 30% were part-time or in insecure jobs or self-employment, and the bottom 30% were marginalised, working for poverty wages or unemployed (Hutton, 1995, p 14). Hutton's view was that, far from education offering opportunities to all, education had become a creator of class division, and in the 1990s the growth in inequality had been the fastest of any advanced state. The plethora of national, European and international reports drawing attention to the growing divide between rich and poor in the UK confirmed the pessimistic conclusion that social justice, equality, economic redistribution and democratic participation were casualties of economic policies (see for example Glyn and Miliband, 1994; D. Acheson, 1998; Hills, 1998; Porter, 1999; Pantazis and Gordon, 2000; Sen, 2000).

The Thatcher governments of the 1980s deliberately followed strategies of inequality in the belief that economic efficiency would follow (Walker and Walker, 1987). What actually followed was an increase in inequality in the distribution of household incomes (Barclay, 1995). A Unicef report, using UK figures for 1997, estimated that one child in five was living in poverty, similar to Mexico, the US and Italy (Dean and Thornton, 2000). New Labour came to power with a commitment to deal with poverty and inequality, but followed conservative spending plans, sanctioned wide disparities in income, asserted that wealth creation was more important than redistribution, and reduced funding for a welfare state, none of which were likely to improve prospects for the poor. Tackling poverty and social exclusion became a matter for mapping areas where the poor lived, and a reliance on area-based policies to improve health, education, and employment in the areas. However, area-based policies had little success in the past and did not appear by 2000 to be much more successful. Labour claimed that by 2000, work-related policies such as the working family's tax credit had moved a million children out of poverty, but the claims were difficult to quantify. Large-scale unemployment and poverty in the UK continued to be located in mainly urban areas, where targeting areas and individuals could not compensate for localised job shortages.

By the 1990s it had become clear that the poor in developed societies were no longer a reserve army of labour, as earlier analyses described it. Modern societies, as Bauman (1998), in another depressing comment, had noted, do not need massive labour forces, profits can be increased while cutting down on labour, and grooming the poor to be a reserve army of labour no longer makes sense. The tragedy for the poor was that modern society engages its members mainly as consumers, and those lacking sufficient income, credit cards and bank accounts were flawed consumers. "Decent and normal members of society, the consumers, want nothing from them and expect nothing. The poor are totally useless ... for them, zero tolerance" (Bauman, 1998, p 91).

A more optimistic and visionary discussion of the prospects for the poor emerged in William Wilson's (1996) account of what happens to the urban poor *When work disappears* in the US. He researched the loss of manual jobs in American society and the 'suburbanization' of employment, which has left the black urban poor in areas of concentrated unemployment, alongside the growth of a black middle class. He demonstrated that the urban poor do not lack aspiration and motivation, but unlike the middle classes their desire for work and a stable life was constrained by lack of job opportunities as well as poor education and training opportunities. Public services and private employers had deserted cities; lack of transport had made journeys to work outside cities difficult. Blaming the poor, a favourite tactic of governments on both sides of the Atlantic, was pointless in the circumstances in which the poor lived, and those addicted to crime and drugs represented only a small segment of populations anxious and willing to work. Wilson (1996, p 238) concluded that "increasing the employment base [in cities] would have an enormous positive impact on the social organization of ghetto neighbourhoods"; Wilson proposed a series of related social and economic policies to enable people to live decently and avoid joblessness, while developing proper social benefit and health care programmes.

The enormous social and economic inequalities existing within countries and between countries remain a source of concern for national governments and international organisations, particularly since the late 1990s when 'global doubts' about the effects of a global economy manifested themselves in local and international protests. A major conclusion reached by commentators on the global economy was that if free market capitalism is to be the basis for a global economy it must be matched by a concern for democratic and civil and political rights for all. Economist and Nobel Prize winner Armatya Sen listed these, plus a free media, basic education and health care, economic safety nets and provision for women's freedom and rights, as crucial to any attempt to alleviate poverty and create a world where employment opportunities exist for all (Sen, 2000, p 29). Similarly Gray (1998) concluded that if market forces continued to be separated from democratic social and political control the age of globalisation would become another turn in the history of servitude for the majority.

The links between education and the national and global economies are not as simple as governments assert. Exhortations to obtain qualifications and skills and learn lifelong will be of use to individuals only if there are economic and political policies which aim for a secure and productive life for all members of society. In the early 21st century in both developed and developing countries, free market policies in both education and the economy continue to have the effect of legitimising continued inequality and the exclusion of weaker social groups.

Conclusion: education in a post-welfare society

[...] An overall conclusion to this review is that since the mid-1970s education has moved from being a key pillar of the welfare state to being a prop for a global market economy.

[...] In the post-war welfare state, education, along with other social policies, contributed to economic stability and attempts to create a more egalitarian distribution of life chances within a growing national economy. An expanding occupational structure and an expansion of opportunity, particularly through the development of comprehensive schooling, led to social mobility for larger numbers of those from manual working-class backgrounds. However, the reproduction of privilege, especially by the upper classes, remained, and the idea that occupation and status would be determined solely by merit remained a myth (Halsey et al, 1997, p 5).

[...] Beliefs in free market capitalism and privatisation led to the dismantling of much welfare state provision, and global economic forces reduced the powers of national governments to control their own economies. In an effort to keep the UK economy competitive, education and training were elevated to key positions; 'raising standards', 'learning to compete' and getting education 'right' became major policy objectives. In the modernised Britain of the late 20th century, private business was designated a major role in the creation of wealth and employment, and government had decided that its role was to encourage competitive markets and equip citizens with skills and aspirations to succeed in a modern flexible economy. Ensuring this meant tighter and tighter central control, the direction of the entire education and training system and an expansion of credentialism. Young people faced some 75 external tests and examinations during their time at school[4]. Those unlikely or unable to join the economy at any but the lowest levels, or whose presence interfered with the prescribed education for the majority, continued to be the recipients of special policies. Social justice was redefined as policy to alleviate the growing divisions and inequalities, which market policies were creating. Education had become narrowed to its economic function, and governments were effectively neutralising schools, colleges and universities as independent and democratic institutions (see Porter, 1999).

Positive aspects

Although the negative effects of educational market reforms have hampered progress since 1979, any long-term view of education over the second half of the 20th century demonstrated widening opportunities and growing aspirations. In 1939 the majority of pupils were still the "elementary schooled proletarians" described by Halsey (*Social Trends 30*, 2000, p 17). By 1946 some 4.5 million English school pupils and subsequently their children were democratically entitled to a secondary education. Gradually the right to prepare for entry to public examinations, further and higher education was extended. By 1998 over 7.5 million pupils were entitled to an education from 4 to 16, with 98% of 4-year-olds in education, and 74% of 16- to 18-year-olds staying in education or training. Some 1.2 million students were enrolled on full-time higher education courses and 1.1 million on adult education courses. Information and communications technology was becoming more equitably shared, with 93% of secondary schools connected to the internet. A National Grid for Learning linking schools, colleges, universities and libraries was to be in place by 2002 (see *Social Trends 30*, 2000, ch 3).

Dramatic shifts in attitudes towards the education of girls over the half-century had led to a closing of the gender gap in school achievement and "in the UK schooling appears to have broken with the traditions of the gender order" (Arnot et al, 1999, p 156). Girls' success was still strongly linked to social class, and educational success had not ensured much wider occupational changes for women. The education of minority groups gradually became a serious issue for successive governments from the 1970s, and some minority groups, overcoming continued racism and xenophobia, began to achieve well. However, a Commission on the Future of Multiethnic Britain, reporting in October 2000, made 18 recommendations to government to counter social racial inequalities in education (Parekh, 2000).

Social class, rooted in economic and power inequalities and partially reproduced through education, remained a powerful predictor of life chances, but working-class attitudes to education were changing. A political consciousness was developing which recognised the importance attached to qualifications and credentials. A final decline in the kind of deference which led pre-war parents to consider education as 'not for the likes of us' ensured that governments would in future need to take working-class educational aspirations seriously. The promotion of lifelong learning was slowly becoming part of what Raymond Williams (1965) had termed *The long revolution*, a process which included an aspiration for universal education and the extension of active learning to all, not just to selected groups.

Civil and human rights awareness and legislation were affecting access to, treatment within and outcomes of education. As always, those affected by inequalities, discrimination and control developed strategies to resist or subvert regressive policies. Short-term ameliorative policies in socially disadvantaged areas, particularly those stemming from New Labour's 'initiatives' post-1997, had positive effects for many individuals. Schools had become less repressive institutions than earlier in the century, and much learning was taking place outside formal educational structures.

Negative aspects

A long-term view of negative consequences of educational reforms during the 1980s and 1990s must give pride of place to the obsession with selection and segregation of children into different schools or different curricula within schools. They were usually based on spurious notions of ability, which effectively mirrored the social class structure. The political project of the right throughout the second half of the 20th century was to avoid any recognition of the limited successes of democratic educational reforms and seek to reintroduce selective mechanisms, which would work for the social reproduction of an hierarchical society. While overt selection had largely become unacceptable by the 1980s, the application of market principles to education proved extraordinarily effective in reintroducing a complex system of selection, passing as 'diversity' in which, as intended, the greatest beneficiaries were the middle classes. The New Labour government pursued market policies, claiming that parental choice, competition, testing, targets and central control of curriculum, teachers and funding were the only route to a 'world class' education system that would retain the loyalty of those middle-class parents who would otherwise use private education[5].

The results of market competition did indeed work to the benefit of middle class and aspirant groups, and despite a rhetoric of inclusion, continued to perpetuate a divided and divisive system. Governments, as Jordan (1998, p 137) pointed out, can announce that opportunities are formally open to all but cannot control jockeying for positional advantage. In the US, the UK and other countries whose educational systems embraced market forces, markets were dysfunctional in terms of 'raising standards' for all. As a wealth of research demonstrated (see for example Willms and Echols, 1992; Gerwirtz et al, 1995; Levačić and Hardman, 1998) the market success of some schools enabled them to select their customers; choice became a sham for many parents. In the UK, under pressure from league table comparisons, schools selected children who would enhance their league table position and were easy to teach. Those with special educational needs, second language needs or learning and behaviour problems were unwanted in oversubscribed schools. Competition for 'able students' exacerbated existing divisions between academic and vocational routes, and vocational qualifications, even to degree level, were still assigned a lower status[6]. A 19th century subject-centred curriculum, controlled and evaluated by central diktat, left schools with a limited capacity for critical reflection. Examination technique, rote learning and revision replaced much substantive teaching.

Education markets did not encourage social balance in schools, equalise opportunities or help the socially excluded, and social segregation in education worked against the possibility of preparing good citizens who care about each other. On the global level in both developed and developing countries, increased numbers of highly educated professional and managerial elites, successful in state school competition or privately schooled, were by the 1990s contributing to what Reich (1991, p 282) described as the politics of secession. This meant "undoing the ties that bind them to their undesired compatriots" and creating new global structures of inequality.

A further major negative aspect of educational reform in the later 20th century was the increasing de-professionalisation of teachers, as they increasingly came under central control and direction, government exerting detailed control of practice hitherto regarded as the responsibility of those teaching in and running schools and colleges. While Etzioni (1969) famously described teachers as 'semi-professionals', the post-war generation of teachers were credited with the major characteristics of professionalism – an ideal of service and a degree of control over their own practice. By the later part of the century teachers had been reduced to technician status, 'delivering' a prepared curriculum, policed by an unpopular inspectorate and publicly criticised by ministers. There was much evidence of lowered morale and a crisis in teacher recruitment. A management ethos dominated schools, or "human service organisations" as one book described them (MacGilchrist et al, 1997, p 111). The creation of a General Teaching Council notionally returned some professional control to teachers, but the drive for centralised control, inspection and direction of activities was extended to all post-16 education and training. University staff were also increasingly de-professionalised, as their activities became subject to measurement, control and external direction.

Market forces, centralised control of education and the subservience of educational ends to economic priorities combined, by the end of the century, to diminish schools as independent, creative and democratising institutions. Schools were places where 'tougher targets' were to raise standards to give "competitive advantage in the modern economy" (Blair, 1998b, p 11). Universities, according to Lord Sainsbury, the Minister for Science, were "at the heart of our productive capacity and are powerful drivers of technological change.... Central to local and regional regeneration" (*Oxford University Gazette*, 3 August 2000, p 1). The notion that educational institutions had any purpose other than an economic function had almost completely disappeared from policy-making discourse.

The future

Predictions about the future direction of education have always proved particularly problematic, change often depending on political prejudice, powerful vested interests and pressure groups. Although as Heller (1988, p 24) remarked, "politics and good intentions do not mix". New Labour's plans for education were replete with good intentions. Barber (2000), describing UK government strategy for education into the 21st century in a speech to policy makers in the US, claimed that "our [New Labour] vision is a world class education service". While few would dispute the desirability of improving the education service for all, a serious question raised by the notion of global competition for world class education is 'Whose world?' ...

The restriction of access to particular forms of education has always acted as a dominant form of social exclusion. New Labour, as with governments around the world at the end of the century, was grappling with a situation in which more and more people were engaged in a competitive attempt to gain qualifications and employment, large numbers were excluded from entering the competition on equal terms, and others, driven by heightened insecurities, were intent on retaining or gaining positional advantage. In this situation good intentions for reducing inequality and exclusion were balanced by the political reality that policies which threatened the middle and aspirant classes could threaten the government's electoral base. But it was becoming possible to predict that all social groups would eventually react against a centrally imposed curriculum, the unfairness of inspection and assessment, control of educational institutions, contempt for local democratic input, and the narrow economistic concept of education which dominated by 2000.

Any real change in the structure, content, governance and organisation of schooling in developed countries in the 21st century may well depend on forces beyond national educational planning. Freeing education to serve goals other than economic will depend on restraint of the global free market system, which Neal Acherson (1998) described as "the most powerful and arrogant order in human history ... a form of capitalism too unfair and callous to last, too unequal to be tolerated and too recklessly greedy to be sustainable". Acherson was optimistic that there are now millions of people worldwide, formerly the 'docile masses' who by now have sufficient education and a sense of their own rights and dignity, to challenge educational inequalities, poverty and injustice. If some form of global cooperation replaced the seemingly irreplaceable economic competitiveness, then it would be possible to consider other functions for education.

Critiques of the narrowing of education to economic ends want to reclaim education as a humanising, liberalising, democratising force, directed, as the UN (1948) Universal Declaration of Human Rights put it, to "the full development of the human personality and a strengthening of respect for human rights and fundamental freedoms". Education must also help people to make sense of the impact of global changes, combat any resurgent nationalism and move beyond a tawdry subservience to market forces.

Notes

[1] Turok (2000) noted the evidence which suggested that most young people participate in temporary training programmes because of a lack of available local jobs. Keep and Mayhew (2000) have analysed the difficulties of matching skills and qualifications to jobs. Weir (1999), director of the Democratic Audit at Essex University, noted that private and business and city interests predominated in New Labour's quangos. Of 320 task forces, 71% of members represented producer interests and 66% of members were male (Weir 1999).

[2] The term 'global outsourcing' began to be used by the end of the 1990s to refer to the use of highly qualified labour overseas who would receive and complete work sent on-line. High-tech industries in southern California became well known for outsourcing work to India.

[3] Robert B. Reich, a Brandeis professor and major political economist in the US, served for a period as US Secretary of State for Labor.

[4] Smithers (2000) commented in *The Guardian* (Education Section) on surveys by teaching unions showing the numbers of external tests faced by school pupils; she also commented that the complex raft of post-16 examinations to be introduced under the Qualifying for Success initiative in October 2000 would exacerbate the 'paperchase'.

[5] This argument was promoted by Hutton (1995), Walden (1996) and Barber (2000) who were either unaware of all the evidence demonstrating the educational advantages permanently accruing to the middle classes in state education and the subtle use made by some of both state and private education, or were supporting a familiar class-based selective system.

[6] In August 2000 the Chief Inspector of Schools, Chris Woodhead, continued to lament the introduction of vocational courses to degree level on the grounds that they were not academically rigorous (Woodhead, 2000).

This chapter was taken from Tomlinson, S. (2001) *Education in a post-welfare society*, Buckingham: Open University Press. The right of Sally Tomlinson to be identified as author of this chapter has been asserted by her in accordance with the 1988 Copyright, Designs and Patents Act.

Daycare: dreams and nightmares

Penelope Leach

Babies and small children have to be cared for every minute of every twenty-four hours. There has to be somebody to feed each baby when she is hungry, cuddle her when she cries, cover her ears when it thunders and show her the rainbow. Somebody must laugh at first joke, applaud first steps, read stories, and steer her between the rock and the hard place of toddlerhood so that she can emerge unscathed into socialised childhood and the new joys of 'my friends' and 'my teacher'. And even then, somebody must be there to welcome her home and then launch her again on each fresh leap into life.

Who is going to do that? Most mothers-to-be answer 'Me, of course' (fathers are more likely to say 'us'), but there is no 'of course' about it. As more and more Western parents find themselves unable to afford to spend with children time that could otherwise earn money to spend on them, pressure for more daycare mounts. A daycare debate is raging from the European Commission to national parliaments, from the White House to Wall Street, from multinational corporation boardrooms to high-street firms, and in political parties, trades unions and women's organisations at every level. But that debate is about big issues like the economy, the labour market and women's votes; it is not about the small people whose care *is* the issue. Starting from the premise that lack of daycare is depriving economies of needed workers and women of needed work, it is assumed that enough daycare to keep children who are not old enough for school safely out of the way during the working week is vital to national, local and family economies. The agenda for debate is simply this: how can daycare be made available, acceptable and affordable to all (and who should pay)?

Childcare: a bigger agenda for a different debate

Post-war changes in families, communities and indeed whole societies, have eroded traditional Western childcare patterns based on an earning male married to a dependent female who nurtured their joint children within a context of extended family support. Settled new patterns have not yet evolved in their place and, because children cannot be left uncared for while a radical rethink goes on, Western policy makers have turned to daycare without first asking the crucial question: how can children's needs best be met within modern socio-economic circumstances?

Daycare is neither an answer to that unasked question about children's needs, nor a new design for family living within which their fulfilment can be assumed. On the contrary, daycare as it is used today and proposed for tomorrow papers

421

over some of the cracks in the old pattern and this defers radical reform. A new design would certainly include some kinds and degrees of daycare to replace, both for children and for parents, some of the companionship, support and social education once offered by siblings, relatives and neighbours, but that does not mean that daycare is the right starting point or the ultimate aspiration.

Daycare frees mothers to earn – and thus lessens their economic dependency on partners and states – but than does not mean that it gives women-who-are-mothers real equality of opportunity in the marketplace either with men or with non-mothering women. Their children, and their feelings for their children, still exist; paying for daycare takes most of their earnings; finding time for loving them limits their availability for advancement and never having enough time for anything puts the mother/worker at the top of the stress table.

Daycare does not give women-who-are-mothers equality at home either, even when they are in a marriage or partnership. Women do almost all the work of household and childcare whether they work outside their homes or not. Women who return to an outside job after a period at home do indeed shoulder a double burden: few can assume that once they are committed to the same outside working hours as their husbands, those men will feel committed to the same hours of work at home as themselves. A recent Italian survey, for example, showed that when mothers added forty hours of paid work to their working week at home, their partners added twelve minutes a week on household and childcare tasks to their working week outside. Those mothers spent 51.5 hours in 'family work' when they had no other job and still spent 31.7 hours if they were also fully employed. The woman who must regularly work a week of seventy-plus hours for forty hours' pay is neither equal to nor equalled by anyone. Recent American analyses suggest that for every extra hour wives work outside the home, husbands work an extra three minutes within it, and that housework directly associated with children's presence at home takes up an extra 5.5 hours a week of women's time and only 1.25 hours of men's Furthermore, while higher-earning couples purchase more help with house-cleaning and catering than couples with lower incomes, it is almost entirely women's earnings which pay for that help. And what *about* their children? While they are babies or young toddlers, even the very best daycare seldom gives them anything they positively need, and being there all day and every day, often deprives them of what they need from mothers. Daycare comes into its own as first choice *for children themselves* only towards the end of the toddler period, when it begins to fulfil developmental needs for extra companionship and education from others.

Agenda item one: what do parents want?

As long as parents are expected to carry the main responsibility for their children's care, childcare planning and practice should be based upon their views and wishes. The current daycare debate does not reflect the way things are in most families and it assumes, rather than asks, how parents would like them to be.

In the Western world as a whole, more children under five (and an even larger majority of children under three) are cared for by mothers (and some fathers) at home than in any form of daycare. Children who are not home-and-parent-based are still usually cared for by relatives. A 1992 survey of 6,000 (mainly middle-class) American parent showed that in 53% of families with a child under five one parent stayed at home, 17% used daycare, 10% had children cared for in a relative's or neighbour's home, 8% had a caregiver in their homes and 12% used a combination of these options. Data from the National Longitudinal Survey showed that only 14% of mothers stayed right out of the labour market until their children reached kindergarten age, but 40% stayed at home throughout the first year and only 15% put children into group care before they were four years old. A 1993 report from Population Trends and Public Policy shows that American fathers now care for 20% of pre-school children during hours when their mothers are at work, compared with grandparents and other relatives, who care for 24%, childminders who care for 23%, and childcare centres and nursery schools, which care for 24%.

While it is clear in most countries that more mothers would go out to work if they had access to acceptable and affordable daycare, it is equally clear that many still would not, especially while their children are infants. In the United States in 1991 58% of women were part of the officially recorded labour force while they had a child below school age (six years). The comparable figure for the United Kingdom (where children start school a year earlier) was around 40%. Daycare is scarce in both countries – notably so in the UK, whose provision compared so badly with most other European nations – and it is widely assumed that this scarcity keeps millions of mothers at home unwillingly. But how many millions and for how long? In other countries substantial numbers of women who do have access both to daycare and to jobs are voluntarily forgoing the financial and other benefits of outside work during their children's first years. The Netherlands, for example, has a lower rate of female unemployment and more daycare than Britain, yet it has fewer 'working mothers'. Denmark has almost universal publicly funded daycare and something approaching genuine equality of opportunity for mothers and fathers in the workplace, but only just over 70% of women are in paid employment before their children reach school age.

Whatever the availability of jobs and daycare, few women have a 'free' choice about going out to work when their children are very young. Choosing to stay at home to care for children always makes people poorer. Many women are too poor to have any real choice: if they can find any work and any way of having their children cared for while they do it, they must. Some, especially in the UK and the US, with their high unemployment levels and low minimum wages, remain poor whatever they choose. So while it is certainly true that more daycare provision would increase the number of mothers in the workplace, it is also true that more financial help with the costs of being a parent would reduce that number, no matter how much affordable daycare was available.

Wherever extensive surveys have been carried out among mothers who are seeking or using daycare in order to go out to work, the results show that many would prefer to remain at home during their children's first years if they could afford to do so. In Britain, for example, a 1990 report by Social Community

Planning Research showed 64% of the exclusively female sample thought that women should be at home with children until they reached school age, while in a 1991 Gallup Poll, two thirds of mothers said that only economic necessity prevented them from being so. In surveys published in 1989 and 1992, almost 80% of American women said that they wished it were possible for them to care full-time at home for their very young children. Of course we cannot assume that every woman who expresses such a sentiment would act upon it if she got the chance. In the politically inconceivable event of being offered financial support for personal childcare, some of those women would doubtless find the provision inadequate, life at home intolerable and the lure of careers and companionship irresistible. But what if a period of home-based, child-centred life was not only affordable but companionable, if deferred or interrupted careers were guaranteed and, perhaps above all, if such arrangements existed not for a special category of women called 'mothers' but for a special category of people called 'parents'? In the UK or North America such a question would probably be dismissed as unanswerably unrealistic, but it is not unrealistic in Scandinavia. In Sweden, parents have a genuine choice between universally available quality daycare and unmatched financial and social support for personal parenting by either sex. About 70% of women and about 30% of men care for babies at home for the first eighteen months. According to a national poll sponsored by the Swedish government in 1987, more than 80% would regard it as ideal to care for those children at home for twice that period, until they reach the age of three.

Clearly, then, the assumption that universally available, acceptable, affordable daycare would fulfil most parents' ideals is premature and may well be unjustified. So where does that assumption come from?

Agenda item two: sources of pressure towards universal daycare

Many mothers, especially in the UK and North America, see only one parenting choice: between staying at home and being broke in a boring backwater, or finding daycare and joining the rich regatta of mainstream work before it leaves them 'out of it' for ever. Of course only those with financial resources that assure them of a home to stay in, and the personal resources to value themselves as people and therefore be confident of their value to their children, will choose to stay at home. And that means that most are going to see leaving their children in daycare as the best option – if only there were enough daycare....

That is the way the people in grey suits with computers for minds want women to choose. Their blinkered bias, conscious and unconscious, fuels the assumption that 'Everybody (or certainly anybody who is ever going to *be* anybody) uses daycare.'

Presentations of official statistics often overstate the overall need for daycare and almost invariably ignore the ages of the children who will receive it. In Canada, for example, a 1987 Labour Force Survey by Statistics Canada stated that 60% of women with children below school age were in the labour force and

40% were not. It was therefore estimated that 60% of Canadian families required daycare centres. Attention to the detailed realities of the survey subjects' lives produced a different picture. Of those 60% of mothers, 6% were currently unemployed – often on maternity leave – and 17% were working part-time, often in the evenings or at weekends, and sharing the care of babies with partners or relations. Of the remaining 37% of 'full-time working mothers', between 5 and 10% were running small businesses or caring for other people's children, at home, while caring for their own. There was therefore a potential demand for daycare places from just over 30% of mothers – half the stated number – and no information on the level of actual demand. A recent American report on fathers' roles in childcare shows that the real picture is at least as complex in the US. Sixty-five per cent of families did not pay for childcare even if both parents were employed, not only because many used unpaid care by relatives but also because many parents worked part-time or worked non-day shifts so as to be home when a partner was at work.

Official forecasts of demand usually assume that the children of any *woman* in the labour force will require formal full-time daycare, completely ignoring all forms of joint parenting, all informal arrangements and the range of work options (such as part-time work and flexi-time) which are preferred by many women wishing to combine working and caring. Furthermore, such forecasts have to be read carefully if questions concerning *women's* participation in the labour force are not to be compounded with questions specifically concerning the participation of women with childcare responsibilities. The European Childcare Network, for example, speaking of the European Community to the year 1995, states that demand for daycare

> ... will increase over time. Even without any additional measure to assist with childcare, labour-force participation rates among women and their share of the labour force are expected to continue to rise.... Demand will also increase because the supply of alternative sources of childcare – particularly relatives and other women caring for children in their own home or in the child's home – will fall as more women enter the labour market.... Demand for publicly funded childcare services will therefore increase even without any attempt to respond to this demand. It will increase still further where the attempt is made....

That statement is not based on the expected increase in the number of mothers participating in the labour force while their children are of particular ages; indeed it is not based on figures that are concerned with *mothers* at all. It is based on the expected increase in the percentage of *all women, aged 15-64*, participating in the labour force by 1995 as compared with 1986. Interestingly, even on that blockbuster basis, the actual predicted increases are surprisingly small: 0.1% in Germany, 1.0% in the UK, 1.6% in Ireland, 1.7% in Spain. The highest predicted percentage increases are around 6% in France, Italy, the Netherlands and Denmark. They will leave a high percentage of women outside the labour force and therefore still theoretically available for childcare at home. Denmark is expected to have 82%

of all women (not only mothers) working by 1995, and France and the UK both expect just over 60%. No other EC country expects much more than 50%. Such forecasts, and the conclusions drawn from them, tend to overestimate the importance of childcare responsibilities in keeping women's participation in the labour force down, and therefore to overestimate the extent to which that participation would be increased by increases in daycare provision. Looking at the 25- to 49-year-old group within which childcare responsibilities are most common, figures for the whole of the European Community in 1991 show that 84% of all single women without children were in the labour force (working or seeking work) but only 67% of married women *without children.*

This difference between being single and married was insignificant in Denmark and the UK but in Spain, Greece, Ireland and Luxembourg it was as much as 30–35%. For all these countries, the fact of being married rather than single reduced women's labour-market activity far more than having children. In fact in Spain, Greece, Belgium, Portugal and France, women with children were *more* likely to work than married women without. Only in the UK and in Germany did having children reduce women's work activity by as much as 10-15%. As the recent report *Employment in Europe* puts it:

> There are various reasons for this difference in labour force participation between single and married women over much of the Community. As well as social and cultural factors, they include the fact that family responsibilities are not confined to bringing up children but extend to caring for a household and carrying out the domestic chores which this entails.

It may also, of course, extend to the care of the old and the sick. The European Childcare Network statement quoted above is no doubt correct in its conclusion that "Such measures [responding to the demand for childcare] will change attitudes and expectations, making employment more acceptable and attractive, and encouraging women with children to enter or remain the labour market". But the difference such measures might make are easily overestimated.

Western media, fed both by those who make and by those who must live with policy, play a substantial part in convincing people that 'everybody goes out to work', and that whatever the ages of her children, and his, everybody should do so. Media have glamorised the career woman who is also a loving mother, and the Supermum who can do everything at the same time. They do not ask who is holding the baby while these admirable females outsmart males in the boardroom. A baby is a big plus to the image of a North American TV commentator but not if she stays off the screen to take care of him or her. Indeed, women's magazines and columns have survived their sexist identity by cleaning babies off their pages altogether except as professional extras or fashion props. Almost all the public role models available to girls and women are now seemingly (though not always actually) childless career models. Parenting, the perpetual and prime concern of millions of adults, becomes interesting only if it is in some way unusual – a gay adoption, perhaps, or a woman who turns the tables by leaving a lone father holding the baby.

Media makes myths and are then just as likely as the rest of us to believe them. There is selection and slant (unconscious as well as sometimes deliberate) to even the most 'factual' reporting of daycare issues. Reports concerning the numbers of mothers working outside their homes, for example, almost invariably draw attention to the vast numbers who do, rather than the (often similar) numbers who do not. Recent New York headlines, typical of many, read "52 per cent of mothers now in the workplace", and the story began, "Homemaking is on the way out. More than half of all American mothers are back at work....". Equally accurate would have been a headline reading "48 per cent of mothers still home-based" and a story that began, "Almost half of all American mothers but many fewer fathers...". Britain's *Guardian* newspaper, in a serious article in its education supplement, recently published comparative statistics of female disadvantage in various European countries. Tables contrasted the numbers of men and women in government and in management under factual headings – "There are no women Cabinet members in John Major's government" and "Men dominate the higher levels of management in all countries". But the table contrasting the numbers of male and female parents of children under four in the workforce was uniquely and unstatedly speculative: "Lack of childcare facilities prevents women, as opposed to men, from pursuing their careers".

When media report, even editorialise, on the effects of daycare on children, they usually pick on positive studies and select their most positive results. Jerome Kagan, author of an important American study of daycare, took pains to explain that his experimental daycare facility was as good as unlimited funding, professional expertise, highly trained staff and (middle-class) parental involvement could possibly make it and that *under those circumstances* the daycare children did as well (*on specific measures*) as the matched group of home-reared children. None of his provisos was widely reported at the time or has been since. The study was interpreted as an authoritative pro-daycare statement and remains a classic for its protagonists. There are equally authoritative, sometimes more subtle and recent, studies that raise serious concerns about the effects of daycare on very young children; none has received comparable coverage. The most recent studies convincingly suggest that neither a pro-daycare nor an anti-daycare stance is tenable because the effects of daycare on children depend on the caring institution and its personnel and on the age, family experiences and characteristics of individual children being cared for. There are many complex questions still to be asked and many subtle answers to be interpreted and tested. Nevertheless, the accepted and acceptable message is that good daycare is OK for kids and more good daycare is better for everybody.

It is easy to see why governments and their institutions are eager to believe that message. They want the best for children; or say they do. But children are nations' 'most precious resource' in more than the obvious sense: their individual care is very expensive. Daycare can offer economies of scale on the one hand and jobs on the other. Naturally parents who are seeking more and more daycare for younger and younger infants are looking for economic improvement in their own lives, but not many would do so if they believed that they earned money at their children's expense. What sad and subtle subtext tells them that money earned away and spent on their children is more important than time at home spent with their children?

People in Western societies still grow up believing that they will and should be important to their children, but not that the importance is manifest in their reliable presence and constant influence. Of course nobody can say, 'At such and such an age your child needs you to be around this many hours a day and any fewer will be disastrous for him or her', but it would be fair to say, 'The more you are around, the better, and the younger the child, the more it matters.' Yet very few people say that. In North America, especially, there is increasing pressure on parents not just to work while children are very young but to work from a few weeks after they are born; and not just to work a few hours but to work as if they were childless, including the commute, the after-work drinks and the all-expenses-paid travel. The snappy American term 'quality time' tells parents that they can pack all the desirable interaction with their children into a single hour of each working day provided it is a *good* hour. There is just enough truth in the idea to convince those seeking reassurance abut what they feel they have to do anyway: of course an hour is better than no time at all and if time is scarce of course it is better not wasted on chores. But still, the concept of 'quality time' is absurd. The younger the child, the more impossible it is to schedule togetherness times. You cannot make a tired baby stay awake for a day's worth of cuddling, and trying may be a selfish attempt to salve adult consciences and conflicts at the expense of overstimulated infants. Yu cannot easily persuade a one-year-old who wanted you to play with him this morning to take his one and only chance and play right now; if he is angry at your desertion he will not let you off the hook that easily. And if you are not there when your toddler's first rhyme is spoken, you will not hear it or see her face as she hears what she has made. Magic moments happen when they happen and the painful truth is that the ones that are missed are gone for ever.

People are expected to feel strongly about their children, but not to act upon those feelings. Everybody sympathises with the pain mothers suffer (only mothers; fathers are seldom mentioned) when they leave their babies to return to work, but there is little sympathy for those who avoid that pain by staying close. Indeed the fact that babies do not have to have their mothers' exclusive care twenty-four hours a day, seven days a week, is increasingly taken to mean that they *should not* have it. There is another snappy term – 'smother love' – for that, and it is just as nonsensical as the first one. It is clearly and certainly best for babies to have something close to full-time mother care for six months at least – conveniently linked with breast-feeding – and family care for a further year and better two. Using financial or career penalties to blackmail women into leaving infants who are scarcely settled into life outside wombs that are still bleeding is no less than barbarous.

People are expected to do their best for their children but not to assume that they know best, or are best. The widespread Western cult of the professional teaches that 'expert' advisers and 'trained caregivers' often know better than parents because parents 'are too involved to be objective'. The last quality children require of parents is objectivity: it is parents' unique tendency to consider their children uniquely wonderful that makes them so special. Professionals can be helpful to parents but they cannot replace them because, however much they know about children in general, they know almost nothing about this particular child. Benjamin Spock opened his famous childcare manual of the forties with the message to parents: "You know more than you think you know". Almost half a century later that message urgently needs elaborating: 'You know more than you think you know *and a great deal more than anyone else*'.

Agenda item three: what kind of daycare?

Most of the parents who must leave their infants with outsiders and most of the governments who encourage them to do so favour professional childcare over the arrangements with private individuals which currently provide most daycare places, especially for babies and toddlers. In recent years many countries have controlled 'other family care' through various forms of regulation and licensing, and there is no doubt that excellent work is being done by some British childminders, North American daycare mothers and variously named European equivalents. But even the best of this type of care is not generally regarded as desirable or satisfactory. Spokespeople – grey-suited or not – generally explain this by referring to scandals about babies being kept confined in cots or tied in chairs, dirty, ill-fed and unattended; about toddlers and older children being crowded into inadequate rooms without toys or supervision; and about physical or sexual abuse. They admit that there have been similar scandals in daycare centres and nurseries, but point out that licensing and inspection are more effective in those contexts. They say that licensing of individual carers cannot easily prevent these horrors because the demand for places outstrips the supply. Thus unlicensed caretakers (who often undercut the cost of licensed places) stay in business, in the US, for example, catering to at least three times as many children as regulated caregivers, according to 1991 estimates. Unlicensed caregivers can provide excellent care, of course, just as licensed individuals, and inspected centres, can provide poor care despite meeting minimum physical standards. But if other family care is wanted the problems of inspecting and supervising it are not insuperable, and the better they are met, the less likelihood there is that a black market in unlicensed care will operate. In the UK, for example, a carer, rather unfortunately known as a 'childminder', has a great deal to gain from registration. She will have opportunities for training and encouragement to specialise, if she wishes, in the care of children with a variety of special needs. Families seeking childcare may be referred to her by health and welfare workers in the neighbourhood. She will receive advice and assistance with matters such as insurance and, in many areas, there will also be various back-up and social facilities available to her, ranging from a toy library, through a play centre for all local carers and children, to emergency back-up in case she, or one of the children, is taken ill. If 'other family care' is wanted, its problems are not insoluble. The truth is that institutional

429

daycare offers advantages to adults that have nothing to do with infants' safety or happiness.

Policy makers assume that there are major economic advantages to institutional care, especially the economy of scale achieved by having one worker looking after, say, five infants or ten pre-school children, instead of an individual caregiver who typically looks after only one or two in addition to her own. Furthermore, nursery workers are fully integrated in the labour market, where individual carers are often peripheral to it. The individual who takes a child into her home frees his or her parent for employment but she is often not fully 'employed' herself in the sense that she is not 'trained', would not take any other kind of job (wishing to remain at home for her own children) and is paid minimal – sometimes undeclared – wages for her childcare services.

These arguments are specious if they are not actually dishonest. The more economy of scale a daycare institution offers, the worse that care will be for the children. Although imaginative organisation can make the best of limited resources, a high ratio of adults to children is crucial to quality of care and the younger the children are, the higher that ratio needs to be. The ideal ratio is certainly one adult to one *baby* or six adults to six. Caregivers, like parents, may be able to meet the needs of a baby and of older children at the same time, but where age groups are closely segregated, even the highest ratio recommended in any country for this age group – one adult to three babies – is too low. Good care does not only depend on how many infants each adult must care for, though. It also depends on the qualities of the adults. High(er) pay is crucial to that, of course. But childcare is so labour-intensive that any increase in salaries has a marked effect on total costs – and rapidly reverses economies of scale. Daycare centres are always expensive to run and the better they are, the more they cost. An expert estimate from the US said that they *ought* to cost $150 per child per week in 1988. At that time parents who were paying for daycare were paying an average of around $55 per week. Perhaps childcare institutions appear economic to policy makers because, unlike state benefits to unemployed mothers, any public funding can be recouped from parents and/or their employers, and because many centres, especially in North America and increasingly in the UK, are commercial, profitable concerns. For-profit nurseries increased by more than 60% in London between 1985 and 1988.

For parents, daycare centres have both practical and emotional advantages over 'other family care'. Children are a centre's business, so parents assume that their child will be basically well cared for by people who know about safety and hygiene, nutrition and health, education and play. Because a centre is a business, it can be more reliable than any individual: always open for its stated hours and days, never down with the flu or pregnant, and unlikely to decide that it cannot keep even the most terrible two. And centres place few personal demands on parents who are already overstretched between home and work. Where a daycare mother has to be made into a friend and kept feeling needed and appreciated, a centre asks little more of parents than their money, reasonable punctuality and a few civil words twice a day.

That relative impersonality may be more important to some parents than they themselves realise. Most parents are ambivalent about leaving children with outsiders. When mothers delegate the care of babies or toddlers, they often feel an uncomfortable mixture of guilt, because there is not enough love between caregiver and infant, and jealousy, because there is too much. Such a mother may find it far more comfortable to leave her child with someone whom she can see as a trained professional in an institutional setting (and therefore quite different from herself at home) than to leave him with someone who is just like herself – except that she is willing to care for the child all day.

Most important of all, though, to policy makers and parents alike, may be the perception of institutional daycare as 'educational' and therefore positively advantageous to children. The popular image of group daycare is a nursery-school image. Whenever daycare issues are publicly debated, television screens are filled with pictures of three- and four-year-olds happily playing together in an enchanting child-scale world of bright rooms, tiny furniture and brilliantly coloured 'educational toys'. These are the images that inform campaigns for more daycare places. This is what people want their children to have.

Parents are right to want their *children* to have that kind of experience, but they are not right to assume that the experience is, or can be, equally valuable for babies. By the time children are around three years old, most of them enjoy and almost all of them benefit from being part of a close-knit group of children; from close contact with non-family adults and trained teachers, and from a wider and more carefully planned range of opportunities, activities and equipment than most private homes can provide. Every child should have the opportunity for pre-school educational experience. Its provision in settings variously termed nursery schools, pre-kindergartens, playgroups, playschools or *écoles maternelles* should indeed be a real priority. Much of Western Europe has made it a priority, but in the UK 'pre-school education' is still one of the many broken promises of the Thatcher years, while in America, less-privileged children, especially the under-fours, are still waiting for the chance of a Head Start.

Babies and toddlers are not waiting for groups to join, though. What is good for most children of three years is not necessarily appropriate for children of thirty months and may be downright harmful to any child of thirteen, let alone three, months. The educational tradition that legitimises pre-school centres has no relevance to infants, and their corporate nature – so desirable to policy makers and reassuring to parents – is developmentally inappropriate for them.

Agenda item four: what infants need

Older babies and toddlers do not need their mothers every minute; the necessity for 'full-time exclusive mothering' has been exposed as a myth of the post-war West. We know that giving their care shared between parents and other adults is not damaging to children and may be enriching; that shared care – albeit of many different kinds – has been the norm in every time and place and remains so in many. And we know that lack of people with whom to share childcare is a major problem in Western maternity. Daycare *is* shared care, so why is it not ideal?

The answer comes from a lot of other things we know about children: things that are being conveniently forgotten in the daycare debate. Perhaps the most important is that infants are *not* children and nor are toddlers – quite. The spiralling strands of development that transform helpless newborns into sociable and socialised small people are plaited into their relationships with known, loved and loving adults. Those adults do not have to be parents or relations but, unfashionable and unpalatable though the fact may be, it is much easier if they are. Mothers start out with an irreplaceable bio-emotional advantage in relating to their infants and fathers start out with a lesser one that still puts them ahead of any outsider. That does not make every natural mother or father a 'good parent' nor handicap every infant raised otherwise, but it does stack the odds and should inform the debate. Whoever it is who cares for infants, they need to have permanence, continuity, passion and a parent-like commitment that is difficult to find or meet outside the vested interests and social expectations of family roles and cannot be adequately replaced by professionalism.

Why continuous individual care matters to babies

If a new baby wants to suck, she will suck your finger or her own, whichever is handiest. She does not know that she is separate from other people; she recognises no boundaries between self and other.

The long, slow realisation of her separate self starts early. As well as using other people as extensions of herself, the baby uses them as mirrors that reflect her own behaviour back to her. In her first weeks, for instance, she smiles and frowns more or less at random, but within a couple of months, she smiles only when she is pleased and sociable and frowns only when she is not. It is the consistently pleased or concerned responses of adults that have taught her which is which.

Responsive and overtly affectionate adults are crucial to all aspects of infants' development. Every time a baby's very existence is celebrated in another spontaneous hug; every time her sounds, expressions and body language are noticed and answered; every time somebody does something just because she seems to want or enjoy it, a tiny piece is added to the foundations of that baby's future self-esteem, self-confidence and social competence. The more of that sensitive, tuned-in experience a baby gets (and the less of its opposite), the better. We cannot measure out 'enough' but we know the likely consequences of strict rationing. After the Second World War, thousands of orphaned and refugee babies were kept in institutions where their care was physically excellent but wholly impersonal. Many of those babies failed to thrive; some died for reasons nobody could quite understand. The researchers of the day eventually concluded that those babies were suffering from 'maternal deprivation', but while being with their mothers would certainly have saved them, it was not separation from their particular blood-mothers that removed their will to live but deprivation of individualised, responsive, sociable care. Western countries learned to avoid residential nurseries when they could, and organise those they had to have differently. But the same syndrome became apparent in 1990 when Romania's packed orphanages were revealed to the world. Impersonal residential care is only the greatest, not the only, risky situation. Any personal indifference is damaging to infants, even that of a potentially loving mother who becomes so submerged in postnatal depression that it is all she can do to keep her baby fed and warm and clean and more that she can do to offer herself to him, respond to him, glory in him. An outside caregiver has less reason that a mother to celebrate an infant and therefore needs less cause to be indifferent to him. A nursery worker has less reason still to celebrate this infant because she has others to care for who may overload her or whom she may prefer. How well an infant thrives despite any of those situations probably depends on how much time he also spends with someone who cares not just *for* but *about* him. Three hours a day in an understaffed nursery where he is special to nobody is far from ideal for a newborn, but nine hours a day is far more likely to damage his development.

By around three months or so, infants realise that they are separate from the mothers and others on whom they are totally dependent, and then only sensitive and consistent responses can protect them from the lonely fear of being abandoned and from anxiety about their needs being met. If circumstances allow her to do so, a baby will now learn to recognise and distinguish all the people who regularly come and go within her small space; learn what responses to expect from each person and, gradually, learn how to evoke the responses she wants. A baby who expects particular people to respond to her particular signals in their particular ways is confused and distressed when they do not. If a mother who has been smiling and chatting to her three-month-old baby suddenly becomes impassive and silent, the infant will quiet, sober, stare and probably cry. It is not that the adult's silent, serious face is frightening in itself (it certainly would not bother the baby is she was studying her mother who was watching TV, for instance). What upsets that baby is her unexpected failure to manage and control the interaction and evoke a response. She reacts as we react if somebody cuts us in the street: as if the mother had snubbed her, hurting her feelings.

Many people dislike the notion of babies 'managing' adults; it makes them sound manipulative and raises peculiarly Western fears that they will become spoiled. But it is only by being allowed, even helped, to find reliable ways of controlling some aspects of adult behaviour that a baby can build vital competence and confidence in her own powers of communication. Whether they are six or sixteen months old, most babies try to keep a beloved adult with them all the time and, while they are awake, many are successful. Once they fall asleep, though, they cannot prevent adults from leaving; like it or not, they usually wake up alone. If a baby is to accept that calmly – neither fighting to stay awake so as to prevent it, nor panicking when she awakens – she needs to know, from repeated experience, that she can get a parent or accepted substitute (not someone unexpected or strange) back again with a cry or call. All babies are physically helpless, but the babies who *feel* damagingly helpless in the longer term are the ones who cannot trust their special adults to be there and to respond to them.

In the first half-year or so babies are seldom alarmed by strangers (though they may be alarmed by what strangers do). Introduced to an admiring male visitor, for example, a baby will usually try to interact with him as she does with her father. If she does not get the responses she expects she may be puzzled, or obviously turned off, but as soon as she is handed back to familiar arms she will switch on again, and after a while she may willingly give the new person another try. That familiar interlude is vital. She can cope with a stranger for a while, but not with an unbroken succession of strangers. Each presents her with subtly different intonations, expressions and body language and, without reconfirmation from someone she knows well, she gradually loses track of who she is. Handed from one stranger to another, a baby may even panic as an adult can panic in a fairground hall of mirrors, seeing a different distortion of himself wherever he turns. When a baby in his third hour in a conference crèche or third day in a daycare centre, suddenly cries and cannot be comforted, he is usually assumed to be crying for loss of his mother; in truth he is more likely to be crying for loss of his own identity and control, vested in his mother and not yet assured by a sufficiently known nursery worker.

Only adults who know, have known and will go on knowing an individual baby can provide that vital sense of trust and growing empowerment. Even the best-intentioned and qualified stranger cannot do it, because however much she knows about babies in general, she knows nothing about *this* one. The baby eats lunch; the caregiver goes to put her down for a nap but she cries. Training or experience suggests questions but not answers: is she crying because she is tried and this is her idiosyncratic way through to the relaxation of sleep? Is she crying because she is not tired and therefore does not, today, want to nap? Or is she crying because some minute difference between the stranger and her accustomed caretaker – her smell, her tone, her arrangement of cuddly toys – has broken the usual progression from full belly to slumber? It does not hurt a baby to have to get to know someone new, especially if someone familiar can stay around while she does it. By tomorrow the stranger will seem less strange, if she is still there in a week or two she will be a known friend. But what if someone else is there tomorrow and someone else next week?

Even beloved adults cannot always understand a baby's messages. When they do understand them, they do not always choose to do or give what the baby wants. That's fine. Babies have to learn to communicate more and more clearly (and eventually to speak) and of course they cannot always have what they want. But adults who are tied to infants in reciprocal affection will always *try* to understand and they will always answer, even if the answer is 'no'. That is what matters; that is what assures infants that they are real, individual people who can act upon other people, and that is the assurance that will keep them going forward. However carefully she is fed, washed and protected, and however many mobiles are hung for her, a baby's overall care is not good enough to ensure her optimal development unless she is constantly with people who know her as an individual and who always have the time (and usually the inclination) to listen to and answer her; to cuddle and play, show and share. Those are the people she will attach herself to and that attachment matters.

Every baby needs at least one special person to attach herself to. It is through that first love relationship that she will learn about herself, other people and the world; experience emotions and learn to cope with them; move through egocentric baby love into trust, and eventually towards empathy and then the altruism that will one day enable her to give another person what she needs for herself now. At least one person. More is better, safer. Babies do not have a fixed quota of devotion: if there are several adults around and available to an infant, she will usually select one for her primary, passionate attachment (and, even today, that will probably be her mother), but each and all of them will be special to her and any one can serve as a life-raft when the mother's absence would otherwise leave her downing in a sea of deserted despair. Every baby will sometimes need a human life-raft. The grieving of a baby who loses her one and only special person – her lone mother who dies, for example, or the lifelong foster mother from whom she is removed – is agonising to see because we know we are looking at genuine tragedy. But the pain of the separations we arrange and connive at every time we change caregivers or leave a baby in the daycare centre that has new staff – again – or with an agency babysitter she has never seen, may not be as different as we assume. In her first six, nine or even twelve months, that baby has no way of knowing that the parent who leaves her will come back; no way of measuring the passage of time; no way of holding the parent's image in her mind so as to anticipate her or his return. Only another known and beloved adult can keep her happily afloat.

Why nurseries and daycare centres seldom meet those infant needs

That vital continuous one-to-one attention can rarely be achieved in group care, however excellent the facility may be. Babies in their first year need one primary adult each, and while that may be inconvenient, it is not very surprising. Human beings do no give birth to litters but almost always to single babies. Women can only just feed two at a time (ask any mother of twins) and cannot single-handedly care for more (ask any mother of triplets). No amount of 'training' enables a nursery worker to do better. If one baby is sucking a bottle on her lap when another wakes from a nap and a third drops a toy from his highchair, she cannot respond adequately to them all. If one is unwell and one is tired, she cannot cuddle them both in a way that makes them feel she cares, let alone keep the third busy and safe. And that is three. How many daycare centres really offer a 1:3 adult–child ratio? A recent survey of eighteen British nurseries produced an average ratio of 1:4.6, while data from the comparative licensing study of American states showed that *recommended* ratios for infants ranged from 1:3 in three states to 1:8 in four states. And as all researchers acknowledge, even these figures may overestimate the adult attention available to each baby; as, for example, when two adults have charge of six infants, one will often stay with them while the other cleans up.

In most countries, the majority of daycare centres for infants are not excellent. How could they be? The work is underpaid and undervalued, as well as demanding, so it neither attracts nor keeps high-quality staff. As a recent report to the European Commission put it: "Childcare workers ... are among the lowest paid of women workers.... The conditions of work are also often very poor.... Often the pressure of work is such that workers are too exhausted to even think about their work, let alone improve it".

Although both parents and policy makers assume that centre care is professional care, this is seldom true for children under three. In this one respect, the UK fares better than much of the European Community, because it has a well-established diploma-level Nursery Nurses' qualification. In those eighteen British nurseries, only 20% of the staff lacked any formal training. In most EC countries, however, it is rare for those who work in daycare centres with this age group to have childcare qualifications of any kind, and in many countries even the basic educational requirements for entry to the work are minimal. In the US, where federal standards have been abolished and each state makes its own childcare regulations, the current situation is best summed up by the researchers who studied comparative licensing: " ... the possibility of having a 'qualified staff' is virtually non-existent.... In a majority of states, the existing regulations allow these very young children to be cared for by a staff that would have a mean age of 18, has not graduated from high school, and has no previous group daycare experience...".

Higher salaries are desperately needed, and might help to attract higher-calibre staff (although they would also raise the costs of care), but a real improvement in standards would also require training, better working conditions and career opportunities. Unfortunately, every such concession to adult needs further reduces fulfilment of the children's. The daycare centre's working day, for example, has to be longer than a full office day to allow for parental commuting. Centre staff's working hours can be reduced by splitting the day into two shifts, but that immediately doubles the number of people with whom infants must interact. As soon as nursery workers are also given proper lunch-hours and breaks, sick leave, holiday entitlement, in-service training, educational leave and encouragement to relocate for promotion, there is such constant staff movement that babies are likely to be handled by several different people each day and are unlikely to be handled by those same people all week: some will inevitably be strangers to some of the children, filling in for the known caregivers who are already filling in for parents. And still nursery workers leave. In North America the annual turnover of childcare staff is around 42%, and aides come and go even more frequently. It is not uncommon for a group of children to have three 'mother figures' in a year. If each baby is not fully attached to each successive caregiver, she will spend many days in limbo; if she is fully attached, she will spend many days in grief.

When infants become toddlers

When somebody of eighteen months in jeans and trainers struts across the room yelling 'No, go 'way!' the unwary onlooker may easily mistake him for a child – and one who is ready to leave his mum. But the autonomy of the toddler is as much an illusion as his toughness. Both are to be fostered but neither can be relied upon. Treated as a clinging baby, he fights, but treated as the sturdy child he sometimes seems to be, he instantly becomes – a clinging baby. The drive to grow up – to become an autonomous child – constantly conflicts with the need for the safe dependence of infancy.

This is the stage in children's lives when adults rightly begin to demand new, socialised behaviour, from using a pot instead of a nappy, to *saying* no instead of grabbing and hitting. Those demands are appropriate (if gently made) because they are within the toddler's developmental repertoire and important to his eventual acceptance in a wider and less tolerant world than family, but they offer him no obvious reward. His socialisation depends on that conflict-laden desire to grow up, and the only way to foster it is to resist pushing him forward but to let him lead the way and fall back when he frightens himself. 'Me do it! Go 'way!' he yells, faced with his coat. But he does not mean 'Don't help me and don't stay with me'; he means something like 'Give me space (about 18 inches) and time (about thirty seconds) to have a try and then help me so that I can feel successful instead of being overwhelmed by frustration and fury'.

Toddlers live on an emotional seesaw between babyhood and childhood, tears and tantrums. They need their special adults to stand on the centre and balance it; to let them try but still be willing to help; to let them express their sharp new feelings but to control their actions when they cannot control themselves; to let them disagree without finding them disagreeable. Out of all that comes yet another kind of trust. The toddler's trust that his special adults will not only control him when he feels like a murderous monster but will go on accepting and loving him when he behaves like one. If unconditional love is important to the biddable baby who means no harm, it is vital to the bolshy toddler who must pit himself against parents to see whether the limits of their patience with what he *does* also mark limits to their acceptance of what he *is*. Only when he is certain that there are no limits to that will he be sure that it is safe to be himself: to become a genuinely autonomous (if still very small and inexperienced) person.

The toddler will not be ready for a classroom (or even a 'toddler room') until he has crossed that bridge of trust into early childhood. Parents and the other people who are special to him are the pilings of that bridge and it will not hold steady beneath him if they keep being pulled up and replaced. Unfortunately, even parents who have given or arranged for individual one-to-one care during infancy are often overwhelmed by the pressures towards group care in the second year. Sometimes a substitute caregiver who loved a baby is unwilling or unable to cope with what she sadly labels a 'terrible two'. Sometimes some of that terribleness looks like boredom and the educational value of the group that would stop him being bored becomes more credible and more tempting. If 'school' is going to be good for him when he is three, won't sending him at two be a head start (as well as a convenience)?

The fact that a toddler is bored with a caregiver (whether or not she or he is his mother or father) does not mean that he is bored of being adult-centred but only that he is ready for new activities. He finds other children fascinating and will enjoy spending time playing near and alongside them, but that does not mean that he is ready to make real friends and be their classmate. His toddler activities mimic those of pre-school children: he, too, wants to paint and climb and sing and cook, but, unlike those three-year-olds, his enjoyment and his learning depend on adult participation or at least adult support and commentary. And, far from being even a partial replacement for that individual adult attention, a group of other toddlers – each as needful of the adult as himself – introduces competition and social stresses he is not yet capable of dealing with. Of course he will have to learn to deal with them: learn to share toys, to take turns, to argue his case with words rather than blows and to give way gracefully, but he cannot do so without the trusted control of his own particular adult until he is capable of putting himself in another child's shoes so as to 'do unto others as he would they should do unto him'. For most children, that is a third-year development. In the meantime, and especially as the numbers of only children and of isolated caregivers increase, there is a real need for places where they can go together to meet and play with others as they can in the UK's extensive (although scattered) network of adult-and-toddler groups and one-o-clock clubs.

Everyone who lives or works with toddlers knows that they are not well adapted to group life. Nevertheless, many people believe that joining a group before he is developmentally ready can accelerate a toddler's readiness: that the experience and the teachers will help him grow up and, above all, help his speech, his independence and his sociability. Research suggests otherwise. A major British study, for example, showed that under-threes talks and are talked to far less in a group than in domestic situations, even where the pre-school teacher was well trained and the mother or caregiver at home was not especially child-centred or communicative. As for learning to be sociable, outgoing and independent, Gamble and Zigler's 1988 paper on the effects of daycare summarises many studies to suggest that early daycare may foster those 'virtues' to excess: "From the research carried out to date, a tentative consensus emerges that … children who have experienced early group care tend towards assertiveness, aggression, and peer rather than adult orientation". A 1990 study from the Institute of Human Development at the University of California even suggests that, beloved though they are of North American adults, those virtues may not be virtues at all in small children. Looking back over the lives of mature adults who had been studied from infancy, the researchers found that "Men who were rated as independent in childhood emerge in adulthood with a quite distinctive catalog of impressive attributes … calm, warm, giving, sympathetic, insightful, undefensive, incisive, consistent across roles, comfortable with ambiguity and uncertainty, and socially poised".

It really does seem that the appropriate use of professionally staffed daycare centres is for children who are well into their third year or more, able to cope with the inevitable discontinuities of care and to benefit from the group life and the educational tradition that are premature for younger age groups.

So who *is* to care for infants and young toddlers when family members are not available?

Agenda item five: buying individual care

There is nothing new about paying women to look after children, but there is something new about using money as the sole motivation for the task. Generations of privileged Western children have been reared wholly or partly by housekeepers and nannies, at home and all over empires. But being a traditional nanny was something closer to a way of life than to a job as we know it, and the tradition depended on an ample supply of women for whom a lifetime spent suspended somewhere between the drawing room and the servant's hall (or the native or slave quarters) was preferable to the available alternatives. A children's mammy in the southern states of America or their ayah in India had contact with, and protection from, the ruling race, and often some advancement of their own offspring too. In Britain, the First World War killed so many men that thousands of women were left with no prospect of marriage and homes of their own, at a time when it was scarcely possible for females to earn and live independently. Becoming nannies – or governesses if they had some education – was a dignified alternative to domestic service. Such women valued their autonomy in the nursery domain and the household's protection and reflected status. Wages were scarcely relevant.

Employing a nanny (or any in-home caregiver) no longer implies great wealth and in countries where wages are low and unemployment rates high, their numbers are booming. It is estimated that there are more than 100,000 trained nannies employed in the UK alone, and according to Fallows, 6% of American under-fives were already cared for in this way in 1985. Many more children in both countries are cared for by 'au pairs'. So is an individual caregiver who comes to, or lives in, the child's own home the answer for women who want to work outside it? It may well answer the childcare needs of fortunate individuals but it cannot answer society's because the system cannot be comfortably translocated into the supposedly equalitarian marketplaces of modern Western life.

Paid one-to-one care by someone brought in from outside the family offers no economies of scale: the mother simply replaces herself with somebody else. If the household is to make anything out of the arrangement, she must pay the nanny less than she herself can earn, after taxes, outside the home. But who is going to want to fill, as a job, the role with someone else's child that the mother does not wish to fill on her own? The answer, of course, is only someone of lower earning potential than the mother and that almost always means someone lower down each society's own educational and status ladder. Whether that matters to the child or not, it does not suggest a high valuation for children as a group, or high respect for the job of caring for them. Perhaps we have not moved as far as we like to think from those old colonialist traditions.

The system does not only affect the employer's children either. Many caregivers have children of their own. What kind of care are those children getting while their mothers care for the children of other people who are doing something different? A pregnant Californian mother of a one-year-old explained to me how the system works with Mexican nannies and added: "I nearly fired her when she got pregnant soon after me, but she's got a sister with five kids and when she's too big to work, she'll take care of them and the sister will come work for me. Then when she's had her baby, she'll leave it with her sister and come back. Bring the baby with her and care for them both together? No way. I'm not paying her to look after her own child, I'm paying her to look after mine". There were eight children, three mothers and one father involved in those arrangements. Was *any* of the children going to have as good a childhood – let alone a better one – than he or she would have had if society had taken it for granted that parents care for their own?

Attempts have been made to dignify the role of paid caregiver by making childcare into a professional, specialised job and, above all, by separating it from domestic responsibilities. A trained British nanny will not expect to undertake anything but childcare and will not expect to work all day and then get up for night feeds and nightmares. So, at the end of the working day the employer finds herself doing household chores that would have been done while the baby napped if she had been in charge, cooking a meal for the nanny who is now off duty, and facing yet another broken night. The truth is that no single salary can pay an individual to do everything mothers are expected to do for love, and no single salary ever has. Traditional nannies had nurserymaids of their own.

So what about the less professional, less specialised 'mother's helper'? She certainly commands less money and accepts more chores; she may even accept a job description that says she will do anything the mother would otherwise do. But why should she want to? Surely she will find being at home with the baby just as lonely and boring as the mother would? There is a difference between them – she gets paid a small wage where the mothers gets paid nothing – but does that really counterbalance the other difference: that it is neither her home nor her baby? Mothers do what they do because, overall, they like it, or like some parts of it enough to put up with the rest. If they do not, nobody else is likely to, and money alone is not going to make them do it well and go on doing it.

Out of all the kinds of purchased daycare that are currently available, the kind that is most likely to meet the needs of infants, as opposed to pre-school children, is not institutional group care, not pseudo-professional care by nannies and their like, but the best of the licensed 'other family care' that parents and policy makers tend to regard as second best.

Women who take children into their own homes on a daily care basis – daycare mothers in North America, childminders in Britain – mostly look after other people's so as to be able to go on looking after their own. They tend, therefore, to be people who recognise the value of their parenting to their own children – which is why they do not want to ration or withdraw it in a hurry – and who are confident that the parenting skills learned on those children can be valuable to others. Such women often see the 'mothering' of one or two other children at a time as the continued exercise of skills they are proud of, within a life-style they enjoy, or at least prefer to other currently available options.

It is often easier for parents to make, and keep, a comfortable relationship with a caregiver in her home than in their own because the caregiver functions more like a member of the extended family than like their employee. The relationship is an equal partnership focused on what really matters – the child's well-being and happiness – rather than diffused over other concerns that can seem to matter (like whether she runs up the telephone bill or uses the best coffee). The baby joins an ongoing household where his new caregiver is clearly in charge and has her own routine into which he is welcomed. It may take him a little longer to settle with her than with a babysitter or nanny who comes into his own familiar home, but once he has done so, her busy household may feel less lonely and strange than his own does without parents. Her household responsibilities can be an advantage too. Any nine-month-old would rather go shopping and then play while watching someone cook than be with someone who has nothing to do but watch him – or the soaps. And her own, older children may enrich his life as brothers and sisters might. Unlike the other infants in a daycare centre, they are not at his age stage and therefore direct competitors for her attention; rather they are objects of fascination and admiration whose comings and goings keep his days varied and interesting.

Such arrangements do no always work out well, of course, but where they do, the similarities with extended-family care are inescapable. Although daycare mothers are paid for their services – and should be paid more – their motivation is only partly commercial and their involvement with individual children and their families is a large part of their reward. Some come to function as extended family not just for children but for their parents, especially for those who are alone. Sometimes the relationship outlives infancy and toddlerhood. Some childminders take children to playgroups, just as their mothers might, and to nursery schools when they are ready for pre-school education. When geography allows, it is even sometimes that original infant caregiver who provides the six- or seven-year-old with after-school care.

Although this is an idealised picture of other family care as it is in many countries, experience in the UK suggests that it need not be unrealistic. Offered training and community back-up, along with registration, some British childminders can, and do, offer daycare that is quality care for infants.

Agenda item six: own-family care

The more closely the search for alternatives to own-family care for infants is studied, the more absurd it seems because the kind of daycare that works best is the kind that most closely approximates to it.

Babies and toddlers need individual care, consistently given by the same known and loving adults.

The needs of the youngest among them can be fully met only if much of that care is given by their mothers. Most daycare protagonists gloss overt babies' need to be breast-fed and to establish the primary attachments on which later development depends, but I am aware of none who denies it. Regular all-day separation in the first six months means that the baby cannot be fully breast-fed; furthermore, it means that the nurseling relationship between baby and mother (which can, of course, be maintained if she uses bottles rather than her breasts) is diluted. The baby will be fine if he has a single, continuously available, long-term alternative person to attach himself to (his father, perhaps, or the rare kind of in-home caregiver who really is psychologically part of his family). The mother will be fine if she feels no sense of long-term loss. But those are large ifs.

As the first months pass, infants' care can gradually be more and more extensively shared with other consistent, individual caregivers, but there is not yet any positive advantage to the infant in it being so, and if the only 'sharing' available to the mother means substituting an outsider's care for her own, there may well be disadvantages. However taxing an infant's care may be for his or her own family, few other caregivers are ever going to do it as well as most parents because nobody will ever do as much for money alone as they will do for that atavistic mystery we call parental love. So why are Western societies so sure that the future lies with daycare rather than with parent care?

If the search for alternatives to parental care is absurd, so is the popular belief that there must *be* widely available alternatives because parents cannot and do not want to care for their own infants. It is true that many two-parent families cannot manage on one income and that lone parents cannot manage on none. It is true that many women, still underprivileged in the workforce, do not want to leave it to be part of a specially underprivileged subgroup called stay-at-home mothers, and that few men even consider it. And it is true that it is difficult for parents to put children first if doing so ensure that they themselves come last. What is not true is that those are the inevitable results of making one or two children the major commitment of two or three years of a forty-year working life.

We need to think again, not from where we are into a nostalgic past, but from where we are into where we could choose to go. How can young children's needs best be met in the socio-economic circumstances of today?...

Part 4: Children, social policy and the future

> For most parents, *our* children are everything to us: *our* hopes, *our* ambitions, *our* future. (Tony Blair, in DfES, 2003, p 1; emphasis added)

In what is one of the most important chapters in this volume, Ruth Lister (Chapter Twenty-Five) discusses 'the social investment state' in the context of 'transformations in citizenship and governance', which refers to the concept of 'partnership' in New Labour's modernising project. In order to understand what is at stake here, it will be helpful to look briefly at the social theory of New Labour as expounded by Anthony Giddens in his influential book, *The Third Way: The renewal of social democracy* (1998). In contrast to neoliberalism, says Giddens, with its emphasis on competitiveness and the generation of wealth and the 'old left' emphasis on redistribution of wealth, the new social democratic polity emphasises the "redistribution of possibilities". In place of "after the event" redistribution, should come "the cultivation of human potential", with the guideline being "investment in *human capital* ... rather than direct provision for economic maintenance"; and in place of the welfare state, "we should put the social investment state, operating in the context of a positive welfare society" (Giddens, 1998, pp 98-101,117; emphasis original).

The reference to 'positive welfare' is crucial to Third Way strategies since it is both a means to and a result of the 'modernisation' of society in at least two respects. First there are those *reordered* relationships between state and citizen, individual and community, and socially excluded and included. Second, 'modernisation' refers to 'new' (a key word in New Labour's vocabulary) social and political principles that underpin the renewal of social democracy in an age of advanced liberal government, namely a globalised capitalism in which citizens must continually compete for jobs and security and are personally responsible for minimising 'risk'. Accordingly, "a prime motto for the new politics" is: "*no rights without responsibilities*" (1998, p 65; emphasis original; this is virtually the catchphrase of New Labour). Thus, "positive welfare" means replacing "each of Beveridge's negatives with a positive: in place of Want, autonomy; not Disease but active health; instead of Ignorance, education, as a continuing part of life; rather than Squalor, well-being; and in place of Idleness, initiative" (Giddens, 1998, p 128; William Beveridge was the author of a report, published in 1942, often regarded as a blueprint for the post-war welfare state, in which he referred to the principal social problems as 'Five Giants': Want, Disease, Squalor, Idleness, Ignorance). To describe this new concept of welfare as one of self-reliance alone, however, would be to underestimate its potency, since in the hands of New Labour there is always an underlying authoritarian imperative.

Besides Giddens, the other important academic architect of 'social investment' is Gøsta Esping-Andersen, who has written extensively about the restructuring of welfare systems for the global age. When he refers to "a child-centred investment strategy" (Esping-Andersen et al, 2002, p 46), he means it in the sense of viewing children as human capital within a comprehensive socioeconomic paradigm that would eliminate social exclusion and produce "a competitive knowledge economy" (see, for example, his economic reasoning in support of 'The case for abolishing child poverty', 2004, pp 54-63). The strategy he has in mind is one that emphasises the necessity for acquiring "cultural, social and cognitive capital" in order to enhance "life chances" and live "a good life". The crucial issue is seen as the "interplay between parental and societal investments in children's development", for only if the latter occurs efficiently can equality and social justice be achieved. Failure to invest in children will leave them at the mercy of "social inheritance", which in the case of the poor reduces their opportunities and condemns them to social exclusion.

There are, then, according to this thesis, a number of reasons why social investment in children is vital for the future (Esping-Andersen et al, 2002, pp 26-67). First, to be a "post-industrial 'winner', strong cognitive abilities and social skills are becoming a must; those without will likely find themselves trapped in a lifetime of low wages and precarious employment". Second, a child-focus is *sine qua non* "for a sustainable, efficient, and competitive knowledge-based production system". With the increasing size of retirement populations, the working-age cohorts of the future will be small and, therefore, will need to perform at maximum ability: "the only real asset that most advanced nations hold is the quality and skills of their people". The third reason refers to family conditions in childhood (particularly in young families and in lone-mother households) and their relationship to social exclusion, which covers a variety of exclusions ranging from being socially isolated through labour market marginality to lack of sufficient financial resources. Given this to be the case, "all ... evidence indicates that (early) childhood is the critical point at which people's life courses are shaped. Remedial policies once people have reached adulthood are unlikely to be effective.... A social investment strategy directed at children must be a centrepiece in any policy for social inclusion" (Esping-Andersen et al, 2002, p 30).

In her chapter, Lister reminds us that the idea of social investment did not originate with the current government; indeed, it has a long historical paternity (for historical consideration of children as 'investments', see Hendrick, 1994). However, New Labour publications and pronouncements are littered with references to children as investment capital:

- "they are 20% of the population but they are 100% of the future";
- "our children are our future and the most important investment that we can make as a nation is in developing the potential of all our country's children";
- "if we do not find it within ourselves to pay attention to them as young children today, they may force us to pay attention to them as troubled adults tomorrow" (quoted in Hendrick, 2003, p 237).

Drawing on the work of two Canadian researchers, Lister frames children in the social investment state as "the child as citizen-in-becoming" or as she refines the description: the child "as citizen-*worker*-in-becoming", "citizen-*worker* of the future" (see also Williams, 2004, pp 414-17). It is this combination of citizenship and 'work' (the government regards the latter as integral to the former) that helps to explain why, under New Labour, somewhat paradoxically given its suspicion of children in almost every other context, the child takes on what Lister calls "an iconic status" with the real value of financial assistance for children nearly doubling between 1997-2002. Since coming to office in 1997, the government has placed a growing emphasis on early childhood education and care, education up to secondary level, and reducing truancy rates. It introduced the Sure Start initiative for the socially disadvantaged and, most significantly, pledged itself to eradicate child poverty. In all, between 1998 and 2003 there were no less than 23 policy initiatives with respect to children and youth (Fawcett et al, 2004, p 2).

The social investment perception of children, however, is in conflict with the dominant view held by those researching within the academic realm of the 'new' social studies of childhood, namely that children should be seen as *beings* in the *present* rather than as *becomings* in the *future* (Lee, 2001; Mayall, 2002; James and James, 2004). This view is also influential in university social policy and social work departments, and among many professionals in Children's Organisations. These two very different understandings of childhood could be said to be evidence of the uncertainty that is alleged to characterise post-modernity. More mundanely, it could be an example of the struggle between competing ethical conceptions of citizenship, regardless of the age of those involved, at a time of 'renewal' for liberal democracy (on children as 'non-citizens', see Cockburn, 1998; Scott, in Franklin, 2002; James and James, 2004).

Nothwithstanding the conflict, the tendency to identify children primarily as human capital (with its futuristic impetus) is, as Lister says, "one way of side-stepping social divisions, even though these frame and shape children's opportunities and adult outcomes". Such a move is not entirely incidental since broadly speaking the child figure can be presented as an homogenous and binding image, thereby eliding the realities of class, gender, race and disability. This is not the place to speculate on the cultural use of *images* of childhood, but much could be made of the focus on children by the New Labour government, perhaps the most avowedly 'post-modernist' in Europe, as it calls on 'children' (as they are being 'finished') in the service of its attempts to reshape civil society and to create a new type of citizenry.

The references to uncertainty, individualisation and post-modern politics are clearly evident in Alan Prout's chapter (Twenty-Six), as he identifies the tension between "self-realisation" and "control" in what he terms "late modernity", which, he says, can best be relieved through a more active and broader participatory role for children in society. Prout describes the growing willingness to acknowledge children's capacity for self-realisation while at the same time many government programmes aim to extend control, surveillance and regulation of them: "Initiatives acknowledging children's personhood and their participation in social life, although present, are scattered and uncoordinated. Instead the self-realisation aspect of modern childhood is channelled into the private sphere, through an intensified political concern with parenthood".

In accordance with the theme of social investment, Prout follows Jenks (1996) in arguing that the current perception of children through futurity is a core feature of modernity. "The modern family", writes Jenks, "enabled the modern state to invest in 'futures'. The ideology of care both lubricated and legitimised investment of economic and cultural capital in the 'promise' of childhood" (Jenks, 1996, p 100). With this in mind, Prout goes on to make the critical point concerning the commitment of the government (and the Prime Minister personally) to reduce and eventually eradicate child poverty: "Absolutely central is the importance attached by government to children as an investment in the future.... The central focus is on the better adult lives that will, it is predicted, emerge from reducing child poverty. It is not on the better lives that children will lead as children". As Prout says, this is not to doubt the existence of a genuine concern for poor children, but to show that "*on its own* a focus on futurity is unbalanced" (emphasis original), and needs to be accompanied by equal emphasis on the well-being of children in the present (for assessments of child welfare under New Labour, see Bradshaw, 2002; Hendrick, 2003; Hallett and Prout, 2003; Fawcett et al, 2004; and James and James, 2004).

There is, however, more to 'the future' than merely 'social investment'. Prout argues that "modernity's project of rational control" has reached its limit with the discovery of 'risk', uncertainty, fragmentation, and insecurity (Giddens, 1991; Beck, 1992), each of which has cast doubt on those old truths (sustained through the welfare state and affluence) that prevailed until, say, the 1960s. Paradoxically, the new relativism (uncertainty) takes the child "as a repository for nostalgic longings for stability" and hence seeks to control the future through children, especially given that they are 'unfinished' – hence the promise of a new creation (on bodies as unfinished, see Shilling, 1993, and for children's bodies, James et al, 1998; Prout, 2000). In a situation where the "normal chaos of love" (Beck and Beck-Gersheim, 1995, 2002) prevails, who (and what) else is truly knowable (and reliable) except children (and childhood) – insofar as they always stand as 'our' beginnings, perhaps they offer the possibility of getting it right a second time around? Or, perhaps we have lost sight of the value of 'intimacy' to such a degree that its death is a foregone conclusion? (Hendrick, 2002, p 281; Martin Jaques, 'The death of intimacy', *The Guardian*, 18 September 2004).

If, claims Prout, control is one side of modernity, the other is self-realisation, for "the belief [that] the world is increasingly subject to rational control creates the conditions in which people can shape their own lives through the formation and exercise of self-consciousness, creativity and agency". (However, this 'life politics' approach is open to a number of criticisms; eg Garrett, 2003). From out of this process, described by Beck (1998) as a "second modernisation" comes the phenomenon of what he calls "individualisation": an awareness of oneself as a unique self-choosing individual, not subject to a fixed identity. Prout quotes Beck to the effect that "The 'biographization' of youth means becoming active, struggling and designing one's own life" (1998, p 78). As to how children should be allowed to proceed towards this goal, Prout advocates greater participation in the public sphere, in contrast to their relative silence in current debates, and compares the UK unfavourably with the Nordic countries (since Prout wrote this chapter in 2000, there have been several government initiatives designed to broaden participation, but only in limited circumstances; see the Special Issue of *Children & Society*, vol 18, no 2, April 2004).

Investing in the citizen-workers of the future: transformations in citizenship and the state under New Labour

Ruth Lister

Introduction

In a recent scientific report, commissioned by the Belgian Presidency of the European Union in 2001, Gøsta Esping-Andersen and colleagues presented "a set of building blocks" for the creation of a "new welfare architecture". The architecture's foundation stone is "a child-centred social investment strategy" (Esping-Andersen et al, 2002, pp 6, 26)[1]. The foundation stone is, in fact, already being laid in some countries – most notably the liberal-oriented welfare states of Canada and the UK. This [chapter] offers a critical analysis of the strategy's genesis and implications in the UK, in the context of a brief overview of the more general transformations of citizenship and the state under New Labour. The [chapter] focuses in particular on the emergent "social investment state"'s construction of children – its main beneficiaries – as citizen-workers of the future.

Transformations in citizenship and governance

"No rights without responsibilities", described by Anthony Giddens as "a prime motto" for third-way politics, sums up New Labour's position on citizenship (1998, p 65).[2] It is reflected in a range of social policies designed to regulate behaviour (Deacon, 2002). These include use of the benefits system not merely to promote the paid work ethic in the name of social inclusion but also to discourage and punish anti-social behaviour. In the words of Alistair Darling (when Work and Pensions Secretary):

> there is no unconditional right to benefit.... It's not only possible, but entirely desirable that we should look at making sure the social security system and the benefits system are matched by responsibility.... It is right that we should ask ourselves if there is a role for the benefits system as part of the wider system in asserting the values we hold and asserting

the kind of behaviour that we want to see. (Address to the Parliamentary Press Gallery, reported in the *Independent*, 16 May)

"Citizenship for the twenty first century" is how Tony Blair (2002b) has described New Labour's governance model of partnership between the individual and the state. This model of governance represents a further development of the managerial state inherited from the Conservatives (Clarke and Newman, 1997; Clarke et al., 2000; Lister, 2002). With partnership "out goes the Big State. In comes the Enabling State" (Blair, 2002b, 2002c). The enabling state is a leaner state, in which brokerage and regulating, as well as enabling, are emphasized over providing (Miliband, 1999). Partnership, while not a novel idea, is, in its multifarious guises and new suits of clothing, the linchpin of New Labour's modernizing governance agenda (Newman, 2001).[3] Although frequently associated in the governance literature with the "hollowing out" of the state, Janet Newman suggests an alternative interpretation of partnerships:

> that they can be viewed as a further dispersal and penetration of state power. The spread of an official and legitimated discourse of partnership has the capacity to draw local stakeholders, from community groups to business organisations, into a more direct relationship with government and involve them in supporting and carrying out the government's agenda .... Labour's emphasis on holistic and joined-up government, and its use of partnerships as a means of delivering public policy, can be viewed as enhancing the state's capacity to secure political objectives by sharing power with a range of actors, drawing them into the policy process. (Newman, 2001, p 125)

The "joined up government" to which Newman refers, with its slogan of "joined up solutions for joined up problems", particularly in tackling social exclusion (Mulgan, 1998, p 262; Miliband, 1999), is combined with a problem-solving, technocratic approach under which "what matters is what works" (Blair, 1998a, p 4). This "dogmatic pragmatism" (Clarke, 1999, p 85) diverts attention from the need for more systemic structural change (Lister, 2001).

If partnerships are the linchpin of the new governance, managerialism, another element in New Labour's inheritance, can be seen as the "organizational glue" that holds it together (Newman, 1998; Clarke and Hoggett, 1999, p 15; Clarke et al, 2000).[4] It is embodied in the government's enthusiasm for target-setting and its plans to "root out waste and inefficiency" and to "provide efficient and modern public services" (HM Treasury, 1998: p 1). Increases in public spending carry a managerialist price tag of value for money, reform, audit and targets. In his 2002 Spending Review statement, the Chancellor emphasised that

> in each area of service delivery ... we are tying new resources to reform and results, and developing a modern way for efficient public services, which includes setting demanding national targets; monitoring

performance by independent and open audit and inspection; giving front-line staff the power and flexibility to deliver; extending choice; rewarding success; and turning around failing services. (Brown 2002b: col 22)

The social investment state

Brown (2002b) presented his Spending Review as addressing "past decades of chronic underinvestment in education, health, transport and housing". The "role of Government", he declared, "is – by expanding educational, employment and economic opportunity, and by encouraging stronger communities – to enable and empower people to make globalisation work for their families and their future" (*ibid.*). With the exception of the absence of any explicit reference to children, this sums up pretty well the main elements of the "social investment state".

The term was coined by Giddens in his articulation of the Third Way. The guideline, he argues, "is investment in *human capital* wherever possible, rather than direct provision of economic maintenance" (1998, p 117; emphasis in original). An earlier template was provided by the Commission on Social Justice (CSJ) in its vision of an "Investors' Britain". Its central proposition was that "it is through investment that economic and social policy are inextricably linked". "High investment – in skills, research, technology, childcare and community development – is the last and first step" in a "virtuous circle of sustainable growth" (CSJ, 1994, pp 97, 103). The emphasis was on economic opportunity in the name of social justice as well as of economic prosperity and the achievement of security through investment in and redistribution of "opportunities rather than just ... income" (CSJ, 1994, p 95).

Although the Commission's report was seen by many as promoting a "modernizing" agenda, within a year of publication (after the death of John Smith, its instigator), its report had effectively metamorphosed from a symbol of New Labour to one of old, as the juggernaut of accelerated modernisation rolled over it. Nevertheless, the influence of its model of an "Investors' Britain" is clear, if unacknowledged. New Labour has rejected the traditional egalitarian model espoused by the Labour Party for a paradigm and discourse of lifelong opportunity and social inclusion (Lister, 2000a, 2001, 2002). This is linked to "a new supply-side agenda for the left". The agenda emphasises "lifetime access to education and training" as part of the necessary investment in "human capital". It is complemented by "an active labour market policy for the left" in which "the state must become an active agent for employment, not merely the passive recipient of the casualties of economic failure" (Blair and Schröder, 1991, pp 31, 35)[5]. Both exemplify Bob Jessop's formulation of the post-Fordist "Schumpeterian workfare state" in which "redistributive welfare rights take second place to a productivist reordering of social policy" in the name of international competitiveness and the need to equip the population to respond to global change (Jessop, 1994, p 24; 2000; see also Holden, 1991).

As well as investment in "human capital", the social investment state is concerned to strengthen *social* capital: "investors argue that investment in social institutions is as important as investment in economic infrastructure" and that "the moral and social reconstruction of our society depends on our willingness to invest in social capital", which is both "a good in itself " and "also essential for economic renewal" (CSJ, 1994, pp 306, 308). New Labour has launched a "national strategy action plan" for neighbourhood renewal animated by the "vision that, within 10 to 20 years, no one should be seriously disadvantaged by where they live" (Social Exclusion Unit, 2001, p 8). According to Blair, a "central goal" and "a key task for our second term is to develop greater coherence around our commitment to community, to grasp the opportunity of 'civic renewal'. That means a commitment to making the state work better. But most of all, it means strengthening communities themselves" (Blair, 2002a, pp 9, 11; 2002c). The appeal to community has played a key role in the third-way differentiation of New Labour from the new right and old left, for it posits "an alternative to both the untrammelled free market (of neo-liberalism) and the strong state (of social democracy)" (Levitas, 2000, p 191).

Children

For the Commission on Social Justice (CSJ), families and children were critical to the strengthening of both social and human capital. "Children are 100 per cent of the nation's future" it declared, and it argued that "the best indicator of the capacity of our economy tomorrow is the quality of our children today" (CSJ, 1994, p 311). A similar message emerges from Esping-Andersen's sketch of a "new welfare architecture", in which he emphasises that "a social investment strategy directed at children must be a centrepiece of any policy for social inclusion" (Esping-Andersen et al, 2002, p 30).

Children emerged as key figures in New Labour's nascent social investment state early in 1991. In his Beveridge Lecture, the Prime Minister pledged the government to eradicate child poverty in two decades, explaining that "we have made children our top priority because, as the Chancellor memorably said in his Budget, 'they are 20% of the population but they are [echoing the CSJ] 100% of the future'" (Blair, 1991, p 16). Around the same time, the Treasury published a document, *Tackling poverty and extending opportunity*, which emphasised the impact of poverty on children's life chances and opportunities (HM Treasury, 1991).

Although the pledge to end child poverty was made by Blair, much of the policy impetus on children has come from the Treasury, which under Brown has become a key actor in the development of social policy (Deakin and Parry, 2000). Brown has described child poverty as "a scar on Britain's soul", arguing that "we must give all our children the opportunity to achieve their hopes and fulfil their potential. By investing in them, we are investing in our future" (Brown, 1991, p 8). He has developed these themes in a series of speeches, together with the argument that "tackling child poverty is the best anti-drugs, anti-crime, anti-deprivation policy for our country" (Brown, 2000a). In his foreword to the pre-2002 Budget report, he states that "our children are our future and the most important investment that we can make as a nation is in developing the potential of all our country's children" (Brown, 2001, p iv). While this report does acknowledge that "action to abolish child poverty must *improve the current quality of children's lives* as well as investing to enable children to reach their full potential as adults" (HM Treasury, 2001, p 5; emphasis added), the point is not developed[6]. Brown went on to present his 2002 Budget as:

> building a Britain of greater enterprise and greater fairness, and nothing is more important to an enterprising, fairer Britain than that, through education and through support for the family, we invest in the potential of every single child in our country. (Brown, 2002a, col 586)

New investment in children

Brown also announced "one of the biggest single investments in children and families since the welfare state was formed in the 1940s" (Brown, 2002a, col 587). He was referring primarily to additional investment in an evolving tax credits system that reflects the influence of the Canadian and Australian models and represents what Sylvia Bashevkin has described as an increasingly "fiscalized social policy" (2000, p 2). Means-tested benefits for children are being replaced by a child tax credit (CTC), which "will provide a single, seamless system of income-related support for families with children" paid direct to the caring parent with the universal child benefit (HM Treasury, 2002a, para 5.17)[7]. In addition, a new working tax credit will incorporate a childcare element (payable to the caring parent). These tax credits represent a further shift in the balance of financial support towards means-testing in the name of the principle of "progressive universalism" that is, "giving everyone a stake in the system while offering more help to those who need it most" (HM Treasury, 2002, para 5.5)[8].

Prior to the introduction of the CTC, the amount of money available for the children of both employed and non-employed parents has already been increased significantly. This includes a phased improvement in the social assistance rates for children so that by October 2002 the real value of assistance for under-11-year-old children had virtually doubled. This improvement deviates from the third way in welfare as initially articulated by New Labour: improvements in out-of-work benefits were dismissed as "dependency"-inducing "cash handouts" to be rejected in favour of "a modern form of welfare that believes in empowerment not dependency" (DSS, 1998, p 19). It has therefore not been trumpeted as loudly as other policy developments, so much so that many people are still unaware of it. It is an example of a wider phenomenon: "redistribution by stealth". Redistribution of resources, as opposed to redistribution of opportunities, does not fit the New Labour template. When pressed on the issue, Brown has therefore described it as redistribution based on "people exercising responsibilities" to work and bring up children in contrast to old forms of redistribution based on "something for nothing" (*Today Programme*, BBC Radio, 29 March 1991).

More consistent with the New Labour template has been the piloting and planned introduction of means-tested educational maintenance allowances to encourage young people from low-income families to stay on at school and a commitment to an experiment in "asset-based welfare" with a universal "child trust fund" under which every new-born child would be given a modest capital sum, accessible only when they reach 18 (Kelly and Le Grand, 2001). Indeed, assets-based welfare has itself been characterised as representing a transition to a social investment state (Sherraden, 2002). The New Labour template also informs a series of service-based initiatives. Of particular significance is Sure Start, which was inspired by the American Head Start programme (see HM Treasury, 2001). Sure Start is to be combined with early years education and childcare within a single interdepartmental unit with an integrated budget. A further injection of funds into the national childcare strategy is promised, in the face of evidence that the policy is flagging. This will involve the creation of children's centres and of an additional 250,000 childcare places by 2005-06 (Strategy Unit, 2002).

For all its weaknesses, the national childcare strategy represents a breakthrough in British social policy. It represents the first time that government has accepted that childcare is a public as well as a private responsibility. Birte Siim has argued that "from the point of view of social policies towards women and children, Britain ... represents an exception to the rule of European social policies", particularly in the area of childcare services (Siim, 2000, p 92). This, she suggests, reflects the dominant liberal philosophy of the separation of public and private spheres and (partial) non-intervention in the latter (see also Lewis, 1998; O'Connor et al, 1991).

This philosophy has framed general policy towards children other than those deemed at risk of abuse or neglect. Despite the introduction of family allowances and their extension and replacement by child benefit, children have been the subject of public neglect. The UK has been described as "a serious contender for the title of worst place in Europe to be a child" (Micklewright and Stewart, 2000, p 23). Arguably, this reflects not only the liberal strand in the dominant social welfare philosophy but also an ambivalence in British attitudes towards children (Lister, 2000b). A tendency to sentimentalise and idealise children has existed alongside a reluctance to accommodate their presence in the adult world and an element of hostility and fear, as reflected in the recent demonisation of "feral children"[9]. In addition, during the Thatcher years there was an increasingly strongly expressed view that having children is "essentially a private matter", akin to other expensive consumer goods (Beenstock, 1984; cited in J. Brown, 1988). Such claims tap deep-rooted attitudes put most crudely in the (male) expression – "why should I pay for another man's pleasure?".

This sentiment underlies some of the hostility that has always existed towards family allowances/child benefit and the fact that child poverty has not been a popular cause in the UK. Keith Banting's analysis, for instance, suggests that, although family poverty became an important issue for the 1964-70 Wilson Labour government (partly thanks to pressure from the newly-formed Child Poverty Action Group), it was a key concern for neither organised labour nor the wider electorate (Banting, 1979). As the former Conservative Chancellor observes, approvingly, in his memoirs, "the moral sense of the nation" is more sympathetic to pensioner than child poverty (Lawson, 1992c, p 595). Such attitudes may help to explain signs of disappointment among some government ministers that "the pledge to end child poverty has not generated the expected political returns", particularly in the "Labour heartlands" (Barnes, 2000, p 1). One consequence has been the bizarre spectacle of the Chancellor calling for an "alliance for children" to put the kind of pressure on him that Jubilee 2000 did with regard to debt eradication in the South. He envisaged "a movement based on faith in the future, a crusade for nothing less than the kind of society our children will inherit" (Brown, 2000b). In response, the End Child Poverty Campaign has been set up by a number of children's charities.

Children as citizen-workers of the future

We are witnessing a genuine, unprecedented, attempt to shift the social priorities of the state and nation to investing in children. What are the implications for citizenship? Jane Jenson, writing in the Canadian context, has suggested that, in the social investment state, children have become the "model citizens" but they are so symbolically because, as minors, they cannot be full citizens able "to employ the force of democratic politics to insist on social reform in the name of equality" (2001, pp 122, 125). In a more recent paper with Denis Saint-Martin she traces a shift in the "ideal–typical representation of citizen" from "citizen-worker" in the "social rights" citizenship regime to "the child as citizen-in-becoming" in the "social investment" regime (Jenson and Saint-Martin, 2001, Table 2).

In the UK, as argued above, the "citizen-worker" is still centre stage. In so far as s/he is being joined there by the child, it is the child as "citizen-*worker*-in-becoming" or "citizen-*worker* of the future". It is the future *worker*-citizen more than *democratic*-citizen who is the prime asset of the social-investment state. Moreover, the future orientation and discourses of the social investment state encourage not just the elision of demands for equality in the here-and-now[10], but also, paradoxically, the partial disappearance of childhood and of the child *qua* child, including the child as a rights-bearer (under the UN Convention on the Rights of the Child). The child as cipher for future economic prosperity and forward-looking modernisation overshadows the child as child-citizen[11].

In many ways, the discourse of social investment in children reflects that deployed by organisations and individuals, in the UK and elsewhere, making the case for better state financial support and services for children[12]. As such, it has arguably proved its utility in persuading politicians. In turn, it may also represent a politically astute discourse for politicians to use in a culture unsympathetic to children and alongside a rhetoric hostile to cash benefits. However, there are also dangers: as Sanford F. Schram has cautioned in the US context, the deployment of the economistic discourse of investment represents "a slippery politics" (1995, p 24). Valerie Polakow warns that if children are seen to "matter instrumentally, not existentially", expenditure on them will only be justifiable where there is a demonstrable payoff, so that there is no room for "expenditure which merely contributes to the well-being or enjoyment of children as children" (1993, p 101).

In the UK, while there is strong support for the commitment to eradicate child poverty, there is also an emergent critique of the social investment paradigm from a child-centred perspective as well as ongoing criticism of the government's patchy record on children's rights. According to Alan Prout, the central focus of policy "is on the better adult lives that will, it is predicted, emerge from reducing child poverty. It is not on the better lives that children will lead as children" (2000a, p 305). Fawcett et al contrast this focus with what has been called a "new paradigm" of childhood:

> For governments, children symbolise 'the future', 'social renewal', 'survival of the nation' or equivalent sentiments. Such a view is at odds with alternative approaches which counsel the importance of seeing *children as 'beings' rather than 'becomings'*, as people to be valued in their own right in the present rather than assessed primarily in terms of how well they will construct the future. (Fawcett et al, 2004; emphasis added)

Prout does not reject the discourse of investment in children but warns that, "on its own a focus on futurity is unbalanced and needs to be accompanied by a concern for the present well-being of children, for their participation in social life and for their opportunities for human self-realisation" (2000, p 300). As the Children's Forum declared in their official statement to the UN General Assembly, "you call us the future, but we are also the present" (cited in Stasiulis, 2002, p 508).

This assertion of their agency as children is supported by a study of childhood poverty from within the new paradigm of childhood. Its author Tess Ridge criticises the focus "on children as 'adults to be', as future investments, rather than as children with their own voices and agency, their own experiences and concerns" (Ridge, 2002b, p 12; 2002a; see also Roche, 1991). Goals and targets are future-oriented rather than focused "on the quality of children's lives – goals of achieving childhoods that are, as far as possible, happy, healthy and fulfilled" (Piachaud, 2001, p 453; see also Thomas and Hocking, 2003). Likewise, in the target-filled world of the managerial state, education is reduced to a utilitarian achievement-oriented measurement culture of tests and exams, with little attention paid to the actual educational experience.

The state is, however, not monolithic and there are spaces within it where children *are* valued as 'beings' and not just 'becomings'. For instance, Fawcett et al (2004) suggest that, on the ground, programmes such as Sure Start do often engage with "quality of life issues in the here-and-now as well as investing in the future". Of particular significance is the Children and Young Person's Unit established by the government in 2000 within the Department for Education and Skills. In 2001 it published a consultation document, *Building a strategy for children and young people*. This set out a vision and set of principles that pays attention to the present as well as the future and that treats children and young people as social actors whose views should be taken into account. An imaginative consultation process was designed to maximise children and young people's own participation. The Unit has also published a guidance document on children and young people's participation in decisions that affect their lives at every level from their own lives to national policy making.

"Promoting citizenship and social inclusion" is one of the arguments put in favour of such an approach (CYPU, 2001, p 6). This conjures up what Daiva Stasiulis calls the "imaginary of the child citizen as an active participant in governance", personified in and promoted by an emergent international children's movement (2002, p 509; see also Roche, 1991)[13]. This imaginary does not, however, have very deep roots in government thinking about children and children's rights, as codified in the UN Convention on the Rights of the Child.

Children's right to express their views and have them taken seriously in all matters affecting them is enshrined in Article 12 of the Convention on the Rights of the Child. Gerison Lansdown (2002) has argued that "it is far from adequately implemented in respect of children in the UK". Her view and that of many children's rights activists is that the appointment of a Children's Rights Commissioner is crucial to the protection and promotion of the human rights of children (Children's Rights Alliance for England, 2002; Willow, 2002)[14]. Hitherto, the government has resisted such calls for an English Commissioner, despite acceptance in the devolved administrations and many other countries and a commitment in Labour's 1992 Election Manifesto (subsequently dropped by Blair) (Lansdown, 2002). This was the subject of criticism in the second UK report of the UN Committee on the Rights of the Child, which highlighted the extent to which the government's approach to children's rights has been piecemeal and partial (CRC, 2002). A particular focus of criticism in the report is the "unequal enjoyment of economic, social, cultural, civil and political rights" by vulnerable groups of children including asylum and refugee children (CRC, 2002, para 22). There has, for instance, been a reluctance to extend to the children of asylum-seekers the welfare and educational rights enjoyed by other children (Maternity Alliance, 2002; Sale, 2002; see also Stasiulis, 2002).

More generally, New Labour has been more willing to countenance rights for children who do not live with their parents than to intervene in the private sphere of the family of those who do. This is most notable in the refusal to remove parents' right to hit their children, again strongly criticised by the UN Committee as constituting "a serious violation of the dignity of the child" (CRC, 2002, para 35). As Fawcett et al (2004) observe, the government thereby "allies itself with older discourses around 'children as property' and sets itself firmly against moves to democratize the family more fully, a rather curious positioning in view of its much-vaunted claims to be 'modern' and its assumptions about gender equality".

Jenson and Saint-Martin (2001) warn that neglect of gender equality issues may be one consequence of the future-oriented social investment state. There is a danger that children's poverty is divorced from that of their mothers and more generally that "questions of gender power ... are more and more difficult to raise, as adults are left to take responsibility for their own lives" (Jenson, 2001, p 125). In Canada, the discourse of child poverty has dominated policy making on poverty for longer. A Status of Canada Women report argues that the discourse has served to make the structural causes of poverty less visible; to encourage a response motivated by pity for the helpless child; and to displace women's issues generally and women's poverty specifically (Wiegers, 2002; Stasiulis, 2002).

A focus on children and social investment does not, however, necessarily have to mean the displacement of gender issues. Esping-Andersen, for instance, makes the somewhat instrumentalist case for treating the development of "women-friendly" policies as themselves "a social investment". He justifies this position on the grounds that "in many countries women constitute a massive untapped labour reserve that can help narrow future age dependency rates and reduce associated financial pressures" and that "female employment is one of the most effective means of combating social exclusion and poverty" (Esping-Andersen et al, 2002, p 94).

It would be wrong to say that New Labour has ignored the issue of gender equality but the consensus is that it has accorded it relatively low priority, despite the establishment of a Women and Equality Unit and a number of specific policies that will improve women's lives. New Labour's avoidance of a systematic gendered analysis and strategy is not, however, simply a function of its child-oriented priorities. It also reflects its association of feminism with "yesterday's politics" (Coote, 2000, p 3) and a related reluctance to acknowledge structural inequalities and conflicts of interest in a concern to promote consensus and cohesion (Franklin, 2000a, 2000b; McRobbie, 2000; Coote, 2001). That said, a focus on the child is one way of side-stepping social divisions, even though these frame and shape children's opportunities and adult outcomes: "because the figure of the child is unified, homogeneous, undifferentiated, there is little talk about race, ethnicity, gender, class and disability. Children become a single, essentialized category" (Dobrowolsky, 2002, p 67).

Conclusion

The design of the new welfare architecture in the UK involves the changing construction of both citizenship and the state. With regard to citizenship, in return for the promise of investment in economic opportunity by the state, increased emphasis is being placed on the responsibilities of citizens, most notably: to equip themselves to respond to the challenges of economic globalisation through improved employability; to support themselves through paid work; to invest in their own pensions; and to ensure the responsible behaviour of their children.

The changing construction of the state has been analysed here from the perspective of both governance and its role. In terms of *governance*, the emergent state can be characterised as "the enabling, managerial, partnership state", a partial inheritance from the previous Conservative government. In terms of *role*, the notion of "the social investment state" captures its essence, both analytically and normatively. While there are some differences of detail and emphasis in the various formulations of the social investment state, broadly its key features are as set out in Box 1.

> **Box 1: Key features of the social investment state**
> - Investment in human and social capital: children and community as emblems.
> - Children prioritised as citizen-workers of the future.
> - Future-focused.
> - Redistribution of opportunity to promote social inclusion rather than of income to promote equality.
> - Adaptation of individuals and society to enhance global competitiveness.
> - Integration of social and economic policy, but with the former still the 'handmaiden' of the latter.

From a normative perspective, as investment in 'human' and social capital becomes a primary function of the social investment state, the child and the community have become its emblems. The child in particular takes on iconic status. However, it is the child as 'citizen-worker' of the future rather than the 'citizen-child' of the present who is invoked by the new discourse of social investment. Thus, despite the prioritising of children, the quality of their childhood risks being overshadowed by a preoccupation with their development as future citizen-workers. At the same time, the poverty of today's citizens of working age is marginalised. Moreover, despite a strong emphasis on the need to integrate economic and social policy, integration has not challenged the traditional subordinate 'handmaiden' relationship of the social to the economic (Titmuss, 1974, p 31; see also Beck et al, 1997).

From an analytical perspective, it is difficult to make sense of current developments using only traditional welfare regime analysis. In some ways the UK is shifting further towards a liberal welfare regime, as conventionally articulated, with increased reliance on means-tested and private forms of welfare provision (Lister 2000a, 2002). In other ways, most notably in relation to childcare, it is inching in the direction of more institutionalised Continental and Nordic welfare states, as the state finally acknowledges that childcare is a public as well as a private responsibility. The idea of the "social investment state" may therefore provide a more helpful analytic framework for understanding the emergent new welfare architecture. Indeed, the suggestion is that it may represent a transformation of some liberal regimes, most notably the UK and Canada, into a rather different – hybrid – animal from that described in Esping-Andersen's original analysis (Dobrowolsky and Saint-Martin, 2002; Jenson and Saint-Martin, 2002)[15].

It may be tempting, therefore, to interpret all policy developments in terms of the social investment state template. We need, though, to be careful. First, not all policy shifts are necessarily *reducible* to the template, even if they are consistent with it. Thus, for instance, New Labour's preoccupation with citizenship responsibility and the obligations associated with the paid work ethic needs to be analysed in its own right as well as simply as an expression of the social investment state. Indeed, it helps us to understand better the true complexion of the model-citizen in that state. Likewise, shifts in governance, characterised here as the emergence of the "managerial, partnership state", cannot simply be subsumed under the rubric of social investment, even if they are associated with it in practice. Second, the state is not a monolith and it is dangerous to assume "unity or integration" or to flatten out complexity (Pringle and Watson, 1992, p 63; Clarke, 2000). New Labour itself has been described as "essentially ambiguous and Janus-faced", reflecting the "often contradictory and conflicting traditions of social democracy, social conservatism, Thatcherism and pragmatism" upon which it draws (Smith 2001, p 267; Lister, 2001). Such ambiguities mean that there are spaces, such as around childhood and poverty, that civil society actors can exploit to argue for a more genuinely child-focused and also more egalitarian approach. Thus, from both a normative and analytic perspective, even if we are witnessing a genuine paradigm shift, analysts and activists need to remain alert to complexities and possible inconsistencies within the specific policy configurations to be found in emergent social investment states.

Notes

[1] A revised version of the report has been published as Esping-Andersen et al (2002).

[2] Interestingly, Amitai Etzioni has dismissed this formulation as a "grave moral error" on the grounds that "basic individual rights are inalienable, just as one's social obligations cannot be denied"; the relationship between the two is complementary not conditional (2000, p 29). For a more detailed exposition of the construction of citizenship under New Labour see, for instance, Dwyer (1998, 2000); Lister (1998); Heron and Dwyer (1999); Rose (1999).

[3] In New Zealand also, partnerships have been identified as a key element in "a post-welfarist, post-neoliberal form of social governance" (Larner and Craig, 2002, p 4).

[4] Under the Tories, managerialism cast welfare subjects as customers and consumers rather than citizens (Clarke, 1997, 1998; Hughes and Lewis, 1998). New Labour has attempted to marry the two in the person of "the demanding, sceptical, citizen-consumer" who expects improved standards from public services in line with those in the private sector (DSS, 1998, p 16). There is the same emphasis on individual customer service and user- rather than provider-led welfare as under the Conservatives (a model which was not necessarily realised in practice and which had more purchase in some arms of the welfare state than others). At the same time, though, there is something of a more collective and democratic approach: examples include the introduction of citizens' juries and various fora for "listening to" particular groups such as women and older people, as well as resident participation in the neighbourhood renewal action plan. Yet, when Blair (1998b) tells us that "in all walks of life people act as consumers and not just citizens" the suspicion is that it is the consumer rather than the citizen who represents the ideal New Labour welfare subject (see also, Gamble and Kenny, 1999).

[5] Fairclough criticises New Labour's use of the 'human capital' discourse, with its 'reification of people' and its translation of learning into an 'economic rather than an educational process' (2000, pp 49, 75).

[6] The November 2002 Pre-Budget Report does acknowledge that poverty "excludes children from the everyday activities of their peers" (HM Treasury, 2002b).

[7] A higher children's tax credit will be paid during the year of a child's birth as part of a package to improve support in the early years of a child's life (see HM Treasury, 2002a).

[8] The government did implement a significant increase in the universal child benefit in its first term, but all the indications are that this will not be repeated. There is considerable criticism of the heavy reliance on means-testing, not least from the former minister, Frank Field, who has described tax credits as "a form of permanent serfdom" (Field, 2002).

[9] The 'feral child' figured prominently in a number of newspaper reports of the acquittal of the young people tried for the murder of the black child Damilola Taylor. See, for instance, the *Daily Mail* (26 April 2002) and Anderson (2002) and, for a critical account of its wider use, Hari (2002).

[10] See Jenson (2001); Jenson and Saint-Martin (2001); Dobrowolsky and Saint-Martin (2002).

[11] According to one participant, when ministers were asked at a seminar in 1998 why they were focusing on children, the response was that "children are the future; we are not interested in the past" (Seminar for Hilary Land, 25 March 2002, London). A similar future orientation can be found in Esping-Andersen's exposition in which he argues, for instance, "minimizing child poverty now will yield an individual and social dividend in the future. And in the far-off future, it should diminish the risks of old age poverty" (Esping-Andersen et al, 2002, p 55).

[12] See, for instance, J. Brown (1988); England and Folbre (1991); Esping-Andersen et al (2002); European Forum for Child Welfare (2002). Indeed, I have used the argument myself, particularly in my former role as Director of CPAG.

[13] The movement was made visible as children took to the streets in March 2003 to protest against war with Iraq.

[14] The case has also been made by Cherie Booth QC in the 2002 Barbara Kahn Memorial Lecture in which she criticised the government for being "halfhearted" about children's rights (*Guardian*, 25 September 2002).

[15] Esping-Andersen himself suggests a bifurcation between "youth-oriented" liberal regimes and a group that is "ever more aged-biased and service-lean" (1991, p 166). He includes the UK in the latter (with the US), but this was before the emergence of New Labour's social investment state.

This is a revised version of a paper given at the American Political Science Association Annual Meeting 2002. It engages with the work of a team of political scientists led by Jane Jenson of Montreal University. It was taken from *Social Policy & Administration*, 2003, vol 37, no 5. The right of Ruth Lister to be identified as author of this chapter has been asserted by her in accordance with the 1988 Copyright, Designs and Patents Act.

Children's participation: control and self-realisation in British late modernity

Alan Prout

Introduction

This [chapter] addresses the idea of children's participation in decision making about matters that affect their lives and, more broadly, their inclusion in institutional, social and political life. It does not set out to make a case for participation: many others have done that, showing its grounds in both principle and pragmatism (see, for example, Flekkoy and Kaufman, 1997; Franklin, 1995; Landsdowne, 1995; Hart, 1992). Rather, it explores the meaning of children's participation within a wider sociological framework. In particular it suggests that the drive towards, and the resistance against, greater participation are caught up in, indeed are an expression of, a generalised tension between control and self-realisation within late modernity. When it comes to children, I suggest, control and self-realisation are both present but in tension. On the one hand, there is an increasing tendency to see children as individuals with a capacity for self-realisation and, within the limits of social interdependency, autonomous action; on the other, there are practices directed at a greater surveillance, control and regulation of children.

The tension between control and self-realisation can be handled in a variety of ways and this, at the societal level, influences the capacity for retaining or opening up space for the representation and participation of children. For reasons beyond the scope of this [chapter][1], some societies, notably but not exclusively the Nordic ones, make greater efforts towards representing children's interests. Although still subject to tensions between the control of children and their opportunities for self-realisation, these societies handle them in ways that seem to create more space for children in public discourse.

The main focus of this [chapter], however, is contemporary Britain. Here the tensions of late modernity seem to be played out in ways that, overall, constrain and limit the interests and voice of children in public discourse. Initiatives acknowledging children's personhood and their participation in social life, although present, are scattered and uncoordinated. Instead the self-realisation aspect of late modern childhood is channelled into the private sphere, especially through an intensified political concern with parenthood.

Childhood, modernity and futurism

In exploring these phenomena I will first draw attention to the way that modernity has emphasised childhood as a period of the life course oriented towards the future. Jenks has suggested that such a constitution of children through futurity is connected to the core features of modernity. He writes:

> The modern family enabled the modern state to invest in 'futures'. The ideology of care both lubricated and legitimised the investment of economic and cultural capital in the 'promise' of childhood. (Jenks, 1996a, p 15)

A contemporary illustration of this can be found in what is, paradoxically, one of the most positive of recent UK policy directions: the renewed concern with child poverty. Sharply rising child poverty, and a worsening position in international comparisons, were the produce of previous decades of neo-liberal social and economic policy (see Adelman and Bradshaw, 1999; Micklewright and Stewart, 1999). Confronted with this inheritance, the UK government has pledged to eradicate child poverty over the next 20 years.

However, welcome though this undoubtedly is, it is important to examine the rationale and motives that are given for this aim. Absolutely central is the importance attached by government to children as an investment in the future. To this end the key government paper on child poverty draws heavily on social scientific evidence, especially the findings of longitudinal studies of children that link childhood circumstances with adult outcomes (HM Treasury, 1999). It is shown that poverty and disadvantage in childhood are precursors to educational and labour market failures in later life. The central focus is on the better adult lives that will, it is predicted, emerge from reducing child poverty. It is not on the better lives that children will lead as children.

In pointing this out I do not question the government's sincerity in its attack on child poverty. Nor do I doubt the need to make a collective investment in children or to reduce resource and opportunity disparities between children: both are notions with which I profoundly agree. My point is that *on its own* a focus on futurity is unbalanced and needs to be accompanied by a concern for the present well-being of children, for their participation in social life and for their opportunities for human self-realisation.

In trying to understand why such a strong emphasis is placed on the futurity of children it is important to remember that, despite the different local and national shapes that modernity takes, a powerful common dynamic can be seen in the attempt to take control of both society and nature through rational knowledge and planning. It is this project of control, I would suggest, that is rather one-sidedly expressed in the concentration that current UK policy has on children as a means of shaping the societal future.

Paradoxically the desire to control the future through children seems to be intensified even as modernity's project of rational control meets its limits and as a new mood of uncertainty, risk (Beck, 1992) and ontological insecurity (Giddens,

1991) replaces the more rigid notions of identity, authority and morality that characterised the earlier part of 20th century. Late modernity has seen the emergence of new patterns of family life, marriage and divorce, labour market participation, work and global economy. The child may act as a repository for nostalgic longings for stability and certainty (Jenks, 1996) or as a figure of redemptive possibility (Popkewitz and Bloch, 2000) but a primary significance of this, I suggest, is that in a world seen as increasingly shifting, complex and uncertain, children, precisely because they are seen as especially unfinished, appear as a good target for controlling the future – and perhaps, therefore, a target that still retains a wide social credibility.

In this scenario the quintessentially modernist (Freeman, 1999, p 234) idea of prevention, especially through 'early intervention' policies, looms large. But prevention, as Freeman argues, is caught in an accelerating recursive cycle. As societies become more complex, prevention becomes more difficult to engineer. The failure of such interventions summons up a renewed commitment to prevention. The cycle is one in which children as a primary target of prevention seem caught in a system that can only respond to its own failure through a ratcheting up of control.

Although this can be seen across a range of policy areas, schooling illustrates this particularly well. Education has, perhaps not unsurprisingly, emerged as a key site for the control of the future through children. The recent intensification of this project did not start with New Labour but it has certainly been continued and enlarged under it (Ball, 1998). While accompanied by a dispersion of power from local authorities to head teachers and parents, more centralised control has been installed in a number of ways: a highly prescriptive national curriculum, in Bernsteinian terms both strongly classified and strongly framed, aspects of which have now been introduced even into pre-school provision; a system of national testing now extended to younger and younger children; and the installation of school league tables that impel teachers towards the efficient transmission of a given content but reduce the time to explore children's own interests. Prescribed curriculum time has come to fill up more and more of the day, during which children are urged to become ever more productive (Christensen and James, 2001).

While the effect of this on teachers and parents have been widely discussed, their impact on children has remained relatively muted in public debate. Implicitly, however, the shaping of children is a fundamental drive within educational policy. Precisely at a time when the intensification of global competition, the speed up of economic processes, the demand for more compliant and flexible labour, and the intricate networking of national economies erode the state's capacity to control its own economic activity, the shaping of children as the future labour force is seen as an increasingly important option. This, after all, is exactly what supply side economics is about.

Self-realisation: the other side of modernity

In so far as current policy sees children as an investment in the future, it is entirely in line with one, but only one, aspect of modernity's view of childhood. However, to allow the relationship between modernity and children to be thought solely in this way is both to misunderstand it and to deny them its promise. For modernity cannot be characterised by an unalloyed concern with the control of society and nature. Modernity also embraces the notion of self-realisation, the belief that a world increasingly subject to rational control creates the conditions in which people can shape their own lives through the formation and exercise of self-consciousness, creativity and agency.

A tension between self-realisation and control has always been a feature of modernity (Giddens, 1990, 1991). The last decades, however, have seen a new social and cultural emphasis on self-realisation. Just as there has been a new understanding that there are limits to the rational control of society and nature, so the self-realisation side of modernity has experienced a renewed vigour. The German sociologist Ulrich Beck (1998) argues that this constitutes a 'second modernisation'. If the first modernisation emphasised the control side of modernity, then this second modernisation emphasises self-realisation. Central to this, he suggests, is a trend towards people coming to think of themselves as unique individuals with chosen rather than prescribed or standard identities. This requires not fewer but different sources of social interdependency because although such individuals are produced through collectivities (such as family, locality and class), they are not bound by them in traditional ways.

In this view the phenomenon of 'individualisation' is the product of new *social* processes rather than a recrudescence of an essential, autonomous individual who exists prior to social relations. A concatenation of factors, rather than a single cause, is said to be responsible for this shift. The emergence of consumption (especially leisure) as a source of identity, the pluralisation of family forms, the decline in the authority of expert knowledge, the distribution of norms about the value of democracy and so on, all contribute to a process that has become self-propelling.

The emergence of individualisation as an important feature of contemporary society has important consequences for the UK, where inequality has been heightened in recent years. The reduced capacity to make choices that poverty and other forms of inequality entail, becomes more apparent. The gap between those with and those without the capacity to form their life is intensified when 'choice' has become a widely distributed expectation. For example, children's ability to join in contemporary consumption patterns has a crucial importance for their identity and their social relations with other children. The experience of social exclusion when growing up poor is partly constituted by an awareness of a reduced capacity to join in with these consumption practices and the identities that go with them (Shropshire and Middleton, 1999).

Individualisation may also have other, perhaps unexpected, consequences. For example, there is a rising incidence of reported mental health problems among young people, an increase that cannot be accounted for by the extension of poverty since the 1970s. Rutter and Smith (1995, p 807) comment that

> ... the shift towards individualistic values, the increasing emphasis on self-realisation and fulfilment, and the consequent rise in expectations, should be studied as possible causes of disorders.

The concept of individualisation does, however, make it possible to see the emergence of ideas about children as persons in their own right in a wider societal and historical context. Young people, Beck writes:

> ... no longer become individualized. They individualize themselves. The 'biographization' of youth means becoming active, struggling and designing one's own life. (Beck, 1998, p 78)

As this process of the young being recognised as having 'a life of their own' continues so the more traditional integuments of childhood become increasingly strained. In this respect the logic of individualisation requires new kinds of institutions in which authority, and allegiance, must be constantly renegotiated, re-established and earned. A recent survey of children's values showed exactly such an attitude on the part of young people (Holland and Thomson, 1999, p 3):

> Authority has been described as legitimate power: power that needs not explain or defend itself. There are few figures or institutions other than parents and families that are able to claim such authority in the eyes of young people. Rather authority has to be earned and negotiated. Young people articulated an 'ethic of reciprocity' arguing that their respect could be won by anyone who respected them.... They tended to be very wary of claims to authority and respect on the basis of tradition, custom or force.

Participation in the public sphere

Whether, how and to what extent these new relations are given expression in the public sphere is, however, another question. European, and especially the Nordic, countries provide examples of public institutions through which children and young peoples' interests can be represented. Although these can take many forms, the creation of an Independent Commissioner for Children, is one institution that is widely seen as among the most successful in placing children and young people on the political agenda. The Norwegian and Swedish examples are widely recognised as successful in fostering a climate of opinion that accepts children's right to a vote, marks their citizenship and their position as a special kind of minority, promotes their integration into society and acknowledges their individuality (see, for example, Norwegian Ministry of Children and the Family, 1996; Moss and Petrie, 1999).

Such attention to the greater inclusion of children's voice in public debate raises many issues. For example, it focuses attention on critical evaluation about the effectiveness of participatory processes. Importantly it also exposes ambiguity in the relationship between control and self-realisation. It, therefore, provokes debate about how in practice and effect they can become difficult to disentangle and distinguish from one another, especially as more diffuse and implicit methods for the formation of subjectivity come into play (see Gulestad, 1996; Dahlberg and others, 1999; Beyer and Kampmann, 1999).

However, one does not need to be uncritical of the Nordic countries in order to recognise that the picture, and the problems, in the UK are rather different and more fundamental. There has been little official interest in measures to render government structures more effective for children (for a detailed prospectus see Hodgkin and Newall, 1996) and existing structures for representing young people's voice to government are under-utilised. It is also significant that in Britain the exclusion of young people from consultation about changes in the educational system have received at best only minor attention in political discussion. Not only is children's voice suppressed in a discursive sense but also policies that have a direct impact upon children have been introduced without any significant consultation of their views, or, indeed, consideration that they might have any (Wyness, 1999, p 358).

The British government has ratified that the United Nations Convention on the Rights of the Child (with certain reservations), an act that committed it both to implementing children's right to a voice in decisions that affect them and to giving the Convention wide publicity, including among young people. However, a recent survey (Alderson, 1999) of over 2000 people aged seven to 17 found that 75% had never heard of it.

Of course there have been admirable efforts, especially at local level, to take up the idea of children's participation (Lansdown, 1995; Freeman and others, 1999). It is notable, however, that where these achieve national or legislative status they tend to concern the individual child in specific, delimited circumstances (usually children in especially disadvantaged circumstances, such as disabled children or those in care). While research shows that even in these cases formal rights often remain a dead letter (Lansdown, 1995; Who Cares Trust, 1998; Shakespeare and others, 2000), when it comes to the representation or inclusion of children per se in decision making about community or school affairs, initiatives have remained local, scattered, ad hoc, fragile and experimental. "Non-participation is endemic in the UK.... Young people are seemingly invisible on the landscape" writes Matthews and Limb (1997), in a survey of local youth councils. They are able to contrast this with the much more extensive participation opportunities for children in Norway, Sweden, Italy and France.

Familialisation and the privatisation of self-realisation

The counter-posing of children's to parent's rights is especially strong in the UK (and also the US), where it is in part an expression of an ideologically and materially embedded (though contested, shifting and problematic) separation of the state and the family, and the 'public' and the 'private' spheres. Arguably these features are also related to neo-liberal welfare regimes (Pringle, 1998) and indirect state intervention in the family (often through children) by means of multiple, diffuse professional practices directed towards the construction of families who will choose to enact dominant values and norms (Rose, 1990).

But if children's voices and interests are muted in a public sphere increasingly dominated by a more explicit control project, then the same cannot be said of the private, familial sphere. Indeed, it might be thought that the private spheres of the family, and in some important respects the peer group, become constructed as the primary locations within which the effects of individualisation processes are channelled and expressed.

A number of sociologists have suggested that the familialisation of childhood, that is the construction of parents as those responsible for the representation of children's interests in the public sphere, is a trend to be found across the industrialised countries (Nasman, 1994; Qvortrup, 1995). Partly because historically there has been an assumption in UK policy that children are the responsibility of their parents unless some serious problem such as abuse arises, the trend to familialisation appears especially marked in the UK. It is evident not only in the simultaneous rise of parents influence on school governance and decline of children's, as mentioned earlier, but has corollaries across the range of services directed towards children and young people. In the policy environment of the 1980s the family increasingly replaced the identification of young people as a group. The family became the government's preferred route to policy interventions and recent policy statements confirm this trend (Home Office, 1998).

There are indications that it is through the private sphere that the processes of individualisation are being produced and expressed. For example, research from economics, marketing, psychology and sociology concur that children have become a substantial group of consumers in themselves (Gunter and Furnham, 1998). It is also clear that children also have a high degree of influence over family purchases and that children develop many different techniques of persuasion in the pursuit of this.

It also seems that a trend begun in the 1970s (Hillman and others, 1990) towards the sequestration of children in the family and the decline of children's more autonomous movement in the neighbourhood, have continued into the 1990s (O'Brien, 1999). This suggests a double effect. First, an incipient exclusion of children from public space, where they are seen increasingly as causing problems and therefore 'out of place'. Children become more subject to regulation and control (see Valentine, 1996; Matthews and Limb, 2000). Second, a simultaneous proliferation of special locations that concentrate groups of children together for activities taking place under more or less adult surveillance and supervision (McKendrick and others, 2000; Furedi, 1997). The effect would seem to be the construction of a way of life for many children that consists of moving from one 'island' of childhood to another. In this sense the space of childhood, literally as well as metaphorically, may be becoming more specialised and more localised.

This 'institutionalisation' of childhood is in some senses quite compatible with familialisation (Nasman, 1994). It is well caught in the image of the parent as chauffeur to children whose week is packed with different activities, to and from which they are ferried by car. Nevertheless, O'Brien (1999) is right to emphasise that only a small minority of children is tightly controlled in the process. For many it involves a high degree of negotiation with parents keen both to protect their children from the real and supposed dangers of the street but also anxious to maximise their children's accumulation of informal cultural and social capital.

It seems, then, that a pattern is emerging in which public institutions are more and more concerned with the control of children, while the private sphere is constituted, notwithstanding the enrolment of parents into elements of the control project discussed earlier, as the place where children are more allowed to express choice, exercise autonomy and work at their individual self-realisation.

The need for institutional responsiveness

Although a tension between control and self-realisation runs through modernity, the play between them can be handled in many different ways and there is no determinant outcome to it. The different ways, for example, that the UK and the Nordic countries consider children is a testament to the possibility that there is room for manoeuvre. From this perspective it would seem that a better balance of the control and self-realisation strands in British policy and practice could be possible. It would, however, require a serious recognition of the imbalance that currently exists.

There are a number of reasons for suggesting that such a recognition is necessary. Certainly, the familialisation of children does not sit easily with the renewed UK concern for overcoming child poverty and its associated inequalities. Indeed, familialisation is likely to have the effect of intensifying inequalities between children. Britain is already a very unequal society. Today's parents may be the keenest sponsors of their individual child but to valorise this phenomenon where there are wide disparities between parents' possession of economic, social and cultural capital is to risk further magnifying the processes through which some children gain advantages in the system. The attempt to limit such disparities in resource distribution between children rests on an acknowledgement of a covenant between society and children that is additional to the bond between the individual parent and child.

In this sense O'Neill (1994) is right to defend the welfare state through the idea of a 'standard' or 'civic' childhood that guarantees all children a decent level of economic, social and cultural resource. As he argues, such a view of childhood cannot be contained in social relations that are modelled on the market contract because this assumes an already extant, independent individual. Rather, it seems to require an appreciation of the network of relationships within which children, families and local communities are enmeshed and a channelling of the economic, social and cultural capital necessary to children's growth and well-being through multiple routes (see also Jack and Jordan, 1999; Smith, 1999).

However, in late modern conditions there are at least two problems with the notion of a civic childhood that require its modification. The first flows from the demography of an ageing population. Trends in the industrialised countries mean both that children are a declining proportion of the population and that the proportion of households including children is also declining (European Commission, 1996; ONS, 1991). This, combined with the emergence of political lobbies for the older generation, must provoke questions about who is to speak for children in decisions about resource allocation and how inter-generational distributive justice is to be achieved and maintained (Sgritta, 1994, p 361). From this point of view public institutions that give representation to children's interests and needs would seem to be increasingly necessary.

Second, if it is true that Beck's second modernisation is in process, then we would expect to find moves towards the disintegration of a standardised childhood, both in the consciousness of individual children and in the diversification of their life conditions. These phenomena are in fact already well known (Clarke, 1996). The implementation of civic childhood, therefore, faces the problem of translating a general commitment to provide children with a decent and fair share of resources into the delivery of public goods and services in ways that recognise children's increasingly diverse and complex life circumstances.

In this situation treating children the *same* may have to mean *different*. This point does not necessarily index an opposition to universal services and benefits but it does require a critical reflection on the way resources are made available and flexibility in their content. It seems unlikely that the provision of a standard childhood to individualised children will be accomplished by the routine methods of welfarism. Rather, the demand is for more responsive institutions that engage in a more creative dialogue with their users (OECD, 1998).

Attempts to build procedures for children's participation in decision making speak directly to these questions of flexibility, institutional responsiveness and engagement. Although more is needed, there is already a growing body of research suggesting that the participation of children in genuine decision making in school and neighbourhood has many positive outcomes (Landsdowne, 1995; Matthews and Limb, 2000; Smith, 2000; Alderson, 1999; Freeman and others, 1999).

This value of participation also needs to be seen in the context of young people's disengagement from public institutions. The disillusionment of the young, compared to their parents or grandparents, with conventional politics has been widely commented upon (Wilkinson and Mulgan, 1995). Similarly, there is much concern with children's disengagement from schooling. Acute manifestations include school exclusions and truancy (SEU, 1998). Although these involve a minority of children, some commentators (see Klein, 1999) argue that disaffection with schools is more pervasive and constitutes a burgeoning crisis for industrial societies.

Qualitative studies show children's attitude to school to be complex and ambivalent. Christensen and James (2001) suggest that, although children value education as a route to a good job, for many children their lack of control over the pace and content of school tasks makes it an experience to be endured. They experience the school environment as one of control and see it as the place where their right to have a say is least respected (Edwards and others, 2000; Mayall, 2000). However, while confirming that school is an anti-democratic environment for pupils, Alderson (1999) found enormous enthusiasm among children for genuine, practical involvement in improving their school. Nationally and internationally such experience is also being gained in a wide range of other contexts including after-school clubs, urban regeneration projects, and environmental planning processes.

Conclusion

There is much more to learn about how to make organisations better attuned to participation, how to engage children in serious dialogue and how to make participation practices appropriate and effective. There is a need for continual reflexivity about how control and self-realisation are constituted, played off and played into each other. In the UK participation initiatives, often scattered in local authorities or through the work of voluntary organisations, need to be brought together in a debate about a new approach to children that recognises the need to include children's voice.

Ultimately, however, what makes such a debate necessary is children's positioning in the complex, unforeseen consequences of the modern age. Children are caught up in this, made by and making it, for good or ill. Being a child is no longer, even if it ever was, simply a matter of being shaped by adult-controlled institutions. If individualisation processes continue then children will become evermore recognised as the active interpreters and co-producers of their own lives and hence of the communities and societies of which they are a part. In this sense good governance in the contemporary world may be compelled to recognise that children provide not a last recourse for controlling the future but simply another indication of modernity's limits.

Acknowledgements

I wish to thank the Economic and Social Research Council for their funding of the Children 5-16 Research Programme and the 22 project teams whose work has illuminated important aspects of contemporary childhood in Britain. I would also like to thank the two anonymous referees and Pia Christensen for their helpful comments on an earlier draft.

Note

[1] Pringle (1998) provides a thought-provoking discussion drawing on Esping-Andersen's categorisation of welfare regimes. Policy and practice towards children in neo-liberal, conservative corporatist and Nordic welfare states (exemplified by Britain, France and Sweden) are compared and contrasted. A useful and wide-ranging comparative discussion

is found in Dahlberg and others (1999). This not only contrasts the British experience to Nordic and European ones but also indicates some of the political issues that emerge when children's interests and voices are given greater prominence.

This chapter was taken from *Children & Society*, 2000, vol 14, no 4. The right of Alan Prout to be identified as author of this chapter has been asserted by him in accordance with the 1988 Copyright, Designs and Patents Act.

Conclusion

> Ethics deals with values, with good and bad, with right and wrong. We
> cannot avoid involvement in ethics for what we do – and what we don't
> do – is always a possible subject of ethical evaluation. (Singer, 1991, p v)

In this Reader I have sought to provide a compilation of chapters that offers
more than a 'balance sheet' approach to children and social policy. On the one
hand, I have chosen chapters which individually raise interesting, controversial
and significant matters concerning a range of conceptual frameworks pertaining
to what we can think of as 'moral agendas for children's welfare' (King, 1999).
On the other hand, my intention has been to reference many of these matters
through child-centred critiques of specific policies or policy areas.

Hopefully, when considered together, the chapters have shown the variety of
ways of thinking about children's well being or, to be more precise, about the
issues that are raised once the 'thinking' gets under way. It will no doubt be
obvious to anyone who has perused just a sample of the material here that 'child
welfare' is a multifaceted subject with a number of different and very often
conflicting interests, meanings and procedures. This should not come as a surprise,
nor should it be seen as an obstacle to clarifying contentious and intellectually
difficult issues.

A first and important step on the way to engaging in reasoned thought about
children and social policy is to be aware of the complex interplay of theories,
values, objectives and ramifications. I should make clear, however, that by 'thinking'
I have in mind, for example, not only the conceptual relationships involved in
trying to theorise who children *are* when they are *in* social policy (Chapter Four),
or what might be termed the epistemological/philosophical questions considered
by King (Chapter Three), but also those which surround (or *should* surround)
policy contexts given that the UK is a deeply adult-centric society: social capital
(Chapter Eight), disability (Chapter Eighteen), housing (Chapter Twenty-One),
social security benefits (Chapters Nineteen and Twenty), daycare (Chapter Twenty-
Four), and social investment (Chapter Twenty-Five). Indeed, these chapters are
illustrative of the *ramifications* of policies, as they demonstrate that children's interests
(including their wishes and anxieties which, it should be remembered are crucial
to individual self-worth) are not only overlooked, but are often suppressed, or
reinterpreted, by those of other and more powerful constituencies.

In many respects, children's well being has never been higher on the social
agenda – it has already been noted that between 1998-2003 there were more
than 23 significant policy initiatives in relation to child welfare (Fawcett et al,
2004, p 2), although it is neither so high as to give cause for complacency nor has
it reached the point where we can safely adopt a late-modern form of arrogance
with regard to the past. However, as I have indicated elsewhere (Hendrick, 2003,
p 252), legislative activity is not in itself a sign of progress and it may well be in
a form that many or most of those affected find irrelevant, oppressive and insulting.

Even a cursory acquaintance with the material in this volume shows that despite a number of benefits accruing to children since New Labour came to power (for a balanced account see Fawcett et al, 2004), many researchers are uneasy, if not downright critical, and feel that there is plenty of scope for further progress. Equally important is the willingness of many of the authors to think conceptually, not only in order to identify and understand the rationale of specific policies and their strengths and weaknesses, but also to identify and understand those ethical stances as they express adult values and principles with regard to children (on values and principles in social policy, see Drake, 2001). The contributors have also made it clear that social policy that is either for, or inclusive of, children is never independent of the more pervasive cultural understandings concerning *who* children are and what childhood *is*. In their different ways Moss and Petrie (Chapter Four) and Prout (Chapter Twenty-Six) raise questions about this issue as, in the context of specific policy areas, do the chapters considering 'rights' (Chapters Six, Nine, and Twelve), and also those which focus on the governmental use of law in order to control young people and quell what is deemed to be 'anti-social' behaviour – the latter being primarily a matter of political objectives (Chapters Thirteen to Sixteen).

Implicit in the conceptualising of *who* children are is the existence of a social context. It is customary to position children within what have been referred to as the "wider social changes associated with the roles of men and women, families and the state" (Foley, in Foley et al, 2001, p 4), but not with reference to their own lives as social actors, however limited that may be depending on their age (for children as social actors, see volumes in the *Future of Childhood Series*, edited by Prout; for an historical consideration, see Hendrick in Christensen and James, 2000). Chapters Seven, Nine, Thirteen, Seventeen, Nineteen, Twenty-Three and Twenty-Four demonstrate that children *do* enter the social context by virtue of their association with adult groups as when, for example, they experience the implications of housing policy, are regarded as being within 'the family' for social security benefits, are seen as hindrances to mothers' participation in the labour market, and are generally considered as secondary figures in strategies for improving health. Children, and their welfare, are also defined with reference to their 'culture' (for race and culture, see Chapter Ten) and to particular social theories (Chapters Seven and Eight for the influence of 'risk' and social capital respectively). But there can be no more vivid illustration of the nature and extent to which children are dependent on adult social change than the ways in which they are being perceived and treated by the New Labour government that came to power in 1997. As an expression of its commitment to 'Third Way' politics (which is intended to deal with globalisation, the emergence of the knowledge economy, and individualisation), the government has moulded together a number of policies – economic, penal, educational, health – under the rubric of 'social investment', a theme that, as we have seen, explicitly identifies children as 'the future'.

The 'Third Way' responses to the transformations that are said to be "altering the landscape of politics" (the above-mentioned globalisation, and so on) regard children as a malleable form of human capital suitable for a variety of purposes: economic, educational, familial, generational and, not least representational, in the sense that with 'proper parenting' they may embody an ideal citizenship. In this respect, social policy embraces children in order to involve them in a kind of lifelong enterprise, usually and disproportionately on behalf of (adult) 'others' (here I am deliberately inverting the conventional use of 'other' to mean *included* rather than excluded or deviant). And it is not only troubled and troublesome children who figure in this programme, although it is they who are regularly exploited by the media (and conveniently so for the government in that the 'anti-social' behaviour of young people – and 'irresponsible' parenting – can be presented as a major concern of the electorate). An increasing proportion of children are being brought into contact with authorised micro social systems, such as Sure Start, expanded daycare and nursery services and, perhaps the principal conduit of social discipline, aside from the family, schooling, which of course is not a new cultural force, but is one that has become increasingly subject to government-controlled curriculum and panoply of tests for even the youngest age groups, together with a growing contractual dimension involving good behaviour, attendance, and homework. It is the view of the government that

> Schools, along with families, have a responsibility to ensure that children and young people learn respect for others and for themselves. They need to appreciate and understand the moral code on which civilised society is based and to appreciate the culture and background of others. They need to develop the strength of character and attitudes to life and work, such as responsibility, determination, care and generosity, which will enable them to become citizens of a successful democratic society. (DfEE, 1997)

Clearly, children are involved here in a comprehensive agenda that looks to the school and the family to provide similar environments in which children can be bound to the goals of the social investment strategies (see Chapters Nine, Twenty-Three, Twenty-Five), the long-term outcome of which is intended to be a consensual state which has successfully minimised discord caused by gender, race and especially social class.

The reference above to a consensual state should remind us that there is more at stake in the present 'restructuring' of welfare than investment in economic competitiveness and social inclusion. Numerous commentators have observed how, in the last decade or so, we have witnessed a trend towards "a 'new' mode of governance, involving the reconfiguration of relationships between the state and civil society, the public and private sectors, citizens and communities" (Newman, 2001, p 4; see my introduction to Part Four and references to Giddens and Esping-Andersen). 'Governance' usually implies "a change in the meaning of government, referring to a *new* process of governing; or a *changed* condition of ordered rule; or the *new* method by which society is governed" (Rhodes, 1997, p 46, quoted in Newman, 2001, p 11; emphasis original; see also Rose, in Barry et al, 1996; Kooiman, 2003). This 'new' mode is embodied in New Labour's 'modernisation' project, which is designed to invoke a 'new' set of moral and civic principles to drive forward the reshaping of civic society (Hendrick, 2003, pp 234-8). But reference to 'civic society' hardly reveals the scale of the undertaking where children are concerned, for what is in process is a 'remaking' of childhood (in concert with that of 'parenthood', 'marriage', 'welfare', 'citizenship' and so on) of the kind deemed by the government to be suitable for what is so often referred to as 'post-modern society' (for a brief account of the 'remaking' of childhood in the late 19th to early 20th centuries, see Hendrick, 1997, pp 9-15).

In some senses this returns us to the theme of the child as human capital, as 'citizen worker-in-becoming' (Chapter Twenty-Five) and to the place of 'child welfare' in the scheme of governance, particularly in its form as 'government at a distance', which occurs in part through disciplined individuals regulating themselves. Nikolas Rose has explained the process as one of the "shaping of the private self", meaning that modern governments (not only New Labour) want populations to govern themselves so that the state does "less of the rowing and more of the steering". Thus 'dependency' is transformed into autonomy, with the individual being capable of self-government, which in turn allows for 'distance' between the government and the governed. Hence the importance of the slogan 'education, education, education', which is concerned not merely with training in skills that may be necessary for many job transitions, *"more important is the development of cognitive and emotional competence"* (Giddens, 1998, p 125; emphasis added). What is referred to here as "emotional competence" pervades all the current strategies that constitute the New Labour agenda: 'welfare to work', 'from social exclusion to social inclusion', 'no rights without responsibilities', 'positive welfare', and 'citizenship for the 21st century', to name but several. No wonder it has been claimed that modern governance is about "governing the soul" (Rose, 1999).

All the matters mentioned above have been discussed in one way or another by the chapters in this volume. However, thinking theoretically (and politically) about child welfare remains in a rather elementary stage of development, although the 'new' social studies of childhood has done much to provide children with both an academic and a policy presence (James and Prout, 1990/97; Alanen, 1992; Qvortrup et al, 1994; Jenks, 1996; James et al, 1998; Christensen and James, 2000; Lee, 2001; Mayall, 2002; Hallett and Prout, 2003; James and James, 2004). Even so, children ('kids') continue to remain marginal figures within public debates and are always at risk of being caricatured, certainly by government rhetoric and the tabloid press. It may well be that part of the difficulty of establishing and sustaining both a more informed and a more just conception of children is the widely (and erroneously) held view that childhood is *simply* a stage in the life course, always in motion as it advances towards adulthood. The child as becoming, as unfinished, is a difficult image to shift – not least because it is *in part* an accurate representation. The varieties of childhood, especially as they are marked out by different ages, seem to be too complex for the popular imagination to grasp (and dealing with them in a fair and reasonable manner would require too much revision of adult prejudice). And as children are unable to create a social movement comparable to that of, say, feminism, they are deprived of an effective political response. It looks as if for the foreseeable future, children will need our empathy, defined sociologically as "the ability to assume or take on the social roles and attitudes of other social actors" (Abercrombie et al, 2000, p 117). In some respects 'child welfare' seems to be not too different from animal welfare: it offers us the opportunity to think and act ethically, but usually on our own terms. And yet, in these morally ambivalent times, perhaps we should keep in mind, with respect to our obligations to children, the cautionary words, written many years ago, of the late James Baldwin, the American novelist and essayist:

> For nothing is fixed, forever and forever and forever, it is not fixed; the earth is always shifting, the light is always changing, the sea does not cease to grind down rock. Generations do not cease to be born, and we are responsible to them because we are the only witnesses they have. The sea rises, the light fails, lovers cling to each other, and children cling to us. The moment we cease to hold each other, the sea engulfs us and the light goes out.

References

Abel-Smith, B. and Townsend, P. (1965) *The poor and the poorest*, London: Bell and Sons.

Abercrombie, N., Hills, S. and Turner, B.B. (2000) *The Penguin dictionary of sociology*, Harmondsworth: Penguin.

Acherson, N. (1998) 'We live under the most arrogant of world orders', *Independent on Sunday*, 25 January.

Adams, J. (1995) *Risk*, London: UCL Press.

Adelman, L. and Bradshaw, J. (1999) *Children in poverty in Britain: Analysis of the family resources survey 1994/95*, York: Social Policy Research Unit, University of York.

Adelman, L., Middleton, S. and Ashworth, K. (2003) *Poorest children: Severe and persistent poverty and social exclusion*, London: Save the Children and Centre for Research in Social Policy.

Advisory Board on Family Law (1999) *A consultation paper on contact between children and violent parents*, London: Lord Chancellor's Department.

Ahmad, D. (1990) *Black perspectives in social work*, Birmingham: Venture Press.

Ahmad, W., Darr, A. and Jones, L. (2000) '"I send my child to school and he comes back an Englishman": minority ethnic deaf people, identity politics and services', in W. Ahmad (ed) *Ethnicity, disability and chronic illness*, Buckingham: Open University Press.

Alanen, L. (1992) *Modern childhood? Exploring the 'child question' in sociology*, Research Reports 50, Finland: University of Jyvaskyla.

Alanen, L. (1994) 'Gender and generation: feminism and the "child question"', in J. Qvortrup, M. Bardy, G. Sgritta and H. Wintersberger (eds) *Childhood matters: Social theory, practice and politics*, Aldershot: Avebury.

Alaszewski, A. and Walsh, M. (1995) 'Literature review: typologies of welfare organisations', *British Journal of Social Work*, vol 25, pp 805-15.

Alderson, P. (1990) *Choosing for children*, Oxford: Oxford University Press.

Alderson, P. (1993) *Children's consent to surgery*, Buckingham: Open University Press.

Alderson, P. (1995) *Listening to children*, Ilford: Barnardo's.

Alderson, P. (1999) 'Civil rights in schools', ESRC Children 5-16 Research Programme Briefing (www.esrc.ac.uk/curprog.html).

Aldgate, J. and Statham, D. (2001) *The Children Act: New messages from research*, London: The Stationery Office.

Aldgate. K. and Tunstill, J. (1995) *Making sense of Section 17: Implementing services for children in need within the 1989 Children Act*, London: HMSO.

Aldridge, J. and Becker, S. (2002) 'Children who care: rights and wrongs in debate and policy on young carers', in B. Franklin, *The new handbook of children's rights*, London: Routledge.

Aldridge, M. (1994) *Making social work news*, London: Routledge.

Aldridge, T. (1994) 'Opinion: repent at pleasure', *Solicitors Journal*, vol 138, p 838, 19 August.

Ali, Z., Fazil, A., Bywaters, P., Wallace, L. and Singh, G. (2001) 'Disability, ethnicity and childhood: a critical review of research', *Disability and Society*, vol 16, no 7, pp 949-67.

Allatt, P. (1993) 'Becoming privileged: the role of family process', in I. Bates and G. Riseborough, *Youth and inequality*, Buckingham: Open University Press.

Allatt, P. (1996) 'Consuming schooling: choice, commodity, gift and systems of exchange', in S. Edgell, K. Hetherington and A. Warde (eds) *Consumption matters: The production and experiences of consumption*, Oxford: Blackwell/ *The Sociological Review*.

Allen, N. (1992) *Making sense of the Children Act* (2nd edn), London: Longman.

Allen, R. (2002) '"There must be some better way of dealing with kids": young offenders, public attitudes and policy change', *Youth Justice*, vol 2, no 1, pp 3-13.

Allsop, J. (1984) *Health policy and the National Health Service*, London: Longman.

Alston, P. (1994) *The best interests of the child: Reconciling culture with human rights*, Oxford: Clarendon Press.

Alston, P. and Parker, S. (1992) 'Introduction', in P. Alston, S. Parker and J. Seymour (eds) *Children, rights and the law*, Oxford: Clarendon Press.

Amato, P. (1995) 'Single-parent households as settings for children's development, well-being and attainment: a social network/resources perspective', in A.-M. Ambert (ed) *Sociological studies of children*, vol 7, pp 19-47.

Amin, K. and Oppenheim, C. (1992) *Poverty in black and white: Deprivation and ethnic minorities*, London: Child Poverty Action Group.

Anderson, B. (2002) 'The time for sentimentalism is over: let us tame these feral children', *Independent*, 29 April.

Anderson, J. (2000) '"Stop smacking us!"', *ChildRight*, no 168, p 15.

Andrews, M. (1994) *Dickens and the grown-up child*, Basingstoke: Macmillan.

Appiah, K.A. (1985) 'The uncompleted argument: Du Bois and the illusion of race', in H.L. Gates, Jr (ed) *'Race', writing and difference*, Chicago, IL: University of Chicago Press, pp 21-37.

Archard, D.W. (1993) *Children: Rights and childhood*, London: Routledge.

Archard, D.W. (2003) *Children, family and the state*, Aldershot: Ashgate.

Archbishops of Canterbury and York (1990) *Faith in the countryside – Report of the Archbishops' Commission on Rural Areas*, Worthing: Churchman Publishing.

Aries, P. (1973) *Centuries of childhood*, Harmondsworth: Penguin.

Armstrong, D. (1983) *The political anatomy of the body*, Cambridge: Cambridge University Press.

Armstrong, D. (1986) 'The invention of infant mortality', *Sociology of Health and Illness*, vol 8.

Armstrong, D. (1995) 'The rise of surveillance medicine', *Sociology of Health and Illness*, vol 17, no 3, pp 392-414.

Arnot, M., David, M. and Weiner, G. (1999) *Closing the gender gap*, Cambridge: Polity.

Arthur, J. (2003) 'Multi-culturalism', in H. Lafolletee (ed) *Oxford handbook of ethics*, Oxford: Oxford University Press.

Ashenden, S. (1996) 'Reflective governance and child sexual abuse: liberal welfare rationality and the Cleveland Inquiry', *Economy and Society*, vol 25, no 1, pp 64-88.

Ashton, D. and Green, F. (1996) *Education, training and the global economy*, London: Edward Elgar.

Ashworth, K., Hill, M. and Walker, R. (1992) *A new approach to poverty dynamics*, Working Papers of the European Scientific Network on Household Panel Studies, Colchester: University of Essex Institute for Social and Economic Research.

Ashworth, K., Middleton, S. and Walker, R. (1997) *Income Support dynamics: Evidence from administrative data*, CRSP Paper 257a, Loughborough: Loughborough University Centre for Research in Social Policy, Social Security Unit.

Association of Directors of Social Services and NCH Action for Children (1996) *Children still in need: Refocusing child protection in the context of children in need*, London: NCH Action for Children.

Atkinson, A.B. (1995) *Incomes and the welfare state: Essays on Britain and Europe*, Cambridge: Cambridge University Press.

Audit Commission (1994) *Seen but not heard: Coordinating community child health and social services for children in need*, London: HMSO.

Audit Commission (1996) *Misspent youth, young people and crime*, London: Audit Commission for Local Authorities and the National Health Service in England and Wales.

Audit Commission (1998) *Misspent youth '98: The challenge of youth justice*, London: Audit Commission.

Audit Commission (1999a) *Safety in numbers: Promoting community safety*, London: Audit Commission.

Audit Commission (1999b) *Children in mind*, London: Audit Commission.

BACCH (British Association for Community Child Health) (1995) *Child health matters: Implementing the UN Convention on the Rights of the Child within the National Health Service. A practitioners' guide*, London: BACCH.

Backett, K.C. (1990) 'Image and reality: health enhancing behaviours in middle class families', *Health Education Journal*, vol 49, no 2, pp 61-3.

Backett, K.C. (1992) 'Taboos and excesses: lay health moralities in middle class families', *Health Education Journal*, vol 49, no 2, pp 61-3.

Backett, K.C. and Alexander, H. (1991) 'Talking to young children about health: methods and findings', *Health Education Journal*, vol 50, no 1, pp 34-8.

Bailey Harris, R., Davis, G., Barron, R. and Pearce, J. (1998) *Monitoring private law applications under the Children Act: A research report to the Nuffield Foundation*, Bristol: University of Bristol.

Bailey, R. (1996) 'Prenatal testing and the prevention of impairment', in J. Morris (ed) *Encounters with strangers: Feminism and disability*, London: Women's Press.

Bailey, V. (1987) *Delinquency and citizenship: Reclaiming the young offender, 1914-1948*, Oxford: Oxford University Press.

Bainham, A. (1990) 'The privatisation of the public interest in children', *Modern Law Review*, vol 53, no 2, p 206.

Baistow, K. (1995) 'From sickly survival to the realisation of potential: child health as a social project', *Children & Society*, vol 9, no 1.

Balchin, P. (1995) *Housing policy*, London: Routledge.

Baldwin, S. and Carlisle, J. (1994) *Social support for disabled children and their families*, London: HMSO.

Ball, S. (1998) 'Education policy', in N. Ellison and C. Pierson (eds) *Developments in British social policy*, Basingstoke: Macmillan.

Bandalli, S. (2000) 'Children, responsibility and the new youth justice', in B. Goldson (ed) *The new youth justice*, Dorset: Russell House Publishing, pp 81-95.

Bane, M.J. and Ellwood, D.T. (1994) *Welfare realities: From rhetoric to reform*, Cambridge, MA: Harvard University Press.

Banting, K. (1979) *Poverty, politics and policy*, Basingstoke: Macmillan.

Barber, M. (2000) 'High expectations and standards for all – no matter what', *Times Educational Supplement*, 2 November.

Barclay, P. (1995) *Income and wealth*, vol 1, York: Joseph Rowntree Foundation.

Bargen, J. (1995) 'A critical view of conferencing', *Australian and New Zealand Journal of Criminology*, vol 25, pp 100-13.

Barn, R. (2002) '"Race", ethnicity and child welfare', in B. Mason and A. Sawyers (eds) *Exploring the unsaid*, London: Karnac, pp 3-15.

Barn, R., Sinclair, R. and Ferdinand, D. (1997) *Acting on principle: An examination of race and ethnicity in social services provision for children and families*, London: BAA/CRE.

Barnardo's (1998) *Children are unbeatable*, Ilford: Barnardo's.

Barnes, M. (2000) 'Editorial: keeping up the pressure', *Poverty*, no 106, p 1.

Barrett, M. and McIntosh, M. (1982) *The anti-social family*, London: Verso-NLB.

Barrett Browning, E. (1843) *Theory of the children*.

Barry, A., Osbrone, T. and Rose, N. (eds) (1996) *Foucault and political reason: Liberalism, neo-liberalism and rationalities of government*, London: University College Press.

Barry, B. (2000) *Culture and equality*, Cambridge: Polity Press.

Barth, R.P. (1997) 'Effects of age and race on the odds of adoption versus remaining in long-term out-of-home care', *Child Welfare*, vol 76, no 2, pp 285-308.

Barton, C. and Douglas, G. (1995) *Law and parenthood*, London: Butterworth.

Baruch, G. and James, K. (2003) *The National Framework for Children, Young People and Maternity Services: The mental health and psychological wellbeing of children and young people. Report from consultation with users of child and adolescent mental health services*, London: DH.

Bashevkin, S. (2000) *Road-testing the Third Way: Welfare reform in Canada, Britain and the United States*, Jerusalem: The Hebrew University of Jerusalem.

Bateman, T. (2002) 'A note on the relationship between the Detention and Training Order and Section 91 of the Powers of the Criminal Courts (Sentencing) Act 2000: a recipe for injustice', *Youth Justice*, vol 1, no 3, pp 36-41.

Bateman, T. (2003) 'Living with final warnings: making the best of a bad job?', *Youth Justice*, vol 2, no 3, pp 131-40.

Bates, P. (1994) 'Children in secure psychiatric units: Re K, W and H – "Out of sight, out of mind"?', *Journal of Child Law*, vol 6, no 3, pp 131-7.

Bauman, Z. (1998) *Work, consumerism and the new poor*, Buckingham: Open University Press.

Bauman, Z. (1999) *In search of politics*, Cambridge: Polity Press.

Beall, J. (1997) 'Social capital in waste – a solid investment?', *Journal of International Development*, vol 89, no 7, pp 951-61.

Beck, U. (1992) *Risk society*, London: Sage Publications.

Beck, U. (1997) 'Democratisation of the family', *Childhood*, vol 4, no 2, pp 151-68.

Beck, U. (1998) *Democracy without enemies*, Cambridge: Polity Press.

Beck, U. and Beck-Gernsheim, E. (2002) *Reinventing the family*, Cambridge: Polity.

Beck, W., van der Maesen, L. and Walker, A. (eds) (1997) *The social quality of Europe*, The Hague/London/Boston: Kluwer Law International.

Becker, H. (1963) *Outsiders*, New York, NY: Free Press of Glencoe.

Becker, S., Aldridge, J. and Dearden, C. (1998) *Young carers and their families*, Oxford: Blackwell.

Beenstock, M. (1984) 'Rationalising child benefit', Paper given at Policy Studies Institute Seminar, London, June (cited in J. Brown, 1988).

Begum, N., Hill, M. and Stevens, A. (1994) *Reflections: Views of black people on their lives and community care*, CCETSW Paper 32.3, London: Central Council for Education and Training in Social Work.

Behlmer, G.K. (1982) *Child abuse and moral reform in England, 1870-1908*, Stanford, CA: Stanford University Press.

Beiner, R. (ed) (1995) *Theorizing citizenship*, Albany, NY: State University of New York Press.

Bell, C. (1999) 'Appealing for justice for children and young people: a critical analysis of the Crime and Disorder Bill', in B. Goldson (ed) *Youth justice: Contemporary policy and practice*, Aldershot: Ashgate, pp 191-210.

Bell, V. (1994) 'Dreaming and time in Foucault's philosophy', *Theory Culture and Society*, vol 11, pp 151-63.

Belsky, J. (2001) 'Developmental risks (still) associated with early child care', *Journal of Psychological Psychiatry*, vol 42, no 7, pp 845-59.

Belsky, J. (2002) 'Quality counts: amount of childcare and children's socioemotional development', *Developmental and Behavioral Pediatrics*, vol 23, no 3, June, pp 167-70.

Bennett, A. (1997) *Talking heads*, London: Faber and Faber Ltd.

Bennett, D.L. (1985) 'Young people and their health needs', *Seminars in Adolescent Medicine*, vol 1, no 1, pp 1-14.

Beresford, B. (1994) *Positively parents: Caring for a severely disabled child*, London: HMSO.

Berkowitz, S. (1991) *Key findings from the State Survey: Component of the Study of High Risk Child Abuse and Neglect Groups*, Washington, DC: National Center on Child Abuse and Neglect.

Berry, L.C. (1999) *The child, the state, and the Victorian novel*, Charlottesville/London: University Press of Virginia.

Beveridge, Sir W. (1942) *Report on social insurance and allied services*, Cmd 6404, London: HMSO.

Beyer, S. and Kampmann, J. (1999) 'Unconventional perspectives on learning and learning sites', Paper to conference on Sites of Learning, Hull University, September.

Bianchi, S.M. and Robinson, J. (1997) 'What did you do today? Children's use of time, family composition, and the acquisition of cultural capital', *Journal of Marriage and the Family*, no 59, pp 332-44, May.

Bignall, T. and Butt, J. (2000) *Between ambition and achievement: Young black people's views and experiences of independence and independent living*, Bristol/York: The Policy Press/Joseph Rowntree Foundation.

Bjørnson, Ø. and Haavet, L.E. (1994) *Langsomt ble landet et velferdssamfunn: Trygdens historie 1894-1994*, Oslo: Ad NotamGyldendal.

Blair, T. (1998a) *The Third Way: New politics for the new century*, London: Fabian Society.

Blair, T. (1998b) 'The government's strategy', *The Government's Annual Report 1997/98*, London: The Stationery Office.

Blair, T. (1991) Beveridge Lecture, Toynbee Hall, London, 18 March, reproduced in R. Walker (ed) *Ending child poverty*, Bristol: The Policy Press.

Blair, T. (2002a) 'New Labour and community', *Renewal*, vol 10, no 2, pp 9-14.

Blair, T. (2002b) Speech to Labour Party Conference, Blackpool, 1 October (www.labour.org/uk/tbconfspeech/).

Blair, T. (2002c) 'My vision for Britain', *Observer*, 10 November.

Blair, T. (2004a) 'Foreword', *Cutting crime, delivering justice: A strategic plan for criminal justice*, London, The Stationery Office, pp 5-6.

Blair, T. (2004b) 'Foreword', *Confident communities in a secure Britain: The Home Office Strategic Plan 2004-08*, London, The Stationery Office, pp 5-6.

Blair, T. and Schröder, G. (1991) 'Europe: the Third Way/Die Neue Mitte', reproduced in *The Spokesman*, no 66, pp 27-37.

Bluebond-Langer, M. (1978) *The private worlds of dying children*, Princeton, NJ: Princeton University Press.

Bluebond-Langer, M. (1991) 'Living with cystic fibrosis', *Medical Anthropology Quarterly*, vol 5, no 2, pp 133-52.

Blumbery, A. (1969) 'The practice of law as a confidence game', in Y. Aubert (ed) (1971) *The sociology of law*, Harmondsworth: Penguin.

Blunkett, D., Falconer, C. and Goldsmith, P. (2004) 'Preface', *Cutting crime, delivering justice: A strategic plan for criminal justice*, London, The Stationery Office, pp 7-8.

Blustein, J. (1979) 'Child rearing and family interests', in O. O'Neill and W. Ruddick (eds) *Having children: Philosophical and legal reflections on parenthood*, New York, NY: Oxford University Press.

Blyth, E (1990) 'Assisted reproduction: what's in it for children?', *Children's Society*, vol 4, no 2, pp 167, 182.

Boisjoly, J., Duncan, G.J. and Hofferth, S. (1995) 'Access to social capital', *Journal of Family Issues*, vol 16, no 5, pp 609-31.

Bojer, H. (2000) 'Children and theories of social justice', *Feminist Economics*, vol 6, no 2, pp 23-39.

Booth Report (1985) *Report of the Matrimonial Causes Procedure Committee*, London: HMSO.

Borland, M. et al (1996) *Parenting in middle childhood*, Glasgow: Report to Health Education Board for Scotland.

Boss, P. (1971) *Exploration in child care*, London: Routledge and Kegan Paul.

Boswell, G. (1991) *Section 53 Offenders: An exploration of experience and needs*, London: The Prince's Trust.

Botting, B. and Crawley, R. (1995) 'Trends and patterns in childhood mortality and morbidity', in B. Botting (ed) *The health of our children*, London: HMSO.

Bourdieu, P. (1984) *Distinction. A social critique of the judgement of taste*, London: Routledge.

Bourdieu, P. (1986) 'The forms of capital', in J.G. Richardson (ed) *Handbook of theory and research for the sociology of education*, New York, NY: Greenwood Press.

Bourdieu, P. (1991) 'Epilogue: on the possibility of a field of world sociology', in P. Bourdieu and J.S. Coleman (eds) *Social theory for a changing society*, Boulder, CO: Westview Press.

Bourdieu, P. (1993) *Sociology in question*, London, Sage Publications.

Boushel, M. (1994) 'The protective environment of children: towards a framework for anti-oppressive, cross-cultural and cross-national understanding', *British Journal of Social Work*, no 24, pp 173-90.

Bowlby, J. (1951) *Maternal care and mental health*, Geneva: WHO.

Bowlby, J. (1969) *Attachment and loss*, London: Howarth Press.

Boyle, D. (2001) *The tyranny of numbers*, London: Harper Collins.

Boyne, R. and Rattansi, A. (eds) (1990) *Postmodernism and society*, Basingstoke: Macmillan.

Bradbury, B., Jenkins, S.P. and Micklewright J. (eds) (2001) *The dynamics of child poverty in industrialised countries*, Cambridge: Cambridge University Press.

Bradley, D. (1990) 'Children, family and the state in Sweden', *Journal of Law and Society*, vol 17, no 4, pp 427-44.

Bradshaw, J. (1990) *Child poverty and deprivation in the UK*, London: National Children's Bureau.

Bradshaw, J. (1993) *Budget standards for the United Kingdom*, Aldershot: Avebury.

Bradshaw, J. (ed) (2001) *Poverty: The outcomes for children*, London: Family Policy Studies Centre.

Bradshaw, J. (ed) (2002) *The well-being of children*, London: Save the Children.

Brandon, M., Thoburn, J., Lewis, A. and Way, A. (1999) *Safeguarding children with the 1989 Children Act*, London: The Stationery Office.

Brannen, J. (1999) 'Reconsidering children and childhood: sociological and policy perspectives', in E.B. Silva and C. Smart (eds) *The new family?*, London: Sage Publications.

Brannen, J. and Edwards, R. (eds) (1996) *Perspectives on parenting and childhood: Looking back and moving forward*, London: South Bank University.

Brannen, J. and Moss, P. (eds) (2003) *Rethinking children's care*, Buckingham: Open University Press.

Brannen, J. and O'Brien, J. (1995) 'Childhood and the sociological gaze: paradigms and paradoxes', *Sociology*, vol 29, no 4, pp 729-37.

Brannen, J. and O'Brien, M. (eds) (1996) *Children in families: Research and policy*, London: Flamer Press.

Brannen, J., Dodd, D., Oakley, A. and Storey, P. (1994) *Young people: Health and family life*, Buckingham: Open University Press.

Breggin, P. (1998) *Talking back to Ritalin: What doctors aren't telling you about stimulant drugs for children*, Monroe: Common Courage Press.

Brian, J. and Martin, M.D. (1983) *Child care and health for nursery nurses*, Amersham: Hulton.

Bromley, P. and Lowe, N. (1992) *Bromley's family law* (8th edn), London: Butterworths.

Brophy, J. and Bates, P. (1999) *The guardian ad litem: Complex cases and the use of experts following the Children Act 1989*, Research Paper no 3/99, London: Lord Chancellor's Department.

Brown, C. (1984) *Black and white Britain: The Third PI Survey*, Aldershot: Gower.

Brown, G. (1991) 'A scar on the nation's soul', *Poverty*, no 104.

Brown, G. (2000a) Speech to the Children and Young Person's Unit Conference, Islington, London, 15 November.

Brown, G. (2000b) Speech to the CPAG Child Poverty Conference, 'Our children are our future', London, 15 May.

Brown, G. (2001) 'Foreword', in HM Treasury (2001).

Brown, G. (2002a) 'Budget Statement', *House of Commons Hansard*, 17 April.

Brown, G. (2002b) 'Spending Review', *House of Commons Hansard*, 15 July.

Brown, J.B. (1993) *The home: In its relation to man and society*.

Brown, J. (1988) *Child Benefit: Investing in the future*, London: Child Poverty Action Group.

Brown, J. (1989) *In search of a policy: The rationale for social security provision for one parent families*, London: National Council for One Parent Families.

Brown, P. and Lauder, H. (1996) 'Education, globalisation and economic development', *Journal of Education Policy*, vol 11, no 1, pp 1-26.

Brynin, M. and Scott, J. (1996) *Young people, health and the family*, London: Health Education Authority.

Buckingham, D. (2000) *After the death of childhood*, Cambridge: Polity Press.

Burman, E. (1994) *Deconstructing developmental psychology*, London: Routledge.

Burman, E. (2001) 'Beyond the baby and the bathwater: postdualistic developmental psychologies for diverse childhoods', *European Early Childhood Education Research Journal*, vol 9, no 1, pp 5-22.

Burns, L. and Smith, A. (1994) *The end of bed and breakfast?*, London: Shelter.

Burrows, L. and Walentowicz, P. (1992) *Homes cost less than homelessness*, London: Shelter.

Butler, I. and Williamson, H. (1994) *Children speak: Children, trauma and social work*, Harlow: Longman.

Butler-Sloss (1988) *Report of the Inquiry into Child Abuse in Cleveland*, Cmnd 412, London: HMSO.

Cadranel, J.A. (1991) 'Paediatrics', in H. Davis and L. Fallowfiled (eds) *Counselling and communication in health care*, Chichester: Wiley.

Cain, M. (ed) (1989) *Growing up good: Policing the behaviour of girls in Europe*, London: Sage Publications.

Calder, A. (1971) *The people's war*, London.

Calouste Gulbenkian Foundation (1993) *One scandal too many ... the case for comprehensive protection for children in all settings*, London: Calouste Gulbenkian Foundation.

Campbell, A. (1981) *Girl delinquents*, Oxford: Blackwell.

Campbell, C. (1997) 'Moving beyond health education: the role of social capital in conceptualising "health-enabling communities"', Draft paper, Gender Institute, LSE, submitted for publication.

Campbell, C. with Wood, R. and Kelly, M. (in press) *Social capital and health*, London: Health Education Authority.

Campbell, J.D. (1975) 'Illness is a point of view', *Child Development*, vol 46, p 100.

Campbell, T. (1992) 'The rights of the minor: as person, as child, as future adult', *International Journal of Law and the Family*, vol 6, pp 1-23.

Cannan, C. (1992) *Changing families, changing welfare*, Hemel Hempstead: Harvester Wheatsheaf.

Cantwell, B. and Scott, S. (1995) 'Children's wishes, children's burdens', *Journal of Social Welfare and Family Law*, vol 17, no 3, p 377.

Cantwell, B., Roberts, J. and Young, V. (1999) 'Presumption of contact in private law: an interdisciplinary issue', *Family Law*, no 29, pp 226-32.

Carling, A., Duncan, S. and Edwards, R. (2002) *Analysing families*, London: Routledge.

Carney, T. (1991) 'Social security: dialogue or closure?', in P. Alston and G. Breenan (eds) *The UN Children's Convention and Australia,* Melbourne: Methuen, pp 202-20.

Carney, T. (1992) '"Reconciling the irreconcilable"?: a rights or interests based approach to uncontrollability? a comment on Seymour', in P. Alston, S. Parker and J. Seymour (eds) *Children, rights and the law*, Oxford: Oxford University Press.

Carney, T. and Tait, D. (1997) *The adult guardianship experiment: Tribunals and popular justice*, Sydney: Federation Press.

Castel, R. (1991) 'From dangerousness to risk', in G. Burchell, C. Gordon and P. Miller (eds) *The Foucault effect: Studies in governmentality*, Hemel Hempstead: Harvester Wheatsheaf.

Chapin, H.D. *The theory and practice of infant feeding*.

Chazan, M., Laing, A.F. and Davies, D. (1994) *Emotional and behavioural difficulties in middle childhood*, London: Falmer Press.

Children's Legal Centre (1991) 'Young people, mental health and the law', *ChildRight*, vol 78, pp 23-5.

Children's Legal Centre (1993) 'Mental health code revised', *ChildRight*, vol 101, pp 7-8.

Children's Legal Centre (1994) 'How schools exclude black children', *ChildRight*, vol 109, pp 13-14.

Children's Legal Centre (1995) 'Consent to medical treatment – young people's legal rights', *ChildRight*, vol 115, pp 11-14.

Children's Rights Office (1998) *A report to the UK government on progress towards implementing the convention on the rights of the child: A summary of the views and concerns of those working with children*, London: Children's Rights Office.

Children's Society, The (1996) *A little voice*, London: The Children's Society.

Children's Society, The (2000) *Guarding children's interests*, London: The Children's Society.

Christensen, P. and James, A. (eds) (2000) *Research with children*, London: Falmer Press.

Christensen, P. and James, A. (2001) 'What are schools for? The temporal experience of learning', in L. Alanen and B. Mayall (eds) *Conceptualising child–adult relationships*, London: Falmer Press.

Christensen, P. and James, A. (2001) 'What are schools for: the temporal experience of learning', in B. Mayall and L. Allanen (eds) *Conceptualising child–adult relations*, London: Falmer Press.

Claflin, C.J. and Barbarin, O.A. (1991) 'Does "telling" less protect more?', *Journal of Pediatric Psychology*, vol 16, no 2, pp 169-91.

Clarke, J. (1991) 'Coming to terms with culture', in H. Dean and R. Woods (eds) *Social policy review 11*, Luton: Social Policy Association.

Clarke, J. (ed) (1993) *A crisis in care? Challenges to social work*, London: Sage Publications/Open University.

Clarke, J. (1997) 'Capturing the customer', *Self, Agency and Society*, vol 1, no 1, pp 55-73.

Clarke, J. (1998) 'Consumerism', in G. Hughes (ed) *Imagining welfare futures*, London: Routledge.

Clarke, J. (1998) 'Thriving on chaos? Managerialism and the welfare state', in J. Carter (ed) *Postmodernity and the fragmentation of welfare*, London: Routledge.

Clarke, J. (2000) 'Governing welfare systems: subjects and states', Paper presented at the Social Policy Association Annual Conference, Roehampton.

Clarke, J. and Hoggett, P. (1991) 'Regressive modernisation? The changing patterns of social services delivery in the United Kingdom', in H. Wollmann and E. Schröter (eds) *Comparing public sector reform in Britain and Germany*, Aldershot: Ashgate.

Clarke, J. and Newman, J. (1997) *The managerial state*, London: Sage Publications.

Clarke, J., Gewirtz, S. and McLaughlin, E. (eds) (2000) *New managerialism, new welfare?*, London: Sage Publications.

Clarke, L. (1996) 'Demographic change and the family situation of children', in J. Brannen and M. O'Brien (eds) *Children in families: Research and policy*, London: Falmer Press.

Cleaver, H., Wattam, C. and Cawson, P. (1995) *Assessing risk in child protection, Final Report submitted to the Department of Health*, London: NSPCC.

Cmnd 9684 (1956) *Report of National Insurance Advisory Committee on the Question of Widow's Benefits*, London: HSMO.

Coady, C. (1992) 'Theory, rights and children: a comment on O'Neill and Campbell', *International Journal of Law and the Family*, vol 6, pp 46-63.

Cockburn, T. (1998) 'Children and citizenship in Britain: a case for a socially interdependent model of citizenship', *Childhood*, vol 5, no 1, pp 99-117.

Coggan, C., Patterson, P. and Fill, J. (1997) 'Suicide: qualitative data from focus group interviews with youth', *Social Science and Medicine*, vol 45, no 10, pp 1563-70.

Cohen, H. (1980) *Equal rights for children*, Towota, NJ: Littlefield, Adams.

Cohen, R., Coxall, J., Craig, G. and Sadiq-Sangster, A. (1992) *Hardship Britain*, London: CPAG.

Cohen, S. (1985) *Visions of social control*, Cambridge: Polity Press.

Cohen, S. and Scull, A. (eds) (1983) *Social control and the state: Historical and comparative essays*, Oxford: Basil Blackwell.

Cohen, S. and Syme, S.L. (eds) (1984) *Social support and health*, Orlando, FL: Academic Press.

Cole, M. (1961) *The story of Fabian socialism*, London: Heinemann.

Coleman, D. and Salt, J. (1996) *Ethnicity in the 1991 census: Volume one: Demographic characteristics of the ethnic minority populations*, London: The Stationery Office.

Coleman, J. (1993) 'Understanding adolescence today: a review', *Children & Society*, vol 7, no 2, pp 137-41.

Coleman, J. (1994) 'Black children in care: crisis of identity', *Runnymede Bulletin*, 4-5 October.

Coleman, J. (2000) 'Young people in Britain at the beginning of a new century', *Children & Society*, vol 14, no 4, pp 230-42.

Coleman, J.S. (1961) *The adolescent society: The social life of the teenager and its impact on education*, New York, NY: Free Press of Glencoe.

Coleman, J.S. (1988) 'Social capital in the creation of human capital', *American Journal of Sociology*, no 94 (Supplement) S95-S120.

Coleman, J.S. (1990) *The foundations of social theory*, Cambridge, MA: Harvard University Press.

Coleman, J.S. (1994a) 'Social capital, human capital, and investment in youth', in A.C. Petersen and J.T. Mortimer, *Youth unemployment and society*, Cambridge: Cambridge University Press.

Colton, M., Drury, C. and Williams, M. (1995) *Children in need: Family support under the Children Act 1989*, Aldershot: Avebury.

Community Care (2000) 'Compulsory treatment risk', *Community Care Magazine*, 9 March

Community Care, Mental Health Foundation and Young Minds (2002) 'Changing minds: better mental health care for children', *Community Care*, July.

Conway, J. (1988) *Prescription for poor health*, London: London Food Commission, Maternity Alliance, SHAC and Shelter.

Cooper, J. (1983) *The creation of the British Personal Social Services 1962-74*, London: Heinemann.

Coote, A. (2000) 'Introduction', in A. Coote (ed) *New gender agenda*, London: IPPR.

Coote, A. (2001) 'Feminism and the third way: a call for dialogue', in S. White (ed) *New Labour: The progressive future?*, Basingstoke/New York, NY: Palgrave.

Cooter, R. (1992) 'Introduction', in R. Cooter (ed) *In the name of the child: Health and welfare, 1880-1940*, London: Routledge.

Coppock, V. (2002) 'Medicalising children's behaviour', in B. Franklin, *The new handbook of children's rights*, London: Routledge.

Coppock, V., Haydon, D. and Richter, I. (1995) *The illusions of post-feminism: New women, old myths*, London: Taylor and Francis.

Corker, M. (2002) 'Sensing disability', *Hypatia*, vol 16, no 4, pp 34-52.

Corker, M. (2003) '"They don't know what they don't know": the social constitution of deaf childhoods in sites of learning', in S. Gabel and S. Lissner (eds) *Disability, culture and education*, New York, NY: Peter Lang.

Corker, M. and Davis, J.M. (2000) 'Disabled children – (still) invisible under the law', in J. Cooper (ed) *Law, rights and disability*, London: Jessica Kingsley Publishers.

Corker, M. and French, S. (1999) *Disability discourse*, Buckingham: Open University Press.

Court, D. and Alberman, E. (1988), 'Worlds apart', in D. Forfar (ed) *Child health in a changing society*, Oxford: Oxford University Press.

Courtney, M., Barth, R.P., Berrick, J.D., Brooks, D., Needell, B. and Park, L. (1996) 'Race and child welfare services: past research and future directions', *Child Welfare*, no 75, pp 99-137.

Coveney, P. (1967) *The image of childhood*, Harmondsworth: Penguin.

Cox, E. (1995) *Truly civil society*, Sydney, Australia: ABC Books.

Cox, R. (1996) *Shaping childhood*, London: Routledge.

CPS (Crown Prosecution Service) (1989) *Annual Report 1987-88*, London: CPS.

CPS (1994) *Code for Crown Prosecutors*, London: CPS.

CRAE (Children's Rights Alliance for England) (2002) 'Report to the Pre-sessional Working Group of the Committee on the Rights of the Child', London: CRAE (www.crights.org.uk).

Crawford, A. (1999) *The local governance of crime*, Oxford: Oxford University Press.

CRC (UN Committee on the Rights of the Child) (2002) *Concluding observations of the Committee on the Rights of the Child: United Kingdom of Great Britain and Northern Ireland*, Geneva: Office of the High Commissioner for Human Rights (www.unhchr.ch).

CRDU (Children's Rights Development Unit) (1994) *UK agenda for children*, London: CRDU.

Cretney, S. (2003) *Family law in the twentieth century*, Oxford: Oxford University Press.

Crompton, R. (1995) 'Women's employment and the middle class', in T. Butler and M. Savage (eds) *Social change and the middle class*, London: UCL Press.

Crowley, A. (1998) *A criminal waste: A study of child offenders eligible for secure training centres*, London: The Children's Society.

CSJ (Commission on Social Justice) (1994) *Social justice: Strategies for national renewal*, London: Vintage.

CSO (Central Statistical Office) (1995a) *Social Trends – 1995 edition*, London: HMSO.

CSO (1995b) *Fighting with figures*, London: HMSO.

Cunningham, H. (1995) *Children and childhood in Western society since 1500*, London: Longman.

CYPU (2001) *Learning to listen: Core principles for the involvement of children and young people*, Nottingham: DfES Publications.

Dahlberg, G., Moss, P. and Pence, A. (1999) *Beyond quality in early childhood education and care: Postmodern perspectives*, London: Falmer Books.

Dahrendorf, R. (1994) 'The changing quality of citizenship', in B. Van Steenbergen, *The condition of citizenship*, London: Sage Publications.

Dalrymple, J. and Burke, B. (1995) *Anti-oppressive practice: Social care and the law*, Buckingham: Open University Press.

Daly, C. and Hamilton, C. (2002) 'Children and mental health', *ChildRight*, vol 189, pp 16-19.

Daniel, P. and Ivatts, J. (1998) *Children and social policy*, Basingstoke: Macmillan.

Dartington Social Research Unit (1995) *Child protection: Messages from research*, London: HMSO.

Davidson, A. (1997) *From subject to citizen: Australian citizenship in the twentieth century*, Cambridge: Cambridge University Press.

Davie, R., Butler, N. and Goldstein, H. (1972) *From birth to seven*, London: Longman and the National Children's Bureau.

Davies, L. and Fitzpatrick, G. (2000) *The Euridem Project, Children's Rights Alliance for England*, London: Children's Rights Office.

Davis, F.G. (1991) *Who is black? One nation's definition*, University Park, PA: Pennsylvania State University Press.

Davis, G. and Pearce, J. (1999a) 'The welfare principle in action', *Family Law*, no 29, pp 237-41.

Davis, G. and Pearce, J. (1999b) 'On the trail of the welfare principle', *Family Law*, no 29, pp 144-8.

Davis, H. and Bourhill, M. (1997) '"Crisis": the demonisation of children and young people', in P. Scraton (ed) *'Childhood' in 'crisis'?*, London: UCL Press, pp 28-57.

Davis, J.M. and Corker, M. (2001) 'Disability studies and anthropology: difference troubles in academic paradigms', *Anthropology in Action*, vol 8, no 2, pp 18-27.

Davis, J. and Ridge, T. (1997) *Same scenery, different lifestyle: Rural children on a low income*, London: The Children's Society.

Davis, J.M. and Watson, N. (2000) 'Disabled children's rights in everyday life: problematising notions of competency and promoting self-empowerment', *International Journal of Children's Rights*, vol 8, pp 211-28.

Davis, J.M. and Watson, N. (2001) 'Where are the children's experiences? Analysing social and cultural exclusion in "special" and "mainstream" schools', *Disability and Society*, vol 16, no 5, pp 671-87.

Davis, J.M., Watson, N. and Cunningham-Burley, S. (2000) 'Learning the lives of disabled children: developing a reflexive approach', in P. Christensen and A. James (eds) *Conducting research with children*, London: Falmer.

Deacon, A. (2002) *Perspectives on welfare*, Buckingham/Philadelphia, PA: Open University Press.

Deakin, N. and Parry, R. (2000) *The Treasury and social policy*, Basingstoke: Macmillan.

Dean, H. (1999) 'Citizenship', in M. Powell (ed) *New Labour, new welfare state? The 'third way' in British social policy*, Bristol: The Policy Press.

Department for Education and Skills (2002) *Statistics of education: Pupil progress by pupil characteristics*, London: Department for Education and Skills.

DES (Department of Education and Science) (1989) *Discipline in schools: Report of the Committee of Enquiry Chaired by Lord Elton*, London: HMSO.

DES (1990) *A survey of the education of children living in temporary accommodation*, HMI Report ref 178/90/NS.

Dewar, J. (1998) 'The normal chaos of family law', *Modern Law Review*, vol 61, no 4, pp 467-85.

DfEE (Department for Education and Employment) (1996) *Learning to compete: Education and training for 14-19 year olds*, Cmnd 3486, London: The Stationery Office.

DfEE (1997) *Excellence in schools*, London: The Stationery Office.

DfEE (2000) 'The Connexions strategy document' (www.gov.uk/strategy.htm).

DH (Department of Health) (1989) *An introduction to the Children Act*, London: HMSO.

DH (1990) *The 1989 Children Act: Guidance and regulations, Volume 2. Family support, day care and educational provision for young children*, London: HMSO.

DH (1991) *Child abuse: A study of inquiry reports 1980-89*, London: HMSO.

DH (1998) *Our healthier nation: A contract for health*, London: The Stationery Office.

DH (1999) *Convention on the Rights of the Child: Second report to the UN Committee on the Rights of the Child by the United Kingdom*, London: The Stationery Office.

DH (2000) *Protecting children: Supporting parents*, London: The Stationery Office.

DH (2001) *Consent – What you have a right to expect: A guide for children and young people*, London: DH.

DH (2002a) *Tackling health inequalities: Summary of the cross-cutting review of health inequalities*, London: DH.

DH (2002b) *Mental Health Bill Consultation Document*, London: The Stationery Office.

DH (2003) *Children's National Service Framework: External Working Groups: Mental health and psychological well-being of children and young people*, London: DH.

DH (2004) *Prescription cost analysis data*, London: The Stationery Office.

DH and Department for Education (1995) *A handbook on child and adolescent mental health*, London: HMSO.

DH/DfEE and the Home Office (2000) *Framework for the assessment of children in need and their families*, London: The Stationery Office.

DH and Welsh Office (1993) *Code of Practice: Mental Health Act 1983*, London: HMSO.

DH and Welsh Office (2000) *Lost in care – The report of the Tribunal of the Inquiry into the abuse if children in care in the former county council areas of Gwynedd and Clwyd since 1974* (The Waterhouse Report), London: The Stationery Office.

DHSS (Department of Health and Social Security) (1982) *Child abuse: A study of inquiry reports 1973-1981*, London: HMSO.

DHSS (1985) *Review of childcare law: Report to Ministers of an Interdepartmental Working Party*, London: HMSO.

DHSS/Home Office (1987) *The law on child care and family services*, London: HMSO.

Diduck, A. (2000) 'Solicitors and legal subjects', in J. Bridgeman and D. Monk (eds) *Feminist perspectives on child law*, London: Cavendish.

Dignan, J. (1999) 'The Crime and Disorder Act and the prospects for restorative justice', *Criminal Law Review*, pp 48-60.

Dingwall, R. (1989) 'Some problems about predicting child abuse and neglect', in O. Stevenson (ed) *Child abuse: Public policy and professional practice*, Hemel Hempstead: Harvester Wheatsheaf.

Dingwall, R. (1994) 'Dilemmas of family policy in liberal states', in M. Maclean and J. Lurczewski (eds) *Families, politics and the law: Perspectives for East and West Europe*, Oxford: Oxford University Press.

Dingwall, R. and Eekelaar, J. (1988) 'Families and the state: an historical perspective on the public regulation of private conduct', *Law and Policy*, vol 10, no 4, pp 341-61.

Dingwall, R., Eekelaar, J. and Murray, T. (1983) *The protection of children: State intervention and family life*, Oxford: Basil Blackwell.

Dingwall, R., Eekelaar, J. and Murray, T. (1984) 'Childhood as a social problem: a survey of the history of legal regulation', *Journal of Law and Society*, vol 11, pp 207-32.

Dingwall, R., Eekelaar, J. and Murray, T. (1995) 'Postscript', in R. Dingwall, J. Eekelaar and T. Murray, *The protection of children: State intervention and family life* (2nd edn), Oxford: Basil Blackwell.

Dobrowolsky, A. (2002) 'Rhetoric versus reality: the figure of the child and New Labour's strategic "social investment state"', *Studies in Political Economy*, Autumn, pp 43-73.

Dobrowolsky, A. and Saint-Martin, D. (2002) 'Agency, actors and change in a child-focused future: problematizing path dependency's past and statist parameters', Paper prepared for the Canadian Political Science Association Annual Meeting, University of Toronto, 29 May-1 June.

Dodd, M. (1999) 'Privacy and the press: the latest stage in the battle', *R v Central Criminal Court ex parte S, Child and Family Law Quarterly*, vol 11, no 2, pp 171-81.

Dominelli, L. (1997) *Anti-racist social work* (2nd edn), London: Macmillan.

Donegan, L. (1993) 'See you in court, Dad', *The Guardian*, date missing.

Donzelot, J (1980) *The policing of families: Welfare versus the state*, London: Hutchinson.

Donzelot, J. (1988) 'The promotion of the social', *Economy and Society*, vol 17, no 3, pp 395-427.

Dore, R. (1976) *The diploma disease*, London: Allen & Unwin.

Dorling, D. (1993) 'Children in need', *Roof*, September/October.

Dornan, P. (2004a) 'Introduction', in P. Dornan (ed) *Ending child poverty by 2020: The first five years*, London: Child Poverty Action Group.

Dornan, P. (2004b) 'How do we treat our children?', *Poverty*, issue 117, p 1.

Douglas, J.W.B. (1964) *The home and the school*, London: Macgibbon & Kee.

Douglas, M. (1992) *Risk and blame: Essays in cultural theory*, London: Routledge and Kegan Paul.

Downie, R.S., Fyfe, C. and Tannahill, A. (1990) *Health promotion: Models and values*, Oxford: Oxford University Press.

Drake, R.F. (2001) *The principles of social policy*, Basingstoke: Palgrave.

Driver, S. and Martell, L. (1997) 'New Labour's communitarianisms', *Critical Social Policy*, vol 17, no 3, pp 27-44.

DSS (Department of Social Security) (1996) *Households Below Average Income: A statistical analysis 1979-1994/5*, Leeds: Corporate Document Services.

DSS (1998) *New ambitions for our country: A new contract for welfare*, London: The Stationery Office.

DSS (1999) *Opportunity for All: Tackling poverty and social exclusion*, Cm 4445, London: The Stationery Office.

DSS (2000a) *Family Resources Survey Great Britain 1998-1999*, London: Corporate Data Services.

DSS (2000b) *Households Below Average Income 1994/5-1998/9*, Leeds: Corporate Document Services.

DTI (1998) *Our competitive future: Building a knowledge-based economy*, London: The Stationery Office.

Dummett, A. (1984) *A portrait of English racism*, London: CARAF Publications.

Dunne, G.A. (1999) 'Opting into motherhood: lesbians blurring the boundaries and redefining the meaning of parenthood', *Gender and Society*, special issue on new families.

Durrant, J. (1999) *The status of Swedish children and youth since the passage of the 1979 corporal punishment ban*, London: Save the Children.

Durrant, J. and Olsen, G. (1997) 'Parenting and public policy: contextualising the Swedish corporal punishment ban', *Journal of Social Welfare and Family Law*, vol 19, no 4, pp 443-61.

Dutt, R. (2000) 'Racism and social work practice', in L. Cull and J. Roche (eds) *The law and social work: Contemporary issues for practice*, Basingstoke: Palgrave.

Dutt, R. and Phillips, M. (2000) 'Assessing black children in need and their families', in DH, *Assessing children in need and their families* (Practice Guidance), London: The Stationery Office.

Dwivedi, K.N. and Varma, V.P. (eds) (1996) *Meeting the needs of ethnic minority children: A handbook for professionals*, London: Jessica Kingsley Publishers.

Dwork, D. (1987) *War is good for babies and other young children: A history of the Infant and Child Welfare Movement in England, 1898-1918*, London: Tavistock Publications.

DWP (Department for Work and Pensions) (2002) *Households Below Average Income: A statistical analysis 1994/95-2000/01*, Leeds: Corporate Document Services.

DWP (2003) *Households Below Average Income 1994/95-2001/02*, London: The Stationery Office.

Dwyer, P. (1998) 'Conditional citizens? welfare rights and responsibilities in the late 1990', *Critical Social Policy*, vol 18, no 4, pp 493-517.

Dwyer, P. (2000) *Welfare rights and responsibilities*, Bristol: The Policy Press.

Dyson, A. and Robson, E. (1999) *Links between school, family and the community: A review of the evidence*, Findings, York: Joseph Rowntree Foundation.

Eade, J., Vamplew, T. and Peach, C. (1996) 'The Bangladeshis: the encapsulated community', in C. Peach (ed) *Ethnicity in the 1991 Census: Volume two: The ethnic minority populations of Great Britain*, London: The Stationery Office, pp 150-60.

Edwards, R., Alldred, P. and David, M. (2000) 'Children's understanding of parental involvement in education', ESRC Children 5-16 Research Programme Briefing (www.esrc.ac.uk/curprog.html).

Eekelaar, J. (1991) 'Parental responsibility: state of nature or nature of the state?', *Journal of Social Welfare and Family Law*, vol 37, no 1, pp 37-50.

Eekelaar, J. (1994) 'The interests of the child and the child's wishes: the role of dynamic self-determinism', in P. Alston (ed) *The best interests of the child: Reconciling culture and human rights*, Oxford: Clarendon Press.

Eekelaar, J. (1999) 'Family law: keeping us "on message"', *Child and Family Law Quarterly*, vol 11, no 4, pp 387-96.

Eekelaar, J. and Dingwall, R. (1990) *The reform of child care law: A practical guide*, London: Routledge.

Eekelaar, J., Dingwall, D. and Murray, T. (1982) 'Victims or threats? Children in care proceedings', *Journal of Social Welfare Law*, March.

Eiser, C., Patterson, D. and Eiser, J.R (1983) 'Children's knowledge of health and illness', *Child Care, Health and Development*, vol 9, pp 285-92.

Elder, G., Modell, J. and Parke, R.D. (1993) *Children in time and place. Developmental and historical insights*, Cambridge: Cambridge University Press.

Elshtain, J.B. (1989) 'The family, democratic politics and the question of authority', in G. Scarre (ed) *Children, parents and politics*, Cambridge: Cambridge University Press.

England, P. and Folbre, N. (1991) 'Who should pay for the kids?', *Annals of the American Association of Political and Social Science*, no 563, pp 194-207.

English, D.J. and Pecora, P.J. (1994) 'Risk assessment as a practice method in child protective services', *Child Welfare*, vol 73, no 5, pp 451-73.

Ennew, J. (1986) *The sexual exploitation of children*, Cambridge: Polity Press.

Ennew, J. (1992) 'It is a wise child that knows its own father: exploring the possibilities of non-biological families', NOSEB Conference on Children at Risk, University of Bergen.

Ennew, J. and Morrow, V. (1994) 'Out of the moths of babes', in Verhellen and F. Spiesschaert (eds) *Children's rights: Monitoring issues*, Ghent: Myes and Breesch.

Ermisch, J., Francescani, M. and Pevalin, D. (2001) *Outcomes for children of poverty*, DWP Research Project no 158, Leeds: Corporate Document Services.

Escott, T.H.S. (1885) *England: Her people, polity and pursuits*, New York, NY: Henry Hott & Co.

Esmail, A. and Everington, S. (1993) 'Racial discrimination against doctors from ethnic minorities', *British Medical Journal*, no 306, pp 691-2.

Esping-Andersen, G. (1990) *The three worlds of welfare capitalism*, Cambridge: Polity.

Esping-Andersen, G. (1991) *Social foundations of postindustrial economics*, Oxford: Oxford University Press.

Esping-Andersen, G., with Gallie, D., Hemerijck, A. and Myles, J. (ed) (2002) *Why we need a new welfare state*, Oxford: Oxford University Press.

Estes, C. (1979) *The ageing enterprise*, San Francisco, CA: Jossey-Bass.

Etzioni, A. (1993) *The spirit of community: Rights, responsibilities and the communitarian agenda*, London: Fontana Press.

Etzioni, A. (1996) 'The responsive community: a communitarian perspective', *American Sociological Review*, no 61, pp 1-11.

Etzioni, A. (2000) *The third way to a good society*, London: Demos.

European Commission (1996) *The demographic situation in the European Union 1995,* Brussels: EC.

European Forum for Child Welfare (2002) 'Eradicating child poverty: fact or fiction' (www.efcw.org).

Fairbairn, G. and Fairbairn, S. (eds) (1992) *Integrating special children: Some ethical issues*, Aldershot: Avebury.

Fairclough, N. (2000) *New Labour, new language?*, London and New York, NY: Routledge.

Fawcett, B., Featherstone, B. and Goddard, J. (2004) *Contemporary child care policy and practice*, Basingstoke: Palgrave Macmillan.

Federle, K. (1994) 'Rights flow downhill', *International Journal of Children's Rights*, no 2, p 343.

Feinberg, J. (1980) 'The child's right to an open future', in W. Aiken and H. LaFollette (eds) *Whose child? Children's rights, parental authority and state power*, Boston: Littlefield, Adams.

Fendler, L (2001) 'Educating flexible souls', in K. Hultqvist and G. Dahlberg (eds) *Governing the child in the new millennium*, London: RoutledgeFalmer.

Fennell, P. (1992) 'Informal compulsion: the psychiatric treatment of juveniles under common law', *Journal of Social Welfare and Family Law*, no 4, pp 311-33.

Ferguson, H. (1990) 'Rethinking child protection practices: a case for history', in Violence against Children Study Group, *Taking child abuse seriously*, London: Unwin Hyman.

Fernando, S. (1991) *Mental health, race and culture*, London: Macmillan.

Fernando, S. (1995) *Mental health in a multi-ethnic society*, London: Routledge.

Ferry, J.-M. (1994) 'Approaches to liberty: outline for a "methodological communitarianism"', *Ratio Juris*, vol 7, pp 291-307.

Field, F. (2002) 'Gordon Brown's invention: a form of permanent serfdom', *Daily Telegraph*, 11 June.

Fielding, M. (2001) 'Taking education really seriously', in M. Fielding (ed) *Taking education really seriously: Four years' hard labour*, London: RoutledgeFalmer.

Fine, B. (1998) 'The developmental state is dead – long live social capital', mimeo, Department of Economics, London: SOAS.

Fine, G.A. and Sandstrom, K.L. (1988) *Knowing children: Participant observation with minors*, London: Sage Publications.

Finer Report (1974) *Report of the Committee on One-Parent Families, i and ii,* Cmnd 5629, London: HMSO.

Fink, D. (2001) 'The two solitudes: policy makers and policy implementers', in M. Fielding (ed) *Taking education really seriously: Four years' hard labour*, London: RoutledgeFalmer.

Fionda, J. (1999) 'New Labour, old hat: youth justice and the Crime and Disorder Act 1998', *Criminal Law Review*, no 36.

Flekkoy, G.D. and Kaufman, N.H. (1997) *The participation rights of the child: Rights and responsibilities in family and society*, London: Jessica Kingsley.

Foley, M.W. and Edwards, B. (1997) 'Escape from politics? Social theory and the social capital debate', editors introduction, *American Behavioural Scientist*, vol 40, no 5, pp 550-61.

Foley, P., Roche, J. and Tucker, S. (eds) (2001) *Children in society*, Basingstoke: Palgrave.

Ford, J. and Kempson, E. (1995) 'No way out', *Roof*, July/August.

Ford, J., Mongon, D. and Whelan, M. (1982) *Special education and social control: Invisible disasters*, London: Routledge & Kegan Paul.

Forsythe, B. (1995) 'Discrimination in social work: an historical note', *British Journal of Social Work*, no 25, pp 1-16.

Fortin, J. (1998) *Children's rights and the developing law*, London: Butterworths.

Fottrell, D. (ed) (2000) *Revisiting children's rights*, Kluwer.

Foucault, M. (1977a) *Discipline and punish: The birth of the prison*, London: Allen & Unwin.

Foucault, M. (1977b) *The 'archaeology' of knowledge*, London: Tavistock.

Foucault, M. (1978) 'Politics and the study of discourse', *Ideology and Consciousness*, Spring, no 3, pp 7-26.

Foucault, M. (1979a) *The history of sexuality, vol i: An introduction*, London: Allen Lane/Penguin.

Foucault, M. (1979b) *The history of sexuality, vol iii*, New York, NY: Pantheon.

Foucault, M. (1986) 'Space, knowledge and power', in P. Rainbow (ed) *The Foucault Reader*, Hammondsworth: Penguin.

Foucault, M. (1991) 'Governmentality', in G. Burchell, C. Gordon and P. Miller (eds) *The Foucault effect: Studies in governmentality*, Hemel Hempstead: Harvester Wheatsheaf.

Fox, L.M. (1982) 'Two value positions in recent child care law and practice', *British Journal of Social Work*, vol 12, no 2, pp 265-90.

Fox Harding, L.M. (1991) *Perspectives in child care policy*, London: Longman.

Fox Harding, L.M. (1994) '"Parental responsibility": a dominant theme in British child and family policy for the 1990s', *International Journal of Sociology and Social Policy*, vol 14, no 1/2, pp 84-108.

Fox Harding, L.M. (1996) *Family, state and social policy*, Basingstoke: Macmillan.

Franklin, B. (ed) (1986) *The rights of children*, Oxford: Basil Blackwell.

Franklin, B. (ed) (1995) *The handbook of children's rights: Essays in comparative policy and practice*, London: Routledge.

Franklin, B. (2002) 'Children's rights and media wrongs: changing representations of children and developing the rights agenda', in B. Franklin (ed) *The new handbook of children's rights: Comparative policy and practice*, London: Routledge.

Franklin, B. and Parton, N. (eds) (1991) *Social work, the media and public relations*, London: Routledge.

Franklin, J. (2000a) 'After modernisation: gender, the third way and the new politics', in A. Coote (ed) *New gender agenda*, London: IPPR.

Franklin, J. (2000b) 'What's wrong with New Labour politics?', *Feminist Review*, no 66, pp 138-42.

Fraser, D. (1984) *The evolution of the British welfare state*, Basingstoke: Macmillan.

Fraser, N. and Gordon, L. (1994) 'Civil citizenship against social citizenship? On the ideology of contract–versus–charity', in B.Van Steenbergen (ed) *The condition of citizenship*, London: Sage Publications, pp 90-107.

Frazer, E. and Lacey, N. (1993) *The politics of community: A feminist critique of the liberal-communitarian debate*, London: Harvester Wheatsheaf.

Freeden, M. (1978) *The new liberalism*, Oxford: Oxford University Press.

Freeman, C., Henderson, P. and Kettle, J. (1999) *Planning with children for better communities: The challenge for professionals*, Bristol: The Policy Press.

Freeman, M.D.A. (1983) *The rights and wrongs of children*, London: Frances Pinter.

Freeman, M. (1987) 'Taking children's rights seriously', *Children and Society*, vol 1, no 4, pp 299-319.

Freeman, M. (1992) *Children, their families and the law*.

Freeman, M.D.A (1993) 'Removing rights from adolescents', *Adoption and Fostering*, vol 17, no 1, pp 14-21

Freeman, M. (1997) 'The new birth right: identity and the child of the reproductive revolution', *International Journal of Children's Rights*, vol 4, pp 273-97.

Freeman, M. (1998) 'The next Children's Act?', *Family Law*, no 28, pp 341-48.

Freeman, R. (1999) 'Recursive politics: prevention, modernity and social systems', *Children & Society*, vol 13, no 4, pp 232-41.

Frosh, S. (1999) 'Identity, religious fundamentalism and children's welfare', in M. King (ed) *Moral agendas for children's welfare*, London: Routledge.

Frost, N. (1990) 'Official intervention and child protection: the relationship between state and family in contemporary Britain', in Violence Against Children Study Group, *Taking child abuse seriously*, London: Unwin Hyman.

Frost, N. and Stein, M. (1989) *The politics of child welfare*, Hemel Hempstead: Harvester Wheatsheaf.

Fuhrmann, G., McGill, J. and O' Connell, M. (1999) 'Parent education's second generation, integrating violence sensitivity', *Family and Conciliation Courts Review*, vol 37, no 1, pp 24-35.

Fukuyama, F. (1996) *Trust: The social virtues and the creation of prosperity*, London: Hamish Hamilton.

Furedi, F. (1997) *The culture of fear: Risk taking and the morality of law expectations*, London: Cassell.

Furstenberg, F.R. and Hughes, M.E. (1995) 'Social capital and successful development among at-risk youth', *Journal of Marriage and the Family*, no 57, pp 580-92.

Gamble, A. and Kenny, M. (1991) 'Now we are two', *Fabian Review*, vol 111, no 2, pp 10-11

Gamble, A. and Zigler, E. (1988) 'Effects of infant daycare: another look at the evidence', in A. Gamble and E. Zigler (eds) *The parental leave crisis*, London: Yale University Press.

Garland, D. (1985) *Punishment and welfare: A history of penal strategies*, Aldershot: Gower.

Garling, T. and Valsiner, J. (eds) (1985) *Children within environments*, New York, NY: Plenum Press.

Garrett, P. (2004) 'The electronic eye: emerging surveillant practices in social work with children and families', *European Journal of Social Work*, vol 7, no 1, pp 57-71.

Geach, H. and Szwed, E. (eds) (1983) *Providing civil justice for children*, London: Edward Arnold.

Gewirtz, S., Ball, S.J. and Bowe, R. (1995) *Markets, choice and equity in education*, Buckingham: Open University Press.

Gibbons, J., Conroy, S. and Bell, C. (1995) *Operating the child protection system*, London: HMSO.

Giddens, A. (1984) *The constitution of society*, Cambridge: Polity Press.

Giddens, A. (1990) *The consequences of modernity*, Cambridge: Polity Press.

Giddens, A. (1991) *Modernity and self-identity*, Cambridge: Polity Press.

Giddens, A. (1998) *The third way*, Cambridge: Polity Press.

Giddens, A. ESRC Tenth Annual Lecture, London: Economic and Social Research Council.

Gilbert, B.B. (1966) *The evolution of National Insurance in GB: The origin of the welfare state*, London: Michael Joseph.

Gill, O. (1992) *Parenting under pressure*, Cardiff: Barnardo's.

Gillies, P. (1998) 'Effectiveness of alliances and partnerships for health promotion', *Health Promotion International*, vol 13, no 2, pp 99-120.

Glennerster, H. (1995) *British social policy since 1945*, Oxford: Blackwell.

Goldson, B. (1997) 'Children in trouble: state responses to juvenile crime', in P. Scraton (ed) *'Childhood' in 'crisis'?*, London: UCL Press, pp 124-45.

Goldson, B. (1999) 'Youth (in)justice: contemporary developments in policy and practice', in B. Goldson (ed) *Youth justice: Contemporary policy and practice*, Aldershot: Ashgate.

Goldson, B. (2000) 'Wither diversion? Interventionism and the new youth justice', in B. Goldson (ed) *The new youth justice*, Dorset: Russell House Publishing, pp 35-57.

Goldson, B. (2001) 'The demonisation of children: from the symbolic to the institutional', in P. Foley, J. Roche and S. Tucker (eds) *Children in society: Contemporary theory, policy and practice*, Basingstoke: Palgrave, pp 34-41.

Goldson, B. (2002a) 'New punitiveness: the politics of child incarceration', in J. Muncie, G. Hughes and E. McLaughlin (eds) *Youth justice: Critical readings*, London, Sage Publications, pp 386-400.

Goldson, B. (2002b) *Vulnerable inside: Children in secure and penal settings*, London: The Children's Society.

Goldson, B. (2002c) 'New labour, social justice and children: political calculation and the deserving-undeserving schism', *The British Journal of Social Work*, vol 2, no 6, pp 683-95.

Goldson, B. (2002d) 'Children, crime and the state', in B. Goldson, M. Lavalette and McKechnie (eds) *Children, welfare and the state*, London: Sage Publications.

Goldson, B. (2004a) 'Victims or threats? Children, care and control', in J. Fink (ed) *Care: Personal lives and social policy*, Bristol: The Policy Press, pp 77-109.

Goldson, B. (2004b) 'Youth crime and youth justice', in J. Muncie and D. Wilson (eds) *The student handbook of criminal justice and criminology*, London: Cavendish Publishing, pp 221-34.

Goldson, B. and Chigwada-Bailey, R. (1999) '(What) justice for black children and young people?', in B. Goldson (ed) *Youth justice: Contemporary policy and practice*, Aldershot, Ashgate, pp 51-74.

Goldson, B. and Jamieson, J. (2002) 'Youth crime, the "parenting deficit" and state intervention: a contextual critique', *Youth Justice*, vol 2, no 2, pp 82-99.

Goldstein, J., Freud, A. and Solnit, J. (1973) *Beyond the best interests of the child*, New York, NY: Macmillan.

Goldstein, J., Freud, A. and Solnit, J. (1980) *Before the best interests of the child*, New York, NY: Macmillan.

Goodhart, D. (2004) 'Too diverse?', *Prospect*, February.

Goodwin, R. and Le Grande, J. (1987) *Not only the poor*, London: Allen and Unwin.

Gordon, C. (1986) 'Questions, ethos, event: Foucault on Kant and Enlightenment', *Economy and Society*, vol 15, no 1, pp 71-87.

Gordon, C. (1991) 'Governmental rationality: an introduction', in G. Burchell, C. Gordon and P. Miller (eds) *The Foucault effect: Studies in governmentality*, Hemel Hempstead: Harvester Wheatsheaf.

Gordon, D. (2000) *Poverty and social exclusion in Britain*, York: Joseph Rowntree Foundation.

Gordon, L. (1988) *Heroes of their own lives*, New York, NY: Viking Penguin.

Gordon, L. (1994) *Pitied but not entitled: Single mothers and the history of welfare*, New York, NY: The Free Press.

Gouldner. A. (1970) *The coming crisis of Western sociology*, London: Heinemann.

Gunter, B. and Furnham, A. (1998) *Children as consumers*, London: Routledge.

Graham, J. and Bowling, B. (1995) *Young people and crime*, Research Study 145, London, Home Office.

Granovetter, M. (1973) 'The strength of weak ties', *American Journal of Sociology*, no 78, pp 1360-80.

Graveson, R.H. (1953) *Status in the common law*, London: Athlone Press.

Gray, J. (1999) *False dawn: The delusions of global capitalism*, London: Granta Books.

Gray, J. and Flores, F. (2000) *Entrepreneurship and the wired life*, London: Demos.

Green, J. (1995) 'Accidents and risk society', in R. Bunton, S. Nettleton and R. Burrows (eds) *The sociology of health promotion*, London: Routledge.

Gregg, P., Harkness, S. and Machin, S. (1999) *Child development and family income*, York: Joseph Rowntree Foundation.

Greve, J. with Currie, E. (1990) *Homelessness in Britain*, York: Joseph Rowntree Memorial Trust.

Griffin, C. (1993) *Representation of youth: The study of youth and adolescence in Britain and America*, Cambridge: Polity Press.

Guevara, J.P and Stein, M.T (2001) 'Evidence based management of attention deficit hyperactivity disorder', *British Medical Journal*, vol 323, pp 1232-5.

Gulestad, M. (1996) 'From obedience to negotiation: dilemmas in the transmission of values between the generations in Norway', *Journal of the Royal Anthropological Institute*, vol 2, no 1, pp 25-42.

Gunter, B. and Furnham, A. (1998) *Children as consumers*, London: Routledge.

Gusfield, J. (1963) *Symbolic crusade*, Urbana, IL: University of Illinois Press.

Hackett, L. and Hackett, R. (1994) 'Child-rearing practices and psychiatric disorder in Gujarati and British children', *British Journal of Social Work*, no 24, pp 191-202.

Hacking, I. (1990) *The taming of chance*, Cambridge: Cambridge University Press.

Hacking, I. (1991) 'The making and moulding of child abuse', *Critical Inquiry*, vol 17, no 2, pp 253-88.

Hagell, A. and Newburn, T. (1994) *Persistent young offenders*, London: Policy Studies Institute.

Haines, K. (2000) 'Referral Orders and Youth Offender Panels: restorative approaches and the new youth justice', in B. Goldson (ed) *The new youth justice*, Dorset: Russell House Publishing, pp 58-80.

Hale, B. (1999) 'The view from Court 45', *Child and Family Law Quarterly*, vol 11, no 4, pp 377-86.

Hall, A. and Wellman, B. (1984) 'Social networks and social support', in S. Cohen and S.L. Syme (eds) *Social support and health*, Orlando, FL: Academic Press.

Hall, P. (1976) *Reforming the welfare: The politics of change in the Personal Social Services*, London: Heinemann.

Hallett, C. and Birchall, E. (1992) *Co-ordination and child protection: A review of the literature*, London: HMSO.

Hallett, C. and Prout, A. (eds) (2003) *Hearing the voices of children*, London: RoutledgeFalmer.

Halsey, A.H., Lauder, H., Brown, P. and Wells, A.S. (1997) *Education, culture, economy and society*, Oxford: Oxford University Press.

Hancock, L. (2004) 'Criminal justice, public opinion, fear and popular politics', in J. Muncie and D. Wilson (eds) *The student handbook of criminal justice and criminology*, London: Cavendish Publishing, pp 51-66.

Handler, J. (1988) 'Dependent people, the state, and the modern/postmodern research for the dialogic community', *UCLA Law Review*, vol 35, pp 999-1113.

Hardyment, C. (1983) *Dream babies*, London: Jonathan Cape.

Hari, J. (2002) 'Yah boo to a Daily Mail myth', *New Statesman*, 23 September, pp 24-5.

Harrington, V. and Mayhew, P. (2001) *Mobile phone theft*, Home Office Research Study 235, London: Home Office.

Harris, B. (1995) *The health of the schoolchild: A history of the school medical service in England and Wales*, Buckingham: Open University Press.

Harris, D. (1987) *Justifying state welfare: The new right versus the old left*, Oxford: Blackwell.

Harris, J. (1993) *Private lives, public spirit: Britain 1870-1914*, Oxford: Oxford University Press.

Harris, N. (1993) 'Social citizenship and young people in Europe', in B. Jackson and D. McGoldrick (eds) *Legal visions of the new Europe*, London: Graham and Trotman/Martin Nijhoff.

Harris, P.L. (1992) *Children and emotion*, Oxford: Blackwell.

Harris, R. and Timms, N. (1993) *Secure accommodation in child care*, London: Routledge.

Harris, R.J. and Webb, D. (1987) *Welfare, power and juvenile justice*, London: Tavistock.

Harriss, J. and De Renzio, P. (1997) '"Missing link" or analytically missing?: The concept of social capital', *Journal of International Development*, vol 9, no 7, pp 19-37.

Hart, R. (1992) *Children's participation: From tokenism to citizenship*, Florence: UNICEF Innocenti Essays.

Hatch, J. Amos (1995) *Qualitative research in early childhood settings*, Greenwood Press.

Haydon, D. and Scraton, P. (2000) 'Condemn a little more, understand a little less? The political context and rights implications of the domestic and European rulings in the Venables-Thompson Case', *Journal of Law and Society*, vol 27, no 3, pp 416-48.

Hayes, M. and Williams, C. (1999) *Family law: Principles, policy and practice* (2nd edn), London: Butterworths.

Haynes, G. (2000) 'New national standards on registered childminding', *ChildRight*, no 170, p 21.

Hawthorne-Kirk, R. and Part, D. (1995) 'Social support and early years centres', in M. Hill, R.H. Kirk and D. Part (eds) *Supporting families*, Edinburgh: HMSO.

Hearn, B. (1995) *Child and family support and protection. A practical approach*, London: National Children's Bureau.

Heathorn, S. (2000) *For home, country and race. Constructing gender, class, and Englishness in the elementary school, 1880-1914*, Toronto: University of Toronto Press.

Heinz, W.R. (1994) 'Social structure and psychosocial dimensions of youth unemployment', in A.C. Petersen and J.T. Mortimer (eds) *Youth unemployment and society*, Cambridge: Cambridge University Press.

Heller, J. *Picture this*, New York, NY: Ballantine.

Hendrick, H. (1990) *Images of youth. Age, class and the male youth problem, 1880-1920*, Oxford: Clarendon Press.

Hendrick, H. (1990/97) 'Constructions and reconstructions of British childhood', in A. James and A. Prout (eds) *Constructing and reconstructing childhood*, London: Falmer Press.

Hendrick, H. (1994) *Child welfare: England 1872-1989*, London: Routledge.

Hendrick, H. (1997) *Children, childhood and English society, 1880-1990*, Cambridge: Cambridge University Press.

Hendrick, H. (2000) 'The child as a social actor in historical sources', in P. Christensen and A. James (eds) *Research with children*, London: Falmer Press.

Hendrick, H. (2002) 'Conceptualising childcare: early childhood education and care in post 1945 Britain', *ZSE. Zeitschrift für Soziologie der Erziehung und Sozialization*, vol 22, no 3, pp 265-82.

Hendrick, H. (2003) *Child welfare: Historical dimensions, contemporary debate*, Bristol: The Policy Press.

Henggeler, S.W., Melton, G.B. and Rodrigue, J.R. (1992) *Pediatric and adolescent AIDS*, Newbury Park, CA: Sage Publications.

Heron, E. and Dwyer, P. (1991) 'Doing the right thing: Labour's attempt to forge a new welfare deal between the individual and the state', *Social Policy & Administration*, vol 33, no 1, pp 91-104.

Hester, M., Pearson, C. and Radford, L. (1997) *Domestic violence: A national survey of court welfare and voluntary sector mediation practice*, Bristol: The Policy Press.

Hewlett, S.A. (1993) *Child neglect in rich nations*, New York, NY: UNICEF.

Heywood, J. (1965 edn) *Children in care: The development of the service for the deprived child*, London: Routledge and Kegan Paul.

Hill, M.S. and Jenkins, S.P. (1999) *Poverty among British children: Chronic or transitory*, ESRC Research Centre of Micro-Social Change Working Paper 92-93, Colchester: Institute for Economic and Social Research, University of Essex.

Hill, M.S. and Jenkins, S.P. (2001) 'Poverty among British children: chronic or transitory?', in B. Bradbury, S.P. Jenkins and J. Micklewright (eds) *The dynamics of child poverty in industrialised countries*, Cambridge: Cambridge University Press.

Hill, M. and Tisdall, K. (1997) *Children and society*, London: Longman.

Hill, M.S., Laybourn, A. and Borland, M. (1996) 'Engaging with primary-aged children about their emotions and well-being: methodological considerations', *Children & Society*, vol 10, pp 129-44.

Hillman, M., Adams, J. and Whitelegg, J. (1990) *One false move: A study of children's independent mobility*, London: Policy Studies Institute.

Hills, J. (1995) *Joseph Rowntree Foundation Inquiry into Income and Wealth, Vol Two*, York: Joseph Rowntree Foundation.

Himmelfarb, G. (1995) *The de-moralisation of society: From Victorian virtues to modern values*, London: IEA Health and Welfare Unit.

Hirst, P. (1981) 'The genesis of the social', *Politics and Power*, no 3, pp 67-82.

HM Chief Inspector of Prisons (1999) *Suicide is everyone's concern: A thematic review by HM Chief Inspector of Prisons for England and Wales*, London: Home Office.

HM Treasury (1991) *Tackling poverty and extending opportunity*, London: HM Treasury.

HM Treasury (1998) *Modern public services for Britain: Investing in reform* (Pocket Guide), London: HM Treasury.

HM Treasury (1999) *The modernisation of Britain's tax and benefit system, Number Four*, London: HM Treasury.

HM Treasury (2001) *Tackling child poverty: Giving every child the best possible start in life*, London: HM Treasury (www.hm-treasury.gov.uk).

HM Treasury (2002a) *Budget report*, London: HM Treasury.

HM Treasury (2002b) *Pre-Budget report*, London: HM Treasury.

Hockenberry-Easton, M. and Minick, P. (1974) 'Living with cancer', *Oncology Nursing Forum*, vol 21, no 6, pp 1025-31.

Hodgkin, R. (1994) 'The right to consent to treatment', *Children UK*, Winter 4-5.

Hodgkin, R. and Newell, P. (1996) *Effective government structures for children*, London: Calouste Gulbenkian Foundation.

Hodgkin, R. and Newell, P. (1998) *Implementation handbook on the Convention on the Rights of the Child*, New York, NY: UNICEF.

Holden, C. (1991) 'Globalization, social exclusion and Labour's new work ethic', *Critical Social Policy*, vol 19, no 4, pp 529-38.

Holland, J. and Thomson, R. (1999) 'Respect – youth values: identity, diversity and social change', ESRC Children 5-16 Research Programme Briefing (www.esrc.ac.uk/curprog.html).

Holland, P. (2004) *Picturing childhood*, London: I.B.Tauris.

Holman, B. (1988) *Putting families first: Prevention and child care*, London: Macmillan.

Holman, B. (1995) *The evacuation*, Oxford: Lion Publishing.

Holtermann, S. (1995) *All our futures*, Barkingside: Barnardo's.

Holterman S. (1996) 'The impact of public expenditure and fiscal policies on Britain's children and young people', *Children and Society*, vol 10, no 1, pp 3-13.

Home Office in conjunction with the DH (1992) *Memorandum of good practice on video recording interviews with child witnesses for criminal proceedings*, London: HMSO.

Home Office (1994a) *National standards for probation service and family court welfare work*, London: Home Office.

Home Office (1994b) 'The cautioning of offenders', *Home Office Circular* 18/1994, London: Home Office.

Home Office (1997) *No more excuses: A new approach to tackling youth crime in England and Wales*, Cmnd 380, London: The Stationery Office.

Home Office (1998a) *Supporting parents: A consultation document*, London: Home Office.

Home Office (1998) *Supporting families: A consultation document*, London: The Stationery Office.

Home Office (1998) *Guidance on statutory crime and disorder partnerships: Crime and Disorder Act 1998*, London: Home Office Communication Directorate.

Home Office (2002) *Criminal statistics for England and Wales 2001*, London: Home Office.

Home Office (2003) *Respect and responsibility – Taking a stand against anti-social behaviour*, London: The Stationery Office.

Home Office (2004a) *Confident communities in a secure Britain: The Home Office Strategic Plan 2004-08*, London: The Stationery Office.

Home Office (2004b) 'The Home Office Strategic Plan and Summary: Putting the law-abiding citizen first' (www.homeoffice.gov.uk/docs3/strategicplan.html, visited 21 July, 2004).

Hood, S., Kelly, P. and Mayall, B (1996) 'Children as research subjects: a risky enterprise', *Children & Society*, vol 10, pp 117-28.

Hood-Williams, J. (1990) 'Patriarchy for children: on the stability of power relations in children's lives', in L. Chisholm et al (eds) *Childhood, youth and social change*, London: Falmer Press.

House of Lords/House of Commons Joint Committee on Human Rights (2003) *Tenth Report of Session 2002-03: The UN Convention on the Rights of the Child*, London: The Stationery Office.

Howard, M., Garnham, A., Finnister, G. and Veit-Wilson, J. (2001) *Poverty: The facts*, London: Child Poverty Action Group.

Howard League (1995) *Secure training centres: Repeating past failures*, Briefing Paper, London: Howard League for Penal Reform.

Howe, D. (1992) 'Child abuse and the bureaucratisation of social work', *Sociological Review*, vol 40, no 3, pp 491-508.

Howells, J.H. (1974) *Remember Maria*, London: John H. Butterworth.

Howitt, D. (1991) *Concerning psychology: Psychology applied to social issues*, Milton Keynes: Open University Press.

Howitt, D. (1992) *Child abuse errors: When good intentions go wrong*, Hemel Hempstead: Harvester Wheatsheaf.

Howitt, D. and Owusu-Bempah, J. (1990) 'Pragmatics of institutional racism: beyond words', *Human Relations*, no 43, pp 885-9.

Howitt, D. and Owusu-Bempah, J. (1994) *The racism of psychology: Time for change*, Hemel Hempstead: Harvester Wheatsheaf.

Hudson, A. (1983) 'The welfare state and adolescent femininity', *Youth and Policy*, vol 2, no 1, Summer.

Hughes, G. and Lewis, G. (1998) *Unsettling welfare*, London: Routledge.

Humphreys, C. (1999) 'Judicial alienation syndrome: failures to respond to post-separation violence', *Family Law*, no 29, pp 313-16.

Humphries, S. (1981) *Hooligans or rebels? An oral history of working class childhood and youth, 1889-1939*, Oxford: Blackwell.

Hunt, J. and Macleod, A. (1998) *Statutory intervention in child protection research project: A thematic summary*, Bristol: Centre for Socio-Legal Studies, University of Bristol.

Hurt, J.S. (1979) *Elementary education and the working classes, 1860-1914*, London: Routledge and Kegan Paul.

Hurt, J.S. (1985) 'Feeding the hungry schoolchild in the first half of the twentieth century', in D.J. Oddy and D. Miller (eds) *Diet and health in modern Britain*.

Hurt, J.S. (1988) *Outside the mainstream*.

Hutcheon, L. (1989) *The politics of postmodernism*, London: Routledge.

Hutton, W. (1995) *The state we're in*, London: Cape.

HVA (Health Visitors Association) and GMSC (General Medical Services Committee) (1989) *Homeless families and their health*, London: HVA and GMSC.

Hyton, C. (1997) *Black families' survival strategies: Way of coping in UK society*, York: Joseph Rowntree Foundation.

Ingleby, D.I. (1985) 'Professions as socializers: the "Psy Complex"', in A. Scull and S. Spitzer (eds) *Research in law, deviance and social control*, no 7, New York, NY: Jai Press.

Inglis, R. (1989) *The children's war: Evacuation, 1939-1945*, London: Collins.

Ingstad, B. and Reynolds-Whyte, S. (1993) *Disability and culture*, Berkeley, CA: University of California Press.

Innes, M. (1999) '"An iron fist in an iron glove?": the zero tolerance policing debate', *The Howard Journal*, vol 38, no 4, pp 397-410.

Ireland, L. and Holloway, I. (1996) 'Qualitative health research with children', *Children & Society*, vol 10, no 2, pp 155-65.

Jack, G. (2001) 'An ecological perspective on child abuse', in P. Foley et al (eds) *Children in society*, Basingstoke: Palgrave.

Jack, G. and Jordan, B. (1999) 'Social capital and child welfare', *Children & Society*, vol 13, no 4, pp 242-56.

Jackson, A.A. (1995) 'The health of the nation: the population perspective', in D. Davies (ed) *Nutrition in child health*, London: Royal College of Physicians.

Jackson, S. and Scott, S. (1999) 'Risk anxiety and the social construction of childhood', in D. Lupton (ed) *Risk and sociocultural theory*, Cambridge: Polity Press.

Jaffa, T. and Deszery, A.M (1989) 'Reasons for admission to an adolescent unit', *Journal of Adolescence*, vol 12, pp 187-95.

James, A. (1993) *Childhood identities*, Edinburgh: Edinburgh University Press.

James, A. (1995) 'Social work in divorce: welfare, mediation and justice', *International Journal of Law and the Family*, no 9, pp 265-74.

James, A. (1999) 'Parents: a children's perspective', in A. Bainham, S. Day Sclater and M. Richards (eds) *What is a parent?*, Oxford: Hart Publishing.

James, A. and James, A.L. (1995) 'Social work in divorce: welfare, mediation and justice', *International Journal of Law and the Family*, no 9, pp 256-74.

James, A.L. and James, A. (1999) 'Pump up the volume: listening to children in separation and divorce', *Childhood*, vol 6, no 2, pp 189-206.

James, A. and James, A. (2001a) 'Tightening the net: children, community and control', *British Journal of Sociology*, vol 52, no 2, pp 211-28.

James, A. and James A.L. (2001b) 'Childhood: towards a theory of continuity and change', *The Annals of the American Academy of Political and Social Sciences*, no 575, pp 25-37.

James, A. and James, A.L. (2004) *Constructing childhood*, Basingstoke: Palgrave Macmillan.

James, A. and Jenks, C (1996) 'Public perceptions of childhood criminality', *British Journal of Sociology*, vol 47, pp 315-31.

James, A. and Prout, A. (1990a) *Constructing and reconstructing childhood: Contemporary issues in the sociological study of children*, London: Falmer Press.

James, A. and Prout, A. (eds) (1990b) 'Re-presenting childhood: time and transition in the study of childhood', in A. James and A. Prout (eds) *Constructing and reconstructing childhood*, Basingstoke: Falmer Press.

James, A.L. and Richards, M. (1999) 'Sociological perspectives, family policy, family law and children: adult thinking and sociological tinkering', *Journal of Social Welfare and Family Law*, vol 21, no 1, pp 23-39.

James, A., Jenks, C. and Prout, A. (1998) *Theorizing childhood*, Cambridge: Polity Press.

Jameson, F. (2002) 'The dialectics of disaster', *The South Atlantic Quarterly*, vol 101, no 2, pp 197-305.

Jarvis, S. and Jenkins, S.P. (1998) 'How much income mobility is there in Britain?', *Economic Journal*, vol 108, pp 426-43.

Jenkins, R. (1992) *Pierre Bourdieu*, London: Routledge.

Jenkins, S. (1975) 'Child welfare as a class system', in A. Schorr (ed) *Children and decent people*, London: George Allen and Unwin.

Jenks, C. (1982) *The sociology of childhood – Essential readings*, London: Batsford Academic.

Jenks, C. (1996a) 'The postmodern child', in J. Brannen and M. O'Brien (eds) *Children in families*, London: Falmer.

Jenks, C. (1996) *Childhood*, London: Routledge.

Jenson, J. (2001) 'Rethinking equality and equity: Canadian children and the social union', in E. Broadbent (ed) *Democratic equality: What went wrong?*, Toronto/Buffalo/London: University of Toronto Press.

Jenson, J. and Saint-Martin, D. (2001) 'Changing citizenship regimes: social policy strategies in the investment state', Paper prepared for workshop on *Fostering social cohesion: A comparison of new political strategies*, Université de Montréal, 21-22 June.

Jenson, J. and Saint-Martin, D. (2002) 'Building blocks for a new welfare architecture: from Ford to LEGO', Paper prepared for the American Political Science Association Annual Conference, Boston, 29 August-1 September.

Jervis, J. 1998) *Exploring the modern*, Oxford: Blackwell.

Jessop, B. (1994) 'The transition to post-Fordism and the Schumpeterian workfare state', in R. Burrows and B. Loader (eds) *Towards a post-Fordist welfare state?*, London and New York, NY: Routledge.

Jessop, B. (2000) 'From the KWNS to the SWPR', in G. Lewis, S. Gewirtz and J. Clarke (eds) *Rethinking social policy*, London: Sage Publications.

Jewkes, Y. (2004) *Media and crime*, London: Sage Publications.

John, M. (ed) (1996) *Children in charge: The child's right to a fair hearing*, London: Jessica Kingsley.

Johnson, A.G. (1995) *The Blackwell dictionary of sociology*, Oxford: Blackwell.

Johnson, N. (1999) 'The Personal Social Services and community care', in M. Powell.

Jones, C. (2002) 'Voices from the front line: state social workers and New Labour', *British Journal of Social Work*, vol 31, pp 547-62.

Jones, M. (1999) *New institutional space: TECs and the remaking of economic governance*, London: Jessica Kingsley.

Jordan, B. (1990) *Social work in an unjust society*, London: Harvester Wheatsheaf.

Jordan, B. (1998) *The new politics of welfare*, London: Sage Publications.

Jowett, S. (1995) *Health and well-being in the 1990s*, Slough: NFER.

Kagan, S., Chen, N. and Neuman, M. (1996) 'Introduction: the changing context of American early care and education', in S. Kagan and N. Cohen (eds) *Reinventing early care and education: A vision for a quality system*, San Francisco, CA: Jossey-Bass.

Kaganas, F. (1999) 'Contact, conflict and risk', in S. Day Sclater and C. Piper (eds) *Undercurrents of divorce*, Aldershot: Ashgate.

Kaganas, F. and Piper, C. (1999) 'Divorce and domestic violence', in S. Day Sclater and C. Piper (eds) *Undercurrents of divorce*, Aldershot: Ashgate.

Kaltenborn, K. and Lempp, R. (1998) 'The welfare of the child in custody disputes after parental separation or divorce', *International Journal of Law, Policy and the Family*, no 12, pp 74-106.

Kamerman, S.B. and Kahn, A.K (1978) *Family policy: Government and families in fourteen countries*, New York, NY: Columbia University Press.

Karn, V. (1997) *Ethnicity in the 1991 census: Volume four: Employment, education and housing among the ethnic minority populations of Britain*, London: The Stationery Office.

Keep, E. and Mayhew, K. (2000) 'Towards the knowledge based economy', *Renewal*, vol 7, no 4, pp 50-9.

Keith, L. and Morris, J. (1994) 'Easy targets: a disability rights perspective on the "children as carers" debate', *Critical*.

Kelly, G. and Le Grand, J. (2001) 'Assets for the people', *Prospect*, December.

Kempson, E., Bryson, A. and Rowlingson, K. (1994) *Hard times*, London: Policy Studies Institute.

Kemshall, H. (2002) *Risk, social policy and welfare*, Buckingham: Open University Press.

Kemshall, H. and Pritchard, J. (eds) (1996) *Good practice in risk assessment and risk management*, London: Jessica Kingsley Publishers.

Killeen, J. et al (1999) 'Education and the labour market', *Journal of Education Policy*, vol 14, no 2, pp 99-116.

King, A., Wold, B., Tudor-Smith, C. and Harel, Y. (1996) *The health of youth: A cross-national survey*, WHO Regional Publications, European Series, No 69.

King, M. (1981) 'Welfare and justice', in M. King (ed) *Childhood, welfare and justice*, London: Batsford Academic, pp 105-36.

King, M. (1991) 'Children and the legal process: views from a mental health clinic', *Journal of Social Welfare and Family Law*, no 4, pp 269-84.

King, M. (1997) *A better world for children*, London: Routledge.

King, M. (1999a) '"Being sensible": images and practices of the new family lawyers', *Journal of Social Policy*, vol 28, no 2, pp 249-73.

King, M. (1999b) 'Introduction', in M. King (ed) *Moral agendas for children's welfare*, London: Routledge.

King, M. and Kaganas, F. (1998) 'The risks and dangers of experts in court', *Current Legal Issues*, no 1, pp 221-42.

King, M. and Piper, C. (1995) *How the law thinks about children* (2nd edn), Aldershot: Arena.

Kitson-Clarke, G. (1962) *The making of Victorian England*, London: Methuen.

Klein, R. (1999) *Defying disaffection: How schools are winning the hearts and minds of reluctant learners*, Stoke-on-Trent: Trentham Books.

Knorr, K., Krohn, R. and Whitley, R. (eds) (1981) 'The social process of scientific investigation', *Sociology of the Sciences*, *Year Book 4*, London and Dortrecht: D. Reidol.

Kohm, L. and Lawrence, M. (1997-98) 'Sex at six: the victimisation of innocence and other concerns over children's rights', *Journal of Family Law*, no 36, pp 361-406.

Kukathas, C. (1999) 'Cultural toleration', in I. Shapiro and W. Kymlicka (eds) *Ethnicity and group rights*, New York, NY: New York University Press, pp 69-111.

Kumar, V. (1993) *Poverty and inequality in the UK: The effects on children*, London: National Children's Bureau.

Kurtz, Z. (1992) *With health in mind: Mental health care for children and young people*, Action for Sick Children in Association with South West Thames Regional Health Authority.

Kurtz, Z. (2003) 'Outcomes for children's health and well being', *Children & Society*, vol 17, pp 173-83.

Kurtz, Z. and Tomlinson, J. (1991) 'How do we value our children today? As reflected by children's health, health care and policy?', *Children & Society*, vol 5, no 3.

Kurtz, Z., Thornes, R. and Wolkind, S. (1994) *Services for the mental health of children and young people in England: A national review*, London: Maudsley Hospital and South Thames (West) Regional Health Authority.

Kymlicka W. and Norman, W. (1994) 'Return of the citizen: a survey of recent work on citizenship theory', *Ethics*, vol 104, pp 352-81.

Land, H. and Parker, R. (1978) 'The United Kingdom', in S.B. Kemerman and A.K. Kahn (eds) *Family policy: Government and families in fourteen countries*, New York, NY: Columbia University Press.

Landrine, H. (1992) 'Clinical implications of cultural differences: the referential versus the indexical self', *Clinical Psychology Review*, vol 12, pp 401-15.

Langan, M. and Ostner, I. (1991) 'Gender and welfare: towards a comparative framework', in G. Room (ed) *Towards a European welfare state*, Bristol: School for Advanced Urban Studies.

Lansdown, G. (1994) 'Children's rights', in B. Mayall (ed) *Children's childhoods: Observed and experienced*, London: Falmer, pp 33-45.

Lansdown, G. (1995) *Taking part: Children's participation in decision making*, London: Institute for Public Policy Research.

Lansdown, G. (1996), 'Implementation of the UN Convention on the Rights of the Child in the UK', in M. Long (ed) *Children in our charge*, London: Jessica Kingsley.

Lansdown, G. (2002) 'Children's rights commissioners for the UK', in B. Franklin (ed) *The new handbook of children's rights*, London and New York, NY: Routledge.

Larner, W. and Craig, D. (2002) 'After neoliberalism? Local partnerships and social governance in Aotearoa New Zealand', Paper presented at the American Political Science Association Annual Meeting, Boston, 28 August-1 September

Lash, S., Szerszynski, B. and Wynne, B. (eds) (1996) *Risk, environment and modernity: Towards a new ecology*, London: Sage Publications.

Latz, L. (1993) 'What can we learn from Reggio-Emilia', in C. Edwards, L. Gandini and G. Forman (eds) *The hundred languages of children*, Norwood, NJ: Ablex.

Law Commission (1988) *Family review of child care law: Guardianship and custody*, Report No 172, London: HMSO.

Laws, S. (1998) *Hear me! Consulting with young people on mental health services*, London: Mental Health Foundation.

Laws, S. (1999) 'Involving children and young people in the monitoring and evaluation of mental health services', *Healthy Minds*, London: National Children's Bureau.

Laws, S., Armitt, D., Metzendor, W., Percival, P. and Reisel, J. (1999) *Time to listen: Young people's experiences of mental health services*, London: Save the Children.

Lawson, E. (1991) 'Are Gillick rights under threat'?, *ChildRight*, vol 80, pp 17-21.

Lawson, N. (1992) *The view from No 11*, London: Bantam Press.

Laybourn, A. and Cutting, E. (1996) *Young people with epilepsy*, Glasgow: Report for Enlighten.

Leach, P. (1999) *The physical punishment of children*, London: NSPCC.

Lee, N. (2001) *Childhood and society*, Buckingham: Open University Press.

Leigh, J. (1992) 'The 1991 Child Support Act: its relationship with the 1989 Children Act', *Journal of Child Law*, vol 4, no 4, pp 177-80.

Leira, A. (1992) *Welfare states and working mothers*, Cambridge: Cambridge University Press.

Lerner, G. (1997) *Why history matters*, New York, NY: Oxford University Press.

Levi, M. (1996) 'Social and unsocial capital: a review essay of Robert Putnam's *Making democracy work*', *Politics and Society*, vol 24, no 1, pp 45-55.

Levitas, R. (ed) (1986) *The ideology of the New Right*, Cambridge: Polity Press.

Levitas, R. (1998) *The inclusive society? Social exclusion and New Labour*, London: Macmillan.

Levitas, R. (2000) 'Community, utopia and New Labour', *Local Economy*, vol 15, no 3, pp 188-97.

Levitt, R., Wall, A. and Appleby, J. (1992) *The reorganised National Health Service*, London: Chapman and Hall.

Lewis, J. (1980) *The politics of motherhood*, London: Croom Helm.

Lewis, J. (1992) 'Gender and the development of welfare regimes', *Journal of European Social Policy*, vol 2, no 3, pp 159-73.

Lewis, J. (ed) (1993) *Women and social policies in Europe*, Aldershot: Edward Elgar.

Lewis, J. (1997) 'Gender and welfare regimes: further thoughts', *Social Politics: International Studies in Gender, State, and Society*, vol 4, no 2, pp 160-78.

Lewis, J. (ed) (1998) *Gender, social care and welfare state restructuring in Europe*, Aldershot: Ashgate.

Lewis, J., Bernstock, P. and Bovell, V. (1995) 'The community care changes: unresolved tensions and policy issues in implementation', *Journal of Social Policy*, vol 24, no 1, pp 73-94.

Lim, H. and Roche, J. (2000) 'Feminism and children's rights', in J. Bridgeman and D. Monk (eds) *Feminist perspectives on child law*, London: Cavendish.

Lind, M. (1995) *The next American nation*, New York, NY: Free Press.

Lindon, J. (1996) *Growing up: From eight years to young adulthood*, London: National Children's Bureau.

Lindsay, D. (1994) *The welfare of children*, New York, NY: Oxford University Press.

Lister, R. (1994) '"She has other duties": women, citizenship and social security', in S. Baldwin and J. Falkingham (eds) *Social security and social change: New challenges to the Beveridge model*, Hemel Hempstead: Harvester Wheatsheaf.

Lister, R. (1998) 'Vocabularies of citizenship and gender: the UK', *Critical Social Policy*, vol 18, no 3, pp 309-31.

Lister, R. (2000a) To Rio via the third way: Labour's "welfare" reform agenda', *Renewal*, vol 8, no 4, pp 9-20.

Lister, R. (2000b) 'The politics of child poverty in Britain from 1965 to 1990', *Revue Française de Civilisation Britannique*, vol 11, no 1, pp 67-80.

Lister, R. (2001) 'New Labour: a study in ambiguity from a position of ambivalence', *Critical Social Policy*, vol 21, no 4, pp 425-47.

Lister, R. (2002) 'Towards a new welfare settlement?', in C. Hay (ed) *British politics today*, Cambridge: Polity Press.

Littlejohn-Blake, S.M. and Darling, C.A. (1993) 'Understanding the strengths of African American families', *Journal of Black Studies*, vol 23, no 4, pp 460-71.

Lobo, E. (1978) *Children of immigrants to Britain: Their health and social problems*, London: Allen and Unwin.

London Borough of Brent (1985) *A child in trust: Report of the Panel of Inquiry Investigating the Circumstances Surrounding the Death of Jasmine Beckford*, London: London Borough of Brent.

London Borough of Greenwich (1987) *A child in mind: Protection of children in a responsible society: Report of the Commission of Inquiry into the Circumstances Surrounding the Death of Kimberley Carlile*, London: London Borough of Greenwich.

London Borough of Lambeth (1987) *Whose child? The Report of the Panel Appointed to Inquire into the Death of Tyra Henry*, London: London Borough of Lambeth.

Lord Chancellor's Department (1993) *Looking to the future: Mediation and the ground for divorce*, Cmnd 2424, London: HMSO.

Lowry, S. (1991) *Housing and health*, London: BMA.

Lyon, C. and Parton, N. (1995) 'Children's rights and the Children Act 1989', in B. Franklin (ed) *The handbook of children's rights: Comparative policy and practice*, London: Routledge.

Lyon, C., Surrey, E. and Timms, J. (1999) *Effective support services for children and young people: When parental relationships break down*, Liverpool: Calouste Gulbenkian Foundation, NYAS, Liverpool University.

Lyon, D. (2001) *Surveillance society: Monitoring everyday life*, Buckingham, Open University Press.

Lyon, J., Dennison, C. and Wilson, A. (2000) *'Tell them so they listen': Messages from young people in custody*, London: Home Office.

Lyons, C.M., Surrey, E. and Timms, J. (1999) *Effective support services for children and young people: When parental relationships break down – A child-centred approach*, London: Calouste Gulbenkian Foundation.

McAdoo, H.P. (1988) 'Transgenerational patterns of upward mobility in African American families', in H.P. McAdoo (ed) *Black families*, New York, NY: Oxford University Press, pp 225-37.

MacCormack, A. and Hall, S. (1995) 'Infectious diseases in childhood', in B. Botting (ed) *The health of our children*, London: HMSO.

McCulloch, A. and Joshi, H. (1999) *Child development and resources: An exploration of evidence from the second generation of the 1958 British birth cohort*, Paper 99-15, London: Institute for Social and Economic Research.

McCulloch, G. (1988) 'Education and economic performance', *History of Education*, vol 27, no 3, pp 203-6.

Macdonald, G. (1993) 'Defining the goals and raising issues in mental health promotion', in D. Trent and C. Reed (eds) *Promoting mental health*, Avebury: Aldershot.

McFarlane, J. (1964) 'Perspectives on personality, consistency and change from the guidance study', *Vita Humana*, vol 7, p 115.

MacFarlane, A. and Mitchell, R. (1988) 'Health services for children and their relationship to the educational and social services', in D. Forfar (ed) *Child health in a changing society*, Oxford: Oxford University Press.

MacGilchrist, B., Myers, K. and Reed, J. (1997) *The intelligent school*, London: Paul Chapman.

McGillivray, A. (ed) (1997) *Governing childhood*, Aldershot: Dartmouth.

MacGregor, B.D., Robertson, D.S. and Shucksmith, M. (1987) *Rural housing in Scotland*, Aberdeen: Aberdeen University Press.

McGuire, J. (2004) 'Reducing offending by young offenders: what does the evidence tell us?', Paper presented at *Children in Trouble with the Law... what works?*, Criminal Justice System Northern Ireland and Department of Justice, Equality and Law Reform Conference, Slieve Donard Hotel, Newcastle, Northern Ireland, March, unpublished.

MacIntyre, A. (1981) *After virtue: A study in moral theory*, London: Duckworth.

McKay, S. and Rowlingson, K. (1999) *Social security in Britain*, Basingstoke: Macmillan.

McKay, S., Walker, R. and Ashworth, K. (1997) *The changing Income Support caseload*, CRSP 261aS, Loughborough: Loughborough University Centre for Research in Social Policy.

McKendrick, J., Bradford, M.G. and Fielder, A.V. (2000) 'The dangers of safe play', ESRC Children 5-16 Research Programme Briefing (www.esrc.ac.uk/curprog.html).

Maclean, M. and Eekelaar, J. (1997) *The parental obligation: A study of parenthood across households*, Oxford: Hart Publishing.

MacMurray, J. (1932) *Freedom in the modern world*, London: Faber.

Macnicol, J. (1986) 'The effect of the evacuation of schoolchildren on official attitudes to state intervention', in H.L. Smith (ed) *War and social change*, Manchester: Manchester University Press.

McRobbie, A. (2000) 'Feminism and the third way', *Feminist Review*, vol 64, pp 97-112.

Maggs, J.L., Schulenberg, J. and Hurrelmann, K. (1997) 'Developmental transitions during adolescence: health promotion implications', in J. Schulenberg, J.L. Maggs and K. Hurrelmann (eds) *Health risks and developmental transitions during adolescence*, Cambridge: Cambridge University Press.

Maitra, B. (1996) 'Child abuse: a universal "diagnostic" category? The implication of culture in definition and assessment', *International Journal of Social Psychiatry*, vol 42, pp 287-304.

Malek, M. (1991) *Psychiatric admissions: A report on young people entering psychiatric care*, London: The Children's Society.

Mallett, S. (2004), 'Understanding home: a critical review of the literature', *The Sociological Review*, vol 52, no 1, pp 62-84.

Malpass, P. and Murie, A. (1994) *Housing policy and practice* (4th edn), London: Macmillan.

Marginson, S. (1999) 'After globalisation: emerging politics of education', *Journal of Education Policy*, vol 14, no 1, pp 19-31.

Marsella, A.J., Devos, G. and Hsu, L.K. (1985) *Culture and self: Asian and western perspectives*, New York, NY: Tavistock.

Mason, D. (1995) *Race and ethnicity in modern Britain*, Oxford: Oxford University Press.

Masson, J. (1991) 'Adolescent crisis and parental power', *Family Law*, December, pp 528-31.

Masson, J. and Winn Oakley, M. (1999) *Out of hearing*, Chichester: John Wiley & Sons Ltd.

Maternity Alliance (2002) 'A crying shame: pregnant asylum seekers and their babies in detention', Briefing paper, London: Maternity Alliance.

Matthews, H. and Limb, M. (1997) 'The right to a say: the development of youth councils/forums within the UK', *Area*, vol 30, no 1, pp 66-78.

Matthews, H. and Limb, M. (2000) 'Children and the street', ESRC Children 5-16 Research Programme Briefing (www.esrc.ac.uk/curprog.html).

Mayall, B. (1986) *Keeping children healthy*, London: Allen & Unwin.

Mayall, B. (1994) *Negotiating health: Primary school children at home and school*, London: Cassell.

Mayall, B. (1996) *Children, health and the social order*, Buckingham: Open University Press.

Mayall, B. (2000) 'Negotiating childhood', ESRC Children 5-16 Research Programme Briefing (www.esrc.ac.uk/curprog.html).

Mayall, B. (2002) *Towards a sociology for childhood*, Buckingham: Open University Press.

Mayall, B., Bendelow, G., Barker, S., Storey, P. and Veltman, M. (1996) *Children's health in primary schools*, London: Falmer Press.

Mayall, N. (1994) 'Children's action at home and school', in B. Mayall (ed) *Children's childhoods*, London: Falmer Press.

Mearn, A. (1883) *The bitter cry of outcast London*.

Mechanic, D. (1990) 'Promoting health', *Society*, Jan/Feb pp 16-22.

Mental Health Foundation (1998) *The big picture: Promoting children and young people's mental health*, London: Mental Health Foundation.

Mental Health Foundation (1999) *Bright futures: Promoting children and young people's mental health*, London: Mental Health Foundation.

Michel, S. and Mahon, R. (eds) *Child care policy at the crossroads*, New York, NY: Routledge.

Micklewright, J. and Stewart, K. (1999) *Is child welfare converging in the European Union?*, Innocenti Occasional Paper, EPS 69, Florence: UNICEF International Child Development Centre.

Micklewright, J. and Stewart, K. (2000) 'Child well-being and social cohesion', *New Economy*, vol 7, no 1, pp 18-23.

Middleton, S., Ashworth, K. and Walker, R. (1994) *Family fortunes: Pressure on parents and children in the 1990s*, London: Child Poverty Action Group.

Miliband, D. (1991) 'This is the modern world', *Fabian Review*, vol 111, no 4, pp 11-13.

Millar, J. and Ridge, T. (2001) *Families, poverty, work*.

Millar, J. and Warman, A. (1996) *Family obligations in Europe*, London: Family Policy Studies Centre.

Miller, P. (1987) *Domination and power*, London, Routledge.

Miller, P. and Rose, N. (1988) 'The Tavistock Programme: the government of subjectivity and social life', *Sociology*, vol 22, no 2, pp 171-92.

Miller, P. and Rose, N. (1990) 'Governing economic life', *Economy and Society*, vol 19, no 1, pp 1-31.

Ministerial Group on the Family (1999) *Supporting families: A consultation document*, London: The Stationery Office.

Mnookin, R. (1976) 'Child-custody adjudication: judicial functions in the face of indeterminacy', *Law and Contemporary Problems*, vol 39, no 3, pp 226-93.

Mnookin, R (1983) 'The "best interests" syndrome and the allocation of power in child care', in H. Geach and E. Szed (eds) *Providing civil justice for children*, London: Edward Arnold.

Modell, J. (1994) 'When may social capital influence children's school performance?', in A.C. Petersen and J.T. Mortimer, *Youth unemployment and society*, Cambridge: Cambridge University Press.

Modood, T., Berthoud, R. and others (1997) *Ethnic minorities in Britain: Diversity and disadvantage*, London: Policy Studies Institute.

Moller Okin, S. (1989) *Justice, gender and the family*, New York, NY: Basic Books.

Monaghan, G., Hibbert, P. and Moore, S. (2004) *Children in trouble: Time for change*, London: Barnardo's, The Children's Society, the Howard League for Penal Reform, the National Children's Bureau, the Children's Rights Alliance for England, NCH, NSPPC and the National Association for Youth Justice.

Montagu, A. (1974) *Man's most dangerous myth: The fallacy of race*, New York, NY: Oxford University Press.

Moody, S. and Tombs, J. (1982) *Prosecution in the public interest*, Edinburgh: Scottish Academic Press.

Morgan, J. (1986) 'Controlling minors' fertility', *Monash University Law Review*, vol 12, pp 161-97.

Morgan, P. (1996) *Who needs parents?*, London: IEA Health and Welfare Unit.

Morgan, P. (2002) *Marriage-lite*, London: Institute for the Study of Civil Society.

Morgan, R. (1994) 'Imprisonment', in M. Maguire, R. Morgan and R. Reiner (eds) *The Oxford handbook of criminology*, Oxford: Clarendon Press.

Morgan, R. (2004) 'Where does child welfare fit into youth justice?', Paper presented at 'Children First, Offending Second?', Nacro Youth Crime Conference, Loughborough University, April, unpublished.

Morris, A., Gillet, H., Szwed, E. and Geach, H. (1980) *Justice for children*, Basingstoke: Macmillan.

Morris, J. (1993) *Independent lives: Community care and disabled people*, Basingstoke: Macmillan.

Morris, J. (1997) 'Gone missing? Disabled children living away from their families', *Disability and Society*, vol 12, no 2, pp 241-58.

Morrison, M. (1995) 'Researching food consumers in school', *Educational Studies*, vol 21, no 2, pp 239-63.

Morrow, V. (1996) 'Rethinking childhood dependency: children's contribution to the domestic economy', *The Sociological Review*, vol 44, no 1, pp 58-77.

Moss, P. and Petrie, P. (1999) 'Rethinking school: a review of three national experiences', Findings, York: Joseph Rowntree Foundation (Summary of a full report, *Rethinking school: Some international perspectives*, London: National Youth Agency).

Moss, P. and Petrie, P. (2002) *From children's services to children's spaces*, London: Routledge.

Moynihan, D. (1965) *The negro family in the United States: The case for action*, Washington, DC: Government Printing Press.

Mulgan, G. (1998) 'Social exclusion: joined up solutions to joined up problems', in C. Oppenheim (ed) *An inclusive society: Strategies for tackling poverty*, London: IPPR.

Muncie, J. (1999a) 'Institutionalised intolerance: youth justice and the 1998 Crime and Disorder Act', *Critical Social Policy*, vol 19, no 2, pp 147-75.

Munice, J (1999b) 'Exorcising demons: media , politics and criminal justice', in B. Franklin (ed) *Social policy, the media and misrepresentation*, London: Routledge.

Muncie, J. (2004a) *Youth and crime*, London: Sage Publications.

Muncie, J. (2004b) 'Youth justice: responsibilisation and rights', in J. Roche et al (eds) *Youth in society* (2nd edn), London: Sage Publications/Open University.

Muncie, J. and Hughes, G. (2002) 'Modes of youth governance: political rationalities, criminalisation and resistance', in J. Muncie, G. Hughes and E. McLaughlin (eds) *Youth justice: Critical readings*, London: Sage Publications, pp 1-18.

Murch, M. and Hooper, D. (1992) *The family justice system*, Bristol: Family Law.

Nacro (1999a) Nacro *Briefing – Putting the community into community safety: Community consultation*, London: Nacro Crime and Policy Section.

Nacro (1999b) *Community safety, community solutions: Tackling crime in inner city neighbourhoods – Summary*, London: Nacro.

Nacro (2003a) *A failure of justice*, London: Nacro.

Nacro (2003b) *Youth crime briefing: Detention and training order early release – the revised guidance and use of electronic monitoring*, March, London: Nacro.

Nacro (2004a) *Youth crime briefing: New legislation – impact on sentencing*, March, London: Nacro.

Nacro (2004b) *Youth crime briefing: Parenting provision in a youth justice context*, June, London: Nacro.

Nacro (2004c) *Youth crime briefing: Some facts about young people who offend – 2002*, March, London: Nacro.

Nasman, E. (1994) 'Individualisation and institutionalisation of children', in J. Qvortrup, M. Bardy, G. Sgritta and H. Wintersberger (eds) *Childhood matters: Social theory, practice and politics*, Aldershot: Avebury.

National Children's Bureau (1999) *Healthy minds: The Newsletter of the Young People's Mental Health and Well-Being Project*, vol 6, November.

NCH Action for Children (1995) *Fact file '95*, London.

Neale, B. and Smart, C. (1997) '"Good!" and "bad" lawyers? Struggling in the shadow of the law', *Journal of Social Welfare and Family Law*, vol 19, no 4, pp 377-402.

Neather, A. (2004) 'Fears haunting New Labour', *Evening Standard*, 5 April.

Nestmann, F. and Niepel, G. (1994) 'Social support in single-parent families: children as sources of support', in F. Nestmann and K. Hurrelmann (eds) *Social networks and social support in childhood and adolescence*, Berlin: de Gruyter.

Newman, J. (1998) 'Managerialism and social welfare', in G. Hughes and G. Lewis, *Unsettling welfare*, London: Routledge.

Newman, J. (2001) *Modernising governance*, London: Sage Publications.

Newson, J. and Newson, E. (1974) 'Cultural aspects of child rearing in the English speaking world', in M. Richards (ed) *The integration of a child into a social world*, London: Cambridge University Press.

Newton, J. (1994) *All in one place*, London: CHAS.

NHS Health Advisory Service (1989) *Bridges over troubled waters: A report on services for disturbed adolescents*, London: HMSO.

NHS Health Advisory Service (1995) *Together we stand: The commissioning, role and management of child and adolescent mental health services*, London: HMSO.

Noble, M., Cheung, S.Y. and Smith, G. (1998) 'Origins and destinations – social security claimant dynamics', *Journal of Social Policy*, vol 27, pp 351-69.

Norwegian Ministry of Children and the Family (1996) *The Ombudsman for children and childhood in Norway*, Oslo: Ministry for Children and the Family.

NOU (Norges Offentlige Utredninger) (1975) *Stønad til enslige forsørgere m.v.*, 18.

Novak, T. (2002) 'Rich children, poor children', in B. Goldson, M. Lavalette and J. McKechnie (eds) *Children, welfare and the state*, London: Sage Publications, pp 59-72.

Nowotny, H. (1991) 'Women in public life in Austria', in C. Fuchs Epstein and R. Laub Coser (eds) *Access to power: Cross-national studies of women and elites*, London: Sage Publications.

Oakley, A. (1980) *Women confined: Towards a sociology of childbirth*, Oxford: Martin Robertson.

Oakley, A. et al (1995) 'Health and cancer prevention: knowledge and beliefs of children and young people', *British Medical Journal*, vol 310, pp 1029-33.

O'Brian, C. (1990) 'Family therapy with black families', *Journal of Family Therapy*, vol 12, pp 3-16.

O'Brien, M. (1995) 'Health and lifestyle a critical mess? Notes on the differentiation of health', in R. Bunton, S. Nettleton and R. Burrows (eds) *The sociology of health promotion*, London: Sage Publications.

O'Brien, M. (1999) Paper to the ESRC Seminar on Postmodern Kinship, Leeds University, 10 December.

O'Connor, J., Orloff, A.S. and Shaver, S. (1999) *States, markets, families, gender: Liberalism and social policy in Australia, Canada, Great Britain and the United States*, Cambridge: Cambridge University Press.

O'Donovan, K. (1993) *Family law matters*, London: Pluto Press.

OECD (Organisation for Economic Co-operation and Development) (1998) *Schooling for tomorrow: Learning and schooling in the knowledge society*, CERI/SFT (98) 8, Paris: OECD.

Office for Criminal Justice Reform (2004) *Cutting crime, delivering justice: A strategic plan for criminal justice 2004-08*, London: The Stationery Office.

Ogden, J. (1991) 'Care or control?', *Social Work Today*, 4 July, p 9.

Okin, S. Moller (1989) *Justice, gender and the family*, New York, NY: Basic Books.

Oldfield, N. (1992) *Using budget standards to estimate the cost of children*, York: Family Budget Centre, University of York.

Oldfield, N. (1993) 'The cost of a child', in J. Bradshaw (ed) *Budget standards for the United Kingdom*, Aldershot: Avebury, pp 177-95.

Oldfield, N. and Yu, A.C.S. (1993) *The cost of a child: Living standards for the 1990s*, London: CPAG.

Oliver, D. and Heater, D. (1994) *The foundations of citizenship*, Hemel Hempstead: Harvester Wheatsheaf.

Oliver, M. (1990) *The politics of disablement*, Basingstoke: Macmillan.

Olsen, R. (1996) 'Young carers: challenging the facts and politics of research into children and caring', *Disability and Society*, vol 11, no 1, pp 41-54.

Olsen, R. and Clarke, H. (2003) *Parenting and disability*, Bristol: The Policy Press.

Olsen, R. and Parker, G. (1997) 'A response to Aldridge and Becker: "Disability rights and the denial of young carers: the dangers of zero-sum arguments"', *Critical Social Policy*, vol 17, pp 125-33.

O'Malley, P. (1992) 'Risk, power and crime prevention', *Economy and Society*, vol 21, no 3, pp 283-99.

O'Neill, J. (1994) *The missing child in liberal theory*, Toronto: University of Toronto Press.

O'Neill, O. (1992) 'Children's rights and children's lives', *International Journal of Law and the Family*, vol 6, pp 24-42 (also in P. Alston et al [eds] *Children, rights and the law*, Oxford: Clarendon Press).

ONS (Office for National Statistics) (1999) *Social Trends 29*, London: The Stationery Office.

ONS (2000) *The mental health of children and adolescents in Great Britain, 2000*, London: The Stationery Office.

Oppenheim, C. and Harker, L. (1996) *Poverty: The facts* (3rd edn), London: CPAG.

Ot prp [odelstringsproposisjon] (1957) *Om lov om forsørgertrygd for barn*, nr 41.

Owen, M. (1992) *Social justice and children in care*, Aldershot: Avebury.

Owusu-Bempah, J. (1989) 'The new institutional racism', *Community Care*, 1 November, pp 16-17.

Owusu-Bempah, J. (1994) 'Race, self-identity and social work', *British Journal of Social Work*, vol 24, pp 123-36.

Owusu-Bempah, J. (1997) 'Race', in M. Davies (ed) *The Blackwell companion to social work*, Oxford: Blackwell, pp 50-6.

Owusu-Bempah, J. (1998) 'The relevance of confidentiality in social work practice across cultures', in .R. Compton and B. Gallaway (eds) *Social work processes* (6th edn), Pacific Grove, CA: Brooks/Cole, pp 151-70.

wusu-Bempah, J. (2001) 'Racism: an important factor in practice with ethnic minority children and families' , in P. Foley et al (eds) *Children in society*, Basingstoke: Palgrave.

Owusu-Bempah, J. and Howitt, D. (1995) 'How Eurocentric psychology damages Africa', *The Psychologist*, vol 18, no 10, pp 462-5.

Owusu-Bempah, J. and Howitt, D. (1997) *Professional abuse of black childhood*, Leicester: School of Social Work, University of Leicester.

Owusu-Bempah, K. and Howitt, D. (1999) 'Even their "soul" is defective', *The Psychologist: Bulletin of the British Psychological Society*, vol 12, no 3, pp 126-30.

Packman, J. (1981) *The child's generation: Child care policy from Curtis to Houghton* (2nd edn), Oxford: Blackwell.

Packman, J. and Jordan, B. (1991) 'The Children Act: looking forward, looking back', *British Journal of Social Work*, vol 21, no 2, pp 315-27.

Page, D. (1993) *Building for communities – A study of new housing association estates*, York: Joseph Rowntree Foundation

Pahl, R. (1997) 'Friendly society', in S. Kraemer and J. Roberts (eds) *The politics of attachment: Towards a secure society*, London: Free Association Books.

Palmeri, A. (1980) 'Childhood's end: toward the liberation of children', in W. Aiken and H. LaFollette (eds) *Whose child? Children's rights, parental authority and state power*, Boston: Littlefield, Adams.

Pantazis, C. and Gordon, D. (2000) *Tackling inequalities*, Bristol: The Policy Press.

Papadopoulos, T. (1996) '"Family", state and social policy for children in Greece', in J. Brannen and M. O'Brien (eds) *Children in families: Research and policy*, London: Falmer.

Parcel, T. and Menaghan, E. (1994) 'Early parental work, family social capital, and early childhood outcomes', *American Journal of Sociology*, vol 99, no 4, pp 972-1009.

Parekh, B. (2000) *The future of multi-ethnic Britain*, London: Profile.

Parker, H. (1998) *Low cost but acceptable: A minimum income standard for the UK*, Bristol: The Policy Press.

Parker, R. (ed) (1980) *Caring for separated children: Plans, procedures and priorities. A report by a working party established by the National Children's Bureau*, Basingstoke: Macmillan.

Parker, S. (1994) 'The best interests of the child – principles and problems', in P. Alston (ed) *The best interests of the child: Reconciling culture and human rights*, Oxford: Clarendon Press.

Parton, C. (1990) 'Women, gender oppression and child abuse', in the Violence Against Children Study Group, *Taking child abuse seriously*, London: Unwin Hyman.

Parton, N. (1985) *The politics of child abuse*, London: Macmillan.

Parton, N. (1991) *Governing the family: Childcare, child protection and the state*, Basingstoke: Macmillan.

Parton, N. (1994) 'Problematics of government, (post)modernity and social work', *British Journal of Social Work*, vol 24, no 1, pp 9-32.

Parton, N. (1995) 'Neglect as child protection: the political context and the practical outcomes', *Children and Society*, vol 9, no 1, pp 67-89.

Parton, N. (1996a) 'The new politics of child protection', in J. Pilcher and S. Wang (eds) *Thatcher's children: Politics, childhood and society in the 1980s and 1990s*, London: Falmer Press.

Parton, N. (1996b) 'Social work, risk and "the blaming system"', in N. Parton (ed) *Social theory, social change and social work*, London: Routledge.

Parton, N. (ed) (1997) *Child protection and family support: Tensions, contradictions and possibilities*, London: Routledge.

Parton, N. and Marshall, W. (1998) 'Postmodern and discourse approaches to social work', in R. Adams, C. Dominelli and M. Payne (eds) *Social work*, Basingstoke: Macmillan.

Parton, N., Thorpe, D. and Wattam, C. (1997) *Child protection: Risk and the moral order*, Basingstoke: Macmillan.

Pascall, G. (1986) *Social policy: A feminist analysis*, London: Routledge.

Pasquino, P. (1988) 'Theatrum politicum: the genealogy of capital – police and the state of prosperity', *Ideology and Consciousness*, no 4, pp 41-54.

Pateman, C. (1989) *The disorder of women*, Cambridge: Polity Press.

Pavetti, L.A. (1993) 'The dynamics of welfare and work: exploring the process by which women work their way off welfare', PhD dissertation thesis, JFK School of Government, Harvard, Cambridge, MA.

Payne, M. (1992) 'Psychodynamic theory within the politics of social work theory', *Journal of Social Work Practice*, vol 6, no 2, pp 141-9.

Peach, C. (1996) *Ethnicity in the 1991 census: Volume two: The ethnic minority populations of Great Britain*, London: The Stationery Office.

Pedersen, S. (1993) *Family, dependence and the origins of the welfare state: Britain and France 1914-1945*, Cambridge: Cambridge University Press.

Perri 6 (1997) 'Escaping poverty: from safety nets to networks of opportunity', *Arguments*, London: Demos.

Perry, A. and Scanlon, L. (1999) 'Children's welfare in divorce', Paper presented at the Annual Conference of the Socio-Legal Studies Association, Loughborough University, 6 April.

Petrie, P. (1994) 'Quality in school-age child care services: an enquiry about values', in P. Moss and A. Pence (eds) *Valuing quality in early childhood services: New approaches in defining quality*, London: Paul Chapman Publishers.

Phillips, M., Shyne, A., Sherman, E. and Haring, B. (1971) 'Factors associated with placement decisions in child welfare', Research Centre, Child Welfare League of America.

Phillipson, C., Bernard, M. and Strang, P. (1986) *Dependency and independency in later life*, London: Croom Helm.

Philp, M. (1979) 'Notes on the form of knowledge in social work', *Sociological Review*, vol 27, no 1, pp 83-111.

Philp, M. (1985) 'Michel Foucault', in Q. Skinner (ed) *The return of grand theory in human sciences*, Cambridge: Cambridge University Press.

Piachaud, D. (1979). *The cost of a child*, London: Child Poverty Action Group.

Piachaud, D. (2001) 'Child poverty, opportunities and quality of life', *The Political Quarterly*, vol 72, no 4, pp 446-53.

Piachaud, D. and Sutherland, H. (2001) 'Child poverty and the new labour government', *Journal of Social Policy*, vol 30, pp 95-118.

Pinchbeck, I. and Hewitt, M. (1969, 1973) *Children in English society*, 2 vols, London: Routledge and Kegan Paul.

Piper, C. (1993) *The responsible parent: A study in divorce mediation*, Hemel Hempstead: Harvester Wheatsheaf.

Piper, C. (1999a) 'How do you define a family lawyer?', *Legal Studies*, vol 19, no 1, pp 93-111.

Piper, C. (1999b) 'Moral campaigns for children's welfare in the nineteenth century', in M. King (ed) *Moral agendas for children's welfare*, London: Routledge.

Piper, C. and Day Sclater, S. (1999) 'Changing divorce', in S. Day Sclater and C. Piper (eds) *Undercurrents of divorce*, Aldershot: Ashgate.

Piper, C. and Kaganas, F. (1997) 'The Family Law Act 1996 s1(d): how will "they" know there is a risk of violence?', *Child and Family Law Quarterly*, vol 9, no 3, pp 363-82.

Pitts, J. (1988) *The politics of juvenile justice*.

Pitts, J. (2000) 'The new youth justice and the politics of electoral anxiety', in B. Goldson (ed) *The new youth justice*, Dorset: Russell House Publishing, pp 1-13.

Pixley, J. (1993) *Citizenship and employment: Investigating post-industrial options*, Hong Kong: Cambridge University Press.

Plant, M. and Plant, M. (1992) *Risk takers*, London: Routledge.

Platt, A. (1969) *The child savers: The invention of delinquency*, Chicago, IL: University of Chicago Press.

Platt, A.M. (1977) *The invention of delinquency*, Chicago, IL: Chicago University Press.

Platt, L. and Noble, M. (1999) *Race, place and poverty: Ethnic groups and low income distributions*, York: York Publishing Services.

Platt, S. (1987) 'The new rural clearances', *Roof*, July/August.

Plumb, J.H. (1975) 'The new world of children in eighteenth-century England', *Past and Present*, vol 67, pp 74-95.

Polakow, V. (1993) *Lives on the edge: Single mothers and their children in the other America*, Chicago, IL/London: University of Chicago Press.

Pollard, A. and Filer, A. (1996) *The social world of children's learning*, London: Cassell.

Pollard, A., Broadfoot, P., Cross, P., Osborn, M. and Abbot, D. (1994) *Changing English primary schools*, London: Cassell.

Pollock, L. (1983) *Forgotten children: Parent-child relations from 1500 to 1900*, Cambridge: Cambridge University Press.

Popkewitz, T. (1998) *Struggling for the soul: The politics of schooling and the construction of the teacher*, New York, NY: Teachers' College Press.

Popkewitz, T.S. and Bloch, M. (2000) 'Administering freedom: a history of present – rescuing the parent to rescue the child for society', in G. Dahlberg and G. Hultqvist (eds) *The changing child in a changing world: Current ways of thinking and practicing childhood*, New York, NY: Routledge.

Porter, J. (1999) *Reschooling and the global economic future*, Wallingford: Symposium.

Porter, R. (1991) 'History of the body', in P. Burke (ed) *New perspectives on historical writing*, Cambridge: Cambridge University Press.

Portes, A. and Landolt, P. (1996) 'The downside of social capital', *The American Prospect*, no 26, pp 18-21.

Powell, M. (1999) *New Labour, new welfare state?*, Bristol: The Policy Press.

Powell, M. (2002) *Evaluating New Labour's welfare reforms*, Bristol: The Policy Press.

Power, A. (1987) *Property before people – The management of twentieth-century council housing*, London: Allen & Unwin.

Power, C. (1995) 'Health related behaviour', in B. Botting (ed) *The health of our children*, London: HMSO.

Power, M. (1994a) *The audit explosion*, London: Demos.

Power, M. (1994b) 'The audit society', in A.G. Hopwood and P. Miller (eds) *Accounting as social and institutional practice*, Cambridge: Cambridge University Press.

Priestley, M. (1998) 'Childhood disability and disabled childhoods: agendas for research', *Childhood*, vol 5, no 2, pp 207-23.

Pringle, K. (1998) *Children and social welfare in Europe*, Buckingham: Open University Press.

Pringle, R. and Watson, S. (1992) '"Women's interests" and the post-structuralist state', in M. Barrett and A. Phillips (eds) *Destabilizing theory: Contemporary feminist debates*, Cambridge: Polity Press.

Prout, A. (1986) '"Wet children" and "little actresses": going sick in primary school', *Sociology of Health and Illness*, vol 8, pp 111-36.

Prout, A. (1996) *Families, cultural bias and health promotion*, London: Health Education Authority.

Prout, A. (1999) 'Living arrows: children's lives and the limits of parenthood', *The Parenting Forum Newsletter*, vol 15.

Prout, A. (2000a) 'Children's participation: control and self-realisation in British late modernity', *Children & Society*, vol 14.

Prout, A. (2000) 'Childhood bodies: construction, agency and hybridity', in A. Prout (ed) *The body, childhood and society*, Basingstoke: Macmillan.

Prout, A. and Christensen, P. (1996) 'Hierarchies, boundaries and symbols: medicine use and the cultural performance of childhood sickness', in P.J. Bush et al, *Children: Medicines and culture*, New York, NY: Haworth Press.

Prout, A. and James, A. (1997) 'A new paradigm for the sociology of childhood', in A. James and A. Prout (eds) *Constructing and deconstructing childhood: Contemporary issues in the sociological study of childhood* (2nd edn), London: Falmer Press.

Pupavac, V. (2002) 'The international children's rights regime', in D. Chandler (ed) *Rethinking human rights,* Basingstoke: Palgrave.

Putnam, R.D. (1993) *Making democracy work: Civic traditions in modern Italy*, Princetown, NJ: Princetown University Press.

Putnam, R.D. (1995) 'Bowling alone: America's declining social capital', *Journal of Democracy*, vol 6, no 1, pp 65-78.

Putzel, J. (1997) 'Accounting for the "dark side" of social capital: reading Robert Putnam on democracy', *Journal of International Development*, vol 9, no 7, pp 939-49.

Qvortrup, J. (1994) 'Childhood matters: an introduction', in J. Qvortrup et al (eds) *Childhood matters: Social theory, practice and politics*, Aldershot: Avebury, pp 1-23.

Qvortrup, J. (1995) 'Children and modern society: a paradoxical relationship', in J. Brannen and M. O'Brien (eds) *Children in families: Research and policy*, London: Falmer Press.

Qvortrup, J. (1997) 'A voice for children in statistical accounting: a plea for children's right to be heard', in A. James and A Prout (eds) *Constructing and reconstructing childhood*, London: Falmer Press, pp 85-106.

Raleigh, V.S. and Balajaaran, R. (1995) 'The health of infants and children among ethnic minorities', in B. Botting (ed) *The health of our children*, London: HMSO.

Randall, V. (2000) *The politics of daycare in Britain*, Oxford: Oxford University Press.

Ratcliffe, P. (1997) *Ethnicity in the 1991 Census: Volume Three: Social geography and ethnicity in Britain: Geographical spread, spatial concentration and internal migration*, London: The Stationery Office.

Raz, J. (1986) *The morality of freedom*, Oxford: Clarendon Press.

RCP (Royal College of Physicians) (1994) *Homelessness and ill health*, London: RCP.

RCP (Royal College of Psychiatrists) (2002) *Parent-training programmes for the management of young children with conduct disorders: Findings from research*, London: RCP.

Readings, B. (1996) *The university in ruins*, Cambridge, MA: Harvard University Press.

Reay, D. (1998) 'Engineering social reproduction: mothers in the educational marketplace', *British Journal of Sociology of Education*, vol 19, no 2, pp 195-209.

Rechner, M. (1990) 'Adolescents with cancer', *Journal of Pediatric Oncology Nursing*, vol 7, no 4, pp 139-44.

Reddy, S.G. (1996) 'Claims to expert knowledge and the subversion of democracy: the triumph of risk over uncertainty', *Economy and Society*, vol 25, no 2, pp 222-54.

Reder, P., Duncan, S. and Gray, M. (eds) (1993) *Beyond blame: Child abuse tragedies revisited*, London: Routledge.

Reece, H. (1996) 'The paramountcy principle: consensus or construct?', *Current Legal Problems*, no 49, pp 267-304.

Reich, R. (1991) *The work of nations*, New York, NY: Simon and Schuster.

Reiner, R. (1988) 'British criminology and the state', *British Journal of Criminology*, vol 29, no 1, pp 138-58.

Ribbens McCarthy, J. and Edwards, R. (2992) 'The individual in public and private: the significance of mothers and children', in A. Carling et al (eds) *Analysing families*, London: Routledge.

Richards, K.D. (1995) *A content analysis of texts in a clinical setting*, Birmingham: Aston University.

Richards, M. (1986) 'Behind the best interests of the child: an examination of the arguments of GFS concerning custody and access at divorce', *Journal of Social Welfare and Family Law*, March, pp 77-95.

Ridge, T. (2002a) *Childhood poverty and social exclusion: From a child's perspective*, Bristol: The Policy Press.

Ridge, T. (2002b) 'Listening to children: their contribution to anti-poverty policies', *Poverty*, no 111, pp 10-13.

Ridge, T. and Millar, J. (2000) 'Excluding children: autonomy, friendship and the experience of the care system', *Social Policy and Administration*, vol 34, no 2, pp 160-75.

Roberts, H., Smith, S.J. and Bryce, C. (1995) *Children at risk? Safety as a social value*, Milton Keynes: Open University Press.

Roberts, I. and Singh, C. (1999) *Using mentors to change problem behaviour in primary school children*, Research Findings No 95, London: Home Office Research and Statistics Directorate.

Roberts, M. (1999) 'R v M: refusal of medical treatment', *Childright*, vol 159, pp 14-15.

Roberts, M. (2000) 'Protecting children, supporting parents: government consultation on physical punishment', *ChildRight*, no 163, pp 3-5.

Robertson, J. and Robertson, J. (1989) *Separation and the very young*, London: Free Association Books.

Robinson, C. and Stalker, K. (1998) *Growing up with disability*, London: Jessica Kingsley Publishers.

Robinson, L. (1995) *Psychology for social workers: Black perspectives*, London: Routledge.

Robinson, P. (1997) *The myth of parity of esteem: Earning and qualifications*, Discussion paper no 34, London: Centre for Economic Performance.

Robinson, P. (2000) 'Measuring the knowledge economy', in D. Robertson (ed) *The knowledge economy*, London: Routledge.

Roche, J. (1991) 'The 1989 Children Act: once a parent always a parent', *Journal of Social Welfare and Family Law*, no 5, pp 345-61.

Roche, J. (1995) 'Children's rights: in the name of the child', *Journal of Social Welfare and Family Law*, vol 17, no 3, pp 281-300.

Roche, J. (1996a) 'Children's rights: a lawyer's view', in M. John (ed) *Children in our charge: The child's right to resources*, London: Jessica Kingsley Publishers.

Roche, J. (1996b) 'The politics of children's rights', in J. Brannen and M. O'Brien (eds) *Children in families*, London: Falmer.

Roche, J. (1999) 'Children's rights: participation and citizenship', *Childhood*, no 6, p 475.

Rodgers, B. and Pryor, J. (1998) *Divorce and separation: The outcomes for children*, York: Joseph Rowntree Foundation.

Roker, D. (1998) *Worth more than this: Young people growing up in family poverty*, London: The Children's Society.

Rooke, P. (1995) '"Uncramping child life": international children's organisations', in P. Weindling (ed) *International health organisations and movements, 1918-1939*, Cambridge: Cambridge University Press.

Rose, L. (1986) *Massacre of the innocents: Infanticide in Great Britain*, London: Routledge.

Rose, N. (1985) *The psychological complex: Psychology, politics and society in England, 1869-1939*, London: Routledge.

Rose, N. (1979) 'The psychological complex: mental measurement and social administration', *Ideology and Consciousness*, vol 5, Spring, pp 5-68.

Rose, N. (1986) 'Law, rights and psychiatry', in P. Miller and N. Rose (eds) *The power of psychiatry*, Cambridge: Cambridge University Press.

Rose, N. (1987) 'Beyond the public/private division: law, power and the family', *Journal of Law and Society*, vol 14, no 1, Spring.

Rose, N. (1989) 'Individualizing psychology', in J. Shotter and K.J. Gergen (eds) *Texts of identity*, London: Sage Publications.

Rose, N. (1990) *Governing the soul: The shaping of the private self*, London: Routledge.

Rose, N. (1991) 'Inventiveness in politics', *Economy and Society*, vol 28, no 3, pp 467-93.

Rose, N. (1993a) 'Government, authority and expertise in advanced liberalism', *Economy and Society*, vol 22, no 3, pp 283-99.

Rose, N. (1993b) 'Towards a critical sociology of freedom', Inaugural lecture, London: Goldsmiths College.

Rose, N. (1996a) 'The death of the social?: re-figuring the territory of government', *Economy and Society*, vol 25, no 3, pp 327-50.

Rose, N. (1996b) 'Psychiatry as a political science: advanced liberalism and the administration of risk', *History of the Human Sciences*, vol 9, no 2, pp 1-23.

Rose, N. (1999) *Powers of freedom: Reframing political thought*, Cambridge: Cambridge University Press.

Rose, N. and Miller, P. (1992) 'Political power beyond the state problematics of government', *British Journal of Sociology*, vol 43, no 2, pp 173-205.

Ross, E. (1993) *Love and toil: Motherhood in outcast London, 1870-1918*, Oxford: Oxford University Press.

Rowntree, B.S. (1902) *Poverty: A study of town life* (2nd edn), London: Macmillan.

Rowntree, B.S. (1941) *Poverty and progress: A second social survey*, London: Longman Green,

Royal College of Psychiatrists (2002) *Parent-training programs for the management of young children with conduct disorders: Findings from research*, London: Royal College of Psychiatrists.

Ruddick, W. (1979) 'Parents and life prospects', in O. O'Neill and W. Ruddick (eds) *Having children: Philosophical and legal reflections on parenthood*, New York, NY: Oxford University Press.

Runyan, D.K., Hunter, W.M., Socolar, R., Amaya-Jackson, L., English, D., Landsverk, J., Dubowitz, H., Browne, D.H., Bangdiwala, S. and Mathew, R. (1998) 'Children who prosper in unfavourable environments: the relationships to social capital', *Pediatrics*, vol 101, no 1, pp 12-18.

Ruskin, J. (1849) *The seven lambs of architecture* (1st edn).

Russell, D. (1995) *Women, madness and medicine*, Cambridge: Polity Press.

Rustin, M. (1997) 'Attachment in context', in S. Kraemer and J. Roberts (eds) *The politics of attachment: Towards a secure society*, London: Free Association Books.

Rutherford, A. (1995) 'Signposting the future of juvenile justice policy in England and Wales', in Howard League for Penal Reform, *Child offenders: UK and international practice*, London: The Howard League for Penal Reform.

Rutter, M. (1977) *Helping troubled children*, Harmondsworth: Penguin.

Rutter, M. and Rutter, M. (1993) *Developing minds*, Harmondsworth: Penguin.

Rutter, M. and Smith, D.J. (1995) 'Towards causal explanations of time trends in psychosocial disorders of young people', in M. Rutter and D.J. Smith (eds) *Psychosocial disorders of youth*, New York, NY: John Wiley & Sons.

Ruxton, S. (2001) 'Towards a "children's policy" for the European Union', in P. Foley, J. Roche and S. Tucker (eds) *Children in society: Contemporary theory, policy and practice*, Basingstoke: Palgrave, pp 65-75.

Sainsbury, D. (ed) (1994) *Gendering welfare states*, London: Sage Publications.

Sainsbury, D. (1996) *Gender, equality and welfare states*, Cambridge: Cambridge University Press.

Sainsbury, D. (1999) 'Gender and social-democratic welfare states', in D. Sainsbury (ed) *Gender and welfare state regimes*, Oxford: Oxford University Press.

Sale, A.U. (2002) 'News analysis', *Community Care*, 20-26 June, p 20.

Sampford, C. (1986) 'The dimensions of liberty and their judicial protection', *Law in Context*, vol 4, pp 29-51.

Sanders, A. (1999) 'Violent fathers, implacably hostile mothers and contact: new directions?', *Family Mediation*, vol 9, no 1, pp 15-16.

Sarat (1997)

Sartorius, N. (1992) 'The promotion of mental health', in D. Trent (ed) *Promoting mental health*, vol 1, Aldershot: Avebury.

Sawyer, C. (1995) *The rise and fall of the third party: Solicitors' assessments of the competence of children to participate in family proceedings*, Oxford: Gulbenkian Foundation.

Sawyer, C. (1997) 'The mature child: how solicitors decide', *Family Law*, January, pp 19-21.

Sawyer, C. (1999) *Rules, roles and relationships: The structure and function of child representation and welfare within family proceedings*, vols 1 and 2, Oxford: Centre for Socio-Legal Studies.

Schorr, A.L. (1992) *The Personal Social Services: An outside view*, York: Joseph Rowntree Foundation.

Schram, S.F. (1995) *Words of welfare: The poverty of social science and the social science of poverty*, Minneapolis, MN/London: University of Minnesota Press.

Scott, C. (2992) 'Citizenship education: who pays the piper?', in B. Franklin (ed) *The new handbook of children's rights*, London: Routledge.

Scott, J., Brynin, M. and Smith, R (1995) 'Interviewing children in the British Household Panel Survey', in J.J. Hox and B.F. Van der Meulen, J.J. Fer ter Laak and L.W.C. Travecchio (eds) *Advances in family research*, Den Haag: CIP-Gegevens Koninklijke, Bibliotheck.

Scott, S., Jackson, S. and Backett-Milburn, K. (1998) 'Swings and roundabouts: risk anxiety and the everyday worlds of children', *Sociology*, vol 32, no 4, pp 665-89.

Scottish Executive (1999) *New Community Schools prospectus*, Edinburgh: Scottish Executive.

Scottish Executive (2000) *New Community Schools: A framework for national evaluation*, Edinburgh: Scottish Executive.

Scraton, P. (ed) (1997) *Childhood in crisis?*, London: UCL Press.

Secretary of State for Social Services (1974) *Report of the Inquiry into the Care and Supervision Provided in Relation to Maria Colwell*, London: HMSO.

Secretary of State for Social Services (1988) *Report of the Inquiry into Child Abuse in Cleveland*, London: HMSO.

Seip, A.-L. (1984) *Sosialhjelpsstaten blir til. Norsk sosialpolitikk 1740-1920*, Oslo: Gyldendal.

Seip, A.-L. (1994) *Veiene til velferdsstaten. Norsk sosialpolitikk 1920-75*, Oslo: Gyldendal.

Sen, A. (2000) 'Freedom's market', *Observer*, 25 June.

Sennett, R. (1998) *The corrosion of character*, London: Norton.

SEU (Social Exclusion Unit) (1998) 'Truancy and school exclusion' (www.cabinetoffice.gov.uk/seu/index.html).

SEU (2001) *A new commitment to neighbourhood renewal*, London: Cabinet Office.

SEU (2002) *Reducing re-offending by ex-prisoners*, London: SEU.

Sevenhuijsen, S. (1999) *Citizenship and the ethics of care: Feminist considerations on justice, morality and politics*, London: Norton.

Sevenhuijsen, S. (1999) *Caring the third way* (Working Paper 12), Leeds: Centre for Research on Family Kinship and Childhood.

Sexty, C. (1990) *Women loosing out – Access to housing in Britain today*, London: Shelter.

Seymour, J. (1992) 'An "uncontrollable" child: a case study in children's and parent's rights', in P. Alston, S. Parker and J. Seymour (eds) *Children, rights and the law*, Oxford: Oxford University Press.

Sgritta, G. (1994) 'The generational division of welfare: equity and conflict', in J. Qvortrup, M. Brady, G. Sgritta and H. Wintersberger (eds) *Childhood matters: Social theory, practice and politics*, Aldershot: Avebury.

Shakespeare, T. (1999) 'Losing the plot? Discourses of disability and genetics', in J. Gabe and P. Conrad (eds) *Social perspectives on the new genetics*, Oxford: Blackwell Publishers.

Shakespeare, T. (2000) *Help*, Birmingham: Venture Press.

Shakespeare, T. and Watson, N. (1998) 'Theoretical principles in disabled childhood', in K. Stalker and C. Robinson (eds) *Growing up with disability*, London: Jessica Kingsley.

Shakespeare, T., Gillespie-Sells, K. and Davis, D. (1996) *Untold desires: The sexual politics of disability*, London: Cassell.

Shakespeare, T., Barnes, C., Cunningham-Burley, S., Davies, J., Priestly, M. and Watson, N. (2000) 'The lives of disabled children', ESRC Children 5-16 Research Programme Briefing (www.esrc.ac.uk/curprog.html).

Shape (2004) *Ignoring the facts is the biggest crime*, London: National Children's Bureau.

Sharpe, S., Mauthner, M. and France-Dawson (1996) *Family health: A literature review*, London: Health Education Authority.

Shelter (1994) *Homelessness – What's the problem*, London: Shelter.

Sherraden, M. (2002) 'From a social welfare state to a social investment state', in C. Kober and W. Paxton (eds) *Asset-based welfare and poverty*, London: National Children's Bureau.

Shilling, C. (1993) *The body and social theory*, London: Sage Publications.

Shropshire, J. and Middleton, S. (1999) *Small expectations: Learning to be poor?*, York: Joseph Rowntree Foundation.

Siim, B. (2000) *Gender and citizenship: Politics and agency in France, Britain and Denmark*, Cambridge: Cambridge University Press.

Silavwe, G.W. (1995) 'The need for a new social work perspective in an African setting: the case of social casework in Zambia', *British Journal of Social Work*, vol 25, pp 71-84.

Silva, E.B. and Smart, C. (1999) *The new family?*, London: Sage Publications.

Silverman, D. (1987) *Communication and medical practice*, London: Sage Publications.

Simey, M. (1951) *Charitable effort in Liverpool in the 19th century*, Liverpool: Liverpool University Press.

Simon, W. (1983) 'Legality, bureaucracy, and class in the welfare system', *Yale Law Journal*, vol 92, pp 1198-269.

Singer, J. (1992) 'The privatization of family law', *Wisconsin Law Review*, vols v-vi, pp 1443-57.

Skellington, R. and Morris, P. (1992) *Race in Britain today*, London: Sage Publications.

Skevik, A. (1998) 'The state–parent–child relationship after family break-ups: child maintenance in Norway and Britain', in P. Flora et al (eds) *The state of social welfare*, Aldershot: Ashgate.

Skevik, A. (2001) 'Family ideology and social policy: policies towards lone parents in Norway and the UK', NOVA report series 07/01, Oslo.

Skolnick, A. (1973) *The intimate environment: Exploring marriage and the family*, New York, NY: Little, Brown.

Smart, B. (1993) *Postmodernity*, London: Routledge.

Smart, C. and Neale, N. (1999) *Family fragments?*, Cambridge: Polity Press.

Smart, C. and Neale, N. (2000) '"It's my life too": children's perspectives on post-divorce parenting', *Family Law*, March, pp 163-69.

Smith, F. (2000) 'Out of school care', ESRC Children 5-16 Research Programme Briefing (www.esrc.ac.uk/curprog.html).

Smith, G., Williamson, H. and Platt, L. (1996) *Youth in an age of uncertainty*, Carnegie UK Trust 'Years of Decision' conference.

Smith, K. and Leon, L. (2001) *Turned upside down: Developing community-based crisis services for 16-25 year olds experiencing a mental health crisis*, London: Mental Health Foundation.

Smith, M.J. (2001) 'Conclusion: the complexity of New Labour', in S. Ludlam and M.J. Smith (eds) *New Labour in government*, Basingstoke: Macmillan.

Smith, T. (1999) 'Neighbourhood and prevention strategies with children and families: what works?', *Children & Society*, vol 13, no 4, pp 265–77.

Smithers, R. (2000) 'You're not alone', *The Guardian* (Education), 15 August.

Social Services Committee (1984) *Children in care*, HC 360, London: HMSO.

Social Trends, 2000, London: The Stationery Office.

Sone, K. (1994) 'The forgotten children', *Community Care*, 30 April, vol 1014, pp 22-3.

Song, M. (1996) '"Helping out": children's labour participation in Chinese take-away businesses in Britain', in J. Brannen and M. O'Brien (eds) *Children in families: Research and policy*, London: Falmer Press.

Spargo, J. ([1906] 1969) *The bitter cry of the children*.

Spencer, N. (1996) *Poverty and child health*, Oxford: Radcliffe Medical Press.

Spencer, N. 'Reducing child health inequalities', in P. Bywaters and E. McLeod (eds) *Working for equality in health*, London: Routledge.

Spring, J. (1994) *Wheels in the head: Educational philosophies of authority, freedom, and culture from Socrates to Paulo Freire*, New York, NY: McGraw-Hill.

SSI (Social Services Inspectorate), Commission for Health Improvement, HM Chief Inspector of Constabulary, HM Chief Inspector of the Crown Prosecution Service, HM Chief Inspector of the Magistrates' Courts Service, HM Chief Inspector of Schools, HM Chief Inspector of Prisons and HM Chief Inspector of Probation (2002) *Safeguarding children: A joint Chief Inspectors' report on arrangements to safeguard children*, London: DH Publications.

Stainton Rogers, R. and Stainton Rogers, W. (1992) *Stories of childhood: Shifting agendas of child concern*, Hemel Hempstead: Harvester Wheatsheaf.

Stasiulis, D. (2002) 'The active child citizen: lessons from Canadian policy and the children's movement', *Citizenship Studies*, vol 6, no 4, pp 507-38.

Statham, D. (1996) *The future of social and personal care*, London: NISW.

Stearn, J. (1986) 'An expensive way of making children ill', *Roof*, vol 11, no 5, September/October.

Stedman Jones, G. (1971) *Outcast London: A study in the relationship between classes in Victorian society*, Oxford: Oxford University Press.

Steedman, C. (1986) *Landscape for a good woman*, London: Virago.

Steedman, C. (1995) *Strange dislocations: Childhood and the idea of human interiority, 1780-1930*, London: Virago.

Steinberg, D. (1981) 'Two years referrals to a Regional Adolescent Unit: some implications for psychiatric services', *Social Science and Medicine*, vol 15.

Stevenson, O. (1998) *Neglect: Issues and dilemmas*, Oxford: Blackwell.

Stewart, A. (1995) 'Two conceptions of citizenship', *British Journal of Sociology*, vol 46, pp 63-78.

Stone, N. (2004) 'Orders in respect of anti-social behaviour: recent judicial developments', *Youth Justice*, vol 4, no 1, pp 46-54.

St meld [stortingsmelding] (1948) *Om folketrygden*, nr 58.

Strategy Unit (2002) *Delivering for children and families*, London: Cabinet Office.

Sutherland, G. (1984) *Ability, merit and measurement: Mental testing and English education, 1880-1940*, Oxford: Oxford University Press.

Sutton, C., Utting, D. and Farrington, D. (2004) *Support from the start: Working with young children and their families to reduce the risks of crime and anti-social behaviour*, Research Brief 524, March, London: Department for Education and Skills.

Swain, J., Finkelstein, V., French, S. and Oliver, M. (1993) *Disabling barriers: Enabling environments*, London: Sage Publications.

Sweeting, H. and West, P. (1995) 'Family life and health in adolescence', *Social Science and Medicine*, vol 40, no 2, pp 163-75.

Taylor, L., Lacey, R. and Bracken, D. (1980) *In whose best interests?*, London: Cobden Trust/Mind.

Teachman, J., Paasch, K. and Carver, K. (1996) 'Social capital and dropping out of school early', *Journal of Marriage and the Family*, no 58, pp 773-83.

Teubner, G. (1983) 'Substantive and reflexive elements in modern law', *Law and Society Review*, vol 17, pp 239-85.

Therborn, G. (1993) 'The politics of childhood: the rights of children in modern times', in F.G. Castles (ed) *Families of nations: Patterns of public policy in western democracies*, Aldershot: Dartmouth.

Thoburn, J. (1995) 'The Children Act 1989 and children "in need"', in A. Bainham, D. Pearl and R. Pickford (eds) *Frontiers of family law*, Chichester: John Wiley & Sons Ltd, pp 219-27.

Thoburn, J., Wilding, J. and Watson, J. (2000) *Family support in cases of emotional maltreatment and neglect*, London: The Stationery Office.

Thom, D 'Wishes, anxieties, play, and gestures: child guidance in inter-war England', in R. Cooter (ed) *In the name of the child: Health and welfare 1880-1940*, London: Routledge.

Thomas, G. and Hocking, G. (2003) *Other people's children*, London: Demos.

Thomas, N. and O'Kane, C (1998) 'The ethics of participatory research with children', *Children & Society*, vol 12, pp 336-48.

Thompson, P. and Warhurst, C. (eds) *Workplaces of the future*, London: Macmillan.

Thorpe, J. (1994) 'Independent representation for minors', *Family Law*, no 20.

Titmuss, R.M. (1974) *Social policy*, London: Allen and Unwin.

Townsend, P. (1970) *The fifth social service: A critical analysis of the Seebohm proposals*, London: The Fabian Society.

Townsend, P. (1981) 'The structured dependency of the elderly', *Ageing and Society*, vol 1, no 21, pp 5-28.

Townsend, P. (1993) *The international analysis of poverty*, Milton Keynes: Harvester.

Townsend, P., Davidson, N. and Whitehead, M. (1992) *The health divide*, Harmondsworth: Penguin.

Triandis, H.C. (1986) 'Collectivism vs individualism: a reconceptualization of a basic concept in cross-cultural psychology', in C. Bagley and K. Varma (eds) *Personality, cognition and values: Cross-cultural perspectives of childhood and adolescence*, London: Macmillan.

Trinder, L. (1997) 'Competing constructions of childhood: children's rights and children's wishes in divorce', *Journal of Social Welfare and Family Law*, vol 19, no 3, pp 291-305.

Triseliotis, Borland, M., Hill, M. and Lambert, L. (1995) *Teenagers and the social work services*, London: HMSO.

Tronto, J. (1993) *Moral boundaries: A political argument for the ethics of care*, London: Routledge.

Tuckwell, G. (1894) *The state and its children*.

Turner, B. (1984) *The body and society*, Oxford.

Turok, I. (2000) 'Inequalities in employment', in C. Pantazis and D. Gordon (eds) *Tackling inequalities*, Bristol: The Policy Press.

Twine, F. (1994) *Citizenship and social rights*, London: Sage Publications.

Ukviller, R. (1979) 'Children versus parents: perplexing policy questions for the ACLU', in O. O'Neill and W. Ruddick (eds) *Having children: Philosophical and legal reflections on parenthood*, New York, NY: Oxford University Press.

Ungerson, C. (1994) 'Housing: need, equity, ownership and the economy', in V. George and S. Miller (eds) *Social policy towards 2000*, London: Routledge.

UNICEF (2000) *A league table of child poverty in rich nations*, Florence: UNICEF.

United Nations Committee on the Rights of the Child (1995) *Eighth Session. Consideration of Reports Submitted by States Parties Under Article 44 of the Convention*, Geneva: United Nations.

United Nations Committee on the Rights of the Child (2002a) *Thirty-first session. Consideration of Reports Submitted by States Parties Under Article 44 of the Convention, United Kingdom of Great Britain and Northern Ireland*, Geneva: United Nations.

United Nations Committee on the Rights of the Child (2002b) *Concluding Observations of the Committee on the Rights of the Child: United Kingdom of Great Britain and Northern Ireland*, Geneva: United Nations.

Urwin, C. and Sharland, E. (1992) 'From bodies to minds in childcare literature: advice to parents in inter-war Britain', in R. Cooter (ed) *In the name of the child: Health and welfare, 1880-1940*, London: Routledge, pp 174-99.

Valentine, G. (1996) 'Children should be seen and not heard? The role of children in public space', *Urban Geography*, vol 7, no 3, pp 205-20.

van den Heuval, H., Heuval, H., Tellegen, G. and Koomen, J. (1992) 'Cultural differences in the use of psychological and social characteristics in children's self-understanding', *European Journal of Social Psychology*, vol 22, pp 353-62.

Vaskilampi, T. et al (1996) 'From catching a cold to eating junk food', in P.J. Bush et al (eds) *Children, medicine and culture*, New York, NY: Haworth Press.

Vleminckx, K. and Smeeding, T.M. (eds) (2000) *Child well-being, child poverty and child policy in modern nations: What do we know?*, Bristol: The Policy Press.

Vernon, A. (1996) 'A stranger in many camps: the experience of disabled black and ethnic minority women', in J. Morris (ed) *Encounters with strangers: Feminism and disability*, London: Women's Press.

Vostanis, P., Cumella, S., Gratton, E. and Winchester, C. (1996) *The impact of homelessness on the mental health of children and families*, Birmingham: Department of Psychiatry, University of Birmingham.

Wadsworth, M. (1996) 'Family and education as determinants of health', in D. Blane, E. Brunner and R. Wilkinson, *Health and social organisation*, London: Routledge.

Wagner, G. (1979) *Barnardo*, London: Weidenfield and Nicholson.

Wakefield, J.C. (1996) 'Does social work need the eco-systems perspective? Part 1: is the perspective clinically useful?', *Social Service Review*, vol 70, pp 1-32.

Wald, N. (1992) 'Antenatal maternal screening for Down's syndrome: results of a demonstration project', *British Medical Journal*, vol 305, pp 391-4.

Walden, G. (1996) *We should know better: Solving the education crisis*, London: Fourth Estate.

Walker, R. with Ashworth, K. (1992) *Poverty dynamics: Issues and examples*, Aldershot: Avebury.

Walker, A. and Walker, C. (eds) (1997) *Britain divided: The growth of social exclusion in the 1980s and 1990s*, London: CPAG.

Walkerdine, V. (1984) 'Developmental psychology and the child-centred pedagogy', in J. Henriques, W. Holloway, C. Urwin, C. Venn and V. Walkerdine, *Changing the subject: Psychology, social regulation and subjectivity*, London: Methuen.

Wall, E., Ferrazzi, G. and Schryer, F. (1998) 'Getting the goods on social capital', *Rural Sociology*, vol 63, no 2, pp 300-22.

Wall, J. (1995) 'The judicial role in interdisciplinary cooperation', *Representing Children*, vol 8, no 2, pp 52-5.

Wall, J. (ed) (1997) *Rooted sorrows*, Bristol: Family Law.

Walsh, C. (2002) 'Curfews: no more hanging around', *Youth Justice*, vol 2, no 2, pp 70-81.

Walsh, C. (2003) 'Dispersal of rights: a critical comment on specified provisions of the Anti-Social Behaviour Bill', *Youth Justice*, vol 3, no 2, pp 104-11.

Warnes, A.M. (1993) 'Being old, old people and the burdens of burden', *Ageing and Society*, vol 13, pp 297-338.

Wates, M. (1997) *Disabled parents: Dispelling the myths*, Cambridge: National Childbirth Trust.

Watson, N., Shakespeare, T., Cunningham-Burley, S., Barnes, C., Corker, M., Davis, J. and Priestley, M. (2000) 'Life as a disabled child: a qualitative study of young people's experiences and perspectives', ESRC Research Programme, Children 5-16: Growing into the Twenty-First Century, University of Leeds.

Weatherley, R. (1994) 'From entitlement to contract: reshaping the welfare state in Australia', *Journal of Sociology and Social Welfare*, vol 21, pp 153-73.

Webb (1926) *My apprenticeship*.

Webster, C. (1982) 'Healthy or hungry thirties?', *History Workshop Journal*, vol 13.

Webster, C. (1985) 'Health, welfare and unemployment during the Depression', *Past and Present*, vol 109.

Weir, D. (1999) 'The city has taken over the quangos under New Labour', *Independent* (Tuesday Review), 23 November.

Weisner, T.S. (1989) 'Cultural and universal aspects of social support for children: evidence from the Abaluyia of Kenya', in D. Belle (ed) *Children's social networks and social support*, New York, NY: John Wiley & Sons Ltd.

West, A. (1999) 'They make us out to be monsters: images of children and young people in care', in B. Franklin (ed) *Social policy, the media and misrepresentation*, London: Routledge

West, P. (1997) 'Health inequalities in the early years: is there equalisation in youth?', *Social Science and Medicine*, vol 44, no 6, pp 833-58.

West, P. and Sweeting, H. (1996) 'Health inequalities: what's going on in youth?', *Health Education*, no 5, pp 14-20.

Weyland, I. (1997) 'The blood tie: raised to the status of an assumption', *Journal of Social Welfare and Family Law*, vol 19, no 2, pp 291-305.

Whelan, R. (1996) *The corrosion of charity: From moral renewal to contract culture*, London: IEA Health and Welfare Unit.

White, S. (undated) *In their own words: Young people's accounts of their experiences as users of child and adolescent mental health services in Stockport*, University of Manchester/Mental Health Foundation.

Whiting, B.B. and Edwards, C.P. (1998) *Children of different worlds: The formation of social behaviour*, Cambridge, MA: Harvard University Press.

Who Cares? Trust (1998) *Still missing? Volume 2: Disabled children and the Children Act*, London: Who Cares? Trust.

Wiegers, W. (2002) *The framing of poverty as 'child poverty' and its implications for women*, Ottawa: Status of Women Canada.

Wilkinson, H. and Mulgan, G. (1995) *Freedom's children*, London: Demos.

Wilkinson, R. (1996) *Unhealthy societies*, London: Routledge.

Wilkinson, S.R. (1988) *The child's world of illness*, Cambridge: Cambridge University Press.

Williams, J. (1993) 'What is a profession? Experience versus expertise', in J. Walmsley et al (eds) *Health, welfare and practice: Reflecting on roles and relationships*, London: Sage/Open University.

Williams, F. (2004) 'What matters is who works: why every child matters to New Labour. Commentary on the DfES Green Paper *Every child matters*', *Critical Social Policy*, vol 24, no 3, pp 406-27.

Williams, F. (1989) *Social policy: A critical introduction*, Cambridge: Polity Press.

Williams, F. (2004) 'What matters is who works: why every child matters to new Labour. Commentary on the DfES Green Paper *Every child matters*', *Critical Social Policy*, vol 24, no 3, pp 406-27.

Williams, P. (1992) 'Housing', in P. Cloke (ed).

Williams, S.J. (1995) 'Theorising class, health and lifestyles: can Bourdieu help us?', *Sociology of Health and Illness*, vol 17, no 5, pp 577-604.

Willie, C.V. (1993) 'Social theory and social policy derived from the black family experience', *Journal of Black Studies*, vol 23, pp 451-9.

Willis, P. (1977) *Learning to labour: How working class kinds get working class jobs*, London: Saxon House.

Willow, C. (1997) *Hear! Hear! Promoting children and young people's democratic participation in local government*, London: Local Government Information Unit in association with the Children's Rights Office.

Willow, C. (2002) 'Lagging behind?', *Community Care*, 12-18 September.

Wilson, D. (2004) '"Keeping quiet" or "going nuts": strategies used by young, black, men in custody', *The Howard Journal of Criminal Justice*, vol 43, no 3, pp 317-30.

Wilson, W. (1994) 'Citizenship and the inner-city ghetto poor', in B. Van Steenbergen (ed) *The condition of citizenship*, London: Sage Publications.

Wilson, W.J. (1996) *When work disappears: The world of the new urban poor*, New York, NY: Alfred Knopf.

Wilson, W.J. (1996a) 'Are American ghetto trends emerging in Europe?', LSE Housing Manual Annual Lecture, June.

Winter, J.M. (1977) 'The impact of the First World War on civilian health in Britain', *Economic History Review*, vol 30.

Wolf, J. (1992) 'The concept of the "best interest" in terms of the UN Convention on the Rights of the Child', in M. Freeman and P. Veerman (eds) *Ideologies of children's rights*, Dordrecht: Martinus Nijhoff.

Wong, D. (2000) 'Relativism', in P. Singer (ed) *A companion to ethics*, Oxford: Blackwell, pp 442-51.

Wonnacott, C. (1999) 'New legislation. The counterfeit contract – reform, pretence and muddled principles in the new referral order', *Child and Family Law Quarterly*, vol 11, no 3, pp 271-87.

Woodhouse, B. (1993) 'Children's rights: the destruction and promise of the family', *Brigham Young University Law Review*, pp 497-515.

Woodroffe, C. and Glickman, M. (1993) 'Trends in child health', in G. Pugh (ed) *30 years of change for children*, London: National Children's Bureau.

Woodroffe, C., Glickman, M., Barker, M. and Power, C. (1993) *Children, teenagers and health: The key facts*, Milton Keynes: Open University Press.

Wooldridge, A. (1994) *Measuring the mind: Education and psychology in England, 1860-1900*, Cambridge: Cambridge University Press.

Woolgar, S. (1986) 'On the alleged distinction between discourse and proxies', *Social Studies of Science*, no 16.

Worrall, A. (1999) 'Troubled or troublesome? Justice for girls and young women', in B. Goldson (ed) *Youth justice: Contemporary policy and practice*, Aldershot: Ashgate, pp 28-50.

Wright, E.O. (1978) *Class, crisis and the state*, London: Verso.

Wyness, M.G. (1999) 'Childhood, agency and educational reform', *Childhood*, vol 6, no 3, pp 353-68.

Wyness, M. (2000) *Contesting childhood*, London: Falmer Press.

Yamamoto, K., Soliman, A., Parsons, J. and Davis, O.L. Jr (1987) 'Voices in unison – stressful events in lives of children in six countries', *Journal of Child Psychology and Psychiatry*, vol 28.

Yeatman, A. (1995) 'Interpreting contemporary contractualism', in J. Boston (ed) *The State under contract*, Wellington: Bridget Williams, pp 124-39.

YJB (Youth Justice Board for England and Wales) and ACPO (Association of Chief Police Officers) (2003) *Sharing personal and sensitive personal information in respect of children and young people at risk of offending: A practical guide*, London: YJB and ACPO.

Yoos, H.L. (1995) 'Children's illness and concepts: old and new paradigms', *Pediatric Nursing*, vol 20, no 2, pp 134-45.

Youth Access (2001) *Breaking down the barriers: Key evaluation findings on young people's mental health needs*, London: Youth Access.

Zigler, E., Kagan, S. and Hall, N. (eds) (1996) *Children, families and government: Preparing for the twenty-first century*, Cambridge: Cambridge University Press.

Index

Court Committee report (1977) 49
court welfare officers 231-2, 245, 246
Cox, E. 149
Cox, R. 24, 30*n*
Crawford, A. 276, 279
Crawforth, Mavis 396
crime
  and control of children 276-9
  see also anti-social behaviour;
    delinquent children; young
    offenders; youth justice system
Crime and Disorder Act (1998) 248,
  251, 257, 260, 265, 276-8, 282, 291
Criminal Justice Act (1991) 291
Criminal Justice Act (1993) 291
Criminal Justice Act (2003) 261-2
Criminal Justice and Court Services
  Act (2000) 260
Criminal Justice and Police Act (2001)
  261
Criminal Justice and Public Order Act
  (1994) 259-60, 265, 291
criminalisation of children 262-4
'crisis of childhood' 209-10, 269, 296,
  298
Crompton, R. 407-8
cruelty to children *see* 'anti-cruelty'
  legislation; child abuse
cultural capital 150, 155
cultural relativism 62
culture
  and best interests of child 59-60, 168
  child-raising practices 61-3, 177-89,
    221
  and disability 330-2
Cunningham, H. 15-16
curfew schemes 260, 261, 277-8
Curtis Committee report 44, 45
custodianship 149
custody of children 163, 164, 169
  child participation 232-4
  see also family justice system
cystic fibrosis 308

D

Dahlberg, G. 90
danger and risk 80-2
Daniel, Paul 214-15, 341, 351, **367-83**
Darling, Alistair 449-50
Darling, C.A. 187
Davie, Ronald 380

Davis, G. 244, 246
Davis, J. 110, 111
Davis, John 211-12, **323-37**
daycare critique 219-21, 421-42
  individual care providers 439-41
  parents choices 422-4
  pressure for universal daycare 424-9
  media myths 426-7
  'quality time' myth 428
  quality of institutional and individual
    care 429-31
  child development perspective 431-8
  quality of staff 435-6
De Tocqueville, Alexis 151
Deaf children 330-2, 334
Dearden, Chris 390-2
death rate *see* infant mortality rate
decision making
  children's contribution 122, 124, 169-
    72, 471
  and morality 79-82
  see also children's participation;
    consultation with children
'deficit theory syndrome' 154
Deleuze, Gilles 103-4
delinquent children
  family-oriented approach 46
  inter-war legislation 41-2
  moral campaigns in 19C 21-2
  and neglect 32
  see also anti-social behaviour;
    disturbed behaviour; young
    offenders
demonisation of children 205-6, 256-7,
  454
Department of the Environment 369,
  375-6
Department of Health
  on consent 294-5
  healthy eating 318
  and young carers 395-6
Department of Health and Social
  Security *see* Review of Child Care
  Law
Detention and Training Orders 260
developmental psychology 104, 286-7
developmental retardation and
  homelessness 378-9
deviance 14, 32, 250
  disturbed behaviour 285-300
  see also delinquent children
dialogic communities 64, 196-7, 197-8

repossession of housing 369, 370
reproductive technology 119–20
research
 culture and child-raising practices
 182–4
 see also child-centred research
resources
 for disabled children 328–9
 for young carers projects 391–2
responsibilities and rights 203, 270–1,
 449–50
 children's health 314–18
restorative justice 205–6, 251, 262
Review of Child Care Law (DHSS)
 136, 173*n*, 223
Richards, K.D. 178
Richards, M. 163, 281
Ridge, Tess 54, **107–16**, 110, 111, 456
Right to Buy scheme 214, 215, 368,
 372, 374, 376–7
rights
 disability rights movement 216–17,
 326, 392–4
 and responsibilities 203, 270–1,
 449–50
 health of children 314–18
 see also children's rights; parents: rights
 perspective; social rights
Rinaldi, Carlina 85, 90
risk
 'at risk' children 228
 risk of offending 258–9, 262–5, 277
 and child abuse 80–2
 focus on assessment and
 management 55–6, 136–42
 demonisation of children 205
 and health of children 210–11, 308–
 12, 380
 risk-taking behaviour 301, 312
Ritalin prescriptions 296
Roberts, DS Phil 297
Roberts, M. 294
Robinson, P. 409, 410
Robson, E. 275–6
Roche, Jeremy 203–4, **223–41**
Roker, D. 110, 111
Rose, Nikolas 32, 45, 56, 86
 disturbed children 42–3
 family and state intervention 101–2
 governance 264, 265, 478
 on individual psychology 286
 mental health services 299

political numbers 95–6
'psy' sciences 103
 rights and psychiatry 299
Rosebery, Lord 25
Ross, Ellen 34
Rowntree, B.S. 342, 360
Royal College of Physicians 379, 380
Royal Commission on the Blind, the
 Deaf and the Dumb report (1889)
 36
Ruddick, W. 158
rules of thumb 247
Runyan, D.K. 145
rural housing 376–7
Ruskin, John 23
Rustin, M. 96
Rutter, M. 289, 467

S

Sadler, Michael Thomas 15
Sainsbury, Lord 417
Saint-Martin, Denis 455, 457–8
Sawyer, C. 231–2, 233
Scarman, Lord 165, 166, 224, 225
school
 child-centred research on 116
 and control of children 273–6, 465
 experience of disabled children
 327–37
 health care 38, 39, 44
 health services 38, 39, 44, 319
 illness at school 316
 New Community Schools 326–7
 and social capital 153–4
 young carers in 389–90, 397
 see also education
school councils 274–5
school meals
 introduction of 23, 38, 39, 40–1, 43
 limitations of 316, 318–19
school medical service (SMS) 39, 44
school-age child care 93
schools' inspectorate 380–1
Schram, Sanford F. 455
Scotland: New Community Schools
 326–7
Scotland's health report 311
Scottish Council Foundation 94
Scottish Law Commission 240*n*
Scraton, P. 269
'second modernisation' 446, 466, 471

Child welfare
Historical dimensions, contemporary debate
Harry Hendrick

"Hendrick has provided us with a book to be appreciated and savoured, one offering students and the general reader a shrewd and intelligent overview of child welfare policy. Here is a standard text, one unlikely to be bettered for a long time." *Youth & Policy*

This book offers a provocative account of contemporary policies on child welfare and the ideological thrust behind them and provides an informed historical perspective on the evolution of child welfare during the last century.

Paperback £18.99 US$29.95 ISBN 1 86134 477 5
Hardback £55.00 US$59.95 ISBN 1 86134 478 3
234 x 156mm 304 pages February 2003

Children, family and the state
Decision-making and child participation
Nigel Thomas

"This book makes a welcome contribution to our understanding of looked after children's experiences of participation in decision-making. The author's findings contain important messages for social workers, managers and policy makers ... It should be essential reading on all courses for those working with looked after children at both undergraduate and postqualifying level. It is a must for anyone committed to understanding and promoting children's rights." *Social Work Education*

Children, family and the state examines different theories of childhood, children's rights and the relationship between children, parents and the state. Focusing on children who are looked after by the state, it reviews the changing objectives of the care system and the extent to which children have been involved in decisions about their care.

Paperback £18.99 US$29.95 ISBN 1 86134 448 1
234 x 156mm 256 pages October 2002

Discovering child poverty
The creation of a policy agenda from 1800 to the present
Lucinda Platt

Discovering child poverty

"Accessible and scholarly, pioneering and timely, this book will be invaluable to students, researchers and professionals seeking to understand the political significance of child poverty, its evolution as a concept and policy, and its importance in contemporary debate on the restructuring of the welfare state." *Harry Hendrick, Institute of History, University of Southern Denmark*

This book charts key British developments in child welfare, child poverty research and state support for children from 1800 to the present day. With direct quotations from key sources, it argues that even in the face of clear evidence of hardship the response of policy makers to child poverty has been ambivalent.

Paperback £13.99 US$23.95 ISBN 1 86134 583 6

234 x 156mm 156 pages January 2005

Studies in Poverty, Inequality and Social Exclusion series

Childhood poverty and social exclusion
From a child's perspective
Tess Ridge

Childhood poverty and social exclusion

From a child's perspective

"The sharp observations of these young citizens on their schooling, on problems in their neighbourhood and on the deficiencies of their leisure opportunities, set an agenda for any practitioner who aspires to tackle family poverty." *Community Care*

Without a deeper understanding of poverty as a lived experience in childhood, policies targeted at eradicating child poverty may fail. Using child-centred research methods to explore children's own accounts of their lives, this original book presents a rare and valuable opportunity to understand the issues and concerns that low-income children themselves identify as important. The findings raise critical issues for both policy and practice.

Paperback £18.99 US$29.95 ISBN 1 86134 362 0

Hardback £50.00 US$59.95 ISBN 1 86134 363 9

234 x 156mm 192 pages October 2002

Studies in Poverty, Inequality and Social Exclusion series

Children caring for parents with mental illness
Perspectives of young carers, parents and professionals
Jo Aldridge and Saul Becker

"With its critique of earlier literature, its new evidence and its useful overview of law and policy, this important book needs to be widely read and translated into practice." *Mental Health Today*

Little is known about the experiences of children living in families affected by severe and enduring mental illness. This is the first in-depth study of children and young people caring for parents affected in this way. Drawing on primary research data collected from 40 families, the book presents the perspectives of children (young carers), their parents and the key professionals in contact with them.

Paperback £19.99 US$32.50 ISBN 1 86134 399 X

Hardback £50.00 US$59.95 ISBN 1 86134 400 7

234 x 156mm 224 pages March 2003

Child protection and mental health services
Interprofessional responses to the needs of mothers
Nicky Stanley, Bridget Penhale, Denise Riordan, Rosaline S. Barbour and Sue Holden

"... will be of value to practitioners, students and teachers for its clarity in examining a very important issue. It does what it sets out to do and can spark off debate about the challenge that still confronts us in creating responsive and integrated services." *Child and Family Social Work*

Health and social care professionals are constantly exhorted to work collaboratively. This book reports on research which examines interprofessional work with families in which mothers have a mental health problem and where there are also concerns about child protection. Breakdowns in interprofessional collaboration, issues of risk and relevant resources are all addressed. Mothers' views and experiences are contrasted with professional perspectives.

Paperback £17.99 US$29.95 ISBN 1 86134 427 9

234 x 156mm 160 pages September 2003

Parenting and disability
Disabled parents' experiences of raising children
Richard Olsen and Harriet Clarke

"... fundamental reading for social workers, healthcare and childhood studies students as well as being an important contribution to disability literature." *Journal of Social Policy*

This book reports on the first substantial UK study of parenting, disability and mental health. It examines the views of parents and children in 75 families. Covering a broad spectrum of issues facing disabled parents and their families, it provides a comprehensive review of relevant policy issues.

Paperback £18.99 US$29.95 ISBN 1 86134 364 7

Hardback £50.00 US$59.95 ISBN 1 86134 365 5

234 x 156mm 208 pages April 2003

Social work and Irish people in Britain
Historical and contemporary responses to Irish children and families
Paul Michael Garrett

"I look forward to reading anything by Paul Michael Garrett because he writes with attitude. His insistent, slightly angry but always well-informed arguments draw attention to issues that the rest of us are content to skim over – in this case the failure of social work to engage in an anti-oppressive fashion with the Irish experience in Britain." *Community Care*

Dominant social work and social care discourses on 'race' and ethnicity often fail to incorporate an Irish dimension. This book challenges this omission and provides new insights into how social work has engaged with Irish children and their families, historically and to the present day.

Paperback £23.50 US$39.50 ISBN 1 86134 411 2

Hardback £50.00 US$69.95 ISBN 1 86134 412 0

234 x 156mm 192 pages June 2004

To order further copies of this publication or any other Policy Press titles please contact:

In the UK and Europe:
Marston Book Services, PO Box 269, Abingdon, Oxon, OX14 4YN, UK
Tel: +44 (0)1235 465500
Fax: +44 (0)1235 465556
Email: direct.orders@marston.co.uk

In the USA and Canada:
ISBS, 920 NE 58th Street, Suite 300, Portland, OR 97213-3786, USA
Tel: +1 800 944 6190 (toll free)
Fax: +1 503 280 8832
Email: info@isbs.com

In Australia and New Zealand:
DA Information Services, 648 Whitehorse Road Mitcham, Victoria 3132, Australia
Tel: +61 (3) 9210 7777
Fax: +61 (3) 9210 7788
E-mail: service@dadirect.com.au

Further information about all of our titles can be found on our website:

www.policypress.org.uk